Risks and Reconstruction

*Experiences of Resettlers
and Refugees*

Risks and Reconstruction

*Experiences of Resettlers
and Refugees*

Edited by

Michael M. Cernea
Christopher McDowell

The World Bank
Washington, D.C.

Cover design by Patricia Hord Graphik Design. The sculpture on the back cover,
titled *Desperadida*, is by a Mozambican artist, Mestre Bata; it was photographed by
Michelle Iannacci.

Library of Congress Cataloging-in-Publication Data

Risks and reconstruction: experiences of resettlers and refugees / edited by
Michael M. Cernea, Christopher McDowell.
    p. cm.
  Includes bibliographical references.
  ISBN 0-8213-4444-7
    1. Refugees — Developing countries. 2. Forced migration — Developing countries.
3. Land settlement — Developing countries. 4. Relocation (Housing) — Developing
countries. 5. Rehabilitation — Developing countries. 6. Economic development —
Social aspects. I. Cernea, Michael M. II. McDowell, Chris.

HV640 .R35 2000
362.87'09172'4 — dc21

                       99-059266

Table of Contents

Part Two   Land Loss and Land-Based Relocation

Part Three   From Joblessness to Re-Employment

Part Four   Homelessness and Home Reconstruction

Part Eight Toward Social Re-Articulation

Figure and Tables

Acknowledgments

The authors would like to acknowledge the assistance provided by the two institutions that cosponsored the work for this volume: the World Bank through its vice presidency for Environmentally and Socially Sustainable Development (ESSD), Social Development Department, and the University of Oxford through its Refugee Studies Programme (RSP). Some of the contributors to the volume had their field research sponsored by the Department for International Development (DfID), the government of the United Kingdom, the government of the Netherlands, the Institute of Social Studies in the Netherlands, the Swiss Development Corporation, or Oxfam.

With one volume editor in Washington, D.C., and the other in Oxford, Ethiopia, and Australia—and both often in the field—and with the volume's co-authors spread across 14 countries, its preparation presented many challenges and relied on all available forms of late 20th century communication. It is therefore important to acknowledge the forbearance and the cooperative spirit with which all the co-authors responded to the editors' requests.

In particular, we would like to thank the book's two main reviewers, Maninder Gill, coordinator of the World Bank's Resettlement Thematic Team (Social Development Department), and Scott Guggenheim of the World Bank's Indonesia office for their insightful comments and support. Many other reviewers helped enrich the volume during various manuscript stages with their comments and suggestions.

We are pleased to acknowledge with thanks the help provided by several others, at various phases. At Oxford, Dr. Barbara Harrell-Bond, founding Director of RSP, and Prof. David Turton, Director of RSP, as well as other members of the RSP team, helped establish a research program on the effects of displacement on refugee and resettlers. The International Conference on Resettlers and Refugees, sponsored by the University of Oxford and cosponsored by the

World Bank, discussed some of the papers in this volume in an initial iteration.

Several social scientists at the World Bank, particularly Lynn Bennett, Shelton Davis, Ishrat Husain, Alexander Marc, Maninder Gill, and Warren Waters, provided valuable support "in the last stretch," when the publication of the volume encountered financial difficulties. Eveline Herfkens and Jean-Daniel Gerber, formerly members of the World Bank's Board of Executive Directors, from the Netherlands and Switzerland, respectively, were very helpful in securing grant support from their governments for research and operational work with resettlers and refugees, some of which is reflected in this volume. Much of the editorial work on this volume's manuscripts was done in the quiet and hospitable premises of the Bethesda Library, Montgomery County (Maryland), and appreciation is expressed to its friendly and efficient staff. Finally, thanks go also to the University of Woologong, Australia, which invited one of the editors for a resettlement teaching and research program during the last period of work on this book.

The coordination of the manuscript preparation effort has significantly benefited from the well-organized help provided throughout by Gracie Ochieng, who processed the volumes' chapters repeatedly, and, in the last stage, by Milan Lin-Rodrigo, sociologist, and Bonnie Bradford, publications specialist. Gaudencio Dizon created the book's layout with unusual speed.

The sculpture reproduced on the back cover of the volume represents a refugee woman, fleeing disaster. It is the work of Mestre Bata, a Mozambican artist, and is entitled *Desperadida*. Its photographer is Michelle Iannacci. To them, too, our grateful thanks.

Editors and contributors alike strongly invite feedback from readers on the issues and recommendations contained in this volume and express in advance their gratitude for such feedback.

The Editors

Notes on Contributors

Jonathan Brown is operations adviser in the Quality Assurance Group, Office of the Managing Directors of the World Bank. From 1990 to 1997, he managed the unit in the World Bank that provided investment lending and policy advice in infrastructure, energy, and environment for Russia, Azerbaijan, and Central Asia. He also held management positions in the Africa Region of the World Bank from 1981 to 1990 and was the Bank's first resident representative in Senegal from 1978 to 1981. Before joining the Bank in 1973, Mr. Brown worked for three years in educational and agricultural projects in Chad. A graduate in history of Yale College, he received a masters degree in communications from the University of Pennsylvania and an MBA from the Harvard Business School. He has written and lectured widely on development issues.

Michael M. Cernea joined the World Bank in 1974 as its first in-house sociologist and worked as the Bank's Senior Adviser for Sociology and Social Policy until 1997. He has carried out social research, policy work, and development project work in many countries throughout Africa, Asia, the Middle East, Europe, and Latin America. Michael Cernea has a Ph.D. in sociology and social philosophy, has taught and lectured in universities in Europe and the United States, has been a visiting scholar at Harvard and other universities, and was appointed honorary professor for Resettlement and Social Studies at Hohai University in Nanjing, China. In 1991, he was elected to the Academy of Sciences, Romania. He is the recipient of the Solon T. Kimball Award for Public Policy and Applied Anthropology, granted by the American Anthropological Association, and of the Bronislaw Malinowski Prize offered by the Society for Applied Anthropology "in recognition of scholarly efforts to understand and serve the needs of the world through social science." He has written and edited numerous books and studies on development, social change, population resettlement, social forestry, grassroots organizations, and participation including *Putting People First: Sociological Variables in Development* (1985, 1991), *Anthropological Approaches to Resettlement: Policy, Practice, Theory* (edited with Scott Guggenheim, 1993), *Social Organization and Development Anthropology* (1996), *Social Assessment for Better Development* (edited with Ayse Kudat, 1997) *Resettlement and Development* (Vol. I and II, published in China, 1996-1998) and *The Economics of Involuntary Resettlement: Questions and Challenges* (1999).

Tiéman Diarra is head of ethnosociology at the Institut des Sciences Humaines in Mali. He has worked widely in the development field, on medical issues and education, as well as resettlement. He is co-author, with Dolores Koenig and Moussa Sow, of *Innovation and Individuality in African Development: Changing Production Strategies in Rural Mali*. His recent articles include "Evaluation of Ivermectin Distribution in Benin, Côte d'Ivoire, Ghana, and Togo: Estimation of coverage of treatment and operational aspects of distribution system" (co-authored), and "Representations et itineraires therapeutiques dans le quartier de Bankoni (Mali)."

Walter Fernandes, a Jesuit priest, is trained as a sociologist, specializing in tribal social research and population displacement and resettlement. Formerly director of the Indian Social Institute, a non-governmental organization, and editor of *Social Action*, he is presently head of the Program for Tribal Studies, Indian Social Institute, New Delhi. Dr. Fernandes is currently preparing an all-India database on population displacements from 1951 to 1995, and coordinating the work of NGOs in the search for alternatives to India rehabilitation policy and the Land Acquisition Act of 1894. Among his published books are *Development, Displacement and Rehabilitation: Issues for a National Debate* (with Enakshi Ganguly Thukral, ed., 1989), *Development, Displacement and Rehabilitation in the Tribal Areas of Orissa* (with Anthony Raj, 1992), and *Development, Induced Displacement and Rehabilitation in Orissa 1951-1995: A Database on Its Nature and Extent* (with Mohammed Asif, 1997).

Reginald Herbold Green is a professorial fellow of the Institute of Development Studies (Sussex), and has been a student of the applied political economy of Africa for nearly 40 years. He has worked, researched, taught, or advised in more than 30 African countries and published extensively. His concern with displacees and with food security arises from his concern with reduction of poverty by the empowerment of poor households and with the provision of basic services integral to sustainable development. His work relating to displacees has been in Tanzania, Mozambique, Namibia, Rwanda, Somalia/Somaliland, and — more tangentially — Angola and Ethiopia.

Roxanne Hakim is an anthropologist, a graduate of the University of Bombay with a Ph.D. from the University of Cambridge. Her research has focused on resettlement and identity, particularly in relation to the Sardar Sarovar Dam in India. She has worked in evaluation of poverty alleviation programs in southern Africa. In 1999, she joined the staff of the World Bank in Washington, D.C., through its Young Professionals Program.

Barbara Harrell-Bond is a research lecturer at the University of Oxford and founding director (1982-1996) of its Refugee Studies Programme. She began her career as an anthropologist conducting research in an urban housing estate near Oxford. She earned a diploma in social anthropology, an M. Litt. and D. Phil. from the University of Oxford. As a member of the Department of Anthropology, University of Edinburgh, she carried out her first research in Africa in 1967, examining marriage among professional groups in Sierra Leone. On the basis of this research she went on to specialize in anthropology of law, joining the Faculty of Law at the University of Warwick. In 1982, she began research on the delivery of humanitarian assistance, particularly by the United Nations and its agencies, and on international and human rights law, especially as it affects refugees, asylum seekers, and other displaced groups, and development, gender, and ethnicity issues. The majority of her research has been conducted in Africa, but she has also carried out fieldwork in the Middle East and in central and southern Europe. In 1996, she was awarded the Distinguished Service Award by the American Anthropological Association.

Renée Hirschon was for many years senior lecturer in anthropology at Oxford Brookes University and, until 1998, a professor of social anthropology at the University of the Aegean. She is currently a research associate with the Refugee Studies Programme, University of Oxford, and honorary research fellow at Oxford Brookes University.

Gaim Kibreab received his PhD. from Uppsala University. He has published extensively on involuntary migration, resettlement, the environment, and refugee issues, as well as on repatriation. He is the author of *People on the Edge in the Horn: Displacement, Land-Use and the Environment* (1996). Dr. Kibreab's current research is on post-conflict reconstruction and reintegration of returnees, internally displaced persons, and demobilized former combatants in Eritrea. He is affiliated with and teaches at South Bank University, London.

Dolores Koenig is associate professor of anthropology at the American University in Washington, D.C. She served as senior social science adviser for Mali's Manantali Resettlement Project and has worked on a wide variety of other development projects. She is co-author, with Tiéman Diarra and Moussa Sow, of *Innovation and Individuality in African Development: Changing Production Strategies in Rural Mali*. She has also written a number of articles including "Women and Resettlement," *Women and International Development Annual* (Vol. 4), and "Competition among Malian Elites in the Manantali Resettlement Project: The Impacts on Local Development."

Véronique Lassailly-Jacob is a French geographer and research fellow at the National Council for Scientific Research in Paris. Her field research includes forced migration and rural development in Africa. She specializes in the study of land-resettlement schemes implemented for involuntary migrants.

L. K. Mahapatra, formerly vice chancellor of Utkal and Sambalpur Universities in India, is professor emeritus of anthropology at Utkal University, a visiting professor at Hamburg University, and a visiting fellow of the Ford Foundation in Indonesia. He is currently a member of the UNESCO-affiliated International Commission on Anthropology in Policy and Practice, and Anthropological Aspects of Global Environment Change, and president of the Anthropological Society of Orissa. He has published widely on a range of issues including rural development and resettlement. Recent work includes *Tribal Development: Myth and Reality* (1994) and *Development for the Underprivileged* (1999).

Sheela Mahapatra received a masters degree in anthropology from Utkal University and is a doctoral candidate at the University of Oxford. She has published various anthropological articles with a focus on rights systems and entitlement to natural resources.

Christopher McDowell is a social anthropologist and social development consultant, currently lecturing on resettlement at the University of Wollongong, Australia. He has been associated with the Resettlement Studies Programme at the University of Oxford, and worked in Ethiopia from 1997 to 1999. He has done extensive field-work in southern and east Africa and in Western Europe, specializing in involuntary displacement and resettlement, return, reintegration, and rehabilitation following emergencies, and in the linkages between migration and sustainable rural livelihoods. His published volumes include *A Tamil Asylum Diaspora: Sri Lankan Migration, Politics and Settlement in Switzerland* (1996), *Migration and Sustainable Livelihoods: A Critical Review of the Literature* (with Arjan de Haan, 1997). He has also edited *Understanding Impoverishment: the consequences of development-induced displacement* (1996) and *Restoring the Land: environment and change in post-apartheid South Africa* (with Mamphela Ramphele, 1992).

Sheilah Meikle is a senior lecturer at London's University College Development Planning Unit. She is a sociologist and town planner with extensive experience in Asia, Africa, and the Middle East. She has undertaken work for a wide range of national and international agencies and organizations. In recent years, this has included training, research, and consultancy assignments in China.

María Clara Mejía, an anthropologist, is an independent consultant. Until 1999 she worked as a resettlement specialist in the Environment Unit of the World Bank's Latin America and Caribbean region office, carrying out operational activities in countries throughout Latin America. Prior to joining the World Bank, she was head of the Unit of Planning and Socio-Economic Studies in the Environment Office of the National Electricity Authority of Colombia. Ms. Mejia was trained in economics and energy planning at the Universidad de Medellin, Colombia and the Instituto de Economica Energetica in Bariloche, Argentina. She received her masters degree in anthropology from Catholic University in Washington, D.C. Ms. Mejia has written several papers on social and environmental aspects of development projects in Latin America.

Ranjit Nayak is a researcher in the Department of Social Anthropology at the University of Cambridge. He is currently working on an examination of the rhetoric of human rights in India. Previous research and publications have focused on displacement and resettlement, indigenous people, poverty, and human rights.

I. U. B. Reddy is a resettlement specialist in the Social Development Unit of the World Bank in New Delhi. He was previously on the staff of the Unit for Urban Studies, Tata Institute of Social Sciences,

Bombay. Dr Reddy obtained his masters and PhD. degrees in regional planning from the Indian Institute of Technology, Kharagpur (India), and an additional masters degree in sociology from Sri Venktreswara University, Tirupathi (India). His research interest is in displacement and resettlement issues, urban problems, and regional development, and he has authored two books on displacement and resettlement.

Christian Sørensen is a development worker specializing in participatory methodologies within development planning and management. He has worked in Tanzania and in Eritrea (1993-1998), where he was responsible for ACORD's program work along the rehabilitation-development continuum with returnees and ex-fighters. He is currently working for Africa Now, a British non-governmental organization, in The Gambia on developing a methodological handbook on village banking.

Eftihia Voutira is an associate professor of anthropology in the Department of Balkan, East European, and Middle East Studies at the University of Macedonia in Greece. She is also a research officer at the School of Geography and a research associate at the Refugee Studies Programme, University of Oxford. As a member of the Refugee Studies Programme she has taught and conducted extensive research on issues of refugee identity, forced migration, and humanitarian assistance in Eastern Europe and the former Soviet Union. She is the author of numerous articles, encyclopaedia entries, and reports on refugees, forced migration, repatriation, and humanitarian emergencies.

Wolde-Selassie Abutte is a doctoral candidate in social anthropology at the Institute of Ethnology, University of Göttingen, Germany. His research has focused on the socioeconomic impacts of rural resettlement in Metekel in western Ethiopia. Over the last decade he has completed consultancy assignments in Ethiopia for non-governmental organization and the government on rehabilitation, relief, and language issues. His publications include articles on agriculture and horticulture in resettlement sites, socioeconomic differentiation, and household food security.

Youxuan Zhu is an independent architect and urban planner. He has worked for five years with the World Bank's China department. He has participated in preparing and supervising various World Bank-assisted projects in China, focusing on issues of environmental planning, resettlement policy, urban transport, urban construction, and urban land-market development.

Reconstructing resettlers' and refugees' livelihoods

Michael M. Cernea and Christopher McDowell

The present volume offers for international discussion the first multidimensional comparative analysis of two large groups of the world's displaced populations: resettlers uprooted by development and refugees fleeing military conflicts or natural calamities. The volume's co-authors — academics and practitioners from both fields — have joined up to explore common central issues: the condition of being "displaced," the risks of impoverishment and destitution, the rights and entitlements of those uprooted, and, most important, the means of *reconstruction of their livelihoods*.

Refugee populations are generated by wars, civil conflicts, ethnic persecutions, or famines and other natural disasters. These populations often cross national borders and become international refugees within a different country. Recently, however, as borders have become less porous, many remain inside national borders and are defined as "internal refugees," or internally displaced people.

Involuntary resettlers are those uprooted by development-inducing programs, such as infrastructure construction for industrial estates, dams and reservoirs, highways, ports and airports, and urban transportation networks. They typically remain inside national borders. Both groups are subsets of a wider category defined by the encompassing concept of "displaced populations."

For decades, the concepts of "human rights," "social justice," and "social inclusion" have not been even uttered in mainstream development discourse. Recently, however, these concepts have started finding their way into the public forum, influencing policies for development and poverty reduction. *"We must act,"* stated the president of the World Bank, *"so that poverty will be alleviated, our environment protected, social justice extended, human rights strengthened. Social injustice can destroy economic and political advances"* (Wolfensohn, 1995). The "new development paradigm" explicitly departs from the limitations of the past "Washington consensus" with its "narrow focus on economics," replacing it explicitly with development defined as "social transformation": "The new development strategy takes as its core objective the transformation of society... (which) will not only raise GDP per capita, but also living standards, ...health and literacy, will reduce poverty, ...will be sustainable, strengthening the environment and ensuring real societal transformation" (Stiglitz 1999). Within such a development perspective, resettlement and the reestablishment of refugee livelihoods are domains in which affirming human rights, extending social justice, and promoting inclusion instead of exclusion gain prominence on the policy agenda.

The world's interest in both population categories—forced resettlers and refugees—each numbering in the tens of millions, has considerably increased during the last two decades. Contrary to the expectations of many, a world that was supposed to grow increasingly more stable and more peaceful keeps erupting in numerous local wars between countries, civil wars within countries, genocidal ethnic massacres, vicious religious persecutions, not to mention natural calamities with disastrous human consequences—all generating wave after wave of refugees. According to recent statistics, there are some 30 million refugees and persons in refugee-like situations in the world. Also contrary to expectations, development programs that are supposed to widely improve living standards have also brought, under the wings of progress, the forced displacement of millions and millions of poor and vulnerable people in many of the world's developing countries, inducing impoverishment and hardships. The number of persons involuntarily displaced and resettled by infrastructural development projects during the last 10 years is between 90 and 100 million.

Responding to the international concerns about the world's growing numbers of forced resettlers and refugees, many governments and international organizations have strengthened during the last decade their policies and assistance programs in this area. All 29 developed country members of the Organization for Economic Cooperation and Development (OECD) have adopted the same set of unified policy guidelines regarding the involuntary resettlement of people under their aid agencies' projects (OECD 1992). The

Copenhagen World Summit for Social Development has incorporated the call to reestablish resettlers' and refugees' livelihoods and rights into its special Program of Action (United Nations 1995). In turn, the World Bank, after having formulated the first international policy on resettlement (1980), has strengthened this policy with new provisions (World Bank 1986, 1988, 1990, 1994, 1998). It also has moved forcefully into refugee assistance work, in partnership with the United Nations High Commissioner for Refugees (UNHCR), providing increased support for the sustainable reconstruction of countries emerging from periods of conflict.

Post-conflict reconstruction "is not an issue we can relegate to the sidelines of development....The Bank and its partners must begin to ask hard questions about how we can best integrate a concern for conflict prevention into development operations....The rationale for Bank action is a simple one: We will not have peace without economic hope" (Wolfensohn 1998).

The Bank has defined its institutional and financial role in reconstruction and has also helped carry out and publish significant research on refugees and involuntary resettlement, such as the important statement *Post-Conflict Reconstruction: The Role of the World Bank* (1998) and policy and field studies (World Bank 1994; OED 1995; Colletta and others 1996a, 1996b; Cernea 1988, 1991, 1999).

Important academic, policy, and operational research on forced population displacements has been carried out by many institutions and agencies, such as the UNHCR, the United Nations Research Institute for Social Development (UNRISD), and the Brookings Institution (Cohen and Deng 1998a, 1998b), while the world's principal hub for such research has been the Refugee Studies Programme (RSP) of the University of Oxford. The RSP has developed a vast program of field investigations and a special series of research publications on refugees.

Responding to burning policy and practical issues, the RSP, with co-sponsorship from the World Bank and other institutions, hosted in 1995 and 1996 two major international conferences dedicated to development-caused involuntary resettlement. The initial results of this effort were presented publicly in the volume *Understanding Impoverishment – The Consequences of Development-Induced Displacement*, edited by Christopher McDowell (Berghahn Books, 1996). The volume explored why and how resettlers get impoverished; it also highlighted emerging patterns of collective opposition to displacement. Soon, the book became a working tool for many researchers. It contributed to increasing the international awareness about the inequities and drama of involuntary resettlement.

The present book is a logical continuation of prior research and an effort to cover new territory. For the first time in international literature, it considers the two large groups of displaced populations, resettlers and refugees, in a systematic comparative way.

The purpose of the large, international group of scholars and practitioners who produced this book is twofold: first, to explore the possible synergies between the two fields — refugee research and resettlement research; second, to focus on the *reconstruction segment* of the displacement-relocation continuum, usually less examined in the scholarly literature. These two goals present significant intellectual challenges.

The book brings to the dialogue a vast amount of new ethnographic material, resulting from new empirical research, and numerous original conceptualizations. Between them, the co-authors report direct field findings from places as diverse as China, India, Ethiopia, Colombia, Argentina, Greece, Sub-Saharan Africa, Azerbaijan, and many other countries. The main focus is on developing countries, but experiences from middle-range and developed countries are also discussed.

Historically, research on displaced populations has focused primarily on reporting failures and the plight of those uprooted. It has been much less interested in the few experiences of successful relocation. By design, this volume has embarked on a complementary effort: while highlighting displacement's negative effects, it deliberately directs more analysis to successful approaches in the reconstruction of livelihoods. The lens is trained on how refugees and resettlers struggle with the risks and hardships of their displacement, trying to reestablish themselves. This deliberate search responds to the need to find and disseminate problem-resolution tools for institutions and practitioners.

To provide intellectual unity to this volume, the editors and authors have generally followed two principles. The first principle is *methodological*: pursuing a comparative approach between refugees' and resettlers' situations and activities. The second principle is *theoretical*: using a common set of concepts as a framework to help interpret and focus on substantive comparisons between similar variables.

As this book demonstrates, there are significant differences between refugees and resettlers. But there are also many similarities in their situations once they are uprooted and on their paths to recovery. The debate in this volume aims to reveal both, not to reduce the two to simplified common denominators. *Differences* are important because it is on their basis that diverse innovative approaches to coping and recovery emerge, and these approaches can possibly be "transferred" in adjusted forms. *Similarities* are equally important because frequently there is more than one solution to the same problem and there is much to gain from exchanging knowledge on various solutions against similar obstacles.

But along which variables should *refugees'* and *resettlers'* situations be compared? This question was answered by using a theoretical model of displacement and resettlement. This is "the impoverishment risks and reconstruction (IRR) model for resettling displaced populations," described in detail in the first chapter and subsequently discussed throughout the book. Significantly, the model itself evolved recently and was enriched through international debate. Initially, when published previously (see Cernea 1996), the model's emphasis was on identifying the impoverishment risks. The present volume goes further, elaborating on the second part of the model that captures the reconstruction process, and defining the multiple functions that can be played by this general model.

The impoverishment risks and reconstruction model provides the conceptual architecture for this volume's organization. Impoverishment is a sincretic and multidimensional process. The model first deconstructs it into its fundamental components: *landlessness, joblessness, homelessness, marginalization, food insecurity, increased morbidity and mortality, loss of access to common property assets, and community disarticulation*. This analytical deconstruction facilitates the understanding of how these subprocesses interlink, influence, and amplify each other. Reconstruction, then, is a reversal of the impoverishment processes and can be understood and accomplished along the same variables, considered in a holistic, integrated way.

Following the main lines of this conceptual framework, the volume's chapters are grouped in several sections. The chapters are written by researchers or practitioners with specialized expertise in dealing with one or another population—refugees or resettlers. The authors often "cross the boundaries" into the other domain, advancing overarching typologies, drawing comparisons, and illuminating differences that cannot be subsumed or commonalities that can.

Part One contains two studies of a general theoretical nature, which set the stage for the following sections that deal with specific components of the reconstruction processes. The two studies articulate the conceptual and methodological premises for defining impoverishment and reconstruction, with respect to resettlers and refugees, respectively. The authors of the two opening studies, who are themselves specialized in each of the two domains (Michael

Cernea for resettlers and Barbara Harrell-Bond and Eftihia Voutira for refugees), call upon scholars in both areas to bridge their knowledge and join their efforts, while warning that the analytical and comparative tasks at hand are far from simple. Cernea's study outlines the magnitude and impacts of development-driven resettlement worldwide and describes the functions that the theoretical model can perform. Harrell-Bond and Voutira offer an overview of the global problem of refugees and emphasize that the *institutional* obstacles to reciprocal transfers of knowledge between refugee and resettlers' experiences are much bigger than the *conceptual* obstacles. The authors of this chapter find it "disheartening" to realize how few researchers have sought to compare refugees' and resettlers' experiences.

The subsequent seven parts of the volume are each dedicated to exploring one or another of the major process-variables for resisting impoverishment and reconstructing livelihoods. Since each section is preceded by a detailed editors' note, we will introduce them here only briefly.

Part Two discusses landlessness and strategies for land-based relocation, or alternatives when land is not available. Ranjit Nayak explores the anatomy of the land deprivation process through an in-depth case study of the Kisan population in India. Veronique Lassailly-Jacob offers a broad synthesis of experiences in Africa based on reestablishment of resettlers and refugees through large-scale land settlement schemes.

Part Three explores joblessness and reemployment options in papers by Sheilah Meikle and Zou Youxuan on resettlers in China and Maria Clara Mejía on the productive reintegration of a group of resettled brickmakers in Argentina. Institutional support for job creation appears essential, yet refugees tend to have less access or entitlement to this type of support than resettlers.

In Part Four, I.U.B. Reddy focuses on urban resettlement and the various urban categories of resettlers needing dwellings and land titles on their house plots, while Christian Sørensen provides a detailed discussion of house reconstruction by refugees. As the authors report the good experience from some new approaches, they also emphasize that home rebuilding, either by resettlers or returning refugees, is only a first step in culturally identifying with the new location and in reconstructing the social fabric of the new communities.

In Part Five, Walter Fernandes analyzes some of the processes occurring for both resettlers and refugees that are most difficult to define, from creeping marginalization of all kinds to social re-inclusion. Fernandes calls attention to not just the economic but also the psychological content of marginalization, showing their interaction as well, and emphasizes that to counteract marginalization, the project-affected people must be enabled to share in the project's benefits.

In Part Six, Roxanne Hakim and Reginald Green analyze the many facets of food insecurity, hunger, malnutrition, and the struggle of displacees to reestablish a sustainable food basis. Hakim explores the depths of one Gujarati population's struggle for its food, health, and livelihood, a struggle confronting a changed environment since, because of resettlement, the Vasava tribal group had to shift from its traditional production of corn and food crops to the new and riskier production of cotton for cash. Yet people live "not by bread alone," as Green writes; his study also discusses health care protection under displacement conditions and undertakes a broad synthesis of African experiences, embracing and comparing refugees and resettlers.

Part Seven is devoted to one of the most important yet least addressed components of displacement and reestablishment in developing countries: the access to assets under common property regime. Two wide-sweeping studies, by Gaim Kibreab and by Dolores Koenig and Tiéman Diarra, comprehensively document the social and economic complexities of losing, maintaining, or regaining access to such resources for both refugees and resettlers. The authors review the theoretical debate about the nature of common property of certain natural resources and their management. Kibreab also develops at length the argument for using the risk and reconstruction model for refugee populations, not only for resettlers, since relevant commonalties between the two populations make such use methodologically legitimate and theoretically advantageous. Governments that overlook the essential importance of commonly owned assets, and typically do not compensate them, will find in these studies a strong argument to reconsider their procedures.

Part Eight brings together many strands that, for analytical purposes, have been addressed distinctly in previous sections. Its four chapters begin with the analysis of social disarticulation and move to what is most difficult both to achieve in practice and to study empirically—social re-articulation. Jonathan Brown addresses reconstruction processes for post-conflict refugees in an integrative manner, highlighting the most important elements of institutional and agency cooperation in carrying out organized reconstruction. Renée Hirshon describes the successful experiences of Greek refugees in an urban community who, despite the odds, have rebuilt their social networks and their well-being. Wolde-Selassie Abutte, in turn, analyzes social re-articulation after resettlement. He focuses on the sociocultural changes in the Beles Valley of Ethiopia, where involuntary resettlers, against even harder odds, have made remarkable progress not only in coping and surviving, but also in rebuilding voluntary associations, re-articulating networks, and reviving community spirit and practices. And a joint study by Lakshman Mahapatra and Sheila Mahapatra concludes the volume with an integrated examination of a resettled community, analyzing how the various components of reconstruction complement each other and converge in a little-known case of successful relocation.

The authors' analyses in the different sections of the volume are interlinked, cross-referenced, and sometimes overlapping, because neither the impoverishment risks nor the reconstruction processes could be treated without these connections. Understanding them is deepened by grasping their interconnection. And the practical attainment of reconstruction objectives depends on integrative, rather than insular, approaches.

Throughout the volume, the contributors place the reader in a position to weigh comparable experiences and sometimes different viewpoints. The basic aims of bringing two perspectives to the forum are to foster complementarity and to avoid reducing one set of problems to the other. There are remarkable coincidences between the co-authors on many issues, and there are also differences in some of the views advanced for public discussion, fostering further debate.

The authors and editors believe that this volume is an important step toward better communication and mutual enrichment of perspectives. The volume also reflects research that has recently made significant progress in the two fields, yet still has apparent unevenness.

We regard this volume as the beginning, not the end, of the dialogue. We hope this work will be seen as the start of a longer intellectual journey, to which we are inviting all those studying resettlement and refugee problems.

PART ONE

Refugees and resettlers:
theoretical considerations

Risks, safeguards, and reconstruction: a model for population displacement and resettlement

Michael M. Cernea

> *We must act so that poverty will be alleviated, our environment protected, social justice extended, human rights strengthened. Social injustice can destroy economic and political advances.*

> *James D. Wolfensohn*

During the last two decades of the previous century, the magnitude of forced population displacements caused by development programs was on the order of 10 million people each year, or some 200 million people globally during that period. Thus, by their frequency, size, and dire consequences, development-caused displacements have become a problem of worldwide proportions.

Social justice and forced displacements

Compulsory displacements that occur for development reasons embody a perverse and intrinsic contradiction in the context of development. They raise major ethical questions because they reflect an inequitable distribution of development's benefits and losses.

Forced displacement results from the need to build infrastructure for new industries, irrigation, transportation highways, or power generation, or for urban developments such as hospitals, schools, and airports. Such programs are indisputably needed. They improve many people's lives, provide employment, and supply better services. But the involuntary displacements caused by such programs also create major impositions on some population segments. They restrict that population's rights by state-power intervention and are often carried out in ways that cause the affected populations to end up worse off. This raises major issues of social justice and equity. The principle of the "greater good for the larger numbers," routinely invoked to rationalize forced displacements, is, in fact, often abused and turned into an unwarranted justification for tolerating ills that are avoidable. The outcome is an unjustifiable repartition of development's costs and benefits: some people enjoy the gains of development, while others bear its pains.

The most widespread effect of involuntary displacement is the impoverishment of considerable numbers of people. In India, for instance, researchers found that the country's development programs have caused an aggregate displacement of more than 20 million people during roughly four decades, but that 75 percent of these people have *not* been "rehabilitated" (Fernandes 1991; Fernandes, Das, and Rao 1989). Their livelihoods have not been restored; in fact, the vast majority of development resettlers in India have become impoverished (Mahapatra 1999b).

But this does not happen in India alone. Such impoverishment, with its de facto lack of social justice and equity, is manifest in numerous other countries throughout the developing world when involuntary resettlement occurs. Material and cultural losses in each case are vast. No less serious a consequence is the political tension that accompanies forced relocation. Forced displacement epitomizes social exclusion of certain groups of people. It cumulates physical exclusion from a geographic territory with economic and social exclusion out of a set of functioning social networks. The concept of exclusion (Rodgers, Gore, and Figueiredo 1995) adds to the understanding of impoverishment. Sen (1997) argues further that various forms of social exclusion are contrary to the very nature of development, defined as increasing freedom.

Development will continue, however, to require changes in land use and water use and thus make various degrees of population relocation at times unavoidable. Yet, this does not mean that the inequitable *distribution* of development's gains and pains is itself inevitable, or ethically justified. Such inequity is, in fact, profoundly contrary to the proclaimed goals of induced development. There is no reason to accept spatial rearrangements and their pernicious consequences with resignation as an ineluctable tragedy. Adherence to social justice and equity norms and respect for civil rights and people's entitlements should remain paramount whenever development brings about risks and exacts predictable tolls.

If impoverishment is the looming risk in displacement, the challenge is to organize risk prevention and provide safeguards. This can increase the benefits of development by eliminating some of its avoidable pathologies. It may not be feasible to prevent every single adverse effect. But it is certainly possible to put in place sets of procedures, backed up by financial resources, that would increase equity in bearing the burden of loss and in the distribution of benefits. It is certainly possible, under enlightened policies, to protect much more effectively then current practices do the civil rights, human dignity, and economic entitlements of those subject to involuntary relocation.

The conventional planning approaches that cause many to be displaced and allow only a few to be "rehabilitated" do not adequately protect against risks and loss of entitlements and rights. Without social safety measures, they have led to recurrent failures. In most cases, they have been incapable of preventing the victimization, decapitalization, and impoverishment of those affected. But the repeated instances of resettlement without rehabilitation point sharply also to congenital defects in the current domestic *policies* of many countries, not just in the planning procedures. We argue that such "development" policies, and the resulting planning methodologies, must be corrected or changed.

There are practical ways to fully avoid specific instances of involuntary displacement, or at least to decrease their magnitude. Although, historically speaking, relocations (as a class of processes) are unavoidable, not every individual case of displacement proposed by planners is either inevitable or justified. Further, even when displacement is planned, mass impoverishment itself is not a necessary outcome and therefore should not be tolerated as inexorable. There are many ways to reduce displacement's hazards and adverse socioeconomic effects.

Redressing the inequities caused by displacement and enabling affected people to share in the benefits of growth are not just possible but imperative, on both economic and moral grounds. Socially responsible resettlement — that is, resettlement genuinely guided by an equity compass — can counteract lasting impoverishment and generate benefits for both the national and local economy. Yet, much too often, those who approve and design projects causing displacement are deprived of an "equity compass" that can guide them in allocating project resources and preventing (or mitigating) the risks of impoverishment (Cernea 1986, 1988, 1996b; Mahapatra 1991;

Scudder 1981). In an attempt to help develop such an equity compass, this chapter proposes a risks-and-reconstruction-oriented
framework for resettlement operations. It argues against some chronic
flaws in the policies and methodologies for planning and financing
resettlement and recommends necessary improvements in policy and
in mainstream resettlement practices.

A model of risks and risk avoidance

We present below a theoretical model for involuntary resettlement
that highlights the intrinsic risks that cause impoverishment through
displacement, as well as the ways to counteract—eliminate or mitigate—these risks. This conceptual model is defined as the *impoverishment risks and reconstruction model for resettling displaced populations.*
In elaborating this IRR model, the aim has been (a) to explain what
happens during massive forced displacements—a task very important in itself, and (b) to create a theoretical and safeguarding tool
capable of guiding policy, planning, and actual development programs to counteract these adverse effects. We believe that this impoverishment risks and reconstruction (IRR) model substantively
adds to the tools of explaining, diagnosing, predicting, and planning for development and thus helps create the knowledge compass needed for complex resettlement situations.

In presenting the impoverishment risks and livelihood reconstruction framework, we first emphasize the need for theoretical modeling in resettlement research and briefly review prior models. We
also raise the issue of commonalities between refugee and resettlement situations and the possible application of this resettlement
framework in refugee research as well. Second, we define the four
basic functions of this model, and, further, identify and document
the principal risks of impoverishment one by one. In the next section, we turn the model on its head, to argue that it intrinsically
points the way to risk reversals and can guide strategies for reestablishing resettlers' livelihoods, based on an "economics of recovery." The last part of this chapter compares some of the current
mainstream resettlement practices and analytical methods with the
new model proposed, and recommends ways to improve resettlement practice and research.

Over the years, students of planned human settlements on new
lands have proposed several conceptual frameworks to describe
planned settlement processes. By the late 1960s, Chambers (1969)
identified a three-stage general model in the evolution of land settlement schemes in Africa. Soon after, Nelson (1973) confirmed this

pattern in a synthesis of many experiences with new land settlements in Latin America. Both models — Chambers' and Nelson's — generalized the experience of voluntary settlers and conceptualized the institutional or organizational dimensions of managed land-settlement programs.

Building upon these earlier concepts, Scudder and Colson formulated in 1982 a theoretical model of settlement processes distinguishing four, rather than three, stages: recruitment, transition, development, and incorporation or handing over. The Scudder-Colson diachronic framework was built around the key concept of "stage"; it focused on settlers' stress and their specific behavioral reactions in each stage. Initially, the model was formulated to apply to *voluntary* settlement processes. Subsequently, Scudder extended it to some *involuntary* resettlement processes as well, but only to those involuntary relocations that succeed and move through all four stages, as the model is not intended to apply to resettlement operations that fail and do not complete the last two stages.

Moving to the domain of refugee studies proper, we find the conceptual framework for interpreting refugee situations proposed by Emmanuel Marx (1990). This model was grounded in the sociological theory of networks and centered on what its author termed "the social world of refugees."

From one theoretical framework to the other, these attempts to distill accumulated knowledge into patterns and conceptual models have created intellectual tools that helped many researchers to interpret their particular field findings. They have helped distinguish regularities and build theories on settlement processes. Beyond their merits, however, these models were less productive in some important respects. None of these models has placed at its center the onset of impoverishment, its unfolding, and the process of escaping impoverishment. Among the conceptual models mentioned above, only one, the Scudder-Colson model, addressed involuntary resettlements as well, and it did so only for cases of successful resettlement. Historically, however, the majority of involuntary resettlement operations have been unsuccessful. The cumulative impacts of failed resettlements were not "modeled" in the Scudder-Colson framework of stages.

There has been further discussion in the literature (de Wet 1988, Partridge 1989) around these conceptual models — yet certainly not enough, as Scudder (1996) rightly observed. But there was, and is, a broad consensus on the need to persevere in searching for theoretical constructs that explain and illuminate the complexities of resettlement.

The call for developing a more comprehensive theoretical model was perhaps voiced strongest by Brenchin, West, and associates (1991) in their massive volume on the displacement of resident populations from nature conservation parks. The authors maintained that many development decisions that involve involuntary relocation are made without the full anticipation of the general impact pattern triggered. Calling for a model that would define and predict the *cumulative* impacts of displacement and would provide a practical guide, they wrote:

> *What is too little understood both by professionals and scholars alike is the social impact of displacement and relocation. When resident peoples are forced to move, certain general impacts can be expected. But the collective social impact on the community or other social organizations differs widely from case to case; to date no model exists to predict the cumulative effect (1991:17).*

The impoverishment risks and reconstruction framework presented in this chapter aims precisely at rendering these "cumulative effects" analytically understandable, both distinctly and in their interconnection. It does so by modeling the constitutive subprocesses of displacement and the mechanisms for "influencing" them — that is, for preventing or eliminating them through deliberate action. The IRR model builds upon, and further advances, the prior modeling efforts summarized above.

The IRR model has been formulated and developed relatively recently, during the 1990s, in a series of studies (Cernea 1990, 1995b, 1996a, 1998, and 1999; World Bank 1994). A preliminary version was first applied on a wide scale in the resettlement review of almost 200 projects carried out by the World Bank in 1993–1994 (World Bank 1994). The origin of this model is both empirical and theoretical. Empirically, it is derived from the extraordinary accumulation of factual findings during the last quarter century, reported by resettlement studies in many countries. Theoretically, it benefits from the new state-of-the-art achieved by resettlement research during the same period.[1]

---

[1]   The state-of-the-art in resettlement research, and the main areas of recent progress in the knowledge of resettlement, are discussed in more detail in Cernea, 1999; see also the "Annotated Bibliography" on involuntary resettlement published by Guggenheim, 1994. Since the publication of this bibliography in 1994, the resettlement literature has continued to grow explosively.

Similarities in refugee and resettlement situations

The IRR model has been embraced and applied in a number of studies and in some operational resettlement activities, as will be shown in the last part of this chapter. However, a question raised recently is whether this model, initially defined for resettlement caused by development programs, can provide research advantages in studying refugee displacements as well.[2] This question came up in the context of efforts and trends towards bridge-building between the two key research domains concerned with displaced population — the research on refugees and the research on development — resettlers; trends that are clearly getting stronger and gaining ground. Indeed, both involuntary resettlers (displaced by development projects) and refugees fleeing violence (wars or armed civil conflicts) confront many strikingly similar social and economic problems. These two groups are the largest subsets of displaced populations worldwide. Research currently carried out separately on resettlement and postconflict reconstruction stands to gain substantial knowledge by breaking out of separation and insularity.[3]

In order to bring these two domains closer, it would be necessary, first, to develop within each more theory building. Abstracting the general from the particular and the individual will help to illuminate what is common in these two categories of situations and people. Each domain must strive to develop overarching concepts, inventories of findings, structured comparisons, and theoretical models as intellectual stepping-stones toward such knowledge articulation (Cernea 1996a). There are also institutional difficulties to overcoming such a reciprocal transfer of knowledge, as Harrell-Bond and

---

[2]   The discussion about using and expanding the IRR model to the condition of refugees was started at the Oxford International Conference of 1996 on Resettlement and Refugees. It continues in this volume in several chapters, conceptually linked to the present chapter, that analyze the impoverishment risks and social disarticulation affecting both populations. Such discussion is enriching the knowledge about both subsets of displaced populations.

[3]   This potential for gains is fourfold. *Empirically*, the two bodies of research could enrich each other by comparing their factual findings. *Theoretically*, they could broaden their conceptualizations by exploring links and similarities between their sets of variables. *Methodologically*, they could sharpen their inquiry by borrowing and exchanging research techniques. And *politically*, they could influence the public arena more strongly by mutually reinforcing their policy advocacy and operational recommendations.

Voutira correctly point out (see this volume) with reference to the practices of major international agencies. But this does not reduce the role of scholars in striving for knowledge integration: in fact, it increases this role. Taking a comparative perspective, Harrell-Bond and Voutira also highlight the challenge and the difficulties of "arriving at a theoretical model of resettlement which applies to different situations of forced migration—those resulting from impoverishment, civil strife, or 'development' projects which uproot populations." Voutira and Harrell-Bond emphasize that impoverishment is a "consequence of virtually all types of displacement.... methodologically [impoverishment] allows for a common denominator in refugee and oustee experience." Yet because the causes of impoverishment and the definition of "success" are not the same, it is necessary to keep score of the differences.

Indeed, the issue is not to take one conceptual framework and "apply" or transpose it *tale-quale* elsewhere, on another category of processes.[4] The challenge is to test the value-added it provides as a research tool and use it creatively for throwing light on other processes as well. In this spirit, Kibreab (see this volume) argues that the impoverishment risks and reconstruction model is a relevant tool for refugee-related research and practical relief work. "In spite of the ostensible dissimilarities between oustees' and refugees' situations," Kibreab writes, "a closer examination of the issues reveals that the so-called differences do not limit the scope of the model, but, rather, make it compellingly relevant."

Four basic functions of the model

The impoverishment risks and reconstruction model focuses on the social and economic content of both segments of the process: the forced displacement and the reestablishment. The model is essentially synchronic, in that it captures processes that are simultaneous,

---

[4]   In this chapter I do not propose to explore in detail the extent to which this conceptual framework can provide investigative advantages in studying refugee displacements as well. I believe that there is considerable potential for this extension, if mechanical "application" of the model is avoided. Occasionally, however, I will point out similarities between resettlers and refugees, which invite a systematic exploration of this model's potential. Specialists in refugee studies are even better placed to test the model and determine, with adequate adjustments, if or how it can help account for refugees' risks and postconflict recovery.

but it also reflects the movement in time from the destitution of displacement to recovery in resettlement.

At the core of the model are three fundamental concepts: *risk*, *impoverishment*, and *reconstruction*. These "building blocks" are further split into sets of specifying notions, as will be shown, each reflecting another dimension, or variable, of impoverishment or of reconstruction, (for example, landlessness, marginalization, morbidity, or social disarticulation). These variables are interlinked and influence each other: some play a primary role and others a derivative role in either impoverishment or reconstruction (largely as a function of given circumstances). Introducing these interlinked concepts considerably broadens the theoretical discourse on resettlement processes, thus helping to illuminate better its nature, inner linkages, pathologies, and socioeconomic remedies.

So constructed, the conceptual framework captures the dialectic between *potential* risk and *actuality*. All forced displacements are prone to major socioeconomic risks, *but not fatally condemned to succumb to them.*

We use the sociological concept of risk[5] to indicate the *possibility* that a certain course of action will trigger future injurious effects — losses and destruction (Giddens 1990). The concept of risk is posited as a counter-concept to security (Luhman 1993): the higher the risks, the lower the security of the displaced populations. Risks are often directly perceptible, and also measurable through science (Adams 1998), as they are an objective reality. The cultural construction of a risk — be it a social risk or a natural risk — could emphasize or deemphasize (belittle) its seriousness, or could also ignore it, but this does not change the objective existence of risks (Stallings 1995).

The modeling of displacement risks results from deconstructing the syncretic, multifaceted process of displacement into its identifiable, principal, and most widespread components. These are:

---

[5]   The literature on "risk" is vast and growing, and the modern society itself is more and more defined as the "risk society" (Beck 1990). Frequently the terms "risk" and "danger," or "hazard" and "danger," or "hazard" and "risk" are used as interchangeable and overlapping. Some sociologists (for example, Giddens 1990) explicitly reject the distinction between risk and danger. Other researchers, however, argue that in some situations a difference exists, and define risk as the probability of an injurious effect resulting from a hazard (Kaplan and Garrick 1981). Consonant with most of the current risk literature, risk may be defined as the possibility embedded in a certain course of social action to trigger adverse effects (losses, destruction, functionally counterproductive impacts, deprivation of future generations, and so on).

a. Landlessness
b. Joblessness
c. Homelessness
d. Marginalization
e. Food insecurity
f. Increased morbidity
g. Loss of access to common property resources
h. Community disarticulation.

Each will be further examined in turn.

Most important is the internal logic of the model. It suggests that preventing or overcoming the pattern of impoverishment would require risk reversal. This can be accomplished through targeted strategies, backed up by adequate financing. Turning the model on its head shows which strategies must be adopted and which directions should be taken:

a. From landlessness to land-based resettlement
b. From joblessness to reemployment
c. From homelessness to house reconstruction
d. From marginalization to social inclusion
e. From increased morbidity to improved health care
f. From food insecurity to adequate nutrition
g. From loss of access to restoration of community assets and services
h. From social disarticulation to networks and community rebuilding.

The model's dual emphasis — on risks to be prevented *and* on reconstruction strategies to be implemented — facilitates its operational use as a guide for action. Like other models, its components can be influenced and "manipulated" through informed planning, in order to diminish the impact of one or several components, as given conditions require or permit. That requires considering these variables as a system, in their mutual connections, not as a set of separate elements.

Understanding the linkages among these variables enables decisionmakers to trigger chain effects and synergies in mitigating or remedial actions. As a conceptual template, the model is also flexible, allowing for the integration of other dimensions when relevant and for adaptation to changing circumstances.

Beyond individual projects, this framework can be employed in general policy formulation. It can inform all the social actors in resettlement, namely governments and decisionmakers, social researchers, project designers, the resettlers themselves, implementation agencies, and other involved parties. This model can be linked with other conceptual frameworks, to achieve complementarity of perspectives and additional knowledge.

The four distinct but interlinked *functions* that the risks and reconstruction model performs are:

1. A predictive (warning and planning) function
2. A diagnostic (explanatory and assessment) function
3. A problem-resolution function, in guiding and measuring resettlers' reestablishment
4. A research function, in formulating hypotheses and conducting theory-led field investigations.

A brief characterization of each function, or capacity, is necessary.

The predictive function

The model's *predictive capacity* results from the in-depth knowledge of past processes stored and synthesized by the model. This knowledge helps predict likely problems "hidden" in the new situations: these are conceptualized as the eight major impoverishment risks. The predictions are, in fact, early warnings of major social pathologies likely to recur, warnings that can be issued long before the decision to displace is adopted. Thus, the model equips management and planners with a power to anticipate that is essential in planning for risk-avoidance or risk-reduction.

The practical utility of this function is that it enables both the planners and the would-be displacees to transparently recognize the risks in advance, search for alternatives to avoid displacement, and/or respond with mitigatory measures, bargaining strategies, and coping approaches. Governments, agencies, and planners that omit the explicit identification[6] of the risks in advance expose themselves, and the populations affected, to more unmitigated negative outcomes.

The diagnostic function

This refers to the capacity of the model to *explain* and *assess*, by converting the general prognosis into a specific on-the-ground diagnosis of the project situation at hand. The model functions as a cognitive tool for guiding assessment fieldwork and "weighing" the likely

---

6   Unfortunately, many agencies adopt an "ostrich position," burying their heads in ignorance by avoiding use of the tools of risk identification at the outset.

intensity (high? moderate? low?) of one or another impoverishment risk in a given context.

The practical utility of this diagnostic function is that it reveals — to policy officials, who decide on triggering displacements, and to the affected populations who incur the consequences — the socio-economic hazards and possible outcomes of the impending displacements. The specific risk assessment (diagnosis) supplies advance information and recommendations crucial for project preparation and planning of counter-risk measures.

The problem-resolution function

The *problem-resolution* capacity results from the model's analytical incisiveness and its explicit action orientation. The IRR model is formulated with awareness of the social actors in resettlement, their interaction, communication, and ability to contribute to resolution. To achieve problem resolution, the part of the model that identifies pauperization risks must be fully reversed, "stood on its head," as will be shown further. As a result, the practical utility of the model increases greatly by moving from prediction and diagnosis to prescription for action. The model becomes a compass for strategies to reconstruct resettlers' livelihoods, "pushing" beyond immediate relief mechanisms and making possible a redevelopment orientation.

The research function

For social researchers, the IRR model provides a conceptual scaffolding for conducting and organizing their theory-led fieldwork. The model stimulates the generation of hypotheses about relations between key variables in both displacement and relocation. It facilitates the exploration of mutual linkages of and the reciprocal reinforcement or weakening effects between related risks.

The research utility of the model comes from its ability to guide data collection in the field and coherently aggregate disparate empirical findings along the model's key variables. It also makes possible comparisons of responses to risks across cultures, countries, and time periods.

Major impoverishment risks in displacement

Despite the enormous diversity of project-specific situations, the empirical findings of many resettlement researchers reveal the presence of several basic regularities. Clear patterns emerge from this evidence. Comparing these empirical findings, we have identified eight common processes and constructed a general risk pattern. The convergent and cumulative effect of these processes is the rapid onset of impoverishment (Cernea 1990, 1995b). Before displacement actually begins, these processes are only impending social and economic risks. But if appropriate counteraction is not initiated, these potential hazards convert into actual impoverishment disasters.

These risks threaten not only the people displaced, they are risks incurred by the local (regional) economy as well, to which they may inflict major loss and disruption. Depending on local conditions, the intensity of individual risk varies. But pattern identification makes it possible *to predict that such risks are typical and are likely to emerge* in future comparable displacement situations.

A concise description of each fundamental risk follows, illustrated by some empirical evidence. Much additional evidence is provided by this volume's co-authors in subsequent chapters.[7]

Landlessness

Expropriation of land removes the main foundation upon which people's productive systems, commercial activities, and livelihoods are constructed. This is the principal form of decapitalization and pauperization of displaced people, as they lose both natural and man-made capital.

Unless the land basis of people's productive systems is reconstructed elsewhere, or replaced with steady income-generating employment, landlessness sets in and the affected families become impoverished. Nayak (see this volume) documents in detail how the Kisan tribe of Orissa, India, has been deprived of its lands, how land compensation failed to restore its land basis, and how landlessness not only set in, but also snowballed into other risks and losses to the tribe. From India's Rengali project, Ota (1996) reports that the percentage of landless families after relocation more than doubled—from 4.6 percent to 10.9 percent—while Reddy (1997) documents that in the coal mining displacements around Singrauli, the proportion of landless people skyrocketed from 20 percent before displacement to 72 percent afterward. A sociological study of Kenya's Kiambere Hydropower project found that farmers' average land holdings after resettlement dropped from 13 to 6 hectares;

---

[7]   The empirical evidence for each of the model's variables is enormous and abundantly available in the resettlement literature. For each variable of the model, I will refer only to selected significant field findings. (See also the extensive bibliography at the end of the present volume.)

their livestock was reduced by more than one-third; yields per hectare decreased by 68 percent for maize and 75 percent for beans. Family
income dropped from Ksh. 10,968 to Ksh. 1,976 – a loss of 82 percent
(Mburugu 1993; Cook 1993). In Indonesia, a survey by the Institute
of Ecology of Padjadjaran University (1989) around the Saguling reservoir found that resettled families' land ownership decreased by 47
percent and their income was halved. Similar evidence is available
from Brazil (Mougeot 1989). Findings from anthropological field
studies show that loss of land generally has far more severe consequences for farm families than the loss of the house.

Joblessness

*The risk of losing wage employment is very high both in urban and rural
displacements for those employed in enterprises, services, or agriculture.
Yet, creating new jobs is difficult and requires substantial investment.
Unemployment or underemployment among resettlers often endures long
after physical relocation has been completed.*

The previously employed may lose in three ways: in urban areas,
workers lose jobs in industry and services. In rural areas, landless
laborers lose access to work on land owned by others (leased or
sharecropped) and also lose the use of assets under common property regimes. Self-employed small producers – craftsmen, shopkeepers, and others – lose their small business. In the Madagascar Tana
Plain project in 1993, for example, those displaced who operated
private small enterprises – workshops, foodstalls, artisan units –
were not entitled to compensation and lost their place of business
and their customers. A survey carried out among tribal households
in five villages at Talcher, Orissa (Pandey 1996), found an increase
in unemployment from 9 percent to 43.6 percent, accompanied by a
large shift from primary to tertiary occupations (when available).
Reported reductions in levels of earnings were between 50 percent
and 80 percent among tribes and scheduled castes. Vocational re-
training, offered to some resettlers, can provide skills but not necessarily jobs. Similar findings come from developed countries. In the
Churchill-Nelson Hydro project in Manitoba, Canada, the economic
activities of resettled indigenous people – fisheries, waterfowl capture, fur processing – were curtailed; field studies found a significant increase in nonproductive time in the community.

Joblessness among resettlers often surfaces after a time delay,
rather than immediately, because in the short run resettlers may
receive employment in project-related jobs. Such employment, however, is short-lived and not sustainable. Evidence compiled from

several dam projects[8] shows that the "employment boom" created by new construction temporarily absorbs some resettlers, but severely drops toward the end of the project. This compounds the incidence of chronic or temporary joblessness among the displaced.

Homelessness

Loss of shelter tends to be only temporary for many resettlers; but, for some, homelessness or a worsening in their housing standards remains a lingering condition. In a broader cultural sense, loss of a family's individual home and the loss of a group's cultural space tend to result in alienation and status deprivation. For refugees, homelessness and "placelessness" are intrinsic by definition.

In the Cameroon-Douala Urban project, more than 2000 displaced families were hindered in their efforts to set up new permanent houses; less than 5 percent received loans to help pay for assigned house plots. According to reports from China's Danjiangkou reservoir project, about 20 percent of those relocated became homeless and destitute.[9] Violent destruction of shelters belonging to people labeled squatters is used in some places as a means to speed up evictions (for example, in Uganda in the Kibale Park area). When governments initiate compulsory villagization schemes and force people to resettle, families lose natural and man-made capital assets and tend to experience a lasting sense of placelessness (see evidence from South Africa reported by de Wet 1995; see also Low and Altman 1992, for the concept of "place attachment"). Resettlers' risk of worsening housing conditions increases if compensation for demolished dwellings is paid at assessed market value rather than replacement value.

Resettlers often cannot incur the labor and financial costs of rebuilding a house quickly and are compelled to move into "temporary" shelters. These resemble the condition of refugee camps, set up overnight. The "emergency housing centers" and "temporary relocation camps" used by some projects as a "temporary" backup (for example, the Upper Krishna dam and irrigation project in Karnataka, India) often make homelessness chronic rather than tem-

---

8   For example, the China-Gezhouba dam, Brazil-Tucurui dam, Turkey-Ataturk dam, Togo-Benin Nangbeto Hydropower dam, and Korea-Chungju dam.

9   China's tragic experiences with Danjiangkou and Sanmenxia Dam displacements in the 1960s and 1970s led to the adoption of new and better resettlement policies, policies that attempt to transform resettlement into an opportunity for development.

porary. At the Foum-Gleita irrigation project in Mauritania, only 200 out of the 881 displaced families successfully reconstructed their housing; the rest lived precariously for two years or longer in tents or under tarpaulins. In the Kukadi-Krishna irrigation subprojects in Maharashtra, India, 59 percent of the displaced families were found living in temporary or semipermanent houses 10 to 15 years after their relocation (Joseph 1998). Yet resettlers' risk of homelessness—related closely to joblessness, marginalization, and morbidity—can certainly be avoided by adequate project financing and timely preparation.

Marginalization

Marginalization occurs when families lose economic power and spiral on a "downward mobility" path. Middle-income farm households do not become landless, they become small landholders; small shopkeepers and craftsmen downsize and slip below poverty thresholds. Many individuals cannot use their earlier acquired skills at the new location; human capital is lost or rendered inactive or obsolete. Economic marginalization is often accompanied by social and psychological marginalization, expressed in a drop in social status, in resettlers' loss of confidence in society and in themselves, a feeling of injustice, and deepened vulnerability. The coerciveness of displacement and the victimization of resettlers tend to depreciate resettlers' self-image, and they are often perceived by host communities as a socially degrading stigma.

The facets of marginalization are multiple. The cultural status of displacees is belittled when they go to new relocation areas, where they are regarded as "strangers" and denied opportunities and entitlements. Psychological marginalization and its consequences (see a detailed discussion by Fernandes in this volume) are typically overlooked in resettlement planning. Yet, cultural and behavioral impairments, anxiety, and decline in self-esteem have been widely reported from many areas (Appell 1986). Relative economic deprivation and marginalization begins prior to actual displacement, because new investments in infrastructure and services in condemned areas are discontinued long before projects start. Partial but significant loss of farming land (for example, to roads or canals) renders some small farms economically nonviable, even though physically they may seem to survive. High-productivity farmers from fertile valley-bottom lands tend to become marginalized when moved uphill to inferior soils. Marginalization also occurs through the loss of off-farm income sources, as found in the Nepal Kulekhani Hydroelectric project (Bjonnes 1983, Pockharel 1995) and in Sri Lanka's Kotmale project (Soeftestad 1990).

For urban resettlers, marginalization is sometimes gradual and may occur after relocation, when, for example, resettlers receive temporary jobs (instead of land) that, in the long term, turn out to be unsustainable as income sources. Government agencies also tacitly accept lasting marginalization of resettlers when they consider it "a matter of course" that the displaced cannot restore their prior standards of living.

Food insecurity

Forced uprooting increases the risk that people will fall into temporary or chronic undernourishment, defined as calorie-protein intake levels below the minimum necessary for normal growth and work.

Food insecurity and undernourishment are both symptoms and results of inadequate resettlement. During physical relocation, sudden drops in food crop availability and incomes are predictable. Subsequently, as rebuilding regular food production capacity at the relocation site may take years, hunger or undernourishment tends to become a lingering long-term effect. In this volume, Green provides an extensive overview of the food-related risks for both refugees and resettlers, notwithstanding significant differences between them. Hakim, in turn, documents these risks and consequences in her insightful analysis of the resettlement of Gujarat's Vasava tribe, which was compelled to shift from food crops to cash crops. Convergent findings are reported from virtually all sites. The adverse effects of the Manantali Dam and water regime management in Senegal were described precisely with the concept "development-induced food insecurity" (Horowitz and Salem-Murdock 1993). At Sri Lanka's Victoria dam project, some 55 percent of resettled families were still receiving food stamps even after a long period (Rew and Driver 1986). Because the area of cultivated land per capita in the Bailiambe reservoir in China decreased from 1.3 mu to only 0.4 mu after relocation, local food production became insufficient, and 75,000 tons of annual food relief had to be provided for several years. Nutrition-related risks reinforce morbidity and mortality risks (see further) and largely depend on whether the primary risks of landlessness and joblessness are effectively counteracted.

Increased morbidity and mortality

Massive population displacement threatens to cause serious declines in health levels. Displacement-induced social stress and psychological trauma are sometimes accompanied by the outbreak of relocation-related illnesses, particularly parasitic and vector-born diseases such as malaria and schistosomiasis. Unsafe water supply and improvised sewage systems increase vulnerability to epidemics and chronic diarrhea, dysentery, and so on. The weakest segments of the demographic spectrum – infants, children, and the elderly – are affected most strongly.

Empirical research shows that displaced people experience higher levels of exposure and vulnerability to illness and severe disease than they did prior to displacement. An unintended byproduct of large infrastructure programs is often increased morbidity also among area groups that are not displaced.[10] Overall, in the absence of preventive health measures, direct and secondary effects of dislocation include psychosomatic diseases, diseases of poor hygiene (such as diarrhea and dysentery), and parasitic and vector-borne diseases caused by unsafe and insufficient water supplies and unsanitary waste systems. In Sri Lanka, an outbreak of gastroenteritis occurred along the Victoria dam reservoir (Rew and Driver 1986), and in Mahaweli's System C resettlement site the incidence of malaria rose from 8.9 percent to 15.6 percent (Jayewardene 1995). In the Akosombo area in Ghana, the prevalence of schistosomiasis rose from 1.8 percent prior to resettlement to 75 percent among adult lakeside dwellers and close to 100 percent among their children, within a few years after impoundment in the 1960s. The Foum-Gleita irrigation project in Mauritania exceeded its anticipated increase of schistosomiasis, reaching 75 percent among schoolchildren; farmers' health also worsened from drinking contaminated water. At Nam Pong reservoir in Thailand, monitoring confirmed that local rates of morbidity – from liver fluke and hookworm infection – were higher than provincial levels, the result of deteriorated living conditions and poor waste-disposal practices.

The interaction between two processes included in the risk model – decrease in health and loss of shelter – has been long established empirically. Research has documented that more vulnerable groups, such as the aged, suffer increased morbidity and mortality rates as an effect of losing their prior homes (Ferraro 1982, Borup and others 1979). Exposure to the "social stress" inherent in forced relocation was highlighted as having differential consequences on mental health across age, gender, and marital and occupational status (Scudder and Colson 1982; Scudder 1985; Turner and others 1995; see Appell 1986 for original suggestions on measuring social stress).

---

[10] This is due largely to the appearance of "boom towns" and uncontrolled labor camps, in which sanitary services tend to be deficient.

Increased mortality rates are reported also as a result either of accidents associated with new reservoirs or epidemic outbreaks around new bodies of water. Lack of proper information and precautionary measures resulted in more than a hundred deaths by drowning at Saguling Dam Lake (Indonesia) during the first 14 months of operation. At Cirata reservoir (Indonesia), 10 people drowned in the first 10 months after impounding (Padjadjaran University 1989).

Loss of access to common property and services

For poor people, particularly for the landless and assetless, loss of access to the common property assets that belonged to relocated communities (pastures, forested lands, water bodies, burial grounds, quarries, and so on) results in significant deterioration in income and livelihood levels. Typically, losses of common property assets are not compensated by governments. These losses are compounded by loss of access to some public services, such as school (Mathur 1998; Mahapatra 1999a, 1999b) that can be grouped within this category of risks.

Kibreab (see this volume) offers a documented conceptual analysis of the linkages between common property resources (CPRs), poverty, and impoverishment risks. Given typical power structures and the vulnerability of the displacees, Kibreab demonstrates that the loss of CPRs has ravaging long-term consequences on their livelihoods and social standing. Empirical evidence shows that in all regions a significant share of the poor households' income comes from edible forest products, firewood, common grazing areas, and public quarries. Loss of these resources leaves a big gap. For example, in semi-arid regions of India, between 91 and 100 percent of firewood, between 66 and 89 percent of domestic fuel, and between 69 and 80 percent of poor households' grazing needs are supplied by lands held under a common property regime (Sequeira 1994). A study of seven projects causing displacements between 1950 and 1994 in Orissa, India, has found that no compensation has been paid for common properties by any of the projects (Pandey and Associates 1998). In the Rengali Dam area in India, prior to displacement all families had access to common grazing lands and burial grounds; after relocation, only 23.7 percent and 17.5 percent, respectively, had such access.

When displaced people's access to resources under common property regimes is not protected, they tend either to encroach on reserved forests or to increase the pressure on the common property resources of the host area's population. This becomes in itself a new cause of both social conflict and further environmental degradation.

Social disarticulation

Forced displacement tears apart the existing social fabric. It disperses and fragments communities, dismantles patterns of social organization and interpersonal ties; kinship groups become scattered as well. Life-sustaining informal networks of reciprocal help, local voluntary associations, and self-organized mutual service are disrupted. This is a net loss of valuable "social capital" that compounds the loss of natural, physical, and human capital (discussed previously). The social capital lost through social disarticulation is typically unperceived and uncompensated by the programs causing it, and this real loss has long-term consequences.

Dismantled social networks that once mobilized people to act around common interests and to meet their most pressing needs are difficult to rebuild. This loss is greater in projects that relocate families in a dispersed manner, severing their prior ties with neighbors, rather than relocating them in groups and social units. A detailed sociological study by Behura and Nayak (1993) on a dam project in India found various manifestations of social disarticulation within the kinship system, such as the loosening of intimate bonds, growing alienation and anomie, the weakening of control on interpersonal behavior, and lower cohesion in family structures. Marriages were deferred because dowries, feasts, and gifts became unaffordable. Resettlers' relationships with non-displaced kinsmen were eroded and interaction between individual families was reduced. As a result, participation in group activities decreased; post-harvest communal feasts and pilgrimages were discontinued; and common burial grounds became shapeless and disordered. A monograph on the Hirakud dam in India found that displaced households whose "economic status had been completely shattered as a result of displacement" did not become "properly integrated" in host villages for many years after relocation (Baboo 1992). "The people may physically persist, but the community that was—is no more" (Downing 1996a), because its spatial, temporal, and cultural determinants are gone.

Historians of migration have also concluded convergently that the costs of population relocation generally go much beyond "simply the financial costs": among the "heaviest costs of all are the severing of personal ties in familiar surroundings, to face new economic and social uncertainties in a strange land" (Sowell 1996). Poverty becomes not just an absence of income and assets—such as land, shelter, and food: the loss of reciprocity networks directly worsens the corollaries of poverty—powerlessness, dependency, and vulnerability.

Differential risk intensities

The major impoverishment risks, identified and described above, must be seen in their interconnectedness, as a pattern of variables. They affect populations frequently described as being risk-averse. Yet this heavy knot of risks is forced upon them beyond their choice. Affected people must deal with these risks virtually simultaneously, as a patterned situation, not just one at a time. The result is a crisis.

Depending on site circumstances, sector (urban or rural), and season when displacement occurs, the intensity of the individual risks varies; at times, one or another risk may not even be experienced by a particular subgroup. Conversely, other risks, site-specific, may emerge. The individual situation is always richer and somehow different from the general pattern. But the general model is present in all situations, despite variations. What is fundamental for positing the problem theoretically and in policy terms is that forced-displacement situations intrinsically contain a basic risk pattern.

To exemplify variance, we note that gender-oriented analysis revealed that women suffer more severe impacts (Feeney 1995, Koenig 1995, Pandey 1998). Agnihotri (1996) signals blatant discrimination against women in compensation criteria. For instance, entitlement to land compensation for unmarried individuals is set in Orissa at age 18 years for men, but age 30 for women! A comprehensive review of the worldwide evidence on indigenous and tribal groups affected by forced resettlement (Colchester 1999) has demonstrated definitively that such vulnerable groups are much more prone than the general population to impoverishment hazards of the kind discussed above. And insightful field research has empirically documented *why* this is happening by explaining the causes of the particular vulnerability of these populations (Fernandes this volume and 1991, Mahapatra 1994; Nayak this volume).

Children, as an age category, are subject to particularly perverse consequences. Elaborating on the risks and reconstruction model in light of evidence from India, Mahapatra (1999a) suggests that "to the eight-fold impoverishment risk model one may add the educational loss affecting children." Relocation often interrupts schooling and for some of these children it means that they never return to school. After displacement, as a result of drops in family income, many are drafted into the labor market earlier than what would have otherwise been the case. Differences characteristic to particularly vulnerable groups clearly call for directly targeted responses.

Risks to host populations

Host populations are a major actor with a stake in good resettlement, particularly within mass displacements caused by either development programs or conflicts. Recognizing the specific risks to hosts is integral to using the risks and reconstruction model and approach.

Obviously, risks to hosts are not identical with the risks to displacees, in substance or intensity, but are related to them and may also result in impoverishment implications. The inflows of displacees increase pressure on resources and scarce social services, as well as competition for employment. Prices of commodities tend to rise and health risks in the host area increase. Cultural clashes (in nonhomogeneous areas) are quite likely, and social tensions tend to endure for a long time. Secondary adverse effects on the environment hurt both the hosts and the displacees.

The most effective safeguard for the hosts' interests is an adequately designed and financed recovery plan for the resettlers. The project-planning stage, when relocation sites and host-area populations are identified, is the appropriate time for considering not only the risks to displacees but also the risks to hosts. Experience has proven that when special opportunities are made available to displacees, it is wise to allow hosts as well, whenever possible, to share such opportunities. This minimizes tensions and competition between the two populations.

In sum, the IRR model captures a broad range of hazards—not only the economic risks, but also the social and cultural ones. It introduces a view on resettlement that reveals the causal mechanisms of impoverishment, its main processes and dimensions. These include income and nonincome dimensions of impoverishment, such as assets impoverishment, housing impoverishment, health, nutrition and educational impoverishment, loss of organization, and powerlessness. During displacement, people lose capital in all its forms—natural capital, man-made capital, and human and social capital. Actions to safeguard against such capital losses[11] are indispensable, but more than only safeguarding is required. We conclude

---

[11]   The implications of the impoverishment risks and reconstruction model in terms of a typology of capital losses during forcible displacement have been recently explored and developed by Juliette Hayes in her dissertation at the London School of Economics (1999). This perspective on impoverishment processes contributes to the argument for multisided post-displacement reconstruction and adequate resettlement financing for restoring the various types of capital loss.

therefore that reconstructive strategies must be *multidimensional*, taking the form of a comprehensive and systematic resettlement program. This is reflected in the second part of the IRR model, which reverts and converts the risks-pattern analysis into a reconstruction-pattern strategy.

Risk reversals: the model as self-destroying prophecy

The fundamental question to answer now is if the resettlement model can help *predict* and *diagnose* the risks of displacement, can it also guide problem resolution?

The answer is affirmative. The risks and reconstruction model complements its risk diagnosis with an explicit framework for the socioeconomic reestablishment of those displaced. The model is not just a predictor of inescapable pauperization; it is a guide toward counteracting the risks and resolving the problems that displacement creates. The risk model has to be read "in reverse," turned on its head, and thus it maps the way for reconstructing the livelihoods of those displaced, as will be shown further.

Robert K. Merton has convincingly demonstrated that the prediction of an undesirable outcome may act as a "self-destroying prophecy" (Merton 1979). It follows that a risk prediction model becomes maximally useful *not* when it is confirmed by adverse events, but, rather, when, as a result of its warnings being taken seriously and acted upon, the risks are prevented from becoming reality, or are minimized, and the consequences predicted by the model do not occur. The predictive-cum-planning capacity of the impoverishment risks and reconstruction model results from the forewarning virtue of the knowledge "packaged" in it. This is how the IRR model "contributes" toward destroying its own prophecy.

Risk recognition is crucial for sound planning. More than offering a general warning, the proposed model serves as a matrix for on-the-ground assessment of how the general risks would vary in each local context. It helps identify the specific configurations of displacement risks for each given population. Such on-the-ground risk assessments can—and, in fact, must—lead directly to the planning of counter-risk activities. Use of this model as a tool for project preparation and actual planning of resettlement has already been reported from the field.[12]

12   Such reports, for instance, came from India (Thangaraj 1996) and the Philippines (Spiegel 1997); others report using this model in field supervision of resettlement operations (Downing 1996a, 1996b; Mathur and Marsden 1998); for other applications, see also the last section of this chapter.

As mentioned earlier, the internal logic of the IRR model suggests that to prevent and overcome the patterns of impoverishment it is necessary to act in time to attack the risks and stop them from becoming reality. Risk identification is not an exercise carried out for academic purposes: it is carried out to *design for action, for risk-reversal.*

Reversing the risk model indicates which directions the action for safeguarding, reconstruction, and development should take. For instance, to prevent landlessness in the wake of displacement, land-based resettlement must be conceived before displacement even begins (relying on options that are likely to fit local land-contingencies). To prevent homelessness, the house-reconstruction program can and must also be designed in advance; it would include not a single method but rather various approaches acceptable to resettlers; and so on.

To formulate this idea more generally, we can say that the IRR model conveys two basic messages: a policy message and a strategy message.

The major policy message embodied in the model is that the general risk pattern inherent in displacement *can be controlled through a policy response* that mandates and finances integrated problem resolution. But this pattern of interlocked risks *cannot* be controlled by piecemeal palliatives.

The strategy message embodied in the model is *that specific re-settlement programs* (plans) are required each time, in order to build the bridge from the general risk model to the particular resettlement circumstances and to mobilize concerted actions by interested institutions and social groups. Single means — for instance, just cash compensation — do not respond to all risks. Compensation alone is not a substitute for the absence of strategy and full-fledged resettlement programs.

While it is incumbent upon the state to pursue a policy of recovery and allocate needed resources — financial, organizational, technical, and so on — it would be unrealistic to conceive of reconstruction only as a top-down, paternalistic effort, without the participation and initiative of the displaced people themselves. The required strategy is not a one-actor strategy, for the state alone; rather, it is an all-actors strategy. Despite the polarized situation to be expected in a displacement context, the participation of all relevant actors (resettlers, local leaders, nongovernmental organizations, and host populations) in reconstruction is indispensable.

Financial and technical means for post-displacement reconstruction differ, of course, between development-caused resettlement and conflict-caused refugee situations. In development-induced displacements, the state is accountable and amenable to provide resources for reconstruction; however, this is not the case when it comes to refugees. Yet, similarities exist: the essential components of reconstruction defined in the model are the same, and such similarities create terrain for experience transfer between postcconflict assistance and development-caused resettlement.

The components of reconstruction

The primary objective of any induced involuntary resettlement process should be to prevent impoverishment and to reconstruct and improve the livelihood of resettlers. In further examining the components of this reconstruction, we will follow a slightly different sequence than in the earlier discussion of risks. First, we will address the basic economic variables – land and employment – and then, those referring to community reconstruction, housing, and social services.[13]

*From landlessness to land-based reestablishment
and from joblessness to reemployment*

Settling displaced people back on cultivatable land or in income-generating employment is the heart of the matter in reconstructing livelihoods. Success tends to be correlated with several options, such as identifying equivalent lands; bringing new lands into production through land recovery; crop intensification or a shift to more valuable crops; diversification of on-farm or off-farm activities; and use of project-created productive resources such as reservoirs, irrigated areas downstream, and so on. Investments for creating sustainable new employment in the relocation zone are essential as well.

Agricultural land-settlement schemes have been frequently employed in Africa for creating a new productive basis both for resettlers and refugees. Lassailly-Jacob documents and compares such experiences in this volume (see also 1994, 1996; Eriksen 1999).

---

[13]   We believe that considerably more empirical research is needed to identify and disseminate existing positive experiences in reconstructing livelihoods. Sociologists and anthropologists have been more concerned with describing and deploring displacement's pathologies than with focusing on resettlement's successes. Because to date good practice has been less frequent than failure, gathering more knowledge on the existing successful experiences is a priority.

In very densely populated areas, land scarcity requires creative approaches. To overcome land scarcity around the Shuikou Dam (China), project officials made a bold effort to convert unproductive hillsides and steep uplands around the reservoir into flat terraces for horticulture or into forested areas. Project-paid mechanical equipment was used for land recovery on a vast scale. Orchards were planted several years in advance of resettlers' relocation, so that trees were close to fruit bearing at relocation time.[14] The approach resulted in some 53,000 mu of fruit trees, 10,000 mu of tea plantations, 26,000 mu of bamboo trees, and more than 200,000 forest trees. This intensified agriculture and changes in cropping patterns provided new land, work, and livelihood for about 20,000 resettlers. Their average income from the new crops is actually higher than the level anticipated in the project's original resettlement plan. Significantly, this improvement in the resettlers' economic situation occurred even though, on a per capita basis, farmland was reduced in the area from 0.98 mu to 0.32 mu. Complementary strategies and diversification benefited the remainder of Shuikou's resettlers; these included animal husbandry, including duck raising and reservoir fishing (6 percent of resettlers), jobs in the service sector and transportation (13.4 percent), jobs in new enterprises (19.3 percent) (World Bank/OED 1998). Resettlers' initiative in Saguling (Indonesia) saved the fertile topsoil about to be lost in the reservoir area, moving it to upland plots and increasing fertility (Costa-Pierce 1996).

Throughout the developing world empirical evidence confirms that replacing land with land—or, in the terms of our model, "land-based resettlement"—is by far a more successful strategy than compensation in cash, which most often fails to lead to income restoration, let alone betterment. In addition, systematic field studies (McMillan and others 1998) have demonstrated that if provided alone, new land is not enough for achieving success even in the case of voluntary settlement. Technical assistance and favorable social policy measures must accompany land-based resettlement.

Project support, combined with resettlers' initiative and resources, can turn the loss of land into an opportunity for "farming the waters," in other words, for organizing fish farms in the new reservoirs. Through aquaculture many new reservoirs have been successfully turned into income sources. In Mexico's Aquamilpa reservoir area, fishing represented a mere 4.1 percent of productive activities among those to be affected in 1989 by the reservoir. But,

---

[14]   Personal observations, Shuikou (1986, 1988, 1990, 1994).

by 1995, about 60.8 percent of that population was engaged in fishing activities. In the Cirata reservoir area (Indonesia), cage aquaculture workers earned about rupees 56,000 more a month than rice field workers in the same area before the dam construction (Costa Pierce 1996).

The creation of national parks and biosphere reserves has repeatedly brought the threat of displacement to the door of resident people. Once again, virtually each empirically described case shows that problem resolution depends primarily on resolving land and employment issues. While eviction from traditional lands has been typically disastrous to those affected (West and Brenchin 1991), the few successful cases of physical relocation, such as that of the Mololtoja National Park in Swaziland, are those where good alternative lands had been allocated to the residents in a culturally sensitive manner (Ntshalintshali and McGurk 1991). These cases again confirm the centrality of land for productive reestablishment. An alternative for avoiding eviction is to combine recognition of land rights with employment creation in conservation works, helping resident groups to gain a vested interest in preservation as an income-generating source for themselves (Raval 1991, Wells and Brandon 1992).

Training resettlers in new skills is an effective strategy only if accompanied by actual employment resulting from firm market demand for new skills or from new investments. In the Dudichua Coal Project in India, 225 of 378 farmers displaced by the new mine were retrained and employed (one job per family), attaining earnings about eight times the average rural wage (World Bank 1995d). With limited project support, a group of brickmakers in Argentina (Yacyretá Project) has succeeded handsomely in resuming productive activities and improving their incomes (see Mejia this volume 2000, 1999). There are important unresolved dilemmas, however, regarding land-based reestablishment not addressed even in otherwise detailed policies, such as the issue of squatters or of the abuses in the overuse of the eminent domain principle. By definition, urban "squatters" reside on public lands, such as reserves of "right of way" lands and other public lots, often with the tacit acquiescence of municipal authorities. Squatters are also among the poorest groups of people. When such lands are needed for new projects, displacing squatters forcibly without providing an alternative location aggravates their poverty and only pushes them to become squatters elsewhere. Solutions that alleviate their condition, without encouraging squatting by others, are not easy and need policy and legislative elaboration.

A controversial issue is also the unlimited application of the eminent domain principle. There is much merit in the argument that, when large amounts of land must be given up by their historic owners for new and promising developments, these landowners should become direct co-owners of the new developments, and co-beneficiaries for as long as the new development remains productive. Or, alternatively, rather than expropriating such owners *en masse,* [15] the state could offer them the option of creating a leasing corporation that will maintain ownership of the land but would lease it to the project for, say, 99 years, or for the duration of the new development. This will make unnecessary the imposition of eminent domain, with its dire result of sudden land dispossession and likely chronic impoverishment. The trade-offs involved in such options (and in others) for all concerned need to be weighed carefully, with flexibility for choosing them when appropriate and without the rigidity of preimposed recipes.

Another excellent option for recovery and *improvement* is resettling reservoir-displaced farmers on land newly irrigated downstream. Nonetheless, it is rarely used. Some states in India (Madhya Pradesh, Gujarat, and others) try to relocate oustees into command areas by enacting land-ceiling laws for newly irrigated land, a good administrative solution that should be reinforced by gaining the cooperation of command-area farmers. Overall, the combination of providing land and employment opportunities is an important strategy for recovery, particularly in those situations where neither one alone — land or employment — can ensure the full use of the labor resources of resettled families.

From homelessness to house reconstruction

Better shelter conditions are one of the relatively easy-to-achieve improvements in resettlers' livelihoods. However, this is much more difficult, in the case of refugees deprived of any compensation for their lost dwellings and assets.

---

[15]   Historically, when the principle of eminent domain was initially crafted, the lawmakers envisaged expropriations limited to isolated individuals or small groups. Given the large-size expropriations required by some infrastructural equipment today, and the absence in law of commensurate remedies designed for full communities rather than isolated families, questioning the limits of applying eminent domain principles is an issue ripe for open discussion.

From empirical research worldwide we distinguish at least two findings common in many cultures. First, it is repeatedly confirmed that impoverishment through worsened housing can be effectively prevented through fair recognition of housing reconstruction costs in the displacing project's budget. Second, throughout the world, resettlers tend to display a strong propensity to improve their living standards over past levels: they do so through incremental investments in kind (labor) and cash. Even amid the bleakness of uprootedness and the anger caused by low compensation, the immediacy of the need for family shelter and the deep-seated aspiration for better lives often coalesce in an all-out effort to build, against all odds, larger and more durable homes. Resettlers use different strategies for this: mobilizing family labor, organizing mutual help, taking out loans to complement the compensation, shifting parts of the compensation for land toward home-building, and staggering reconstruction — first laying out foundations for larger houses and rebuilding them in stages, as the family masters resources and time.

Abundant empirical evidence about resettlers' investment behavior indicates that many use a part of the cash compensation received for their productive assets toward housing. They spend more than the house compensation proper for rebuilding a better dwelling than they had before.[16]

Actual improvements in family housing take one or more of the following forms: more square footage per capita; better-quality housing materials, particularly for roofing; connection to services (electricity, water); safer sanitation facilities; space for house gardens; and others. Typical constraints on house reestablishment processes are longer average commuting distances and transportation costs in urban areas, affordability issues and long-term loan (mortgage) burdens, and differential entitlements for the housing of former squatters.

---

[16]   Such shift of meager compensation resources from restoring *productive* assets (such as land) to restoring *consumption* assets (the house and its equipment) may restrict the family's income-generating capacity for awhile. Its rationale requires cultural and economic analysis; it may, or may not, be vindicated in the long run. Values and aspirations, and factors, such as family size and structure, intervene heavily in guiding resettlers' decisions. My field research in China (Shuikou Dam, 1986, 1988, 1990, 1994) and Nepal (Kali Gandaki Dam area) found that some resettlers *deliberately* rebuild large houses with the goal of using them not only as "consumption assets," but also as structures apt to yield income through partial lease, use as shops, roadside restaurants, and so on (see also Sapkota 1999).

Gains in living standards through improved housing conditions, rather than just "restoration," have been documented in numerous projects: in Argentina, by the initial cohorts of resettlers from Yacyretá Dam; in Nepal, by the majority of those displaced by the construction of the Kali Gandaki dam and its access road (Khodka 1999, Sapkota 1999); in China, by those displaced by the Shuikou dam, who increased their floor space with about 25 additional square meters per family (World Bank/OED 1998); in Kenya, by the resettlers from the Export Development project (World Bank 1995a); and others. In Shanghai, families displaced by a Sewerage Project were able to choose between state apartments offered for rent or private apartments made available to resettlers at only one-third of the construction cost (see also Reddy, this volume, for the reconstruction of urban dwellings in India). Field studies have reported innovative approaches employed in house reconstruction, such as vouchers in the Republic of Korea. Daily transportation of resettlers by project vehicles to new sites in Togo's Nangbeto Project enabled them to expand the project-supplied core house–unit for each family by adding additional rooms.[17] In sum, evidence worldwide confirms that homelessness is not an unavoidable risk of impoverishment; in fact, house reconstruction allows room not just for restoring prior standards of living, often very low, but for reconstructing at improved levels.

From social disarticulation to community reconstruction,
from marginalization to social inclusion, and from expropriation
to restoration of community assets and services

The reconstruction of communities, networks, and social cohesion is essential, yet seldom is it deliberately pursued in current government approaches. Planners tend to overlook these sociocultural and psychological (not just economic) dimensions, and are rarely concerned with facilitating reintegration within host populations or compensating community-owned assets.

The above three dimensions are partly distinct and partly overlapping. The reason for grouping them is to emphasize that manipulating model variables can achieve synergistic effects in reconstruction programs intent on using this potential synergy. Community reconstruction refers to group structures, including informal and formal institutions, while overcoming marginalization refers primarily to the individual family or household level. On-the-ground

---

[17]   Personal observation, Togo, 1989.

approaches would differ when villages or neighborhoods are created as *new social units* that need community assets and public services, or when *fill-in operations* insert scattered resettlers within preexisting communities, increasing pressure on existing services and host-owned common resources.

Re-creating community structures and community-owned resources is a complex endeavor that cannot be accomplished overnight. Research on the Mahaweli resettlement program in Sri Lanka (Rodrigo 1991) has concluded that the *initial* allocation of resources to resettlers, including access to common property resources, is virtually decisive for resettlers' successful "takeoff" at the new site. If access to resources is below a critical limit (on a per-family or percapita basis), the takeoff is jeopardized, but if it provides a minimal but viable basis, post-resettlement development can build upon it and be successful. Thus, because of its incrementality over the family-owned resources, the access to community-owned resources, in some form or another, often becomes critical for overall successful reconstruction. Findings elsewhere have confirmed this conclusion.

Some of the most interesting experiences in the deliberate preservation of community structures or assistance for the formation of new community networks are reported from China, Ethiopia, Greece, and Mexico. By law, project authorities in China must negotiate with displacees simultaneously as individuals and as community groups. The government resources for financing resettlement are divided in some proportion between households (for individual family purposes) and community bodies represented by township committees (for group purposes). Community-owned assets lost in displacement are valued and financially compensated by the state to enable the reconstruction of the same, or of comparable, community assets, which contribute to the livelihoods of resettlers (Shi and Hu 1994). Thus, by design, some patterns of the social organization of the displaced village are empowered to have a function in resettlement, and thus to continue their existence and role. Furthermore, the Chinese approach is also unique in that it fosters community solidarity in sharing some of the losses (particularly land) and requires some redistribution of nonaffected village lands used by the nondisplaced farmers to the village members who are displaced and lost land.[18]

Enabling the rebirth of community institutions is paramount for successful resettlement and livelihood reconstruction. From Ethio-

---

[18]   These interpretations are based on personal observations of actual resettlement practice in several provinces of China, and on discussions with community leaders and members, central and local officials, and so on.

pia, Wolde-Selassie (see this volume) reports the profoundly positive effects of restoring religious village associations and customs
after displacement. Organized collective help to the most vulnerable and marginalized community members accelerates reinclusion.
And the experience of Greek resettlers, as analyzed by Hirschon
(see this volume), shows that in re-articulation and reintegration
processes, common cultural values can overcome material deprivations, economic disadvantage, and inadequate physical provisions.
Thus, community re-articulation is not necessarily a function of regaining economic well-being — it can precede it. Mexico's Aquamilpa
resettlement program not only restored prior community services,
but also built several new community facilities (Johns 1996). Such
experiences are precious especially because the restoration of access to community resources tends to occur less frequently than the
replacement of private assets, leaving room for competition and
conflict between resettlers and hosts. Overall, all three facets of the
reconstruction processes require institution building and concur-
rence from the host area population.

*From food insecurity to adequate nutrition and from increased
morbidity to better health care*

Nutrition levels and health will depend in the long run on progress
in resettlers' economic recovery (see above, land and/or employment). But in the short run, reconstruction requires that sudden disruptions in food supply and risks to health and life are arrested
through immediate counteraction, even before full economic reconstruction is undertaken. Borrowing from successful experiences of
organized assistance to refugees (emergency relief) can be highly
effective for offsetting immediate nutritional and health risks to
resettlers and for focusing on most vulnerable groups (such as children, the elderly, and pregnant women). Sustainable reconstruction,
however, requires long-term planning as well, beyond immediate
relief measures, together with information and education, to foster
needed changes in resettlers' behavior and their ability to cope with
the circumstances of the new habitat.

Existing evidence indicates that the food scarcity risks are more
readily recognized by resettlement agencies than the health-related
risks incurred by resettlers. Long-term planning is seldom done.
Resettlers' coping response tends also to address first the immediately perceivable food needs. A World Health Organization (WHO)
study of four countries in the lower Mekong basin (Thailand, Vietnam, Laos, and Cambodia) showed that the most effective long-term

strategy for reducing the adverse health impacts of dam reservoirs is institution building in the health and sanitation sectors. The study recommended that all four countries incorporate "a human health component into all integrated river basin development projects" as a safeguard against higher risks of morbidity and mortality (Mather, Sornmani, and Keola 1994). Togo's Nangbeto Dam project offered a replicable example of such good practice: it introduced a continuous health-monitoring studies program throughout the construction years. This helped protect the resettlers' and host population's health (Michard, Adam, and Aziablé 1992).

The constitutive elements of livelihood reconstruction have been addressed above in subclusters, and it is important to repeat that the model inherently emphasizes their interdependence. Therefore, optimizing the reconstruction strategy requires pursuing these directions simultaneously, with internal priorities dictated by local project circumstances.

Overall, the reconstruction part of the IRR model provides the broad chart for pursuing the reestablishment of resettlers along several clear indicators. The evidence quoted demonstrates that:

a. Impoverishment risks can be successfully attacked and reversed.
b. Livelihood reconstruction, however difficult, is feasible along the specific directions identified.
c. The body of replicable positive experiences is growing continuously.

Necessary improvements in current resettlement practices

How does the IRR model compare to today's mainstream practices in involuntary resettlement operations generated by development projects?

Evidence indicates that the IRR framework is in some important respects ahead of current mainstream practices,[19] and its wider adop-

---

[19] Within "mainstream practices" we can, of course, distinguish various levels and standards. The bulk of resettlement operations occur under various types of national (domestic) programs. Field research by many evaluators has concluded that under these operations, standards tend to be, unfortunately, very low and detrimental to most displacees. Resettlement operations under development projects assisted by international aid aim to achieve higher standards, formulated in the policies of multilateral development banks, U.N. agencies, or bilateral donor agencies like those of OECD countries. But there is much to be changed and improved even in the methodology of this group of projects.

tion would significantly improve standards and performances. It brings a set of new elements, different from conventional approaches and methods. It builds upon the more advanced scholarly analyses of resettlement to date and proposes to development programs an improved way of diagnosing, costing, planning, financing, and implementing resettlement. This can substantially correct many of the current analytical flaws and implementation weaknesses, widely and legitimately criticized.

The model is fully compatible with the most advanced resettlement policies in existence today and offers a methodology capable of vastly increasing consistency and effectiveness in the implementation of these policies. The World Bank's policy guidelines in resettlement, adopted first in 1980 (and formally strengthened in 1986, 1990, and 1994), have been gradually adopted, in essence, by other organizations, such as the aid agencies of the Organization for Economic Cooperation and Development (OECD) countries (OECD 1992), the Asian Development Bank (ADB) (ADB 1995), and others. Yet more institutional emphasis and incisive monitoring are required for their consistent application. [20] For instance, the economic analytical methodology employed in the preparation of projects under these guidelines is often operationally inconsistent with the guidelines themselves, leaving ample room for cost externalizations and very incomplete risk analysis. The impoverishment risks analysis methodology is still to be generalized in such projects, including many co-financed by the World Bank, ADB, or OECD donor agencies. For the vast majority of developing countries, and some developed countries, which do not have any explicit policy for involuntary resettlement, the IRR model can serve as one of the building blocks for formulating such overdue policy guidelines.

As a planning and monitoring tool, the IRR has started to be used in the last four to five years in a number of projects in various countries. From India and the Philippines, its use has been reported in resettlement preparation and planning (Thangaraj 1996, Spiegel 1997). Others have used the model in field supervision of resettlement operations and in project implementation monitoring work (Downing 1996a, 1996b; Sapkota 1999). For Lesotho, Scudder has

---

[20] Deficiencies in adherence to policy standards appear, especially during implementation, because implementation depends primarily on the political will and institutional capacity of borrowing governments and their project execution agencies. Such agencies often do not feel a strong "ownership" of these aid policy standards, despite project legal agreements, because of the absence of national policy standards.

developed operational indicators for measuring impoverishment risks and their actual impacts under the country's large Water Engineering project (Scudder 1999). A workshop of resettlement planners and practitioners from various states of India explored the model's planning potential, with analytical contributions reported in detail in Mathur and Marsden's book (1998).

For the most part, however, the risks of impoverishment are currently not addressed explicitly and systematically during the planning of very many projects that cause displacement. This occurs frequently in domestic projects that are not subject to in-depth and multisided screening; but to a considerable extent it has also been true in projects assisted by various bilateral or multilateral donor agencies or by credit-export entities.

The IRR model is to be used in conjunction with other analytical project tools, and it can help correct and improve some of them. We emphasize primarily the need to correct three entrenched flaws in the routine methodology of planning for such projects, flaws that account for the recurrent undertreatment of impoverishment risks. These include:

a. The flaws and incompleteness of the conventional methods for project risk analysis
b. The over-reliance of project justification on the cost-benefit analysis (CBA) despite its glaring insufficiencies
c. The absence of genuine consultation and involvement of the affected populations

A few comments on each one are in order.

Flaws in conventional risk methodology

Formal "risk analysis" is a subset of project economic and financial preparation methodology, and is carried out routinely. Yet the risk that displacement inflicts upon affected people are not part of the routine risk and sensitivity analyses carried out by planners during project economic and financial analysis.

Conventional project risk analysis evaluates the sources and magnitude of risks that may adversely influence the rate of return to project investments. It estimates the switching values of key variables (such as duration of project implementation, cost overruns, and availability of local co-financing) and the sensitivity of the project's net present value to possible changes in these variables. A sensitivity analysis is usually carried out for each one of these variables because they can threaten project outputs and the returns to investors. When necessary, the sensitivity tests are developed into alternative project scenarios and contingency actions, all in the effort to minimize financial risk and maximize returns to investments.

But risks to the people affected by the project are not part of the conventional economic risk analysis. While conventional project economic analysis and sensitivity tests are generally designed to identify, estimate, and help prevent the major risks to projects' rates of return and to project investors, they are not designed to also identify and measure the risks posed by the project to the other project stakeholders such as those displaced. This, quite simply, is a basic flaw in the pattern of current project risk analysis. The methodological bias is obvious: while risks to project investors, and to the invested capital, are analyzed and weighed carefully, the risks posed by the project itself to some of the project population, such as the displaced groups, are not subjected to similar rigorous, explicit, and systematic analysis. The risks resulting from displacement are only indirectly risks to investments and they remain out of the "classic" type of investment-risk analysis.[21] This conflicts with the goal of safeguarding people's interests and welfare. It conflicts also with the general policy objective of reducing poverty.

The conclusion, therefore, is that the conventional project risk analysis must be substantially reformulated and broadened, to cover risks to affected people who are stakeholders in these projects. In other words, project risk analysis must *explicitly* include the risks of impoverishment highlighted in the IRR and design insurance measures, as well as, to the extent possible, risk safeguards and social safety nets.

The optimal response to predictable impoverishment risks is to search for project alternatives that could eliminate altogether the need to displace people, or could at least reduce the number of displacees. Such alternatives are sometimes technically feasible: for instance, by modifying the routing of a planned highway to circumvent existing settlements; by changing the location of a dam; or by reducing the dam's height. When it is not possible to fully avoid displacement, however, policymakers and planners are guided by

---

[21]   One kind of "social" risk that routine economic analysis does consider is defined in economics as "behavioral risk." The term refers to risks to the project, not the people. This includes risks that can be incurred by investments because of modifications in people's general behavior (such as behavioral changes in consumption patterns, in employment preferences, and in support for the project altogether). For the safety of project investments, anticipating this kind of risks is, of course, necessary. But this is only a unidirectional consideration of the relations between people and projects. It does not add anything to the social safety of people that the project itself puts at risk.

the model to conceive special measures targeted against each of the predicted impoverishment risks. These measures could be of an economic, financial, technical, legal, or cultural nature. They should be commensurate with risk intensity. An experienced planner would identify which risks loom larger in each case, how they interact, and which to counteract first to achieve positive chain effects.[22]

Why cost-benefit analysis is incomplete

Furthermore, the overreliance on cost-benefit analysis to justify projects that cause displacement is another fundamental source of mistreatment of the impoverishment risks inherent in such projects. CBA is utterly insufficient because it is only a macroeconomic tool that does not explore *the distribution* of either costs or benefits *among project stakeholders.*

The cost-benefit methodology justifies project investments by determining that the *aggregate* of a project's benefits outweighs the sum of project costs by an acceptable margin. But this justification is not sufficient for several reasons. First, losses and harm caused to the displaced individuals are not compensated by the aggregate benefits of development, because the distribution of these benefits is not tailored accordingly. The displacees are seldom among the direct beneficiaries of such projects. [23] Because the CBA method cannot predict and channel the allocation of a program's future benefits

---

[22]   In the Philippines Batangas Port Development project, for instance, a social planner has introduced the IRR model to sharpen the perception by project staff of risk intensity and accordingly calibrate the reconstruction strategy (Spiegel 1997). He used a simple five-point Lickert scale to hypothesize the risk intensity for Batangas relocatees (that is, low risk potential, moderately low, medium, moderately high, high) for each one of the eight risk variables: landlessness, joblessness, homelessness, and so on. The goal was to tailor a comprehensive risk-response package that allocates differential resources commensurate to each risk intensity, in ways attuned to specific circumstances in that location.

[23]   Mohan Mathur gives the example of electricity generated by projects in the Singrauli region of India, which is available to people hundreds of miles away in Delhi and other north Indian cities, while those who gave up their lands for the construction of power plants often have no access to electricity. "In fact," he writes, "planners' view of projects as a means of eradicating poverty makes little sense to those who lose their lands and livelihoods. ... Development programs are increasingly being seen as inimical to people's interests and responsible for their worsening, not improving, situation" (Mathur 1999).

with reasonable certainty, the wholesale accounting of costs and benefits covers up a morally fallacious and haphazard distribution of these benefits. [24] Second, the real losses and full costs of displacement are typically not valued and measured properly. Therefore, they are not included and accounted for fully in projects' CBAs.

As the economic justification of projects is based on cost-benefit analysis, compensation levels tend to be brought down as much as possible to obey the cost-minimizing commandments of CBA. The frequent response to displacement, therefore, is to pay the least compensation possible, to externalize a large part of real costs, and to abandon the displaced people to fend for themselves after being uprooted. Even though this response has allowed impoverishment to run rampant in so many cases, it continues to be practiced widely.

The analysis of capital losses (physical, natural, human, and social capital) in the first part of this chapter documented many of the socioeconomic costs that are routinely overlooked under current procedures. A large part of these real costs is treated as "externalities" in current costing practice. Externalized out of projects' budgets, these costs are left to be borne by those who suffer the displacement. This is why the "justification" of costs to individuals through aggregate cost-benefit accounting is logically crude, and glosses over the real impoverishment impacts. It devalues individuals' losses and leaves many negative socioeconomic effects unaddressed.

The fact that development projects often produce real long-term gains for beneficiaries does not make the uprooting less painful for the displacees. In real-life terms, personal costs are neither fully subtracted from the aggregate benefits, nor paid for by the project's beneficiaries. These costs are covered only in small part by the meager compensation for expropriated assets and are borne in disproportionately large part by the population group victimized in the name of the "greater good for the greater numbers." This kind of spurious rationality conflicts with social justice. It vitiates both development philosophy and planning practice. Moreover, tolerance vis-à-vis this incomplete methodology in project economic analyses does not en-

---

[24]   The randomness and inequities of access to the "gains or pains" of development become obvious on the ground, when by some "wheel of fortune" — as in the case of downstream irrigation development vis-à-vis upstream inundation and destruction — the program generates benefits for certain population segments while it inflicts adversity upon other population groups (unlucky enough to live upstream). Thus, the absence of distributional analysis in CBA legitimizes by default — and helps perpetuate — situations where some people share the gains, while others share the pains.

courage planners to seek genuine alternative solutions.[25] In sum, the CBA methodology, and its distorted application, are responsible for unnecessary tolerance of risks and, by omission, the magnification of perverse effects that otherwise could be counteracted.

To overcome the incompleteness of CBA, explicit distributional analysis should be introduced as mandatory in the methodology of development projects. Projects that involve displacement are a special subcategory of projects, more complex in their effects than others, and they should therefore include a special economic and financial analysis, distinct from CBA. This analysis must be focused on distribution. The "equity compass" requires that *cost and benefits be calculated distinctly for each population category affected, positively or negatively* (rather than indiscriminately for the society at large or for the project as a whole). This requirement flows from the principle that *differential* impacts must be recognized. This is, in fact, the principle that led to adopting safeguarding policies, such as the resettlement policy. This principle should therefore be translated in analytical economic methodologies able to make such differentiation.

The survival of improper methodologies for costing resettlement is due in many countries to the absence of national (domestic) policy and legal frameworks that define the rights and entitlements of people affected by state-imposed displacements or private-sector investments that cause displacement. Within such policy vacuums, arbitrariness easily sets in. Instituting equitable policies, as well as revising outdated policy provisions affecting resettlement (such as land acquisition or eminent domain law), needs to occur through a process of open public debate on development's goals and means, so that not only procedures but also entrenched mind-sets among decisionmakers, politicians, and technicians can be influenced and modified.[26] It will take policy debates and policy decisions within

---

[25]   I analyzed the economics of involuntary resettlement in a more detailed way elsewhere (see Cernea 1999). Also, for a detailed discussion of methodological fallacies in the economics of resettlement, see Pearce 1999.
[26]   The broad changes needed "make indispensable a wide participation of the civil society in such 'debate' on the viability and justifiability of projects themselves. This is precisely why the formulating and drafting of a policy and legislation needs to be converted into a *process* of generating wider public debate on the projects and the very patterns of development that create widespread displacement. If, after the due process outlined above, displacement becomes inevitable, resettlement must become an opportunity, a mandate for reconstructing production systems, raising standards of living, restoring community and kinship relations and minimizing the conflict with the host community" (Kothari 1995).

many countries and development agencies to mandate changes in the way project economic analysis, risk analysis, and CBA are applied to projects entailing involuntary resettlement.

Perhaps the most damaging consequence of applying only, and often distortingly, the cost-benefit analysis is *the underfinancing of resettlement components* in projects. If the losses to displaced people are not calculated fairly for compensation, and if the economic and financial analysis does not budget the investments needed (above simple compensation) to restart productive activities and trigger development, the resulting financing for resettlement is necessarily insufficient. Consequently, the impoverishment trends cannot be stopped.

In contrast, we argue that the response to displacement/impoverishment risks resulting from the model must be predicated not just on an "economics of compensation" but on an *"economics of recovery"* and development (Cernea 1999). The difference is fundamental. It requires the full internalization of resettlement costs *and* the allocation of growth-supporting investments, in addition to compensation. It implies an economic analysis of resettlement that goes beyond CBA and would lead to different patterns of financing resettlement.

It must be stated clearly: the cost of productively reestablishing a displaced family and a community is bound to exceed the strict market value of the physical losses imposed on that family or community. By definition, compensation alone is never sufficient for reestablishing a similar socioeconomic basis for resettlers. As long as resettlement planning will be centered on asset-compensation alone, it will not be able to achieve the policy goal of restoring and improving resettlers' livelihood. [27] This is why it is necessary to build a new economics of resettlement, transforming what now is essentially a compensation-based economics into an economics of recovery. The new economics of recovery would justify growth-enhancing investments in resettlement operations, in addition to providing compensation, to support resettlers' development. Formulating such an economics of recovery, with its set of analytical tools and measurements, is a professional challenge to economists. But ultimately, affirming and implementing a new economics is a political matter (see also Cernea 1996, 1999), part of a public policy response to hard dilemmas of development.

---

[27]   "The key to development-oriented resettlement is to adopt a people-centered approach, not a property-compensation approach" (Serageldin 1994).

The conclusion is inescapable: Because government agencies use the weight of the state and the force of the law to impose expropriation and displacement, it is incumbent upon governments to enable those displaced to get back on their feet and share in the benefits made possible by their displacement.

Budgetary resources for enabling livelihood reconstruction can indeed be significantly supplemented through policy decisions for mandating that resettlers would share in the stream of benefits from the projects they make possible. Van Wicklin (1999) has identified a vast range of options for providing such access to benefits. Such sharing is not only an equitable way of financing the true costs of reconstruction but also a necessity, given the limitations of other available resources.

Resettlers' participation in risk analysis

Finally, the lack of consultation with the populations likely to be displaced during project preparation and before final decision-making compounds the fallacies introduced by inadequate economic analytical methods. It is correctly argued that participation through consultation with potentially affected people is indispensable for "resettlement in development mode" (Bartolome, de Wet, Mander 1999). The weak institutional capacity of state agencies for resettlement planning and implementation in many developing countries (Gill 1999) make participation of affected people even more necessary.

Information and communication between planners and resettlers is instrumental, in this respect, for early warnings and for making possible joint preventive activities. However, transparent information is still a rare occurrence. Dysfunctional communication between decisionmakers and groups affected by displacement are one of the roots of resettlement failure. As Mairal and Bergua (1996) have convincingly demonstrated, the risk-perception of would-be resettlers differs considerably from what technical experts and agencies tend to think about risks resulting from displacement. Their research has confirmed the hypothesis that agencies' failure to grasp what is socially perceived as risks has "played an essential role in the escalation of conflict in the Zaragoza dam area" in Spain.

For resettlers themselves, the predictive (warning) utility of the IRR model is that it enables them, and their organizations, to be informed for conscious participation, negotiation, and adoption of coping (resource-mobilization) strategies, with lead time. Resettlers must receive information in a timely and transparent manner, understand well the impending displacement, and overcome disbelief or the tendency to denial. By forecasting the chain effects of displacement, the IRR model helps informed participation and prompts resettlers to search for alternatives, to resist inadequately prepared displacements before they occur, and to pursue their entitlements when displacement is unavoidable.

Conversely, breakdowns in information and communication tend to result in "reverse participation," that is, in active opposition movements against development programs (Oliver-Smith 1994, Dwivedi 1997). The ill-advised position taken by some agencies, which maintain an information embargo about likely displacements and resettlers' entitlements, virtually guarantees such opposition. Withholding information, instead of participation and transparency, is often "justified" by officials to prevent panic and stress. In fact, however, this is deceptive and self-defeating. It preempts the early mobilization of resettlers in the reconstruction of their own livelihoods. Their energy is an exceptionally important factor, which even the resettlement literature has seldom highlighted.

Resettlement research and the IRR model

To conclude the presentation of the IRR framework, it is important to briefly outline its use in recent research practice and research literature since this model was first formulated.

During the last several years, the IRR model has been increasingly discussed by researchers and practitioners and is currently "at work" in numerous development and research projects. A large study carried out by the Institute for Socioeconomic Development (ISED) in Orissa, India, took the IRR model as its conceptual and methodological basis in exploring resettlement processes caused by seven major projects (in dam construction, thermal plants, mining, and industry). The sample included 31 villages and 441 households with 2,274 people, selected from among 95 affected villages with 1,977 households. That study produced one of the most comprehensive and integrated surveys of displacement impacts published to date in India (Pandey and others 1998), confirming the framework under the practical demands of a large-scale field investigation. Pandey's research findings are structured along the model's impoverishment risks.

Another study focuses on "countering the impoverishment risks" reported research on India's Rengali dam (Ota 1996; see also Ota and Mohanty 1998). The study measured actual impacts of each risk variable, analyzing counterrisk measures and formulating recommendations about what needs to be done on the ground. Research on impoverishment risk and impacts was also started in Lesotho, at the request of the international panel monitoring the Water Engineering Project (Hitchcock, Scudder and others 1999). In Nepal (Kali Gandaki Project) the application of the model in several ongoing impact evaluation resettlement studies has revealed positive resettlement experiences and produced operational recommendations (Sapkota 1999).

The theoretical implications and potential of the IRR have also been discussed during the last four to five years in several international scientific conferences that took place in Colombia, South Africa, India, the United States, and elsewhere, as well as in print in numerous publications. Several books and studies have been devoted to discussion of the validity of the model, tested its applicability, or proposed developments in its variables.

A book published in 1999 by an Indian resettlement scholar, L. K. Mahapatra, reports on an original test to which he submitted the model: the author undertook a vast secondary analysis of virtually the entire empirical research literature on resettlement published in India during the last 20 to 30 years, to explore whether or not the IRR model is validated by the findings reported in the research literature. His analysis fully confirmed the model. Parasuraman (1999:45) discussed the impoverishment risks identified by the IRR model in his book on displacements in India and concluded that in India the "loss of land is the single most important cause of postdisplacement impoverishment. M. Basu (1994) explored the linkages between the IRR model and the "basic needs" framework, emphasizing that people's basic needs are retrieved and addressed within the IRR model. Juliette Hayes derived and developed from the risks part of the IRR framework a "capital loss model" in displacement processes, with intriguing implications for further economic research on capital losses.

Several scholars proposed expanding the IRR by including other risk variables and losses, such as the loss of access to public services (Mathur 1998, 1999), loss of civil rights (Downing 1996a), or temporary loss of access to schooling for school-age children caught in the throes of displacement (Mahapatra 1999a, 1999b). Whether or not these or other risks should be added to the general risk model is a question deserving reflection, but the very proposals exploit the flexibility and adaptability of the model itself, which is prone to refinements.

As this chapter goes to print, Robert Hackenberg's article in the journal *Human Organization* has opened up a "public discussion" in that journal among anthropologists around the impoverishment risks and the economics of involuntary displacement and reconstruction (Hackenberg 1999).

Significantly, also, the first full-scale research project on conflict-caused refugee populations that explicitly tests and applies the IRR model has been completed by Robert Muggah (1999) in Colombia. This study generated important new findings about internally displaced refugees. It recommends policy and strategy measures for reestablishing or creating institutional capacities necessary for resettling refugees (Muggah 1999). Crisp, in turn, undertook a critical review of the United Nations High Commissioner for Refugees (UNHCR) program for Mozambique's huge postconflict refugee population, in light of the IRR framework. In that "shattered society coming together again," Crisp revealed causes of successes and failures in the itinerary "from social disarticulation to social reconstruction" (Crisp 1996).

In short, the IRR is being increasingly used operationally, and proving its worth, in project preparation, appraisals; monitoring and evaluation work; in designing indicators or formulating recommendations; as well as in theory-led basic research. Further use of the risks and reconstruction model will certainly test its potential in more ways and will explore its relevance for various types of displacements and reconstruction approaches.

Having myself done considerable research and operational work on resettlement, I cannot emphasize enough the difficulties involved in actually preventing and mitigating its impoverishment risks and moral hazards. This is why forecasting impoverishment trends is crucial for adopting and implementing policies that avoid displacement and counteract undesirable outcomes when resettlement is unavoidable. Failure to acknowledge and make known the economic and cultural risks inherent in displacement only allows them to unfold unimpeded in every case. Conversely, equitable policy, plus planning, financing, and implementing resettlement with the participation of those affected, can create the premises for the improvement of resettlers' livelihoods.

Acknowledgments

The formulation and refinement of the IRR model has much benefited from discussions around earlier papers in which it was presented. I am grateful, in particular, to R. Cernea, D. Aronson, T. Downing, D. Gibson, M. Gill, S. Guggenheim, L. K. Mahapatra, H. H. Mathur, M. C. Mejia, V. Lassailly-Jacob, W. Partridge, M. Lin-

Rodrigo, T. Scudder, I. Serageldin, A. Steer, P. Streeten, and H. van der Tak for their valuable comments, which have helped strengthen the argument, and to Gracie Ochieng for her work in processing the chapter. Parts of this chapter were presented as the Keynote Address at the International Conference "Towards New Approaches to Resettlement," University of Oxford, RSP, September 1996, and at several other international conferences — at Rhodes University, South Africa; in New Delhi, India; Harvard University, Cambridge; and Yale University, New Haven — or were published in earlier, preliminary versions. Debates in these conferences have enriched the synthesis presented in this chapter, and I thank all who made a contribution.

The views expressed are the author's own and do not necessarily reflect the view of the institutions with which he is associated.

CHAPTER 2

"Successful" refugee settlement: are past experiences relevant?

Eftihia Voutira and Barbara Harrell-Bond[1]

At the transition from the 20th to the 21st century, different causes of uprootedness have left many population groups in what are described as refugee-like situations. A major underlying challenge for the contributors to the present book is the feasibility of arriving at a theoretical model of resettlement that applies to different situations of forced migration — those resulting from impoverishment, civil strife, or "development" projects that uproot populations.

At the core of the debate is Cernea's conceptual model of resettlement represented as a clash between "impoverishment risks" and "livelihood reconstruction" (see Cernea, this volume, and 1995b). Cernea builds the model upon the development-induced type of displacements, but highlights impoverishment as a consequence of virtually all types of displacement. This is certainly true, and methodologically it allows for a common denominator in refugee and "oustee" experience (Cernea 1996a: 296-7).[2] His interest is in bridging the research and policy divide concerning interventions on behalf of both sets of displaced populations and in encouraging a

---

[1]   The authors wish to thank all those who commented on this paper, particularly Professor Elizabeth Colson. We also wish to acknowledge the work of Anna Schmidt and Aimé Sangara, who assisted with both substantive and technical aspects of the production of this paper.

[2]   The term "oustee" is used in the conventional sense of describing populations that have been forcibly displaced by planned development projects and as shorthand for the expression "development displaced" people (Cernea 1995b).

two-way transfer of successful experiences (1996a:293; also see Cernea 1990b; Cernea and Guggenheim 1993). But how feasible is such "bridging" and experience transfer?

The difficulty, as we will show, is that not only are the causes of the impoverishment different, but also definitions of "success" are not the same. For Cernea, and, in general, for development agencies such as the World Bank, success would find the resettlers' livelihoods not only restored, but also, if possible, improved from their previous situation. In contrast, the United Nations High Commissioner for Refugees (UNHCR) seeks, instead of integration in the host economy, the elimination of the refugee situation altogether through repatriation (HRW 1997). The incompatibility of the two current "solutions" to displacement has increased.

This chapter argues that the major obstacle to a reciprocal transfer of knowledge from refugee and oustee settlement experience is not just conceptual, residing in one-sided research, it is *institutional*, originating in the practices of major agencies. There are separate bureaucracies operating under separate budgets that are responsible for these two categories of displaced people, and they maintain a radical division of labor between them. Moreover, they each define their roles and their relationships vis-à-vis the host and the donor states differently. They function under different legal and regulatory regimes, and, in some instances, promote incompatible long-term objectives as to what constitutes a "successful" solution for the particular beneficiary populations. Instances of good institutional cooperation, which overcomes the idiosyncrasies of separate bureaucracies, do exist, as Brown (see this volume) reports from postconflict reconstruction work in Azerbaijan. However, such cooperation is not yet as frequent as it should be.

Aligning the goals for resettlers and refugees

As we already noted, current multinational efforts aim to eliminate the problem of cross-border refugees through repatriation. Until this "solution" can be realized, refugees are the recipients of relief programs, described now as "care and maintenance." These interventions are never sufficient to allow for the restoration of livelihoods. However, oustees from development project areas require temporary income support, but resettlement programs are, from the outset, designed to be "developmental." The World Bank policy demands attention to the rights of oustees and their entitlements. What results from applying this conceptual model of "reconstructing livelihoods" (see Cernea, this volume) to refugees is that their settlement, whether in the country of asylum or as returnees in their own home country, is not considered successful unless it also entails the restoration of their livelihoods, if not an improvement of their former conditions, as this also is the objective in the case of assistance to development oustees.

Most importantly, as we will show, the role of national governments in making policy concerning refugees and oustees vis-à-vis new international agents has fundamentally changed. This change has a direct impact on our capacity to assess the relevance of "successful" historical examples and, therefore, their transferability in contemporary contexts.

States can still determine policy concerning oustees, given that oustees are citizens, while, with very few exceptions, today it is the international humanitarian community that defines policy *for* sovereign states in relation to the refugees they host. As will be shown, the few examples of "successful" refugee settlement from which policymakers concerned with oustee settlement could learn are those where the host government was fully in charge of policy.

This chapter shows that, although there are examples of "successful" settlement of refugees and that these are instructive in providing an understanding of the relationships between refugee and oustee experiences, not every type of "success" is transferable from one kind of displacement to another. Transferability is largely dependent on the contingent historical and contextual conditions that have made the "success" cases. More or less similar contextual coalitions may sometimes exist elsewhere, but frequently the contextual definitions differ. These conditions cannot be reproduced, given the emergence of a new global political economy in which the observance of the rights of refugees, which include their right to physical protection, non-*refoulement*, and integration in their host society, has deteriorated. In this respect, contemporary refugee policy does have a lot more to learn from policies about development oustee entitlements than it had in the past.

Successful refugee settlement: rerooting the uprooted

One of the most commonly held assumptions today is that incoming cross-border refugees are a temporary phenomenon, while development oustees, being citizens of their own country, are to be permanently resettled. This was not always the case. In its original conception, first under the League of Nations and then under the United Nations (U.N.), the policy for refugee settlement — integration in the country of asylum — was *also* intended to provide the basis for their *permanent rerooting*, leading ultimately to their full social and economic participation in the new country as citizens. In formal terms, then, the category "refugee" was expected to disappear, as they became naturalized in their arrival country as citizens, like all oustees already are.[3] Underlying this approach is the principle that all uprooted people should be viewed as resources for national development (see, for example, Zetter 1992; Harrell-Bond 1996; Voutira 1997a; Weighill 1997).

The case of resettlement of approximately 1.5 million Greek refugees from Turkey in post-World War I Greece is a paradigmatic case of a "successful" example of national integration, boundary consolidation, and the reconstruction of livelihoods through investment in the rural economy.[4] This large-scale refugee settlement was the result of the forced exchange of populations between Greece and Turkey as part the Lausanne Treaty (1923). This is a case in which the concept of refugees is broadened to include a group that was an ethnic minority in its country of normal incidence and, through an exchange of population, was dislocated and sent back to the nation-state where that ethnic group was in the vast majority. Their rehabilitation has been described as the greatest peacetime achievement of the modern Greek State (Mavrogodatos 1992:9). The common objective of the Greek government and the Refugee Settlement Commission (RSC), which was the main organization supervised by the League of Nations, was the creation of rural settlements in northern Greece and particularly in Macedonia. The primary role of the RSC was to manage the two foreign loans advanced with the explicit purpose of *rural* refugee rehabilitation. The composition of the RSC included two government officials and two "foreigners," representatives of the creditors, which were the governments of the United States and Britain. The work of these foreigners was to

---

[3]   The view of the limited nature of the refugee "problem" was mirrored in the provisions of the U.N. in establishing the Office of the United Nations High Commission for Refugees as one whose tenure as well as geographical mandate was limited (Holborn 1975, Vol. 1:68). The 1967 U.N. Protocol made UNHCR's mandate global, but it continues to be renewable by the U.N. every five years.

[4]   See also Hirschon in this volume for a critical approach to this success story.

participate in the planning and oversee the expenditure of the funds (Voutira 1994, 1997a).[5]

The complex social engineering devised by the RSC was tailored to the interplay of distinct local, social, economic, and political factors; for example, the availability of Muslim properties and large estates in the region that could be expropriated. It also involved the targeting of resources for the improvement of the agricultural sector, which was highly undeveloped. Thirdly, the particular national security concerns required that the northern border be secured from both the threat of communism from the north and irredentism from other newly established Balkan states (Mavrogodatos 1983).

Refugees were divided into two categories: rural and urban (Hirschon 1989; see also Hirschon, this volume). These distinctions did not refer to their origins, but to the place of their resettlement. Loans for rural settlement were made under the condition that the money was to be used in projects that were "irreversible and long-term": *no funds were to be used for temporary relief purposes*. Rehabilitation was largely accomplished through agriculture and home industries. These were financed through loans and compensation (or reparations) for property left behind. In establishing the amounts to which people were entitled, a critical role was played by refugee associations, which were organized on the basis of the localities from which they originated (Pentzopoulos 1962). Their primary aim was to document the exchange value of losses and write petitions on behalf of the members of these communities that they now represented in Greece.[6]

---

[5]   These were Hans Morgentau (U.S.) and Charles Eddy (U.K.). Their memoirs and assessments of the success of the Asia Minor refugee settlement are important documents because we see not only the priorities of the international community but also the way in which their conclusions have been integrated in modern Greek representations about the "refugees" representing the "progressive" forces in Greek society, by injecting "new blood" in the Old Greece (Voutira 1995).

[6]   In the Greek language, there are two terms for the money used for the resettlement program. First, *apozimiosi* is the term for compensation for loss of property and livelihood (which might be better described as "reparation"). This term refers *to the debt owed by the state to the refugees for their losses*. The other term, *apokatastasi*, refers to the money given to the refugees by the state that was given as a loan that had to be repaid. The wave of Pontic Greek "repatriates" who have recently arrived from the Soviet Union

(Note continues on the following page.)

What made this successful resettlement unique? First was the magnitude of the population movement: 1.5 million people arrived within a space of four years (Hirschon 1989). Second, it was the speed in which they were accommodated: "In three years, from 1923–1926, the largest part of the refugee resettlement had been accomplished" (Mavrogodatos 1992:10). Possibly the most important dimension was the way in which refugees were used to serve multiple political and economic interests of the Greek state. One of these was the creation of a culturally homogeneous population: before the arrival of the refugees from Asia Minor, the population of the region was 42.6 percent Greek; by 1926, it had risen to 88.8 percent (Pentzopoulos 1962:134). Another was the strategy of investment in the impoverished rural economy. The third was the imposition of the revolutionary measure of radically redistributing the land in central and northern Greece, where the majority of refugee rural resettlement took place. By giving land titles to the newcomers, the government ensured the creation of a *petit-bourgeois* class with an interest in maintaining liberal democracy against the threat of communism.

Another historical particularity contributing as a factor was the quasi-feudal political economy of Greece, at the time with a government in power that was *willing to take the risk* of redefining the institution of property by expropriating the rural lands for distribution to the refugees. This policy of redistributing the land involved, in fact, a type of social revolution *from above* that undermined the possibility of revolution *from below*. As Mavrogodatos notes, the introduction of these radical measures was not done by the refugees, it was done *before* them and *for* them by the Greek state (1992:12).

A comparable type of national consolidation and postconflict economic reconstruction was carried out in Cyprus after the events of 1974 when 180,000 Greek Cypriot refugees from the Turkish-occupied north had to be resettled in the south, in this case largely in an urban setting (Zetter 1992). Like Greece in the 1920s, at the time of the war in Cyprus, the island's economy was based on "small-scale entrepreneurial capitalism" (Zetter, 22). Some 70 percent of

---

feel cheated; when they fled Pontos toward the Caucasus they were never compensated for their losses and are now demanding they receive *apozimiosi* (Voutira 1991). See Lee (1986) for a detailed discussion on the right of the refugees to compensation and how its neglect has allowed states to create refugees with impunity.

the prewar economy had depended on earnings from the north, from which the refugees had been expelled.

The logic of this "successful" settlement was based on deploying refugees in the restructuring of the economy. An urban housing program was established, with refugees building houses for themselves and employed in the postwar reconstruction projects. They were paid for their labor, and with this money they were able to buy their own food, thus stimulating local production. Analysis has shown that Cyprus's current economic boom can be traced to the government's calculated and strategic use of this disaster as an opportunity: "The catastrophe of 1974 had turned the government of Cyprus into an engine for economic development and social change" (Kliot and Mansfeld 1994:354; Zetter 1992). For example, the government took this opportunity to establish a social welfare system that provided free social services on the basis of need rather than refugee status. Free public education was introduced at all levels, together with a scholarship and loans for study abroad.

Crucially, as in the Greek andAsia Minor refugee case, the government behaved in a strongly interventionist manner: "Faced with a radically new context for public policy, evidence suggests that the government was at least opportunistic, at most distinctly instrumental and managerial in its approach to the potential offered by the crisis" (Zetter 1992:13–14). External funding was made available through loans and grants; all of the humanitarian funds raised by the UNHCR were channeled into the national assistance program. In the Greek-Cypriot government's own words:

> Success was based on a number of exogenous and endogenous factors. Endogenous factors, such as the booming Arab markets, the Lebanese crisis of 1975, favorable weather and the international market prices for some of the major Cypriot agricultural products, together with foreign aid provided some of the impetus that lifted the economy. An additional element has been the availability of credit facilities, which helped bridge the financing gap. Internally, the aggressive and expansionary fiscal and monetary policies, the acceptance by the trade unions of a substantial cut on wage levels, entrepreneurial ability, which exploited the export opportunities that came along, the diligence, perseverance, self-sacrifice, and hard work of the people formed the front which helped lift the economy out of decline, pushing it along the path of recovery (Republic of Cyprus, n.d.:16).

The same belief—that the uprooted can become a resource for national economic and political development—underpinned the approach to the resettlement of an estimated 9 million people, refugees from World War II, living in desperate conditions in the center of Europe. Refugees were promoted as the instrument to fuel the economies of the receiving states, which were mainly Australia, New Zealand, and those of North and South America (Harrell-Bond 1985). Further advantages anticipated included regional economic integration and democratic cooperation among Western states. In fact, for the allies, the dispossessed were seen as the seeds for advancing liberal democracy and as votes for maintaining it.

In contrast to the Greek and Cypriot examples, these refugees could not be construed as co-ethnics with the host population; the explicit criteria used in promoting this "era of migration," that is, the settlement of refugees in Europe, was the fact that they were *white*. Such racial ideology is evident in the stated views that "reception countries overseas will clamor for white population," and in the expression of regret that "The Union of South Africa with its dangerously small white population is actually calling a halt to immigration" (Harrell-Bond 1985). In the Greece and Cyprus cases, the hosts and the refugees shared one common enemy in national terms, the Turks. And, as with the European refugees, they were expected to share a categorical rejection of another potential enemy, communism. This was articulated in the last report of the RSC, which argued that:

> if the patriotism of the ruling classes and the good sense of the refugees continue to hold in check those doctrines which claim that the happiness and the progress of the nation can only be acquired by submitting to the rule of a group of fanatics, enemies of all enlightenment, persecutors of all liberties and all initiative; if in several thousand years...a strong race of peasants born out of the mixing of all of the elements of Hellenism secures the prosperity of Greece, that result will have been due to the impulse originally given by the RSC (*Bank of Athens Bulletin*, December 1930:1868).

In the preceding cases, the significant variables that allowed for the assessment of refugee settlement as "successful" are permanence of residence and status as citizens; strong government intervention in devising and implementing policy; ethnic and/or ideological affinity between newcomers and hosts that allowed for the emergence of a sense of solidarity and the acceptance of sacrifice on the part of the receiving populations; an emphasis upon rehabilitation rather than relief, with "compensation" and the use of humanitarian assistance functioning as an integral part of national social and economic reconstruction. In all of these cases, the underlying approach of the host governments was to conceptualize the disaster as both a challenge and a development opportunity (see Setter 1992:13).

Tibetan refugees: another variant of "successful" refugee settlement?

Upon the invasion and occupation of Tibet by the Chinese in 1959, Tibetans fled to India, Nepal, and Bhutan (Norbu 1994). A small group of Tibetan refugees in Nepal was purposely resettled in Switzerland.[7] Today there are very small numbers of Tibetans living in other parts of the world. They are self-governed through Dharamsala, the seat of their government-in-exile, have their own constitution, have diplomatic representation in several countries, and members pay taxes from wherever they live in exile. Before flight, Tibetans lived in scattered hamlets, speaking mutually incomprehensible regional dialects. From the beginning they were encouraged by their own leadership to anticipate a very long period of life in exile.

In addition to their own self-assessment, there is a general consensus among scholars and humanitarian organizations that the Tibetan refugees constitute a case of "success" (Norbu 1994). Like in Greece and Cyprus, refugee policy was an issue for attention at the highest levels of government. In India, Nehru himself took a personal interest and granted asylum to the Dalai Lama on March 30, 1959, allowing him to set up a government-in-exile in Dharamsala. Furthermore, Nehru exercised pressure in persuading Bhutan to provide land for Tibetan settlement and recognize the Dalai Lama's political authority over his people. As in the previous cases, Tibetan refugee settlement also served to justify political agendas (Norbu 1994). In Nepal, the king made a Swiss geologist, Dr. Toni Hagen, responsible for policy concerning the Tibetan refugees and, with support from the International Committee of the Red Cross (ICRC), he was able to channel the refugees' cultural capital into income-

---

[7] This was arranged by Dr Toni Hagen. When asked why, he replied that he believed it would be good for the Swiss to be exposed to the Tibetan culture (personal communication with Harrell-Bond).

generating projects, including creating a carpet-making industry that today accounts for the single largest source of Nepal's foreign exchange and employs more Nepalese than refugees (Hagen 1994).

In India, all external sources of humanitarian assistance to the Tibetans, including funds from UNHCR, were coordinated through Dharamsala, which was responsible for identifying priorities and allocating resources. In the early period of their exile, the Indian government employed Tibetans in road construction projects until they were able to establish the economies of their own communities. An anthropologist, Melvyn Goldstein, reports that in south India the Tibetans had become an economic success within five years of starting a settlement. He also observed, "very little manifestation of the dysfunctional behavior commonly associated with the 'refugee' syndrome. There was little incidence of mental and emotional disorders and no incidence of alcoholism" (Goldstein 1978:403, as cited by Norbu 1994:12). Another study of the Tibetans in northern India found them to have "successfully emerged from a self-sufficient barter economy into a competitive economy, and have adjusted to the new situation" (Saklaini 1984:216, 13).

Educational services for Tibetan refugees in India are managed by the Central Tibetan School Administration, described as "an autonomous organization set up by the Government of India, Ministry of Education, Social Welfare and Culture" (Nowak 1977). Facilities include both residential and day schools located throughout India. Students are offered a modern curriculum that will allow them access to the institutions of higher education in India. At the same time, courses specifically designed for Tibetans in language, religion, history, and customs are provided to ensure that the students "cannot fail to acquire a strongly Tibetan self-image in the process of their education" (Nowak 1977:191–198). Thus, unlike the previous cases of "successful" refugee settlement that have been considered above, which were predicated on an understanding that the refugees would "assimilate," the Tibetan case is an example of successful adaptation of refugees in their host societies while maintaining their identity and engaging in nation-building in exile.[8]

In fact, the essential characteristic of Tibetan refugee settlement, noted by all observers, is the fact that Tibetans have done more than

---

[8]   By "nation-building," we refer to the acquisition of a collective sense of membership and belonging to a distinct group. In this context, nation-building can be considered distinct from "nationalism as a political program that aims at the congruence of cultural and political sovereignty over a territory (Gellner 1983).

maintain a distinct group identity. They have promoted and developed a Tibetan culture that was increasingly suppressed in their home country, achieving in exile what has been described as "the renaissance of Tibetan civilization" (Haimendorf 1990 as quoted by Norbu 1994). As Haimendorf, an anthropologist, puts it: "The ability of homeless and impoverished groups of refugees to build and fund in foreign lands numerous monasteries of a remarkably high architectural standard and their success in developing viable monastic communities similar to those of Tibet is one of the miracles of the twentieth century" (Haimendorf 1990 as quoted by Norbu 1994, 2).

The Saharawi refugees:
another case of nation-building in exile

Like the Tibetans, the Saharawi also provide a model of "successful" refugee adaptation without assimilation. The war for self-determination began in 1975 when Morocco invaded and occupied what was the Spanish Sahara, a colony of Spain. As refugees, they have settled in three areas in the desert region of Tindouf and have been granted autonomy and self-government by the Algerian government.[9]

Life in the camps is both regulated and managed by the Sahara Arab Democratic Party. The organization of aid originates with the Algerian Red Crescent which, together with the Saharawi Red Crescent, assesses all needs and mobilizes support from the Algerian government, UNHCR, and other foreign donors, including a network of support groups that exist in many Western countries. The logic of the organization of aid is guided by the general concern with social transformation and the modernization of their economy, which, before colonialism, was based on cattle raising and nomadism.

Even though the population depends on foreign assistance for survival, the community-controlled self-management of the settlements means that there are no experts, advisers, foreign aid workers, and volunteers in them. At the center of the administration are women whose position of equality is the dominant motif of Saharawi social organization, which is explained as:

> Our women were never veiled. They always worked, but the difference today is that women are politicized and

---

[9]   The Sahara Arab Democratic Republic is recognized by many countries around the world, including the Organization of African Unity (OAU).

are at the base of our national culture...every woman learns to drive and to shoot the rifle. Military training used to be taught by men but now these instructors have been replaced by women. Each woman goes through the entire curriculum, but after taking exams is allowed to specialize in whatever she chooses (Harrell-Bond 1981).

In contrast with the Tibetans, at least those in India, whose education is based on the national curriculum and supplemented with classes on Tibetan history, language, and culture, the Saharawi have been developing their own curriculum based on the Arabic language, with additional training in French and Spanish. Both Tibetans and the Saharawi are aiming toward self-determination and the establishment of an independent, sovereign state. However, unlike the Tibetans, who are pacifists by creed, the Saharawi have been engaged in armed conflict with Morocco. Like all the cases discussed above, providing a safe haven for the Saharawi was compatible with the political aims of the host state.[10]

"Invisible" refugees: host-state sovereignty and international assistance

As was noted in the Introduction, one of the obstacles to the transferability of experiences and lessons learned from the settlement of oustees as compared with refugees is the question, "Who decides refugee policy — the refugees, the host government, or the international humanitarian regime?" The answer to this question will also inform the definition of successful resettlement of refugees, that is, from whose point of view it is judged to be a success.

We saw in the case of Greece that it was under the auspices of the RSC that government and representatives of foreign aid worked together for some seven years to settle the refugees. It is from *their* standpoint that refugee settlement was judged to be a success. In the case of Cyprus, the government assumed *full* responsibility for policy, management, and implementation of the assistance program for refugees. Neither country relied at any point either exclusively or extensively on external sources of funds. Success, in the case of Cyprus, was determined to be a success through objective economic criteria,

---

10 From the founding of the OAU, Algeria has supported the independence of colonies in Africa, including its military support for the Saharawi. It has also had a long-term border dispute with Morocco.

such as the gross domestic product (GDP), levels of unemployment and foreign exchange transfers (Republic of Cyprus n.d.). However, Tibetan and Saharawi refugee settlement represents a variation, where the host government worked with the refugees to effect their resettlement, allowing for the full autonomy of the refugees in the planning and management of their affairs. All international aid was channeled directly through the refugee organizations. In the case of Tibetans living in India, success is measured in terms the extent to which refugees were able to support themselves and maintain their identity. In Nepal, it is measured by the capacity of the Tibetan refugees to contribute to the national economy of the host (that is, foreign exchange earnings and expanding employment). For the Saharawi, success is measured by the extent to which they are able to maintain control over their own social development in exile and promote their longer-term democratic goals, which include the equality of women.[11]

Today, all of these cases constitute an exception because of what has become the norm in refugee policymaking and implementation since the expansion of UNHCR's mandate in 1967 beyond the confines of Europe. Given that since the 1970s, the majority of refugees are found in the South, refugee policy is typically decided outside the country that hosts refugees: notably by those who hold the purse strings—donor states. Normally, when a host country receives refugees, it requests international assistance from UNHCR, whose mandate includes the power to *administer* any funds, public or private, received for assistance to refugees and to distribute them among private and public agencies deemed best qualified to administer such assistance (Lee 1986). Once it began working in the South, its own role as the "guardian" and protector of refugees was reinterpreted to make the administration of material assistance through nongovernmental organizations, rather than through host governments, its *method* of protecting refugees (Holborn 1975).[12] Progressively, the conjunction of protection with material assistance became coextensive with the refugee camps where refugees were required to live to receive aid. States wanting to receive international assistance in the form of relief for refugees on their territory were required

---

[11]   The promotion of gender equality in the context of *contemporary* Algeria introduces a new variable of potential tension between the values of the refugee community and those of the host state that are worthy of further research.

[12]   Recently, Nicholas Morris has defended the UNHCR against the common accusation that its role as the protector of refugees suffers from its association with assistance (1997:4993-4).

to provide the land for the establishment of the camps and to recognize the organizations, whether foreign or local, designated by the UNHCR as most qualified to administer them (Voutira and Harrell-Bond 1995).

There are two examples of refugee settlement since that time that are instructive to examine because they help to clarify the relative space and room to maneuver that is left to governments that host refugees. The flight of the tens of thousands of Fula-speaking people throughout the 1960s and 1970s to Sierra Leone from Sekou Toure's Guinea is a case in point. When, in the late 1960s, Sierra Leone was offered international assistance for refugees, the president, Siaka Stevens, rejected it.

Instead, the Sierra Leone government permitted the Fula to settle themselves throughout the country. Some Fula were employed in urban centers as unskilled laborers, others involved themselves in trade, many in the diamond industry, and most were cattle-herders. As "breadwinners" and earners of income, they were subject to the same fiscal obligations as ordinary Sierra Leoneans. Their leadership was absorbed into the Muslim religious community; one was even elected as the head of all the Fula-speaking population of Freetown, the capital city. Although there were incidents of conflict between local farmers and Guinean cattle-herders over land use, these were settled in the mosques or local courts (Harrell-Bond and others 1978). These refugees only became "visible" years later when Sekou Toure fell and many returned to Guinea and when UNHCR announced this movement to be a "successful" repatriation (*Refugees* 1984).

Another example of "invisible" refugees were those fleeing the anticolonial war in Guinea Bissau, a struggle that was actively supported by Organization of African Unity (OAU) members. Those who went to Guinea were, like the Fula in Sierra Leone, allowed to settle freely among their hosts. Like Siaka Stevens, when UNHCR offered to assist refugees in Guinea, Sekou Toure also refused their help. However, the many other people from Guinea Bissau who fled to Senegal were assisted by UNHCR in refugee camps located in southern Senegal.[13]

---

[13]   According to Gilbert Jaeger, head of refugee protection at the time, during their mission to Conakry they had established that the refugees were not in need of relief assistance and were being protected by their hosts. However, for the UNHCR, which was just beginning to work in Africa and had already established itself in Senegal to work with the refugees from the Guinea-Bissau war, Sekou Toure's refusal to allow them to establish its program in Guinea was "extremely embarrassing."

It can be argued that one of the main advantages that refugees in Sierra Leone and Guinea had over those in Senegal is that they did not receive international aid. If they had, they would have to be labeled as "refugees" and placed in camps and remain isolated from the host society. Moreover, the policies of these governments allowed the refugees freedom of movement and, at least in the case of the Fula in Sierra Leone, access to documents so they could travel internationally.[14]

Like the Greek, Cypriot, Indian, and Algerian cases, where hosting refugees also served political agendas, the Government of Guinea supported the refugees in their anticolonial war for independence from Portugal. Sierra Leone, however, seriously risked its relations with Guinea by hosting the Fula, who had an active interest in the overthrow of Sekou Toure's regime. The two countries were bound by a mutual defense pact at the same time, and Guinea soldiers came to Sierra Leone in the early 1970s to provide Siaka Stevens with personal protection. Thus, *unlike* the previous cases we have considered, hosting the Fula was a political liability for the Sierra Leone government. Yet, *like* the previous cases, hosting refugees and maintaining control over policy required strong political will on the part of the Sierra Leone government.

From refugees without international policy to an international policy "without" refugees

The preceding discussion focused on what were "successful" cases of refugee settlement from the standpoint of the refugees' long-term interests and the ability of the host states to preserve their sovereignty over policymaking and implementation. In all these cases, the main financial burden was carried by the host state and, when international aid was made available, the state and the refugees were in control of its distribution. The aim of Tibetan refugee settlement was to facilitate the refugees' self-sufficiency as a distinct group in host states, whether or not they would eventually return to Tibet. While maintaining their distinctiveness as a group was not one of the main preoccupations of the Fula in Sierra Leone, they were also expected to support themselves without international relief assistance and to contribute to the economy as ordinary citizens as long as they remained in the country. Similarly, for the refugees from the

---

[14]   When a Fula wanted to leave Sierra Leone, the Ministry of the Interior issued them "alien" documents.

anticolonial war in Guinea Bissau, the objective was to support themselves within the economy of Guinea independently of the outcome of the war.

It is clear from all of these cases that "successful" refugee settlement is contingent on the host state's capacity to determine its own policy for refugees vis-à-vis international aid so that these resources, money, and people can be used in the interests of national development. So far, so good. From this standpoint, refugees and oustees have the same fates: they are both contingent on the government's development priorities. At the same time, refugees exist, survive, and flourish *independently of international policy* since they are subsumed under the host state's direct authority. At what point did states lose their capacity to formulate and implement policy so that decisions about national development or development *simpliciter* no longer include refugees as a factor?

The internationalization of refugee and oustee policy: development at the core

Throughout the 1960s, the main ideology that informed views about development were drawn from modernization theory. As implemented by the World Bank and other donors who were determined to modernize Africa, the main method was the introduction of integrated rural agricultural capital-intensive development projects. The underlying assumption behind this approach to the promotion of planned settlements adopted by the World Bank was that uprooting, whether forced or not, is actually good for people: displacement makes people more susceptible to new change (IBRD 1961:131, as quoted by Daley 1989:205).

Initially, when UNHCR began to be involved in providing material assistance to refugees, its approach to refugee settlement mirrored the World Bank's integrated rural agricultural development projects and thus still viewed refugees as active participants and resources for the development of the host state.[15]

Like World Bank policies, UNHCR's program for refugees was to promote integrated zonal development as part of "multi-sectoral development projects" aimed at "strengthening infrastructural project and [providing] services [for refugees] in education, train-

---

[15]   In fact, early on in UNHCR experience in Africa, the idea was mooted that the World Bank itself should take over responsibility for developing a "refugee affected" area in Togo (interview, Jacque Cuenod, September 1997).

ing, health and agriculture" (Betts 1984:13, as quoted by Daley 1989:130). Although these parallel services were established to meet the needs of the refugees, it was believed that these could be "handed over" to host governments once self-sufficiency was achieved by the refugees. As Daley notes, this involved the belief that "both the refugee community and the local population would therefore share in the benefits accruing from the new financial investments in the area, thus avoiding friction between the two groups" (Betts 1984:13, as quoted by Daley 1989:129).

The success of this approach to the settlement of refugees, which was premised on the full integration of refugees into the socioeconomic structure of the host society, was contingent upon the willingness of host states to provide secure land tenure to refugee farmers and to follow the spirit of the 1951 Convention that promotes the naturalization of refugees as citizens. The turning point was the establishment of the OAU and the implementation of its own regional legislation, which includes provision for voluntary repatriation and calls on the international actors to assist returnees in the process of reintegration. Thereafter, in the 1970s UNHCR began, in relation to refugees in the South, to talk of "durable" rather than permanent solutions. As formulated by UNHCR, these "durable" solutions were, in order of desirability, voluntary repatriation, integration in the country of first asylum, and "resettlement" in a third country.

Resettlement in a third country, that is, to one of the traditional immigration countries in the West, was available to only a tiny minority of refugees in the South. Throughout the 1970s, voluntary repatriation was not considered a viable option for most refugees since the conditions that led to their flight had not changed. The emphasis was on "integration" in the host country. At the core of the policy was a particular construction of refugee livelihood understood as "self-sufficiency," in isolation from the host population. Donors had elaborate schemes for targeting and earmarking aid to refugees with a view, as noted above, toward "handing over" after this desired state of self-sufficiency had been achieved.

The internationalization of refugee policy: relief at the core

By the end of the 1970s, UNHCR's attempts at achieving the "self-sufficiency" and "integration" of refugees were shown to have failed (for example, see Clark and Stein 1985). Efforts to ameliorate refugees' increasing impoverishment and suffering depended on the restitution of relief programs as a temporary measure against starvation. Since that time, aid to refugees continues to be premised on their presence being *temporary* and in isolation from the host society, demarcated and symbolized by the boundaries of the refugee camp that became coextensive with aid to refugees (Voutira and Harrell-Bond 1995). International donors have never committed to the long-term investment required to respond to the maintenance of rural settlements for refugees, and states have not been encouraged to absorb these populations into their national development plans (RSP 1991).

By the 1980s (see Coles 1985), the promotion of voluntary repatriation had become the international priority. Repatriation as a solution was particularly attractive to the donors because of its potential for reducing costs (Harrell-Bond 1988). Furthermore, it was argued that most refugees would repatriate if aid were reduced or moved across the border to their country of origin (Ruiz 1987; De Waal 1988).

The adoption of repatriation as the best solution for refugees entails an unbridgeable gap between oustee and refugee experiences; the only thing that policy cannot do for oustees is return them "home." From the standpoint of repatriation, therefore, policies pertaining to each group are only comparable from the standpoint of displacement rather than settlement.

Ironically, however, the implementation of repatriation as the best solution *at all costs*, even against the refugees' own free will, makes their experiences essentially comparable. Like oustees, returnees, where forced to repatriation, undergo "involuntary resettlement," fall under the jurisdiction of their own state, are likely to be more impoverished than before they fled or even during exile, and are likely to suffer serious psychological traumas upon return, similar to the ones experienced by oustees in radically new environments. They are also confronted with similar if not greater challenges of integration in a hostile social environment, where refugee return is seen, those who stayed behind as a threat to the socioeconomic order, if not the political order, which it very often is.

Ethnic migrants, repatriates, or refugees: the relevance of the past

The *enforcement* of repatriation from Tanzania to Rwanda in December 1996, an example par excellence of the ultimate solution to the refugee problem, redefines the policy challenge by identifying the post-Cold War refugee problem as not that of original displacement, but one of coercive return (Schoepf 1997).[16] As noted in our discussion, the need to address the requirements for the successful settlement of co-ethnics are no less acute than settling refugees. It also raises the question of who is responsible for policy decisions concerning *when* refugees are to be forced to repatriate, and who is responsible for them once they have returned. One answer to this question is who pays for what. An examination of UNHCR's expenditures in 1996–97 shows that the largest expenditure has been on "care and maintenance" of refugees, and mainly in Africa. Its projections for 1998 include plans to almost double expenditures for special programs on repatriation for African refugees in 1998 (Schmidt 1997).

The current emphasis of the international policy on involuntary repatriation, as stated at the 1997 meeting of UNHCR's Executive Committee (EXCOM), has two implications. Firstly, it divorces international refugee policy from refugee welfare *per se*. Secondly, from the standpoint of this chapter, it would appear to make our discussion on successful refugee settlement in host states a superfluous exercise. This observation would be reinforced if one also looks at the rising numbers of coerced ethnic return migrations throughout the world, such as the sobering figure of 25 million ethnic Russians threatened to be forcibly returned from the "near abroad" (Voutira 1996). Yet such a conclusion would be premature, particularly if one examines the variables that accounted for the "success" of refugee settlement in the first place.

The least contested examples of successful refugee settlement examined thus far were Asia Minor refugees in Greece and Greek Cypriot refugees in Cyprus. The critical variables identified as the determinants of this success were permanence of residence and status as citizens; strong government intervention in devising and implementing policy; ethnic and/or ideological affinity between newcomers and hosts; a collective enemy that allowed for the emergence of a sense of solidarity and the acceptance of sacrifice on the part of the receiving populations; an emphasis upon rehabilitation rather than relief, with "compensation" and reparations; and the use of humanitarian assistance functioning as an integral part of national social and economic reconstruction. In both examples, the underlying approach was to conceptualize the

---

16   The prohibition of *refoulement* notwithstanding, this exercise was carried out in December by the Tanzanian Army, who, in turn, submitted an "invoice" for US$2.7 million, which UNHCR covered through its Tanzanian budget (Schoepf 1997).

disaster as a national development opportunity (see Zetter 1992:13). Seen from the standpoint of the current challenges for settling "returnees" rather than "refugees" in the most common sense, these cases become doubly relevant, not only because they were successful, but also because they were, in fact, successful cases of involuntary "repatriations."

Research on refugees and oustees: are there lessons to be learned?

A major obstacle to the transferability of knowledge to practice is disciplinary division within academia and fields of knowledge. In translating research insights from one discipline to another, a major barrier is the conceptual and theoretical baggage of each discipline, which undermines the possibilities of scientists talking to each other across corridors. But it is within the power of the research communities themselves to either stubbornly maintain or gradually demolish such barriers.

Even more divisive and dysfunctional are funding practices for research. Until recently, conventional sources of social science research funding did not accept applications from academics interested in displacement and assistance practices.[17] Most research on both oustees' and refugees' issues has been funded by the institutions that have been allocated responsibility for them. Over the years, each of these institutions, the World Bank and the UNHCR, have attracted distinct sets of academic "followers." There have been problems for academics who undertake contract research, as they are usually not allowed to publish their findings. Only a very few have conducted contract research for *both* organizations, and one of these, Art Hansen, expressed amazement at his own failure to cross-reference his own research on oustees with that of his work on refugees (personal communication, Hansen 1996). Unnecessary mental compartmentalization still undercuts conceptualization and research.

It is disheartening to note how few researchers have sought to compare the refugee and oustee experiences that could have informed and changed policy (for example, see Loizos 1981, Colson

---

[17] Ironically, there has been a radical shift in the policies of funders such as the U.K.'s Economic and Social Research Council, which now tends to be mainly interested in socially relevant research. Refugees, migration, and displacement are also now major interests of the social science councils of Scandinavian countries.

1991, and Scudder 1993). What might be the relevant factors to compare? Are the differences in how people cope in the first period of exile (through conservatism or risk-taking) related to their age? However, language skills and linguistic affinity may also be a determining factor in whether settlers or refugees are prepared to take risks. What determines successful settlement from the standpoint of the relationships that obtain between oustees or refugees and the members of the host society among whom they are settled?

One of the obstacles both to theory-building and policymaking is that neither oustees nor refugees represent homogeneous populations, although there is a tendency to treat them as such. As we have seen, agricultural settlements were "the solution" for integrating African refugees, on the basis of the assumption that all of them knew how to farm and with little appreciation for the variety of vocations that are inherent to any rural economy (Harrell-Bond 1986; also Lassailly-Jacob, in this volume). We know from the literature that displacement affects subgroups of people differently, depending on many factors, including losses, cultural background, gender, age, education, social class, political affiliation, and past experiences of displacement (Voutira and others 1995).

All of these differences (and others) could translate into either resources or liabilities in the process of guided resettlement. In addition to these social factors that resettlers and refugees bring with them, there are innumerable other variables relating to the context in which resettlement takes place. These variables include, for example, the ecology; the economy; whether resettlement takes place in an urban or a rural environment; intergroup relations, including past interactions; and so on. Such complexities seriously challenge the possibility of arriving at a unified theory.

And yet despite these complexities that cannot be accommodated under one "grand theory" in the human sciences (Skinner 1990), it is nevertheless important to acknowledge *how much we do already know* about the varieties of human experiences under conditions of forced migration and involuntary resettlement. We could derive more practical benefits from this accumulated knowledge. Such a recognition implies that it would be pointless to lament the lack of theory in refugee studies. What should be acknowledged, instead, is the inability to implement this knowledge in practice and to influence policy effectively. It is this inability that masquerades as our collective *ignorance.*

PART TWO

Land loss and land-based relocation

Editors' For most refugees and resettlers alike, regaining ac-
Note cess to productive land is essential. Displacement
from their homeland takes away the foundation of
productive activities and also derails the functioning
of community institutions. At relocation sites, both refugees and
resettlers must scramble foremost to secure their daily food
through access to land by whatever means necessary — be it purchase, lease, sharecropping, or illegal squatting — in order to start
on the hard, uphill road to recovery.

For refugees, the short-term goal is temporary access to land,
with a view to the hoped-for return to their land of origin. For
development resettlers, since return to their previous lands is impossible by definition, alternative and sustainable land-based options are necessary. Uncertainties are numerous in both situations.

The studies by Ranjit Nayak and Véronique Lassailly-Jacob included in this section illuminate the effects of landlessness in the
aftermath of displacement, and outline some of the ways of providing access to land. The authors focus on the establishment of
land-settlement schemes for refugees and development oustees.

Nayak draws upon data from his field research among the displaced Kisan tribe of Orissa (India); in that situation, the government took some measures to compensate the Kisan settlers for
their lost lands. His chapter carefully examines all three methods
of compensation: "land for land, cash for land, and employment
for land." Of these approaches, land-based resettlement is essential
for the mass of the Kisan, since most are not prepared to use cash for
investing sustainably in alternative income-producing activities. The
author's research reveals how and why cash for land failed to reconstruct the prior livelihood levels of the Kisan dislocatees.

The major risk of landlessness can escalate, expanding the
hazards and affecting the overall economic, psychological, and

political conditions of the displacees. Nayak details, for example, the exposure of the Kisan to wage labor exploitation and the decline in their practice of traditional ceremonies and other community activities. The symbolic and emotional relationship between the Kisan and their land could not be "compensated," and the consequences of land loss on their overall social status are analyzed, as are the specific vulnerabilities related to gender and age. Finally, the author argues that inadequate analytical methods are a significant cause of poor settlement planning, and that routine cost-benefit analyses fail to capture the losses associated with the landlessness and multifaceted impoverishment of dislocated populations. He suggests that greater compensation—and participation—of displacees in planning their move could help diminish some of the impoverishment risks.

Veronique Lassailly-Jacob, for her part, focuses on both refugees and development displacees and deals with land-based resettlement in Africa. The chapter offers an overview of some of Africa's largest agricultural land settlement programs, including those in Sudan, Egypt, Ghana, Zambia, and other countries. The strategy of planned long-term settlements had initially been used for resettlers, and, more recently, efforts have been made to integrate refugees. The United Nations High Commissioner for Refugees (UNHCR) has pioneered rural settlements in Africa as durable solutions for refugees: over a period of some 30 years, from the early 1960s to the late 1980s, more than 200 agricultural settlements were opened in Africa to assist one million refugees, short and long term, in the Sudan, Zaire, Tanzania, Uganda, Botswana, and other countries. The chapter compares the circumstances, processes, and problems of settling development resettlers ("oustees") and settling "refugees" in sub-Saharan Africa, bringing out valuable implications for resettlement planning and research.

The similarities and differences between refugees and oustees highlighted in this chapter help to better assess the complex problems associated with resettling refugees. Lassailly-Jacob compares the psychosocial stress felt by oustees, forced to accept the loss of their ancestral land, with the trauma of refugees, for whom persecution is followed by a sense of fear, alienation, and uncertainty about the future. She also argues that the political attitude of governments and the organizational support given to the inhabitants of settlement schemes, resettlers or refugees, are crucial factors behind the success or failure of relocation.

CHAPTER 3

Risks associated with landlessness: an exploration toward socially friendly displacement and resettlement

Ranjit Nayak

This chapter was inspired by a conference at the University of Oxford, organized around Michael Cernea's risk impoverishment and recovery model. The purpose of the chapter is to discuss issues associated with the risks arising out of landlessness, especially those that need to be considered in any land-based reconstruction of livelihood. At the outset, a brief attempt is made to define some of the concepts and the way they would be used in the chapter and to clarify certain misconceptions and confusion surrounding frequently used concepts in displacement and resettlement studies. This is followed by an introduction to the Kisan tribe of eastern India and a brief description of their predicament as a consequence of land alienation, drawing upon the author's anthropological fieldwork between 1991 and 1995. The empirical investigation collected both quantitative and qualitative evidence.[1]

Before the socially unfriendly transformations and the dangers encountered by the Kisan are outlined, some details of the project, the modus operandi of the authorities in charge of resettlement and its deficiencies, the survival mechanisms employed by the affected people, and the costs faced by the landless Kisan are described. The

---

[1]   During a household survey conducted in 1994, 158 households in 21 villages, including resettlement colonies, were investigated. Qualitative methods included observation, participant observation, recorded interviews, and group discussions.

chapter then elaborates on the dangers or potential risks that come with the severance of people from their land and the experience of landlessness, especially those situations that do not lend themselves to easy identification or quantification. While some of these are covered by the risk impoverishment model, others are not and need to be considered. The chapter closes with a call for rethinking the research methods employed in displacement studies, since most of the dangers and vulnerabilities, as the Kisan case reveals, cannot be detected through currently operative research and survey methods that tend to generate only specific kinds of information.

The landless

Landlessness as a human condition occurs as a consequence of the alienation of people from the land; it assumes that an association with land is innately associated with being human. This chaper concentrates on those people for whom landlessness is about deprivation of livelihood. People directly dependent on land for their livelihood are at risk of landlessness whenever the event of the alienation of land arises. The problem of such landless people is acute. Refugees, indigenous peoples, ethnic minorities, and other groups that depend on land for their subsistence are frequently victims of these processes and are the *landless people* discussed in this chapter. Landlessness is a social hazard for such people because it brings with it a cluster of vulnerabilities that give rise to impoverishment.

Landlessness is one of several risks widely recognized in our "risk society" (a term borrowed from Beck 1992), where risks may be seen as "the probabilities of physical harm due to given technological *or development* or other processes" (Lash and Wynne 1992:4). Notwithstanding generational or spatial distinctions, risks have swept through humanity along with modernization, frequently appearing through social institutions and organizations where they are triggered. Moreover, these institutions and organizations (such as governments) are the very ones that are expected to check and control the risks. This implies that the main risk arises from, or rather is, social dependence on such institutions and organizations, which increasingly in the modernizing process are becoming remote and inaccessible to the people affected by risks. This phenomenon has raised issues of credibility and trust in issues of risks, though potent, positive attempts at repairing and restoring eroded trust are still tasks to be undertaken. Repair and restoration is a difficult concept since it involves the awkward and fundamental questioning of power and authority involved in the context.

Displacement and landlessness

Resettlement as a process has been and remains a historical feature of humankind. Furthermore, every displacement is involuntary in that populations shift because of reasons that are relatively unsuitable or detrimental to their livelihood in a certain context. The reasons may include war, natural calamities, persecution, discrimination, economic insecurity, lack of opportunity, development projects, and so on. Movement of populations may or may not be induced externally. While there are external factors such as the environment, available resources, or development projects, there are also internal factors in a population that may induce displacement. Differentiation within a population along lines of beliefs, class, age, gender, or generation are possible sources of schism, conflicts, and separation, and large sections of populations may be displaced as a result. Whatever the factors, external or internal, no population shift is voluntary and the term involuntary is superfluous. The same holds true of the resettlement of displaced populations. Can one settle voluntarily wherever one desires? Ownership laws, property laws, land ceiling and land consolidation laws, and other complex legalities involving land do not make doing so feasible.

States and other powerful agencies throughout the world routinely displace populations during the implementation of development programs. Indeed, it is generally accepted that displacement and resettlement as concepts were initiated in the language of the state, especially in administration (see Das 1996). Inevitably, these concepts became the subject matter of development studies, policy studies, sociology, social anthropology, and development economics, with each of the disciplines as well as the state privileging certain issues of displacement over others, because of either paradigmatic and disciplinary orientations in the case of the former or the nature of administrative processes in the case of the latter. Needless to say, the different treatment of such concepts as "resettlement" or "rehabilitation" by different authorities as well as academic disciplines causes complexities in the analysis of particular instances of displacements and in the framing of policies. Interventions toward changing, halting, or even improving the displacement process are, therefore, partly dependent on justifications drawn from past experiences. Of course, experiences of the present during the displacement process, if detected and acted upon, may transform the experience or suspend it, though such events are rare.

At the present time there is a serious concern for the welfare of those displaced or about to be displaced, and increasingly this is becoming the focus of displacement and resettlement studies. The "people-centered" focus is a valid approach; however, while focusing on the human side of the process, there may be a tendency to avoid a holistic or an interdisciplinary approach. Whatever the dominant paradigm, the field of displacement and resettlement is an established subject of investigation across disciplines in the social sciences and has the potential and resource to be an independent discipline in its own right. Recent efforts to bring together the fields of refugee studies and development-induced displacement studies signify a movement toward the generalization and relative independence of the field.

Experiencing landlessness: the Kisan of India

The people and the project

The Kisan are a tribe settled in the four Indian states of Orissa, Bihar, West Bengal, and Madhya Pradesh. According to the 1981 census (data from the 1991 census were not available at the time of writing), the population of Kisan in Orissa was 227,992 people, accounting for more than 90 percent of the total Kisan population. No comprehensive anthropological, sociological, or economic study of the Kisan had been published prior to 1995. The recent attempt at stating some of the general features of the Kisan in a volume called *The Scheduled Tribes* (Singh 1994) is useful because of its statistics based on the 1981 census of India. In all available records, the Kisan are documented as settled agriculturists along the banks of the Sankh River.

The Kisan were displaced from their traditional environmental in the postcolonial period as part of the Nehruvian thrust toward development and self-reliance. As part of the project of the Rourkela Steel Plant at Rourkela (built with German assistance), in Orissa, the Mandira Dam and Reservoir[2] was built on the river Sankh to

---

[2]   The reservoir was expected to have a capacity of 257,000 cubic feet volume of water, considered adequate to meet the minimum demand of 125 cubic feet per second (cusecs) of the steel plant (inclusive of the provision of recycling water). The flow of the river during the dry season could supply only 20 cusecs, which was deemed inadequate. This being the rationale behind the project, the construction of the dam and reservoir was taken up by the Hirakud Project Administration, which had looked after the completion of the Hirakud Dam (for the largest multipurpose river valley of Orissa, on which construction began in 1948). See Viegas "The Hirakud Dam Oustees: Thirty Years After" in E.G. Thukral *Big Dams, Displaced People: Rivers of Sorrow, Rivers of Change* New Delhi: Sage Publications.

meet the water requirements of the steel plant,[3] especially during the dry season. The commencement of the construction of the Mandira Reservoir began after 1957, 16 kilometers upstream from Mandira, and was enclosed by an earthen dam 1,365 feet in length and a spillway dam provided with 11 radial gates to enable a discharge of 100,000 cusecs of water during the monsoon. Land acquired for the Mandira Dam and Reservoir by the government, through a specially established organization called the Mandira Land Organisation during 1955 and 1956, totaled 11,871.30 acres.[3]

No less than 100,000 Kisan were affected by the operation. The project alienated the land (both homestead and agricultural) of the Kisan, who were residing in 15 villages. The government of Orissa attempted to resettle the Kisan in six resettlement colonies, namely, Lachada, Khandapahar, Laing, Ursamandalla, Bankibahal, and the Jaidega. Bankibahal and Jaidega are located near the reservoir, Laing and Ursamandalla are situated near the dam, and Lachada and Khandapahar are located about 150 kilometers away from the dam in the remote hills. The notification for displacement was given in 1954, though the Kisan claim to have been notified during 1955. Failure to persuade the Kisan to resettle led to the shifting by force of the Kisan to the new resettlement sites in lorries that arrived in their villages without prior notice. They were disembarked in the colonies, which had only makeshift wooden enclosures to live in and no available source of water or food. The authorities supplied food and water to them during the initial stages. The Kisan themselves had to transfer their cattle by foot, which took several days.

Compensation and rehabilitation

The officials of the government of Orissa, who were in charge of implementing a rehabilitation program (see Fernandes and Raj 1992), registered on paper several development activities in the resettlement colonies since their inception in 1957; however, names of the

---

[3]   In addition, 19,785.22 acres were acquired at the same time for the steel plant, and 1,132.35 acres for mining minerals such as limestone and dolomite as well as iron ore. A total of 32,788.87 acres were taken over between 1954 and 1956 by the Rourkela Steel Plant Authorities for the construction of the plant, dam, mines, and quarries. In the case of the Mandira Dam and Reservoir, private land totaled 6,159.81 acres, and government land, 5,711.49 acres. All private land belonged to the tribes residing in that region, primarily the Kisan, the Oraon, the Munda, and the Kharia. The Kisan were the worst affected, losing almost all of their land.

resettlement colonies where such development was apparently carried out do not figure in the records.[4] It is believed by the Kisan that the projects detailed were never actually begun. My own field observations do not indicate an extensive development or rehabilitation program. Most infrastructure activities (such as building houses, wells, and walking paths) done immediately after the resettlement, I am led to believe, were done by the few physically able people at a time of dearth of food, when the Kisan had to rely entirely on meager government-supplied food grains.

The government had a compensation scheme that exchanged acquired land with one, two, or all three of the replacement strategies of land, cash, or employment. There are no records of compensation received by individual families with the government of Orissa, the government of India, or the steel plant. My attempts at locating them were fruitless, and I was told that the officially existing records had been consigned to the record room of the office of the District Magistrate of Sundergarh (Orissa) and that access to such records is possible only in the event of an official inquiry or a special investigation such as a judicial inquiry. Until then, they remain the secret of the state and therefore inaccessible.

---

[4]   The government records indicate that plots of land for construction of houses were made available to every displaced family in the resettlement colonies and that a housing subsidy ranging from rupees 200 to rupees 400 had been disbursed per family. Recent government papers of 1992 further indicate that extensive development programs had been executed in the resettlement colonies under the categories listed below. But these programs have never been implemented. Among these are *Health care* (seven medical aid centers in seven villages, four of which were provided by the Rourkela Steel Plant); *Education* (93 classrooms in 25 villages; eight classrooms renovated in eight villages; nine classrooms electrified in three villages); *Drinking water* (27 wells dug in 27 villages; 32 tube wells dug in 20 villages; two overhead tanks in two villages; two tanks renovated in two villages; two wells renovated in two villages; initiated piped-water schemes; *Communication* (tar road of 5 kilometers linking 3 villages constructed; three bus-waiting sheds made in three villages); *Recreational facilities* (14 village community centers provided in 14 villages; village community centers renovated in three villages; *Cultural activities_and sports* (organization of tribal dances, and hockey tournaments in 73 villages; sports materials supplied in three villages); *Agricultural development* (seeds, fertilizers, lift-irrigation points, and subsidies to three villages); *Dairy and poultry development* (materials and transportation subsidies); and *Cottage industries* (subsidies in three villages).

Land for land

In its land-for-land scheme, the government records claim to have allotted wasteland totaling 4,110.22 acres to the displaced people in lieu of fertile land acquired, subject to a maximum of 33 acres of wasteland provided per family. It provided each family[5] with a reclamation subsidy of 100 rupees per acre as well. The Kisan claim that the reclamation subsidy has not been received 40 years after the promise. As per my survey, the proportion of alienation of land ranges from 59 to 100 percent per household, with the maximum land alienated from a household being 35 acres and the minimum being three acres (the latter being the total amount of land owned by a household in a certain instance).

Close to half of those interviewed said that their land had been taken away through oral agreements rather than through administrative procedures. This is supported by the fact that documents confirming such agreements, such as affidavits or official letters are not in the possession of the Kisan, and official documentation in regard to agreements are absent in the relevant government offices. Some of the elderly Kisan allege that the officials in charge of distribution kept certain land to themselves, which they later sold to the non-Kisan. There is no evidence obtainable to prove the allegation, but the way in which the distribution of land was organized suggests that most agreements, oral or written, were not upheld.

The Kisan continue to pay an annual tax on alienated land because pre 1957 administrative records still hold good. About 65 percent of the total households are victims of this serious administrative oversight that has not been recognized, despite the fact that several members of the Kisan have been complaining about it to the administrative officers over the years. Attempts to stop paying the land tax have not been successful as officials threaten to take away their current homestead land. It is the general opinion among the Kisan that none of the successive official incumbents wish to change the scheme of things or rectify the error.

---

5   The government have not clearly defined what they mean by "family" for the purposes of compensation. As an anthropologist it was difficult for me to clearly identify the boundary of the "family," since several nuclear units of the same and different generations reside along with members of different lineages and sometimes clans under the same roof and for a certain ego there could be, among others, nephews, nieces, cousins twice removed, wife's cousins etc. I found it useful to identify the "household" as a unit rather than the "family."

Cash for land

For the purposes of compensation, the government of Orissa classified land into four classes according to the degree of fertility and available irrigation, with payments ranging between 200 and 900 rupees per acre. The Kisan were told by the authorities in charge of cash compensation that the rates per acre in each of the respective classes of land accounted for a year's loss of crop. The Kisan never agreed to the compensation, not because it was too little or included only a year's loss of crop that they had already sowed, but because they did not wish to part from their land in the first place. Indeed, the rates of compensation officially allocated per acre in each of the classes of land were adequate and level with the market prices of 1956 and 1957.

Class I land constituted the riverbanks where the Kisan collectively cultivated paddy and shared the produce. When they did so, the production of food grains from this region alone was sufficient to feed the Kisan population in the years when climate conditions for food production were favorable. There were instances, as some of the elderly recall, when they bartered rice for pulses or cattle with neighboring tribes and castes. It was only in certain years, especially those when there were spells of drought, diseases affecting crops, floods, or untimely changes in season, that the Kisan had to cultivate on Class II land if feasible, or seek financial support in the form of loans from the local money lender (who usually belonged to the *Teli* caste[6]) to purchase food grains from the market. Rarely were state-subsidized food grains made available. In addition, loans from money lenders were difficult to obtain and on many occasions had to be pawned with a certain piece of agricultural land or with cattle.

According to the Kisan, most of the members (more than 80 percent) who had been promised cash compensation never received it. Those who did receive cash compensation either in full or in part do not recall how it was spent. They are worse off than some of their fellow tribe members who were compensated with wasteland, as the compensation money was exhausted while seeking short-term benefits. Only a minority among the Kisan bought land elsewhere, moving away from the resettlement colony. However, the majority

---

[6]   Caste is used here in the local Kisan sense of *Jati*. The *Teli* are believed traditionally to deal with oil and related products. They are among the relatively well off Hindu castes in the region.

spent their compensation money on substance abuse in the confusion and disorientation created by the abrupt displacement. It is also well-documented by tribal studies in India that cash as compensation for land is used differently by tribal peoples, and most often is wasted on nonproductive uses.

A significant part of compensation money was held back by the officials in charge of the distribution of compensation money. This amount was sometimes as high as 40 percent and was unofficially taken as bribes for the release of the compensation money. Those compensated were helpless because they were dependent on the officials. The officials who made their "cuts" appear to be part of the official procedures for compensation easily deceived the Kisan. Many of the elderly Kisan males who received cash compensation reported that the officials, by making available the compensation money, were helping them at least get something when the Kisan had given up hope of receiving anything in return for alienated land. Some of the young Kisan are convinced that giving bribes is an essential feature of coping with the local bureaucracy and is necessary to achieve individual or collective goals in life.

Employment for land

The government had announced a policy of preferential reservation in government services for the displaced. Every displaced family was issued a locally displaced person (LDP) certificate. Presentation of the certificate at recruitment interviews conducted by the various departments of the state administration guaranteed employment in state services.

However, more than half of the LDP certificate holders have never received any employment from the time they were issued the certificate in 1957 until the time of our field research from 1991 to 1995. The government officials are aware of this, though their records state that 496 displaced families have been provided with one job per family. According to the officials, the T. N. Singh formula of *one job per one displaced family* failed to be implemented for two reasons. The first was a matter of administrative delay whereby the list of persons displaced because of the Mandira Dam was received by the government authorities after the government had changed its recruitment policy. In 1978, the government realized that recruitment potential had become limited and it could no longer absorb the LDP certificate holders. The second was a managerial issue, especially concerning quality control. The bulk of displaced persons qualified for neither semi-skilled nor skilled jobs. Furthermore, the Bureau of

Public Enterprise issued instructions in February 1986 that any understanding, formal or informal, in regard to the offer of employment to one member of every dispossessed family in the project was considered withdrawn. By July 1992, about 7000 employees of the Rourkela Steel Plant were found to be surplus because the plant was undergoing a massive modernization program. The upgrading of technology through computerization and roboticization led to recruitment of highly specialized personnel and a substantial number of semi-skilled and unskilled workers were made redundant. Among other reasons for the failure of the LDP certificate holders to obtain employment was the fact that some had sold their certificates to members of the surrounding Hindu population for cash. At a time of disorientation in the resettlement colonies, some of the non-Kisan talked the Kisan into selling these certificates for small sums of money and used the certificates to illegally gain employment, in all cases taking on the names stated on the certificate. A handful of such Kisan have realized that it is too late to recover their certificates. They do not have the capacity to go to court and they cannot afford the legal costs involved in filing charges.

Effects of landlessness or potential risks

Becoming landless — apart from disastrous economic, ecological, and political effects — has profound transformative effects on people's behavior, practices, psychology, and emotions. To the Kisan, the effects were turbulent, inhuman, and extreme because of their absolute involvement and historical intimacy with land. Some of the important effects are outlined below; however, it should be kept in mind that these effects act concurrently and overlap in terms of their causes and dynamics. Some of the effects of landlessness are revealed by Cernea's risk impoverishment model; others, though specific to landlessness in this instance, may cause the same extent of vulnerability as the main risk of impoverishment emphasized by the model. These vulnerabilities as an outcome of landlessness are also risks in future displacements, especially for agricultural and farm-based societies and should be avoided in order for any land-based reconstruction of livelihoods to be successful.

Economic consequences

Land received in compensation by the few Kisan, officially classified as wasteland, was inadequate and unsuitable for agriculture. The Lachada and Khandapahar resettlement colonies are on hill slopes of the Kisan on which it is impossible to grow paddy, traditionally the staple food. Mines surround the Jaidega and Bankibahal resettlement colonies on one side and the Mandira Reservoir on the other. Land in this region has been subjected to several quarrying and refilling processes over the years. The absence of the technology for appropriate refilling of quarried land in the past has made it impossible for the Kisan to undertake any form of agricultural activity because chunks of rejected metallic and residual ores take the place of topsoil. Such lands had been unsaleable until recently.

The inability to engage in agriculture left the Kisan with the option of earning their livelihood through wage labor. Laboring, in the neighboring private and public sector limestone quarries, iron ore mines, cement factories, and local mineral transport services, is the current occupation of about half the number of previously settled agriculturists. Labor contractors who conduct business with the mines and factories pay wages that are lower than the minimum wage fixed by the government. Women are paid lower wages than men by convention, though this is not permissible by law. About 87 percent of Kisan households engage in more than just wage labor to survive. Selling crafts and fish, trading with local non-Kisan retailers and wholesalers, masonry and construction work, and seasonal work in the fields of neighboring Hindu castes for nominal wages are some of the other income-generating activities.

More than half of the surveyed households are in debt to moneylenders, shops, banks, and fellow Kisan. The average number of dependents per household is more than 7.2, and at least one member of the household contracts an illness every month resulting in expenditures on health. Wages earned by one male member is just enough for two main meals a day for three members of the household and the frequency of intake of a nonvegetarian meal is less than two meals per month. Households are obliged to live predominantly on supplies of food grains rationed by the Department of Food and Civil Supplies of the government of Orissa.

If the Kisan were compensated with arable land instead of wasteland, cash, or perhaps even steady employment, they would have probably been able to subsist with relatively less distress and inconvenience. The Kisan would have also had an opportunity to rebuild their traditions and customs, most of which center around land. This is an important aspect to be considered in any displacement venture. The availability of training facilities for skilled occupations could have helped some of the Kisan to obtain employment. We should bear in mind while framing policies that such training and employment opportunities ought to be made available for at least two generations to make up for certain land losses.

Ecological repercussions

The Kisan, in the pre-displacement period, were extensively dependent on their landscape (including agricultural land, forests, streams, river, and so on) for food crops (such as paddy, millets, mustard, vegetables, pulses, potatoes, sweet potatoes, turmeric, ginger, and so on), wild game (boar, deer, rabbits, and so on), construction of their houses (wood, special clay, and so on), naturally growing food (mango, tamarind, bamboo, arrowroot, wild honey, pepper, blackberries, and so forth), medicines (such as *satabari* and *amla*), firewood and crafts (ropes from suma grass, brooms, or fula jhadu from piri grass, leaf plates or khalli from the leaves of *Shorea robusta*, and other domestic items from *chiro* grass). Post-displacement, they are deprived of this elaborate life support system, being compelled to manage significant changes in patterns of diet, animal use, utilization of implements, and so forth.

In the new context, the Kisan are faced with deforestation of the meager surrounding vegetation; their landscape is increasingly barren, as a result of overgrazing, occasional forest fires, building and maintaining houses, selling wood to support themselves, and so on. As a consequence, they are unable to breed animals for milk and meat, though there has been a movement toward cultivating horse gram, potatoes, sweet potatoes, and certain tuberous roots. The climatic conditions have proven detrimental to the health of resettlers, particularly after the monsoons and until the dry season. Low-lying areas hold stagnant water that sometimes serve as a water source for both domestic use and to meet the water requirements of the cattle. Moreover, they become breeding grounds for mosquitoes, leading to outbreaks of malaria, various bacteria-based and waterborne diseases, and other harmful cyclical infections that pass between humans and animals.

Under normal circumstances, concepts and practices with regard to the environment are internalized in Kisan society through a complex set of relations, or *sambandh*, in their world, or *merha*. Specifically, the Kisan world features a profound intimacy between various entities such as the landscape (forests, fields, rivers, settlements, the habitat of the spirits, animals, and so on) and everything above (the sun, the moon, the air, the moving spirits, and so forth) and below it (the place of their origin, the habitat of ancestor spirits). All entities are constituted in each other with none privileged over another (see

Croll and Parkin 1993 and Hirsch and O'Hanlon 1995). According to their beliefs and practices, they are born from the land, live with the land, and return to it when they die. Land is their mother and the sun their father. Everything that grows on the surface is the work of ancestors who live under it, and the landscape is the home of all their spirits. There are extensive oral traditions in the form of myths, stories, and poetry and songs, and elaborate customary practices of rituals, grand sacrifices to their father or Supreme Being and spirits.

The deep sense of mutuality and reciprocity among the various entities in the Kisan world was abruptly severed by displacement, and landlessness caused serious disorientation and anomie as the Kisan complex was not successfully reproduced in the new context. Along with that there was a sense of loss of their knowledge of the forests and the location of all resources that had been passed from one generation to another. Learning about an unfamiliar landscape could not be achieved instantaneously, and this thought was disturbing to the Kisan. During the years after the resettlement, there would appear to have been a decline in traditional beliefs, and certainly in the observation by the Kisan of traditional practices.

Resettlement in an unfamiliar landscape and environment can be alienating and traumatic because of a range of reasons, as pointed out above. If resettlement sites are to be located in environmentally unfriendly regions, then reconstructing environments should be made part of any resettlement package. Respect of traditional beliefs and practices can build the foundations for good resettlements. If resettlement authorities do not take appropriate care, then the risk is not only economic impoverishment but also spiritual impoverishment.

Impairing human relations

The sudden social and psychological crisis caused by landlessness split the tribe. The movement to the resettlement colonies itself disintegrated households that consisted of a multiplicity of blood and marriage relations; schisms were along random lines separating husbands from wives, biological children from their parents, siblings from each other, and so on. During the post-displacement years, however, there has been a gradual rearrangement of family patterns, though there are instances in which residential reunions have not yet taken place. At the same time, outward migration has increased, especially by the youth that leave in search of economic opportunities.

Changes in the sphere of social activities are noteworthy. The institution of the *akhda*, which involves social singing, dancing, theater, storytelling, social games, and so on, has significantly declined, according to the elderly. Most of the members stay indoors or meet in small gatherings to gamble, drink, or smoke. Participation in other similar customary festivities and social ceremonies has declined markedly.

The uncontrollable and chaotic social fissioning only confirms the widely recognized view that displacement is an extremely potent divisive and alienating force that weakens human bonding and sometimes obliterates it, to the extent that carefully nurtured or ascriptive bonds disintegrate randomly. As concluded by several social scientists, such effects can be prevented by ensuring that families remain together during and after the process of displacement. One way of securing this aim is by choosing sensible transporting procedures, using indigenous knowledge and approaches to movement, seeking the help of social workers toward providing support during and after the movement, allowing time after notification for social reconciliation to the idea of resettlement, and creating conditions that enable the authorities to deliver upon their promises to the people.

Incapacitating beliefs and norms of living

The traditional Kisan belief pantheon, in brief, consists of the Supreme Being *Dharmes*, spirits, and ancestor spirits. *Dharmes* the creator is *Bhagwan* (God) and *Baba* (father), and *Biri* or *Suraj* (sun) is his symbol. He is omnipresent, all-knowing, and above every *Manus* (human being) and *Bhut* (spirit). Prayers and sacrifices are offered to him on special occasions such as birth, marriage, death, and festivals. The Kisan world features several spirits, most of them female; moreover, each of them is associated with the landscape and is propitiated through regular offering of sacrifices. Some of the important spirits are the *Sarna Budhia*, the lady of the grove; *Pat*, the *tola* protector; *Darha*, the *tola* defender and his wife *Deswali*; the *Mahadania*, the great gift; the *Devimai*, the mother goddess; the *Mahadeo*, the village procreator; the *Chaparbudhia*, the old lady of the roof of the houses; the *Gairahi bhut*, the spirit of the surface; the *Bansakti*, the power of the forests; the *Garhadhorachaturseema*, the collective spirits of the river, stream, and the four directions; the *Chandi*, the spirit of hunting; the *Joda* and her companion *Achrayal*, the spirits of the women; the *Khunt bhut*, the land spirit; the *Baranda pacho*, the lady of the households; the *Chulhaina*, the spirit of the hearth; and *Goyesalinad*, the spirit of the cattle. These are then the ancestor spirits, who come into existence with the death of every human being and who live under the land. They are significant in the everyday existence of the Kisan, for they are the continuation of their human existence, only in a different form.

Landlessness brought about a sense of normlessness and incoherence as the Kisan world of fluidity, unification, and familiarity could not be immediately reproduced in the new environment. The absence of ancestor spirits, spirits, myths, stories, songs, and other environmentally associated and embedded cultural patterns was distressing. It was around the time of displacement that Catholic missionary activity began to make significant inroads into the beliefs of the alienated Kisan. The pre-displacement situation was characterized by the coexistence of both the Kisan religious practices and Catholicism introduced by the missionaries; however, the latter had marginal effects. Today more than half of the Kisan households are church-going Catholics. Intensified missionary activity in the resettlement colonies led to the incorporation of such Christian rituals as baptism, holy communion, the marriage ceremony, and the funeral rite into their religious practices, without necessarily putting an end to their own traditions. Landlessness and the consequent fragile psychological disposition and emotional vulnerability, however, in some ways facilitated the expansion of Christianity. While some members immediately proclaimed themselves Catholics, others proclaimed themselves Hindu.

The Kisan demonstrate that landlessness entails deprivation of a society's norms, values, morals, beliefs, and all things that go into making life and giving life to a person and a collective. All these are risks and losses of development-induced displacement, with bearings on all spheres of human life.

Undermining trust and political participation

Attempts by the Kisan to reverse decisions of the state, or at sustaining any protest movement for compensation, or against the newer forms of exploitation have been sporadic and have failed to gather the momentum required to become significant and effective. Space limitations prevent us from repeating in more detail our analysis of what undermines or limits more forceful forms of political participation by the Kisan, or the various forms of human rights violations to which they were subjected. However, it is important to emphasize that some forms of political protest have been kept alive, including nonviolent procedures of letters to administrative heads, and complaints to administrative officials, politicians, and other people in a position to influence the state.

Significantly, the Kisan are currently attempting to textualize their demands in Hindi, the national language; Oriya, the official language of the government of Orissa; and English. The first English document of the Kisan protest, in which the term "human rights" was featured, was a letter addressed to the president of India in 1981.[7] The letter sums up the Kisan status and feelings as follows:

> The poor original inhabitants have been pushed out... and have not been provided with the basic amenities of life till this day. Their means of existence is being crushed at the outset. They are made subject — race, *refugees* and *slaves* (in their home...). It is happening in *bharat,* i.e., *india,* which is the champion of *human rights* ... it is needless to point out that the Adivasis and other weaker sections are now facing gradual *extinction....*
>
> Till now Govt. of Orissa and Rourkela Steel Plant Management have not shown the attitude to redress the genuine grievances of the indigenous people.... State Govt. is applying irrational, fraudulent and unscrupulous *job reservation policy* in the compact tribal district.... Present... *policy* adopted so far... is wrong, unjust and unfair. This is destroying the ethnic, linguistic, sociocultural fabrics and the regional way of the Adivasis[8] and other weaker section....
>
> It is quite evident that long 24 years have already passed, but the problems of *displaced persons* have not yet been dealt with sympathy and understanding as such we can very well assume that the state authorities have adopted a slow Mass Murder Policy. It is a dangerous threat to the Tribal lives and properties. The Adivasis and other weaker sections are often humiliated and terrorised. They are living in indignity and anxiety... the indigenous Tribals and other weaker sections of Sundergarh District

---

[7]   The letter dated May 29, 1981 was signed by Mr. Gregory Ekka, a member of the Kisan tribe and the only political representative of recent times to represent the Kisan in wider society. Copies of the letter were sent to the prime minister of India, the Union minister and joint secretaries for home affairs, the governor and the chief minister of the state of Orissa and several other senior officials — yet all these authorities failed to take action.

[8]   The term *adivasi* translates as "original inhabitant" and is used in the nontribal population to refer to tribal peoples.

earnestly appeal to your honour to *dismantle* the colonies of non-tribals set up on the land acquired for Steel Plant, Rourkela, restore them the illegally alienated land, stop forcible occupation of land and withdraw aggressive, repressive and oppressive measures from the Tribal belt of Orissa. It is the paramount duty of the Union Government to preserve their ethnic linguistic and socio-cultural identity, and save them from *injustice* — social, economic and political — and *oppression* social economic and political. It is also mentioned here that the Union Government and the State Government will be wholly responsible if untoward incident will take place in future. (Emphasis by *italics* in the original).

An issue that is inadequately addressed in the resettlement literature concerns the role of authorities in charge of the practical upholding of human rights. Can the same authorities that have been directly responsible for violations of human rights be made to see what the violated need? And do they have the right to decide what is moral and right for the disenfranchized?

The answer could possibly point to alternative structures, for instance, to independent institutions with greater capacity to mediate between different value systems, such as nongovernmental organizations, or the church in the case of the Kisan. It is, however, essential for centers of power to create conditions in which such mediation can occur. Social scientists interested in development have a primary responsibility for militating against preconceived judgements on the value systems of the cultures involved. This can assist in the creation of socially friendly policies of displacement and resettlement and in the reconstruction of shattered livelihoods.

Deterioration in mental health

The Kisan who experienced the uprooting of 1957 are testimony of the state of mental health of displaced peoples and illustrate another one of the main risks of impoverishment through displacement: the risk of increased morbidity and mortality. The severance of the Kisan bonds from their traditional lands and environment is a fundamental factor in their acute depression and possibly in increased mortality rates, including infant mortality. A continuous pining for lost land characterizes the elderly. Anxiety, grieving, various neuropsychiatric illness and post-traumatic stress disorders feature among the Kisan. In essence, they suffer from profound cultural and landscape bereavement for their lost origins.

Stress and depression trickle up and down the generations, affecting people often irrespective of age or gender. An example of this effect can be seen among the children brought up in the resettlement colonies. The children can narrate the displacement and resettlement experience in minute detail as if they had themselves experienced the process. The children have been shown the sites of the traditional villages by the elders, who have taken them by boats on the reservoir and frequently narrated the stories of their own sufferings as children and adults themselves caught in the traumatic experience. One can foresee that these experiences, which became part of their identity, would be transmitted to following generations through various forms such as songs, stories, legends, or myths.

It is striking that mental health issues have been virtually absent in displacement and resettlement studies, even though there is almost universal agreement that dislocation is stressful and gives rise to social pathologies.[9] According to the World Bank's *World Development Report 1993: Investing in Health,* health indicators are as good as economic indicators in measuring socioeconomic development, and investments in health ought to be made along with investments in development. However, it fails to take adequate account or provide appropriate directives in regard to mental health as a widespread illness particular to refugees and other displaced populations.

It is not easy to attribute direct indicators of psychological effects of displacement, and social surveys can easily fail to grasp the workings of the human mind (see also Fernandes, this volume). The only way to know about mental health impacts of displacement is to focus research on variables. The absence of such research by default would eliminate mental health issues from policy and planning considerations. Therefore, displacement authorities ought to recognize mental health as a high-risk factor, and secure mental health services not only in the post-displacement period but also much before the displacement process is initiated, in order to prepare for a transition with minimal levels of stress and psychological disorder. Mental health ought to be an important indi-

---

[9]   See Good (1996).The author makes the observation at the outset of his paper and appeals to researchers, planners, and policymakers to explicitly consider the mental health dimensions of resettlement and relocation.

cator while ensuring a minimum standard of "quality-of-life index" for the resettlers.

Failure in entitlements and social security

Amartya Sen's entitlement theory[10] for the analysis of poverty and famine provides a useful tool in the analysis of certain risks faced in displacement and resettlement, especially landlessness, and ties in with the theoretical framework on impoverishment risks and reconstruction. The displaced belong to the most vulnerable segments of society, and landlessness frequently increases the risk of further impoverishment by exposing the displaced to newer and increasing forms of vulnerability. In the case of the Kisan, the risk of impoverishment through landlessness is significantly accentuated by the development of the open market economic system chosen by India, and capitalistic relations can be heavily implicated in this risk.

In line with Sen's argument, a person's "entitlement relations" constitute the set of relationships between persons and commodities that define a particular person's entitlement set.[11] They include a range of social relations, such as those that are binding, customary, or moral, or based on transfers or inheritance entitlements, own-labor or production-based entitlements (that is, what one is accorded or is able directly to produce through one's own labor) and trade-based entitlement (that is, what one obtains by trading something one owns with a willing party). An analysis of entitlement effects of capitalistic transformation of a previously noncapitalistic (or at best partially capitalistic) economy, such as that of the Kisan, naturally involves a focus upon trade-based entitlements. Furthermore, it may involve considering other forms of entitlement insofar as capitalistic transformation affects, and in most cases erodes, such entitlements as well. For example, the capitalist development of the Kisan involves the disintegration of a system of barter and alternative socioeconomic arrangements such as institutionalized pooling of food and other resources that to a greater extent protect the vulnerable Kisan in times of food scarcity. The breakdown of customary gift entitlements such as the *jajmani* relations of village India is another example.

---

10 See Sen (1981).
11 Sen defines an individual's entitlement set as the set of commodities that an individual is practically capable of gaining access to. Capitalist, as well as precapitalist property relations, are thus subsumed under this title.

Displacement, combined with capitalist development, has entailed the proliferation of wage relations for the Kisan, who are becoming increasingly dependent upon their "exchange entitlements." This implies that members of the Kisan face a new source of vulnerability in the form of "exchange entitlement volatility," the important form of which is the volatility of prices caused by fluctuations in supply and demand of wage labor (which in turn is dependent on such factors as technical development, increase or reduction in mining ventures, cement industries, and so on).

An open market system implies the incorporation of local economies in larger spheres such as the regional, national, and global ones. On the one hand, this provides multifold and new specializations, as well as earning opportunities. Furthermore, through improvements (via earnings and via trade in capital goods) in the character and efficiency of the means of production, it implies significant increases in aggregate productivity and thereby in the wealth of a community. On the other hand, the same process of incorporation in larger spheres implies that local communities are subject to the vicissitudes and imbalances of even larger forces beyond their grasp and control. The particular commodity in which the local community invests and specializes, such as bamboo baskets or ropes in the case of the Kisan, continues to collapse in value because of shifts in the demands in the larger economic sphere (in this case the reason being the mass proliferation of artificial fibers). Similarly, the Kisan engaged in wage labor in the mines for their livelihood are severely affected by modernization of methods of mining, and others who are engaged in unskilled work in the steel plant are continually being made redundant by technological innovation and roboticization. These processes are potential factors for food insecurity, as the people would not be able to purchase commodities at the prices they are able to pay.

The most important relationship in determining the survivability of particular communities, in other words, is in the capitalist context—the relationship of members of these communities with the relevant markets and commodity prices. Moreover, this is not to deny that other conditions, for example, natural conditions in the form of drought, may exercise their own dramatic and direct influence on prices. Capitalist development, for the very reason that it makes productive improvements of an altogether new order possible (that is, the exploitation of specialization and comparative advantage through spatial and temporal integration), creates new forms of vulnerability, particularly for communities that come face-to-face with and predominantly dependent upon exchange relations. The vulnerability is particularly acute for those who face such relations abruptly. One solution, given that the capitalistic process is inevitable and unstoppable, is to develop safety nets and strengthen mechanisms of social security (see Sen and Dreze 1992) for the affected, which, in this case, should respond also to the specific roles, constraints, and losses experienced by the displaced Kisan.

Limits of administrative procedures, concepts, and legalities

Socially responsible *policies* alone do not automatically result in successful land-based reconstruction of livelihoods. Socially responsible *implementers* and *administrators* of policies are of crucial significance in any reconstruction of livelihood. Administrative delays, bottlenecks, corruption, inefficiency, and insensitivity are some of the risks to be encountered by displaced peoples, especially in many developing countries where bureaucratic structures tend to be massive, powerful, and lethargic. The administration experienced by the Kisan in their course to landlessness from self-sufficient land-based existence provides an eloquent instance of the maladies of administration.

The Kisan were motivated by the state to move to the resettlement sites through incentives such as bribes of cash and alcohol. The failure in persuasion through such methods saw the administrators cheat the Kisan by indicating to them an extremely fertile patch of land downstream of Sankh River as the proposed resettlement site, and then forcibly transporting them to wasteland in lorries. Furthermore, the adopted modes of compensation and the procedures through which compensation was discharged by the authorities were inappropriate under the circumstances. Compensation with land for land was inept not only in terms of the quality of land set aside for the purpose, the quantity of land, or the procedures of compensation, but also in terms of the principle governing acquisition and compensation adopted by the authorities. The compensation procedures neither ensured justice in their administration nor left the Kisan as equally well off as they were before, let alone better off. They were not explicitly aimed to do so in the first place. In fact the administration of compensation was self-defeating in that it fostered corruption in the administrative system itself, even though it was supposed to ensure equality and fair procedures in regard to the people who stood deprived of its power and resources at their time of crisis. Over the years following displacement, the administration has failed to undertake any significant development activity and even failed to respond to their complaints.

The following is an account that illustrates the unbelievable procrastination perpetrated by the administration vis-à-vis the Kisan. In the years 1965 and 1966, there were strong complaints by the tribes to the government of Orissa and the Rourkela Steel Plant that the reservoir had given rise to problems of waterlogging and sand casting in certain areas, directly affecting eight villages. In 1967, the government forced the Rourkela Steel Plant to rehabilitate the affected people. A joint inspection team involving the government and the Rourkela Steel Plant surveyed the area on December 24, 1974, and May 20, 1979, and calculated the affected area to be 466.65 acres. The steel plant was informed by the government that the cost of acquisition of the area was 2,898,000 rupees.

The steel plant authorities, after clearances from the board of directors and the government of India (Ministry of Steel and Mines), only initiated rehabilitation in 1982. However, a fresh intimation by the government of Orissa notifying of a change in the amount of the cost of acquisition from 2,898,000 to 9,686,000 rupees was used as a reason to withdraw again from the principle of rehabilitation and to again stall the process. The Rourkela Steel Plant decided to withdraw from the project on June 4, 1989, for two reasons, the first being that the newly calculated sum was more than three times the previous amount, and second, it was under no obligation to acquire the affected land as it had not been acquired as part of its plan of construction of the plant, the Mandira Dam, or the reservoir.

The government of India (Ministry of Steel and Mines) issued directions for a fresh joint inspection team to obtain information on the existing cropping pattern, damage to land, flooding, and siltation, in addition to reassessing the affected area. The survey was carried out on April 18, 1991, by the AGM Town Services and the Additional District Magistrate-cum-Special Officer Land Acquisition and Reclamation. The report indicated that the affected area was 478.31 acres and featured sand casting and waterlogging. The Ministry of Steel and Mines responded in February 1992 by pointing out that the report provided insufficient information regarding the legal implication of not pursuing with the acquisition of the affected land; the exact nature and extent of damage to the land; the alternative usage of the land; the suitability of agricultural activities on the land; the neighboring Koel-Karo Project (a hydroelectric project in southern Bihar) and its effects on the land; and whether acquisition of land is necessary and inevitable, as opposed to some form of mediation for resolving the issue. The ministry also pushed for the consultation of the Steel Authority of India and mentioned that the final decision of the government of India rested on the views of the Steel Authority, which had to judge whether the acquisition of the land was in its best interests or not. No decision has been arrived at yet, the last reminder to the authorities having been made on November 13, 1992. The Kisan continue to suffer, falling victim to the administrative vicissitude of lack of coordination between administrative departments, shifting responsibilities, and administrative irresponsibility.

In such systems, the local or international nongovernmental systems of support and securities remain devoid of powers to effectively come to the aid of displaced peoples, if they so desire. International commercial and development agencies, however, may yield certain power, especially if they fund the development project that causes displacement. In such contexts they are capable of influencing policies that may potentially help the displaced. While recognizing that bureaucracies have immense powers that can positively transform peoples' lives, it may be said that seldom do such alterations occur in the case of displaced and resettled peoples. Part of the problem lies in the way bureaucracies are structured. The rigorous formalization of statuses, their segmentation and stratification, and the multiplication of "guarantees" given to the diverse strata and their occupants simultaneously render the tasks of coordination and control both indispensable and extremely difficult.

Crozier has coined the term "bureaucratic viscous circle" to describe how bureaucratic control and surveillance mechanisms become increasingly cumbersome as their scope extends, and yet increasingly more necessary as their efficiency declines. They are hardly calculated to provide a high level of motivation to employees of such an organization, who are more inclined to follow "strategies of safety" rather than "strategies of initiative" (see Crozier 1964). There are ways in which the bureaucracy can be made effective, such as through appropriate delegation of power in the bureaucratic structure, decentralization of power, reduction in the span of control, changes to enable speedy communications between bureaucrats in the hierarchy, lateral intervention in policymaking from specialists and technocrats, streamlining of the bureaucratic work force, and so on. However, it remains to be seen whether these often advocated prescriptions by public administration specialists are actually implemented to alter the bureaucracy and potentially minimize the risks that impoverished people might encounter.

The displaced are frequently at the mercy of rigid administrative concepts and processes, one of which is compensation. Compensation as an administrative device used in procedures of displacement presumes the notion of an arrangement that replaces (or counterbalances) alienated goods, property, or employment, and so on. In the case of the Kisan, replacements were made for alienated land (as well as one year's produce) with varying extents of land, cash, and employment. The basic principle of recompense in administration is equity of value. Thus, deprived goods or property can be converted to cash or goods or material benefits. It is frequently the case that the fixation of exchange value rests on the compensating authority. Rarely are people consulted in regard to the compensation goods or benefits they would like, or invited to negotiate equity for deprivations inflicted on them. Even if the displaced have a role in the latter, the outcome may not necessarily be satisfactory in the long run, for the displaced may be subject to the vagaries of wider economic forces beyond their control or to administrative procedures that may work against compensation.

On many occasions, the compensated stand to lose in the long run because of the above-mentioned factors, though there may be an apparent gain at the time when the compensation is made. The practice of handing out compensation as a once-and-for-all event by the authorities is in many ways an approach that fails to take account of the forces at work in the resettlement sites that are or become crucial in the long run, let alone natural forces (such as adverse climatic conditions, floods, and earthquakes) that can significantly alter an economy. Thus, the value of land or property may increase in time disproportionately to the income gained through the provided employment or cash benefits in compensation, resulting in further impoverishment.

If compensation is made in the form of a one-off payment rather than installments over a period of time, it works to the advantage of the compensating authorities. There are significant losses in the forms of cost overruns, debt servicing liabilities, and escalation of other costs with time lags that work against the interests of authorities. Indeed, this raises a question relating to costs and benefits for both authorities and victims as both parties wish to benefit from compensation in the long run. Much complexity is involved in counterbalancing in such a way that enables both parties to benefit through the reciprocity, and this is seldom achieved.

The principle of equivalence intrinsic to compensation is limiting. As long as we are trapped with the administrative concept of compensation, we would continue to seek arrangements based on equivalence, frequently in terms of monetary values. By definition, therefore, things that cannot be evaluated; that is, cannot be converted to monetary or numerical values, would be excluded from compensation, and furthermore, things whose value cannot be assessed appropriately would be compensated inappropriately. A range of significant losses, for example, in regard to mental health, can never be compensated under the prevalent policies of resettlement. Compensation leaves much to be desired and is unfair as the equivalence is quickly lost if grounded on purely monetary value. The displaced surely deserve more than just compensation, as it is a concept and procedure that is inflexible, imprecise, and unjust.

The landless or the displaced have to be provided for over and above what was taken from them, in order to recover and reconstruct their livelihood, if they can, at least at their pre-displacement or traditional level. Resettlement, while integrating people into a wider economic arena, should create conditions that would aid the people to cope and benefit in the new circumstance. Any settlement with the displaced on a basis of equivalence does not enable coping, adaptation, development, or prosperity. There are several instances that prove that resettlers are worse off compared with their pre-displacement circumstances. Implementing compensation is another way of conferring social and economic injustice. We should discard concepts such as compensation that have inherent limits within themselves, and instead use a set of alternative, positive, and flexible concepts in administration that would aid resettlers to maintain or improve their livelihood rather than face impoverishment.

Further displacement

People uprooted once are not free from being uprooted again. Future development projects may displace people from the resettlement sites, and these may or may not be the same activity that caused them to be displaced in the first instance. Many of the Kisan have been doubly displaced because of mining, waterlogging, sand casting, floods, and other hostile environmental conditions, such as dry and lifeless land. Thus, any restored or reconstructed livelihood is again put at risk of another displacement. It is in such contexts that one realizes the wastes in public expenditures, the futility of certain long-term projects, and the needless human and economic costs. Caution should be exercised when framing any policy of resettlement to take into account all proposed activities in the future in the vicinity that could displace the resettled population. This requires coordination between the various government departments.

As mentioned earlier in the chapter, certain occupations taken up by the resettlers, such as wage labor, may involve further displacement. These occupations are taken by the chronically landless not by choice, but because of compulsion to earn their livelihood.

For the Kisan, wage labor does not facilitate in the creation of additional assets through savings, and hence there is nothing to fall back on.

Further displacement can also occur from a general failure in social or environmental adaptation. Social conflicts, religious differences, and political alliances can coerce people to separate. Unstable psychological dispositions may prompt meaningless movements. A small fraction of the Kisan was found to be always on the move in search of a suitable place to live over the years, spending under a year at some places and up to 10 years at others.

The landless can be further displaced as a result of natural calamities (which are universal in their effects and can inflict people independent of their being displaced or not) if their resettlement site is proximate to impending calamities, natural or man-made, such as landslides, earthquakes, floods, desertification, and so on. It is, therefore, important that the resettlement site chosen be sensitive to all the above factors in order that any form of socially friendly resettlement program can be pursued. This also implies that resettlement policies with a long-term view are necessary, rather than a policy of one-time "compensation," as is the case in many instances.

Inadequate research methods

One of the further questions that needs to be asked is whether the available, or rather the used, research and survey methods are adequate to the task of assessing any instance of landlessness. This question is important in light of the kind of information being generated in the field of displacement and resettlement, the nature of investigations that are being carried out in resettlement or impending displacement sites, and approaches to framing policies for future displacements. A popular approach has been the cost-benefit analysis method, which is believed to be a comprehensive tool for evaluation and has been adopted by various governments and development agencies to determine the socioeconomic viability of large-scale development projects affecting huge populations. However, it seems to have eroded its credibility in the face of several harmful human experiences (see the reverse critique of cost-benefit analysis in resettlement projects in Cernea, this volume). The Kisan have been a victim of this calculation, and it is important to point out that such a method itself can be a "risk" that victims of displacement frequently encounter.

We speak about improving "resettlement performance" (see Mathur and Cernea 1995) when we do not have the tools to assess such performance. The "quality of life"[12] index is an attempt at performance assessment, though it is not without limitations. We need a new range of indicators that ought to be germane to the Kisan context. A few from the Kisan would include indicators relating to mental and physical health, nutrition, poverty, scarcity of land, economic and personal security, workload and work conditions, age and gender vulnerabilities, social activities and leisure, consumption, communication, human rights, environment, children and adolescents, social prejudice effects, political participation, the disabled, and the elderly. We need a new "multidisciplinarity" to take account of diverse quantifiable and nonquantifiable indicators. We should also speak about the performance of authorities and governments in charge of displacement, with the affected people given the rights to assess a government's performance (not only through the available means of political elections), and these should be considered seriously.

There are other dilemmas plaguing research on displacement and resettlement in general. These are related to the observation that "social scientists all too often speak to themselves: historically they have been much better at recording development's tragedies than helping prevent them" (Cernea 1996b:1515). There is an apparent reluctance to be positively oriented in the academic community. This is not because scientists are incapable or lack a certain imagination to realize that their reluctance is a limitation or even an opportunity to demolish constraining boundaries and explore policy-oriented work, but because it touches upon the problem of academic authority. The authority that derives from neutrality and objectivity stands at risk of being eroded at the prospect of positivist or applied work. Helping prevent disasters are, in our postpositivist times, the exclusive domain of the biased, such as the nonacademic or ex-academic person, the social worker, the activist, or the politician. The academic researchers are not the appliers or activists; in fact, researchers and activists examine each other's work suspiciously and rarely generously. The chameleons that shuttle in between, though rare, generate mixed reactions from both camps. However, in my view, these are the people best placed to have the insight and orientation that is lacked by the "pure" researchers and activists.

---

12 See Fürntratt-Loep (1995), in which the author provides an alternative to the generally accepted "quality of life" index and proposes an elaborate framework of assessment investigating 152 countries.

Brief conclusions

Finally, the stated risks related to landlessness, though contextual, can be faced by any community that encounters the prospect of or the process of displacement. Needless to say, with every new development process, newer forms of hazards come into existence. Some of these, as mentioned earlier, are subtle and do not easily lend themselves to identification through the procedures of investigation we are familiar with. They are sometimes as potent as the easily detectable dangers in their impoverishing effects. Cernea's eight main risks, namely, landlessness, joblessness, homelessness, marginalization, increased morbidity and mortality, food insecurity, loss of access to common property, and social disintegration, are a consolidated attempt at identifying and counteracting the harmful consequences of several of the manifest (see Merton 1968) and immediate dangers encountered in development-induced displacement. The model has the capacity to be operational in a range of impending resettlement sites in the developing world and covers in its scope quantifiable impoverishment processes in resettlements. Indeed such quantifiability is vital, as it is the *sine qua non* of the framing of development policies in general or resettlement policies in particular, independent of whether they are "people-centered" or "property-compensation"[13] types.

Policymaking has always been more dependent on concrete evidence that can be quantified or converted to statistics than on unquantifiable, qualitative evidence. Grounding themselves on such selective evidence, policies at best rely on partial information about resettlement processes. This is one of the possible explanations for the failure of policies. Cernea's general theoretical model, while excelling in the identification of relatively visible or "main" impoverishment processes (and these are vital in policymaking), should be complemented in each specific case by analysis that takes adequate account of certain relatively latent processes, some of which may be seen in my research on the landlessness of the Kisan. These latent processes are by their nature unquantifiable and remain invisible in many empirical studies, most of such studies being nonparticipant and observation-oriented. Subtleties can be made visible either by the vocal or educated among the victims or through intensive interactions. One of the customary ways through which such interaction

---

13   See Serageldin (1995), who makes a distinction between "people-centered resettlement policy" and "property-compensation policy."

can be achieved is by anthropological fieldwork. Other ways of detection can be achieved through interdisciplinary exercises or, more important, through informal networks, living with the victims, or sheer intensive observation. Socially dedicated volunteers or missionaries or travelers may sometimes furnish information that may otherwise escape the trained eye of the sociologist, economist, engineer, or anthropologist.

The impoverishing risks of landlessness, substantiated in the Kisan context, do not account in full for the entire range of risks that generally come with landlessness. However, they are some of the essential ones that must be considered in any event of displacement or resettlement. As shown, they have the potential to become major additional impoverishment factors in development-induced displacement. Together with the basic risks outlined by Cernea, they form a formidable guide and checklist for policy framers, authorities in charge of implementing displacement and resettlement, funders of development projects that cause displacements, nongovernmental agencies, activists, and researchers.

CHAPTER 4

Reconstructing livelihoods through land settlement schemes: comparative reflections on refugees and oustees in Africa[1]

Véronique Lassailly-Jacob

Land access and tenure rights are major issues when rural populations are forcibly displaced and relocated. Loss of land has been identified as the most significant of eight risks of impoverishment related to forced displacement (Cernea 1996d).[2] Despite their great impacts on settlers' livelihood, land issues have too often been neglected in both refugee and "oustee" settlement studies.[3] This chapter intends to discuss *landlessness and recovery through land-based relocation,* one dimension of the new conceptual model of impoverishment developed by Michael Cernea (see Chapter 1 in this volume).

Involuntary population displacements have occurred in Africa for centuries. Slavery, compulsory labor and forced relocation under colonial rule, tribal conflicts, wars, and anticolonial warfare, as well as natural disasters, have uprooted massive populations and scarred African history. Today, there are three main causes for dis-

---

[1] My grateful thanks go to Michael Cernea and Noal Mellot for their highly valuable comments and suggestions for rewriting this chapter.

[2] The other fundamental impoverishment risks intrinsic to forced displacement are joblessness, homelessness, marginalization, increased morbidity and mortality, food insecurity, loss of access to common property and services, and community disarticulation. These are discussed in this volume.

[3] The term "oustees" is used extensively for people forced off their land in the name of development. It is borrowed from the Indian literature on involuntary population displacement.

placement of population in Africa: development programs and processes; wars, persecutions, and political turmoil; and droughts, famines, and natural disasters. Although political violence and famines are the major causes of mass exoduses, development-induced displacement is rising rapidly because of the accelerated laying of infrastructures in the context of growing demographic pressure. In addition, the causes of mass exoduses of populations are increasingly interrelated and include demographic, ecological, or economic factors.

In 1996, there were an estimated 5.2 million registered refugees in Africa (U.S. Committee for Refugees 1996). Over the last decade, 13 major dams have forced more than 500,000 people out of their homes, and many more have been uprooted to make room for infrastructure projects, urban development, and transportation programs. The number of people evicted from game reserves, forest reserves, and national parks is escalating as well (Cernea 1997b). Droughts and famine have also forced thousands of people off their land. Kane (1995) reports that, during the 1968 to 1973 Sahel drought, about 20 percent of Mauritania's population was uprooted: more than 250,000 people fled to towns. Again, during the mid-1980s, another Sahel famine drove more than 2 million people out of Chad, Mali, Mauritania, Burkina Faso, and Niger.

Because of a lack of reliable data, the full extent of such population movements is unknown, but it is substantial. The number of refugees is far greater than what is counted in official statistics. For one thing, many persons are displaced within their home country and, therefore, do not show up in international refugee statistics. For another, even more persons spontaneously settle or hide along the host country's border. As for development-induced and disaster-related displacements, most of the statistics come from various, dispersed agencies and provide inaccurate assessments at best.

This chapter focuses on refugees and oustees in rural sub-Saharan Africa. As stated by Cernea, "both populations undergo a major disruption in their patterns of social organization and culture. They are facing the same task of physically and culturally surviving this disruption by reorganizing their economy and their ways of life" (1996b:295). Both groups suffer from the trauma of being forced to reconstruct their livelihood elsewhere.

Forced to move, they may be labeled "involuntary" or "forced migrants." However, given the nature of their displacement, they form two distinct groups: refugees generally move voluntarily while oustees are removed. For refugees, the decision about when and where to move rests with themselves, even though they "choose" under extreme stress. Most African rural refugees can be called "mass distress migrants." In contrast, oustees are "displacees" or "evacuees" who are moved as a result of administrative decisions. They are therefore entitled to compensation. As a result, assistance and coping strategies differ between the two groups.

Types of settlement

Because the vast majority of refugees and oustees come from rural areas, land is the most valuable asset that they lose through displacement. For farmers, herders, hunters, or gatherers, land is the foundation of their system of economic production and the basis of both their livelihood and identity. Regaining an appropriate piece of land so as to reestablish one's livelihood can be an extremely difficult, even impossible, goal. Four types of resettlement arrangements can be identified.

First, people may regain land by themselves without any assistance, that is, self-settled refugees or oustees. Most spontaneously settled refugees have ethnic affinities, clan relations, or kinship within a region or across a border. They reestablish themselves either by opening new land and establishing their own settlements or by sharing land and villages with hosts. Angolan refugees who fled into Zambia's North-Western Province between 1966 and 1972 mixed with the local population and became well integrated (Hansen 1990). This was also true of Mozambicans who settled in border villages in Zambia, Tanzania, and Zimbabwe. In these countries, self-settled refugees "hide" among locals to avoid being registered and regrouped in controlled settlements.

The second type of resettlement assists people in regaining land locally. For example, the United Nations High Commissioner for Refugees may adopt a program to assist the region within which people become hosts to refugees. In Guinea, about half a million refugees from Liberia and Sierra Leone have settled spontaneously in border villages and small towns since 1989. In agreement with the Guinean government, the UNHCR decided to support the host villages. As a result, "this refugee influx and the relief it attracted created an economic boom in the Forest Region of Guinea. The refugees gave a boost to rice production by increasing the cultivation of the lower swamp areas, a common practice in Liberia but hardly known in Guinea" (Van Damme 1995:361). The same policy has been applied in both the western region of Cote d'Ivoire, which is hosting thousands of self-settled Liberian refugees, and the Kigoma region in Tanzania, where approximately 13,000 refugees are spontaneously settled in 22 villages (Scott Wilson 1988). As long as an area's carrying capacity is not exceeded as a result of the number of newcomers, assisted self-settled refugees may contribute to local development.

Third, people (mostly refugees) might relocate but without regaining any land. Most refugees are put up in reception centers, transit camps, or care-and-maintenance camps where they survive on food rations and a few income-generating activities. Internally displaced refugees and many returnees survive in the periphery of main cities. This landlessness situation may also exist among evacuees. Following the implementation of the Kiambere project in Kenya, an estimated 6,500 oustees received cash compensation to buy land and resettle, but many of them used their cash compensation for school fees, payment of debts, aid to relatives, bride price, or current consumption. Only 14 percent of those compensated used the money to buy new land. As a result, most of the displaced had no further sources of income, and impoverishment followed (Mburugu 1994).

The fourth type of resettlement includes those who are given land by the authorities in order to rebuild their livelihood. Most African displaced communities have been relocated on new land as a result of dam construction and the formation of man-made lakes. As for refugees, an objective in UNHCR's strategy during the past 30 years has been to help some of them build a decent future in their land of exile. Agricultural settlements have been established for refugees and oustees who receive land for farming, as well as implements and technical assistance (compare Lassailly-Jacob 1994a).

This chapter deals with planned land settlement schemes established in order to reconstruct the livelihood of refugees and oustees. Comparing these schemes may help to (a) "bridge the gap"[4] between refugee and oustee studies and (b) bring to light some of the key issues that make such land settlement schemes so difficult to implement, especially in the case of refugees.

Land settlement schemes for refugees and oustees

Since the 1960s, the construction of big hydroelectric dams and the formation of large artificial lakes have been the most frequent cause

---

[4]   M. Cernea (1996a) calls for more exchanges between two fields of research that have seldom been brought together: refugee studies and "development oustee" studies. Comparative studies would enrich each field empirically, theoretically, and methodologically. Contacts between these two fields could shed light on similarities and differences in the behavior of these populations, their adaptation strategies, and the reception that authorities grant them.

of the forced displacement of African rural communities. Akosombo, Kossou, Kariba, Kainji, Aswan, Nangbeto, and Manantali are among the major dams that have disrupted thousands of lives by forcing people to move. Governments have usually resettled the uprooted on planned sites, where the relocatees could benefit from agricultural programs. In these government-sponsored resettlement schemes, new settlers have received, in compensation, land and assistance to help them regain self-sufficiency or even raise their standards of living.

With the help of international aid, government-sponsored resettlement schemes have also been extended to populations displaced by war. Since the early 1960s, the UNHCR has pioneered agricultural settlements in Africa as a durable solution for long-term rural refugees. Some host governments, with the help of international agencies (World Bank, Food and Agriculture Organization of the United Nations [FAO], and the United Nations) and numerous nongovernmental organizations (NGOs), have attempted through those settlements to locally integrate refugee communities and help them reach self-sufficiency. Between 1961 and 1978, approximately 60 rural settlements have been installed, most of them in Burundi, Uganda, and Tanzania (Christensen 1985). In the 1990s, nearly a quarter of all refugees in sub-Saharan Africa were estimated to be living in 140 organized settlements, mostly in the eastern and southern regions (Mathieu 1991). Among the countries that have accepted this sort of aid are Sudan, Tanzania, Uganda, Zaïre, Botswana, Burundi, and Zambia. Tanzania has allocated more than 6,000 square kilometers of land for settling refugees on 16 organized settlements, including Ulyankulu, Mishamo, and Katumba (Armstrong 1991). Planned land settlements have long been considered the best means for promoting refugee self-sufficiency and local integration. Despite the 28 agricultural settlements established in Uganda since 1989 to house some 100,000 Sudanese refugees (UNHCR 1996), the international community has now determined that this sort of solution is too costly. Host governments, too, are more and more reluctant to let refugees become long-term settlers.

Government-planned settlements for development oustees and internationally sponsored sites for war refugees are similar in some respects. Both sorts of schemes are carefully supervised and implemented in order to create viable, modern rural communities. Most of them benefit from heavy investments in infrastructure (such as access roads and drinking water) and community facilities (including schools and health centers). Both sorts of schemes emphasize agricultural development. Settlers are assisted in regaining self-sufficiency and restoring income through farming, usually through small-holder agriculture. Plots are demarcated and allocated to each household, along with tools, seeds, modern input, and extension advice.

Despite heavy investments, both sorts of schemes encounter numerous and often similar difficulties. Overall, results have not met expectations. For example, Stein and Clark (1990) have stated that out of 117 refugee settlements set up between 1961 and 1982 in Africa, only 59 were still operating in 1990. Eleven had been abandoned, and 47 closed as a result of repatriation. Among those still operating, 32 had "sporadically" been considered self-sufficient, usually thanks to additional international aid. The other 27 settlements had not yet attained self-sufficiency by 1982.

In the case of settlements for oustees, the results are no better despite a higher level of aid. To cite an example: although sizeable investments were made to develop intensive agriculture, the irrigated scheme of Khasm El Girba has not met production objectives. Planned in the early 1970s as a site for Nubian farmers who had been forced out of the Nile Valley by the lake behind the Aswan Dam, this area has had increasingly disappointing results, even though a new development plan went into effect in 1980 (Salem-Murdock 1989). In some cases, resettlement is followed by massive exodus, as in the Akosombo project. In other cases, it may take several years before the original level of subsistence is reached.

What are the typical constraints that these land settlement schemes encounter in their attempt to create long-term viable communities? Highlighting similarities and differences in planners' interventions and settlers' recovery difficulties may help us detect the obstacles that keep such schemes from becoming viable.

Planners' interventions

Planning departures and arrivals

Planning is a key factor for establishing viable new communities. Good planning involves adequate timing for the settlers' departure from their area of origin. In development-induced displacement, departure and resettlement are most often planned too late. Planners usually underestimate the burden of what is often a huge undertaking. The size and nature of the population to be displaced are poorly estimated because of a lack of previous censuses and transport difficulties. Too often, resettling oustees is considered to be an "unavoidable by-product" of development projects. While dam construction usually proceeds on time or even ahead of schedule, the displacement of the affected population occurs as a "last-moment salvage operation" leading to the inappropriate outcome of "cash resettlement programs" (Cernea 1997b).

However, in the case of oustee resettlement, planners have opportunities for making plans well in advance. If that is done, the population can be informed and consulted before displacement. People can prepare themselves mentally for that traumatic event, even if it seems beyond imagination up until the last minute. Planners have the means to undertake detailed baseline surveys such as a census and study of the population's means of livelihood in both the homeland and the resettlement area. In the Kossou Resettlement Project in the Côte d'Ivoire, evacuees were informed two years before the lake was impounded. All local chiefs were called to a meeting held in Yamoussoukro by President Houphouet-Boigny, who personally led the campaign. These oustees were consulted about where they wished to be resettled, and their demands were taken into account (Lassailly-Jacob 1994b).

In contrast, refugees move in an emergency. Host-country governments and the international community are suddenly—without warning—faced with a massive arrival of people. In a few days during July 1994, the Zairian government received 800,000 Rwandese. Planners have to find quick solutions for an already disrupted population under stress. They have no baseline data about the newcomers' ways of life. Given this lack of premovement data as well as the emergency procedures, stereotyped contingency plans—and therefore inappropriate responses—are applied everywhere. During the first years following the arrival of refugees, the host government establishes reception centers and transit camps, but it hopes that the refugees will soon return to their homeland. Only when it realizes that peace is not at hand does the host government decide—sometimes still under emergency conditions—to organize rural settlements.

Planning the new sites

Second, good planning entails selecting a proper agro-ecological and geographical location for the new sites. This includes considerations about market proximity, the availability of fertile land, sufficient clean water supply, and adequate rainfall. These are critical factors for a settlement's viability. Sites for oustees are not always well selected. For example, sites for villagers displaced by the Nangbeto

Dam, Togo, were located on slopes with poor drainage; the land was not cleared ahead of time, and there was insufficient arable land (Cernea 1997b).

Emergency pressures and poor planning have been major obstacles to viable refugee land settlements. Many refugee settlements, especially the older ones, were selected without adequate baseline studies or land feasibility surveys. As a consequence, these sites may have poor soil, be infested by tsetse flies, or have water and sanitation problems. Armstrong (1991:218) describes the site of Burigi in Tanzania as being "remote, inaccessible, with unreliable water supply on the edge of an extensive forest reserve. It was infested by the tse-tse fly. The refugees themselves were nomadic cattle refugees..." Another example is the selection of Ulyankulu, a refugee settlement in Tanzania. A faulty land survey resulted in the transference of 25,000 out of 60,000 refugees to a new settlement called Mishamo. It had been discovered, much too late, that the soil at the original site was unsuitable and the water supply inadequate (Gasarasi 1987). Other refugee settlements, such as those established in eastern Sudan for Eritrean refugees, have been located in areas with poor soil (see Sorensen, in this volume). At the resettlement sites in a semibarren area of Kassala Province, Sudan, rainfall is sporadic; the land has little farming potential and is better suited for pastoral livelihoods. No serious preliminary assessments were made about the sites' farming potential. Pedological and hydrological surveys were conducted in haste, if at all. Authorities had selected several sites despite warnings from prospection teams sent by international organizations. Furthermore, the remoteness of these sites has impeded trade and thus keeps settlers from securing a livelihood (Stein and Clark 1990).

Controlling settlement size

Thirdly, good planning necessitates controlling the number of newcomers. Oustees can be moved together all at once or in planned stages. They can start their new lives at the same time and enter successive adaptation phases at the same pace. Resettlement planners have the means to know when the displacement will occur, how many people will be moved, and what the size of the new settlements will be.

By contrast, refugees arrive in unpredictable, successive, and unexpected waves. Their numbers increase and decrease quickly in response to political events in either their country of origin or the host country. Continual new arrivals or sudden departures disorganize the settlement process and disrupt the smooth implementation of aid programs. This leads to a confusion between the emergency relief and development aid phases of settlement.

Good planning also means populating new settlements as a function of the land's human-carrying capacity. For planners, relocation is often an opportunity to group the uprooted in large settlements so as to facilitate administration and community services. As a result, land settlement schemes often house too many people who have to survive on insufficient resources. As a consequence, arable land is in short supply, and pressure mounts on the environment.

In the case of oustees, a selected site's population-carrying capacity can be studied in advance, after conducting soil surveys. But this does not happen often. In the Zambian part of the Kariba Project, the relocation of Tonga oustees in the Lusitu area has increased the population density fourfold. As a result, this area has become a dust bowl (Scudder 1980).

Most refugee settlements are overpopulated because "once a settlement has opened, there is a great temptation to continue to send newly arrived refugees (or spontaneously settled refugees who have been rounded up by the host government) to the site. Ndzevane in Swaziland and Meheba in Zambia recently doubled in size to accommodate new arrivals" (Stein and Clark, 1990:24). Such practices threaten a settlement's viability and its relations with the host community. In many cases, the UNHCR declared a settlement "self-sufficient" only after part of the population was moved elsewhere. Only then could available resources be brought into balance with the number of refugees and their hosts (Clark 1987). One of the reasons behind the success of Etsha, a farming settlement established in Botswana for Angolan refugees, is its small size: about 3,800 people were put up in 13 villages over a large area (Potten 1976).

Reconstructing livelihoods

Fourthly, sound planning calls for restoring productive capacities by allocating new means of production. Land is the most important means of production for rural settlers. However, acquiring and reallocating new land is an almost insurmountable task for planners (see Lassailly-Jacob 1996). In Africa, two overlapping systems of land tenure operate: national law and customary laws that prevail in rural areas. Before displacement, most farmers held only customary rights on their land. After displacement, most settlers have lost their customary rights without having gained any formal legal title to the new land.

Even if new settlers are located on "vacant" lands, these lands are generally governed by informal customary rights. Vacant lands may be used extensively by shifting cultivators, pastoralists, or hunter-gatherers whose livelihood is affected in the case of a re-settlement project. Land acquisition procedures with former users are usually neglected because of the lack of legal framework. These procedures take time and should be worked out well before the arrival of the resettlers. As a result, oustees usually suffer from a lack of arable and communal lands. In the Nangbeto Project, Togo, the land allocated per family has matched what the family previously farmed during a year, but no fallow land was added. In their study of resettled Malinke villages following the construction of the Manantali Dam in Mali, Horowitz and others (1993) have shown that the inadequate preliminary analysis of the land needs for the various activities of these farmers-herders-gatherers led to insufficient allotments. This brought on poverty. In the reinstalled Ciskei village studied by de Wet (1993), the reduction in farm size along with the attraction of urban employment accelerated rural flight.

Refugees generally have easier access to vacant land than do oustees. Refugees "borrow" the land with UNHCR's administrative assistance; they are given a right of usufruct as long as they remain in the country. It is assumed that after repatriation, this land will return to local communities.

Planning community reconstruction

Fifthly, sound planning should reconstitute socially viable communities on the new sites. In the case of oustees, planners have the means to resettle people in groups as in their home area. This way, the spatial identity of each social unit, clan, village, ward, or kinship group can be preserved. Whole former villages can be relocated as units to new settlements. Oustees thus maintain at least some of their former social networks, helping them cope with the new situation. New neighbors are already close by and are thus more willing and able to assist each other. Planners have, therefore, the potential to reduce and mitigate another key risk in the "risks and reconstruction model": social disarticulation (see Cernea in this volume).

However, community reconstruction is seldom achieved. In New Nubia, Egypt, rows of houses of about the same size were built in the new settlement. Houses were assigned as a function not of kinship but of family size. The arrangement of families in their former hamlets came undone, and family networks were broken up (Fahim 1983).

By contrast, refugees assigned to an agricultural camp are usually grouped by date of arrival and not by family or clan. They come from different areas and do not know each other when grouped in wards or village units. Nuclear families and isolated individuals without any ties have to start a new life together. In Ukwimi, Zambia, Mozambican families arriving in the same trucks were grouped in village units. Since members of the same family did not always arrive together, they were put up in different villages and not allowed to regroup. This policy split up many families (Lassailly-Jacob 1993). For such reasons, the building of a new community in a refugee settlement may be a difficult, long-term process. Another reason for the success of the Etsha settlement in Botswana was that people were grouped as they had been previously in Angola: the 13 new villages corresponded to the initial regrouping of the refugees when they entered Botswana (Potten 1976).

Planning and assessing the future

Once deemed self-sufficient, land settlements for oustees are handed over to local authorities. This cuts them off from outside assistance and integrates them in local administrative structures. At this stage, many settlements have experienced difficulty in maintaining infrastructure and services; future viability becomes uncertain. In Tanzania, Ulyankulu and Mishamo refugee settlements reached the handover stage in seven years, while in Katumba this took five years; the handover of these three settlements has been seen by the UNHCR and other agencies as an example of successful absorption of refugees in a host country. However, recently the UNHCR has found it necessary to renew aid to these three settlements (Scott Wilson 1988).

Once handed over, these settlements tend to be forgotten by the outside world. While most studies undertaken have focused on early stages of land settlement projects, too few follow-up studies are made about their long-term sustainability. As Clark (1987:14) has pointed out about refugee settlements: "research on rural settlements has focused almost exclusively on the time period when international assistance is being provided. Once the outside agencies leave, such settlements tend to be virtually forgotten unless aid is renewed or some major crisis befalls the settlement. Thus, longer-term issues tend to be ignored, and the longer-term impacts of aid programs are rarely evaluated." And when repatriation occurs, very little attention is paid to the impact of the mass departure of refugees on the host area, in particular, the future of settlements that have been planned and managed at high cost.

Oustee studies face a similar situation. Apart from Salem-Murdock's work (1989) on Nubian resettlers in the Khasm-El-Girba Scheme and the follow-up studies by Scudder (1993) of Gwembe Tonga resettlers in Zambia, little information is available about what happens to oustee settlements and settlers in the long term. Resettlement is not sufficiently seen as a long-term dynamic process. More investigations, especially longitudinal studies, are needed to draw lessons from successes and failures. This would help us to develop methodologies and models for understanding the processes of social, economic, and political change linked to resettlement in the long run.

Reflections on land settlement planning

Good planning is crucial to implementing viable resettlement programs. In the case of oustee resettlements, state agencies have the means for adequately planning new sites in appropriate agricultural areas if they take the time to establish an adequate legal framework and allocate enough financial resources. However, they frequently miss the opportunity to do either. In the case of refugees, establishing viable communities is a much more arduous task owing to the lack of time for planning and to the attitude of the host government.

Host governments make the major decisions that affect the resettlement of oustees as well as refugees. When a government perceives oustees as victims for the good of the nation, it compensates them and tries to reintegrate them as citizens. Selecting suitable sites, acquiring and clearing the land, giving deed to it, and building concrete houses are criteria of permanency and integration.

In contrast, refugees tend to be seen as a temporary burden. Settlement in overcrowded sites in remote areas, with land unsuitable for farming, are indications of marginal, temporary, and provisional arrangements. The host country's asylum policy treats refugees as transients. Hence, their settlements are less viable, and their integration is considered undesirable. Host-country authorities often provide asylum to masses of refugees in the hope that the international community will share the burden and provide assistance for developing peripheral areas (Kibreab 1989).

Recovery difficulties: comparative observations

In addition to planners and host governments, settlers also play an important part in the success or failure of resettlement programs.

One difficulty is linked to settlers' origin and activities. Most, but not all, new settlers come from rural areas. Many refugees put up in agricultural settlements may have been educated urban dwellers or herders, fishermen, gatherers, hunters, or traders. As new agricultural settlers, they are nonetheless given plots of arable land for growing crops. Not used to working the land, these settlers cannot become self-sufficient soon. The pastoralist Rwandese Tutsis who fled to Tanzania with large herds of cattle were directed to settlements threatened by the tsetse fly. They were given plots and forced to farm. When their cattle started to die, many abandoned the settlements (Armstrong 1991).

Both refugees and oustees often survive thanks to unprogrammed, spontaneous activities rather than the planned but unprofitable farming programs. The Eritrean refugees in Kassala Province, Sudan, though grouped on farming settlements, survived mainly through parallel activities: they worked as laborers on state-run or private farms, raised livestock, or became petty traders (Asfaha and Lassailly-Jacob 1994). In the case of the people displaced by the Akosombo and Kpong dams in Ghana, Adu-Aryee observed that "spontaneous" economic activities such as fishing or draw-down farming on the lakeshore were more developed than the costly planned activities.

A second difficulty is related to the household structure. In the case of development displacees, entire families are moved to new sites; therefore, the family labor force is potentially maintained as before. By comparison, refugee households have usually been disrupted or even destroyed before or during the move. Among the new arrivals are many fragmented nuclear families, individuals, and vulnerable people such as orphans and the disabled. In refugee as compared with oustee settlements, more households are headed by women or have nonproductive members. Split-up families, vulnerable individuals, and nonproductive members reduce the chances for viability and make it hard to reach self-sufficiency.

A third difficulty is settlers' behavior. Both refugees and oustees are similarly involuntarily uprooted from their homes and land; however, they behave differently with regard to long-term settlement.

Both are involuntary settlers because they are pushed by external forces toward the new settlements; they are not recruited and selected according to predetermined criteria as in the case of assisted voluntary settlements. Many refugees relocate to rural settlements reluctantly for three reasons. First of all, sites are usually located far inside the host country because authorities seek to protect border areas from insecurity. In 1987, the Zambian army rounded up self-settled Mozambican refugees along the border and drove them to a new agricultural settlement called Ukwimi, located 100 kilometers from the border. Refugees experience anxiety in an unknown environment. They also fear that the distance from their homeland will impede repatriation. Secondly, the sites are heavily supervised and tightly controlled. Many refugees prefer settling on their own among kin (or groups with ethnic or tribal affinities) where possible. Those who have settled a few years among locals feel once more uprooted when they have to move on, this time, to a settlement site. Thirdly, refugees never have a choice of sites; they are assigned to a settlement where they have to go.

Both refugees and oustees are traumatized settlers, but for different reasons. Most refugees have fled in an emergency after having been exposed to violence or persecution. They are under the shock of flight to another country. They may have lost family members and left most of their belongings behind. They face an uncertain future in exile. Development oustees stay in their own country, but they experience the trauma of being permanently deprived of their main social, cultural, and economic foundation: their ancestral lands. They are powerless in decisions made outside their control, as well stated by Mathur, "One unfortunate outcome is a feeling of alienation, helplessness, and powerlessness that overtakes the displaced. This stems from the way in which the people are uprooted from homes and occupations and brought to question their own values and behavior, and the authority of their leaders" (Mathur 1995:18). This feeling of marginalization and powerlessness mainly stems from the lack of cultural mechanisms for coping with this new kind of disruption. In the case of a community displaced by the Rengali Dam in Orissa, India, Behura and Nayak (1993) have shown how these people who have cultural defenses for coping with life-cycle crises, epidemics, and natural disasters were suddenly helpless. Unable to handle this rupture, their standard of living at the resettlement site fell, and their society came apart.

But refugees and oustees behave differently with regard to long-term settlement. Most rural refugees see their exile as being transitory. They have left kin, assets, and farmlands behind. They try to remain informed about events back home, and hope to return as soon as possible. This feeling of being transient settlers is germane to the refugee status. Having crossed a border endows their flight with legal and political significance. Recognition as an international refugee brings entitlement to protection and assistance from the international community, but it also places the concerned under special laws. For example, under Sudanese law (the 1974 Regulation of Asylum Act), refugees have no political rights. Moreover, they are prohibited from leaving settlements without permission, from buying land, and from working outside settlements. Nor do they have any land rights. They receive farms in usufruct only; the land belongs to the host government (Asfaha and Lassailly-Jacob 1994). In brief, scheme-settled refugees are protected, assisted settlers, but they are not granted the basic rights of citizenship. For this reason too, and despite the suitability and viability of any new settlement, refugees tend to return to their homeland as soon as the violence there has ceased. Out of the refugee land settlements in eastern and southern Africa that were closed because of repatriation between 1962 and 1982, seven had already been declared self-sufficient (Kibreab 1989). In 1994, nearly all Mozambican refugees in Ukwimi, Zambia, accepted repatriation, in spite of the satisfactory living standard most of them had attained. This suggests that achieving self-sufficiency does not retain refugees in a host country.

Typically, refugees live from day to day—especially during the first years of exile—and hope to return as soon as peace is restored in their homeland. Prospects for repatriation may hinder or even disrupt farming programs. In Meheba, an agricultural settlement set up for Angolan refugees in Zambia, Powles and Clark (1996) report that many refugees do not consistently work the land because they see themselves as being in Meheba temporarily. They behave as visitors; Angola is still their home. For them, reconstruction means returning to where they came from. Uncertainty about the future and the desire to ultimately return to the place of departure makes short-term income activities more attractive than long-term development.

Whereas refugees keep roots in their homeland, oustees have to put down new roots in the new settlement. Having lost their land for good, they may be more willing to make an effort to resettle permanently, provided that the resettlement plan matches their needs. In this case, long-term development programs are feasible. Despite the many similarities of their situation as forcibly displaced populations, refugees and oustees have quite different reasons and motivations and thus react differently to the programs planned for them.

Future for land settlement schemes

Given the accelerated provision of infrastructure, the magnitude of development-induced population displacement and resettlement will increase. As long as the multiple dimensions—especially the legal ones—of such transfers are not taken into account, resettlement will remain a cause of impoverishment. In most developing countries, eminent domain laws exist as a legal framework in case of expropriation; however, these have no means for solving the many legal problems that arise from the displacement of a population. National rules of law for assessing the value of lost property, compensating the displaced, allocating vacant land, and assisting host communities should be established. Vacant land cannot be made legally available to resettlers without political will at a national level.

Nowadays, as opposed to the 1960s and 1970s, there are far fewer land settlement schemes established or operated for refugees. Organized rural settlements used to provide a "durable" solution for accommodation of long-term rural refugees. They allowed hundreds of thousands of persons in eastern and southern Africa to live decently in exile. However, the reality of self-sufficiency and local integration did not always live up to the expectations established by the UNHCR. Facing more and more emergencies, the international community no longer has the means to provide a decent future to persons in exile. The days are past when many rural refugees could be assisted toward achieving self-sufficient in exile. Going into exile now means hiding among locals or surviving in transit camps, where the living conditions are so poor that few wish to stay on. The international community is no longer focusing on the host countries but on the country of origin. It is trying to facilitate repatriation, or to prevent the crises that trigger mass refugee movements. Not so long ago, the right to flee one's homeland and seek refuge was respected. Nowadays, the demand to stay put has taken priority. But will it hold up under the pressure of events to come?

PART THREE

From joblessness to re-employment

Editors' Regaining wage employment is needed in both urban
Note and rural displacements. Those who lose jobs include
landless laborers, enterprise or service workers, artisans, and small businessmen — the self-employed. Creating new jobs is difficult and requires substantial investment. Thus,
unemployment or underemployment among resettlers often continues long after physical relocation was completed.

The chapters in this section report positive experiences with job
creation in two quite different political and economic settings.
Sheilah Meikle and Zhu Youxuan address the implications of
China's shift from a command to a market economy for resettlement operations, while María Clara Mejía assesses economic recovery programs for brickmakers displaced by the Yacyretá Project
on the Argentina/ Paraguay border.

More than 30 million people in China have been involuntarily
displaced by planned development over the past 40 years. This,
note Meikle and Zhu, has led to the evolution of a new and sophisticated legal and procedural system for dealing with resettlement that, they argue, "can be seen as equitable in ethos and
approach." The authors also argue, however, that for displaced
farmers, shopkeepers, enterprise employees, and illegal migrants,
the more recent transition and related reforms have weakened the
protection of the rights to employment and the ability to create
employment.

In addition, resettlement locations are often at a great distance
from previous locations, meaning longer commutes and inferior
quality of life. The authors argue that in order for Chinese authorities to maintain high standards in resettlement, a better understanding of the full impact of the economic transition on resettlement is
necessary; new policy provisions regarding compensation and livelihood reconstruction must be explored; and, finally, new man-

agement capabilities for resettlement negotiation within the private sector must be identified.

Mejía focuses more sharply on a specific case: the construction of a reservoir on the border of Argentina and Paraguay that resulted in the flooding of clay deposits, previously the essential raw materials for the livelihoods of displaced communities of brickmakers, or *oleros*. Mejía identifies the *oleros* as particularly vulnerable people, living on the edge of the economy, dependent on natural resources, and distrustful of government.

The author was charged with devising a Resettlement and Rehabilitation Action Plan (RRAP) for the displaced artisans and did so based on economic reconstruction principles framed in a wider social development strategy. The main objective was to ensure an integral recovery of prior conditions while at the same time promoting significant improvements in the livelihoods of the *olero* population. The strategy allowed those affected to decide whether to continue their activities, return to rural areas, or receive cash compensation based on the packages on offer. A partnership approach was adopted, and, following a long period of negotiation and implementation, a range of strategies to reduce the risk of impoverishment were effectively put in place.

Mejía offers a series of recommendations, which may serve to improve employment and income restoration for those whose economic base has been eliminated by development projects.

CHAPTER 5

Employment for displacees in the socialist market economy of China

Sheilah Meikle and Zhu Youxuan[1]

This chapter examines how the movement to a socialist market economy in China has been changing the operational environment for involuntary resettlement, and, in particular, its implications for displacees' employment opportunities. Employment is analyzed especially in regard to farmers, shop owners, employees of town and village enterprises (TVEs), and illegal urban immigrants. There are already indications that unless account is taken of the changed operational environment, any future employment creation for resettlers will be less equitable and effective. Further research has supported this argument.[2] Moreover, while transition to a market economy may lead to a more efficient resettlement process, this too will depend on policy developments taking account of the changed operational environment. It thus supports the opinion that "early recognition of and response to the changing environment will help... maintain China as a model....of resettlement."[3]

The chapter starts with a brief introduction to the Chinese context, a consideration of the nature and strengths of Chinese involuntary resettlement and of the characteristics of the transition process

[1]   The authors would like to acknowledge the assistance of Julian Walker, Research Assistant (DPU).
[2]   Meikle and Walker. 1998. "Resettlement Policy and Practice in China and the Philippines." Unpublished report funded by U.K. Department for International Development, Escor Research Scheme Number R6802.
[3]   World Bank. 1993. "China Involuntary Resettlement." Unpublished report, p. 58.

in China. These opening sections will help illuminate the impact of transition on the rights of displacees to employment and the creation of employment opportunities, with specific reference to case studies in Shanghai. The chapter continues with an assessment of the change in resettlement equity, effectiveness, and efficiency in relation to compensation and job opportunities for involuntary resettlers resulting from the transition to a market economy. The final section considers the way ahead.

Background

China has the distinction of being the third largest country in area (after the Russian Federation and Canada), covering 3,700,000 square miles, and the most populous country in the world. With well over 1 billion inhabitants, one person in four of the world's population is Chinese.

Since its foundation in 1949 as the People's Republic of China (PRC), the country has been undergoing a process of economic and social development. Initially, during the revolutionary period, it was in transition from a feudal to a socialist command economy. Since 1978, it has been in transition to a socialist market economy.[4] This development has required, and continues to require, massive investment in infrastructure, which in turn has resulted in extensive resettlement.

The scale of involuntary resettlement during the last 40 years has been enormous, involving well over 30 million people. Homes and jobs have been lost to reservoirs behind the 86,000 dams constructed between 1952 and 1990, for the rights of way for 30,000 kilometers of railroad and 90,000 kilometers of roads, and to newly constructed canals, airports, and factories, as well as to urban development projects.[5]

Since 1990, the pace of investment has continued. World Bank–supported projects alone in China, at a conservative estimate, have or will have accounted for more than 750,000 resettlers. When the loans and credits of other agencies, which are supporting 17 proposed hydro and thermal projects as well as other infrastructure projects, and those projects internally generated and funded are

---

[4]   The date of the Third Plenum of the 11th Central Committee, 1978, is generally acknowledged as the start of the reform period and can therefore be seen as the beginning of the transition to a socialist market economy.
[5]   World Bank. 1993. "China Involuntary Resettlement." Unpublished report, p. 3.

added to the total, then the full significance of resettlement in China can be appreciated.

The Chinese resettlement process

Types of resettlement

Involuntary resettlement in China results from water reservoirs, transport, infrastructure, and urban construction:

Reservoir development, although once the leading cause of resettlement, now displaces no more than 10 percent of the people resettled each year. Reservoir resettlement impacts are much greater and more difficult to deal with than any other type of project, as illustrated by the case study discussed by Ranjit Nayak in this volume. Entire villages, even townships, are overtaken by reservoirs. These populations must frequently be placed on land already used by others, often in a new political jurisdiction. This can result in host-resettler tensions, and all incomes may decline. Rich fertile land is lost and replacement options depend on fragile soil and less dependable water supplies. New cropping patterns have to be mastered, and land scarcity may force people to look for non-agricultural employment.

Transport infrastructure investments displace primarily, but not solely, rural people located in transport corridors and at the sites of airports, bridge abutment, and so forth. This displacement is therefore limited in scale and may vary from as few as a handful of families to hundreds or thousands, depending on circumstances. Transportation displacements also take place in the urban areas. In the 1980s about 12 percent of overall involuntary resettlement was caused by the construction or upgrading of railroads and roads. In these cases, villages rarely lose all the village land and are able to redistribute the remaining lands to ensure more equity of land use. When the village loses too much land to provide sustainable holdings for all residents, those with smaller holdings may be given employment in local TVEs. In more extreme cases they may be given an urban passport and resettled in the nearest town.

Urban resettlement now accounts for the majority of all Chinese resettlement. All urban land is owned by the state and therefore only usufruct rights rather than ownership rights are lost. Any resettlement project must compensate individuals for lost use rights by providing substitute housing of equal or higher standards, and by providing alternative places for doing business and the means to replace lost assets. The discussion of employment in this chapter generally draws on experience from projects in Shanghai and its periphery, and is therefore focused on the last two of the three generic types of resettlement.

Equity and resettlement

Government attitude toward resettlement has been changing since the founding of the PRC. Since 1980, China has responded, within the more relaxed post-1978 political environment, to increasing internal resistance from potential resettlers, and aimed to develop good resettlement practices. The result is that there is now an established legal and procedural system for the implementation of involuntary resettlement, which is substantially in accord with the World Bank's operational directive on resettlement and the Organization for Economic Co-operation and Development's resettlement guidelines.[6] With this increased concern for and emphasis on the needs of individuals and fair compensation for all aspects of their disruption, resettlement policy in China can be seen as equitable in ethos and approach.

The strength of Chinese resettlement

The strength of Chinese resettlement, whether rural or urban, has traditionally derived from the nature of the operational environment in which it has been undertaken. Specifically, "from the persistence of planning elements in the Chinese economy, coupled with collective ownership...and the importance of local government in shaping investment. When combined, these factors allow accurate identification of affected people, protect rights to employment, and foster the ability to create that employment."[7]

With some notable exceptions (such as a failure to provide compensation for illegal residents, even where they may have been on project sites for more than 20 years), resettlement has thus been both equitable and effective. Whether it has also succeeded in being efficient—the third management tenet—is more problematic. This is because efficiency implies the completion of an undertaking with

---

[6]   Key law 1986—Land Administration Law of the People's Republic of China, as amended and amplified in 1988 and by subsequent resettlement laws and regulations; Organization for Economic Cooperation and Development. 1991. "Guidelines for Aid Agencies on Involuntary Displacement and Resettlement in Development Projects"; World Bank. "Operational Directive 4.30, Involuntary Resettlement."

[7]   Ibid., 58.

the optimum use of resources. A tendency for the various arms of government to underwrite any financial shortfall in resettlement makes it difficult, if not impossible, to determine the true amount of resources required to undertake any resettlement.

The transition process

The nature of the process

In order to assess how the transition to a socialist market economy is affecting the strength of resettlement procedures in China, it is necessary first to consider the nature of the transition process.

Transition means change and is the term applied to the current stage of economic and political development in such formally planned economies as China, Vietnam, the states of the former Soviet Union, and Eastern Europe. It describes the move from a centrally planned command economy to some variety of market economy. The principle focus of "transition" is on the fostering of free markets, the logic being that "the freeing of markets is the basic enabling reform from which all the potential benefits of transition flow."[8]

Unlike transitional reforms that began in 1989 in Eastern Europe and the former Soviet Union, the transition in China since 1978 has not been linked to economic crisis or structural political reform. In the case of China, there is consensus only that the broad direction of gradual economic change toward a more open economy will give the market increased responsibility for various services; this reform is far from the almost complete disengagement of the state that has taken place in the republics of the former Soviet Union and in Eastern Europe. The Chinese objective is a socialist system that also includes a market economy. The changes in the roles and responsibilities of various actors in the resettlement process are associated with the Chinese transition and appear particularly relevant.

First, the role of the state as a universal employer and provider of social welfare support has fundamentally changed. In China since the late 1970s there has been growing emphasis on the economic efficiency of state-owned enterprises (SOEs), which is leading toward a disengagement of the state from the provision of welfare support, such as health, housing, and the provision of unemployment support by a reduction of hidden unemployment in state

---

8   World Bank. *From Plan to Market: World Development Report 1996*. New York: Oxford University Press.

enterprises. Such changes have a very marked implication for the welfare of displacees. In its changed condition the state is increasingly performing the role of "enabler," creating the conditions which make it possible for the private sector to function effectively and undertake many of the roles that had previously been vested in the public sector. In China this is demonstrated, for example, by the growing private retail sector and the opening up of markets in land, housing, and employment. From the point of view of resettlement this means that procedures must take account of more complex processes of compensation to deal with the expansion of private ownership.

Second, the increased economic efficiency required of SOEs and TVEs often results in unemployment. Certainly, these enterprises cannot be expected to act as employers of "last resort." It can also be anticipated that such institutions will be requiring staff with appropriate qualifications and skills. Thus, guaranteed new employment for displacees is becoming increasingly unlikely.

Third, closure of state organizations and transfer of their responsibilities to the private sector created a free employment market and left no overall government responsibility for TVEs. This makes it more difficult to guarantee employment for displacees and complicates the resettlement compensation procedure.

Fourth, since the commencement of the transition process in China, the various tiers of government, which had previously been under strong central control, have obtained much greater autonomy. Such changes result in greater diversity among the various regions and within regions in terms of available resources for supporting resettlement as well as in the speed and quality of resettlement practice.[9]

And last, there is increasing mobility of the population and labor force. In China, as in other centrally planned economies, mobility of labor was restricted. Access to welfare benefits, jobs, and housing was dependent on holding the relevant internal residence documents. Such restrictions on movement made each community like a small "country."[10] Workers therefore were forced to "effectively sacrifice...mobility for greater individual security," through guar-

---

[9]   Gu Jian-Guang. 1996. "The Process of Rural Industrialisation in China." Rural Community and Government, Shanghai Institute of Economic Development, Processed.
[10]   Gu Jian-Guang. 1996. "The Process of Rural Industrialisation in China." Rural Community and Government, Shanghai Institute of Economic Development, Processed.

anteed jobs (or access to land) and social benefits through the work-place, while "in a market system employees move between employers, between types of work and between places—and they may experience unemployment."[11]

This increase in labor mobility presents a particular problem in China, where mobility exists in practice, but institutions have been, or are, operating on the assumption that it does not, so that the "floating" population moving to seek work is not cared for by state institutions. Indeed, such institutions may be responsible for returning these populations to their places of origin. "The floating population, mostly single men and women," which make up "20 to 25 percent of the population in most cities," and more in cities such as Shanghai and other growth centers in the coastal south, may at best be tolerated but will not receive any state benefit. Thus, they are generally not eligible for state compensation if they reside, without proper documents, in an area subject to resettlement.[12]

Implications of the economic transition for the employment of displacees

Having highlighted, through an examination of the changing roles and responsibilities of a number of actors involved, the evolving nature of the environment for resettlement in China, this chapter now considers how the operation of a market rather than a command economy has weakened the previous strengths of resettlement in China, specifically the protection of the rights to employment and the ability to create employment.

The following review of the position of displaced farmers, shop-keepers, enterprise employees, and illegal migrants illustrates the impacts of the transition on these groups, as well as the new responsibilities placed on resettlement project staff. The picture that emerges is that resettlement is also clearly in a process of transition. Much of the administrative framework, which has traditionally underpinned the system, is in a state of flux. There is increased autonomy of all actors, who now must operate in an increasingly complex environment, and are faced with new and more demanding responsibilities. For project staff, this means developing imaginative local approaches and involvement in longer and more complex negotiations.

---

[11]   World Bank. *From Plan to Market: World Development Report 1996*. New York: Oxford University Press.

[12]   Confirmed in discussion with a number of resettlement officers.

Displaced farmers

Farming is becoming less secure in China. With increasing development and urbanization, there is extensive land requisition in peri-urban areas, and land is becoming scarcer and hence more valuable. Although villages are still tied to the land, many villagers are now no longer farming but are employed in a variety of enterprises.[13] Incomes continue to be lower in rural than in urban areas. Farmers, or more accurately village residents, have increased expectations, and are no longer satisfied merely with re-registration from rural to urban status upon resettlement. They also require well-paid employment. Shanghai illustrates these points very well.

Because the central government's 1990s policy is reviving Shanghai as a large international city, investment in the urban infrastructure as well as in housing and other real estate sectors increased rapidly. These changes have inevitably resulted in large amounts of land being requisitioned, and in extensive demolition within the urban area. One estimate suggests that a total of 300,000 households, or 1 million people, were relocated in Shanghai over the past five years.[14] In Shanghai's peri-urban areas, extensive land requisition has not only caused relocation of farmers, but also resulted in the conversion of many farmers from a rural status as agricultural workers to urban status as nonfarm workers.

The high population density and low land-to-labor ratio in the peri-urban area of Shanghai make things particularly difficult. For every hectare of farmland requisitioned, between 15 and 30 people have to be given new nonagricultural employment. Under the old system, if a village's per capita land was below 0.5mu, after land requisition at least some farmers had to be re-registered as urban, so that the existing per capita land ratio could be maintained.[15] Those farmers who changed their status to urban were provided with jobs in the city by the city labor bureau.

There is ample evidence that farmers were, in the past, enthusiastic about their changed status because it provided them with legitimate access to better-paid urban employment, as well as better-

---

[13]   Gu Jian-Guang. 1996. "The Process of Rural Industrialisation in China." Rural Community and Government, Shanghai Institute of Economic Development, Processed.

[14]   Discussion with resettlement project officer in Shanghai.

[15]   There are fifteen mu. to the hectare.

quality health, education, and recreational facilities.[16] Now, in the increasingly complex rural and peri-urban environment, the government is still obliged to ensure jobs, if not land, for farmers who are involuntarily resettled. However, it has become more difficult to acquire replacement land for displaced farmers because of both the shortage and cost of land. Additionally, the possibility of obtaining non-land-linked jobs has also become administratively less certain now that the government labor bureau no longer has the sole responsibility to find work for displacees. Furthermore, former government enterprises no longer have the welfare role of acting as an employer of "last resort" in the interest of becoming more economically efficient. As a consequence, jobs increasingly must be found through the private job market and with direct action by the resettlement project staff.[17]

Securing employment for displaced farmers

The provision of secure employment for displaced farmers is one of the most difficult tasks for resettlement project staff, particularly in the instance of urban infrastructure projects such as road building, where the project itself cannot provide long-term job opportunities. One approach increasingly adopted by those projects that can afford it is provision of cash compensation that the village or township can invest to provide an income basis for the resettlers.[18] The cash sum available in rural areas has been up to 10,000 *yuan*. In exceptional cases in Shanghai, the cash sum has amounted to about 100,000 *yuan* (US$18,000–$18,750).[19] Given the current interest rate of 10 percent, this can currently generate an annual income of 10,000 *yuan*.[20] The real value of such an income however, can be expected

---

[16] The authors' discussions with numerous resettlement officers and re-registered farmers at the site of the new Lukou airport near Nanjing, in Jiang Yin at the site of the new bridge over the Yangtze River and in Shanghai.

[17] Cernea gives a further discussion of the impact of landlessness and loss of employment on resettlers elsewhere in this volume.

[18] Authors' discussions with Shanghai project staff.

[19] Approximately 8.1 *yuan* to the U.S. dollar. Annual income for a farmer 1,000–2,000 *yuan*.

[20] According to Davis Langdon and Seah International (1996), "Asia Pacific Construction Costs Handbook," London: E. and F. N. Spon, the 1994 rate marked a steep increase over the average annual inflation rate for the period 1980–1993, which was 7 percent.

to erode very quickly, given annual inflation rates. However, if the resettlers use the compensation to develop collective economies (for example, expand existing enterprises and build new ones), then the affected village members could be expected to benefit both from work in new factories and from dividends paid on their investments. This approach could be very useful for villages with capacity where there is past experience with TVE and where local industry is advanced. Poor areas with limited or no experience in development of such factories, however, would be particularly disadvantaged.

Two Shanghai projects, the Shanghai Sewerage II and the Shanghai Waigaoqiao projects, have adopted other approaches.[21] The Shanghai Sewerage project has had to pay the district labor administration of the Pundong District Government approximately 80,000 *yuan* per person to find secure jobs for the farmers displaced by the project. Whether this approach will result in satisfactory results remains to be seen.

A key problem is the low ratio of labor-intensive to capital-intensive industry in Shanghai, making it difficult to find jobs for unskilled and semi-skilled workers, however efficient the administration. The size of the waiting list—at the end of 1995, between 30,000 and 40,000 people—indicates just how difficult it is for the district labor administration center to place the unemployed.

The Waigaoqiao Power Plant has adopted a different approach. Instead of relying on local government to find jobs for the 1,200 farmers displaced by the project, the power supply bureau of Pudong took responsibility for organizing a service company to provide jobs for the displacees. A total of eight factories and companies, some of which rely on a subsidy from the power bureau, have been created with the assistance of the Shanghai Electricity Power Bureau and the Public Power Supply Bureau. These factories, as part of the power sector enterprises, provide good wages, and the displacees are happy with their new occupation. An indication of the difficulty of this task and the effort involved is the fact that it took between four and five years to provide all the displacees with jobs. Not surprisingly, given the burden of such an approach, the power bureau officials are not prepared to adopt the same approach for the second phase of the project. Instead, they wish to see local government take over these employment-finding responsibilities.

---

21   Both are co-financed by the World Bank.

Small private shopkeepers

Increasing numbers of private retail outlets demonstrate the success of China's reform policy in enabling greater participation of the private sector. More and more of these outlets are also found in communities that have been and are being designated for resettlement. Many individuals with business skills and houses fronting onto streets have converted part of their residential space into small shops, such as convenience stores, small restaurants, barbers, and car repair shops. These shop owners have worked hard to establish themselves and, for some, their shop is their only source of income. Their property and employment are tied to their shop's location and the local catchment area it serves. Unfortunately, most of these shop owners, although they have business licenses to operate, do not have documentary evidence of the change of use of their building, which for the purpose of any evaluation remains residential. The existence of these small private enterprises — in the second stage of the Shanghai Inner Ring Road project they represented 320 of 6,000 households relocated — proves to be a difficult issue for resettlement projects to handle under the existing legislation. Resettlement project officers' concern and awareness of the difficulties associated with this issue were made clear in a recent Overseas Development Association/World Bank resettlement monitoring and evaluation training workshop by the content and the emotional energy released during a training role-play game, in which an "appraisal interview" by "resettlement officers" and a "World Bank representative" was undertaken with "a shopkeeper."

Because of this lack of legal status, internal resettlement agencies have not been able to treat small shops as businesses. They have therefore, during the 1980s and 1990s, adopted three main strategies in a bid to resolve the shopkeeper dilemma. Shops have been closed and shopkeepers compensated for losses with cash and/or additional residential space at the new locations, or offered lease of government-built units at the new location. In some cases, shopkeepers were relocated in alternative street front houses in the original location so that business could be continued.[22] These approaches have limitations and are in one way or another unsatisfactory for either the project or the shopkeeper.

---

[22]   In such cases, compensation is usually based on an annual income reported on the tax return. It could reach between 20,000 and 30,000 *yuan*.

It is not satisfactory for the shopkeeper to have buildings converted into shops treated as residential structures. Where this is the approach the shopkeeper loses the opportunity for self-employment. Even when an alternative job is available, it may not be acceptable. The relocation of shops to a new area, which may be perfectly acceptable to employees of government-owned shops, is generally not a satisfactory solution for the private shopkeeper. It will involve losing the benefit of an established location and may frequently result in higher expenses in terms of rent or other overhead. In the case of the Shanghai Ring Road, because of relatively high rental costs and lack of customers in the new area, many shopkeepers have given up their businesses and taken new jobs, as taxi drivers, for example, or as employees in joint venture enterprises.

The third solution of negotiating an alternative street-front property sounds very reasonable in theory, but in practice may well prove to be unsatisfactory, as it usually involves a lengthy and time-consuming exercise, with uncertain results. In recent years, in Shanghai at least, the resettlement of shopkeepers has been by negotiation. Shopkeepers in more prosperous areas have been offered 20,000 to 30,000 *yuan* compensation, plus the transfer of their business to a new location. This is a well-accepted approach for more prosperous business districts, but in less prosperous districts the smaller and less vocal shopkeepers do not have the same influence.

In Shanghai, many resettlement officers are requesting a change in practice so that differences in land values due to location are recognized in the calculation of resettlement compensation budgets. This approach would reduce the current difficulties by ensuring that there are adequate funds available to compensate for location that are commensurate with the size of the business.

Town and village enterprises

Unlike private shop owners, affected enterprises or institutions in urban resettlement areas were and continue to be recognized under the law. However, since almost all of these units were either state-owned or collectively owned, for many years their compensation and rehabilitation was administratively determined and was not therefore the direct responsibility of the enterprise or local resettlement office. For example, in the case of the Shanghai Inner Ring Road project, as part of city policy, all affected units were expected to internalize part of the costs of the impact of the development. Thus, the city compensated only for the loss of structures and made some contribution to the cost of lost equipment. But no compensation was given for the loss of land or for lost revenue. Such losses were required to be absorbed by the relevant enterprise and their supervising bureaus. For example, the concerned bureaus were responsible for reassigning affected workers and for waiving taxes. Now, with the dissolution of the superior industrial bureaus as part of the market transition, the enterprises have effectively become independent agencies responsible for their own financial situation and are required to individually absorb any losses. Under this situation it has become more and more difficult for enterprises, regardless of whether they are state-owned or collectively owned, to absorb the cost of the impact of resettlement. In the main this tends not to happen. Rather, inefficient and loss-incurring enterprises now see the resettlement process as an opportunity for resolving their financial problems. This means that the responsibility for absorbing the costs of resettlement, including finding work for those who may have lost their jobs, is no longer clearly the responsibility of the TVEs and becomes the project's responsibility. The result is that resettlement project officers are required to negotiate with enterprises on a case-by-case basis. Such negotiations tend to be lengthy, time-consuming, and particularly difficult to resolve in the absence (under the current resettlement laws) of any clear operational guidelines regarding enterprise compensation. In this situation the employment position of those displaced is problematic.

Illegal migrants

Illegal migrants in urban China are those people who do not have residential permits to live in the cities, but still live and work there. Under the current laws and regulations, urban resettlement compensation and rehabilitation covers only those people who have legal urban status. Even those who as individuals have urban status but whose full household is registered in another location are usually not covered. Nor are those who do not have urban resident status, such as temporary workers and visitors. Since most of them rent spaces from individuals (mostly suburban farmers) at market rates, it is their individual responsibility to renegotiate their leases after relocation has been completed. The government deals only with those private landlords who have local resident permits, and provides them with replacement accommodation. Thus, there is the possibility, if mutually desired, for those landlords to continue to lease to temporary residents. The World Bank, where it is involved, frequently requires that temporary residents be given assistance in finding new accommodation. This is not the practice for domestic projects. As has been the situation in the past, the project continues to have no responsibility for finding new work for this disadvantaged group.

Conclusion

The changes wrought by the transition from a planned to a socialist market economy, as demonstrated by the Shanghai projects, have already begun to have an impact on both the resettlement process and the quality of life of resettlers. The indications are that these changes have not yet resulted in a dramatic decline in the *effectiveness* of achieving the required resettlement objectives—namely retaining or improving the quality of life for the resettlers, as measured by the success of establishing them in employment that ensures an equal or a better standard than before. Despite the dependency on a private job market and efficiency pressures on state agencies, resettlers in Shanghai have to date been unlikely to suffer unemployment caused by their forced relocation, although it may take an extended period of time before they are settled in new jobs. However, the evidence also suggests that ensured jobs for displacees may be becoming a thing of the past.

The need for resettlement in new accommodations some distance from the original homes (given land-cost constraints) may also frequently lead to a longer work commute and thus an inferior quality of life. This, however, may be partially compensated by vastly superior accommodations. There is some evidence that the resettlement process is less *efficient* in terms of the extended effort and time needed by resettlement officers to carry out sometimes prolonged negotiations around the issues of resettlement. We cannot be more specific about efficiency without further research.

The issue of *equity* is also problematic. Since the beginning of the transition there has always been an effort to make resettlement equitable. However, as with any process of development, some have benefited more than others. Certainly this will continue to be the case. An increasing number of development players and a greater devolution of responsibility from the center are likely to result in a greater variety among projects in terms of provisions for resettlers. The changes in the environment of projects causing resettlement, whether intentionally or unintentionally, result in a growing need for a systematic review of existing methods of resettlement and guiding policies. In particular, it is necessary to strengthen the negotiation skills of resettlement officers in an increasingly open market, with all that this entails.

There can be no doubt that the transition from a command to a market economy will continue to affect and change resettlement options and procedures. It has already changed the roles and responsibilities of the key actors involved. It is necessary to counteract some of the negative impacts of these changes to avoid the erosion of China's good practices in the field of resettlement. The Shanghai case studies described in this chapter show that if China is to continue to have equitable and effective resettlement procedures and to make the most of the transition to a socialist market economy for improving resettlement practice, it is necessary to further explore the issues raised in this chapter. By so doing it will be possible to clarify, in more detail, the impacts of the transition on resettlement policy and practices in China; explore the need for new policy provisions regarding compensation and the reconstruction of resettlers' livelihoods; and identify the new management capabilities required for resettlement negotiation within the private sector context.

There is enough information available to start asking new, pertinent questions, but we do not, as yet, have many of the answers. These questions require further exploration on the ground. Since this chapter was written, the authors[23] have undertaken further comparative research on resettlement policy and practice in China and in the Philippines. Although the political economy of the Philippines is markedly different from that of China, it was selected for this comparative study because, as proved to be the case, it was anticipated that the experience of resettlement in the Philippines — an established market economy which draws on civil society and private sector organizations — would cast some light on the changing situation in China.

The study's findings further support the initial impressions set out in this chapter by illustrating in more detail the significance of the political economic transition for resettlement. In both countries the study identified a number of areas where political and economic changes have had, and are continuing to have, an impact on the nature and performance of resettlement practice. A significant implication of these changes in both countries, although for somewhat different reasons, is that more time is now needed to achieve equitable packages of compensation and livelihoods for those being resettled.

---

[23]   In collaboration with Southwest Jiaotong University, Chengdu, China and Alabanza Associates in the Philippines, with funding from ESCOR, the research arm of the U.K. government's Department for International Development.

In China this need for time is a function of the need to cope with new economic mechanisms and patterns of ownership, which make established patterns of compensation inappropriate. In the Philippines it is a result of the move to a more democratic state that promotes the rights of resettlers — a positive move in itself, but one that has a side effect of costly delays. This means that resettlement negotiations are taking longer than they were previously. While currently this is a lesser problem in China than in the Philippines, there is every indication, as evidenced by the Filipino case, that with the growing withdrawal of state agencies from specific aspects of the process the situation is likely to deteriorate further.

The research further indicated that one of the principal results of changes in the political economy for resettlement in China is an increasing disjunction between policy and practice. There are two main areas of divergence between policy and practice in regard to resettlement administration. The first is in the area of compensation for the acquisition of collectively owned (village) land, and the second is in the compensation of private enterprises. Undervaluation of land occurs particularly in peri-urban areas where the economic value of land is much higher than its agricultural output value. According to legislation, the acquisition of collectively owned (village) land should be compensated according to the agricultural output value of the land, with a ceiling 20 times the average annual output. However, in practice, it is acknowledged that this figure frequently does not equal the economic value of the land, particularly in suburban areas with a high development value. Therefore peri-urban land is normally compensated at a higher rate than rural land located farther away from cities. For example, in the case study examined during the research the peri-urban villages were compensated for land at rates exceeding 20 times the annual agricultural output ceiling. This higher compensation was made possible by creating requirements for payment of fees for development activities, such as "road building," which legally do not require such payments. [24]

The second mismatch is in the compensation of private enterprises. Legal guidelines do not take account of the lost profits

---

[24]   Thus, for example, in the Kunming Environmental Monitoring and Evaluation Station the resettlement and land acquisition fees were bolstered by fees not listed in the State Land Administration Law, such as the "Wulong river reconstruction fee," "road building fee" and "fee for township development."

encountered by businesses during resettlement [25], but in practice these enterprises are normally dealt with on a case-by case basis, allowing more leeway to take account of lost profit during resettlement. The study has also highlighted six other main areas in which changes in the political economy of each country is having an impact on resettlement policy and practice. These include approaches to compensation, participation of resettlers and their community reorganizations, the role of the private sector, capacity for building livelihoods for resettlers, and the trade-off between resettlement equity and effective infrastructure development. The study further suggests that there are aspects of resettlement practice in each country that have relevance for the other.

These specifically relate to the role of local government, which is stronger and more effectively managed in China than in the Philippines. In China, resettlement compensation is available only for those with permanent registration, which, in the context of a sizable "floating" urban population, has serious implications for equitable compensation. In the Philippines, in contrast, legislation has been adopted to give legal rights to informal occupants or "squatters" affected by resettlement. Approaches to participation also differ. In the Philippines grassroots participation in the resettlement process is fostered through the involvement of nongovernmental organizations (NGOs) and other groups and is enshrined in the legislation for resettlement. In China, by contrast, while the legislation and implementation regulations call for consultation and participation, resettlement is engineered through the local government and party apparatus and therefore without the participation of an independent civil society.

Clearly the findings of this research support and further clarify the argument set out in this chapter. The findings also indicate that there is now a need to extend the body of knowledge about good practice for resettlement in a context of transition, and to explore the scope for providing a forum for different countries in the region to learn from each other's good practice.

---

[25]   Interview with Director of Demolition and Relocation Office, Sichuan Corporation for Real Estate Development.

CHAPTER 6

Economic recovery after involuntary resettlement: the case of brickmakers displaced by the Yacyretá Hydroelectric Project

María Clara Mejía

One of the most difficult challenges in the resettlement of populations involuntarily displaced by development projects is the reestablishment and improvement of prior economic activities and income levels. This chapter presents the main features of an economic rehabilitation program put in place to help protect the way of life and improve the living conditions of brickmakers affected by the construction of the Yacyretá Hydroelectric Project. An outstanding characteristic of this case is that the clay deposits, which are the primary source for brickmaking, will be flooded by the reservoir, which is associated with the operation of the hydropower station. The chapter underscores lessons learned during implementation of the program, and makes recommendations for similar cases in the future. However, it should be noted that because the relocation and economic rehabilitation program for the population displaced by Yacyretá project is still ongoing, the results presented in this paper are preliminary. Careful monitoring and evaluation of changes in the livelihoods of the population are necessary before making definite conclusions.

The original document on which this chapter is based reflected field work done in 1997. It therefore does not include the recent evolution of the cases presented here. As needed, in some cases the author has introduced an updating footnote to either inform the reader on recent results or qualify a comment or conclusion, in light of current events.

The project

The Yacyretá Hydroelectric Project includes construction of a dam and a 3,100-megawatt power-generating station on the Paraná River, the international boundary between Argentina and Paraguay. It has been under construction for almost 15 years and is expected to be completed by the year 2003, when the reservoir will reach its final elevation. The reservoir and civil works related to the project displace around 80,000 people living in three cities and various peri-urban and rural settlements.

In 1992, with help from the technical and social team of the Entidad Binacional Yacyretá (EBY), which owns the project, I formulated the Resettlement and Rehabilitation Action Plan (RRAP) in accordance with the World Bank's Operational Directive on involuntary resettlement (OD 4.30). The RRAP contained policy principles for the resettlement program and recommendations for alternative relocation and rehabilitation strategies for each of the affected groups, as well as specific action plans and institutional arrangements for implementation.[1] During the same year, the Bank approved the requested financial support for the project, and the RRAP became an integral part of the Bank's legal agreement with the Government of Argentina. Of the groups affected by the project, the poorest, most contentious, and most economically sensitive were the artisanal brickmakers, known locally as *oleros*, located on both sides of the Paraná River.[2]

---

[1]   The RRAP is available from the Entidad Binacional Yacyretá in Buenos Aires and Asunción, as well from the World Bank's Information Services Center for Latin America and the Caribbean (in Washington, D.C.).

[2]   While this chapter does not compare the relocation of Argentine and Paraguayan *oleros*, there are many differences between the two populations in terms of the history of the settlements, cultural and ethnic characteristics, the economic importance of their activities, and so on. For example, the majority of Argentine *oleros* affected had lived in the area for only 7 to 12 years, and the earliest had come to the region no more than 15 to 20 years ago, whereas the Paraguayan *oleros* established their settlements about 80 years ago and are considered part of the region's historical tradition. Some of the differences are pointed out by the RRAP and in many other documents available from the Entidad Binacional Yacyretá. However,. for the purpose of this chapter, I will highlight the commonalities and characteristic features of *oleros*.

Why are *oleros* particularly vulnerable?

At its final elevation, the Yacyretá project will displace about 849 families that use clay deposits along the banks of the Paraná River to make bricks for the local market.[3] The brickmakers are dramatically affected by the involuntary displacement because the reservoir will flood not only their homes and production sites but also the critical clay deposits.

Oleros were identified in the RRAP as a highly vulnerable group at risk of impoverishment as a consequence of the involuntary displacement.[4] This risk is mainly due (1) to the double impact of losing homes and jobs; (2) to the strong dependence of the *oleros* on communal natural resources (clay deposits, cheap or even free firewood, and abundant water) affected by the project, which are key to their survival; (3) to dependence on localized kinship relations and social networks, as well as proximity to markets, which are again key factors to lowered production costs; (4) to lack of legally recognized ownership rights to housing sites, production units, and clay deposits; and (5) to low education and organizational levels that make self-relocation more difficult and limit the *oleros'* ability to negotiate with the nations and governmental agencies in charge of the project.

In terms of origin, technology, land tenure, productive capacity, and other such features, *oleros* are a very heterogeneous group. But they do share some basic characteristics. They use a common production system that generates very low income from the manufacture and sale of bricks for local construction in the riverside cities of Posadas, Argentina, and Encarnación, Paraguay. They constitute a sort of "floating" and unstable population located on the outskirts

---

[3]   This figure includes the total *olero* population that will be affected when the reservoir reaches its final elevation of 84 meters. So far about 70 percent of this group has been directly or indirectly affected.

[4]   It should be noted that the term *olero* does not include the medium- and large-size industrial ceramists (*tejerías*) who, while also affected by the project, are not considered vulnerable to impoverishment because of their economic resources and political influence. The alternative offered to these affected industries consists of cash compensation for material and economic losses to permit their self-relocation. This includes the cost of relocating the *tejerías* and salvaging a 10-year supply of clay. This self-relocation strategy ensures continuity and avoids job losses (in Paraguay, 1,000 jobs depend on the affected industry).

of the cities, and frequently lack access to public infrastructure and services. Their settlements are best described as precarious, as they are situated in low-lying areas that are vulnerable to the same annual floods that deposit the raw material from which they derive a living. They depend on very simple machinery (if any) utilizing human and animal power for the extraction of clay and the fabrication, firing, and curing of bricks. Land tenure status includes legal owners, occupants, renters, and squatters. A few have licenses for exploitation of specific sites or buy the material from the maker, but the majority is made up of illegal occupants and squatters on private or public lands that have clay deposits.

As a marginalized group, continually threatened by the existence of too many producers, lack of property rights, and periodic floods of the Paraná River, the *oleros* distrust government and colleagues, to the extent that each one prefers seeking his own solutions to problems. An exception to this pattern is the settlement called Mboi Cae (Paraguay), where *oleros* appear to constitute a more stable community in close proximity to industrial ceramists who occupy higher ground. In this area, a particularly large, permanent clay deposit has been mined by both groups for many decades. In all other areas, however, mobility and rotation seem to be the norm because the river is constantly eroding its banks, shifting its course, and altering access to clay deposits. Brickmaking is also dominated by very poor rural migrants to the city, since the activity does not require capital, specialized skills, or property rights.

In sum, the *oleria* (the workshop for making bricks) is an often transitional and complementary activity that bridges rural migrant families and the urban economy and society. Because of the periodic floods affecting the clay deposits, *oleros* frequently supplement their family income with fishing, construction, and other tempo rary jobs. On average, they devote eight months a year, during the dry months, to brickmaking. In addition to brickmaking's seasonal and natural constraints, there is a fluctuating demand for construction materials, which makes the activity unprofitable for long periods when market prices are low.

Key characteristics of brickmaking

The history of ceramic activity on both sides of the Paraná river carried out by indigenous *Guarani* and other groups dates to pre-Columbian times. The Jesuit missions of the Spanish colonial period also promoted and supported the activity. However, there is no evidence linking current *oleros* and *olerias* affected by Yacyretá to the cultural legacy of indigenous groups. In my view, the recent flourishing of brickmaking activity is related to the modern processes of rural-urban migration and precarious settlements, stimulated, perhaps, by the demand generated in the region during the economic boom produced by the construction of the Yacyretá project itself. Whatever its origins, the activity has become a sort of transitional stage in urban settings for immigrants from rural areas and unemployed in general. The fact that clay deposits are frequently the only "free resource" available explains why landless people depend upon the artisanal brickmaking industry for their survival. However, in the long run, *oleros* would prefer having access to an economic activity that is more secure, better paid, less conflict-prone, safer, and less difficult.

The clay deposits along the banks of the Paraná River can be compared to cases of common pool resources studied by several scholars (Eggerston 1990; Libecap 1989; Ostrom 1990). Phenomena such as rent dissipation, free riding, difficulties in defining and defending boundaries, and so forth, are characteristic of the clay-mining process. One of the most notable characteristics is the relatively open access to clay deposits. They are located in lowlands along the Paraná River, whose periodic flooding prevents private owners from demarcating their properties and establishing permanent structures or production sites. Thus, the boundaries of the deposits vary with each year's flood, and it has become customary that anyone can exercise the right to exploit the deposits. In other words, although there is private property all along the river, the clay deposits are a sort of *tierra de nadie* (no man's land) that permits the survival of thousands of people who have no property, no capital, and no other skills to survive in the peri-urban environment. The use of family members in the production process is a common way to reduce costs and compete with semi-mechanized *olerias*.

From the environmental point of view, the activity constitutes a threat to both natural habitats and humans. The activity is usually carried out on flood-prone lands. Therefore, malaria, dengue, skin sicknesses, and other water-borne diseases are common. In addition, since the activity requires intensive consumption of firewood for "cooking the bricks" in artisan ovens, skin and respiratory diseases are also common among *oleros* and their families. The activity is harmful both to humans and the environment, and is not considered sustainable or ecologically desirable. To make things worse, the lives of *oleros* are plagued with such pathologies of severe urban poverty as alcoholism, domestic violence, and so forth.

The challenge of rehabilitation:
countering the risks of impoverishment

The challenge in designing a resettlement and economic rehabilitation plan for brickmakers was not so much to replicate an unsustainable production system and degrading living conditions as to assist the affected people in developing more environmentally sustainable, productive, healthy, and socially stable and healthy economic alternatives to the extent possible.

Defining a sound strategy for the economic recovery of the *olero* population was a difficult task. On the one hand, *olerias* were considered a local patrimony, and there was a legitimate need to preserve them as the only productive activity families were prepared for. On the other hand, there was a need to shift economic activities since *olerias* were not environmentally sustainable or economically sound in the long run. Clay deposits were going to disappear under water, and the job entailed a permanent risk of impoverishment for *oleros* and their families.

Several questions had to be weighed at the time the RRAP was prepared. First, is it feasible to promote continuation of an activity that has intrinsically unacceptable economic, social, and environmental consequences? Second, is it right to promote its replacement regardless of the *olero* population's expectations, capabilities, and desires? Third, is it possible to design a strategy that combines both continuity in the short to medium term and developmental change in the long term? And, finally, is it possible to pursue a long-term strategy in the context of a development project that does not guarantee ongoing social programs once the relocation process finishes and the hydroelectric project starts operation?

Strategy adopted in the RRAP

The strategy initially recommended by the RRAP was based on the following policy principles: guaranteeing the right of those affected to make the decisions that are relevant to their lives; guaranteeing continuity of the brickmaking industry while creating alternative economic opportunities for the future; locating houses as close as possible to production sites to avoid family disruption and increased labor costs; maintaining community relationships in both spatial and productive terms; recovery and improvement in all cases of prior family income level; and provision in all cases of social and technical assistance to ensure the affected population's reestablishment and improved living standards.

These principles for economic recovery clearly would not succeed unless framed in a wider social development strategy. Thus, the economic recovery program was conceived as a part of the mitigation/development action plan for the displaced population. To that extent, in addition to a housing replacement and economic program, the RRAP recommended three complementary programs on health, education, and community development. The main objective was to ensure an integral recovery of prior conditions and to promote significant improvement in the livelihoods of the *olero* population. Below is a brief description of the components of each of the aforementioned programs.

The health program included vaccinations and preventive campaigns, sanitary control, environmental education, epidemiological studies, and diagnosis and treatment of the most common diseases affecting *oleros*. The education program included adult reading and writing courses, provision of courses and teaching materials related to social and environmental problems, and short training courses on micro-enterprises, family business, and marketable labor skills. And, finally, the community development program was aimed at the promotion of such communal activities as sports and entertainment, improvement of communal assets, leadership development, and strengthening of existing grassroots organizations. A special module was developed to help children and elders in the postrelocation adaptation process. These three programs were designed to start one year prior to the relocation process and last for at least three years after.

Based on previous experiences, the RRAP did not recommend cash compensation to *oleros* unless they were legal owners, had no intention to continue making bricks, and preferred to establish a new economic activity. Recognizing that many of the affected families were recent impoverished migrants coming from failed agricultural enterprises, the RRAP suggested that a return to agriculture under better conditions might be an option offered. In all cases, the RRAP strongly recommended a participatory approach for the design/selection of the different alternatives, and a monitoring system to follow the process, assess the final outcomes, and extract lessons for similar cases in the future.

In sum, the strategy recommended for the economic recovery of *oleros* consisted of several alternatives: (a) providing opportunities to continue the activity, with technical assistance to improve their production system; (b) providing opportunities to return to rural areas, with assistance to restart farming on a viable basis, where they had relevant experience; (c) providing cash compensation for their self-relocation in the urban area and starting new businesses, with a compensation package large enough to permit the recovery and/or improvement of prior family income levels. Regardless of the option chosen, indemnification to cover material losses, including temporary losses due to the moving and reinstallation of the production unit in the new settlement, were offered.

Resettlement planning as an iterative process

Although the RRAP contains basic, broad principles, it had to be contextualized and adapted to specific cases and subgroups, whose circumstances and requirements varied. Thus, the RRAP was conceived not as a document but as a living process that entailed change and adjustment to keep pace with events on the ground. In practical terms, this means that the participatory strategy of the RRAP was utilized to fine-tune, plan, and negotiate its application and included affected groups, government agencies in both countries, and the World Bank. As a complement, a monitoring system and an independent evaluation program were put in place to follow up and assess the implementation of the RRAP and the main outcomes of the resettlement process.[5] The independent evaluation report, as well as periodic monitoring reports, have provided field evidence, documented success and failure, and demonstrated the pros and cons of the strategies adopted.

Table 1 presents a summary of each of the economic recovery programs offered to the affected brickmakers, illustrating the application of the general principles. The description is followed by my own observations based on the preliminary outcomes and lessons learned. A total of five alternatives were offered and freely selected by each *olero* and his family, according to their capacities, expectations, and preferences. The five cases briefly discussed here are as follows:

Case 1 – provision of private lots with no clay, with traditional riverbank material supplied to each unit by the project-implementing agency

Case 2 – provision of private lots issued by lottery, some with clay deposits (but of inferior quality compared to the original deposits) and others without clay, to be exploited by the individual producer, with technical assistance for adapting the production process

Case 3 – provision of communal deposits and machinery to be managed through legally incorporated cooperatives

---

5   See Scombatti and Carvalho 1994.

TABLE 1: RESETTLEMENT AND REHABILITATION OPTIONS FOR
BRICKMAKERS AT YACYRETÁ

Description of options	Number of families	Program details
Case 1—*Oleros* given private plots without clay, but supplied with riverbank material by the implementing agency (San Pedro, Paraguay).	72	• 0.5 hectare plot (no clay deposits) with water, electricity, and infrastructure services necessary to establish production sites (industrial park of San Pedro) • plot and house (45 square meters) near the production area, with all services • five-year supply of clay provided in periodic deliveries to each *oleria* • technical assistance to improve production and commercialization • food support during the transition • compensation for material losses, loss of income during transition, and cost of reinstalling production unit (US$2,500)
Case 2—*Oleros* given communal land with inferior-quality clay, but chose to divide it into private plots allocated by lottery, some with clay and some without, to be exploited by individual production units. Technical assistance provided for adapting the production process (Nemesio Parma, Argentina).	94	• 1.5 hectare plot with clay deposits (different kind of clay) for the relocation of the *oleria* to the industrial parks of Nemesio Parma and Campo Bahuer, with water, electricity, and infrastructure • plot (2,200 square meters) and house (45 square meters) near the production unit, with all services • food support for the transition period until reinstatement of *oleria* • compensation for the construction of a provisional wooden house (US$2,500) • compensation for material losses, loss of income during transition, and cost of reinstalling production unit • transportation service for firewood and clay from the river (until the reservoir is filled) • technical assistance for one to two years to improve production, commercialization, and marketing, to diversify final products, and to di-

TABLE 1 *(continued)*

Description of options	Number of families	Program details
		versify economic activities (family gardens, domestic animals, etc.) • restricted land title[a]
Case 3a—*Oleros* facing loss of both clay and production units (*olerias*) are given communal clay deposits and equipment to be managed through legal cooperative arrangements (San Cosme and Coronel Bogado, Paraguay).	5	• indemnification for material losses • cash compensation for reestablishment of individually owned production units • plot (2,123 square meters) with water and electricity services • provision of clay for five years (at each family's production capacity)
Case 3b—Same as 3a, except families only lost clay deposits and not *olerias*.	58	• social support for establishing the Brickmakers Associatio of Coronel Bogado • communal clay deposits (10 hectares) owned by the Brickmakers Association to be used on a quota basis by the cooperative members • two trucks and a tractor to haul clay to individually owned production units
Case 4—*Oleros* that chose cash compensation (Argentina and Paraguay).	491	• cash compensation based on production capacity (US$6,000–US$16,000) • plot (300 square meters) and house (45 square meters) with all services in urban areas (for those that lost their house) • technical assistance for productive investment of the indemnification • monitoring of a sample to detect economic recovery, continuity of the activity, establishment of new business, or risk of impoverishment
Case 5—*Oleros* that elected reestablishment as small farmers (Santa Tecla, Argentina).	10	• 7-hectare plot with water and electricity for establishing the farm • domestic animals (hens, cows, and mule), agricultural tools, seeds, and inputs

(continued on next page)

TABLE 1 (continued)

Description of options	Number of families	Program details
		• materials for building a wooden house (transitional) to be replaced later with a concrete block house with all services
		• US$800 for building a well and latrine
		• US$600 for building fences around the property, and food support for six months
		• technical assistance for two years until production is stable
		• social assistance to the family during the transition period (1–2 years)
		• land title

a. Titles are withheld for five years as a way to prevent sale of the property and to allow enough time for the reconstruction of the community. Families that opt for this receive a document that consigns their rights on that plot as affected by the Yacyretá Project. However, they are not allowed to sell it for at least five years. Under extreme circumstances, such as death of the household head, a different arrangement can be negotiated with the agency in charge of the project.

Case 4 – cash given in compensation for effect on production unit and clay deposits

Case 5 – reestablishment as small farmers.

Results of Case 1: provision of private lots with no clay, with traditional riverbank material supplied to each unit by the project-implementing agency

This was the strategy adopted by a group of *oleros* in the city of Encarnación, located on the Paraguayan side of the Paraná River. *Oleros* were given houses with services, as well as productive units (individual workshops) located near the new settlement in a place known as *Parque Industrial San Pedro*. To secure continuation of the activity, they negotiated the delivery of clay to their workshops in an amount sufficient to produce for five years, estimated to be the equivalent of the clay available at the prior site.

By 1997, 72 production units had been reestablished and were in full production. Brick production per family averaged about 15,000 per month, which exceeds the average prior to relocation. However, an unexpected problem arose: very low market prices for bricks, due to increased supply and changes in demand. In order to increase income levels, gain control of the market, and guarantee better prices for the bricks, EBY assisted in the creation of a brickmakers cooperative. For *oleros* in this group, land, homes, and job security were guaranteed, and social networks were preserved. Some prosperity was felt in the new site, now called the industrial park.

The strategies applied in Case 1, as well as in Case 2 following, were aimed at securing continuation of the brickmaking activity for at least five years while increasing productivity and savings capacity, whether through a move toward industrial production (if associative and local market conditions permit that) or to a more lucrative and sustainable income-generation activity.

Results of Case 2: provision of private lots (some with clay deposits of inferior quality compared to the original ones and others without clay) to be exploited by each individual producer, with technical assistance for adapting the production process

This is the case of *oleros* relocated in Nemesio Parma, located on the Argentinean side of the river. Here, local government officials dictated that communal production was the only technically viable solution. This assumption guided the purchase of land for the resettlement/rehabilitation of Argentinean *oleros*. The program proposed by local government was based on communal exploitation of a clay deposit (50 hectares) and organization of the affected people into a cooperative of producers as a way to ensure equitable access to clay and distribution of the excavated material to be deposited in each member's plot. In principle, the affected people were in agreement. The strategy required clear rules of the game, willingness to pay transaction costs, and a very complex monitoring process for which the producers were not prepared. The strategy also required social assistance to help *oleros* create the cooperative.

The government's proposal failed for three reasons. First, producers had prior negative experiences with cooperatives and were skeptical of giving control over their futures to "leaders" of these kinds of units. Second, the required agreements on ownership of the clay deposits, transference, and inheritance of rights were impossible to reach among all *oleros*. Third, they feared facing the necessary changes in the production process imposed by the different quality of the clay deposits. Overall, dependence upon provision of this service through the cooperative was not attractive to these very individualistic producers.

After a protracted negotiation process, the *oleros* decided that the communal land should be divided into individual plots to be given to each of the affected families. They took the chance of finding insufficient or inferior clay in some of the small plots, and agreed to the allocation of plots by lottery. In the author's view, they took this risk because (a) the real intention of many of them was to become legal owners of a piece of land, which in Argentina has very profound social and cultural implications in terms of legitimization and recognition as a citizen with consequent access to services; (b) in practice, some of them had other undeclared sources of income (especially the young) and most had been looking for an opportunity to shift to another job; and (c) some of them, especially women, considered a big plot near the city as a good opportunity to cultivate vegetables for the local market, have domestic animals, and so forth. For those that were lucky and found clay on their plots, continuing the brickmaking activity appeared to be a possibility for income generation. However, they encountered problems adapting to the different type of material that required more firewood, longer time for burning bricks in the oven, and other changes in the production system. Others were not so lucky and found insufficient or unsuitable clay. They had to find jobs in the so-called informal market or became workers in others' *olerias*.

At present, 70 of the 94 *olerias* displaced have been reinstalled. The remaining 24 families are now dedicated to other economic activities. Fifty-five brickmakers are using river clay deposits and are already selling their products at local markets. Preliminary assessments indicate that family income has not deteriorated. This is due in part to the fact that the brickmakers were given permission to exploit the riverbank deposits near the new settlement until the reservoir elevation reached 78 meters (1998). This provided two additional years to work with the original materials, and saves their own deposits for future use. However, it created an additional problem since the technical assistance for the necessary changes in the brickmaking process will only last for one more year, and it is possible some will miss the opportunity. Part of the assistance being given is dedicated to diversification of family income sources through activities such as gardening and raising domestic animals. Some experimental production has been done with the new clay, but the *oleros* do not seem very interested in that option because, in their view, they do not want to "eat the only family patrimony."

As of August 1996, 74 percent of the relocated *oleros* had recovered their previous production levels and enjoyed improved access to their production units, to services not previously available (drinking water, sewage, and electricity), and to technical assistance for enhancing income. Equally important, sanitary and environmental conditions have dramatically improved. The final outcomes are not clear yet because the process is still ongoing, and the *oleros* are still using the original clay deposits. But it is clear that they want to keep the property intact and reserve it for future uses. I believe that ownership of the land itself is more important to the *oleros* than is its utility for brickmaking, especially since the clay deposits on the new land are limited and nonrenewable.

Results of Case 3: provision of communal deposits and machinery to be managed through legally incorporated cooperatives

The economic recovery program initially recommended by the RRAP did foresee the possibility of finding new deposits outside the affected area, in spite of the fact that the *oleros'* representatives alleged that there were no other clay sources in the area. In fact, a group of *oleros* (60 families) in Coronel Bogado (a small city in nearby Encarnación) found new, rich sources of clay. Helped by EBY, they joined a legally established cooperative of brick producers. They requested EBT to buy the land and transfer the property to the association. This group reestablished its previous production level. As of 1996, the association was working well, and the quality of the final product and market prices were very satisfactory.[6]

---

[6]   As of January 1999, some interesting developments have taken place for this group of *oleros*. With the assistance of EBY, they created an association and were trained in the administration of communal enterprises. To guarantee their emancipation and self-management, *oleros* exchanged a pending compensation package for machinery and clay. After two years of additional technical assistance, they are ready to manage their own enterprise. At present, they are facing the challenges that are common to this kind of producers' association, such as the search for financial sustainability, the need to plan ahead on the basis of future market behavior, the need to assure diversification and better quality, lack of loyalty among members, and so forth. Far from being closed, the process of economic rehabilitation is still going on and is being monitored and independently assessed. The reader interested in more details should refer to documents and reports produced by EBY since 1996.

Results of Case 4: cash given in compensation for affectation of the productive unit and clay deposits

Despite the fact that the RRAP did not recommend cash compensation, it was expected that a small number of families, because of age, health problems, shortage of family labor, and so on, were not going to continue the activity. That might also be the case of those who thought they could do better on their own. This group would only settle for cash compensation. In practice, the number of families that elected for cash compensation was substantial. Under pressure of the deadline for filling the reservoir, the implementing agency gave in to the demands of "representatives" of the *olero*s to increase cash compensation cases. These representatives were middle-class political aspirants exploiting the fears of the affected people. The cases arose before the relocation took place, in an atmosphere of distrust and pessimism on the part of the *olero*s caused by delays in implementing the resettlement programs. Had the resettlement program been implemented on time, the representatives would have had more difficulty convincing the affected families not to cooperate. But beyond political manipulation, it is clear that the *olero*s were looking for the opportunity to shift into other economic activities, and saw the relocation as their chance to do so. In addition, it turned out that many *olero*s affected by the project were not real *olero*s. Political interference and failures in the definition of those entitled to be relocated or compensated distorted the process.

Preliminary results of the independent evaluation report have concluded that the money was invested in land, clay, machinery, and animals, or in merchandise to be sold at the local market. Based on a sample of 25 percent of those who received cash compensation in San Cosme, the independent evaluation report found that in 40 percent of the cases the money was invested in productive assets, and in 20 percent it was deposited in interest-bearing saving accounts. However, in 30 percent of the cases the money was used to pay previous debts.

But the results are not always positive. In another group, 30 percent of those who selected cash compensation spent the money on housing or transportation improvements, while another 30 percent dedicated the money to buying food and addressing immediate needs. Only a few of them invested in the restoration of their brickmaking production, and a small number deposited the money in a bank that failed. Today, some of those that lost money are working as paid labor in the *olerias* that were relocated, and others have returned to the banks of the river, the area already cleared, hoping for a second resettlement package. The monitoring system in place in each country will track the evolving economic situations of those who chose cash compensation and enable us to learn more.

Results of Case 5: reestablishment as small farmers

This is the case of a small group of *oleros* in Argentina. Once established in a peri-urban setting, going back to the farm is not a return to the bucolic romanticism imagined by urban planners. It implies hard and highly risky work. However, the alternative of returning to rural areas as agriculturalists was considered among the compensation/relocation alternatives for *oleros* who were legal landowners in their place of origin. Only 10 chose this alternative, and their dream of reintegration into the rural economy has yet to be realized. Four of them accepted the farm but did not take possession of the plot, and two others moved to rural plots but do not cultivate the land. Instead, they continued their traditional brickmaking activity by using clay found near the river and will probably continue doing so until the deposits are flooded or until they find other employment in the city. Others have found alternative jobs in the new locality, and some are renting out all or part of the property, taking advantage of the close proximity of the new settlement and the scenic view of the reservoir. The failure to assess the effective productive capacity of the families that chose rural relocation has been correctly pointed out by the independent evaluation report.

Vicissitudes of the implementation process

The negotiation and implementation process has lasted for about six years. Dialogue, de facto solutions, complaints, renegotiations, political interference, delays, mutual distrust, and economic changes (at the macroeconomic and microeconomic levels) have occurred at different times during the process. But in the end, reasonable agreements were reached among all involved parties. As a result of the negotiation process and the active participation of the affected people in the decisionmaking process, a wide range of strategies to reduce the risk of impoverishment and to recover and improve socioeconomic conditions were effectively put in place by the implementing agency. Planning and implementation interacted with one another in an iterative way, and the options finally agreed upon clearly went beyond what was expected when the RRAP was prepared, confirming once again the endless richness of social reality in comparison with general models and plans. Some of the additional difficulties encountered in the process, noted below, complete the general overview and will assist the reader in understanding the complexity of these cases.

New migrants continued to settle in the affected area throughout the planning process because of persistent delays in finishing the hydroelectric project, absence of legal regulations, lack of control of the riverine lower area, poverty and economic crisis in rural areas (especially in Paraguay), and corruption of local authorities and community leaders. This complicated the entire process and made census-taking problematic because any cutoff date for resettlement eligibility seemed arbitrary and entailed judicial resolution and enforcement that were impossible to guarantee.

Despite recommendations made by the resettlement, which requested an assessment of the economic, environmental, and social sustainability of brickmaking activities, the research was never done. Therefore, important information about the *oleros'* lives and expectations, characteristics of the production system, and so forth was missing (see Scombatti and Carvalho 1995). In other cases, studies were biased and no objective analysis was possible.

Last-minute solutions made under pressure to continue filling the reservoir resulted in temporary and unsatisfactory arrangements, and acted in favor of cash compensation instead of relocation of the productive units for a large portion of *oleros* affected on the Argentinean side. Because of the nature of the production activity as explained above and the number of families that were indirectly affected by loss of open access to clay deposits but not previously surveyed, it was difficult to count the real number of people affected and to administer an equitable solution for all parts. Political interference also caused permanent distortion of the entitlement system. Paternalism in provision of assistance as a way to reduce last-minute conflicts created inconsistencies in implementation of the resettlement policy. In addition, the inherent difficulty in defining the exact extent and limits of the implementing agency's responsibility to improve the *oleros'* living conditions contributed to the challenges and uneven results of the economic recovery program. To make things more difficult, local governments (especially in Paraguay) did not accept responsibility for continuing assistance to the already relocated population, once the implementing agency fulfilled the agreements reached with the *oleros.*

During the 12-year resettlement process, the implementing agency lost credibility in the eyes of the affected population because of mounting delays. Political opportunists at all levels (sometimes even involving local nongovernmental organizations) sought to exploit the fear and distrust of the *oleros*. The binational agreements favored different treatment of similar problems, creating inconsistencies in the rehabilitation process.

Lessons learned

Economic rehabilitation of an affected human group depends on open access to common pool resources for its survival imposed an additional level of difficulty on an already complex and challenging process. This is even more the case if the resource is totally affected by the project and not possible to replace, at least not with the same characteristics.

Establishing new rules, with greater constraints on individual flexibility and mobility, requires greater investments of time and resources to assist a traditional activity and culture (such as the *olero* culture) to adapt to a completely new social and economic context. Reproducing an economic activity that might not be sustainable entails structural risks of failure that have little to do with a good resettlement plan or policy and more to do with the inherent extractive nature of the activity.

Under the conditions of dependence on open access to nonrenewable resources, high mobility, and lack of sustainability, the economic rehabilitation process is not a matter of mitigation and reconstruction but rather of the creation of an entirely new development project, rarely faced as such by both project implementation agencies and social scientists working on resettlement and economic rehabilitation.

In the author's opinion, more worrisome than all the constraints described above is the perverse effect of continuous delays in the project schedule, which entail dramatic alteration of the conditions foreseen by the RRAP, speculation, and sudden changes in people's expectations. All of this creates a complex double situation for relocatees who are potentially affected and yet not affected by the loss of clay.

Recommendations

Based on the experience with planning and implementation of economic recovery programs for the brickmakers affected by the Yacyretá Hydroelectric Project, it is highly recommended that a wide variety of alternatives be designed. These alternatives would be based on the heterogeneity of the affected population, preferences, and specific characteristics of the mining and manufacturing activity. A consultation process to refine and contextualize the agreed general policies and principles must be put in place. And, given the uncertainties of such cases, it is useful to conduct small pilot operations to demonstrate the advantages and disadvantages of the various rehabilitation alternatives before selecting final strategies for economic recovery. Written records of the agreements reached with community representatives, local governments, and other partners are also highly recommended. Mediation by a trustworthy third party also prevents opportunistic interference.

Regarding the nature of the new economic activity, I would also recommend communal production. Arrangements in the absence of previous experience risk failure. Existence of a communal resource does not necessarily mean there is a communal system for its exploitation. However, it would strongly depend on the existing economic situation and family productive capacity of each of the affected groups. There is a need to develop a detailed database in order to assess the social and economic feasibility of each resettlement alternative. Whenever there is self-capacity for starting new enterprises, cash compensation accompanied by technical support might be an interesting alternative, but one that would demand a great deal of time and effort to reduce the risk of impoverishment.

It is evident that detailed technical studies on the nature of common pool resources — and the associated cultural and socioeconomic characteristics of the exploitation and appropriation systems that are likely to be affected or used — are needed. A risk analysis should be conducted on the economic and environmental viability of the productive activity before defining the strategy for its recovery. In particular, attention should be paid to the urbanization process promoted by the project itself, and the feasibility of rural agricultural solutions for peri-urban slum dwellers should be carefully assessed. Underpinning this is the need to fully understand the sustainability of the resource in both environmental and economic terms (productivity and future possibilities of the activity). And finally, it is of paramount importance in the implementation of rehabilitation activities that the monitoring and evaluation reports, based on a sound and systematic *ex-ante* database, are available in a timely manner to permit continuing adjustment to the general policy principles of the agreed resettlement plan.

Questions remaining

In the short term, it is clear that the great majority of affected *oleros* displaced by the Yacyretá Hydroelectric Project who chose a resettlement option (as opposed to cash compensation) have reestablished their production units and show no evidence of impoverishment. Moreover, there is good evidence of improved livelihoods and living conditions, including improved housing and environmental health conditions, secure property ownership, access to public services, receipt of technical assistance, and, in some cases, continued access to previous resources that augment short-term incomes.

The prospects for the long term, however, are less clear. In the case of those who depend on external agents to provide primary brickmaking material from the eventually-to-be-submerged riverbanks, it is uncertain whether they will be able — or will want — to secure clay from other sources once the reservoir is filled. Although recent discoveries of new clay deposits have brought some optimism, their location relatively far from the cities will require additional investments and costs in transportation, with a potentially negative effect on costs of production and final prices. Likewise, current trends toward lower prices for artisanal bricks and demand constraints add additional uncertainties to their future. In the case of those who have been given access to inferior clay deposits, the question remains whether they will be able to adapt their traditional technology to the requirements of the new material in a commercially viable way (for example, given increased costs of firing). For those who have committed to a cooperative arrangement, the question is whether the social institutions (such as control of free riders, managing transaction costs, and so forth) will be sustainable or effective. For those who selected cash compensation, it remains to be seen whether they will recover or improve their prior living standards, whether such recovery is sustainable, and whether some of them will be at risk of impoverishment. In the case of the *oleros* who returned to rural areas, it remains to be determined whether they actually can produce agricultural products for subsistence and commercial purposes.

It is my hypothesis that the economic strategies of the relocated *olero* families will ultimately be based on their land ownership rather than on the *oleria* activity. That is, they might abandon brickmaking and use the land to establish other businesses or divide the plots and rent out all or part of the property. Current pressures for obtaining definitive legal title are an indicator of their willingness to sell the property, or part of it, in order to raise a small amount of capital with which to start new activities. That trend is reinforced because the date for filling the reservoir has been postponed for at least two more years, thus opening the possibility of reinvasion of the cleared area and continuation of previous activities if new land is used to raise capital or for purposes other than brickmaking.

Finally, in view of the facts that the implementing agency has given assistance for more than six years and that the local government authorities are not willing to take responsibility for further assistance or investments in favor of the already relocated *olero* population, the major question that arises is whether the brickmaking activity will continue once Entidad Binacional Yacyretá withdraws.

PART FOUR

Homelessness and home reconstruction

Editors' Note Reconstructing a poor family's new house is often the first step on the way to post-displacement recovery. But it is always a difficult process — financially, technically, and emotionally.

Throughout the world, development resettlers tend to display a strong propensity to improve their houses. They do so through incremental investments in labor and cash. Abundant empirical evidence about resettlers' investment behavior indicates that many shift part of the compensation received for their land to supplement the house compensation and rebuild a more spacious and more durable dwelling whenever possible.

For refugees, the threat of absolute homelessness is more acute and likely to endure longer. They face the double need to first build some kind of dwelling at their place of refuge, and then, most often, to build again a home if and when they return to their areas of origin.

This section contains two chapters that illuminate the process of containing the risk of homelessness and highlight transferable experiences in house reconstruction. One, from India, explores recent approaches to relocation and reconstruction in urban resettlement, a particularly difficult process. The other addresses home reconstruction in the context of refugee return in rural Eritrea.

I.U.B. Reddy analyzes home reconstruction in urban India, where the challenges have to do with high population densities, high land values, the distance between place of resettlement and place of work, and the loss of employment opportunities. Especially daunting are the processes of resettling squatters inhabiting public lands to which they do not have legal title. Urban displacees are often forcibly relocated to distant sites where conditions deny them the opportunity for previous economic activities.

In recent years, however, state governments and municipal administrations have developed new approaches to urban resettlement that significantly improve rehabilitation operations, and reduce the resettlement risks faced by oustees. These include the incorporation of resettlement action plans in the first stage of project design, the allocation of secure funding, the provision of suitable housing, security of tenure for resettlers, alternative employment opportunities, and a greater environmental awareness. Supporting these efforts are the methods of needs assessment of affected people (before and after relocation), consultations over shelter design, the establishment of cooperative housing societies, and institutional capacity building for resettlement management at various levels.

In a refugee context, Christian Sørensen describes the centrality of home reconstruction within the multisided process of restoring the livelihoods of returned Eritreans who were formerly refugees in Sudan. Working alongside government agencies in the planned settlement site of Alebu close to the Sudan border, Sørensen observed the ways in which both informal and formal associations stimulated a cooperative effort among returnees to construct new homes. Government agencies developed a close working relationship with returnee associations, consulting with them about preferences for shelter construction in terms of the types of materials used and the layout and size of plots. Returnees, while given technical assistance in some engineering aspects, were largely responsible for the labor; where possible, materials were purchased locally.

Through such consultation and self-management, returnees constructed "homes" rather than houses, which were simple in design and suited to their needs, and were in a "village" layout conducive to maintaining the familiar patterns of social organization. At first returnees were reluctant to take on the responsibility for building their own homes, believing that houses would be provided as part of the return package; however, over time, the "mood" changed toward greater self-reliance characterized by an enthusiasm to organize for positive change. The impressive positive experiences of refugees in Alebu suggest once again that community organizations can be resilient and adaptive in situations of displacement and return resettlement, and are crucial for mobilizing refugees' own initiative-driven home reconstruction. Development resettlers from both urban and rural areas display, in turn, enormous resourcefulness in rebuilding their dwellings. House reconstruction practices emerge — as the two studies in this section amply show — as a domain of vast potential for reciprocal transfer of experiences and lessons learned.

CHAPTER 7

Restoring housing under urban infrastructure projects in India

I. U. B. Reddy

This chapter describes recent approaches developed in various urban infrastructure projects to address problems associated with involuntary resettlement. The main thrust of these new approaches is to improve the overall living standards of project-affected people in the post-resettlement period and to prevent their further impoverishment through planned development.

These evolving new approaches include among others advance planning, detailed social assessments, baseline socioeconomic surveys, preparation of resettlement and rehabilitation action plans, formulation during the early stages of project preparation of policy and legal frameworks for entitlements and benefits, options for entitlements, and integration of resettlement and rehabilitation cost into overall project costs. They also include institutional capacity-building, changes in compensation packages, participation and consultation of project-affected people in planning and implementation, grievance redress mechanisms, and issue of identity cards. Other measures see the inclusion of income-generation schemes and the creation of community development funds; cutoff dates for determining eligibility; recognition of squatters, tenants, and pavement dwellers for various benefits; special measures for speedy recovery of vulnerable groups; and increasing involvement of nongovernmental organizations in planning and implementation.

In this chapter, by focusing on the Bombay Resettlement and Rehabilitation (Second Bombay Urban Transport Project), Private Infrastructure Finance, States' Road Infrastructure Development,

167

Tamil Nadu Urban Development, and Bombay Water Supply and Sewerage projects, some of the new approaches will be explored.

Background

The problem of population displacement is a growing one in India mainly because of accelerated infrastructure development in large, medium-sized, and small towns. For those affected, involuntary re-settlement means a drastic disruption fraught with the risks of im-poverishment. The displacement of families and economic units, such as small business establishments, workshops, food stalls, and fruit and vegetable stalls, deprives people of employment opportu-nities, site-related mutual help networks, and access to basic ser-vices (Cernea 1993c:28). Therefore, appropriate policy measures and implementation plans are necessary to improve the living stan-dards of project-affected people in the post-resettlement period and thus to prevent them from being marginalized in the process of development.

There are few state-level policies and acts in India for resettle-ment of people affected by development projects. Generally, these policies have been created to address rural issues. Applying them to urban areas will require incorporating considerations of effects of high population densities, high land values, the distance between residence and workplace, and the presence of tenants, squatters, and illegal occupants.

In urban areas, the demographic, organizational, and occupational structure is different from that of rural areas. These project-affected persons are mostly employed in industry, services, petty business, and street vending, indicating that they depend on a variety of dif-ferent sources for their livelihood.

Slum dwellers and squatters without title are the most vulner-able. There is no comprehensive policy for resettlement and reha-bilitation of project-affected persons in urban areas, and the problem is more complex there, as large numbers of people do not have any legal title to occupied structures and properties. Existing policies conceived in terms of rural projects are in need of revision to ad-dress urban project issues.

In the above context, this chapter attempts to describe urban re-location approaches of the past and analyze the new approaches and practices that are being developed to tackle resettlement and rehabilitation problems in some of the urban infrastructure projects in India.

Evolution and development of urban relocation in India

Rapid urbanization during the 1960s and 1970s caused the relocation of low-income populations and slum dwellers in large cities.
Several slum-improvement and relocation programs were initiated.
These included clearance, improvement, upgrade, and redevelopment schemes, all aimed at improving living conditions by providing additional facilities or upgrading existing ones. Elsewhere, slum
dwellers were moved to new localities with the offer of alternative
plots and creation of minimum basic amenities. Two major slum
relocation schemes were initiated in Delhi and Bombay as long-term
strategies to improve the living conditions of slum dwellers.

In Bombay, the Bombay Municipal Corporation established 15
resettlement colonies during the 1970s and 1980s to rehouse about
20,000 families. This scheme aimed at providing alternative developed plots and creating minimum civic amenities in new colonies
established in the extended city suburbs. Under this scheme, all slum
dwellers residing on plots needed for urgent civic amenities were
relocated.

In Delhi between 1975 and 1977, the Delhi Development Authority (DDA) implemented a scheme to move encroachers from different parts of the city in order to release the occupied sites for various
designated uses. Alternate plots in resettlement colonies were provided with minimum infrastructure and rental tenure as part of the
process. During those years, the DDA developed 14 large settlements
with 139,520 21-square-meter plots each (Khan 1995:60–79). An
estimated population of 5.97 *lakh* was resettled. The aim in developing resettlement colonies was to provide improved conditions
for human habitation for those disadvantaged sections of the population previously clustered in squatter settlements without basic facilities and services.

Both schemes described above were initiated in order to relocate
squatters and make available the vacated plots for development of
civic amenities in the city. People were shifted to far-off places, which
had the effect of depriving the affected people of previously established mutual-help networks and employment opportunities. There
was no advance planning or consultation with the affected population in the selection of sites or design of basic amenities.

The impact study carried out in Delhi brought out the comparative living standards in the new colonies versus the previous location (Mishra and Gupota 1981). The study found that the overall
living conditions deteriorated in the new colonies: incomes dropped,

opportunities for employment—particularly for women—decreased, average travel time to work increased, and the overall living conditions were generally worse in the new colonies.

Avoiding displacement through urban renewal

A different approach, characterized by the avoidance of involuntary displacement of people living in old and dilapidated buildings, was followed in Bombay. Most of the occupied dwellings had completed their expected life span and their condition had deteriorated rapidly because of lack of repair and maintenance. Realizing the gravity of the situation, the government of Maharashtra set up the Bombay Housing and Area Development Board with responsibility for structural repairs to dilapidated and dangerous buildings and for reconstruction where required. The statute provided for the levy of a tax (*cess*) on the owner of the property relative to the rental value of the land, and the proceeds of the tax were paid into a fund into which the state government and municipal corporation also made annual contributions. This fund was supplemented by institutional loans to undertake structural repairs, to rebuild properties beyond repair after their acquisition, and to ensure the reaccommodation of the original allottees (Sundaram 1993).

Since 1969, the board has identified about 20,000 buildings that were in need either of repair or reconstruction. The scheme's progress was not very satisfactory. Only about 7,000 buildings were structurally repaired, while another 300 were demolished and only 150 reconstructed. Various reasons contributed to the slow progress, including lack of funds, development plan reservations, and delays in acquisition of lands and removal of tenants (Muttagi 1988).

Because of the prohibitive cost of repairs, a law was passed in 1986 enabling the board to acquire *cessed* buildings on the application of 70 percent of the occupants by paying 100 times the rent and handing it over to the tenant cooperative for the conservation of the building.

Slum redevelopment and rehabilitation schemes

In order to tackle the growing problem of slum and squatter settlements, as well as the requirement of lands for expansion of various infrastructure needs, the government of Maharashtra adopted a new method of resettling people with the incentive of granting additional floor space index (FSI). This new scheme, which was introduced in Bombay in 1991, was known as the Slum Redevelopment Scheme (SRD).

A further scheme called the Slum Rehabilitation Scheme (SRS) was launched to provide free housing to those slum dwellers whose names appeared in the 1995 electoral rolls. The scheme was financed primarily by private builders in return for additional FSI.

Slum dwellers were able to form cooperative societies, build tenements for themselves, and make use of remaining FSI to finance their effort. Builders were expected to provide transit accommodation to slum dwellers and construct flats for them on a portion of the plot vacated by them. The balance area of the plot was used by the builders to construct flats for sale on the open market. Under this scheme, the slum dwellers were offered 225 square feet of carpet area free of cost. Thus, about 80 percent of the slums were rebuilt *in situ*, and the remaining buildings were leveled to provide space for essential civic infrastructure. The Slum Rehabilitation Authority (SRA) was set up under the Maharasthra Slums (improvement, eradication, and rehabilitation) Act in 1971 to coordinate the implementation of the scheme, and it was anticipated that around 11 *lakh* dwelling units would be built.

Transfer of development rights

The concept of Transfer of Development Rights (TDR) was adopted in Bombay in 1991 as an additional method to acquire lands required for infrastructure development. The TDR involved a negotiated arrangement under which a private landowner transferred land required for a public purpose to the government in exchange for development rights elsewhere on a one-to-one basis. Under this approach, the owner was responsible for shifting the encroachers or occupants and delivering the unencumbered land to the government. So far, 74 TDRs have been granted.

The owners employed various methods to remove current occupants. These included moving them to nearby vacant spaces or offering them nominal monetary compensation to make their own arrangements for resettlement. In other instances, the owners themselves arranged alternative sites for relocation (Muttagi 1996). Under this scheme the responsibility for resettlement rested with the property owners, and operations were conducted on an unsatisfactory ad hoc basis.

New approaches to involuntary resettlement in current urban infrastructure projects

An examination of earlier urban improvement schemes reveals that resettlement efforts have been narrow and mostly restricted to moving people to a new location and providing only minimum civic amenities. This approach has invited protests from NGOs and also seen growing resistance from the affected communities. In order to meet the growing need for improved infrastructure, the implementing agencies are now giving increased attention to avoiding delays in implementing schemes. Resettlement and rehabilitation are increasingly treated as inseparable components of the earliest stages of project design and are being given priority in terms of advance planning, institutional support, and adequate budgetary resources.

Various innovative approaches and practices have recently been formulated in a number of urban infrastructure projects aimed at addressing resettlement and rehabilitation issues more systematically in order to improve the living standards of project-affected persons. The new approaches include:

Advance planning: to ensure that displacement issues are included in the earliest stages of project preparation and to explore alternative options to avoid or minimize resettlement. For instance, in Bombay, in the road-development sector, resettlement issues are examined much earlier than the technical components in order to tackle the resettlement and rehabilitation issues effectively.

Social assessment: to identify key stakeholders and establish an appropriate framework for their participation in preparation, development of action plans, implementation, and monitoring and evaluation.

Baseline socioeconomic surveys: to collect data on income sources and levels, resource ownership patterns, demographic characteristics, properties to be affected, and overall living standards to form a basis for measuring changes at regular intervals.

Preparation of resettlement and rehabilitation action plans: for identifying at the micro level the exact needs and possibilities for relocation and to deal with the problems in a realistic manner during implementation.

Policy and legal framework: to define rights and entitlements and to describe the procedures and resource allocation for implementation. This way, it is possible to ensure that the standards of living of project-affected persons are improved or at least restored.

Options for entitlements: to provide opportunities to project-affected persons to choose from more than one option according to their preference and suitability.

Changes in methods of compensation evaluation: shift in assessment of lost assets from measures based on market value to measures based on replacement value to enable project-affected persons to replace their lost assets.

Institutional capacity-building: to strengthen the capacity to plan, manage, and monitor resettlement and rehabilitation operations.

Participation and consultation: to understand the needs, resources, and preferences of project-affected persons and prevent costly mistakes. Participation and consultations are important means of ensuring acceptable resettlement and rehabilitation packages.

Recognition of squatters, tenants, and pavement dwellers for resettlement and rehabilitation benefits.

Grievance redress mechanisms: to seek redress of grievances through established procedures.

Issue of identity cards: for recognition and prevention of ineligible persons' claiming the benefits.

Special measures for speedy recovery of vulnerable groups, who have limited resources and skills to cope with new and threatening environments.

Integration of resettlement and rehabilitation costs into overall project cost: In the past, the costs of resettlement and rehabilitation were not included in the overall project budget. As a result, the funds available for resettlement and rehabilitation were too small for proper implementation. However, in a number of recent projects, resettlement and rehabilitation costs have been internalized. As a result, the funds available have increased substantially for timely implementation of resettlement and rehabilitation components.

Increasing involvement of NGOs: NGOs assume many different roles in the resettlement and rehabilitation process responding to the needs of project-affected people. Their involvement is important because they can articulate the resettlers' needs and defend their entitlements. Their involvement also facilitates communication and mobilization of group resources.

Monitoring and evaluation: for follow-up actions and midstream alterations. This will also serve as a warning system and channel for understanding project-affected persons' needs and reactions to resettlement execution.

If incorporated by planners, financiers, and practitioners, the measures listed above would have the potential to significantly improve resettlement and rehabilitation operations, thereby reducing the risks of resettlement faced by development oustees.

In urban resettlement, the provision of suitable housing, security of tenure, and alternative employment opportunities are important criteria for judging success. In the case of housing, much depends on the distance between the new location and the place of employment and its affordability. In the case of economic rehabilitation, the opportunities for site-related employment, provision of credit and loans to start new occupations, and the relocation of small businesses and commercial establishments require further attention. The various measures planned in some urban and infrastructure projects are described in the following sections.

Bombay resettlement and rehabilitation project

The main objective of this project is to assist in poverty reduction by establishing and implementing a comprehensive program of action for dealing with resettlement and rehabilitation of people to be affected by various infrastructure developments in the metropolitan city of Bombay. Currently, the second Bombay Urban Transport Project is under preparation. This involves the construction of a series of fly-overs; pedestrian subways; road improvements, extensions and upgrades; the elimination of some level crossings, quadrupling of railroad tracks, and construction of link and new roads.

The success of this ambitious program will depend on the adequate and planned resettlement and rehabilitation of people living in the corridor of the impact area. The proposed investment under this project will involve the displacement of about 20,000 families who are mostly illegal squatters and pavement dwellers. The proposed Bombay Resettlement and Rehabilitation Project will establish a framework for resettlement and rehabilitation management through policy changes, institutional capacity-building, and assistance to project-affected persons to improve their living standards.

A high-level steering committee was appointed by the government of Maharashtra in 1995. It prepared a resettlement and rehabilitation policy framework with community participation as its main focus. The committee had members consisting of senior government officials, planners, architects, lawyers, and representatives of voluntary organizations. The policy evolved after a series of discussions and deliberations consisting of cross-sections of individuals with knowledge and experience in resettlement and rehabilitation operations. The committee identified various categories of people who would be affected by the engineering activities and proposed suitable entitlements for resettlement and rehabilitation. The policy is now under consideration for approval by the government of Maharashtra. It provides scope for community participation and consultations at various stages of project preparation and implementation.

Various categories of potential project-affected people were identified by the task force on the basis of ownership, land use, and type. These included the structure owners, absentee owners, tenants and subtenants, pavement dwellers, squatters, lessees, and employees working in affected commercial establishments. Though the squatters and pavement dwellers were entitled to assistance under the legal provisions, the policy proposed an alternative option for resettlement and proposed a wide range of activities for economic rehabilitation for those affected economically.

The resettlement proposals included provision of equivalent floor space — subject to a maximum of 70 square meters — irrespective of use of floor space to those who are resident owners, lessees, and lessee tenants, in addition to compensation payable to lost structures. The project-affected persons are obliged to pay 15,000 rupees for the first 16.75 square meters of floor space and the actual cost of construction for floor space in excess thereof. However, the resident lessees, tenants of subtenants, will be provided the ownership rights free of cost. Squatters and tenants were offered the option of either a fully built house of 16.75 square meters or a developed plot of at least 25 square meters, depending on the area currently occupied by them. In the case of shops and business establishments the construction costs in excess of 16.75 square meters were to be charged to the resettlers. There was also provision to pay a monetary supplement equivalent to the cost of the lost structure to the squatters and pavement dwellers. Such a monetary supplement is calculated in terms of a typology of structures that will be developed on the basis of baseline survey data. The cost is updated every year and used for calculating and paying the monetary supplement before the community moves to the new location.

Those who opted for a developed plot (instead of a 16.75-square-meter built house) were provided a developed plot with a minimum size of 25 square meters based on a "site and services scheme." In the sites some plots are reserved for high-income housing or commercial activities to be sold at market prices to recover project costs. The project-affected persons are expected to build their houses with the monetary supplement and are allotted plots at least one year before actual shifting. The new sites will have developed civic amenities including water supply, drainage, and electricity.

The economic losses likely to be incurred by the project-affected persons were identified as (a) increased travel time and cost to the place of work as a result of change of residence, (b) loss of site-related employment opportunities and absence of similar opportunities at the new site, (c) loss of employment by those working in business and commercial establishments that are to be moved, and (d) problems faced by retail traders and those involved in personal service caused by increased distance from places of wholesale trade and by loss of existing clientele. The various measures proposed included (a) when economic loss is due to increased travel, a lump sum amount or a suburban train pass for a period of three years will be offered for adjustment process and (b) in the case of those who lose their occupations, training opportunities will be provided to improve their skills through various ongoing government programs and the provision of community-based credit to support new economic activities. As a part of the economic rehabilitation process a Social Development Fund was proposed to undertake income-generating activities, vocational training, counseling, community banking, and the creation and management of community assets. The fund would be used for providing small loans to community members for a variety of purposes.

The innovative feature in providing alternative housing was the use of a participatory shelter design approach to plan, develop, and construct low-cost housing units. In this approach, the project-affected persons are involved in finalizing the shelter design to take into account their needs and preferences. The various factors to be taken into consideration while designing are suitable site selection, optimum carpet area to built-up area ratio, design that is amenable to multiple uses, cost-effective structural design, adequate light and ventilation, privacy, cost-reduction measures, adaptability, and provision of built-in furniture.

Community Environmental Management Plans (CEMPs) were also prepared to ensure proper siting of housing and compliance with building codes, such as those for water supply, sewerage, light and ventilation, and maintaining the service standards for garbage and sewage disposal. Furthermore, through the cooperative housing societies, residents were encouraged to adopt sound practices to improve environmental conditions in their neighborhood. These included composting, drain cleaning, recycling, planting and raising trees, and properly maintaining the common areas.

Baseline socioeconomic surveys have been carried out by NGOs working in the slum settlements to generate data for the 20,000 households involving 10 subprojects. The key information collected in the survey has been made available to the communities for verification to create trust and confidence. The preparation of Resettlement Action Plans (RAPs) with the involvement of NGOs and project-affected persons has been completed. In addition, those affected are being organized into cooperative housing societies to ensure proper maintenance of the new houses and related services.

Another noteworthy feature of the project is the development of institutional capacity for resettlement and rehabilitation management at various levels. Currently a major study on Institutional Arrangements for Resettlement and Rehabilitation Management in Bombay was undertaken to develop appropriate institutional arrangements to plan, develop, and manage resettlement and rehabilitation arising out of all infrastructure projects in the city. This capacity-building included (a) establishing an institutional framework for planning and managing resettlement and rehabilitation in the context of infrastructure development programs, (b) identifying the needs of various implementing agencies in terms of staffing, training, and logistical support, and (c) identifying the changes required in the administrative procedures for speedy implementation of resettlement and rehabilitation programs, and (d) assessing the capacity of NGOs for undertaking resettlement and rehabilitation activities within their potential roles.

Private infrastructure finance project

This project will assist Infrastructure Leasing and Financial Services (ILFS) in financing projects such as major bridges, urban bypasses, port facilities, water supply and effluent treatment plants, and integrated development of small- and medium-sized cities. These projects will be implemented on a "build-operate-and-transfer" (BOT) basis. In order to tackle the issues of resettlement and rehabilitation, ILFS has prepared an Environment and Social Report (ESR) (ILFS 1995) that outlines the environmental and social impacts of each project. The report covers all possible concerns, regulations, and obligations that need to be addressed in the areas of environment and resettlement and rehabilitation. The aim is to avoid needless controversy, protests, and delays that have surrounded many projects in the past. It also makes the categorical statement that ILFS will comply with the environmental and social regulations and legal requirements in spirit, not just in letter, with due credence to global, domestic, and local concerns.

In cases of involuntary displacement of people, the ESR is committed to ensuring proper evaluation of land values and restoration of standards of living of displaced persons. The entitlements proposed in ESR also cover the details of benefits to be provided to the squatters, pavement dwellers, and tenants who are normally not eligible for compensation under local laws. The packages include replacement cost of lost assets, provision of developed plots, transitional allowances until residences have been reestablished, employment in reconstructed enterprises or packages for reemployment or starting businesses, and a maintenance allowance equivalent to one year's income for losses during the transition period. Serious implementation will go a long way in improving the living standards of project-affected persons and thus counter the impoverishment effects.

The greater emphasis on social and environmental issues by a private enterprise shows that there is a shift toward paying more attention to issues of environment and resettlement in infrastructure projects, issues that in the past were not given due recognition and importance.

State road infrastructure development projects

Road construction has been identified as a major development prerequisite to ensure future growth in India. Several states, such as Andhra Pradesh, Haryana, Rajasthan, Gujarat, Tamil Nadu, Orissa, and West Bengal, are in the process of designing road improvement and upgrade projects with World Bank assistance. These projects involve strengthening, widening and geometric improvements, and the construction of bypasses and bridges. All these activities will necessitate displacement of people, as the roads pass through small and medium-sized towns. Businesses of all sorts that have roadside locations, squatters, kiosks, and other informal activities are also likely to be affected.

In order to deal effectively with the resettlement and rehabilitation of project-affected persons, the state governments have undertaken impact-identification and assessment exercises to measure the magnitude of adverse impacts and the number of people to be affected, with the aim of proposing suitable resettlement and rehabilitation steps. As part of social-impact assessment, strip maps are being prepared for all roads to be included in the project to establish the legal rights of way and document the existing structures, land plots, and other physical assets on the rights of way. Based on the width required for each project, the project-impact area will be defined, and then all properties to be affected in the impact area will be identified and these will be categorized by type of land, activity, persons, temporary or permanent, legal or illegal. Subsequently, a baseline socioeconomic survey will be undertaken to establish current living standards in terms of ownership of resources, income sources and levels, properties to be acquired, and other socioeconomic characteristics. Considering the socioeconomic data, a resettlement and rehabilitation plan will be prepared for implementation of resettlement and rehabilitation measures. During this process vulnerable sectors of the population — the aged, those living below poverty line, tribal populations, and female-headed households — will be given priority.

One of the distinguishing features of road projects affecting small and medium towns is the presence of large numbers of squatters and informal business establishments along the roadsides — those who are not normally eligible for legal compensation. Therefore, appropriate measures are being proposed in the policy to provide assistance to the affected persons so that they are not substantially disadvantaged. The benefits include provision of house plots, opportunities to get the benefits under government-sponsored income and employment programs on a priority basis, and allowing the business establishments to shift beyond the impact area.

While devising ways of dealing with encroachers on the right of way, there was opposition in Haryana State as a result of a ruling by the High Court of Haryana and Punjab to the effect that encroachers on the right of way of national highways should be shifted and not paid any compensation for lost assets. However, efforts are under way to resolve the issue of encroachers from the point of view that they will not paid any legal compensation for land they are occupying. Instead, they will be assisted in securing house plots and extended benefits of economic rehabilitation under various government-sponsored income- and employment-generation schemes.

Allocation of alternative house sites under government programs and extension of vocational training and grants for starting self-employment vocations are among the measures being proposed by the Andhra Pradesh government (Government of Andhra Preadesh 1996). These provisions have also been extended to the squatters and tenants of small businesses to be affected. Another feature is the development of suitable institutional arrangements to carry out the resettlement and rehabilitation activities and to follow up procedures for effective monitoring and handling of grievances of project-affected persons.

This approach of advance planning, systematic identification of encroachers on the right of way, formulation of the entitlement framework, and involvement of people in devising the action plans was not adopted in earlier road projects. Therefore, these ways of dealing with resettlement are innovative in road projects.

Tamil Nadu Urban Development Project

The World Bank–financed Storm Water Drainage subproject in Madurai is one component of the Tamil Nadu Urban Development Project. The objective of the project is to clear 14 storm-water drainage channels that were silted and clogged with both sewage and solid waste. The operation involved eviction of a large number of families, about 2,000 of which were illegal encroachers. The majority of the families to be displaced are from the poorer sections of society, consisting of daily wage earners, rickshaw pullers, rag pickers, and so on. The resettlement packages offered to those displaced are aimed at preventing them from becoming impoverished during the post-resettlement period.

The package includes provision of two options for alternative housing for those who are owner-occupants of the houses. Under the first option, those willing to move to ready-to-occupy apartments of smaller size would be offered them at the highly subsidized cost of 27,000 rupees against the estimated cost of 52,000 rupees. The cost of the house is to be repaid in installments spread over a period of 15 years. Alternatively, the affected persons have the option of choosing a larger developed plot of between 32 and 40 square meters at a nominal cost of 1,600–2,800 rupees. The estimated cost of the plot is around 35,000 rupees. Those who opt for the latter will be assisted in securing a house-building loan from the Tamilnadu Housing Board for house construction at 8 percent interest, repayable over a period of 20 years. The replacement cost of the house structure will be deducted from the price to be charged. Those who choose this option will also be provided temporary accommodation for a period of eight months (Government of Tamilnadu 1995).

The important lesson to be learned from the project was the imaginative planning of ways to minimize the numbers of people displaced. By following the strict technical norms of channel width and carrying out the enumeration studies, the number of families to be displaced was brought down considerably to 116.

A baseline socioeconomic survey was carried out and a Resettlement Action Plan (RAP) was prepared and is currently being implemented. In terms of economic rehabilitation, the measures adopted included employment for affected persons in construction activities in the resettlement colonies themselves, as well as the provision of skill-enhancing training and the eventual extension of benefits under various government income- and employment-generation schemes.

Third Bombay Water Supply and Sewerage Project

The Third Bombay Water Supply and Sewerage Project comprised major expansion of water supply distribution and sewerage systems to expand water supply and sanitation facilities to the people of Mumbai. One of the sites proposed for construction of a reservoir had been occupied by a small number of tenants in Municipal Corporation houses for several years. In order to prevent these people from becoming homeless, the corporation offered them a resettlement package consisting of a free plot and temporary accommodation for a period of two years in the corporation's quarters. Both the temporary accommodation and the site for the construction of a house were in close proximity to their former residences. Another feature of resettlement was that about 100 encroachers who were supposed to be temporarily displaced for about six months were provided all assistance necessary to shift to a place nearby for the duration. Once the construction was completed, the project authorities assisted these people in returning to their previous sites. All necessary assistance during transition was provided. This approach marked a shift toward addressing all project-affected people irrespective of their legal status.

DfID-Financed Slum Improvement Projects

The British government's Overseas Development Administration (now Department for International Development), through the government of India, funded slum-improvement projects in five cities—Calcutta, Hyderabad, Vijayawada, Vishakapatnam, and Indore. The main objective of the project was to integrate the slum communities into the physical fabric and social and economic networks of the city and thus ensure that slum improvement did not cause involuntary displacement. Under the program, slum families staying in dangerous areas—those at risk of flooding, for example—or in areas where future improvements to infrastructure or road-widening projects were being proposed—were relocated to safer places. The relocation program in Vijayawada, for instance, included the development of relocation sites and in-situ development (see Slingsby 1995:39–42). In cases where relocation sites were being developed, development was by demarcation of plots and included the provision of roads and footpaths, storm-water drainage, street lighting, sanitation facilities, water supply, a multipurpose community hall, and health services. Wherever the slums were being improved in-situ, the basic services were upgraded and some additional facilities were also developed. In order to ensure that the resettlers had access to the full range of project components, a wide rage of activities were carried out. These included education, health, marketing facilities, employment opportunities, basic services, housing, and space for animals and cultural buildings.

Conclusions

Evidence presented in this chapter indicates that increasing attention is being paid to various resettlement and rehabilitation issues in the early stages of project design and preparation. Most of the described methods were not followed in the past and are new and innovative ways of dealing with resettlement and rehabilitation issues. The close involvement of World Bank staff and imposition of stringent requirements have led to improved methods of addressing the concerns of project-affected persons. The World Bank has also paid increasing attention to strengthening the capacity of borrowers in order to alleviate poverty and thus promote sustainable development. Because of this change in direction, resettlement and rehabilitation now occupy a more central position, and there is a shift from ad hoc efforts and welfarism to a more systematic, planned, integrated, and participatory approach.

Stronger World Bank requirements have also encouraged implementing agencies to experiment with new ways of ensuring that the living standards of project-affected people are improved in the post-resettlement period. I would further argue that in order to consolidate these gains it is essential to enhance supervision and monitoring mechanisms, improve professional competence through training programs, and provide sufficient resources.

Acknowledgment

The author is grateful to Dr. David Marsden for his valuable comments on an earlier version of the chapter.

CHAPTER 8

Alebu: Eritrean refugees return and restore their livelihoods

Christian Sørensen

This chapter examines the case of Eritreans who have made their home in the planned settlement of Alebu near Tesseney close to Eritrea's western border with Sudan. These particular returnees have experienced two major relocations: the first when they fled Eritrea for Sudan during a struggle for liberation, and the second upon returning home to an independent Eritrean state. Relocations were accompanied by the loss of means of livelihood—including loss of land, jobs, homes, and also often livestock.

Both displacements marked the beginning of long and difficult periods of restoration. While it took several years for Eritrean refugees in Sudan to build what was perceived to be a "satisfactory livelihood in exile," research in Alebu shows a remarkably rapid restoration of returnee livelihoods.

This chapter describes how, soon after arriving back in Eritrea, the Alebu returnees reactivated their social networks, including a range of informal associations, enabling them to pursue a number of strategies that, combined, accelerated the restoration process. It is argued that the strength and nature of this cooperative effort was probably underestimated by planners and should be given much more attention in future rehabilitation efforts.

In Alebu, timely and appropriate assistance and resource inputs based on a listening approach by a good nongovernmental organization, the Agency for Cooperation and Research in Development (ACORD), as well as by the government site staff from the Commission for Eritrean Refugee Affairs (CERA), helped to facilitate the process of livelihood rebuilding. This author argues that the experience from Alebu shows that the social fabric of the Eritrean returnee communities was largely retained during the many years of exile, both for those living in camp situations and for refugees living in towns. Instead of being undermined by monetization and urbanization, which is the prevailing view, the social cohesion and spirit of cooperation within the refugee communities survived, and was perhaps even strengthened under the conditions of exile in Sudan.

Several factors may have contributed to community rearticulation in exile, and this chapter explores some of those factors. In general, it can be argued that "success" in this return and resettlement experience can be attributed to several factors: the proximity of the Eritrean refugees in Sudan to Eritrea and the direct ties they maintained with their country of origin; their social and psychological makeup; their strong nationalism, and their deeply rooted and long experience with survival strategies, pursued under different economic conditions in both Sudan and Eritrea.

The process of restoring the livelihoods of Eritrean returnees may be viewed as an application of a sophisticated strategy for short-term survival and longer-term adaptation under different conditions based on a peasant and/or pastoralist economy with a strong social basis of cooperation, mutual help, and self-help.

While the initial displacement, and the conditions for Eritrean refugees living in Sudan, has been relatively well researched and documented, much less is known about the return phase, the repatriation and rehabilitation process, which started soon after the fall of the Eritrean port town of Massawa to the Eritrean People's Liberation Front (EPLF) in 1990. This chapter is based on research and general observations at the Alebu resettlement site.

By 1996 Alebu had been transformed, with remarkable speed, from a relatively barren part of Eritrea, known mainly for its weekly livestock market, to a thriving town with around 6,000 inhabitants, numerous shops, hotels, grinding mills, a school, a clinic, and hundreds of *neem* trees shooting up between the houses. Alebu is, among other planned resettlement sites in Eritrea, exceptional in the way in which resources have been made available and plans have been drawn up and implemented in close cooperation with the returnees. The results of planning and interventions seem to have matched returnees' expectations.

Some notions and predictions

The planning and execution of a resettlement program for returnees, on the part of both the Eritrean government and the international agencies involved in the repatriation and rehabilitation process, challenged two dominant notions: that of inevitable social disarticulation and that of dependency among long-time camp refugees.

In an introductory document for the Second International Conference on Displacement and Resettlement held in Oxford in 1996, McDowell wrote: "Forced displacement tears apart the social fabric and the existing patterns of social organization.... Life-sustaining informal social networks of mutual self-help among the people, local voluntary associations, self-organized service arrangements, etc., are dispersed and rendered inactive" (McDowell 1996 quoting Cernea 1996). In the literature on Eritrean refugees in Sudan, there are echoes of Cernea and McDowell's analysis and of ways that the social cohesion of Eritrean collectivities was dismantled by urbanization and an increasingly market-oriented and individualized life in exile. It can be argued, primarily, that throughout their long stay away from Eritrea (many Eritrean refugees have been in Sudan for some 20 to 30 years since the first wave of refugees started in 1967) they have been fully integrated into a market economy either by cash crop agricultural production, wage labor, or other "urban"-related trades.

The aim of this chapter is to retest the finding from other processes studied elsewhere, which showed that periods of exile and exposure to different political economies lead, with a certain inevitability, to the rupturing of social organization or the social disarticulation of displaced communities. The chapter focuses on shelter reconstruction in Alebu during 1995 and 1996, which in the minds of the refugees and returnees was a crucial element of the concept "home" and which is one of the eight major elements identified by Cernea in the model of risks and livelihood reconstruction (see this volume).

ACORD's shelter approach in Alebu

When ACORD[1] started working in Alebu in early 1995, the returnees were immediately consulted about their preferences for shelter. This happened informally as well as in convened meetings. Three

---

[1]   ACORD is an NGO consortium working in 17 African countries. In Eritrea, ACORD has four programs, one of which is the Eritrean Rehabilitation Program (ERT-3). As part of this program, ACORD works (together with CERA) in one of the largest returnee settlements, Alebu near Tesseney on the Sudanese border, with almost 6,000 inhabitants. An integrated approach has been adopted that includes shelter, sanitation, tree planting, income generation, and institutional development.

different model houses were built. The preferred design was a simple 4-meter-by-4-meter house built with stabilized soil blocks and covered with cement-fiber tiles.

The returnees produced their own soil blocks, while a production unit on site provided tiles. Stone, sand, soil, lime, and water were available locally. The only raw materials that needed to be brought from Asmara were imported timber for roofs, door and window frames, cement, nails, and fittings.

Alebu is a planned settlement constructed under the Pilot Phase of the PROFERI—the Eritrean government's comprehensive rehabilitation program[2]—and situated near the Tesseney-Barentu highway 25 kilometers from Tesseney. The houses in Alebu were constructed on 15-meter-by-25-meter plots. The layout of the household compound was decided upon and organized by each family. A skilled mason oversaw the overall construction of the house including the laying of the roof, with the family taking responsibility for digging foundations, plastering, and assisting in general labor activities. By June 1996 more than 600 houses had been built on the basis of self-help, assistance, and community participation in Alebu.

But a house is not only a physical structure, and shelter is not merely a technical issue. Much planning went wrong or proved futile in Eritrea, while a heated debate took place, making "shelter" a contentious issue. By the end of my fieldwork this debate had not been concluded.[3]

---

[2]   PROFERI (Program for Refugee Reintegration and Rehabilitation of Resettlement Areas in Eritrea) is the Eritrean government's rehabilitation program for refugees. It has 11 elements: repatriation and initial relief, food aid, agriculture, environment, fisheries, education, roads, health, water, shelter- and capacity building. The program focuses on settling returnees in planned settlement villages, especially in the lowlands of Eritrea, which had been devastated by war and where many of the refugees originally came from. It is thus more than a repatriation program: it has the aim—through establishing such settlements—of contributing to the rehabilitation of the worst-affected areas.

[3]   Before the PROFERI was launched in June 1993, *shelter* was a contentious issue and has remained a subject of heated debate among all the actors involved—including, not the least, CERA. In the initial PROFERI document five specific objectives in relation to the shelter component were stated: to ensure that returnees settle in well-planned villages; to develop technical and administrative capacity to produce building materials; to

(Note continues on next page.)

Some technicians, architects, and planners suggested placing doors and windows according to the sun and prevailing wind directions. Other suggestions referred to joining houses—to save walls—by creating two-room houses facing opposite courtyards (a solution actually implemented in some settlements for spontaneous returnees, such as Ghatelay in the Red Sea Zone). There was even at one stage the possibility raised of constructing four-room houses in the middle of four adjacent compounds; this model was implemented in Areda-Gash-Barka, but received a very cool response by the returnees there. Such an arrangement is generally unacceptable in Eritrea, and referred to as *campo*, indicating the camp-like nature of compounds with shared houses in rows.

But in Alebu the returnees rejected such suggestions from the outset. They preferred a simple, uniform house design, within which they could determine the layout of their compound without interference and could place the house in the compound in a way best suited to their needs.

The final layout of the houses, in most cases, placed them at the back of the compound with the doors facing inward into the courtyard. The neighbor (to the back) would place his or her house in a similar way, so that both households had the benefit of the back wall of the neighbor's house. "This is good for making a kitchen" was the argument.

In spite of earlier protestations, the preferred layout retains, for the outsider, a camp-like effect, but the derogatory term *campo* was replaced by *adi*, meaning a village or town, thus striking a positive note. The difference is, in fact, one of consultation and delegation of decisionmaking from planners to the house owners themselves.

The idea of a house, or home, in Eritrea is not that of a single building, but of a homestead with a number of different buildings including a kitchen; veranda or *baraka*, used for receiving guests and for outdoor sleeping; a shed for small animals and calves; a latrine; and, in some cases, a separate house, or in most cases a *tukul*, for separate sleeping of men or women.

---

develop income-generating activities, based largely on block-making and production of fiber-reinforced cement roofing tiles; to explore options at the community level based on cost-sharing and cost-recovery principles including credit mechanisms for house construction and improvement; to ensure that both returnees and other households have equitable access to program benefits in the long run; and ensure that priority is given to the most vulnerable groups such as the disabled, female-headed households, and the aged.

It is the whole compound that is "home" — not the house itself. When the words *abaiti* or *gezauti* are used for "housing" (both words are plural), what Eritreans have in mind is not a single- (or doubled-) roomed house, but a homestead with several functional buildings and structures. That is what they were dreaming about in Sudan when they talked about establishing a "home" back in Eritrea.

The layout of these structures is extremely important, and that is where some of the more tenacious traditions are seen to survive. Ethnic Beni Amer and Nara may lay their compounds out slightly differently from, for example, Tigrinya families, but the basic requirement of adequate space remains (CERA[4] has calculated locally defined "adequate" space at 375 square meters).

From the beginning, the guiding principle was to enable the returnees to contribute to the building of their own houses. In the first PROFERI documents, a degree of cost recovery was suggested, but interestingly, when the issues of self-help and community participation were considered, it was argued that housing is an emergency need, which cannot await community participation. Community participation, it was believed, would be too slow. This argument was made by CERA in 1993 and 1994 to outside donors, leading to the construction by contractors of several hundreds of houses in settlements for spontaneous returnees — Areda and Ghahtelai, for example, as mentioned above. Second, it was argued that because of the high number of "vulnerable [people] who could not be expected to contribute labor or other resources, housing should be provided for them, rather than being self built."[5] Third, the view was expressed that it was unlikely that returnees, who had become

---

[4]   CERA was created before liberation, and operated among refugees in Sudan to prepare them for their repatriation. After liberation (1991), CERA became the main planning, coordination, and implementation body dealing with repatriation of Eritrean refugees. By the end of 1995 CERA merged with the other big Eritrean rehabilitation body, ERRA (Eritrean Relief and Rehabilitation Agency), which had likewise during the liberation struggle — since 1975 — been working in Sudan — and throughout the world — under the name ERA. The new organization is called ERREC — Eritrean Relief and Refugees Commission. it addresses the rehabilitation needs of refugees, demobilized fighters and other displaced groups in an integrated approach.

[5]   Vulnerability: at one stage, CERA defined vulnerable groups as all households receiving relief, which meant that all planned returnees would fall into this category. Another definition included female-headed households, and the latest definition talks about those who are not physically able-bodied. Overall, around 30 percent of all households under the Pilot Phase were female-headed. This is also the case in Alebu.

accustomed to living off handouts in Sudan, could be mobilized for any substantial self-help contribution and community participation at all. However, in Alebu all three arguments proved misguided.

Self-help and community participation

One hundred and eighty-eight families arrived in Alebu in January and February, 1995, and they were initially reluctant to contribute to shelter construction. They came from different sites in Sudan—mostly from camps like Shagarab, which is known for its lack of economic opportunities for refugees. It may be true that they were suffering from a "dependency syndrome" or "refugee mentality" after many years of having received relief; certainly, people had come with high expectations. They claimed that when approached by representatives of the United Nations High Commissioner for Refugees and CERA in Sudan, they had been promised a house and food for one year, but were not told that they had to build those houses themselves.

There was therefore some delay before construction could begin. Several meetings were held between ACORD and CERA and the returnees, and a great deal of discussion took place, mostly about the expectations of the refugees and the assistance ACORD was able to offer. This finally convinced a small group of returnees to begin building on their own. First, 10 houses were constructed by two groups of returnee households. They produced their own compressed soil blocks and assisted with their manual labor in the construction of the house itself. When these first 10 houses appeared, the mood among the returnee community changed.

This change of heart coincided with the arrival of the second batch of settlers in May and June, 1995—more than 1,000 families primarily from the Semsem area in Sudan,[6] who were less reluctant to

---

[6]   Alebu is situated strategically by the Tessenei-Asmara road. It lies 330 kilometers west of Asmara and 30 kilometers east of Tessenei, the Sudan-Eritrean border town. The area has low rains and poor soil. The Alebu and Gash rivers make the area better for irrigated horticulture than for rain-fed agriculture. Alebu was initially planned to be the home of 500 returnee families. The first returnees were certainly among the poorest; most came from Shagareb, Fao and a small number—15 families—from Om Sagata (QEN) in Sudan. The ethnic breakdown was Nara (131 households), Tigre (30), Tigrinya (15), Kunama (5), Hedareb (4) and Saho (2). Thirty-seven households were female-led, and 60 of those had elderly household-heads.

undertake self-help initiatives and helped in getting the entire community mobilized. Subsequently, a small group of settlers, familiar with ACORD and its activities, arrived from Qala en Nahal.

The returnees organized themselves in groups of five households, volunteering to build houses collectively. The members of these households knew each other well from Sudan. They mobilized the young men to produce stabilized soil-blocks. An ACORD technician stationed in Alebu gave them instruction and supervised their work—which began early in the morning and lasted until dark.

Within a short time 14 soil-block presses were active in Alebu. Once the first two groups of five began building their houses, more and more people became interested. Soon there were waiting lists of people who had organized themselves in work groups and wanted to produce blocks.

A team of four or five youngsters can produce around 500 blocks per day (the daily record was 635)—half the blocks needed for one house. Hence, a team would need to work for around 10 days to produce blocks for five houses. At first it took nearly two weeks to construct a house. However, with experience—and the training of around 30 young returnees—construction time was reduced to around 9 to 10 days per house. During the month of May 1996 alone, a total of 95 houses were constructed. An outside contractor would not have been able to match such speed.

This approach, which got off the ground well in Alebu, did not take cost-recovery into consideration. It was, in a sense, a uniform solution, because the people chose one model only: the square, one-pitched roofed house, primarily based on the two "ACORD materials," fiber-cement tiles and compressed soil blocks.

The key to ACORD's approach, however, was not wholly technical, but rather was composed of the following elements:

- People were involved in the design and choice of house type.

- The self-help component was voluntary.

- Tile production took place on site and generated income for those engaged in the production.

- On-the-job training was made available in house construction for owners.

- Tree planting was linked to house grants, and the connec-

tion between use of roof timber and future wood resources
was clear to the occupants.

■ People made their own plot designs.

The ACORD approach in Alebu involved, in part, actual participation, in part, consultation, and, in part, service delivery; and, although the approach proved to be a workable one, it also had its
constraints and shortcomings. For example, there has been — and
still is, to some extent — too strong a technical, male bias among both
ACORD's and CERA's staff in Alebu. The focus was more on
"house building" — considered the domain of men — rather than
"homemaking," which is women's responsibility. Initially, women
were actually left out of the participatory process. The important
lesson, however, has been that people can be mobilized for a self-
help idea, even when coming from many years of camp life in Sudan.

Vulnerable groups

Shelter construction for vulnerable and weak groups raises two key
questions. How can a distinction be made in terms of those who are
"vulnerable," and therefore cannot contribute to the construction
of a house, and those who were not "vulnerable"? And how should
shelter construction be organized for such "vulnerable groups"?

ACORD and the CERA site management chose to leave these
questions to the returnees themselves. Meetings were held and it
was decided that the able-bodied households would produce building materials for the households who did not have any young men
available to join the work teams. It was decided that Sundays would
be used for this activity.

Following the introduction of this plan the inhabitants of Alebu
worked every Sunday from morning (starting at 6:00 a.m.) until night-
fall. Each Sunday 3,000 blocks were produced, sufficient for three
houses. The workers received food from the vulnerable families for
whom they worked. Initially the Nara took the initiative and started
Sunday *"wefera"* — a pattern of collective community work to assist
the elderly and vulnerable members of the community. But later the
system was generalized, the vulnerable households were listed, and
the list was kept by ACORD and CERA staff. Young men from all
ethnic groups provided the Sunday labor.

When it was realized that all vulnerable households could not
be reached by construction of only three houses per week, the

returnees decided to do community work on Saturdays too, doubling capacity. This is another example of the widely practiced Eritrean system of *"wefera"* (*"nafir"* in Sudan).

Wefera and other informal associations

As mentioned above, doubt has been cast on the vitality of community self-help systems among Eritrean refugees. The Alebu example shows that they have survived displacement and life in refugee conditions, and are still very much alive. But how have they survived, and should they be seen as examples of a traditional, or new, forms of solidarity?

First, and in this regard this author agrees with Kibreab (see this volume), it is doubtful that these systems ever died out—even during the many years of exile. It is true that camp life, urbanization, wage labor, and agricultural mechanization were characteristics of Eritrean refugee life in Sudan. *Wefera* was, however, still practiced, though under different forms. An ex-ACORD staff member from Qala en Nahal, which is known for its mechanized agriculture, reported that *wefera* disappeared from plowing, which tractors now undertook on a hire basis, but was instead shifted to weeding and trashing (of sorghum) as well as the harvesting of sesame, all of which were nonmechanized, labor-intensive processes.

Mechanization thus removed one labor constraint, but created additional ones, which the Eritrean peasants overcame by using the methods of social organization they knew. Mechanization had not removed *wefera*, and may even have strengthened it.

In camp situations with no productive activities, *wefera* may, as Bascon (1992) reports, have become "dormant" but never died. It is worth noting that immediately upon return to Alebu, informal organizations, networks, and mutual self-help systems sprung to life. Similar observations have been made about refugee populations in other settlement camps (see Kibreab in this volume).

During his research in Alebu in March 1995, only two months after the first 188 families returned, Karadawi (1995a) noted the existence of several customary patterns of social activities: *shimagilles*, an institution of elders geared toward maintaining harmony and peace within the community; *nafir*; a form of rotating savings associations named *sanduk* (practiced by the Tigre and Nara) and *equb* (by the Tigrinya); and women's neighborhood units organized around coffee making and coffee drinking, cooking and eating together, fetching fuel wood, and making mats from *doum* palms. Fur-

thermore, there was a youth club with 30 members and three formal committees—for agriculture, school building, and an overall
"three-man committee" to represent the community in its dealings
with the Eritrean authorities.

These committees were all male, and, as is characteristic, female
organizations were noticeably more formal than those composed
exclusively of men. However, both the more formal and the informal organizations evolved at the same time. This level of organization showed that even in a camp, the social fabric had not been torn
apart by either the forced displacement to Sudan or the voluntary
repatriation to Eritrea.

As suggested before, several factors may have contributed to keeping these networks and social structures intact: the proximity and
direct ties of the Eritrean refugees in Sudan to Eritrea, the social and
psychological make-up of the Eritrean refugees in Sudan, their strong
nationalism, and their deeply rooted survival strategies.

There are numerous examples of Eritreans crossing the Sudanese
border—in both directions—during the many years of liberation
struggle and exile. On the occasion of the funeral of an Eritrean in
Port Sudan, not only would relatives and kinfolk from Eritrea send
money, there would also be representatives from back home who
had dared the dangerous journey to attend the occasion. After liberation in 1991 occasional visits to Eritrea by individual family members were often made before a decision on permanent return would
be taken. Economic integration and reorientation of the Eritrean
refugees in Sudan seem not to have significantly altered their deep
links to their places of origin.

With very few exceptions, Eritreans in Sudan, even those who
had lived there for a generation, held inferior positions and enjoyed
inferior living conditions than the Sudanese. Even the self-settled
urban Eritreans, normally regarded as those with the best social
and economic positions, did not compare favorably with the
Sudanese. In Kassala, a town with a large number of Eritreans
(153,000 in 1986), only 4 percent of Eritreans owned their own houses,
compared with 77 percent of Kassala's Sudanese inhabitants
(Kuhlman 1990).

During their many years of exile, Eritreans were always made to
feel that they were temporary visitors. Their movement was restricted and controlled—for example, they needed travel papers to
make the journey to Khartoum—and they encountered difficulties
obtaining the licenses necessary to open businesses (some Eritreans
paraded as Sudanese to get easier access).

It is evident that Eritreans—despite economic integration in Sudan—have retained a strong psychological identification with Eritrea as "home." "At home you are free to behave in all senses," one refugee would note, while another stressed, that in Sudan "you are always a guest." Nationalism and support given to the liberation struggle also played an important role in unifying the Eritreans and keeping the feeling of a common identity alive. After the liberation of Massawa in 1990 by the EPLF, large numbers of Eritrean refugees in Sudan began urging CERA to help them return to their homeland (Habte-Selassie 1992).

The question of whether the visible solidarity and community spirit among the returnees is based on traditional values or is a "modern" and more ideological trend and, as many suggest, only a temporary phenomenon is difficult to answer.

In Alebu, unlike Sudan, community leadership tended not to be based on ethnic organizations. Certainly in Sudan, as Kibreab (this volume) has noted, ethnically based leadership systems were in evidence during the early years. However, over time such structures were weakened. During the period of my research in Alebu it was clear that the settlement was very much a multi-ethnic community, where informal neighborhood groups of women cut across ethnic lines and *wefera* was not exclusively practiced for members of one's own ethnic group (or clan); however, *sanduk* and *equb* still tended to be predominantly ethnic.

Certainly the EPLF played an important role in organizing the returnees in what may be termed "modern" or "ideological" organizations, such as a youth club initiated by a group of ex-fighters.

The egalitarian spirit of the fighters and the spirit of nation-building played an important role in binding the community together. When, for example, the agricultural committee called people for work to clear land, the CERA staff in Alebu, who were all fighters or ex-fighters, led the work parties and sweated along with the rest in the scorching sun from dawn to dusk—a far cry from most of the ACORD staff or other government bureaucrats the refugees had known in Sudan.

It is thus probably a mixture of the "traditional" and "modern" that gave shape and form to the social fabric of Alebu resettlement society: as one writer predicted, based on observations in Sudan, a combination of "cooperative efforts rooted in 'survival' imperatives, social relationships and political associations" (Bascon 1992).

The important fact here is that the strength and nature of this cooperative effort has probably been underestimated by some planners and, I would argue, should be given much more attention in future rehabilitation efforts.[7] Whether the spirit of solidarity and self-help will be a temporary phenomenon, which will fade away, as some observers suggest, is doubtful. Its survival during many years of exile indicates that it has a strong base. While it is true that *wefera* (or *nafir*) survived in Sudan in one form or another, it is also true that Eritreans in Sudan did produce commodities for markets, did live in towns or camps (rather than villages), and did work for wages or salaries (those living in towns).

To understand this apparent contradiction, it may be useful to change the perspective and look upon the process from a perspective closer to the people involved—the refugee or returnee household itself.

Household survival strategies in Sudan and Eritrea

Evidence has been collected that documents the survival strategies adopted by Eritreans under various conditions as refugees in Sudan.

In towns, Eritreans would take jobs and/or be engaged in informal sector activities. Often one job would not be sufficient for sustaining a family, so the same person would have two or more jobs. In the rural areas, subsistence cultivation would be combined with trade and migrant labor. In organized settlements where land was allocated, such as Qala en Nahal, Eritreans would farm and sell their produce at the market, but they would also invest in livestock, often maintaining grazing land at some distance from the settlement. In the absence of land distribution, survival in camps depended on supplementing relief supplies with sharecropping and wage labor (Karadawi 1995a).

This pattern of creating a livelihood based on a variety of very different activities and income sources, and also of seeking several options for investing surpluses, is what Eritreans have always been used to doing. The marginal natural resources of Eritrea have forced

---

[7] International aid for rehabilitation: In 1993 the government presented donors with the US$ 262 million PROFERI program (in Geneva). The response was very disappointing. Only $32 million in pledges and confirmed commitments were received and some $17 million was for food aid alone. Because of this shortfall, the government allocated funds that would normally have been invested in economic programs. A substantial element of voluntary labor was also devoted to rehabilitation, for example, work by the National Service.

people into developing survival strategies based on a combination of production, trade, and migration. No socioeconomic group in Eritrea, not even the "farmers" of the relatively fertile Southern Highlands, could expect to attain a sustainable livelihood through the adoption of a single strategy, but rather through a combination of strategies.

This is a refined and strong system that does not break down during drought, but instead has emerged from the understanding that rainfall is erratic and agricultural investment is highly risky. Only when drought is combined with war or other factors that limit trade and migration, which are vital to this system, do famines occur.

Sudan was already a familiar place for many of the Eritrean refugees, before their forced displacement during the war in Eritrea. Eastern Sudan and western Eritrea were bound together by trade routes, grazing land, and substantial seasonal migration under "normal" circumstances. People belonging to the same ethnic groups, clans, and religious sects lived on both sides of the border.

On becoming refugees in Sudan, Eritreans activated their social networks and their inherent ability to diversify and adapt to new circumstances for survival. A herdsman in Eritrea, for example, became a tractor driver in Qala el Nahal or a petty trader, or both.

Such strategies require excellent organization, trust, and solidarity within the family and the community. If, for example, money or livestock is entrusted to one member, who will migrate temporarily, it is vital that this person return with both the initial capital and the surpluses generated. Families, kinship, and community structures of various kinds all play pivotal roles in the member's success. This also requires interaction between different modes of production, for example, a constant exchange between agriculturalists and pastoralists. Diversification and adaptation are the roots of success, and household and community survival are the goals.

Livelihood restoration in Alebu

The process of restoring livelihoods may thus be viewed as the application of a sophisticated strategy for coping under different conditions based on a peasant and pastoralist economy with a strong social basis of cooperation and mutual self-help.

Upon return to Alebu these mechanisms were immediately reactivated by the ex-refugees, whether they came from a "camp experience" or as "returnees from spontaneous refugee settlements or towns." This could be one reason why the returnees in Alebu were able to restore what they perceive as "satisfactory livelihoods" in a relatively short time. Another is that ACORD and CERA in Alebu made appropriate resources and assistance available.

It is interesting to look closer at the process of livelihood restoration. For all of the returnees it was the second time, or perhaps even the third or fourth time, they had been required to adapt their skills and knowledge to restore their livelihoods following upheaval.

A research of the changes in livelihood over time for 37 returnee households in Alebu was undertaken in May 1996. It was conducted as a "household time line" exercise,[8] where each major change in one of each of the four elements of material livelihood — income, home, livestock, and land — was recorded.

It revealed a sharp drop in livelihoods in connection with the first relocation — going into exile from Eritrea — as well as in connection with the second — returning from exile to Eritrea. The first relocation was caused by persecution and displacement in Eritrea as a result of war. For all respondents there was a decline in livelihood satisfaction before they left Eritrea, which meant that they lost means of livelihood — jobs and land. Some respondents reported how their livestock was looted by the *Derg* (the former Ethiopian military leadership) and their houses burnt. This pre-displacement impoverishment made it impossible for many of the respondents to stay in Eritrea. Others left as a result of persecution for political activities and sympathies.

The restoration of livelihoods in Sudan took time. Only five of the 37 respondents (14 percent) recorded improvements to pre-relocation levels after three to five years of exile, while 16 households (43 percent) recorded such improvements after 6 and up to 20 years of exile. Among those, four households (11 percent) actually recorded overall better livelihoods in exile than before leaving

---

8   Household time-line: A PRA "time-line" tool was used to interview a limited group of 37 households, and a special visualization technique was developed to focus on four aspects of the households' livelihood basis during the last 20–25 years — land, livestock, home, and income. It was clear, however, that "livelihood" is not based on material elements only, but is also psychological. It was therefore left to the households themselves to determine whether their livelihoods at different times were "satisfactory" or not. Four different levels of "livelihood satisfaction" could be chosen from "fully satisfied," "acceptable (but not fully satisfied)," "not acceptable, but bearable" to totally "unacceptable/unbearable." The research was designed and coordinated by Christian Sørensen and carried out by five ACORD staff in Alebu — Fatna Humaned Hamed, Saliha Osman, Hawa Hajaji, Teclebirhan Tewolde, and Gerezgeher Idriss.

Eritrea. These four were all long-time refugees from the 1967 or 1971 movements. The remaining 16 households claimed not to have achieved a level of livelihood satisfaction in exile corresponding to their experiences before leaving Eritrea. After having suffered the "crisis of persecution and displacement," they suffered a prolonged "crisis of exile." They "survived," but did not "cope."

Before the second relocation—the return to Eritrea—the pattern was by and large repeated. Eighteen households (49 percent of the respondents) specifically recorded losses of means of livelihood before leaving Sudan. This process seemed to start in 1989 and was especially marked after 1991. Apart from the 18 households that recorded such decline in livelihood satisfaction, there were another six (making the total 24, or 62 percent of all households) who reported the lowest level of livelihood satisfaction during their whole stay in Sudan.

From this analysis, therefore, it could be argued that pre-repatriation impoverishment had three causes. First, there was a deterioration of the Sudanese economy in the 1990s whereby savings were lost through inflation and entrepreneurial Eritreans reported declining businesses. Second, since late 1994 it was also evident that Eritreans suffered from various degrees of persecution as a result of deteriorating relationships between the governments of Eritrea and Sudan. And third, during relocation, Eritreans were obliged to sell many of their assets, those that they could not transport with them to Eritrea, such as their houses. Where only the physical structure would be sellable (for example, *tukuls* in Shagareb and Qala en Nahal), these were sold in the range of 4,000 to 8,000 Sudanese pounds.

It is perhaps partly myth that returnees left a lot of livestock behind in Sudan. Several of the respondents in Alebu reported that they had to sell their livestock at very low prices before they returned in 1995. They would also be taxed at the border, a factor that, during the first months of 1996, reduced the number of spontaneous returnees to Eritrea.

In Alebu, however, the restoration of livelihoods, as has already been argued, took a relatively short time. All households reported sharply improved livelihood conditions within one year after arrival.

ACORD staff conducted the research and there may have been, of course, an element of trying to please the researchers, but other indicators pointed in the same direction. Research conducted in 1995 examining the prospects for starting income-generating activities in Alebu showed that hardly any of the inhabitants had initially chosen Alebu as their preferred place of settlement, but after having stayed there for some time they came to see it as an ideal residential town with good housing, health and education facilities, and prospects for some local income generation. In addition, it was regarded as an excellent base for undertaking migrant labor and more general trade, with the advantage of a good road system.

The decoration of the people's homes and the care taken of the trees planted in their compounds also indicate a certain degree of satisfaction and a desire for long-term settlement.

While Alebu presents an example of successful resettlement, the findings may contain a measure of short-term optimism, which may not be sustained in the long term. It is possible that an increase in household incomes could be credited to the activities of ACORD, which, for example, gave employment to 120 as casual laborers or subcontractors, such as donkey cart owners selling water to construction sites. After the phasing out of ACORD's construction activities, a drop in general money income may be experienced. Other research findings and observations from Alebu on the food security situation indicated how fragile the livelihoods were. After the Eritrean government stopped its food relief distributions as a result of its decision to go over to food aid monetization early in 1996, people in Alebu reported severe food shortage and cases of starvation.

It is likely in such resettlement operations that a short period of food aid will be necessary, at least until the first successful harvest has been collected for those who have been allocated land. In Alebu there remains a question over the suitability of allocated land, and its ability to produce sufficient crops without negative environmental costs. Without some kind of food aid, people may not have the energy and time (because they have to search for food) to engage in productive and income-generating activities to sustain those livelihoods that they have otherwise so successfully started to restore.

One further factor, which had the potential to derail the restoration process, was the closure of the Eritrean-Sudanese border. The survival strategies of Alebu's inhabitants (as for most returnees who have settled in Gash-Barka) depend to a degree on the movement of people and goods across the border. The deteriorated relationships and the threats of war between Eritrea and Sudan came to pose the most serious threat to Alebu's survival.

Conclusion

Refugees returning to Eritrea arrive short of economic or financial capital (cash, credit, savings, and other resources), but their social and human capital (networks, social claims, social relations, and associations) and accumulated knowledge are considerable. Their optimism and nationalism (political capital, perhaps) also constitute a strong resource. The strength and nature of the returnees' cooperative effort was probably underestimated when their settlements were planned and should be given much more attention in future rehabilitation efforts. It is important that "outsiders," including the government and humanitarian agencies, build on refugees' own initiative-driven strategies for survival and reconstruction of livelihoods instead of imposing preplanned packages.

Alebu stands out among many settlement schemes in Eritrea. The conditions in Alebu are probably close to optimal. The settlement area offers good conditions for home reconstruction and also, to some extent, for income generation; the returnees have been met with a listening approach by "outsiders" (ACORD and the government site staff); and jointly the two partners have arrived at workable methods and solutions to solving problems such as shelter, sanitation, and income generation. The services promised in the PROFERI rehabilitation package—such as water, education, and health—have largely been made available together with the needed physical resource inputs and the allocation of land for farming and plots for residence. All this has facilitated a process of accelerated livelihood restoration.

In most other settlement sites, one or more of the above factors have been missing. This does not mean that livelihoods of the returnees are not restored, but that it takes much longer. Eritrean refugees are now experiencing their second major relocation. During the first, when they went to Sudan as refugees, they started with nothing and struggled for many years before their livelihoods reached acceptable levels. Returning to Eritrea they again more or less start with nothing, but with higher expectations and motivation.

This second process of livelihood restoration is psychologically different in the sense that it is a homecoming, but otherwise it requires the same combination of activation of social and physical resources, as well as cooperation between external actors and the returnees themselves.

The approach that this chapter has tried to adopt is to look at the experience of the refugees and returnees at home and in exile—and now at home again—as a continuum and not as separate experiences. That is how they look upon it themselves.

Rehabilitation is a social, not a technical, process. It is just the name for a phase in the process of general, ongoing human and social development.

PART FIVE

From marginalization to re-inclusion

Editors' Note Marginalization occurs when families lose economic power and slide downward: middle-income farm households do not become landless, but become smaller landholders; small shopkeepers and craftsmen are downsized and slip below poverty thresholds. Many individuals cannot use their previously acquired skills, which may be obsolete upon relocation, and human capital is lost or rendered inactive and useless. The coerciveness of displacement is perceived as a loss of social status and causes a psychological downslide in confidence in society and self, a sense of injustice. Relative economic marginalization begins long before actual displacement; for instance, when lands are condemned for future flooding and are implicitly devalued, new infrastructural investments are prohibited, and the expansion of social services is undercut.

The chapter by Walter Fernandes explores the dual process of economic and social marginalization of project-displaced people through an examination of the linkages between the state of oustees before their displacement, and the deterioration of their self-image subsequent to it. The author pays particular attention to the position of women and Indian "tribals." For Fernandes, marginalization is characterized, at worst, by economic and social deterioration, a crisis of social and cultural identity, and increasing powerlessness and subordination.

In order for oustees to overcome the risks of marginalization and to achieve re-inclusion and "total rehabilitation," Fernandes argues, development oustees must become beneficiaries of the projects that lead to their resettlement.

For this to happen, in addition to jobs, land, and monetary compensation, benefits to displacees should include compensation for psychological and cultural loss, the reconstruction of disintegrated social networks, and human capital investments such as technical training. Practical measures, according to the author, must include access to knowledge about and participation in the decisionmaking processes concerning displacement and resettlement, fair and equitable compensation, action to counter gender discrimination in the labor market, and accommodation of traditional skills and knowledge.

CHAPTER 9

From marginalization to sharing the project benefits

Walter Fernandes

Because of the ongoing impoverishment of involuntary settlers and other project-affected persons, development-induced displacement has become a major issue on the human rights agenda and among socially conscious scholars. A major reason for this is the marginalization of the displaced or project-affected persons, a substantial number of whom are dependent on common property resources (CPR). Since the laws of most developing countries do not formally recognize the right of these communities over these resources of their livelihood, they are deprived of their livelihood without compensation and without an alternative. Women suffer the most among these communities.

Clearly identifiable classes pay the price of development, while its benefits reach other equally identifiable classes. That is the basis of impoverishment and marginalization. An obvious implication is the need to ensure that the displaced persons are the first beneficiaries of projects that displace them. But apart from the indifference of the project authorities, the psychological effects of displacement are a major obstacle to displaced persons' accessing the benefits.

In this chapter I will attempt to explore in depth the meaning of marginalization as part of the impoverishment risks framework (see Cernea, this volume). I will discuss the obstacles confronted by displaced persons in sharing in the project benefits, and suggest some possible solutions. The answer I attempt is not definitive but is an input for discussion aimed at a consensus on new and innovative approaches to rehabilitation to ensure that the displaced or project-affected persons become its beneficiaries.

Economic factors and impoverishment

The first area of consensus required is the very understanding of displacement-induced impoverishment. By this I mean the deterioration in the status of individuals and communities after displacement, not the economic status prior to displacement. In defining it, I go beyond the economic factors, particularly of the formal type, which those inclined to justify displacement use as the sole criterion (see Kar 1991). They calculate losses and gains on the basis of monetary income alone, and conclude that the status of the displaced persons has improved after displacement since in many cases their monetary income rises.

The latter view ignores, firstly, the fact that a large number of displaced or project-affected persons are CPR dependents. Others live by rendering service to the village as a community. For example, out of an estimated 21.3 million displaced persons in India between 1951 and 1990, no fewer than 40 percent are the predominantly CPR dependent tribals who form 8.08 percent of the country's population (Fernandes 1998:251). Another 40 percent are estimated to be from other rural poor communities. Most persons displaced by the Mount Apo project in the Philippines, by the dams on the Bio-Bio river in Chile (Downing 1997), and by James Bay in Quebec (Comeau and Santin 1990) are indigenous peoples. Many of them belong to the nonmonetized informal economy. But only land owners and the marketable commodities are compensated. What individuals once obtained from the informal economy is not compensated for.

Consequently, even when monetary assets rise after displacement, in practice displaced or project-affected persons are impoverished also in economic terms. For example, the more than 100,000 persons displaced in the 1950s by the Hirakud dam in Orissa in eastern India were pushed without transition from their barter economy into a monetized system. Moreover, vested commercial interests and moneylenders take advantage of their lack of market savvy and inexperience in handling large sums of cash, luring the displacees into nonproductive spending of the cash compensation they received for their productive assets. Empirical studies in Hirakud and other places have documented situations in which people dispossessed of their income-generating assets are influenced to buy useless artificial jewelry or pay for expensive "festivals." They were thus left with little or no productive assets except some trinkets that the merchants had sold to them at an exorbitant price (Viegas 1992:40-42). They were absorbed into the dominant economy by being reduced to the condition of suppliers of cheap labor and raw material.

Going beyond economic factors

Studies point to two facets of displacement-induced impoverishment: (a) economic deterioration and (b) loss of the economic, social, and psychological infrastructure that makes it impossible for displaced or project-affected persons to rebuild their lives, let alone improve their lifestyles (Fernandes and Raj 1992:135). Economic indicators are useful to understand the first, namely impoverishment, but not the second, which can be called marginalization in the fullest sense of the term, because it ensures not only that those who are poor remain poor, but also that their status deteriorates further and that they are deprived of an opportunity to improve it. No benefit sharing or alternative to rehabilitation is possible without attending to these features.

Most researchers studying displacement, or persons working among the project-displaced and affected people, have long discarded as insufficient the exclusively economic measurement of impoverishment. They look for a conceptual framework that includes social, psychological, cultural, and health parameters. The impoverishment risks and recovery model formulated by Cernea (see this volume) include all these dimensions, as well as social factors like health, informal economic elements like the CPRs, and the cultural, psychological, and economic factors in community disarticulation and reconstruction.

These aspects are certainly crucial. But for an understanding of impoverishment, one has to examine each factor and interpret social marginalization in even broader terms. The most important area of marginalization that has received inadequate attention is *psychological*. Understanding this feature is essential because most displaced or project-affected persons belong to the classes that are kept at the lowest level of the socioeconomic totem pole. As a consequence of a project, they are brought face to face with the dominant society without adequate preparation, throwing them into a crisis of cultural and social identity and an even greater position of powerlessness. They were already powerless before displacement. By pushing them without preparation into a day-to-day interface with the formal system and the powerful classes, the project increases their sense of powerlessness. They are unable to cope with this encounter with the powerful system. So as a coping mechanism they internalize an ideology of their own powerlessness. Many lose confidence in themselves and in the possibility of reestablishing or improving their condition. In the resettlement literature, this has often been described as "aversion to new risk taking" (Heredero 1989); the process is, in fact, even more complex, as it involves a devaluation of their traditional culture.

What benefits?

Before discussing psychological obstacles, I will identify the benefits the displaced or project-affected persons should receive and the principles on which they are based. The basic issue is their right to assistance for full rehabilitation. Such rehabilitation should result in an improved livelihood after displacement, because they pay the price of development. Rehabilitation is not a welfare scheme planned by good-willed project authorities, but a right of the displaced and project-affected people. Therefore, many enunciate as nonnegotiable the principle that project-affected persons should have a proportionate, predetermined share in all the benefits accruing from the project. When such benefits do not accrue (for example, in military defense establishments that cause displacement), the state must accept complete responsibility for compensating and rehabilitating them on a long-term basis (Fernandes and Paranjpye 1997:17–18).

Compensation and transition

The first benefit is compensation. In most cases the norm used for it is market value. Experience in India shows that this criterion goes against the weaker sections, many of which live in the "backward" regions where the price of land is low. But the assets taken over are their livelihood. The low price given for them results in their impoverishment (Fernandes 1993). Experience in Brazil, Kenya, and elsewhere also shows that monetary compensation is not a solution but a step in rendering displaced and project-affected persons homeless and prone to starvation or food insecurity (Cernea 1995).

Many suggest replacement value as the norm. It should not be limited to individual assets or even CPRs. Instead, the landless should be compensated for loss of their livelihood because adequate compensation is the first prerequisite in the transition of the displaced persons to a new lifestyle. Its calculation should find ways to also value the "intangibles," because such intangibles are nevertheless real. These include the psychological and cultural losses they suffer, the breakup of their social systems, the cost of preparing them psychologically to cope with a new life, and the cost of training them technically to access its benefits.

The displaced and jobs

The second benefit is permanent jobs in the project, not temporary substitutes. Jobs given to the displaced persons can also be viewed as a mode of reducing displacement. For example, in India project townships are built for persons who come from outside the region for a job in the projects, most of which are in isolated areas. So the township has amenities like clubs and theaters, to attract such workers. The township takes up much land, in some cases — for example, the fertilizer plant at Talcher in the Angul district of Orissa — as much as 40 percent of the total land acquired (Fernandes and Raj 1992:34).

Apart from permanent benefits reaching the displaced persons, giving them as many jobs in the project as possible becomes a way of avoiding excessive land acquisition. With the displaced and project-affected persons being trained for the jobs and such other components as supply of provisions to the project, the influx of outsiders will decrease substantially. The few who come can rent houses in the locality, thus adding to its economy, instead of turning the locality into an extraction zone alone (Dhagamwar 1997:115). This approach can also reduce displacement since a township will not be required. Training is feasible because, in most cases, there is a time lag between the announcement and the implementation of the project. As soon as a decision is taken about a scheme, priority can be given to make all the prospective project-affected persons literate and to equip them technically for the jobs.

In addition, one has to question the type of technology introduced in a labor-intensive society. In India, for example, the Coal India Rehabilitation Policy (CIL 1994), as well as the policy of the National Thermal Power Corporation (NTPC 1993), speak of self-employment as a mode of rehabilitation. The reason given for it is mechanization that has reduced the number of unskilled jobs.

This goes against the displaced and project-affected persons. For example, in the mid-1980s, around 50,000 persons were displaced by the Upper Kolab dam and 6,000 by the NALCO plant in the Koraput district of Orissa. The hill that has now become the NALCO mine was the CPR of 70 villages. The mine is fully mechanized and has created about 300 skilled jobs taken by outsiders. Had the traditional means of transport been used, it could have created between 8,000 and 10,000 jobs that would have gone mostly to those displaced (Pattanaik and Panda 1992:208–209).

Displaced and project-affected persons as shareholders

Many go beyond compensation and jobs to question the ownership pattern. Today those who invest capital claim ownership. But the CPRs acquired for the project are the livelihood of many communities. Displacement has become a mode of transferring these assets to the corporate sector, for which they become a source of profit. Those who pay the price get no benefit.

Amerindians whose land was being taken over for the James Bay project in Canada demanded that they not be paid compensation but that the land be considered their investment in the project and that their community receive annual royalty for it (Comeau and Santin 1990:59–61). Because displacement has become a process of impoverishing the CPR dependents, some persons in India (see Sharma 1993:115–117) think that even royalty is inadequate. The communities should own the CPRs even after acquisition, to ensure that their livelihood is not lost. Instead of monetary compensation that is not of much relevance to them, the CPRs should be quantified and turned into shares in the project. The project would thus be owned jointly by the capital investor and the CPR dependents.

To achieve this, project-affected persons have to be given adequate training before becoming involved in ongoing decisions in the project. They may also have to employ professional managers to run the project. But it has to be their decision because they, as a community, own the CPRs. The training given will then be based on the principle of improving their livelihood after displacement. As such, its cost can be considered social investment by the project.

Share in the product

Equally important is a share in the product of the project. Resettlement of the displaced persons is often perceived as an event independent of the project thus created. This perception and the decisions that follow from it go against the principle that the displaced and project-affected persons should be its first beneficiaries. So if the project has a marketable product, a part of it can be used for rehabilitating those who pay the price.

This too requires much training since a very high proportion of those displaced are illiterate and inadequately exposed to the society outside their region. If they are resettled through self-employment as the Coal India and NTPC rehabilitation policies suggest, they will not be able to deal effectively with the economic vested interests that control production and marketing in the region. They would thus be unable to enjoy the fruits of the project built on their assets.

Training them to deal with production and marketing on a cooperative basis is a possible solution. They can form cooperatives or production units using the power, irrigation facilities, and other products, like aluminium and minerals, that the project produces, or be trained to supply provisions to it. We do not state that the entire product should go to them. We only reenunciate the principle that project-affected persons should have a proportionate, predetermined share in all the benefits accruing from the project (Fernandes 1995:278–279).

This solution is possible because many marginalized groups living in the informal sector have a community ethos. One can build on it and turn them into legally recognized cooperatives. It would require the project authorities to work jointly with community leaders and NGOs who understand the culture and can help the people upgrade their social systems. This effort too is to be viewed as social investment.

Rehabilitation as a right

These principles can be upheld only if rehabilitation is recognized as a fundamental right of the project-affected persons. It is not a concession from the project but rather what it owes to them in justice. As such, it has to be the legal obligation of the project authorities to rehabilitate those affected. The fundamental principle is that there can be no displacement without rehabilitation's being an integral part of the project. One refers here to total rehabilitation, not merely the economic component of resettlement. Its cost should be included in the project budget.

In reality, hardly any country legally recognizes the right of the displaced and project-affected persons to get a share in the benefits of the project, much less in its ownership. We have seen it in the case of James Bay in Canada, Mount Apo in the Philippines, Khagan in Pakistan, Narmada in India, and elsewhere. The rehabilitation packages in these and many other schemes were formulated only after the people struggled or because the funding agency made it a condition of funding. Even within these schemes, many limit themselves to the economic component or self-employment. In so doing, the policymakers forget that most displaced persons are illiterate, and are inadequately exposed to the formal economy. They are pushed overnight, with no transition, from a sustenance to a competitive economy, without help to deal with the psychological trauma they suffer because of the changeover. They cannot deal with the dominant forces they will have to confront in their new situation.

The psychological component

In other words, displacement has social, economic, cultural, and *psychological components*. But very few have studied the last of these components. The social and environmental impact of impoverishment has been studied somewhat extensively: for example, the disintegration of the social systems that sustain the displaced and project-affected persos as the basis of their marginalization (see Mahapatra 1994:42–45); the weakening of the sustainable culture that had traditionally ensured the renewability of their resources and equitable distribution (Reddy 1995); their consequent dispossession (see Areeparampil 1989:20–24); the deterioration of their health that weakens them physically and affects their motivation for improvement (Ramaiah 1995). Others have attempted to draw attention to the close link between these factors: what Cernea (1995), for example, sees as impoverishment risks, Areeparampil (1996) as dispossession, and Pathy (1996) as marginalization.

Thus a strong case has already been made to show that even when the focus is on economic factors, the interlinkage of all the elements has to be understood. In other words, impoverishment is not an accident but intrinsic to displacement. So measures should be taken to prevent it. But very few have dealt with the psychological component. Only a few scholars have understood that they should deal with a "broadly defined mental health perspective, one that incorporates an understanding of social and behavioral problems along with mental illnesses, as well as quite specific models of prevention" (Good 1996:1504).

In other words, the main consequence of their marginalization is loss of not only social but also psychological infrastructure. Most researchers have failed to see the link between the marginalized state of the displaced persons before displacement and the deterioration of their self-image subsequent to it. Such deterioration prevents them from gaining awareness of their own strength, which is indispensable for them to perceive themselves as a community capable of being fully human and of demanding a share in the benefits.

The triple foundation of unequal societies

This low self-image is an offshoot of what John Gaventa (1980:3–5) calls the triple base on which unequal societies are founded. Its first step is legal equality combined with denial of access to the poor. While making institutions and systems legally available to all, the dominant society ensures that the weak are denied access to them, through aspects such as the language used, the culture prevalent in them, and the expenses that are beyond reach. The court of law, for example, is, in theory, available to all, but given its physical distance from the village, the expenses involved, and the language used, "we know which people can go to courts for their rights; the poor do not go but are usually taken to courts" (Baxi 1983:103).

The second step is to accord access to a few individuals, without making a dent on the system. For example, a few poor individuals may gain access to schools meant for the rich. Many of them drop out for economic or cultural reasons. The middle and upper classes assume that the poor, who have no choice but to drop out, do so because they are unable to come up to expected intellectual standards. Thus they interpret their action resulting from cultural and economic factors as a consequence of their low intellectual caliber. Victim blaming is thus used to justify discrimination against the victims (Naik 1975:8–13).

Such limited access also results in the double alienation of the few who survive until the end. They reject their own community as inferior, but the dominant society does not accept them as equals (Sharma 1978:12–14). This is the third foundation. No unequal society can survive without the subalterns' internalizing the dominant value system (Gaventa 1980:25–30). For example, it is the mother who socializes the girl child into accepting her subordinate status. Political colonialism was maintained not through force alone but also by the leaders of the colonized internalizing the ideology of "civilizing education" (de Boschere 1967:65–68). Today, the same class has internalized the ideology of the economic superiority of the rich countries and the "inability" of the "Third World" to come up to their technological standards, thus reinterpreting "civilizing education."

Displacement and self-image

So we shall focus on the psychological components or self-image. Most displaced and project-affected persons belong to the marginalized groups. If they are from a "low caste," as in South Asia, or a subordinate race, as in the Euro-American societies, a low self-image is intrinsic to their status. Others, like the tribals, are not brought up with a low self-image. But, having little exposure to the external world, they are unable to cope or interface with it without adequate preparation. They develop a low self-image as a result.

This process is visible at every stage. The manner in which decisions are taken about the project, the low compensation paid, the failure to rehabilitate the displaced and project-affected persons, and the manner in which these people are forced to encounter the dominant society confirm in them a low self-image. The consequent low self-perception ensures that they accept their subordinate status and do not compete for benefits. We shall study the steps that thus ensure the continuation of their subordination.

The decisionmaking process and self-image

The process of self-image deterioration begins with the decision concerning a people-displacing project. Most national constitutions recognize the right of every citizen to inhabit any part of his or her territory. In reality, hardly any country recognizes the right of the displaced and project-affected persons to be involved in the decision concerning their displacement. Thus, the democratic principle is applied selectively and the constitutionally guaranteed right is violated by the imposition of a new lifestyle on a group of people without their informed prior consent. In the name of national development, the poor, particularly those to be displaced, are excluded from their democratic right. Thus, by taking displacement for granted and assuming that the displaced persons, most of them poor and powerless, should adjust themselves to the situation once a decision to displace them is taken, countries abrogate the rights of the poor.

This failure intensifies the unequal power relations and the domination-dependency syndrome in the life of the powerless. The fact of their exclusion from a decision concerning their very survival confirms them in their self-image of being incapable of making decisions for themselves. With motivation for progress lacking, the displaced and project-affected persons take recourse in destructive coping mechanisms (Good 1996:1505).

Knowledge and power

Displaced people are excluded not merely from the decision but also from information about the project. Knowledge is power. The powerful project authorities render the affected populations further powerless by keeping them ignorant of their future situation. Within the people to be displaced, such ignorance creates a sense of insecurity that becomes a barrier to their preparing themselves for a better life or getting project benefits.

To begin with some examples in India, a study done in 1987, three years after work on the Narmada dam commenced, in Madhya Pradesh, one of the three states affected by it, showed that the people did not know which villages would be submerged, when they would be submerged, how many of them would be displaced, whether they would be resettled, or what compensation would be paid (MARG 1987). Since official development projects had been halted in this region, banks would not give loans. Restrictions were put on cultivation. But the people, being ignorant of other details, had developed a sense of fatalism and powerlessness. Similar were the findings of studies among the displaced persons of the NALCO plant (Stanley 1996), the Salandi dam in Orissa (Fernandes and Raj 1992:140–143), and the coal, uranium, and other mines in Bihar (Areeparampil 1996:40–43). Two notifications were issued in October and November 1992 for the Military Test Firing Range in Southern Bihar. The 238,000 persons to be displaced or otherwise affected by it came to know of it from a journalist in March 1993, long after the two-month period for objections had expired.

Such examples can also be found elsewhere. For example, the encounter of the native people of Australia with the white settlers resulted in the creation of the Aborigine myth. The stereotypes of their features, as conceptualized by the whites, were internalized by the natives, who began to perceive themselves as being capable of being only subordinates (Wilcken 1992:55–57). Similar are the conclusions reached by those who have studied persons displaced by the Kulekhani hydroelectric project in Nepal (Pokharel 1995:140-143), James Bay in Canada (Tulugak 1996:20–21), Agumilpa and Zimapan hydro schemes in Mexico (Gallart Nocetti 1992), and others.

While those affected are kept ignorant of the reality that overtakes them, merchants and moneylenders from outside, who have access to the formal economy, get more information. By spreading rumors, they force the people to sell their land at a low price, declare themselves displaced persons, and get most of the benefits that should go to genuine displaced and project-affected persons (Ganguly-Thukral 1992:15–17).

Studies also confirm that the insecurity thus created leaves the project-affected persons unprepared for a new life. They begin to view themselves as inferior beings without rights. Many of them lose hope in their future and develop a fatalistic attitude. People who had until then preserved trees begin to cut and sell them at a throwaway price. They neglect their land and other assets. The ignorance of the "mainstream" society and the fear of the unknown adds to their self-perception of inadequacy, and intensifies their feeling of being incapable of looking after themselves (Fernandes and Raj 1992:74–76).

Low compensation and self-image

This feeling is confirmed by the low compensation offered for the assets they lose. Such a low price is based on the attitude of the dominant society toward the subalterns, expressed in the principle of eminent domain on which most land laws are based, particularly in the Anglo-Saxon tradition. Only individual land documents are considered valid. What does not have such a document is *terra nullius,* that is, nobody's land, and as such can be occupied by anyone. The occupation of Australian and American indigenous land by white colonizers was legitimized under this principle, which has since been struck down by the Australian judiciary as unconstitutional (Brennan 1995:4–5). But the law in most countries does not recognize the long-established traditional community rights that are basic to the livelihood of the natural resource-based communities. For example, such disruption could have been avoided in the Navajo-Hopi resettlement in the United States, had the lawyers and lawmakers given any recognition to the use rights of families long settled as legitimate. Family traditional use areas were classed merely as "communal" property of the tribe, and the families were compensated for something that might be called use rights (Brugge 1993:8).

The second facet of this principle is that the state alone has the right to define the public purpose and displace people. In most countries such a legal system creates two types of citizens: those living on individually owned land and the CPR dependents. The latter cannot claim ownership even though they might have lived there for centuries before the colonial law was enacted. For example, in Thailand the hill tribes that were relocated in the plains on the assumption that the shifting cultivation they practiced was solely responsible for deforestation got no compensation because the forests that were their livelihood were considered government property (Kesmanee 1995:245–248).

Market value, which is the criterion for compensation, and the low price given, render the displaced and project-affected persons further powerless. For example, in Gujarat in western India, 22,171 hectares of land were acquired from 15,560 families in the 1980s for irrigation projects co-financed by the World Bank. But Indian government agencies paid as compensation an average of rupees 8,780 per hectare, when the market rate was rupees 16,000 (Fernandez 1990:36). Thus, decisions taken without involving the affected populations change even the "market value" to the advantage of the project. Such low prices also seem to be the norm in countries as far apart as Brazil, Kenya, and Nepal (Cernea 1996).

Most displacements from dams, roads, and so on tend to be in "backward" (that is, administratively neglected) regions. Besides, much of the livelihood of those communities is natural resource-based under a common property regime. The little private land owned gets low compensation because of the "backwardness" of the regions. For example, in the 1980s, NALCO built two units in Orissa, one in the medium-size farmer-dominated Angul district and the other in the tribal-majority Koraput district. In the first, only 18 percent of the land acquired was common, and included schools, roads, and so forth. In the second, more than 60 percent of the tribal land acquired was CPRs. For the private land they owned, the displaced persons in Koraput received an average compensation of rupees 2,700 per acre compared with rupees 25,000 in Angul (Fernandes and Raj 1992:92).

One can, therefore, ask with Singh (1989:97) whether the low price is a major deciding factor in choosing who is to be displaced for a "public purpose" in India. The cost of executing a project where the least cost is involved in compensation, the least resistance is likely from the local people, or the displaced and project-affected persons have the least legal capacity to demand their due seem to become important factors in project design and execution.

What is said about India applies to most other countries. To the market economy the CPR assets are of little value. But they are the livelihood of those who are the most deprived and have the least assets under private ownership. Besides, the economy, culture, social institutions, and political systems of communities like the tribal communities are based on the the CPR assets. As a result, their dispossession results in a total crisis in the life of tribal communities (Fernandes, Menon and Viegas 1988:233-244). They come face to face with the dominant society in a situation of crisis. The dominant society considers them inferior and wants them only as cheap labor. A sense of helplessness is the consequence of this unequal encounter (Reddy 1993:49–52).

The technology mix

We have stated above that even after losing their livelihood, very few displaced and project-affected persons are given a job in the project. Mechanization is the main reason for high investment and low employment generation in such projects. Other factors apart, one can question the advisability of mechanization and labor-saving devices in the labor-intensive economies of poor countries. This, too, has a consequence on their self-image. Their traditional techniques, like their culture and social life, are ignored while the assets they own get low compensation. Such an approach to their livelihood and their reduction to the status of cheap labor, mostly daily wage earners and, at times, bonded laborers, confirm them in their low self-image (Heredero 1985:99–102).

While mechanization is destructive of the marginalized in general, it is much more so of women. Even when only unskilled jobs were available, they were given mainly to men since in most cultures the man is deemed to be the breadwinner. When mechanization threatens the unskilled jobs of both men and women in one unit of the project, the man is often lured away with the offer of a permanent job elsewhere and the woman is forced to give up her job "voluntarily" in order to accompany her husband (Sen 1992:392–394).

Resettlement and self-image

Since most countries do not consider rehabilitation a right of displaced persons, its nature and extent depend on the power relations of the affected community. For example, during a mid-1992 visit to the Santa Catarina State, Brazil, I saw a well-worked-out resettlement colony that had been completed even before work on the dam began. The displaced persons had accepted resettlement after a long struggle. For many young couples among them it was an opportunity to gain the ownership of 20 hectares of land. Thus, they had adequate motivation to be resettled. According to one version, this scheme is based on recent changes in the resettlement policy in the Brazilian power sector (Fernandes Serra 1993:69–77), which is reinforced by the co-financing agency, the World Bank, and its insistence on rehabilitation. On close scrutiny, I realized that those resettled in this scheme were descendants of post–World War I Italian immigrants who could make their voice heard. The voiceless Amazonian indigenous populations have been displaced before without organized resettlement. In Chile, too, the indigenous populations threatened with displacement by the seven dams on the Bio-Bio River stated that they had not been told about any resettlement plan. A package seems to have been worked out recently (Downing 1997). In Mexico, there have been changes in the official policies (Guggenheim 1993). In the projects I visited there, powerful communities had been resettled with mitigation measures because they agitated against their displacement, and improved resettlement was one of the conditions for funding. But the Amerindians had until then been displaced without mitigatory rehabilitation.

These are but a few examples that show that in most countries, displaced persons are rehabilitated only when they struggle against the project, or for getting more benefits, or when international funding agencies insist on resettlement, or, exceptionally, when a socially conscious administrator works out a scheme. If one or more of these conditions do not exist, the weak among the displaced persons get little out of the schemes. For example, Maharashtra, a western India state, has had a rehabilitation act since 1976. Out of 220 dams implemented during the decade that followed, only 133 were brought under the act; 94,387 displaced families were eligible for land but only 28.5 percent of them were allotted land. Of these, 31.4 percent are nontribals and 15.18 percent are tribals who were deprived of their land. The landless were left out (Fernandez 1990:36).

Even when a socially conscious bureaucrat works out a scheme, adequate resettlement tends to be viewed as a welfare concern, not as a right of those who are paying the price of development. Thus, despite constitutional norms to the contrary, the poor are considered people without a right to a life with dignity. They can thus be forced into a new life without transition and without adequate preparation, and further confirmed in the self-perception of being communities incapable of looking after themselves.

This sense of powerlessness often forces them to seek out coping mechanisms. Drunkenness is the commonest form taken, and it is visible among men as well as women. We saw it even in the NALCO resettlement colony, which is a fairly successful example of rehabilitation (Fernandes and Raj 1992:150–151).

Forced displacement was a deliberate policy of the U.S. government with the Amerindians. The enormously high rates of depression, suicide, alcohol addiction, demoralization, and ill health, which continue today on many American Indian reservations in the United States and Canada, are stark reminders that we know all too well how severe the mental health effects of involuntary resettlement can be. These effects are likely to persist for generations (Good 1996:1505).

Dominant values, self-image, and women

Even among these communities, displacement without transition has a greater negative impact on women than on men. Women in most subaltern classes enjoy a higher status than their dominant counterparts do. The natural resources over which they had some control were the basis of this status. The project deprives them of these resources. As mentioned already, jobs are given almost exclusively to men. So women are reduced to being housewives dependent on the husband's single salary. Through interaction with outsiders in the project township, men from the subaltern classes absorb the dominant consumerist value system as a step toward upward social mobility. They spend much of their income on clothes, entertainment, and other trivia, leaving little for the housewife to run the household with. So even while earning more than in the past in financial terms, the real family income decreases. As a result, the family's nutritional standard deteriorates, as does women's status.

The internalization of the dominant value system also has greater consequences on women than on men. For example, we saw in our studies in Orissa that once women in the middle-size farmer-dominated Angul district were confirmed in their subordinate status, since only men got jobs, and tribal women in other districts were forced to take up low-paid daily-wage unskilled jobs in the mines, men as well as women slowly began to believe that the woman's natural place is the house, that they are not as intelligent as men, and that as such they should not aspire to any other employment (Fernandes and Raj 1992:153–155).

Transition and alternatives

We have identified the factors that deprive the displaced and project-affected persons of the motivation required to improve themselves. We shall now attempt to find alternatives to this situation. Studies and field experience point to the basic principle that the involvement of the poor in decisions that affect their lives and livelihoods is an essential step in building up their self-confidence and their empowerment. Such participation should not be limited to planning rehabilitation, as in most projects, but should begin at the stage of decisionmaking concerning the project. It has to continue in the task of identifying the displaced and project-affected persons, the assets to be taken over, and the criteria for compensation. Only such involvement can function as a healthy transition to recovery.

People's democratic rights

An important cause of a low self-image is the displaced persons' feelings of being denied the right to be human, since they are displaced without their consent. The solution would then be to recognize that a developmental process must be based on the rational choice of the people and must provide legal protection of their democratic right to participate in every step that affects their future. No other benefit makes sense without recognizing them as citizens with equal rights.

That means that prior informed consent is essential for a people-displacing project. This principle has many implications. If most displaced and project-affected persons are illiterate, they may not understand the detailed project. The solution is not to ignore them. Rather, the project authorities have an obligation to translate the details of a project in a language and manner that people understand and to prove, to their satisfaction, the importance of the public purpose for which it is being implemented. Only then can those affected be considered equal citizens with human rights. This is an essential step because knowledge is power that has to be shared with the people.

Compensation and replacement value

This involvement also implies that the assets acquired are recognized as their livelihood. In that case, replacement value, not market value, becomes the norm for compensation. It also means that those without an individual land ownership document, be they CPR dependents or service providers, must be compensated. The landless have to be compensated because in a village, land is not only a site, it is the prime means of production. As such, it supports the owner, his servants, the village artisans, the merchant who buys the produce, and a host of others. "When the cycle of agriculture is disturbed, all these activities are disrupted and the livelihood of all the landless endangered" (NCHSE 1986:ii).

Others add that since forced relocation is a traumatic experience, the trauma suffered has to be quantified and compensated. A motor vehicle accident victim is liable to be compensated not merely for the financial loss suffered, but also for pain and suffering. So financial compensation is the least the project owes to those who are forced to change their lifestyles.

Thus, compensation becomes a mode of replacing the assets, particularly of those who depend on land or forests for their livelihood. This requires the project authorities and funders to move away from a project- and money-centered approach toward providing a combination of productivity and social justice. The good of the people affected is as important as the productivity of the project. With this in mind, rehabilitation has to be turned into people's development (Cernea 1996:1522). This thinking should influence compensation and turn it into a mode of replacing livelihoods lost to projects. The quantum has to be such that it pays for the land the affected persons want to buy, or other modes of beginning a new life. Recognizing their assets as their livelihood, not merely as a marketable commodity, is an important step in revaluing their humanity and society. It can also be a basis for their recognition as part owners of the project.

Transition to a new economy and the right to rehabilitation

Such a new beginning is possible only if displaced and project-affected persons go through a transition before the changeover from an informal to a formal society. Among the steps required, we have mentioned literacy and technical training required for the project-affected persons to take up jobs in the new project. In order to be involved in the decision concerning the project and give their prior informed consent, the future displaced persons should be prepared to understand the project, without which they cannot be involved in the decision concerning it, and identify the displaced persons and project-affected persons, the assets to be acquired, or to fix the criteria for compensation. This transition is the responsibility of the project authorities. But, in most cases, the performance of the officials is judged according to the speed and cost with which they implement the project, not the development and rights of the displaced and project-affected persons. The officials will live up to the social demand for adequate resettlement only if the satisfaction of those displaced is made a prerequisite for project approval.

It is possible to attend to such transition because in most cases there is a time lag between the decision and implementation of the project. For example, the decisions on projects like Sardar Sarovar in Gujarat and NALCO in Orissa in India were made in the 1960s. They were implemented in the 1980s. During this 20-year period an effort could have been made to make all the displaced persons literate, impart to them job-oriented skills, and help them to deal with the psychological trauma of forced eviction. The time gap between decision and displacement continues to be long in many other projects being implemented today; for example, Mount Apo in the Philippines, Three Gorges in China, and James Bay in Canada. It is possible to prepare the displaced persons for the transition. It only requires an ideology of rehabilitation as people's development and political will.

An offshoot of such an ideology is recognition of rehabilitation as a right of the displaced and project-affected persons. We are referring here to rehabilitation, not resettlement alone, though often project authorities as well as researchers identify the two. Resettlement is a one-time event, while rehabilitation is a long process. It implies a change of entire lives in the economic, social, cultural, and psychological areas. It includes replacement of the CPRs and reconstruction of social systems as steps to help people get over their impoverishment and marginalization.

Self-confidence and struggle

The principle of people's involvement in the decision concerning the project, which is basic to this process, has not been recognized until now. But studies show that even partial transition to a new life can be supportive of the weak. For example, the displaced persons of NALCO in Orissa went through a six-month struggle demanding higher compensation and benefits like jobs in the project. Some arrangements were made to avoid their marginalization and enable them to share in some project benefits: their compensation was doubled, and they were promised relocation in a resettlement colony and a job per family. Moreover, they have been grouped and resettled according to their original village. Even the names of the old villages have been retained. This has helped them to rebuild some of the old social systems. In addition, an NGO trained some displaced persons for semi-skilled jobs. So not all of them were confined to the lowest rung on the job ladder, though most remained unskilled laborers. They were given permanent jobs, not temporary ones as happens in most packages of a job per displaced family. Only 82 percent of the families had been given a job each by March 1992, six years after displacement. However, the landless have been ignored. Thus, many conditions of total rehabilitation have not been met. But the partial success achieved through a struggle and the support received from an NGO have given the displaced persons a feeling of being a community with rights. Their self-confidence is seen, among other ways, in the fact that they have been demanding that they be shifted to the project township and not kept in the resettlement colony, because they are full-time employees of the project (Fernandes and Raj 1992:140–145).

Studies indicate that the legal victory won after a long struggle by the Australian Aborigines on land rights in the Mabo case improved their self-image; many of them perceived themselves as human communities with whom the whites had no choice but to negotiate (Eddy 1992:17–18). Though the Canadian Amerindians did not meet with similar success in their legal battle, the very fact of their coming together to demand their rights and the support they received from Amerindians and other friends in the rest of the continent gave them a feeling of a new humanity (Brunelli 1993:170–173).

Conclusion

We have studied in this chapter the causes and manifestations of marginalization, the nature of benefit sharing in development projects, and the obstacles to sharing. Based on this understanding we have searched for new approaches to rehabilitation. The examples given show that displaced persons need something more than economic support for resettlement. Their social systems have to be rebuilt. They need self-confidence that they cannot acquire if they are treated as people without rights. Even when a fairly good economic resettlement scheme exists, they need transition that builds up their self-confidence and skills required for the new situation to cope with the changes.

Past experience also shows that one cannot speak of either displacement or rehabilitation as a one-time event. They are two important parts in a long process that begins long before physical displacement and ends many years after resettlement. So for rehabilitation to be meaningful, one has to begin by questioning the very decisionmaking process about displacement. Otherwise, the future displaced persons are forced to depend on rumors spread by those who want to acquire their assets and capture the benefits that are their due. The insecurity that absence of information generates is an important premise in the process that results in marginalization.

New approaches have, therefore, to be found to rehabilitation. The main feature of an alternative in rehabilitation is that it ensures that the benefits reach the displaced and project-affected persons, that their right to total rehabilitation is recognized, and that they are helped to rebuild their self-image as human communities with a right to a life with dignity. It has material components such as jobs, a share in the ownership and product of the project and re-placement value for compensation.

While these steps are an integral part of this process, basic to them is an ideology of people's development and an understanding that the benefits are tools of a counter-process meant to help them to get over the negative consequences of the dehumanization set in motion by their displacement. The alternative should, therefore, begin with the decision concerning the project and continue through all its stages—like identification of the displaced persons and assets to be acquired, criteria for compensation, and transition to a new life. The goals must become the displacees' economic and social self-reliance and their psychological self-confidence.

PART SIX

Regaining food security
and overcoming health risks

Editors'　Resettlers and refugees alike experience a risk pat-
Note　tern of food insecurity and malnutrition that is closely
interwoven with their vulnerability to disease and
epidemics. Virtually all field studies report that these risks have
much more catastrophic results for refugees than for resettlers. *Even
before full economic reconstruction* the practical commandment is to
arrest by all possible preventive and quick-response measures the
sudden disruption in food supply and tragic increases in morbidity and mortality.

This section combines two perspectives on these complex issues that complement each other: a case rendition of the pursuit of
food security and self-sufficiency by a specific population, the
Vasava hill tribe, by Roxanne Hakim; and a general synthesis of
policy goals and strategy dilemmas in restoring food security health
and sanitation by Reginald Green.

Hakim perceptively chronicles the struggle against food insecurity by a particular human collectivity, resettled from a low-risk
forest context to a higher-risk market-oriented agricultural environment. The resettlers' odyssey "from corn to cotton" epitomizes
the multifaceted and diverse transitions that so many resettlers
have to accomplish, while the richness of Hakim's minute ethnographic depiction captures resettler life in its daily drama. Not only
the means for but also the meaning and parameters of food security change in the new environment. And it is not the meager gov-
ernment-provided compensation but the tenacious energy and
creative coping of the people themselves that hold the hope of
gradually making their hard life whole again.

Green's study comparatively discusses five subgroups of population, from "classic" refugees (international and domestic) to de-

mobilized ex-combatants and development displacees, including as well host residents affected by refugees. The author first emphasizes the intimate linkages between food security, health, nutrition, sanitation, and clean water supply. Against this background, he demonstrates how livelihood recovery is fraught with enormous collective and individual impediments. Institutional distortions, "much more muddle than madness" as Green describes them, compound the obstacles. He criticizes the "tunnel vision" that breaks the continuum between disaster relief and development, and counters this tunnel vision with a full arsenal of possible macro strategies and operational avenues for reaching reconstruction objectives in terms of food, water, and health standards.

Both studies also discuss the relationship between host communities and displacees as an important factor in reestablishment. Hakim documents how the high expenditures entailed by settlement agriculture compel the Vasavas into sharecropping and wage labor within the host community. However, Green focuses on host country macro-policy, attitude and treatment of refugees and displacees as crucial in empowering them to rebuild their livelihoods. The underlying idea of both chapters is that proper planning and genuine participation of the displacees themselves are essential for effectively countering food insecurity and related health and economic risks.

CHAPTER 10

From corn to cotton: changing indicators of food security among resettled Vasavas

Roxanne Hakim

The production of a crop not only satisfies physical needs, but also expresses power relations and social identities.

Persoon 1992

The Sardar Sarovar Dam Project on the Narmada River in Gujarat, India, and its irrigation canal network are estimated to cause the displacement of over 200,000 people, a good part of whom belong to scheduled tribe categories. A massive campaign against the project, both in India and abroad, focused largely on the problem of resettlement. The active involvement of nongovernmental organizations (NGOs), together with demands from the World Bank, resulted in the Gujarat Government's design of an improved resettlement package. On paper, this package is one of the most comprehensive to date, although its implementation has met with certain serious problems.

My research focuses on the resettlement experience of the residents of the hill village of Makhadkhada, situated on the banks of the river Narmada, in the Satpura hills, in Bharuch district of Gujarat. I spent 15 months during 1992 and 1993 in this submerged village, collecting baseline data in the form of ethnography for my doctoral thesis. The six hamlets of Makhadkhada, made up of members of the Vasava tribe, were resettled in five sites in the plains of the Vadodara district, Gujarat, just before the village's submergence in July 1994. I spent another year (1995-1996) with the villagers in the new site of Vadaj as part of my postdoctoral research fellowship with the Royal Anthropological Institute, London. Thus, unlike most writings on resettlement, which focus on the post-resettlement period (Scudder 1996:8), pre-resettlement data forms an important part of my study. My post-resettlement study, then, took place in the initial stages of resettlement. I hope to conduct similar studies over the next 10 years before any firm conclusions about the "success" or "failure" of resettlement can be made.

Cernea's (1997) risk and reconstruction model for resettling displaced populations must be considered as a major milestone in resettlement literature as it provides a framework within which resettlement costs can be assessed and addressed. In this chapter, I look at the issue of food insecurity which is one of the risks developed within the above framework. "Forced uprooting increases the risk that people will fall into chronic undernourishment...and food insecurity...[which] is both a symptom and result of inadequate resettlement" (Cernea 1997). My paper discuss the adjustments the Vasavas have had to make in terms of food production and consumption. After describing the two villages of Makhadkhada and Vadaj, I outline the changes in agricultural cultivation techniques required by the move from hills to plains and the resulting change in diet (caused by new crops and cash crops), and explore the community's apparent reluctance to switch to a more market-dependent economy. Interwoven are issues of taste preference, grain hierarchy, and food stigmas associated with the host communities; the impact on ritual and festival food; and the restructuring of social relations. My earlier work concluded that self-sufficiency is an important component of Vasava community self-identity, which distinguishes them from the plains populations (Hakim 1995, 1996a). The current research addresses the impact that decreased self-sufficiency has had on the identity of the resettled Vasavas in the initial years. This paper is not a summary of the "before-and-after" experience of resettlement concluding with a "success" or "failure" analysis of the policy, but rather an examination of the process of the community's adjustment with a strong ethnographic focus.[1] As I am writing this paper from the field, it also has a field-oriented and local focus. [2]

---

[1]   Pearce (1999:58) argues that before-after comparisons are inadequate for understanding resettlement.

[2]   Time restraint away from the field and limited access to academic material has reduced the scope of comparative data.

From Makhadkhada to Vadaj: the geographical move

The 600 or so Vasava Bhil tribals who inhabited the geographically isolated hill village of Makhadkhada were basically agriculturists who supplemented their agriculture with forest hunting and gathering. They were self-sufficient, eating only what they grew or gathered from the forest. Salt was bartered for *bhindi* (*Hibiscus sabdarifa*) seeds. Cash was raised from the sale of *asitra* (*Bauhinia racemosa*) and *timbru* (*Diopyros melanoxylon*) leaves gathered from the forest, string made from *bhindi* and *otari* (*Portulaca olearaceae*) fiber, and, very occasionally, the *tuver* (*Cajanus cajan*) crop. The Vasavas used cash primarily for buying clothes and tobacco during infrequent visits to market towns, and occasionally spent on "luxury goods" such as jewelry, watches, or flashlights. Makhadkhada had no electricity, and travel by foot was the best means of transport. A jeep road was only recently built to facilitate the transportation of houses to the new sites. There was no post office or shop nearby. A trip to the market town from Makhadkhada was a one- or two-day outing. Water was obtained from clean, flowing streams and often involved a strenuous climb. Land was plentiful and large bamboo and teak houses were scattered over the hills, each surrounded by a *vaddo* (garden) where corn was planted in the rains.

Vadaj, with a population of about 2,000 people, is approximately 90 kilometers from Makhadkhada, in the plains of south Gujarat. The two places support very different lifestyles. Land around Vadaj is much more densely populated than the Satpura hills where Makhadkhada is situated. While Makhadkhada (being interior) was almost exclusively Vasava, the host village is inhabited by people of several caste and tribal groups. Gujarati, the state language, must be spoken in Vadaj, as none of the host communities understand the hill Vasava's own language. Many Vasava women no longer wear their traditional hill dress, having adopted instead the Gujarati short blouse, long skirt, and sari, especially when they go into the host village or nearby town. These changes have been more rapid in Vadaj, being a small settlement close to the host village, than in larger resettlement sites such as Karnet where women still wear the traditional dress. Visits to the market town of Dabhoi (nine kilometers) are frequent, as Vadaj is connected by regular bus and meter-gauge train service. The host village has a few small shops selling essentials, though most people shop in Dabhoi. Electricity came to the new site in June 1996. Water is pumped by hand from a boring pump within the site itself. The teak and bamboo hill houses have been replaced by smaller tin sheds that lack good ventilation.[3] The houses are aligned in rows and placed closer together than in the hills.

A comparison of Vasava life in Makhadkhada and Vadaj reveals that change has already touched many areas of life. I expect the pace of change to increase in the next few years as the community gains confidence in their new surroundings and begins to experiment more and take greater risks with regard to agricultural methods.

Self-sufficiency — at what cost?

My fieldwork in Makhadkhada concluded that self-sufficiency in food production and consumption was an important part of Vasava self-identity (Hakim 1995,1996a). Over the years, hill Vasavas had learned to exploit their land and forest to enable food self-sufficiency and security. As with most poor communities, "filling one's stomach" was a primary concern. However, self-sufficiency itself was not the aim. The emphasis was on low-risk activities, which embodied itself in food self-sufficiency.

In Makhadkhada, it became obvious that the community's apprehensions about new land centered mainly on food production (Hakim 1996b).[4] Life in the new sites is not conducive to maintaining the high level of self-sufficiency possible in the isolated villages of the Satpura hills. An important factor requiring the restructuring of agricultural production patterns is the availability of land. In the hills, agricultural land was plentiful, and cultivation methods were not very labor-intensive. A family cultivated as many hill slopes as its labor could handle. Labor, and not land, was the limiting factor. Customary land rights were respected, and often families with less labor would "lend" land to a family with more labor to cultivate. Forest land was encroached upon as forest law rarely reached these

---

[3]   Although the resettlement policy provides for the transportation of houses to the new sites, bamboo is not available in the new sites (for repairs). Tin sheds are the temporary shelter given by the government. This material is incorporated onto the teak house skeleton. A base plinth (worth rupees 10,000) and replacement roof tiles are also provided through the resettlement package.

[4]   To some extent, the issues or risks surrounding food insecurity are social costs that are relatively measurable, making this an area where rigorous economic analysis could substantially contribute to an improved resettlement policy. See Cernea (1999) for a persuasive argument calling for increased collaboration between social scientists and economists.

hills. In the new sites, access to cultivable land is limited by legal land deeds: the resettlement policy gives every adult male five acres. Although plains land has a higher yield per acre than the hills, a household must maximize production in order to meet its basic nutritional needs. Land and not labor determines production, thus discouraging even small families from "lending" land to others. Land shortage demands very different planning from hills agriculture, where the cost of having a child is invariably less than the benefit because "more hands" are an asset rather than a liability (as in the plains). This change in land availability has disabled many institutions that were responsible for food security in the hills.

Land availability in the hills made it possible to grow a variety of crops. Besides adding to the variety in the diet, this is an important strategy for reducing risk and enhancing security: If some grains do not yield, there are others to fall back on. Although plains land has the potential to grow a wider variety of food and cash crops than the hills, access to limited land (and the need to maximize yield) means that a household has to prioritize the production of a few high-yielding crops, thus reducing the scope for self-sufficiency.

In addition to limited access to cultivable land, changes in methods of cultivation and choice of crops have also contributed to resettlement-related food insecurity. Land in the two areas lends itself to different techniques of cultivation. The black, water-retentive soil of the new sites (ideal for growing cotton) is very fertile, provided the right crops are grown with the right techniques. With hill cultivation, on the other hand, much more is left to nature and chance. In the plains, plowing, sowing, and weeding are best done when the soil has the right water content. In the hills, the sloped, stony ground allows agricultural activity to take place on a relatively loose time-bound schedule within the monsoon months, as excess rainfall never results in water logging. Because plains soil is water-retentive, agriculture must follow a strict time schedule, following the pattern of the monsoons, with optimum time for certain activities being highly restricted and often limited to just a few days. "The secret of plains farming in this area lies in correctly assessing when a particular activity needs to be done and being able to do it within that time span. Bad timing can lead to terrible losses" (Kantilal Seth, former headman of Karnet host village). This concept of disciplined, time-bound agriculture is alien to hill Vasavas and has resulted in less than optimum yields and increasing insecurity.

Satisfaction with hill cultivation makes the Vasavas reluctant to accept the increased effort demanded by plains agriculture, especially since it doesn't necessarily result in a proportionate yield increase. In the new sites, fields must be plowed and weeded several times, and most activities require extra effort. For example, it would take one woman six days to weed an acre of land in Vadaj (as roots sink deeper and cannot be pulled out by hand), while in the hills this task could easily be undertaken in a day. Whereas agricultural work in the hills was completed by January, leaving five months free for other activities, in the plains that work is spread throughout the year. Limited access to plains land means that the monsoon crop has to be supplemented by a winter crop (and sometimes a summer crop, too), thus increasing the duration of agricultural labor.

Maximizing production (in view of limited land availability) on black, water-retentive plains soil raises the question of which crops to grow. Among the Vasavas, risk, cost, and taste regulate the choice of grains for production. An important factor driving food security in the hills is that hill agriculture (based on subsistence crops) requires no cash input and minimal market exchange, if any. The need to maximize yield, along with new cash-based demands, means that cash cropping is inevitable in the new sites.[5] High-yielding cash crops involve high cash investment in the form of seeds, fertilizer, pesticide, irrigation, and labor, as well as a high level of risk. Their market prices fluctuate with changes in the economic and political climate of the country. A fall in price, crop failure, or destruction by pests results in tremendous losses (since investment is high), and Vasavas do not feel they have the cash to invest extensively in cash cropping, nor the security to absorb huge losses. Most families have invested over 15,000 rupees in their agricultural plots since coming to Vadaj, but none have earned back any significant portion of that cash expense through their land.[6]

Since food security among the Vasavas is based on lessened risk rather than high profit, subsistence farming is viewed as a more secure option to cash cropping. However, among host farmers, cash cropping[7] is preferred and *tuver* and white *jowar* (*Sorghum bicolor*) are the only two food crops grown (if at all). Some host farmers boast that an acre of banana plantation (cash crop) can yield up to

---

[5]   Colchester (1999) highlights an interesting point that cash cropping often lowers the status of women, especially in cases where women had access to their own fields prior to project impact.

[6]   Most of the cash investment has come from wood taken from the hills and sold for a good profit in the new land, as well as from earlier savings. Some families have also sold a cotton crop.

45,000 rupees, but even such huge profits haven't tempted many Vasavas to venture into cash cropping seriously. Vasavas plan their agriculture to ensure that their family's food consumption needs are met through subsistence crops to the maximum extent possible. Excess land is devoted to cotton, and currently about 50 percent of the resettled in Vadaj are growing cotton on some of their land.

A study of the impact of resettlement on production patterns reflects this attempt to balance subsistence (low risk and cost) and cash (high yield and price) crops in order to achieve food security. During the first 15 months following resettlement (May 1994), most families lived off the grain stocks they had brought with them from the hills. In fact, many families continue to supplement their new site produce with now dwindling hill grain stocks. The production pattern of the Vasavas in their first year of cultivation (1995-96) reflects a tendency to retain their original pattern of hill agriculture as much as possible. (However, average yields were far lower than in the hills, and, in most cases, the crop was consumed within three to four months.) As in the hills, corn was planted as the main monsoon crop, inter-cropped with *bhindi* and vegetables like *bhinda* (*Abelmoschus esculentus*), *papdi* (*Dolichos trilobus*), and *chowli* (*Vigna unguiculata*), and followed by *urad* (*Phaseolus mungo*) and *tuver*. *Bhadi* (*Panicum pilosum*), *bunti* (*Echinochloa crus*), *muu* (*Panicum pilosum*), and *kodri* (*Paspalum scrobiculatum*), which are important security grains in the hills (due to their long storage life), have not been experimented with at all. These grains are unknown to plains people and rank very low in the grain hierarchy (see below). However, new crops are quickly replacing the hill varieties that are not yielding well in the new land. White *jowar* has replaced corn as the community's main grain for the base of their meal; its popularity stems from its good yield in plains soil, coupled with such factors as low cost, risk, effort, and familiarity.[8] *Tuver* continues to be an important grain due to its good yields and high market price (if the need arises to sell some). Other grains, such as hybrid *jowar*, *chana* (gram), *gahun* (wheat), and *bajri* (*Pennisetum typhoides*) as well as vegetables like eggplant, tomato, and coriander are becoming increas-

---

[7] Cotton and castor seed are very popular, with sugarcane, banana, and vegetables like chilies and tomatoes increasing in acreage.

[8] They have been cultivating this crop since their introduction to their new sites, over five years ago. Being a winter crop in water-retentive soil, it needs no irrigation, nor much weeding. Its only expense is some fertilizer and threshing costs.

ingly popular, while corn and *urad* have decreased in importance due to low yields. These experiments are focused around subsistence food crops grown primarily for self-consumption and reflect the community's attempts to recover their earlier food security (based on lower risk), despite the breakdown of self-sufficiency.

Access to the forest, which was the Vasavas most important resource base, was also crucial to maintaining self-sufficiency and security in Makhadkhada. It influenced, in addition to production and consumption patterns, their religion, myths, social behavior and their understanding of such concepts as space, distance, and possession. The forest provided wood (teak) for houses, agricultural implements, and fuel; bamboo for walls, baskets, brooms, and so forth; grazing ground for cattle; game for hunting and fishing; and leaves, roots, flowers, and fruit for consumption and medicinal purposes. I documented over 90 varieties of edible forest produce during my stay there.

NGO and government workers have argued that the community's dependence on forest edibles is often exaggerated and that the actual meat, fish, or leaves consumed in a meal is calorically insignificant. Although this is often true, I have found that forest edibles have two very important functions for maintaining food security (through self-sufficiency). First, they provide a fallback during times of food shortage and crop failure. It is the security of knowing that the forest is there as an insurance against hunger that is so important for the Vasavas. Second, though forest edibles do not form the basis of many meals, they add flavor and variety to what is an otherwise monotonous diet. Thus, forest food is used even when alternative food is available. In addition, Vasavas spent hours fishing or hunting not only for the catch, but also the pleasure they got from the activity itself.

The new land has almost no forest area accessible to the community, and the loss of forest edibles has been a major cause of food insecurity following resettlement. Related to this issue is the loss of common property, a resettlement "risk" (Cernea 1997) that "is usually not compensated under government relocation schemes" (Mahapatra 1999:208).[9] Makhadkhada had a larger variety and quantity of edible leaves, flowers, and fruit than the new sites. Those available in the new sites are sparsely scattered and often in host

---

[9]   This is a classic area where a cost of resettlement is ignored due to the difficulty it may pose in classical economic cost-benefit analysis (see Cernea 1999 for a discussion of this issue).

farmer's fields.[10] Although the Vasavas had customary rights to cultivate their fields around Makhadkhada, the rest of the land was used collectively. All forest produce except the *mahuda* (*Madhuca indica* or *Bassia lactifolia*) tree was common property, and children freely collected what they wanted. Hunting for small game like squirrels, birds, mongoose, and rabbits continues in Vadaj, but the activity has lost much of its attraction, as it has to be done in secrecy, in the early hours of the morning, caused by fear of ridicule from host communities. Fishing and fish are sorely missed, as there are no rivers, and prices are prohibitively expensive on the market. The loss of access to forest produce has a significant impact on children, who spend much time in activities such as cattle grazing and hence derive a significant proportion of their nutrition from grasses, fruit, and other forest produce such as honey.[11]

The forest also provided income, especially to women who sold and used *cheekh* (tree gum), string made from *otari* and *bhindi*, and leaves of the *timbru* and *asitra* tree for rolling into *beedis*. *Khakhra* (*Butea monosperma*) seeds and *mahuda doolis* (seeds) collected in the forest were bartered for onions and rice. *Mahuda doolis* were also pressed into a delicious oil. In the new sites there is minimal income from forest produce. *Cheekh* is collected and sold by women and children, but it fetches a lower price and involves long hours scrambling among thorns. *Asitra* leaves are available is smaller quantities, and their collection is severely restricted by the hosts. Besides, the extended months of agricultural activity do not leave much free time even in summer, during which most forest-based activity can be carried out. Many of these needs have now to be fulfilled through market purchases, which increases the need for cash.

Cattle are regarded as indicators of wealth and security among hill Vasavas. Since grazing land was freely available in the hills, Vasavas aimed at increasing their stocks of cows, bulls, buffaloes, goats, and chickens. Bulls helped with agriculture while the rest were valued for milk and meat. Lack of common grazing ground

---

[10] However, the Vasavas can freely collect wild grasses that grow around the edges of the host's irrigated fields, since the latter do not consume these.

[11] Ramiah's (1996) study showed that children in displaced families are particularly victimized by food insecurity and that skewed intra-household distribution patterns meant that the ability to buy adequate food for a family did not ensure equal distribution of food among all household members (Ramiah as discussed in Mahapatra 1999:208).

and susceptibility to disease in the new sites has drastically reduced cattle stocks, further adding to resettlement-related insecurity.[12] Families that had more than 25 goats in the hills have just 2
or 3, if any, in Vadaj. The little uncultivated land that is available is
full of thorny scrub. Unlike in Makhadkhada, where cattle grazed
freely outside the monsoon months, agriculture in Vadaj is carried
out throughout the year. Free grazing is restricted and has to be
supplemented by stall feeding. Cash expenses are further increased,
as now goats and cocks needed for rituals, festivals, and guests
have to be bought at high prices.

In the hills, there were times when the grain stock of a household
may have been low and the forest could not meet all their consumption needs. That is, the food security (based on self-sufficiency) of a
household as a single unit broke down. Vasavas still avoided buying grain or borrowing money from a *deshi* (outsider).[13] At such
times, the community as a whole acted as insurance against the
individual's losses. The person in need borrowed grain, cash, or labor from another Vasava (normally from his hamlet, clan, or an af-
fine) which was repaid within the loose margins accepted by all. No
security or interest was needed, and no formal institution existed to
record the deal or punish the defaulter. However, if the borrower
failed to return help to the lender, then he would find it difficult to
get help in the future. The difference between inability to repay and
refusal to repay was recognized clearly, and it is the latter that reduced credit worthiness. Informal checks were effective, as life in
the hills demanded cooperation, and the support of kin and neighbors was highly valued. The rationality of this system (which still
operates among those Vasavas remaining in the hills) lies in the very
unpredictable conditions of hill agriculture that result in localized
disasters.

This is in contrast to Nayak's (1996) observation that undisplaced
kin did not continue to help the displacees from the Rengali Dam
Project, as the latter were unable to reciprocate the help due to their
impoverished status following relocation. The reason for this could
be the particular nature of Vasava lending and borrowing, where
the primary purpose is the assurance of the future help of the borrower rather than the actual repayment of the "loan." However,

---

[12]   The policy provides every adult male with a choice of two bulls or a
bullock cart as part of the resettlement package.
[13]   Here, *Deshi* refers to a person from the plains, but it is also a general
term used to refer to the less isolated world beyond the hills.

this positive scenario may be seen to be a short-term insurance net, as resettlement and the differing agricultural patterns in the hills and plains is eroding the ability of resettled Vasavas to work as effective support structures for their kin in the hills.[14]

Differences in crop yields among families reflect short-term gains or losses, and in the long run, the vagaries of nature ensure that all families have a similar series of setbacks, and so every family is more or less compensated directly or indirectly. An understanding of the universality of their vulnerability had resulted in the community developing a system whereby those currently at an advantage helped out those in trouble. Lending to someone created debt, valued in terms of the security it provided rather than the actual transaction. In this way, community solidarity enhanced food security, even when an individual household's self-sufficiency broke down.

The Vasava case highlights the need for a system of "risk insurance" or "insurance products" within the agricultural package (Downing 1998). New production patterns arising from resettlement have resulted in a diversification of production among the community, which, while in the hills, had almost homogenous production patterns. In the plains, human factors such as appropriate or inappropriate techniques, individual entrepreneurship, degree of inputs, access to capital, and building links with hosts and fellow Vasavas are factors that cause variations in both quantity and variety of production. Thus some farmers may do far better than others, even in the long run. This increasing heterogeneity in economic wealth means that the earlier system of reciprocal help would not work in the plains. Sharecropping (see next section) and land pressure means that "lending" new site land has a "cost": that of the produce that it would have yielded from sharecropping. The need for establishing debt and security within the community is not as important here, as new insurance institutions such as cash stocks, relationships outside the community, and knowledge of market trends have developed as alternatives to the old system, where isolation and high dependence on nature made it imperative to have community support. The resettled community can no longer effec-

---

[14]   The impact of kin separation goes beyond its immediate economic implicationsfor women, who, being less mobile in India, are more affected by the breakdown of village and social units (Colchester 1999, Hakim 1995, 1996b).

tively stand as insurance against individual losses, as its economy is now vulnerable to outside factors.

The above factors (land pressure, increasing cash inputs, loss of forest, nonacceptance of barter transactions in plains shops), along with the development of new wants, has decreased self-reliance by escalating the resettled community's need for cash. In the hills food self-sufficiency meant that cash was saved and spent on "luxury" goods such as clothes, jewelry, and tape recorders. The sudden access to cash from wood sales, along with exposure to new goods following resettlement has meant that many commodities are now viewed as "necessities," and lack the novelty and pleasure that marked their occasional purchases in the hills. "In the new sites we have to wear proper pant and shirt even when we go into the fields and so need more clothes." Accessibility to shops in nearby Dabhoi has exposed them to many wants. Besides agricultural expenses, money is spent on clothes, ornaments, and new prestige items like household appliances and bicycles.

Although food bought for cash was negligible in Makhadkhada, trips to town occasionally called for some food purchases like bananas, which had a novelty value. Buying grain (the daily food) from necessity was almost unknown before resettlement. Now it is accepted as a way of life for many of those relocated who have exhausted their grain stocks or whose new site yields are insufficient for their needs. Land pressure and loss of forest and cattle means that variety in diet has to be provided from bought foods. Although Vasavas love food and are proud of their large appetites, they are reluctant to change their diet. Items like tea, sweets made of ghee (refined butter), ice cream, and cold drinks, which are considered "treats" by most Gujaratis, do not rate high on the community's food preferences, though some young men and boys (who are quicker adapting to new foods) indulge in these because of the status and novelty attached to them. Taste is therefore an important factor that dictates what food to purchase. This, however, has to be regulated (and often sacrificed) with affordability. Most Vasavas choose to purchase wheat in large quantities, though they prefer the taste of corn, as it is sold at subsidized prices in government shops. The consumption of rice, oil, and spices has greatly increased in the new sites, especially for special occasions and for guests. The novelty attached to these foods in the hills is slowly decreasing as their consumption increases. Getting accustomed to *deshi* food and being familiar with the use of *deshi* objects (such as rigging up an electrical wire, riding a bicycle) has status value, as it reflects the extent to which the Vasavas have succeeded in merging into *deshi* life. These new demands means that self-sufficiency is slowly losing its appeal and being separated from food security, which is being given a new basis.

This increased need for cash, which is exaggerated by the loss of cash income through the forest, is met through cash cropping and agricultural labor (*majdoori*) available in the host communities' fields. Although there is much labor available in the hosts' fields, the rate is far lower (20 rupees per day) than what was offered by the forest department in the hills. Vasavas prefer to invest their labor in their own fields, but the increased need for cash (and the temptation of market goods) means that women and girls work as laborers when they have a respite from their own fields.

Many families of poorer host communities (like the Tadvis) in Vadaj, survive only on *majdoori*. In fact, some families told me that they had given up tilling land and now relied solely on labor. "It is less tension and responsibility. You wake up, work, buy your food, cook it, and sleep without any worry or major decisions to make." But to the Vasavas, nothing is worse than being landless, as this implies a total breakdown of the food security they try so hard to maintain. Money earned from *majdoori* has always been regarded as "extra, pocket money." However, those families with depleted grain stocks have had to work as labor to survive during the initial phase of resettlement.

The increased need for cash erodes food security by increasing dependence and vulnerability to outside factors and relationships. Although Vasavas realize that total self-sufficiency is no longer possible, their attempts to restore food security aim at reducing dependence on cash for subsistence. Resettlement policy, too, can help lessen the apprehension associated with the new production methods. However, as highlighted by Pearce, resettlement assistance is often limited to the time span necessary to complete the project's civil works components, with no account taken of the time needed to establish agricultural enterprises and stabilize the income restoration process" (Pearce 1999:116). I had suggested to the government and to the NGO ArchVahini that an agricultural training package would help to familiarize the resettlers with the new land and increase their confidence in decisionmaking. However, NGO workers are of the opinion that left on their own, the Vasavas would learn from the host communities, thereby creating friendly ties with them, though this has resulted in unnecessary low yields in the initial years, and has sometimes led to the host communities taking advantage of the Vasavas' ignorance when crop sharing with them.[15]

The resettlers' vulnerability to outsiders can be decreased by increasing self-reliance. For example, Vasavas in the Sitpur new site have overcome the problem of high irrigation costs (where water is bought from private tubewells at exorbitant rates) by building and maintaining their own tubewell with a government subsidy. However fields in Vadaj, which are scattered among host fields, are spread over too large an area to be covered by one tubewell. In the long run, irrigation costs will drastically decrease as canal waters from the project are made available to the new sites at nominal rates.

The community is increasingly accepting the impossibility of a permanent return to the hills and is exploring strategies aimed at reestablishing food security in new surroundings.

The impact of changing consumption patterns on social relations

The breakdown of self-sufficiency has created the need to restructure relationships between Vasavas, as well as to establish new relations between the resettled Vasavas and the host communities. Changes in agriculture have encouraged new economic relationships with host farmers. The community's unfamiliarity with plains agriculture, along with its preference for lower risk, makes sharecropping an attractive proposition and an important strategy toward reestablishing food security. In the hills, many Vasavas gave their new site land to host farmers to cultivate and accepted whatever part of the produce was given to them. The attraction of this system lay not in its profit (as the Vasavas were often cheated by the host sharecropper), but in its lower risk, and was acceptable as long as the Vasavas' basic needs were still being met by their land in the hills.

With resettlement, families have to get the most out of their five acres to survive. The above form of sharecropping (where the landholder gets one-third of the produce, and the tiller, who bears the cost of all inputs plus labor, gets two-thirds) is feasible only for those few families who have more land than their labor can handle. Another form of sharecropping (equal crop shares), where the tiller provides all the labor and the cash inputs are shared equally with

---

[15] I suggested that the hosts could be successfully incorporated in the training package as teachers.

the landowner, is more popular with land-owning Patels (a high-caste, wealthy host group) who have the cash capital to invest but will not get their hands dirty doing labor. A third form of share-cropping has become popular with resettled Vasavas, as it fulfills their need for cash support. Here, the Vasava tills his own land. Cash expenses such as irrigation, pesticide, fertilizer, and threshing are fully or partly paid for by a host farmer (usually a Patel who owns a tubewell and so cuts his irrigation expense) who is given about one-third of the produce.

The economic relationships that have developed between the Vasavas and their hosts add to food security, but rarely become social ones. With Tadvis and other groups that work for the Patels, social relationships are slowly beginning to form, though this is not so with richer farmers. In one situation where there was reciprocal labor between a Vasava and a host Tadvi household, the economic relationship encouraged a social one, too, as they often eat together in the fields and discuss matters outside the workplace. Though social visits by Tadvis to the new site are rare, the majority of contact continues to revolve around work; inter-dining is extremely rare, if it exists at all. These relationships, especially around the residential areas, are limited only to men. Vasava women are developing acquaintances with Tadvi women working in neighboring fields and at the water pump, but these remain superficial. Younger girls who occasionally work as wage labor in the Patel's fields are becoming more confident about mixing with Tadvi laborers. There is no contact or rapport with host women who do not work as agricultural labor.

Resettlement has also restructured social relationships among Vasavas. New sites differ in what their soil is suited to and enable heterogeneity in production. Hence, economic links with Vasavas in sites with different crops, and with families who continue to reside in the hills, increases food security by enhancing variety in production and the sharing of risk. With resettlement, in-laws have become important economic partners, adding a dimension to what was earlier primarily a social relationship. Since Vasava marriage alliances are usually made with families of another village or hamlet (following clan exogamy), in-laws become a valuable economic link. The initial years of resettlement found many families short of seed grain and food (because of unsuccessful plantings and depletion of grain stocks), and in-laws were instrumental in helping out.

The resettled community's link with its old land has been maintained and is instrumental in retaining some level of food security. The hills continue to be regarded as an insurance against poverty.

Many younger men who are not entitled to resettlement land have returned to cultivate land in the hills, as it assures them food and reduces cash expenses. Even for men cultivating their own land in Vadaj, having kin in the hills has definite advantages. It provides an escape into an environment they continue to miss and provides an opportunity to drink *mahuda*, *toddy* (sap of the palm tree — *Borassus flabellifer*) and eat hill food. More important, a home in the hills also gives access to forest produce: wood, edibles, *mahuda*, fish, leaves of *asitra* and *timbru* for rolling into *beedis*, bamboo for making brooms and baskets, and a place to keep cattle without a fodder problem. The above items, which are no longer accessible in the new sites, have gained a new value to the resettled Vasavas. Dried fish, *hegva* (*Moringa concanensis*), and *mukha* (*Schrebera swieteniodes*) leaves, dried mango, and other items brought back from the hills are eaten with great relish and regarded as a special meal. It is interesting that most of these forest goods would be very low on the host's food hierarchy, but within the resettled Vasava community, their importance has increased with resettlement, as they have gained renewed value as security foods.

Relations with in-laws in nearby new sites also enhance food security, especially if the two new sites grow different crops. For example, Vasavas in Vadaj who have in-laws in Karnet sharecrop rice (which gives high yields in Karnet). However, sharecropping between resettled Vasavas who grow a similar range of crops is not common, as limited land access means that one can rarely afford to share produce.

Agricultural labor among Vasavas (based on clan or territorial links) continues to be paid for in grain, and this cuts agricultural cash expenses and increases security by creating reciprocal bonds for help. Vasavas are quite willing to work for grain payment, as it gives access to a grain, which they normally would not have bought for cash. (Tight reserves of cash means that cash payment for labor, especially amongst family, is invariably a less lucrative deal than grain payment). Helping another Vasava to winnow *chana* gives the helper a share of the produce, which provides him with an alternative to *tuver*, which may be the only lentil his family produces (because of limited land holding). If he worked for cash, it is unlikely he would buy *chana*, but would go in for a cheaper grain. However, cash payment is valued (especially by young girls), as it buys clothes, jewelry, and other consumer goods.

Another imperative strategy to rebuild food security is the knowledge of market trends and the creation of support systems with other farmers. Market exchange has become inevitable with cash cropping and new cash demands. Vasavas are slowly beginning to learn about market fluctuations and regulate sales accordingly, although pressing cash demands and lack of storage facilities often result in distress sales. Here, too, special education through resettlement policy could help reduce food-related insecurity.

Grain hierarchy, food and drink stigmas, ritual and festival foods

Besides changes in actual production patterns, social institutions and behavior associated with food have had a strong influence on restructuring food-related behavior. Resettlement has further exposed the hill Vasavas to plains (*deshi*) communities who articulate their identity (and self-proclaimed superiority) against the Vasavas in terms of consumption patterns, with special reference to food. Host culture stigmas therefore have a strong influence on food production and consumption: Food cultivated, hunted, and bought for cash, ritual and festival foods, and manners associated with eating, thus have an impact on food-related insecurity.

Along with crop yield, cost, and risk, taste also determines production patterns. Food is often a factor that differentiates communities, and nowhere is this more explicitly evident than in Gujarat. The concept of "grain/food hierarchy" emerges from the belief that some communities consider themselves higher and purer than others due to the food they consume, thus giving some foods higher status. Higher castes like Patels and Rabaris (cattle herders) articulate their "purity" over lower castes largely in terms of the food they consume. The latter often achieve upward mobility by giving up "polluting" occupations and foods like meat, fish, eggs, and alcohol. In Gujarat, this is sometimes referred to as becoming a *bhagat*, the concept also assuming a simultaneous increased closeness to God. Food taboos are quite strictly observed between castes, though constitutionally, untouchability and caste-related stigmas are illegal.[16] Theoretically, tribes like the Vasavas do not fall into the caste structure, although in practice they are incorporated into its lower rungs.[17]

---

[16] Caste stigmas are less strictly observed by the educated younger generation.

[17] In Hakim (1996a), I have argued that the categories of *dungri* (hill) and *deshi* (plains) are more useful to understand the popular images traditionally associated with the tribe-caste divide.

The concept of "food or grain hierarchy" was an important factor regulating the relationship between the hill Vasavas and the *deshis* even before resettlement. Outsiders visiting Makhadkhada often said to me, "The most difficult part of living in the hills must be the food. These *dungris*[18] eat food without oil or spices. They apparently don't even drink tea nor have rice." Even in the new sites, the first question asked to me by host villagers was whether I cooked separately from the Vasavas.

The kinds of grains grown in the hills are either not consumed in the plains, or are of a superior, high-yielding variety. The black *jowar* of the hills has been substituted by the refined variety of white *jowar* (which has replaced corn as the resettled community's main crop). *Bunti, bhadi, muu,* and *kodri,* unknown in the plains, are dismissed as "coarse hill grains." The sour *bhindi* plant, which is so useful and important to the Vasavas, is not consumed by plainsmen (but is grown in the new sites), nor is most of the forest produce eaten by the community. New high-status crops such as wheat (and rice), which were previously absent from (or negligible in) the Vasava diet, are being experimented with by an increasing number of families. The higher the consumption of cash-bought foods in a household (because of depleted grain stocks), the higher the consumption of high-status foods like wheat and rice (and forest produce), as availability and subsidized prices take into account the food preferences of most of the host community.

In Gujarat, there are strong stigmas against eating meat and fish and drinking alcohol, all of which rank high in the Vasava food hierarchy. In the new sites, though the consumption of chicken and goat has become almost negligible (due to decreases in animal stock), the consumption of buffalo meat has increased, as it is cheaply available in Dabhoi. Hunting of birds, squirrel, rabbits, and monkeys continues in the new sites, but it has to be carried out secretly, as it can be used by hosts to justify their superior attitudes and their rationale that "the Vasavas can never improve their lot." In the hills, the Vasavas had no such inhibitions and openly hunted. Some "lower" host communities such as the Tadvis will sometime admit to eating chicken and goat meat, but any other meat, especially cow, is taboo. Before resettlement, Vasavas were aware of this stigma; men who were more traveled would rarely admit to eating beef, though others, especially women and children, did not consider the

---

[18]   Literally meaning "people of the hills," but its popular usage in the plains has derogatory connotations.

cow any more sacred than the buffalo or goat, and its consumption was not hidden. In the new sites the consumption of cow continues, but is done in the utmost secrecy. Although resettled Vasavas are not willing to completely accept a new value system (meat, fish, and alcohol continue to be served at special occasions), they acknowledge the importance of food stigmas in determining social position. Vasavas now avoid publicly eating foods that aren't readily consumed by the hosts. However, Vasavas resettled in the state of Maharashtra (those from submergence villages across the river from Makhadkhada) eat meat and even cow flesh openly. This is because the host villagers (Vasavas Pavras and Vasave, who have similar customs, dress, and language as Vasavas) do not have strong stigmas associating nonvegetarian food with low status.[19]

Vasavas are aware that much of this emphasis on being pure and vegetarian is a farce. In Makhadkhada, deshi truck drivers and forest officials, many of whom would normally look down upon the hill tribes for consuming meat and alcohol, themselves indulge in these "vices," in the isolation of the hills, away from the prying eyes of their families. In the new sites, too, many higher-caste men, like the Patels, do eat meat, though never in their own homes or in the presence of their women folk or community members who are vegetarian.[20] These Patels bring a goat, spices, oil, and alcohol into the fields (or to the new site) at night and have a party there. They often ask the Vasavas to kill and clean the animal for them and help cook it.

The influence of host food consumption patterns is clearly seen at public feasts like weddings. In the hills, wedding feasts consisted of corn bhadki (semi-crushed and boiled) with tuver dal (lentils), and for smaller crowds a goat was often killed. In hill villages where Vasavas lived with more Hindu communities like Tadvis, rice, being more prestigious, often replaced corn, as Tadvis look down on eating bhadki. In the new sites, everyone serves rice with tuver dal at public feasts. An increasing number of Vasavas are copying host Tadvis by adding eggplant, potatoes, and a sweet made of wheat, oil, and jaggery to the wedding feast. Food is generally cooked with oil and spices by a specially employed Tadvi bhagat, and everything (except tuver) is bought for cash, whereas in the hills there was no cash expense. At smaller functions (such as the giving of bride price),

---

[19]   A similar observation was made by Patnaik (1996) in his study on the Paraja displaced by the Upper Kolab Project.

[20]   It is very rare to find a Patel women eating meat or drinking alcohol.

goat is still served with rice, as there are rarely any non-Vasavas present.

Unlike changes in production patterns, which adjust to external factors (for example, soil type), the community has greater control over ritual change. There has not been much change in the content of ritual since resettlement. Objects and foods used as offerings, which are important status markers, are only just beginning to show signs of future change. Cocks, hens, chicks, and goats continue to be offered, but as these now have to be bought, many Vasavas have postponed the fulfillment of larger *mantas* (rituals). *Bhuas* and *badvos* (medicine men, witch identifiers, and priests) are taking this expense into account and often reducing the amount of sacrifice needed. Coconuts and incense have increased in importance as offerings, as have rice and *jowar*, which are replacing *bunti*, an important ritual grain in Makhadkhada.

Alcohol remains an important part of any ritual or festival, and is always offered to guests. Drinking is a social activity enjoyed by all Vasavas (regardless of age and gender), and drunkenness sometimes results in violence and witchcraft accusations, especially at large gatherings. In the hills, alcohol was distilled from the *mahuda* flowers which were gathered in April and dried for use through the year. *Mahuda* alcohol remains a popular and accepted method of payment for kin labor, as well as for wedding gifts. It is a necessary part of a wedding proposal and other negotiations, such as bride price, and a vehicle through which relationships are established and strengthened. (For example, some alcohol, referred to as *pat*, is annually given by a man to his wife's family, in acknowledgement of her value.)

The new land has very few *mahuda* trees, and Vasavas have no access to the flowers of even those trees not on private land. Resettled Vasavas now distil alcohol from *jaggery* (*gul*) purchased in Dabhoi, though they prefer *mahuda*, which is purer and believed to have medicinal properties. As Gujarat is a dry state, there is much profit in alcohol sales, and though drinking continues to be a social activity within the community, many households have turned it into a lucrative business. Thus distilling alcohol becomes only a means to an end: the cash profit. Its distillation (in the privacy of the house) lacks the ambience that accompanied the process by a shady stream in the Satpura hills, where the product was shared freely with all those around. Since alcohol now involves a cash investment, accounts are kept of exchanges even among kin, and payment is made at the regular cash rate or with an equal amount of alcohol. Whereas in the hills drinking was limited by *mahuda* stocks, and its distillation was organized around work patterns, in Vadaj, alcohol is always available for cash, and so the incidence of drunkenness has increased.

Alcohol carries less of a social stigma than does the consumption of meat (especially among poorer host communities). Tadvis and migrant labor form the bulk of the Vasavas' clientele for alcohol. Some drink openly, while others consume the alcohol in the resettlement site rather than taking it home. Moreover, being creditors in alcohol exchanges, the Vasavas gain some power, which compensates for the occasional rude remark made by higher castes about their "sinful fondness for vices like alcohol."

In addition to their influence on actual food consumption, host stigmas also regulate behavior associated with eating. Though Vasavas are proud of their healthy appetites, in the presence of *deshis* they consciously avoid eating a lot. Timings of meals differ, and Vasavas try to delay their meal, which was normally consumed by 9 or 10 in the morning, since the hosts break work from noon to 2 p.m. for their meal. Vasava girls try to hide the morning meal, which they carry to the fields, to avoid comments by some hosts, and many now return home to eat it. Food for large feasts is no longer served on *khakhra* leaves (as in the hills), nor does each guest bring his or her own bowl. At the new site, wedding food is served on *bhajis* (plates made from dried leaves sown together) which are bought for cash, adding again to wedding costs and emphasizing the "superiority of *deshi* food habits."

Resettled Vasavas appear to be conditioning many of their practices to fit in with the customs of the hosts. However, this is not the result of an overwhelming sense of inferiority as much as the belief that one must accept the ways of the *deshi* to happily coexist, along with a desire not to stand out. They realize that much of the fuss over eating habits is based on double standards. "If the Patels think we are so uncivilized in our eating habits, then why do they drink our alcohol. Often they won't drink our water, and go directly to the pump to drink it, but they see no objection to drinking alcohol from our glasses, when they are too embarrassed to take it home."

Conclusion: food security, self-sufficiency, and Vasava identity

Vasava self-identity in the hills was based on self-sufficiency in food production and consumption, which was the basis of a secure lifestyle and served to distinguish hill Vasavas from plains farming communities. This relationship between food and identity explains the community's apprehension toward resettlement-linked changes in food production patterns that would increase their dependency on other communities and on market exchanges. However, *deshi* clothes and ritual were never viewed as a direct threat to community identity and were readily adopted even in the hills (Hakim 1996).

While the Vasavas articulated their self-identity with regard to the other (that is, *deshi*) in terms of self-sufficiency in food, *deshi* communities articulated their identity as separate from the Vasavas in terms of consumption and religion. Plains communities openly stated that they were superior to the "backward, hill Vasavas who indulged in drinking alcohol, hunting animals and birds, worshipping stones, and leading uncivilized lives." In the opinion of most *deshi* villagers and many government workers, resettlement provided a "great opportunity to the backward *dungri* to lead a more developed and civilized life in the plains of Gujarat."

Self-sufficiency in the new sites is impossible and inefficient — and therefore undesirable — because of land scarcity, changing production patterns, loss of forest and barter transactions, and greater cash-based wants. The community's reluctance to abandon earlier levels of self-sufficiency is not expressed in terms of insecurity stemming from lost identity, even though it was an important criterion of community identity with regard to the other. It is, rather, fear of the risk associated with a market-dependent system of production that results in insecurity, and not simply the breakdown of self-sufficiency. Rather than self-sufficiency itself, it is the security, familiarity, and lower risk (that embodies itself in self-sufficiency) associated with hill production that is valued.

Resettlement has shown that the new land can enable a comfortable lifestyle, provided the correct inputs are developed. "The new land is good, but the question is whether we can get the best out of it. It needs money for agricultural inputs, for it yields as much as one puts into it. The hosts are right about that. We do not have the security to invest in it properly." Many years of experience ensured that the Vasavas were getting the most out of their land and forest in the Satpura hills. One cannot expect the same in just two years of resettlement. The resettlers have to develop the skills, material resources, and the confidence (based on experience and familiarity) to apply these resourcefully. Agricultural loans and training would definitely help toward increasing productivity and confidence.

Goody and Goody (1995) maintain that food practices are not "permanently embedded in culture." Vasava dietary changes arising from resettlement can be attributed to three processes mentioned by them. First the "advent of new crops...and larger yield," second "hierarchical emulation," evident in the concept of "grain hierarchy" discussed above, and, third, the situation where a "minority adopts most of the practices of the majority by a process of accommodation or incorporation." The authors claim that if such "culinary incorporation is to be avoided, then specific strategies have to be adopted" (Goody and Goody 1995:2).

The initial years of resettlement have shown that although self-sufficiency decreased, it has not resulted in total impoverishment, either materially or nonmaterially.[21] The community has shown exceptional ability to adapt to new ways, and the young make huge efforts to merge into *deshi* life. Clothes and language are important indicators of this effort. Agricultural production patterns also appear optimistic. Although these initial years haven't yielded bumper crops, there is evidence that Vasavas, through trial and error, are changing their production patterns to find a balance between yield efficiency and personal preferences (for example, subsistence farming through food crops). Thus, while corn remains an important crop, its importance has decreased; some are experimenting with different cultivation timing and techniques to improve *urad* yields; and more attention is being paid to the cultivation of cotton in terms of technique and quality of inputs. Limited access to land, the large size of families, and high risk and cost factors discourage total cash cropping, and subsistence agriculture continues to be the main occupation.

However, total subsistence farming in the new sites becomes less viable in the long run. Food crops will not yield without cash inputs, and the yields are not good enough for substantial sales. Some source of cash income has to be found to redress this imbalance and finance new cash-based wants. Cash cropping is preferable to *majdoori*, which is the only other alternative in the absence of forest-based income. In the long run, efficient cash cropping along with subsistence farming appears to be the best strategy.

The change in production patterns following resettlement means that food self-sufficiency will no longer serve to differentiate Vasavas from other plains communities. Food security in the plains cannot viably be associated with self-sufficient farming as it was in the hills. Food security however, is still associated with low-risk farming, as against quick gain, high-risk strategies. Once the resettled Vasavas find their balance between cash cropping and subsistence farming suited to land and family size, and increase confidence in market

---

21   For example, resettled Vasava girls are quickly learning wedding songs sung by the host communities in the state language.

exchanges, it is likely that food security will be reestablished. As they become more familiar with their physical environment, they will also be better able to exploit its edible resources. This, along with sharecropping, knowledge of market trends, *majdoori* (which gives them access to immediate cash), and kin ties in the hills (which remains an insurance during times of need) will somewhat replace the insurance that the forest earlier provided.

Food self-sufficiency now serves as a criterion to differentiate re-settled Vasavas from their kin left in the hills. The Vasavas appear keen to merge into *deshi* culture—their fast adoption of language, dress, and rituals like weddings bearing testimony. To this extent, their emphasis on consumption and ritual as indication of their self-identity is increasing. At this early stage of resettlement, it is not clear whether new criteria will emerge to differentiate resettled Vasavas from their plains brethren as the differences in production patterns continue to diminish. Before, the uniqueness of a self-sufficient food production system based on low risk and cost provided food security to hill Vasavas. With resettlement, the emphasis on low risk embodies itself in production patterns adjusted to somewhat resemble host communities.

In these two years of resettlement, the Vasavas have not regained their earlier level of food security. However, current changes in agricultural patterns show that the community is slowly moving toward greater food security. This pace will accelerate now that they have accepted the impossibility of returning to the hills and as their confidence in decisionmaking increases with every year of experience accumulated. In view of the new circumstances, new resources available, and new needs, food security based on self-sufficiency would not be viable.

CHAPTER 11

Food security in refuge and return: some aspects of entitlements, markets, and modalities

Reginald Herbold Green

Development is about human beings. They need four things. First is water. It is the first thing needed to live. Without it a plant, an animal, or a baby dies. Second is food. Without enough of it, life is miserable and short. Third, once water and food are won, is health — otherwise the human being becomes sick. Fourth is education, once a human being has water, food, and health he needs to learn to open new horizons and unlock new possibilities. And there is a fifth — peace and order. Without those none of the four basic needs can be sustained.

Somali Elder,
Baidoa, 1995

Displaced, disempowered, distressed: food insecurity in crises

Food security and displaced persons is a more complex topic than it appears. Its aspects are rarely covered comprehensively with respect to all of the groups distressed by war (sometimes prettified into "complex political emergencies") or natural catastrophes (usually drought). Five main groups can be identified: *international refugees*

253

from catastrophes (man-made) and life-threatening calamities (natural); *domestic displacees,* who differ from the first group by not having crossed an international frontier and who, as a result, receive much less average international support and attention; *demobilisees,* or ex-combatants, basically analogous to the second cluster and rather less similar to other structural adjustment redeployees into livelihood insecurity (or absence); *refugee-impacted residents* in areas swept over and into by very large numbers of refugees (or, in principle, displacees); *development displacees,*or households turfed-out to make way for projects ranging from dams and game parks through concessions and plantations to urban "renewal" (or "tidying up").

Not only are these five groups rarely considered or analyzed together, action for and with them is usually uncoordinated. Academic work in most cases concentrates on one or two groups, as does most applied research. The same is true of social and political conceptualization and of government and international programming. In addition, the interpenetration of household economic (including food) security, moral economy considerations, and macroeconomic recovery and renewed development (food, gross domestic product [GDP], fiscal and export) analysis and action is usually vestigial or absent. In the case of refugees, short-term survival dominates and economic strategies are usually notable by their absence.

Reintegration into society, and the rehabilitation of livelihood for ex-combatants, is often a low-priority aspect of demobilization, totally walled off from other social and economic thrusts and refugee-impacted community and household programming (especially at long-term household, zonal, and macro levels). Project displacees (like drought displacees) are created in non-war or postwar contexts but these displacements are particularly likely to lead to household food insecurity and to dangerous levels of sociopolitical discontent.

In this chapter, refugees and displaced persons from both calamities and catastrophes are considered together and as central to overall displacement. The centrality turns on their greater numbers. *Demobilisees,* refugee-impacted hosts, and development displacees are the subjects of separate sections. Food security (over time and by source) is linked to other necessities, to participation and governance, and to gender in place of refuge, during and after return.

Return and return home are used in preference to resettlement unless that form of social engineering, characterized by outside planned and imposed new settlements, is dominant, as it often is in the case of development displacees and less generally for demobilized persons and wartime rural displacees resettled in new plot and village security-provided areas. The practice is also common in some countries in respect to ex-combatants, but tends to be suspect from its historic use to hold down newly conquered areas (for example, by the Ethiopian New Empire from Tewedros and Menelik through Mengistu). Most internally displaced and international refugees do wish—quite literally—to return home. Even of those who do not (perhaps 20 percent), self-selected new areas, whether as households or mini-communities, are preferred by most to government- or donor-picked and -designed new settlements (not least because the latter raise negative memories of "secure villages," among the tactics of coercive control and/or proven to be very insecure indeed).

Of necessity, the analysis is at a relatively general level but seeks to stress the critical nature of contexts in strategic design and articulation as well as in refuge and return food security and livelihood empowerment and support. To suppose that the political realities of participation in Rwanda refugee camps resemble those in former Namibian camps would be the beginning (and rather more than the beginning) of unwisdom. So too, that the mechanics of return for Rwandan Hutu refugees under *Interahamwe* (genocide provider) control to present Tutsi-governed Rwanda can usefully resemble those of return of Mozambican refugees to Mozambique in a context in which Maputo wished to be a "government of all the people" and almost all Mozambicans were unwilling to fight again.

In describing institutions, policies, and known dynamics, there is a danger of overlooking four facts. First, 80 percent to 90 percent of return is usually household or community self-help (whether of refugees or of displaced persons). Second, a significant number of refugees are living in communities with family and broader kinship ties and are not recorded. Third, cross-flows into and out of refuge frequently characterize war situations, as rural security (especially for food production) ebbs and flows differentially by area, with wide swings around any trend and indeed often with no discernible trend until well after the event. And last, household livelihoods in camps are frequently substantially more complex than just receiving food and other items; sometimes, as a result, implying that commerce with host areas is near-ubiquitous and often significant.

Parametric concerns: life, livelihood, governance, and sustainability

Food security for refugees and returnees is not a simple dichotomy of physical provision of rations in refuge and of growing for household provisioning upon return; nor does a schematization of survival in place of refuge and development upon return home and upon resettlement clarify as much as it obscures.

Staying alive is the first priority of food security as perceived by households and, at least verbally, by governments, international organizations, and aid agencies. That is correct, for those dead (because of famine, lack of water, exhaustion, sickness, or other aspects of war and flight) there can be no temporal future in refuge, no resettlement, no return home.

Rebuilding livelihoods follows once survival is ensured. But there is no reason to determine the initial time for this as necessarily the moment of return. Indeed, to do so is likely to impede the process of return and of livelihood rehabilitation.

Physical availability is the first condition for food security. It is likely to be crucial in places of refuge (initially for logistical and thereafter for financial reasons). However, it may be equally problematic during the early stages of return unless a "refugee friendly" mode of return is adopted—not unless a detailed arrival area food safety net (or "wages fund'"') is in place.

Entitlement with respect to rations means meeting external registration or estimation criteria to "prove" existence and, sometimes, sociopolitical acceptability to internal refugee governance groups. Thereafter—in refuge as in return—it also relates to growing crops and collecting fuel for household self-provisioning or for sale, to food for work and to work for wages for food programs. In practice, these interact with ration and other goods entitlements because the inevitable partial mismatch of those with needs and preferences inevitably (and usually desirably) leads to two-way trade, including food and often labor, with neighboring communities.

The distinction in refuge and during or after return (or resettlement) is not unreal even if it is a very broad-brush categorization. A camp, or even a less formal set of arrangements, is not perceived as permanent. Even with the best will by all involved (including hosts) and adequate resources, neither of which can be assumed, a place of refuge affords limited opportunities for sustainable livelihood, food production, and rebuilding of self-organization, participation, and governance. "Help them grow food not hate and build new lives not plots" is sound advice, especially when resettlement, not return, is the plausible long-term (a decade or more) prospective. But in camps it has distinct limitations—as seen in the United Nations High Commissioner for Refugees and postrefugee status phases of the 1959–1960 Rwandais Tutsi community in Tanzania, which necessarily involved "villagization," plus social, economic, and legal (citizenship) integration, a solution very few sub-Saharan African countries have been willing to envisage on a large scale and as a formal process. Within return, the during phase has elements rather more analogous to "in-refuge" than to postreturn (when crops are harvested, homes rebuilt, and some services and local infrastructure restored).

Knowledge, logistics, and procurement: security of food supply

Providing food security for displacees, including both calamity- and catastrophe-impacted households, requires knowledge of who is, or is about to become, food-deprived, where they will move, and whether the move caused the food security loss or vice versa. To know how much food to procure, where to move it, and by when requires that knowledge.

From this fact flows the importance of early-warning systems providing analysis—from meteorological and ground-level crop, household food supply, social and (in catastrophe cases) political data—on probable food shortfalls, possible uses of home village distribution to avert displacement (the optimal drought solution if water is accessible at home), and probable displacement locations. In this area, substantial experience has been built up nationally throughout sub-Saharan Africa and also regionally in the case of the Southern African Development Coordination Conference's (SADCC) Food Security Unit, which centralizes, analyses, reports on, and mobilizes response to national system results.

Early-warning systems are most effective in a context of accessible, physical, national food stocks (whether state- or enterprise-held) and of funding to handle emergency distribution and commercial imports until external finance, procurement, and shipment can, if necessary, be mobilized, because the process rarely takes less than 10 months from initial early-warning reports to the arrival of external food to outlying impacted household cooking pots.

In fact, the problem today is not so much that early-warning systems do not warn but that they are often not responded to adequately or in a timely way. One reason is clear. To be adequate in providing response time a system must flash at least an amber light so early that late or erratic rainfall and temperature patterns can reduce a wipeout to a lean year (or even an average harvest), as happened in parts of central and northern Mozambique and southern and northern Tanzania in 1992. To react early risks wasting resources. To react somewhat late (forcing shortcutting on procurement and in extreme cases airlifting) also wastes some resources. To react late (when disaster is ensured or even visible in food intake) guarantees wasting lives. If losing $200,000 is a lesser loss than 1,000 tons of delivered maize (which could be put into a rolling, quick-response reserve) and still less serious than a loss of 10,000 lives, early response is prudent. Given the macroeconomic costs of dislocation and death, even hardheaded macroeconomists might logically accept this ranking.

Linked to hesitancy to cry "drought disaster" until it is too late is the absence of early-response mechanisms that could take initial steps on amber lights, which would save time, money, and lives if the lights went red, but cost little if they stayed mild amber or reverted to green. In these contexts, planning plus mobilizing pledges, working out tentative procurement and logistics, speeding up noncrisis, "in pipeline" flows can be carried out at relatively limited cost. If initial shipments need to be set in motion before certainty of need exists, these can either be put into rolling reserves for early (or isolated drought pocket) use or be absorbed by slowing down normal pipeline flows.

In addition, such coordination structures might reduce the agency and donor suspicion (not always wrong) of data that forces multiple rechecks and delays action.

Catastrophe early warning is inherently problematic but not quite so problematic as it might appear at first glance. How many Rwanda refugees there would be in 1994 was not clear until they came. That there would be very large numbers to Tanzania, Burundi, and Zaire, however, was certain two to four weeks earlier, when the assassination of Rwanda's president returning from potentially successful (so his assassins feared) peace talks led both to genocide by extremist Hutu leaders and to an unstoppable advance by the Tutsi's Rwanda Patriotic Front (RPF), which had initially invaded in 1990 and could clearly defeat the then Rwanda official army. While Rwanda gave more of an early warning than most new catastrophes do, ongoing ones do afford time to plan how to respond to likely or potential new flows. Insight and process, not information, time, or even funding, appear to be the main gaps.

Logistics differ significantly between calamity and catastrophe cases, as well as within both. One factor is the location of the displaced persons—is it peripheral and at the end of weak transport links, or more readily accessible? Catastrophe victims, on the whole, are in more inaccessible areas, although those who have fled to the environs of secure towns (as on the Mozambique coast) may be exceptions. Another factor is the security of handling and transport against pilferage (or worse) in ports and en route, and, in catastrophe cases, against the violence that caused the displacement, since food relief convoys are only occasionally accepted to be "zones of peace." In such cases the delivery exercise bears a distinct resemblance to trying to carry water in a liter tin with the bottom rusted out. Only either a broader food and entitlement supply system, or food ration payments to all the low-income workers in the food aid logistical chain, can reduce losses to single-digit levels.

There is also the question of availability of transport (public or private) in both cost and physical terms. Procuring vehicles is likely to take longer than procuring grain, and setting up new operating units longer than either. There may be preexisting capacity and experience with respect to response to calamities and catastrophes in the past, including communication and liaison networks; vehicles; physical and financial stocks; and coordination links among governments, the domestic social sector, NGOs, and donors.

The warning time determines how well prepared — or how Jerry built (or West African lash-up job) — logistics can be. Dearth following drought should have six to nine months' warning. The mass movements of refugees from war rarely do, and keeping capacity at hand for all potential areas of sudden flow is impracticable. The availability of stocks (public or private) and pipelines (commercial or aid) to be used until resource and food mobilization (national, NGO, donor, or mixed) can replace them is crucial to having food in the hands of hungry displaced people. Even commercial orders for landlocked African countries (such as Botswana) often require six months from global-market-order-placing to arrival in country and even longer to users, especially if up-country distribution systems are insecure. Politics play a major role in logistics for military and control as well as ideological reasons.

The last point requires expansion because there is a myth that food aid can be apolitical and that logistics are purely technical. Humanitarian concern, desire to avert unrest, treating famine as a matter of national dishonor, and averting it as a strategic priority (or an element in baseline good housekeeping) are political. The fatalism in the face of famine, and low priority to averting or even mitigating it, which characterized the New Empire in Ethiopia; the cynical appearance of concern to raise external resources and facilitate population movement to drain rebel areas by the Last Emperor (Comrade Ras Mengistu); the firm declaration that averting famine is a matter of national honor backed by priority allocations of personnel, attention, and resources by the present government are equally political, even if one's normative judgements on the three political stances may be very different.

In time of war, access to food (for troops and key supporters) is one of the sinews of war. Therefore the logistics of who gets food — and where and how — are not purely technical. The political and public relations concerns of "starve them out" versus "let all civilians eat" — qualified in the latter case by the fact that feeding civilians but not troops is not practicable, whatever the stated conditions — are real and have logistical implications.

Governments prefer national channels, sometimes including domestic social sector institutions (as in Tanzania, Namibia, and — in a sharp switch since 1988 — Mozambique) and local government (pre-1982 Mozambique with subsequent partial recentralization more donor- than government-driven). Large-scale external food security supply (beyond funding or delivery to ports) is only welcomed *faute de mieux*, when the *mieux* is mass starvation, and not always then (even, for example, in the Sudan). Part of the reasoning does relate to economies of coordination, coherent strategy, and scale. Part may be, depending on the government, a genuine assertion of accountability to citizens, including beneficiaries. But part is the flip side of the external actors' control "coin." One answer lies in whether a Mozambican church or World Vision is, at present, more technically able to handle food logistics. Whether the former is inherently accountable to Mozambicans (and the state) and the latter is inherently unwilling (or, in terms of its own goals, unable) to be so brings different answers. In a sense, the latter is logistical, too, but only in terms of internalized country logistical capacity development and the political logistics of state leadership and user accountability, not in terms of short-term delivery efficiency.

Procurement: enabling, eating, and warning

The first priority of procurement is to have enough food in time. That is especially important — and hard to achieve — in the first weeks of displacement and camp arrival and in subsequent mass inflow periods. New arrivals are often (not always, for example, Rwanda's in Tanzania) debilitated by the events forcing flight and by transit. Without adequate basic food, medical attention and drugs, and supplementary feeding, many will die of the ferocious interaction of stress debilitation, disease, and dearth.

What that priority implies is contextual. It might be local purchases, if cash and a food surplus are available. It might be regional if a nearby state with large stocks, easy logistics, and export experience exists (such as South Africa and, to a degree, Zimbabwe). But usually it means donor-funded northern grain (perhaps supplemented by beans, canned fish, sugar, UNIMIX, and milk powder), provided largely via the World Food Programme (WFP).

The role of WFP as global grocers to those greatly at risk is an important one. Combined with their global presence and generally close liaison with and response to national early-warning systems and coordination mechanisms is, in most cases, a real, palpable commitment to saving and improving lives of real people, by no means evident in all technical assistance personnel or all international agencies. This combination tends to propel the organization into ubiquitous presence at displacement disasters (whether refugee or internal), either as main procurer or logistician or in a supportive role as one of a clutter of channels.

Following the initial phase, procurement shifts—fragments in many cases—and has, but rarely uses, more options to link short-term feeding to displaced person, host, and regional food security. The standard pattern is to increase the number of procurement and distribution channels and erode both the coordinating role of the state and its ability to relate food aid to broader strategic macroeconomic issues, including food security. The first—usually justified on the grounds of limited host capacity, but having the result of further eroding that capacity—leads to the second.

Multiple sources are not a bad thing per se, especially if this means multiple funding mediums allowing domestic and regional procurement and payment for labor in cash to buy as well as in food to eat. Nor are multiple distribution channels necessarily inappropriate, even though small parallel ones (for example, external NGOs) are probably better focused on feeding into domestic social-sector organizations and into programs focusing on capacity building, empowerment, and rehabilitation, not emergency survival support to displacees.

The problems of multiplicity are, rather, first, the loss of overall strategic and coordinating focus for displacees logically based in the host state with an external supporter liaison link (probably optimally co-serviced and co-led by WFP). Second, there is an increase in cost, loss of economies of scale, and the use of high-cost expatriates on routine in-country logistical and distribution operations. Third, there is a failure to empower (or reempower) government, the domestic commercial sector, the domestic social sector, local producers, or the displacees themselves. The fourth problem is the consequential creation of a permanent crisis context with unnecessary deepening of dependence and very little built-in incentive, or time and communications, to move on from keeping alive to making whole again.

These problems do not relate solely to displacees and camps. However, regional trade and linked reserves, national commercial and surplus-area production-strengthening, and national plus domestic social-sector analytical and managerial capacity-building are indirectly highly relevant to the future of displacees. If achieved, they create a macroeconomic, a macrogovernance, plus a civil society–enterprise context much more conducive to opportunities for poverty reduction, reabsorption and reempowerment, and internalized household food security entitlements (whether from self-provisioning production, producing to sell and buy, or a mix of the two).

In the camp context proper, several procurement-related issues arise. First is a relaxed (or even positive) attitude toward commerce in the form of selling food rations to exchange a nonpreferred for a more satisfying diet. There is no merit in Rwandans eating maize and beans rather than selling them and buying plantains and vegetables. Promoting production of secondary crops (such as fruit, vegetables, perhaps oilseeds, poultry, and perhaps small stock) by securing land-use access and providing seeds, tools, and advice, has both nutritional and empowerment benefits. Employing displaced persons in service provision (such as primary education, health, nutrition, and water supply) and small-infrastructure building within camps and, perhaps, infrastructure-building around them as part of an offset agreement with host governments (central or local) create greater entitlement-food security and markets for host- area food.

These options, as noted, arise once the initial arrival, physical rehabilitation, and averting starvation phase is achieved. The longer a camp is likely to be in operation, the more potentially important they are. Since calamity displacees can and should be empowered to go home soon (or preemptively assisted to stay home and avoid displacement), they relate almost exclusively to catastrophe (war and close affines) displacement. In that context, they serve social, political-economic, and political purposes. These can be encapsulated in the phrase "better to grow food and build new lives than to grow hate and build plots." The detailed articulations are highly contextual, and the overall implications much more general.

Not by bread alone

Food security cannot be bound by food alone, still less by food-aid rations. Water, sanitation, nutrition, primary health care, shelter, and education—training and extension—all figure, or should figure, prominently.

In calamity (nonwar) cases such as drought, the greatest single cause of flight is frequently not access to food but to water for household consumption or preservation of livestock vital for pastoral livelihoods. How much can be done during a crisis varies, usually to some degree even in a one-year drought and more in a longer drought cycle or a wartime calamity situation.

In drought cases, better water access before the event is key to reducing displacement (and limiting livestock losses). In the cases of broken pumps or fractured pipelines and, perhaps, in those of clogged wells or boreholes, something can be accomplished (though it rarely is) during the early-warning window of opportunity. What can be done during displacement is the provision of wages for work to buy food (or food for work) and labor-intensive water facility restoration and enhancement to reduce future vulnerability. Ironically, but predictably, this is greatly hindered by the division of donor budgets into development and emergency. As one frustrated donor said (quite literally in regard to future drought vulnerability reduction proposals), "But you do not understand. What you are proposing is development not disaster relief. Disaster is our bread and butter." That kind of tunnel vision facilitates plenty of bread and butter for disaster-relief specialists, but decreases future bread and butter (food security) for vulnerable rural households. Hard as this may be for Africa's victims to believe, it is much more often muddle than madness or malice.

During return, the water issue normally focuses on "rehabilitation plus." In most rain-fed areas with limited access to perennial streams, rivers, or lakes, reduction of vulnerability to future droughts should be built into the drought and return period's labor-intensive works and/or larger-scale pipelines and boreholes. Vulnerability reduction is as relevant to calamity as to catastrophe refugees. The end of war does not result in the end of drought. This factor is not usually considered in planning return by refugee managers, even though it is of considerable concern to refugees themselves, as evidenced by the rapid return in 1993 of Mozambican refugees except to certain drought-afflicted districts. In some cases, urban areas are as vulnerable to multiyear droughts as rural areas. For example, in 1993 the supply situation was within weeks of forcing the evacuation of Bulawayo and of Beira and its exurb camps, involving 1 million persons in each case.

Linked to water is sanitation. The concentration of population and, at least initially, disorder and poor housing of camps create massive health risks to their inhabitants and to host areas. Environmental sanitation (including but not limited to improved latrines), water protection, and easy access to water for cleansing can ameliorate these risks.

However, a more basic reduction of risk would also involve limiting medium-stay camps to 50,000 residents and long-stay ones to not more than 10,000. Both are relevant to issues of land access, food production, livelihood restoration, and security. With respect to transit camps (for return), this case implies a goal of zero use and, at most, a week's stay when timing of return and preparation for assistance in the home area do not mesh. Both sanitation and food-security conditions posit either organized refugee households or official direct places of refuge/home or return, not wasteful expenditure on transit camps that are likely to aggravate food and health problems.

Sanitation upon return is problematic. Without education—and even then not in low-population density areas—latrines are not a user priority. Given the very high return-period workload, that time is probably not optimal for improved pit latrine campaigns, unless there was substantial preflight use. Keeping compounds and houses clean and tidy is usually a rural African priority; its maintenance in camps is one quick, independent check of morale.

Health facilities—preventive, nutritional rehabilitation, educational, and primary curative—are crucial to achieving safe camps. They should be in camp as soon as possible after the initial influx and staffed by refugees (with training if necessary) for reasons linked to user-friendly provision, dignity, participation, and livelihood. If practicable, there is a case for hiring domestic secondary and tertiary facility access (whether from central or local government or domestic social-sector units) and, of necessity, using a primary level during the initial crisis phase and then "making whole again" in cash, kind (for example, drugs, vaccines), facilities, and/or training.

Health, as for water return, involves rehabilitation of facilities. It also , includes repatriating not merely the personnel but the ongoing operations—presumably in coordination with home country central and local social-sector health authorities, especially if refugee staff-based programs have been set up. Rehabilitation may or may not mean replication and, in most cases, should include enhancement of preventive-educational-primary access. However, unless health posts and clinics were grossly misplaced, the "simpleminded" approach of rebuilding may save more time than it costs in marginal nonoptimality of location. For health posts, as for schools, water sources, and primary roads, an assumption to recreate checked against overlay facility and population maps (prewar or return intent) and user-preference surveying has substantial time and cost gains, as opposed to a *tabula rasa* approach that seeks (in a context of very incomplete data) to create a "New Jerusalem" of physical planning optimality.

Water, health, sanitation, and nutrition (rehabilitative and educational) do relate directly to food security when defined in human terms. Their absence either wastes calories or renders persons unable to use them. The same is true of fuel, which is a major problem because collection in the context of large-camp household self-provisioning is very time- and energy-intensive, as well as often environmentally disastrous — quickly, and potentially, irrevocably. Distribution by camp organizers, with rare exception, is logistically difficult and financially burdensome because local purchase is ruled out for environmental reasons. Fuel conditions in home areas vary so widely that no generalizations are possible.

Education, training, and extension relate more to morale, future livelihoods, and rehabilitation on return than to short-term survival and food security. Some extension advice, such as the degree of toxicity and methods of safe preparation of local cassava for refugees driven from a home zone with low-toxicity, easy-preparation cassava to high-toxicity, complex preparation, relates to survival, though it is perhaps as much health education as extension training. Some training and education and most extension training relate to livelihood restoration in camps as well as upon return, especially if they can be staffed by hired refugee personnel. As with health, the return phase ideally involves repatriating programs as well as personnel.

Access to resources: beyond handouts

Financial (and food-security) prudence, respect for refugee dignity and desires, and, above all, ongoing rehabilitation for return (or resettlement in a new home) call for rapid expansion of refugees' resource base beyond camp handouts. The problem in calamity cases is somewhat different from that in catastrophe cases. It turns on either facilitating access to home farms to ready them for the next season, facilitation of rebuilding of devastated herds, or resettlement. Thus, camp-based livelihoods are unlikely to play a large role. In catastrophe cases, or large ex-pastoralist groups whose capital stock (animals) has been wiped out by drought and who therefore cannot go home (a fairly common and significant subgroup in the Sahel), the in-camp development of resource access is important. Most refugees certainly view it as such. As soon as the initial shock of flight has passed, many begin to look for ways to earn (often to the considerable annoyance of camp organizers and sometimes of hosts).

Many camps, even in unpropitious circumstances, bear out Adam Smith's claim that "the propensity to truck and barter" — or rather the propensity to seek to improve one's condition by exchange — is deep-seated and pervasive. Camps without visible commerce — whether because of isolation, draconian regulation, physical debilitation of residents, or other less evident reasons — are also typified by very poor morale, pervasive pessimism, and deep dependence. The problem for managers is that the most available stocks in trade are rations, tools, and building materials given to refugees to meet basic needs. On the face of it, trade in these items suggests oversupply. However, this is usually simplistic, single-entry bookkeeping. No judgement can be made without a clear view of what is received in return.

The most obvious means of resource broadening in the context of food security is the ability to grow food. However, especially in refuge, this is not as straightforward as it may appear. Household self-provisioning in staples supplied by camp organizers would not add to real incomes of households. Growing supplementary crops for nutritional balance or dietary preference — whether for household use or for sale — is likely to prove much more attractive to many refugees. Cropping (and small-stock keeping) requires land access and, realistically, avoidance of mega-camps. How easy it is to secure such access from hosts is a contextual issue, but in most cases it will prove problematic unless there are close cultural links or other affinities between refugees and hosts, land is not very scarce, and the circumstances of the arrival of the refugees does not make them feared. For example, Mozambican refugees in northern Malawi and southern Tanzania had access, but not in southern Malawi (land scarcity). In 1959–1960 Rwanda and Burundi refugees were accepted as "new villages" in Tanzania, but in 1994 they were not (because of the holocaust they fled and the extreme violence they inflicted upon each other). While, in theory, refugee production of grain for sale to camps might be welcomed by some refugees, it is very problematic in terms of donor reaction, acquisition and allocation of land rights, agronomic suitability, and competition with host growers who might have access to camp procurement (rare) or to trade with refugees (ubiquitous).

Three other income sources are trade, small-scale production of nonfood commodities, and wage employment. Each offers considerable scope, even though refugee administrators have tended to frown on the first and third sources when carried out on a large scale.

Waged labor out of camp is common, unless refugees are in a nearly unpopulated area or one with a war-devastated economy. Locally, low-wage, unskilled work, including but not limited to seasonal agricultural demand, usually dominates. Long-distance employment depends on refugee skills, domestic (or even adjacent-country) labor market needs, and host government attitudes. In the extreme case of pre-1990 Somalia, camps had become a modern variant on migrant Somali pastoralist base camps with working-age men and, to a substantial extent, women working in Somali towns or over the water in Saudi Arabia and Yemen.

There are several reasons why international agencies and donors are somewhat ambivalent: a flood of cheap seasonal labor disadvantages the poorer host community families; camps with more than half of household incomes from remittances by long-distance workers are not readily politically saleable to donors.

Resource recovery: modalities of return

The return (from calamity or catastrophe) process has resource-access problems significantly different from those experienced during a stay in a place of refuge. These are almost universally under-perceived and even more underfinanced; problems are compounded by the legal limitations and country-focused programming of UNHCR. UNHCR in, for example, Maputo has no operational relationship to Mozambican refugees in Malawi who fall under the metro-political jurisdiction of UNHCR's office in Lilongwe. The lines of authority and responsibility during and after return are, to say the least, obscure and problematic.

The main barriers to return, except in cases of unusually long (more than 200 kilometers) distances, do not turn on transport, still less on transit camps, but on working capital and on facilitation of livelihood and daily life rehabilitation in place on arrival. These barriers are compounded by the reality that at least with respect to the second—and arguably for the working capital as well—the needs of international refugees; domestic dislocated households; and remaining, but pauperized in-place households in previously insecure and devastated areas are not best served by separate schools, clinics, administrations, extension services, or labor-intensive infrastructure or employment projects. Joint financing (UNHCR is empowered to finance return and rehabilitation so that could contribute on a pro rata basis) would appear to be the way forward, rather than a plethora of fragmented, overlapping, cost-inefficient, and donor-driven projects.

The working capital needed is primarily for food security until the first normal harvest (what would be called a "wages fund" for rehabilitating a plantation) and secondarily for tools, seeds, and household equipment to enable direct (from one's own production) and indirect (from the sale of other products to buy food) food security and home restoration.

Camp circumstances are rarely favorable for amassing any such working-capital fund. Trade, casual labor, and holding back on ration use (or seeking to secure "extra" rations) can provide something but rarely enough. Unless it is provided on return and for up to 24 months after, return home may involve even more deprivation than displacement. Well-placed noncamp refugees with land access may be much more able to build up food reserves to begin rehabilitation and to shuttle between the temporary farm and home during rehabilitation and/or reconstruction.

Where? How? What? are relevant questions. Where can normally be answered quite simply: on registration after coming home (not in camp before starting). This answer, and the one to the question of "How?" assume that a functioning reception and local governmental and basic services system has been set up. Doing so is a priority that rarely seems to receive adequate attention from donors or agencies, and is underfunded even where identified by the home government. Returnees registered for purposes of access to land and to working capital and for articulating basic service redevelopment are in a better position to be supported on arrival, especially if prereturn surveys in camp can give at least rough indications of how many, how fast, and where, broken down by district.

The answer to "What?" includes food as well as tools and basic household supplies. How much physical food is needed and for how long depends on the time needed for restoration of the domestic commercial system and local food production. But the basic "what" should be cash (if necessary, generated by commercial sales of food aid) to hire returnees for labor-intensive restoration of infrastructure (such as roads, wells and water pipelines, schools, clinics, staff housing, and offices). The cash route facilitates commercial revival and enhances worker dignity and household resource allocation efficiency, and, given the value of the infrastructure built, may be very cost-efficient in contrast to a food ration plus a contractor-constructed program.

Land access in cases of return home, the dominant pattern for most refugees, should not pose massive problems. In fact, it is likely to because of poor (if any) formal record-keeping, land grabbing (or the grabbing of best land) by those who stayed or the first return-ees, historical anachronisms limiting female head-of-household access, and problems of identifying genuinely vacant or abandoned land as opposed to rotational reserve and late returnee lands. Only in the 6- to 18-month absence drought or flood calamity cases can a smooth, largely nonproblematic process be expected.

In the absence of a working capital and a friendly basic services return support system, refugee camp managers should at least turn a blind eye to, and preferably support, refugee household or community-operated systems that facilitate meeting the food or labor funding and basic service needs of return by gradual shifting from camp to home.

One such system, consisting of scouts, pioneers, first wave, women and children last, has typified much of the return to northern and central Mozambique (from displaced person as well as refugee camps). In the first phase, scouts go out to home areas to determine whether return is safe and what the farm-rehabilitation, home-re-building, food-supply, and water-access conditions are. Pioneers follow to begin land clearing and home rebuilding and to get a first crop planted (probably both to demonstrate land-use right claims and to supply food). Larger bodies of able-bodied adults (including more women who are less represented in the first two stages) return for a planting and again for a harvest season, while many women and, especially, children remain in camp. Finally, assuming the success of initial main crops, full return follows.

In this context, camp rations (or other sources) for all household members are drawn to provide supplies to scouts, pioneers, and first wave. Necessarily, this involves rations being used for "non residents" and in the large circular flow from and to camps, which so puzzled observers in southern Malawi and central Mozambique in 1993 and 1994. Blocking it as fraud, as several NGOs sought to do, is unrealistic and highly detrimental to food security and/or to return, if no home-area support system is in place for returnees. Facilitating it with, for example, seed distribution or nurseries to help female-household heads take part as pioneers, would be a more food security–friendly response.

Participation, gender, governance: refugees as human beings

There are arguments for participation, gender consciousness, and partial self-governance in regard to refugee communities based on managerial convenience and survival (including food security) efficiency. However, for present purposes, these are subsumed into a focus on refugees as persons, not merely victims (let alone devious individuals whose chief aim is to cheat donors, a surprisingly common and strong feeling, if not an undercurrent, among many refugee administrators), and as households working toward new lives not as objects of charity sitting passively in an externally created and managed setting.

Refugee participation in camp organization, for example, registering residents and procedures for providing material support, and camp operation, for example, actually distributing general food rations and special interventions such as nutritional supplements for malnourished children, is clearly convenient for camp managers (or returnee support managers). In the initial phases of camp creation, getting this participation is often so urgent that any apparently useful "offers" are accepted without much time to consider longer-term implications or those for governance (as opposed to facilitation of operations). Spontaneous self-help, abiding extended family or residence group, and focused political actors (whether SWAPO of Namibia or *Interahamwe* of Hutu Rwanda) are — in haste and with a lack of contextual knowledge — vaguely conflated as similar and equally useful in getting jobs done, irritating in wanting to do it "their way," and infuriating when they clash with each other for, to the uninformed outsider, often "inexplicable" reasons.

There is a case for multiple-function committees with an overall coordinating group. This is helpful for new functions, such as nutritional rehabilitation and well-child clinics at Bonaco Camp in Ngara. Because they are new, they facilitate drawing a broader section of refugees, not the least of which are women, into leadership and communication roles. A similar approach to growing and trading for food (beyond camp rations) would seem worth more frequent exploration, and would provide another avenue for involving new people, again in particular (but not only) women, as well as averting or limiting "coordination" by camp elites looking remarkably like protection racketeering.

Participation has been used here in a narrow sense, meaning the design, operation, and monitoring of programs. The broader (and perhaps more basic) aspects of participating in food security — receiving, preparing, producing, and trading — are considered elsewhere. Participation, morale, and physical conditions interact. Participation can improve morale by improving conditions in user-friendly ways. As a pure public relations exercise, however, it is likely to lead rapidly to cynical estrangement. There has to be a material as well as an emotional payoff.

Gender, women, and interventions

With respect to refugees, gender issues, conflicts, and dynamics more or less, by definition, include all those pertaining to the societies from which they come, and cannot all be rehearsed as an aspect of food security in refuge and upon return. What follows is a brief checklist of issues necessarily gendered and necessary to face directly in refugee and returnee contexts:

(a) *Food preparation,* except for initial periods of exhaustion and cases of severe debilitation, family preparation of meals (by women) enhances diet and helps restore female refugees' role and self-esteem.

(b) Because *food procurement* is also primarily a female responsibility, ration allocation and delivery should be by household (related to size) with issue to the senior woman in the household. Apart from defending women's status as food procurers, this approach is likely to reduce leakages of nutritionally needed food into sale for purchase of nonfood nonnecessities. Women are in objective reality (not just myth) more concerned with adequate meal provision relative to other uses of resources than are men. These will be opposed by protection racketeering elites and governance groups seeking a revenue base or food for troops. No general answer to those problems is possible, but understanding their existence and facing them squarely (if not necessarily with a high public profile) is often crucial.

(c) *Child nutrition* (educational and supplementary feeding) is important for health and survival and provides fairly nonconflictual opportunities for women's self-organization). Interestingly, UNIMIX (child food supplement) is the refugee distribution item most rarely sold, even though a local market would usually exist.

(d) Proportions of *female-headed households* rise, especially in catastrophe (war) cases, with the need to work through consequential implications since in many preconflict rural African societies (at least outside West Africa) female-headed households were relatively few and had historically been virtually nonexistent.

(e) Households with highly *unfavorable mouths to feed/hands to work ratios,* that is, a single adult with multiple dependents, are, in practice, predominantly female-headed because a man with children or other dependents who loses his spouse will, in most sub-Saharan African societies, virtually always remarry. They require special attention, especially in terms of livelihood rehabilitation in camps and on return home because access to work or land, by itself, cannot result in adequate household food security.

(f) *Land access* (especially on return, small-camp plot allocation to women may not prove contentious) requires attention because historically land-use rights were allocated by head of household. While all adult women had valid claims, these were via a male head of household. That system has often disintegrated as to women's claims via males without parallel improvement of their access as heads of household.

(g) Access to camp and return *public works employment* (and perhaps for health, education, and clerical jobs) will not be gender-equitable unless specific action is taken, for example, by giving preference to heads of household or their nominees and/or guarantees of, say, three months a year to all applying adults. Unwillingness to apply or social barriers to accepting employment are much rarer and less intense than often claimed, but women are all too literally "invisible" to many hiring officers not given specific instructions.

(h) Recognition that particular *activities and sources of income are gendered,* though not identically in all African societies, so that specific interventions are rarely gender-neutral. Water and fuel collection rest primarily on the backs (and heads) of women and girls. Programs to reduce time needed for procurement, therefore, primarily benefit them. While the time saved neither will nor should all go to food production and preparation, much will, so that a direct link to food security does exist. Household-food provisioning, as well as often secondary crop for sales, are also predominately female, so that initiatives (tools, seed, land access, and extension training) focused on them will increase not only the female workload, but also income (in cash and kind) and status.

Arguably, only the first two points are specifically refugee-related. The others arise even in noncrisis, stable-residence pattern situations. However, recognizing these issues, analyzing their implications, and acting on them are particularly likely to be crucial in refugee and return contexts. Mainstreaming gender issues presumably include taking account of them in refugee and return as well as "normal" contexts.

From participation to governance: refugees to people

Participation in refugee contexts is usually about helping being helped. When this topic is deepened to include how to be helped, how to become more self-reliant, and, especially, how to return and/ or build new lives in the area of refuge, it becomes governance. This could also be seen as the process of refugees becoming self-governed, self-serviced communities. This issue rarely arises in cases of short-term drought displacees. Speedy return is normally practicable and desirable, while setting up new governance structures is not.

Privatizing war and dearth: demobilization without reintegration

Demobilization of combatants, and especially of child soldiers, is a standard feature of the end of wars in Africa, whether by negotiated means or by total military conquest. Reintegration into society and livelihood for ex-combatants is sometimes, though by no means always (taking Ethiopia as an example), a key policy, but one not usually considered in the overall displaced person and food security context. That is probably both a conceptual and an applied strategic policy mistake.

Ex-combatants demobilized (or, as in the case of disintegrated armies, are, like Mengistu's, simply thrust into extreme poverty with little chance of achieving adequate livelihood or food security) are very likely to seek to continue to secure their living by the use of weapons, which are usually only too easily available in a disorderly postwar period. Demobilizing into destitution (or a cease-fire in place with no provision for feeding, sheltering, clothing ex-combatants, as in Sierra Leone and, earlier, Liberia) causes grave risk of privatizing rather than ending war.

The food security of ex-combatants is a valid concern. They and their families are human beings, and the vast majority cannot usually be held responsible for the horrors of the war (the ex-Rwanda and current Burundi armies would be exceptions). Even if a normative approach might give low priority to ex-combatants from the insurgents who fought a continuing government, common prudence and concern for the security and particularly the food security in rural areas of civilians strongly counsels demobilization and assistance in societal reintegration and livelihood rehabilitation for them, too. This is the view taken by, for example, the government of Mozambique.

It can be argued that *démobiliseés* are not refugees, but analogous to other structural adjustment employment terminees. That would not make a case against termination benefits or training, but would take them out of the displacee-refuge category. However, *démobiliseés* are predominately from rural areas, have family ties there, and wish to go home. They are leaving one institutional and occupational context in one set of locations for totally different ones (unless retrained as civil police). And they have been as uprooted and dislocated by war just as other refugees and displacees have.

Programmatically, there is a case for including ex-combatants in general displacee and refugee return programs, if these are in total much larger, as in Mozambique, but less so if they are either small or geographically pocketed or if demobilization comes substantially after refugee return (for example, as in Zimbabwe and Namibia). In that case, ex-combatants should be eligible for home area reception (and included in estimates of numbers of expected homecomers) and for access to basic services and to public works supplementary employment as well as—unless there is a less austere set of benefits for *démobiliseés*—any working capital food, tools, and materials grants.

For prudential reasons and out of a sense of obligation toward ex-combatants of a continuing or conquering government, a case for special programs for ex-combatants can be made. The parameters include training (especially for those not opting for family small-scale farming as a new or regained livelihood), pay and/or rations for some period (up to two years), and vocational tool kits (whether for farming, carpentry, or tailoring).

Programs initiated and operated by international agencies, such as those in Liberia, have tended to be ineffective. This is partly because the absence of a functioning government tends to parallel the absence of a functioning economy and the presence of extreme insecurity in many rural areas. But time-bound cash or food aid that is not linked to training that would lead to work hardly facilitates the achievement of peace. *Démobiliseés* drift back into being militia or bandit combatants as fast as new ones opt for a try at a peaceful life.

Child soldiers pose special challenges. Because of their age they have become socialized into violence and the military without any strong prior socialization into community or civilian society and with little or no formal education. They have frequently engaged in horrendous activities and experienced traumatic shocks. In many cases, their own officers, who usually exert some, but imperfect, control over them, are frightened by them.

Family reunion and social service care are logical approaches. But to work well, they require registration and a period in demobilization camps to allow medical (including mental) screening and relative location (and counseling). These are damaged human beings, often deeply damaged to the point of anomie and/or psychotic rage. For many, tender, loving care and school (preferably, at first special school, as the tendency to disruptive conduct, even by former child soldiers who can be resocialized, is very severe) are options. For others, at least initially, institutional care is needed. The risk to the community and to other ex-combatant and/or street children of a small minority running amuck or forming raider or killer bands is not one to be accepted lightly or absentmindedly.

As stressed, *démobiliseés* are persons whose war experience makes them, in many respects, similar to other displaced persons. Most wish to return home, although the urban drift element appears to be stronger than for other dislocated persons or households. As persons, most face food insecurity and absolute poverty if not included in initial support programs. If dumped into destitution and desperation, many will turn to privatized war because guns have been their way of "earning" and no other means appears to be available, with very negative impact on the food security of others in rural areas and on household personal security in both urban and rural areas. There is justification for their inclusion in overall returnee facilitation and probably for specific training, interim food and funding, working, and capital tool kit provision. Finally, among ex-combatants, former child soldiers are a special case because of their age and the lack of any deep premilitary socialization.

Refugee and resident food security interactions

There is little agreement on what the impact of refugees on host populations' food security is. The assertions — usually backed by one or a few temporally and geographically bound examples — range from seeing refugees as a horde of locusts (or even as the Four Horsemen of the Apocalypse) to perceiving them (or rather those who provide for them) in terms analogous to the widow's curse. Among the reasons for this farrago of perceptions is that different institutions are responsible for international refugees and host populations, and each has a vested interest in stressing spillover gains and costs respectively. Even in domestic displacee and "informal" cases (who are, for the most part, not internationally registered and supported), there are institutional divisions and interests, albeit to a lesser extent. Systematic studies focusing on the host community are relatively unusual; the actual balance of costs and gains for hosts varies widely with contexts and also among initial arrival, continued residence, exodus, and long-term, postdeparture phases. When receiving effective international support, refugee populations may in fact be less badly off than either displacees at home or host populations. The high-profile attention they (as contrasted with hosts) receive can lead to very substantial alienation unless the refugee community is both culturally close to its hosts, relatively peaceable in exile, and perceived as "innocent" of causing its own plight. Very large camps of violent refugees, whose preflight conduct was highly problematic (or unproblematically vile) and whose presence near borders incurs real risks of trans-border spillover violence are among the ultimate NIMBYs (not in my backyard).

During initial influx periods, displacees and refugees, whether from political crises or calamities, do create food security risks for hosts. They move into areas that usually have limited household and commercial stocks, poor transport and communications infrastructure for bringing more in, and limited national and international logistical bases for rapid response, even if financial and personnel resources are adequate and rapidly transferable (which is not usually the case). Initially they do, sometimes literally, eat out of the same pot, which is often not very full to start.

The medium-term results are much more complex and variable. If rations to camps are adequate and host production is partly market constrained, then trade with camps will raise overall host access to food (via entitlements). However, if rations are inadequate and/ or host production is physically or ecologically constrained, the results can be negative. Even if overall food entitlement positions improve, some host households may be disadvantaged, for example, poor small farming households who are net food buyers and depend on seasonal or casual labor wages competed for by refugees. Fixed-wage earners are likely to be somewhat adversely affected, as local food prices are likely to rise faster than the national rates because of refugee demand, though this may not be true for staples in the refugees' ration basket. For example, in Ngara in late 1994, the prices of maize and beans (a ration staple not widely consumed locally and one in glut because of the loss of the Rwanda export market) were the lowest in Tanzania, whereas those of plantains and banana beer were at Dar es Salaam levels, having at least trebled over the year. Wage-earning households, unless severely affected by refugee competition, may be better off if camps, agencies, and associated administrations hire locally and provide purchasing power for expansion of commerce. While rental and commercial incomes are likely to rise substantially, these households do not usually represent cases of food insecurity, and a high proportion may be coming in from other districts or towns.

The long-term impact of refugees, normally after they have gone home, on food security is largely ecological. Regarding water, normally ending extra offtake will stabilize or allow restoration of water tables. In regard to overcollection of fuel (by de-treeing and de-bushing) and to erosion and overtillage of land adjacent to camps, the results may be much longer-lasting and, in the absence of early, sustained targeted interventions, lead to downward spirals. This is especially true of very large camps, which have a devastating impact on vegetation because their short- term — hopefully — residents are not very environmentally conscious. For example, marking trees not to be cut within 20 kilometers of Bonaco Camp in Tanzania and explaining the reasons does result in Tanzanian women and girls' sparing them, but refugees cut them down to the mark (and claim linguistic confusion if challenged). If prevention is desired, camps should provide fuel. However, wood and charcoal are expensive to procure and to transport long distances, coal poses combustion and pollution problems, kerosene is highly risky in the context of flimsy, closely packed, and flammable camp housing, bottled gas is expensive (especially with respect to equipment to use), unfamiliar, and a fire hazard. Experiments with sustainable charcoal production in nearby-to-moderate distance forest zones would be more likely if camp administrators were less financially and logistically limited and more responsive to long-term impact on hosts.

The environmental point, in fact, relates back to short- and medium-term food security. Overload on health services, pollution of water sources (in transit or from camps), epidemic escapes, and additional women and girls' work time to procure water and fuel from farther away (as a result of refugee depletion of nearby sources) may have a greater negative impact on food security than either refugee use of food out of a short-term fixed-area supply or the provision of additional income and supply through trade. These impacts on food security — like refugee transit and supply convoy damage to transport infrastructure — are rarely systematically canvassed, estimated, or factored into programs by refugee and displaced person supporters or the governments of affected areas. Mozambique, in terms of infrastructure and services with respect to the impact of displacement, and Tanzania, in terms of infrastructure and ecology's making Ngarans whole again after hosting hordes of refugees, are among the exceptions. Initiative here would appear to need to come from hosts (including source and host governments with major medium-term internal displacement) and agencies and donors working with them. Agencies and institutions working directly with refugees and displaced persons cannot reasonably be expected to give host problems priority attention (as opposed to responding to them when posed), and lack the expertise for conceptualizing and analyzing them. Further refugee programs are ubiquitously underfinanced, even with respect to refuge and (*a fortiori*) return needs without host expenditure lines.

Developing diaspora: project push processes

Persons and communities displaced by projects are not usually fully comparable to calamity or catastrophe refugees. They are disproportionately outsiders — geographically, culturally, politically, and economically — from the start. Nor are means of their food security and problems relating to those needs likely to be as similar as might be supposed. While project displacement offers much better preknowledge of numbers, and timing and is likely to be in a less-fraught context than is war or drought, its specificity — given that not everybody or even large swathes of the population is or is likely to be affected — and the outsider nature of those affected, and often afflicted, may more than counterbalance the positive factors.

Displacements involving limited numbers of people who can resettle within their own community are less problematic. For example, while the Tazara Railway displaced several thousand households along its 1400 kilometers in Tanzania, the rural displacees seem not to have had major food security or other problems. Compensation and access to similar land were the reasons for that achievement. Even the most contentious issue — burial places — is almost always solvable by paying for appropriate ceremonies and/or moves. The smaller number of urban displacees faced greater problems, but because they received compensation and access to residences not notably further from livelihood opportunities than their initial locations, they too probably faced limited problems in sustaining entitlements (cash income) to food.

Larger urban projects resulting in "people dumping" in exurbs — for example, Senegal's second largest "city," Pekine — damage food security because they annihilate communities in moving, remove access to health, education, and water (rarely adequately provided in exurbs), and destroy entitlements (because of distance from earning opportunities that is usually exacerbated by high cost and limited availability of transport). In principle, compensation, transfer of neighborhood community processes, prepositioning of basic services (including access to roughly surveyed and leveled plots as part of the compensation package), and low-cost or destination-friendly transport could reduce negative impacts and create new opportunities. However, the cost — in terms of policy attention and specialist personnel as well as financial resources — combined with the peripheral positioning (to the urban redevelopment goals and projects) of resettlers ensure that such an outcome is unusual.

Large rural projects entailing resettlement of many households and whole communities are usually perceived as the main nonwar, nondrought displacement challenge in sub-Saharan Africa. The most common project types are dams (with or without irrigation projects) and natural parks (when these involve extruding existing small-farming and hunting-gathering communities).

The perceived problems can be grouped by period. Ill-prepared, chaotic, and uneven movement and arrival, when combined with inadequate compensation, lead to immediate food insecurity, though usually far short of famine levels. Lack of ready access to livelihood opportunities and/or resources to exploit them and poor or lagged provision of basic services leads to medium-term production and entitlement food levels below national and local averages. Over time this gap may close, depending on whether whole communities have moved in a way that sustains their self-organization, integrated into preexisting village and local governance patterns, or, as is surprisingly common, become atomistic or even anomistic. In the long term, both displacees and hosts may face declines in food security if their access to services and to infrastructure proves disproportionately vulnerable during a period of national economic failure. Increasing populations (resulting from post-resettlement demography, but reaching carrying capacity faster as a result of it) undermine both cropping and herding capacity. Both sources of post-recovery decline have characterized Kariba resettlee households and communities on the Zambia side, although apparently less so on the Zimbabwe side.

A checklist of key problems may offer some guidance to more mover-friendly resettlement:

(a) Land, grazing, water, fuel, and fishing access are crucial to resettlees, which implies need for a premove agreement involving host communities.

(b) If such a settlement process is to endure, future household-to-natural resource ratios need to be projected and, if future trouble is apparent, either resettlement shifted to a broader front or specific resource conservation and higher levels of sustainable utilization programs set in place promptly.

(c) Compensation is more sensibly (and humanely) related to what resources (including land, water, grazing, fuel, and fishing access) are needed to reconstruct livelihoods than to valuation of existing nonportable assets, unless the latter would yield a substantially larger figure. To be effective, compensation needs to be paid at the time of the move (or part of it in advance).

(d) Infrastructure and basic-service capacity in the receiving area will be overburdened and become a cause of "in-comer" or existing resident controversy unless it is augmented during or soon after the move.

(e) The survival of community interactions and institutions appears to be an important factor in household welfare. Therefore either moving whole communities to become new villages or genuine integration into existing villages (hardly inherently impossible if of the same broad community) needs specific attention before and during resettlement.

(f) If livelihoods in settlement areas will need to be significantly different from previous ones (because of new opportunities as well as lost ones), specific extension training and initial input provision (possibly involving hiring successful long-term resident households' services) will facilitate and speed such shifts.

(g) Monitoring of outcomes is likely to be more effective if it is built into both project and local government ongoing operations beginning before resettlement and continuing for at least five years after the move is completed.

Four procedural and institutional factors impede achieving these goals. First, social science analysts, other than economists and political economists, are frequently reluctant to give advice in usable and relatively unconditional form. If economists are seen as all too prone to "two-handedness" ("on the one hand ... or the other"), sociologists tend to be seen as "octopods" offering eight alternatives, being far readier to warn of the drawbacks of each than to back any and to shift between highly conceptualized principles and highly specific, contextual artifacts with a missing middle of intermediate programmable content. The economists may be unwise, even foolhardy, and the sociologists wise, but advisers who do not advise clearly on how to do something are never popular and rarely influential. Second, neither officials nor social science experts have, at least until very recently, been prone to seeking such information from potential displacees or hosts as their perceptions of needs, capabilities, problems, and aspirations, a point of process not limited to, but particularly pronounced in the case of, resettlement. Third, peripherality of location, of central economic and political concern, and of the people affected (frequently hosts as well as displaced households) reduces both the priority to achieving a user-friendly result and the knowledge base for doing so. Fourth, among project, resettlement agency, basic service, and infrastructure ministries and local government, there is near-infinite room for actual (or blame passing) confusion on who should do what, and serious conflict on who should pay, especially for ongoing or new crisis costs after the initial exercise, and once the building or external finance stage of the project has been completed.

They do it better on their own

Before succumbing to despair, it is worth remembering that rural-rural migration in Africa is large, frequent, and ongoing. Most is outside officially structured contexts and thus is less evident than project displacement. Certainly outcomes vary but, on balance, it can be said that they do not usually involve major losses with respect to food security or livelihood or to major, continuous in-comer and resident conflicts but rather to episodic and resolvable tensions.

Tanzania Masai pastoralists have moved in large numbers to several distant southern and western districts. They do not constitute either a deprived or a rejected minority. More spectacularly, large-scale Akan cocoa farmers have migrated all across Ghana's forest belt with notable success and with few clashes with preexisting communities, which, while they were Akan, were socially and politically distinct. Yoruba cocoa and other tree crop farmers have moved into neighboring Middle Belt and Western Niger Delta states. In Tanzania, whole districts, such as Ngara, and zones, such as Usangu Plains, have had immigration over the past three decades far in excess of their mid-1960s population with improvement of livelihoods for both in-comers and longer-term residents. In Ngara, the movement has been predominantly by other Wahaya from adjacent districts of the Kagera Region, but no such contiguity (geographic or cultural) is evident in Usangu. The latter also features a household- and community-driven technology system shift to small-scale irrigation and a livelihood makeup/dietary one to rice, with positive food security, nutrition, and income impacts.

Problematic cases do exist. The migration of Ibo households from the overcrowded, eroded Owerri Plateau to the less-crowded Jos Plateau has led to tensions, at times flaming into pogroms against the in-comers. While macro-political contexts contributed to these tensions, conflicts related to culture, local government control, and land access have been persistent and severe.

Generalizations are risky, and not necessarily helpful for learning from any one country's voluntary migration history how it or others could better facilitate project displacee migration. However, several points appear frequently and may be relevant. The desire to take advantage of perceived opportunities and lack of opportunity at home play a part in determining who goes when and where. As a result, migrants (to other rural areas) probably have above-average initiative and access to resources to establish themselves, as well as in a frame of mind to effect change. Unless natural resources are scarce or the in-comers are from an unpopular, not just "stranger" group, existing communities are usually willing to accept moderate numbers of in-comers and to accommodate them in political and resource allocational processes. The existence of established home bases — family and community — is often important to in-comers psychologically (because there is somewhere to go back to), and as a working-capital mobilization opportunity (many have their initial land-right acquisition or other resource needs funded by their families) and a means of food security during transition (for example, returning refugees split the household with food growing, and spouses and children continue at the home base until the new one is firmly established).

The absence of whole community shifts (with the result of a remaining base to go back to) is usually not replicable in project displacement. Nor is the voluntary element — one cannot stay in an underwater village behind a dam. But the concept of whole village shifts as the only or the only supported option in the case of project displacement needs questioning. Why should everyone move to the same area? Or at the same time? Would displacee or host relations be easier and integration and self-organization faster if there were more of a scatter of destinations? If compensation packages are provided, can these not be portable so a household could, if it so chose, move to an area quite different from the new resettler community or project zone?

Political perorations and outcast groups

The political and political economic micro and provincial contexts may have an important effect on how well, or, more usually, how badly, the resettlement is conducted from the perspective of those resettled. In many cases, those required to move are minority communities on the fringes of mainstream society, economy, and polity — their voice, leverage, and even visibility are low. There are usually larger, more mainstream groups who will, or believe they will, benefit from the project and who are "in a hurry" to have it done. Even with no ill will or ill intent, those two factors make it likely that compensation and resettlement will be on the fringes of planning, will be handled late, and will be a low priority if, as is usually the case, resources are scarce. Cash compensation without assured access to land that is relatively similar to that lost is inherently inadequate in terms of the horizons, capacities, and goals of the community being required to move. All of which is exacerbated by the fact that unwilling, demonstrating, resisting groups, especially the "small" ones "out there," are viewed at best with irritated condescension by those focusing on the project and its benefits. Emotions are even less amiable if, as is often the case, the group is already unpopular with its neighbors and/or the central and local governmental authorities for other reasons.

A case in Tanzania, which traditionally has been able and inclined to deal sympathetically, and not totally ineffectively, with displaced communities (domestic, drought, external civil war/war or project) and with their impact on hosts, illustrates. It relates to a small, isolated (geographically, culturally, and politically) pastoralist people and a large wheat farming development.

The first problem has been reaching agreement on how many land rights (grazing, water, and residence more than tillage for the outgoers) were lost. This has been harder than in cases, which admittedly cover smaller areas individually, that affected the Masai, who have been much more able to reach agreements on what they have lost and on what compensation was minimally acceptable to them.

The second has been an unwillingness or inability to use compensation either to adapt or to move. The former problem parallels Masai cases, albeit melding cropping and craft-producing elements into their household and community economies has been taken further. The latter is distinctive: Masai have successfully migrated to virtually all four corners of Tanzania and have usually been able to find areas in which pastoralist in-comers were not unwelcome and to develop viable relations with longer-term residents and with local government.

The third problem has been repeated clashes among displacees, or those perceiving themselves as potential displacees, and managers and residents of the project, other nearby villages (including but not only in-comer ones drawn by what were to them spin-off economic opportunities), local government, and police sent in or stationed to preserve order. The rights and wrongs of particular clashes are obscure. The context of abiding ill will and endemic low-grade confrontation is not. That too is unusual. In this case, neighbor community relations are very poor, quite independently of and indeed worse than, district government or police ones.

Fourth, apparently practicable ameliorative measures have not been taken, designed, specifically sought, or systematically explored. Stepped-up attempts to provide access to primary health care, household and livestock water points, primary education, though admittedly all problematic in quasi-nomadic pastoral contexts, are absent. This is in clear contrast with Masai cases, as is the absence of specific demands for and suggestions on ways to design them. Apparently, permanent dry season-water-access sources have been lost in the plateau area now under wheat. Why corridors of access and terms of use have not been negotiated (as they have been for Masai communities historically using Ngorongoro Crater watering holes and mineral licks) is a more basic question; neither the concept nor its moderately effective articulation and implementation are strangers to Tanzania.

The research to date is generally very much from the optic either of the project and government or, more usually, the affected community. Neighbor perceptions and preproject relationships have been less studied. The conclusion tends to be one of pastoralist's and fixed-land user's political and socioeconomic clashes, with the pastoralists either (depending on researcher perception) unwilling to adapt or driven to the wall by forces that are either not understanding or uncaring. A problem with this perception is that it does not explain Masai-government-neighbor interactions, which one might have expected to be similar if anti-pastoralist bias or simple incomprehension of pastoral society were the dominant factors.

No definitive answers are available, but several points are suggestive:

- The displacees' community is not (almost uniquely) viewed as a valid community (or at least not an acceptable one) by its neighbors.
- As a result, neither broadening economic activities (which would entail commerce and contact with neighboring groups) nor finding new pastoral areas for displacees is perceived (correctly) as an option.
- The proportion of community members displaced is larger than for the Masai, so the core home base is seen as threatened, especially because the wheat zone has been expanded at least twice and might be again.
- The government, both because its relations with other communities are good and because many of its officers come from them and share their perceptions, is not well disposed to the displacees or their community, and is more inclined to respond to arson and trespass with police and assault than with proposals for water-point access corridors or boreholes, especially

as the latter do not appear to have been systematically proposed.

■ Unwelcoming government personnel (very few of whom could be from the community, given its low education levels and limited apparent desire to alter them) limits both the priority given to provision and the level of use of basic service facilities, compared to neighboring communities.

The short- and, more important, long-term food security (direct and indirect) problems of development displacement are real. More people, including displacees on less land (still at risk from wheat zone extension) with few opportunities to move out physically or economically, will erode direct (milk, blood, and meat) and indirect (purchased with proceeds of meat and animal sales) food entitlements. Poor (and worsening) water access, combined with limited or nonexistent ability to negotiate access to alternative grazing and water sources in drought years, adds to the downward ratchet, as does the probable pasture degradation arising from attempts to herd beyond carrying capacity. Abnormally low access to education, extension, and health services worsens the physical and economic food supply impact on nutrition in the short run, and prejudices economic and structural change to create new opportunities in the medium or long term.

Any solution would seem to require going back several steps to the basic question of why this community relates with such hostility not just to the state but even more to its neighbors, with state relations more a reflection than a cause. Answers will not in themselves provide better relationships or more productive negotiating contexts, much less water, pasturage, education, or health. But addressing food insecurity without them, or, at a slightly deeper level, looking only at specific gaps in provision or response is likely to treat superficial symptoms ineffectively, while the underlying "infection" worsens.

Doubtless the example is extreme, but it may be illustrative of the roles played by multidirectional absence of knowledge or of perceived options (perceived by protagonists even if an outsider might espy a broader menu), and by lack of basic empathy with, or even acceptance of the legitimacy of, the other party. These are more basic than technical problems of food security or broader services access, and, until understood and addressed, make efforts at those levels of limited success or totally nugatory.

Strengthening displacee food security: a resumé

Food security — by rations, by production, by earning — during displacement, during return, and after return could be enhanced by analysis on a broader perspective. This would take in all groups of displacees, including those displaced by calamity or catastrophe and the refugee-impacted, demobilized, or "development displaced." The time period considered is from the threat of displacement (and food security action with potential to avert) through initial and established displacement to return (or integration into the new country) and after return. Food security would be related to basic services — water, health, sanitation, education, and (at least during and after return) extension and market access — and to empowerment, including camp-, as well as return-period trading and production. The perspectives of several disciplines are needed, not the least of which is applied macro political economy, not just physical food security and nutrition, and especially not only food and displacee management. Analysis should include the implications of a strategic policy of systematic reempowering rather than a rolling short-term one of caring.

There is some work on each of these themes but, on balance, the emphasis is on physical food security and managing displacees and food for them over the short term. More holistic relationships — with hosts or with home macro economy and reconstruction on return — are relatively rarely addressed.

Quite clearly, one purpose of such research is to improve crisis response and management and displacee protection and reempowerment. Part of research should, therefore, be built into the structures of government and agency work with refugees, calamity and catastrophe displacees, distressed host communities, those demobilized and the "development displaced," and be both monitored and evaluated regularly to strengthen that work. However, the very tunnel vision, myopia, and fragmentation, which characterize much of official displacee policy and praxis and are among its chief weaknesses, create a strong case for independent research, including studies commissioned by governments and agencies.

Knowledge, particularly in terms of early warning, is needed to allow lead time to respond to shocks both by planning response on the basis of projected requirements and by prepositioning and mobilizing resources on an earmarked or tentative basis when early-warning amber lights go on.

In the case of calamity (dominantly drought) displacees, the timely response can allow them to be "virtual" rather than actual displacees by ensuring that emergency food entitlement (ration and/or work) and strengthened drought-period water access are put in place.

Development project displacees should be known in advance with respect to numbers, but this knowledge is not necessarily achieved in practice. Further participatory discussions on options as to postmove locations and occupations are rather more the exception than the rule, and provision of land-use (or in urban cases livelihood access) compensation to offset project-caused losses is relatively rare.

Coordination—from analysis and initial response to early warning on through return and reintegration—is frequently weak. Except in the case of refugees, the home government, via a coordinating unit (probably in a key macroeconomic ministry or the prime minister's office), is logically responsible for coordinating its own operations and presenting a coherent position to desired external actors. How formal the internal or external committee need be and whether it should be nationally chaired or co-chaired with the United Nations Development Programme or the WFP depends in large part on how substantial the external role in providing funding and, especially, in onshore operations is.

The refugee situation is rather different. While refugee and home government links should be facilitated (where this is not a self-evident, long-term political non-starter) they can hardly be central until the return phase. What is crucial is a coordinated external actor and host government forum, probably co-chaired by the UNHCR (or the UNDP) and a senior host official or minister. One major topic on its agenda would be "making whole again," that is, meeting the household, local, infrastructural, environmental, and related costs to the host and its people, not just the direct burdens on its treasury. If the host is expected to police camps and to provide military security (whether for or from refugees) at least partial cost reimbursement should be on the agenda. The UNHCR's other roles make it ill suited to running heavy-duty police forces, let alone mini-armies to protect refugees from outsiders or vice versa.

Operationally, too, there is a case both for coordination and for limiting fragmentation, duplication, and diseconomies of small scale. Ideally (except again for refugees) the main channel should be the home country, and the supporting ones the domestic social-sector institutions (for example, churches and mosques and their national councils). Donors, agencies, and external NGOs should seek to provide offshore services and specialized personnel and programming, as well as finance as junior partners to and through them. In refugee cases, either UNHCR or UNDP leadership of all agencies and NGOs is appropriate, but in a context that normally includes refugee representatives (including health, education, water, sanitation, and nutrition providers).

Food security has a physical side. Unless adequate quantities are procured, moved, and delivered, displacees will become debilitated and, in many cases, die. However, food security goes beyond that even on the nutritional side, for example, special interventions or education with reference to children and debilitated arrivals worn out from reaching a place of food and/or physical safety. But, beyond that, the questions of dignity and reempowerment arise, especially during return, but also in the place of refuge. Land and working capital (seeds, tools, and food) are crucial to these and their forward planning and prepositioning at the places to which it has been found that refugees, displacees, and *démobilisées* intend to go home needs far more attention than it has received, with less attention given to usually largely irrelevant transit camps and undesired "new settlements."

Food security can be direct (household provisioning by growing) or indirect (entitlements from producing sales, or from commerce, and/or from waged labor). The desirability of refugee-provided basic services in camp and of labor-intensive infrastructure rehabilitation and development on return (or near the homes of "virtual" calamity displacees when prompt early response enables them to stay at home) fit into this pattern of reempowerment.

Return is as important a part of relating to displacees as support during (or to avert) displacement. For *démobilisées* and "development displacees," indeed, return or resettlement is the whole of the process, since creating even medium-stay camps is a waste of resources and an obstacle to reempowerment. The general points on early warning, prepositioning, institutional structuring, and personnel deployment apply. This is an area in which coordination is probably particularly crucial (with the logical field-level coordinator being the district commissioner or governor or his senior specialist officer) because all arriving households need to be served along similar lines, not by half a dozen separate reempowerment programs depending on prior refugee, displacee, or *démobilisée* status.

In general, return planning and support are too little and too late. Up to 90 percent of displacees return on their own, even though up to 75 percent do stay in organized or semi-organized facilities in places of safety (and/or food provision). In part, this reflects "short-term-ism," in part failure to recognize that food is the key working capital input needed to restore rural production. If a functioning official system in areas of return does not exist, then phased, displacee-driven return programs involving use of complete household ration flow at camps and eventually both back home should be encouraged, not viewed askance as probable fraud.

Participation is crucial to acquiring knowledge of displacees, which only they can provide, to building up sustainable service provision (refugee staff are much less costly than expatriates), and to morale and dignity. Co-governance of programs and especially the overall places of overall refuge governance (applying almost solely to catastrophe refugees or catastrophe-displaced refugees behind the lines of conflict on the side they at least passively favor) pose more problems. These cannot safely be overlooked or treated as outside humanitarian operations, or for that matter food security operations, since refugee macro-governance bodies usually have political, and often personal, projects, frequently requiring use of food for purposes other than civilian household sustenance. Here three nonhumanitarian points do need to be faced squarely. First, is the governance group reasonably acceptable and accountable to the refugees and does it have a political project that is at least not clearly normatively abhorrent or certain to be unsuccessful? Second, what are the group's likely relationships with hosts? And, finally, what are the implications of its political project for speed, ease, and success of return?

These criteria do not give read-off answers. SWAPO was widely felt to qualify on all three points. The Saharan Liberation Movement is queried primarily on the third point; that is, the international community is not committed to forcing a free and fair referendum on Morocco so that the Saharan Liberation Movement (SLM) governance project and return are incompatible. *Interahamwe* failed on the first and third points and was problematic on the second, unless reconsolidating President Mobutu's personal power in eastern Zaire was seen as crucial.

Finance—amount, early availability, and channeling—is a major barrier to improved response. However, early knowledge and response should in fact save money (domestically and internationally), as well as reduce suffering (and death) and enhance food security. Early warning—early preparation and prompt response (including averting most drought displacement)—would raise the quality of assistance (or, if one prefers, its cost-effectiveness) enough to do more for less. Similarly, multiple channeling and maximum use of expatriates are very expensive as well as debilitating for national capacity; focusing on supporting national governmental and social-sector institutions could often yield substantial cost-efficiency gains.

In the case of return, more initial funding is needed. However, if this finance averts the privatization of war into banditry, restores local infrastructure (especially but not only rural) and basic services, and reempowers household production, including direct and/or indirect food self-sufficiency, then it is a bargain in macro as well as in household economic and humanitarian terms. Reempowerment, not just survival, should be the overall strategic response for macroeconomic just as much as household well-being reasons.

PART SEVEN

Regaining and securing access to common property resources

Editors' Note   For poor people, particularly those without land or other assets, income and asset impoverishment can be caused by the loss of access to the nonindividual, common property resources (CPRs) that belonged to communities that are relocated. This kind of loss is systematically overlooked and uncompensated in government recovery schemes. Rarely does project risk analysis include efforts to measure the economic, social, and cultural value of CPRs, which include grazing lands, wastelands, forests and woodlands, surface water and reservoirs, wildlife, fisheries, and riverbeds. Because analysis of common property rights in the context of local customary notions of entitlement is generally not undertaken, the implications of loss of common property assets on the sociocultural and ecological integrity of resettled communities are not fully understood.

In Part Seven of the volume, chapters by Gaim Kibreab and by Dolores Koenig and Tiéman Diarra provide a detailed and comprehensive discussion of the theory of CPRs. Through a range of examples, the authors examine the role of such assets in the livelihoods of the rural poor, and the consequences of losing those assets. The chapters are forward looking in that they consider the possibilities of reviving CPR institutions in areas of relocation in both refugee and development oustee contexts, or of absorbing the resettlers within the existing community resource arrangements in the host areas. The authors concur that CPRs play a key role in the efforts of displaced households to regain a sustainable livelihood and argue that the collective management of resources can offer viable resource protection in resettlement situations.

Kibreab reviews the sustained controversy surrounding CPRs and the "tragedy of the commons," and questions whether or not it is sensible for resettlement projects to revive CPR management systems if those systems may cause, as some contend, resource depletion. The author reasons that the "tragedy of the commons" paradigm, when applied to communally held resources, is misconceived, and that it is not only sensible but essential to reconstruct CPRs at the place of relocation and to stimulate the formal and informal institutions that regulate common assets. By not doing so, he argues, projects that eliminate CPRs without making good the loss to those dependent on such resources inevitably set in motion a process of impoverishment and powerlessness.

But what can be done to compensate oustees for the loss of CPRs? Kibreab contends that monetary compensation is not usually the solution, and proposes instead that CPRs be made available at the new destination and that the necessary conditions to encourage oustees to reinstate effective resource management systems be recreated. Such reconstruction, he argues, requires legally enforced exclusive property rights, the preservation of leadership structures, and maintenance of group cohesion.

Koenig and Diarra highlight the particular problems associated with reconstituting livelihoods after resettling people who live mainly from collectively held natural resources. Drawing on their research on resettlement entailed by the Manantali Dam in Mali, the authors stress the political dimensions of access to CPRs. As a precondition to calculating fair compensation, they highlight the need for governments to recognize the customarily legitimate claims that indigenous people have to CPRs. They also highlight the urgency of addressing the political conflicts that arise between oustees and host communities, particularly where resettlement leads to competing claims to CPRs. The chapter proposes an improved methodology to correctly evaluate the quantity, quality, and diversity of resources in order to avoid underestimating the resources previously available and overestimating the potential of the new site. Efforts should be made, suggest the authors, to involve host organizations.

Finally, Koenig and Diarra propose ways to improve relocation outcomes. These include increasing the political rights and the participation of oustee communities, as well as the transparency of government and implementing agencies. The authors also recommend options for diversifying the ways in which people earn their living, in order to avoid overexploitation of CPRs.

CHAPTER 12

Common property resources and resettlement

Gaim Kibreab[1]

Infrastructure is the physical scaffolding that shoulders economic growth and widens people's access to electricity, clean water, transportation, communication, and other services.

Michael M. Cernea (1994)

Before any developmental project is taken up, the social cost involved must be evaluated with a view to balancing the advantages ... every developmental program must provide for the simultaneous rehabilitation of the persons who are thrown out of their land and houses on account of acquisition of land for such developmental projects. No developmental project, however laudable, can possibly justify impoverishment of large sections of people and their utter destitution.

Supreme Court of India[2]

---

1   The author is affiliated with South Bank University, London.
2   *Lalchand Mahto & Ors vs Coal India Ltd.* in Supreme Court of India, Civil Original Jurisdiction, MP No. 16331 of 1982 (emphasis added).

Overview

On the modern research agenda, population displacement and re-settlement understandably occupy a rather prominent position. This surge of academic interest is, among other things, due to the magnitude of the problem, and the desire to understand its causes and potentially ameliorate the deleterious consequences suffered by the affected populations. As of January 1997, there were, according to the United Nations High Commissioner for Refugees, 13,200,000 refugees; 3,075,000 persons in refugee-like situations;[3] and around 20 million internally displaced persons worldwide (UNHCR 1997:2–3). An average of about 10 million people are also displaced per year by "development projects" and programs such as dam, reservoir, and roads and railway line construction, and urban development (Cernea 1995a; 1995c). Expansion of mechanized agriculture (irrigated and rain-fed) also causes displacement of millions of subsistence farmers and pastoral groups. The number of people displaced by wildlife and forest conservation is also increasingly becoming a serious problem. This is exacerbated by nationalization of land and associated renewable common property resources (CPRs) by governments that allocate such resources to investors in anticipation of higher returns.

Development is inconceivable without optimal utilization of a nation's natural resources. However, the increasing complexity of "development projects" and programs, as well as inadequate and unplanned resettlements informed by misguided and deficient policies or lack of policies, seem to create yet more unwanted social and ecological consequences. In the absence of remedying measures, they may reduce or sometimes even annul the overall net benefits and dividends accruing from such "development projects." Thukral summarizes the experience in India, where there are a large number of big dams (1,500 by the late 1980s) and about 20 million persons affected (1980s data), stating:

> [T]ill a few years ago they [the river valley projects] were being heralded as the symbols of our country's march towards development and progress. Somewhere along the way, that perspective underwent a change. These harbingers of progress began to be viewed as temples of doom spelling disaster for man and nature. The rivers destined

---

[3]   These are people who are not recognized as refugees in spite of the fact that they risk persecution if returned to their countries of origin.

to bring change became the rivers of sorrow. People were no longer willing to pay the price of progress. They began to ask: Who pays the price? Who benefits? (Ganguly Thukral 1992).

The main reason why the rivers that were initially hailed as rivers of hope and opportunity later turned into rivers of sorrow and despair was, among other things, due to the failure by policymakers and planners to create multi-faceted development programs. These should be designed to restore those who were displaced, thereby abandoning their arable land possessions, CPRs, and old way of life — the edifice on which norms and codes of conduct governing economic cooperation and social interaction rested — to an augmented or, at a minimum, their previous socioeconomic status. As Scudder argues, however, the aim of resettlement should be to raise living standards above pre-relocation levels. Mere restoration of previous standards of living will only exacerbate the condition of the majority (Scudder 1997:13).

In most countries, river valleys constitute the bulk of CPRs both in terms of quality and quantity, including water; their loss without replacement has a devastating impact on the livelihoods of the rural poor. For example, in Lesotho, even though the proportion of grazing lost to inundation resulting from the construction of the Lesotho Highlands Water Project (LHWP) may be small, the valleys are critical in the country's seasonal grazing cycle. The valleys are warmer than the highlands in winter and are the habitat for more nutritious and more palatable vegetation (LHWP 1986). Most of the arable lands are also located in the valleys, and crop residues constitute a critical supplement to animal fodder and fuel. The loss of the valleys "due to flooding will reduce the area of winter grazing and the amount of winter fodder significantly ..." (LHWP 1986). In Lesotho, a land-scarce country, the possibility to make good the loss by allocating natural resources (CPRs) in other areas is slim (LHWP 1986, Putsoane 1996). It is these bleak experiences and the desire to circumvent such unwholesome consequences that motivate academics such as Cernea to question the conventional approach to resettlement of populations ousted from their place of origin or habitual residence by "development projects" (Cernea 1990b; see also Cernea 1990a; 1996c; Cernea and Guggenheim 1993; Ganguly Thukral and Singh 1992; and Scudder 1997).

The risk model (see this volume) postulates that in the absence of countervailing intervention, population displacement caused by "development projects" results in the unfolding of a set of scenarios of impoverishment reflected in "landlessness, joblessness, homelessness, marginalization, increased morbidity and mortality, food insecurity, loss of access to common property resources, and social disintegration." The first question that comes to mind is whether it is appropriate to refer to projects that impoverish millions of people directly or indirectly as "developmental." According to Cernea, in India about 20 million people have been displaced by development programs and about 75 percent of these people are worse off compared to their previous status.

The major aim of this paper is to underscore the importance of a development policy that endeavors to counteract the process of impoverishment that may result from the loss of CPRs by people forced to abandon their place of origin or habitual residence because of establishment of "development projects." After a definition and a discussion of the theory of CPRs, the paper examines first, the role of CPRs in the livelihoods of the rural poor and on sustainable resource use; second, the impact of the loss of CPRs on displaced communities; and third, the possibility of reviving CPR institutions in the area of relocation. Last, an attempt is made to expand the scope of the model to cover resettlement of refugees.

The risk model is not based on the principle of compensation of losses. It is about filling a policy vacuum which is a *sine qua non* for adequate planning to prevent the scenario of impoverishment attending displacement from unfolding. This, to a large extent, represents a reversal of previous practices.[4] For example, Brokensha and Scudder argued, "[A]t Kariba we do not think it is unfair to state that the ... government viewed the lake as merely a by-product of the dam, relatively unimportant in itself, and the people requiring relocation as an expensive nuisance" (Brokensha and Scudder 1968).

Before the 1980s, with few exceptions, planning for oustees took place after displacement had already occurred. The literature on the subject is replete with examples in which no adequate planning was exercised to meet the needs of oustees. For example, in India the potential oustees in Rihand and Pong dam (Bhanot and Singh 1992) projects were not informed in advance, and when the hour of displacement struck, they were caught unawares (Ganguly Thukral 1992). In the case of Koyna dam, oustees reported, "there was no time to bring our household goods. The waters rose so quickly that

---

[4]   Before the World Bank's change of heart in the beginning of the 1980s, population displacements resulting from development projects were treated as side effects which had to be accepted for the good of the nation and responses were haphazard. For a discussion see Cernea (1993a and 1999) and Vaswani (1992).

we had to run for life. The water came and everyone cried run! run!" (Karve and Nimbkar 1969). These examples may represent extreme cases, but there is still reluctance among national policymakers and planners to design development programs that will improve the living conditions of oustees or at least enable them to enjoy a socioeconomic status comparable to that of pre-displacement.

As I understand it, the *raison d'être* of the risk model is to predict the set of scenarios of impoverishment that are likely to unfold by "development projects" that cause population displacements, and, consequently, accentuate the need for development of a policy that incorporates countervailing or cushioning programs into the planning and implementation processes of such projects. Only then is it possible to prevent the unfolding of the above stated set of scenarios from taking place. Implicit in the parameters of the model is that the deteriorating living conditions of populations displaced by development projects are not always inevitable consequences as such.[5] They are rather the consequences of failure to intervene in a manner that pre-empts the conditions of impoverishment from unfolding. The developmental implication of this is that as long as remedial measures, designed to offset the pernicious consequences of development projects that *absolutely* require relocation of populations,[6] are made integral parts of such projects, it may be possible for countries to harness their natural resources — water and land — optimally without necessarily incurring immense social and ecological costs. Thus, the effectiveness of the countervailing programs undertaken to circumvent the detrimental effects of displacement and resettlement is measured by their degree of success in rendering the predictions of the risk model inoperative.

Common property resources: definition and theory[7]

Common resources refer to grazing lands, including permanent

---

[5]   "[W]hile some degree of population territorial rearrangements is unavoidable, such inequitable distribution of benefits and losses is neither mandatory nor inevitable... socially responsible resettlement ... can prevent impoverishment and can generate benefits for the regional economy and host populations" (Cernea 1996c:5).

[6]   The emphasis on the word "absolutely" is deliberate because population displacement should be a last resort. The policy of the World Bank, for example, states "[I]nvoluntary displacement should be avoided ... whenever feasible..." quoted in Cernea (1993a:24).

[7]   Part of what follows represents a necessary digression. This is because without such a digression no analysis of CPRs would be complete or interesting.

pastures, uncultivable wastelands, fallow lands, and postharvest grazing areas; forests and woodlands, including religious groves; threshing and waste-dumping grounds; surface water and reservoirs; livestock and human migration routes; ponds and tanks; wildlife; fisheries; watershed drainages and riverbeds; and so on (Jodha 1986:1169; Kibreab 1996b). As used here, the concept of CPRs applies to the above-enumerated resources, provided that access and use are regulated through formal or informal institutions. Formal institutions refer to rules which human beings devise, and informal institutions refer to conventions and codes of behavior.[8] Institutional constraints include "both what individuals are prohibited from doing and, sometimes, under what circumstances individuals are permitted to undertake certain activities" (Jodha 1986:1186; Kibreab 1996b). Thus, "institutions are the framework within which human interaction takes place" (Jodha 1986:1186; Kibreab 1996b). In the absence of resource-regulating institutions, the resources enumerated above are not CPRs. They are nonexclusive, "open-access," or "free-rider" resources in which there are no exclusive property rights. As we shall see below, this distinction is absolutely critical to a proper understanding of the concept of CPRs and to the formulation of appropriate policy guidelines that could inform planning and implementation of development programs designed to meet short- and long-term needs of displaced communities.

The debate on CPRs in natural resource management is one of the most sustained controversies in the social and human sciences, and after centuries of discussions, the debate still looms large. The debate on the commons dilemma is central to the aim of this paper because the desirability of preserving, reviving, revitalizing, reinstating, or reconstructing CPRs among displaced communities is inextricably linked to the type of theory of management of CPRs and alleviation of rural poverty we subscribe to. At the heart of the debate on CPRs lie two issues, namely the difficulty associated with exclusion of potential users of a common resource, and subtractability in the sense that every potential user of a common resource is capable of subtracting from the welfare of others who are dependent on a common resource, hence the "potential divergence between individual and collective economic rationality in joint

---

8   "Informal constraints come from socially transmitted information and are a part of the heritage that we call culture" (North 1990:37). According to Boyd and Richerson culture is defined as the "transmission from one generation to the next, via teaching and imitation, of knowledge, values, the other factors that influence behaviour," quoted in North (1990).

use" (Gordon 1954). In the mainstream literature on natural resource management, resources held in common are said to be subject to overexploitation (Hardin 1968:3859; Cheung 1970; Demsetz 1972; North and Thomas 1977). This axiom is an old one. For example, Aristotle emphatically argued, "what is common to the greatest number has the least care bestowed upon it. Everyone thinks chiefly of his own, hardly at all of the common interest.[9] In 1832, Foster Lloyd also repeated the same truism by comparing the impact of grazing of a given number of stock in two pastures, one owned privately and the other held in common. He predicted that the number of stock in the common would be increased "to press much more forcibly against the means of subsistence," while in the enclosed pasture, there would be a limit beyond which any rational person would cease increasing the size of his herd. He envisaged that the inevitable consequence of the increased stock size on the common pasture would be the depletion of the resource owned in common (Lloyd 1977). The same theory was further developed by Gordon's and Scott's contributions (Gordon 1954, Scott 1955).

The debate took a sudden leap forward following Hardin's contribution. In a discussion of the same subject as Lloyd—the world population problem—Hardin took the example of common pasture used by all members of a community or "open to all" to show what he called the "tragedy of the commons," which obtained in the case of grazing too many cattle on a given common grazing area of land. Hardin argued that since the private benefit of grazing an additional head of cattle on a common pasture with the consequent damage to the common property exceeds the private cost because the cost is shared by all the members of the community, the rational herdsman will add another animal to his herd and the same decision will be reached by all members of the collectivity; thus overuse and abuse are inevitable (Hardin 1968). He stated forcefully that:

> [E]ach man is locked into a system that compels him to increase his herd without limit—in a world that is limited. Ruin is the destination toward which all men rush, each pursuing his own best interest in a society that believes in the freedom of the commons. Freedom in a common brings ruin to all (Hardin 1968:1244).

In his view, the existing incentive structure and the consequent absence of control encourage the individual to increase the size of

---

9   Quoted in Ostrom (1988).

his herd, resulting in resource overexploitation — destruction of the common pasture. Hence the famous parable, "tragedy of the commons." Hardin argues that the herdsman's gain is a function of the size of the herd he grazes on the commons. Because he does not need to internalize the costs or the externalities created by the "assumed" heedless use of the common resource, he need not bother himself about the collective impact of overgrazing. In a similar fashion to Hardin, Picaredi, and Seifert attributed the disaster that afflicted the Sahel to what they call the "tragedy of the commons syndrome," resulting from exploitative traditional pastoral land use practices, which they assume are inherent in the pastoralists' culture (Picaredi and Seifert 1976).

The assumptions underlying the property rights paradigm on the question of CPRs are also similar to those espoused by the exponents of the "tragedy of the commons" model. The central thesis in the property rights paradigm concerning resources owned in common is that resources that are subject to common property rights will sooner or later be depleted because of overconsumption and underinvestment. Demsetz, for example, states that in communally owned land,

> [E]very person has the right to hunt, till, or mine the land. This form of ownership fails to concentrate the cost associated with any person's exercise of his communal right on that person. If a person seeks to maximize the value of his communal rights, he will tend to over-hunt and over-work the land because some of the costs of his doing so are borne by others. The stock of game and the richness of the land will be diminished too quickly (Demsetz 1967:354).

This is due to the fact that when there is collective ownership of a scarce resource, there is an externality that "... occurs whenever an action taken by an economic unit has a *direct* impact on the welfare or productivity of some other economic unit" (Dorfman 1974). For example, if an individual catches an animal, he receives the whole benefit of the catch, but the costs are shared by all members of the user community, i.e. there will be fewer animals for the rest of the members of the user community to catch, and, consequently, the effort involved in hunting will increase. He further argues that the structure of the situation is such that individual members of the user community will have no incentive to invest either to conserve the resource or to replace the off-take. The outcome is, therefore, an incentive to overuse and underinvest in the common resource (Demsetz 1967:354).

Cheung also argues that with unlimited entry of users to a non-exclusive resource, for example, fishery, catching of fish will go on until, to use his own formulation, "rent is completely dissipated." In his view, it is the nonexclusive nature of the resource that precludes stipulation of the conditions of its use in the form of a contract. He argues that the opportunity to stipulate conditions of resource use does not exist in the absence of exclusive rights. The consequence is inevitable depletion of the resource (Cheung 1970:49–50). North and Thomas also use the same theoretical construct to describe the behavior of prehistoric man toward a common resource, namely migratory animals. In their view, the individual band will thoughtlessly continue capturing the commonly held animals before their rivals capture them. The tendency is, therefore, to overexploit the resource until exhaustion because there is no incentive to conserve the resource and because of the failure to internalize the social costs of overexploitation (North and Thomas 1977). Johnson also sees exploitative land use practice as inevitable in conditions of communal ownership of resources because, in his view, the communal land tenure system is inherently inefficient and is devoid of an incentive structure that would encourage people to utilize the land for optimal use (Johnson 1972:271).

The solution to the commons "dilemma," according to the "tragedy of the commons" model and the property rights paradigm, is either privatization or state intervention (Hardin 1978:314). It is postulated that "if ruin is to be avoided in a crowded world, people must be responsive to a coercive force outside their individual psyches, a 'Leviathan', to use Hobbe's term" (Hardin 1978:314). Ophuls had earlier argued, "... because of the tragedy of the commons, environmental problems cannot be solved through cooperation... and the rationale for government with major coercive powers is overwhelming.... even if we avoid the tragedy of the commons, it will only be by recourse to the tragic necessity of Leviathan"(Ophuls 1973:228–229).

Critique of the theory of common property resources

The question that springs to mind is that if the assumptions underlying the "tragedy of the commons" model and the property rights paradigm concerning CPRs are sound and correct, why should a resettlement project aim to revive, revitalize, or reconstruct CPRs? Why should funding and development agencies and governments be expected to expend their scarce resources in efforts designed to conserve and revive resource management systems that are said to lie at the heart of the problem of resource depletion? Exponents of the "tragedy of the commons" parable who are probably overrepresented in international financial and development organizations such as the World Bank, United Nations, and so forth as well as in government bureaucracies (both in donor and receiving countries), may instead see the breakdown of CPRs precipitated by development project-related displacement as a blessing in disguise and consequently be reluctant to allocate scarce resources for their revival or reconstruction. Thus, the task of changing the mind-set of these powerful and ideologically motivated groups may not be easy.

However, for those who are sensitive and willing to embrace empirical knowledge, it is easy to see that the "tragedy of the commons" parable when applied to communally held resources is awry. Despite their preeminent place in policymaking, the "tragedy of the commons" model and the property rights paradigm concerning resources owned or utilized in common have been subject to scathing criticisms over time for lack of theoretical vigor and empirical evidence.[10] For example, Repetto and Holmes among many others state the "tragedy of the commons" "has almost become myth. Rarely has there been so influential a paradigm with so shaky factual and conceptual bases" (Repetto and Homes 1984:615). Circiacy-Wantrup also states that the "catchy phrase" of community property resources has created confusion and argues that whether common property of natural resources represents a tragedy in terms of environmental depletion depends on "what social institutions...are guiding resource use" in both common or private property (Circiacy-Wantrup 1971:43). He further states that agricultural land held in common by villages in medieval Europe was "conserved by institutions based on custom and law before private property and the profit motive broke up these decision systems."

It is argued here that the building blocks or the assumptions on which the "tragedy of the commons" model stands are misconceived.[11] First, the model does not recognize the ability of users of a common resource to limit intensity of use to sustainable levels in the interest of the common good by instituting rules based on cus-

---

[10]   See Runge (1983; 1984); Bromley (1985); Sudgen (1984); Brubaker (1975). Further examples, which reject the tragedy of the commons parable, can be found *ad infinitum*.

[11]   An elaborate critique is beyond the scope of this chapter. Only a few aspects of the theory of the commons will be raised here. For more elaborate discussion and empirical evidence against the "tragedy of the commons" parable see Kibreab (forthcoming-b).

tom, proscriptions, and social norms. Members of the user group observe these rules; otherwise those who try to ride free or break the rules have to bear the cost of nonobservance. Second, no distinction is made between "open-access" resources and CPRs. This distinction is central to the concept of CPRs in which there are social regulations that provide for exclusion of nonmembers and regulation of use (see Berkes and others 1989; Circiacy-Wantrup and Bishop 1975). In the case of "open-access" resources, there are no property rights. A resource without property rights is nobody's property. Thus, entry is unlimited and use is not regulated. Not surprisingly, therefore, the result is deleterious to the resource itself and to those who depend on it. It is the realization of the confusion resulting from the failure to distinguish between "open-access/free-rider resources" and CPRs that prompted Ciriacy-Wantrup and Bishop (1975) to state:

> [E]conomists [this is true in all social science disciplines] are not free to use the concept of "common property resources"...under the conditions where no institutional arrangements exist. Common property is not 'everybody's property.' The concept implies that potential resource users who are not members of a group of co-equal owners are excluded. The concept of 'property' has no meaning without this feature.

Cox also compares the "tragedy of the commons" with Tonypandy.[12] She argues it is not only in history that Tonypandy occurs. In her view, a prime example of Tonypandy in the field of economics is the "tragedy of the commons." Cox equates the "tragedy of the commons" parable with Tonypandy and admonishes academics to feel repugnance for it (Cox 1985:65).

In the corpus of knowledge accumulated over time on the subject, the term "common property" has become a "catch-all" phrase. The confusion could substantially be reduced if a distinction is made between the resource itself and the property rights regime under which it is held (Ostrom 1986; Bromley 1989). This is because a resource can be held under more than one property rights regime, namely communal property (*res communes*), state property (*res publica*), or private property. A resource held outside any of these property rights regimes is "no property," thus it is an "open-access" (*res*

---

12   In Cox 1985:49 Tonypandy refers to "the regrettable situation which occurs when a historical event is reported and memorized inaccurately but consistently until the resulting fiction is believed to be the truth."

nullius) resource. The likely outcome of the activities of multiple users in the latter is often "tragic," mainly because exclusion is impossible, thus entry is unlimited and access to, and use of, the resource is unregulated. This constitutes an essential difference between a resource held under communal property rights regime and a "free-rider" or "open-access" resource. Hardin and like-minded academics do not make this important distinction. This failure is clear in Hardin where he urges his readers to assume a pasture "open to all." The reality of a resource held communally, however, is that it is not "open to all." It is exclusively accessible to members of a socially recognized group of users, among whom there are formal and informal constraints; outsiders are excluded unless they obtain prior permission from the rights holders. Not only are the latter able to deny outsiders entry, but they can also impose conditions of entry. That is what the concept of property rights essentially means.

Common property and the institutions that regulate joint use are quite old, dating in certain instances to prehistoric times. They were well established in formal institutions such as Anglo-Saxon common law, German land law, Roman law, and their successors. They were also well established in informal institutions based on custom, tradition, norms, and so on. Taylor, for example, traces the origin of the open-field system in Western Europe to the time when "nucleated villages were formed during the ninth, tenth, or eleventh centuries" (Taylor 1981:21). Thirsk also traces the earliest case of CPRs in the form of regulated cropping by a whole village to around 1156 (Thirsk 1964:23). Some of the resources and the institutions that regulated access and use centuries ago are still in existence even in countries that have undergone profound structural transformation. For example, England and Wales still have about 1.5 million acres of communally held CPRs (Ciriacy and Bishop 1975:719). The Alpine meadows in Switzerland, Austria, and southern Bavaria are still communally owned, whereby access to, and use of, the CPRs is regulated through old customary rules (Netting 1978). In Japan there are still about 3 million hectares of forests and uncultivated mountain meadows still held and managed in common by villagers (McKean 1986). Many other case studies also show the ability of users of a common resource to devise institutional arrangements to exclude outsiders and to limit the level of exploitation by members to a sustainable level. To mention a few examples, hunters in James Bay; lobstermen in Maine; trawlermen in the New York Bight area; communal forest users in Nepal; irrigation water users in south India (Berkes et al. 1989); water managers in West Basin, California; fishermen in

Alanya, Turkey (Ostrom 1988); and many other user groups have been able to exclude outsiders and to devise binding institutional arrangements that regulate access to, and use of, resources used in common. In many developing countries, CPRs exhibit a high degree of resilience in spite of nationalization and privatization.

These data clearly show that privatization and state ownership of CPRs are not the only viable policy options in the sustainable management of renewable resources. Among rural communities with established institutional arrangements such as kinship, custom, and social norms, communal ownership is equally if not more appropriate than the two property rights regimes mentioned above.

Limitations of privatization of CPRs

The experience of privatization, including individual allocation instead of government control of CPRs, has not been successful. For example, in India, a study of more than 80 villages in 21 districts in the dry region of seven states shows that the large-scale privatization of CPRs has led to a considerable deterioration of the economic conditions of the rural poor (Jodha 1986:1172). In the early 1950s, a far-reaching land reform program was implemented in which most of the CPRs were distributed to individual households, including the poor. Not only has the area and the productivity of the CPRs declined as a result, but most of the poor who had received land soon thereafter have lost their allocations to the well-off. In the dry regions of India, "between 63 and 91 percent of the land distributed to the poor under welfare programs subsequently changed owners" (Jodha 1986:1179).

In rural India, the contribution of CPRs towards the income of the rural poor as well as rural equity was much higher before privatization than at present (Jodha 1986:1178; Pasha 1992:2499). There are many studies that show the depletion of CPRs both in terms of area and productivity subsequent to privatization (see Blaikie and others 1985; Chopra, Kadekodi, and Murty 1989; Damodaran 1988). Since land reform (early 1950s), the area of CPRs had declined by 26 to 63 percent (Jodha 1986:1169). The causes of the decline are (a) physical loss of resources as a result of development projects such as submersion of CPRs in irrigation dams, roads, and buildings; (b) deterioration of physical productivity caused by degradation of pastures and forest lands after privatization; and (c) privatization of rights of usufruct and ownership of CPRs (Jodha 1986:1178) and uninterrupted encroachment by the well-off (Pasha 1992:2499) on what was left as CPRs as a "consequence of government-sponsored privatization" (Karanth 1992:1685).

This is not only true in India, but also is generally the case throughout most of the Asian and African countries.[13] For example, in Botswana, the government's policy of dividing the previously communally held range lands and water into individual holdings and communal grazing has led to depletion of range lands resources and to deterioration of the living conditions of the rural poor (Mufune 1995). This land policy was implemented to conserve the environment and to help the tribal communities, but the outcome has been disastrous on both accounts (Selolwane 1995; Monu 1995).

Limitations of state ownership of CPRs

The belief that common ownership and use of CPRs are the causes of resource depletion has not only generated advocacy for privatization, but also for state intervention. As pointed out earlier, there are those who argue that the "tragedy of the commons" cannot be counteracted without heavy-handed state intervention. This view is uncritically embraced by many postcolonial Asian and African governments. Thus, state intervention in the management of CPRs is widespread. Most researchers who have addressed this issue in the African and Asian contexts generally point out with regret that state intervention has been a recipe for depletion of CPRs and deterioration of the living conditions of the rural poor.[14] Governments may not be innately bad managers of natural resources, even though the historical record of state ownership of CPRs in developing countries has been dismal and leaves no room for optimism. The problems associated with state intervention are twofold. First, in many poor countries, governments view themselves as the sole providers of services and as vehicles of economic development and social progress. In the process, the drive for revenue maximization tends to lock them into a system that forces them to over-exploit the CPRs, disregarding their long-term sustainability. This is done in the name of development. Thus, developmental use of CPRs and their preservation, instead of being perceived as complementary to each other and as constituting parts of the same continuum in national resource management regimes, are traded off with each other by governments

---

[13]   In view of the limited scope of this paper, only a few examples are discussed.
[14]   For an elaborate discussion and the critical literature see Kibreab (forthcoming-b, Chapter 10).

as if they represent a dichotomy. In the trade-off decisions, the developmental use of CPRs prevails over their preservation. Most governments, desperate to earn foreign exchange, find exploitation of forests and other CPRs an easy option too difficult to resist. In many countries this has led to serious problems of environmental degradation.[15]

Second, government ownership of CPRs is exercised by forfeiting the ownership and usership rights of traditional resource users; this often leads to the breakdown of historically evolved resource-regulating institutions based on traditions, customs, kinship relations, moral pressures, and restraints. Thus, enforcement and preservation of the newly acquired (through legislation) state property rights requires continuous policing and monitoring. For governments with poor revenues, these costs become prohibitive, and no effective control is exercised (Bromley and Chapagain 1984; Kibreab 1996b). This is exacerbated by widespread incompetence and corruption of the bureaucracies. As Ghai perceptively observes:

> [W]hile the state took over formal responsibility for the management of commons and other resources previously governed by customary rules, it was rarely able to exercise effective control. This created the worst possible situation from the point of view of resource conservation: the traditional system of resource management was effectively undermined but nothing was put in its place. The result was uncontrolled and shortsighted exploitation of common property resources that further accelerated environmental degradation.

In many developing countries, government ownership has led to the abolition of the traditional resource management systems. Worse still, the governments have been unable to establish viable substitutes for what existed before. The consequence is that the CPRs, which were previously governed by historically evolved, culturally prescribed, and socially sanctioned institutional arrangements, became *de facto* open-access resources. In many countries, government intervention has set in motion a process of encroachment on the sources of livelihood of the rural poor: illegal seizure of CPRs by powerful members of local communities, commercial farmers, and charcoal producers who come from distant areas to expropriate from the poor the source of their livelihoods (Kibreab forthcoming-b).

---

[15]   For detailed examples, see Kibreab (forthcoming-b).

It will be argued below that in view of the failed experiences of holding CPRs under private or state property-rights regimes in traditional communities displaced by development-related projects or other events, the most appropriate resettlement policy with regard to CPRs is one that aims to preserve and develop the latter within a communal property-rights regime. This approach is rational in terms of sustenance of livelihoods, protection of local environment, efficiency (in terms of minimum disputes and speedy and cost-effective resolution), minimization of transaction costs associated with defining property rights, devising and enforcing of resource-regulating rules, and policing of compliance and preservation of community cohesion and a cherished way of life.

The role of communally held CPRs in the livelihoods of the rural poor

In most rural areas in developing countries, CPRs that are subject to regulatory institutions play significant roles in terms of environmental sustainability, sustenance of rural poor, and in fostering and maintaining communal organization and group cohesion. Berkes and Farvar, for example, argue that the diverse traditional resource management systems have been the main means by which societies have managed their natural resources over millennia on a sustainable basis. "It is only as a result of this that we have any resources today to speak about."[16] This is achieved, among other things, through exclusion of outsiders, through limiting intensity of resource use by members

---

[16]   See Berkes and Farvar (1989:6). On the basis of different case studies worldwide, the authors listed a sampling of 18 traditional resource-allocation and use-regulating institutions which have survived the forces of change both in the developed and the developing worlds in the areas of communal irrigation, water run-off management, grazing, fishing, forests and meadows management, wildlife hunting, shifting cultivation,and so on. These are the *boneh* in Iran (irrigation); *huerta* in Spain (irrigation); *zanjera* in Philippines (irrigation); *subak* in Bali, Indonesia (irrigation); *jessour* in Tunisia (water runoff management); *hema* in Arab Middle East (pasture reserves); *agdal* in Morocco (range/ pasture); common pasture in England (range/pasture); *dina* in Mali (grazing, fishing and farming); *iriaichi* in Japan (village forests and meadows); *iriai* in Japan (coastal fishing); *valli* in Adriatic, Italy (lagoon fishing); *tambak* in Java, Indonesia (brackish water fish ponds); *acadja* in West Africa (lagoon fishing); *nituhuschii* in eastern subarctic Canada (wildlife hunting territories); *jhum* in northeast India (shifting cultivation); *ladang* in Malaysia; and *kaingin* in Philippines. To this, one may add *dar* in the Sudan and *diesa* in Eritrea. The list could be increased ad infinitum.

of the rights holders to sustainable levels, and through undertaking conservation activities on a family or mutual help basis to counter problems of soil erosion, deforestation, overgrazing, and siltation.

CPRs benefit rural people, especially the poor, in terms of supply of fodder, wood fuel, construction materials, furniture, food (fish, fruits, roots, barks, nuts, and vegetables), handles for weapons, fibers (for making mats, ropes and baskets), containers for water and milk, raw materials for agricultural implements, musical instruments, glues, gums, flowers, honey, medicinal herbs, small game (meat and skins), clay for making pots, mulch, manure, and so on. Some resources held in common are also useful for ritual purposes.

Through the supply of forage and grazing space, CPRs enable farmers, especially those who suffer from land shortage, to devote all of their arable land possessions to crop production (Jodha 1986). In the absence of fodder and grazing space provided by CPRs, these farmers would be forced to use part of their arable land for grazing. In most developing countries, the rural poor are dependent on mixed farming—crop and animal husbandry. CPRs are instrumental in these farming systems. In such economies, livestock are sources of supply of draft animals for traction, manure for fertilization, and milk and meat for sale and self-consumption. Livestock also represent storage of wealth and are often symbols of high social status. Crop residues are used for animal feed during the dry season.

In view of the physical constraints prevailing in the arid and semi-arid regions, livestock production would be difficult or virtually impossible if farmers, especially the poor, were solely to rely on their own individual plots. One of the central coping strategies adopted by people living in the arid and semi-arid regions is mobility designed to take advantage of the variations in the environment. Livestock change locations several times per year in search of pasture and water and in some places to escape the scourge of biting flies and muddy and sticky soils during the rains (Kibreab 1996b). This would have been impossible if watering points, migration routes, and pastures were not held in common. As opposed to CPRs held in common, experiences from different Asian and African countries show that nationalization and privatization invariably tend to weaken long-standing traditional resource management systems and result in undermining production systems based on pastoralism and mixed farming. To mention a few examples, in the Sudan and Somalia, nationalization of arable land and CPRs has led to spontaneous and unplanned horizontal expansion of large-scale mechanized rain-fed agriculture and excessive tree felling by commercial charcoal producers resulting in dramatic reduction of grazing areas, disruption

of nomadic routes, blocking of access to watering points, displacement of small farmers, and decline of CPRs (Shepherd 1989; Kibreab
forthcoming-b). This had led to not only a concentration of pastoral
herds and humans with detrimental environmental and welfare consequences, but also to increased confrontation between commercial
farmers and pastoral groups because of the trespass of animals into
cropped areas. Bromley and Chapagain's (1984) findings in South
Asia also show that nationalization set in motion the forces of resource degradation partly because villagers were deprived of CPRs
(and hence encroachment was inevitable) and partly because the states
were unable to enforce the new institutional arrangements.

In most of the arid and semi-arid rural areas, livelihoods are
dependent on subsistence agriculture where the distribution of soils
and water, including rainfall, is often quite random over both time
and space (Runge 1986). Joint rights of access to the basic natural
resources ensure fair distribution and consequently foster equality
between common property rights holders. If these resources were
owned individually, some households would be better-off to the
detriment of others because of variations in the quality of the soils,
availability of irrigation water, and distribution of rainfall. In most
arid and semi-arid areas, the amount and distribution of rainfall
and the qualities of soils vary considerably even over short distances
(Kibreab forthcoming-b).

For example, in the Eritrean plateau, arable land and CPRs have
always been owned communally by groups related by common de-
scent or common residence. The available historical evidence suggests that ox plough cultivation was in use as early as 500–1000 B.C.
(McCann 1995). Eritrea is located in the arid and semi-arid region
of sub-Saharan Africa. The inhabitants have always been aware of
the fragility of the environment and of the variation in the quality
of the soils and in the quantity of water and rainfall distribution
even over very short distances. In response to this physical constraint, they developed an institutional arrangement which ensured
equitable distribution of the common resources. One of the dominant systems of land tenure in the country is village ownership
known as *diesa* where land and the associated renewable CPRs are
conceived as the common property of a village. Every member of
the village (*gebar*) who has a habitation (*tisha*) in a village is entitled
to a share in the village land (Nadel 1946). Members of the community receive their share of the communal land by means of a periodical redistribution of the village land, called *warieda*, carried out
by lot. In order to avoid abuse, this is supervised by a village chief,
village priest, and three chosen elders.

To ensure an almost mathematically exact division, the available village land is graded according to its fertility. In the most common system of grading we meet with three categories (though some communities have adopted more numerous grades). They are known as *walakha* (the most fertile land), *dukha* (land of medium quality), and *gereb* (poor land). The drawing of lots is repeated for each category of land, every *gebar* receiving his share of each (emphasis added) (Nadel 1946:13).

Such distributions made possible by communal land tenure ensured that every qualified member of the user group received an equal share of the village land in terms of quality and quantity. This traditional system of communal tenure left no room for initial inequality.

Runge (1986:621) also argues that poverty, in combination with randomly distributed natural resources, creates uncertainty with respect to income streams. In the developed economies, he posits that the randomness of nature and the level of uncertainty resulting from the same are either controlled or minimized by the development of techniques of production such as irrigated crop production, feedlot livestock operations, or by the development of food distribution chains that allow pooling of risks and hence reduce uncertainty. One of the consequences of this high degree of uncertainty in a developing country rural setting is that individuals live under a permanent threat of failure. Unpredictable events, such as floods or drought, may strike and bring calamity.

In the face of this environmental uncertainty, "common property institutions ... [are] innovated; when they emphasize the right to exclude, they provide for the right to be equally included as a hedge against uncertain prospects. The expectation that when one is in need, aid will be forthcoming from others in return for a like commitment, may be more agreeable than 'going it alone' in the face of nature" (Runge 1986:621).

These factors foster unity and promote cooperation among groups of CPRs users.

In the arid and semi-arid regions in which the occurrence and distribution of rainfall are concentrated in a few months per year, riverbeds, water catchments, and streams provide opportunity for irrigated horticultural production during dry seasons. In the drought-prone areas, not only does the produce from these irrigated plots provide income to cultivators, but also contributes to the improvement of the nutritional status of the communities at large. If these were owned privately, the benefits would accrue to a few families and the poor would be excluded.

During periods of crop failure, CPRs constitute important sources of food collected from forests, ponds, rivers, lakes, and other sources. For example, in western Sudan, during the drought years, collected fruits from wild trees were more important in the sustenance of life than relief aid (Rees 1990). CPRs also promote self-employment of poor rural people either in gathering or processing of CPRs (see Johri and Drishnakumar 1991). The proceeds from these activities supplement their incomes in normal years and become critical in tiding over crises resulting from destruction of crops by insects, floods, diseases, drought, and so on. CPRs also mitigate rural inequality when poor farmers are able to supplement their incomes (Jodha 1986; Karanth 1992; Chopra and others 1989). Thus, not only is the revival and revitalization of CPRs among displaced communities indispensable for reconstructing viable livelihoods at the area of relocation, but the question of determining the property rights regime under which to hold these resources is equally critical. The preceding analysis clearly suggests that the most appropriate property rights regime for reconstructing CPRs among relocatees from the point of view of equality, social justice, environmental sustainability, sustenance of social cohesion, community organization, efficiency, and so forth, is neither private nor public, but through communal property rights.

Political vulnerability, displacement, loss of CPRs, and resettlement

Given the inequitable nature of the production relations and power structures prevailing in most societies, those who are adversely affected by development projects are those who are excluded from direct or indirect control over state power and from decisionmaking. These are invariably the downtrodden and the powerless. One of the consequences of this powerlessness is that they are unable to "make their voice heard and force the adoption of better policies" (Cernea 1993a:19; Scudder 1997). Consequently, not only is there lack of "explicit and rigorous norms about how to carry out involuntary displacement and relocation" (Cernea 19983a:119; Scudder 1997), but also the decision as to where to locate dams, roads, relocation sites, and so forth whom to displace; or whose property or rights of usufruct to expropriate for construction or establishment of such projects is seldom a neutral decision dictated purely by resource availability. For example, in India, studies on the composition of people displaced by development projects reveals that the majority belong to the poorer sections of society. According to government estimates between 40 and 50 percent of those displaced by development projects are poor tribal communities (Government of India, quoted in Ganguly Thukral 1992:8). A fairly large proportion also belong to the scheduled castes (Fernandes and Ganguly Thukral 1989). As Thukral perceptively argues this does not imply that resources are available only in areas where the poor live. *"More significantly, these are the areas where the powerless live"* (Ganguly Thukral 1992). He gives examples in which valuable deposits of scarce resources such as cooking coal and oil have not been exploited because of the reluctance of those in authority to displace more powerful groups in society. Research findings also show that those who suffered the most were those who had "lost all and gained nothing" (Ganguly Thukral 1992). In other words, the dams have made the rich richer and the poor poorer (Singh, Kothari, and Amin 1992:188). Those who are displaced have not benefited from the projects that have caused their displacement.

As we saw before, CPRs play a key role in the livelihoods of rural poor. For example, a study of more than 80 villages in the dry regions of 21 districts of seven states in India shows that between 80 and 100 percent of the poor gather food, fuel, fodder, fiber, and many other useful items from CPRs. The corresponding figures for the large farmers show that only between 10 and 28 percent depended on CPRs for the same items (Jodha 1986:1172). Thus, since the overwhelming majority of the rural poor are dependent on CPRs for fodder, fuel, timber, water, manure, silt, supplementary food, income, employment, and so on, and since a large proportion of those who are displaced by development projects are the poorer sections of society, they are those most adversely affected by loss of CPRs in the process of displacement and resettlement. Thus, a development project, be it a dam, a road, a railway, or an agricultural project that absorbs CPRs without making good the loss to those whose livelihoods are dependent on such resources, inevitably sets in motion a process of impoverishment and powerlessness. There are, therefore, compelling reasons for development of a policy that aims at ensuring access to CPRs by oustees at the place of relocation.

Hitherto, in spite of their significant role in the livelihoods of the rural poor and sustainable resource management, CPRs have been either neglected or their significance has been underestimated by policymakers and planners of development projects that cause loss of such resources. For example, Brokensha's and Scudder's findings show that in Nigeria, international experts consistently belittled the agricultural and fisheries potential of the Kainji Lake Basin population in spite of the fact that over 10,000 of the people were involved in intensive farming systems (Brokensha and

Scudder 1968:22). In the countries where there have been displacements and resettlements linked to development projects, only those with title to arable land are compensated. The rest, including those whose livelihoods depend on CPRs and other economic activities, have no legally enforceable right of compensation. Landless laborers, land-poor farmers, sharecroppers, nomads, forest produce gatherers, handicraftsmen, artisans, water sellers, and so forth have no entitlement to compensation in cash or kind simply because they lack formal title to land (Vaswani 1992:158). Those who receive no compensation are likely to drift to different parts of the country in search of livelihoods instead of joining their fellow villagers in the resettlement site. Not only does the exclusion of these groups represent deprivation of sources of livelihood and a form of sociocultural dismemberment and loss of long-established social relations and community networks, but also negatively affects the private property resource-based economic activities at the destination.[17] It is in an attempt to rectify this detrimental situation that the World Bank admonishes those concerned, stating:

> [I]ndigenous people, ethnic minorities, pastoralists, and other groups that may have informal customary rights to the land or *other resources* taken for the project, must be provided with adequate land, infrastructure, and other compensation. The absence of a formal legal title to land by such groups should not be grounds for denying compensation (emphasis added) (Cernea 1993a:25).

It remains to be seen how far this guideline would influence future actions because, as Cernea argues, governments whose policies caused population displacements in the past have not been receptive to research findings and new knowledge (Cernea 1993a:19).

Other social groups that are most adversely affected by loss of CPRs upon displacement are women and children. In most of the developing world's rural areas, women and children are responsible for collecting fuel wood, fodder, water, and other products.[18]

---

[17]   Without artisans, agricultural laborers, sharecroppers, handicraftsmen, and so on, those who receive land at the destination may not be able to make the best out of it.

[18]   Recent studies show, however, that beyond a given distance, the participation of women in firewood collection and carrying decreases because of conflicting demands for women's labor for household chores. For a detailed discussion and empirical evidence see Kibreab (1996b).

Not only do women suffer as a consequence of loss of CPRs, but in countries such as India, "an adult woman who is either unmarried or divorced and who does not hold any land in her own right is neither considered to be a displaced person nor part of the family of such a person. Consequently, she is not to be entitled to any relief" (Vaswani 1992:162). The situation elsewhere is not likely to be different.

The reasons why CPRs are neglected by policymakers and planners in resettlement projects may vary from one region or country to another. However, the norm in most countries is that, development planning emphasizes private or government ownership of resources to the neglect of resources owned in common. This is because of the dominance of the "tragedy of the commons" model and the property rights paradigm, which represent the central plank of the canons of conventional resource management models, the wisdom of many contemporary managers of common property resources, and the models of development exported to developing countries (Berkes and Farvar 1989). However, in the past few years there has been a surge of academic and administrative interest in the preservation, development, use, and management of CPRs. This surging interest is not only due to increasing concern with ecological sustainability, but also to increasing disillusionment with past development projects that emulated the resource management techniques of the industrialized countries. There is also awareness about the significant roles common property systems can play in the development process by providing an efficient, cost-effective, stable, and adaptable institutional framework for sustainable resource use (Gibbs and Bromley 1989; Kibreab 1996b; Kibreab forthcoming-b).

This renewed interest in the role of CPRs in the life of the rural poor has also contributed to a better understanding of the survival strategies of the poor and of the symbiotic relationship that exists between CPRs and private property resource-based economic activities in rural areas. The increasing awareness of the problems suffered due to loss of CPRs and exclusion from the benefits deriving from the projects that cause displacement has over time generated willingness on the part of the victims and their sympathizers to organize themselves in order to articulate and protect their interests. For example, "the oustees of Chaskaman in Maharashtra had organized themselves under the leadership of Baba Adhav, one of the most eminent and respected social workers in Maharashtra" (Ganguly Thukral 1992).

In many developing countries, CPRs, including arable land, are *res publica* suggesting that "legally" the state can allocate such resources for alternative uses at any time without payment of any compensation in cash or kind. For example, in Lesotho, all land, including CPRs, is de jure state property, and the state is not required by law to compensate those who lose their land possessions and access to CPRs (LHWP 1986). The question of state ownership of land and CPRs in this respect is nothing more than a legal nicety. Depending upon its political character, a state may be able to pass a law to entrust upon itself the ownership of all natural resources by violating the principle of due process of law, or it may even expropriate a given resource on the basis of the principle of eminent domain, but no state is justified to invoke these principles to destroy peoples' livelihoods. Thus, livelihoods of all people adversely affected by displacement should be protected. This principle should guide state action, notwithstanding the formal legal rights of people ousted by development projects. This principle is adopted by the Lesotho Highlands Water Authority, which states:

> There are existing mechanisms for directly compensating people for loss of dwellings and structures, but because land is held by the state, there is no compensation for the loss of land. Nevertheless, in order to sustain communities and individuals adversely affected through the loss of their arable and grazing land base, some means of compensation has to be devised to ensure that these communities do not fall below their standard of living.[19]

Because there is no unoccupied land in the country, the aim is not to base compensation on the principle of land for land, but rather to create a new economic framework, probably based on small-scale cottage industries (LHWP 1986).

By now it must have become clear that CPRs play a significant role in the livelihoods of the rural poor; consequently their loss may deprive the latter of important sources of income, biomass, raw materials, and way of life. Failure to make good on this loss is a recipe for impoverishment and social disintegration. The importance of CPRs to the rural poor is succinctly described by Agrawal as follows:

> [T]he vast majority of the people of the world—the poor of the Third World—live within a biomass-based sub-

---

[19]   Lesotho, as a latecomer, seems to have learned through a negative example.

sistence economy. Fundamental needs like food, fuels, building materials, fertilizers, raw materials like bamboo, the various types of grasses for traditional crafts and occupations are all forms of biomass, most of which are collected freely from the immediate environment. For these biomass-dependent people ... [who] do not benefit much from the gross national product, there is another GNP which is far more important, and this is what I call the Gross Nature Product (Agarwal 1989:33).

Thus, the question of reconstructing or reviving CPRs in a post-displacement period is not only a means to development, but is one of the goals of development. Among traditional communities, CPRs are a way of life and they have their own intrinsic values. The extent of the economic, social, and cultural costs incurred by communities that lose access to CPRs due to development projects or other reasons cannot, therefore, be simply measured in economic terms. Notwithstanding the fact that CPRs play a critical role in the economic life of the rural poor, they constitute an integral part of a rural way of life that combine social, legal, and economic institutions in a cultural unity, more than a way of earning incomes.

This suggests that the loss of access to, and control of, CPRs cannot be made good through payment of monetary compensation. In fact the available evidence suggests that payment of monetary compensation to some categories of oustees for loss of arable land does not make economic sense. Cash in the hands of the poor, especially the tribals who have little or no exposure to the outside world, has very little meaning. Dhagamwar's findings show that the cash compensation paid to oustees "ran through their inexperienced hands like water from a sieve" Dhagamwar 1992:189). Viegas's study among the Hirakud Dam oustees also shows that the tribals were easily hoodwinked by greedy petty businessmen selling consumer items such as transistors, watches, and other colorful trinkets (see also Nayak in this volume). Others lost their money in gambling and drinking (Viegas 1992). Not surprisingly, therefore, most of these people were reduced to destitution without any prospect for self-sufficiency. For many, prostitution and thieving become the only means of earning a living. In most cases, as de Wet argues, not only is compensation for loss of land often inadequate, but payment is often delayed "leading to outright loss, and to indebtedness" and as a result "people may never recover their former standard of living" (de Wet 1995:13).

Conditions for reconstructing common property institutions

The question that arises is: What is to be done to avoid loss of CPRs by oustees? There can be no single universally valid way of doing this, but whenever possible the best way to avoid loss of access to CPRs is to make these resources available at the new destination. As pointed out earlier in the discussion of the theory of CPRs and the critique of the same, CPRs can be held in three forms of property rights regimes. It was also pointed out that the most appropriate property rights regime for holding CPRs among rural people, especially the poor, is under communal property. We also saw that the concept of common property does not only refer to natural resources, but also to institutions that regulate allocation and use of such resources. Thus, a mere physical replacement of natural resources at the destination without recreating the necessary conditions that encourage oustees to revive those institutions held in abeyance during the displacement process that regulate access to, and use of, the common property would inevitably lead on the one hand, to depletion of the resources and on the other, to deterioration of the living conditions of those dependent on them. As we saw before, it is these institutions that avert the threat of the "tragedy of the commons" from occurring.

It is assumed in most of the literature that not only do displacement and resettlement disrupt systems of production, social networks, structures of social organization, and so on, but also the informal institutions, including those that regulate resource allocation and use. Whether resource-regulating institutions break down as a result of displacement and relocation is an empirical question. It cannot be determined a priori. Not only is this dependent on the way displacement and relocation are managed, but informal institutions unlike formal institutions are extremely resilient and resistant to change. If the processes of displacement and relocation are sensitively and conscientiously planned and managed with full cooperation and direct participation of the affected populations,[20] in-

---

[20]   This presupposes first, that the communities concerned (both oustees and hosts) are involved in the process from the outset and that the project in question is an outcome of negotiation rather than an imposition; second, they are made beneficiaries rather than benefactors; third, the new site is located in a familiar environment that can allow oustees to make use of their skills, land use practices, and so on;. and fourth, the communities are not left worse off than before in terms of access to and control over resources.

formal institutions may not break down during the process of displacement and relocation. It is reasonable to assume that they remain, rather, in abeyance. If the necessary conditions are recreated in the area of relocation, the communities concerned may be able to revive them. As North perceptively argues, "[A]lthough formal rules may change overnight as the result of political or judicial decisions, informal constraints embodied in customs, traditions, and codes of conduct are much more impervious" (North 1990:6).

As pointed out earlier, it is necessary to distinguish between natural resources and institutions. Loss of access to natural resources caused by inundation or changes in patterns of land use precipitated by introduction of a development project has to be replaced physically at the resettlement site. This is a function of availability of unoccupied natural resources and political will. The latter is important because if political will is lacking, a government may be reluctant to allocate natural resources for such a purpose. The question of reconstructing institutions is more complex than the physical replacement of natural resources. If the natural resources at the resettlement site are to be managed communally, there are certain requirements that should be put in place. The following are some of these requirements.

Exclusive communal property rights

CPRs at the resettlement site should be exclusively accessible only to members of a given community. As pointed out before, property rights refers to the "power to limit the ability of other persons to enjoy the benefits to be secured from the use and enjoyment of a material good" (Bates 1989:28). This may be expressed in terms of communal ownership or communal rights of usufruct. As long as the primacy of the rights of the community in question is recognized and is legally protected against arbitrary eviction or encroachment, the distinction between communal rights of ownership and usufruct in a rural setting is seldom significant. The exclusive rights of the community should also be enforceable at law. The community should be empowered and be independent of outsiders, including government intervention. It should also be free to work out rules of sharing the produce of communally held resources.

Such exclusive rights are the key to sustainability of CPRs, because nonmembers are excluded and access to, and use of, common resources are regulated. This form of property rights is obviously easier to enforce among communities with such a tradition because of their customary practice of acceptance and adherence to collective rules and norms. Common property institutions can also be imposed from outside provided they embody needs felt by the communities concerned. As Gibbs and Bromley state, "[C]ommon property is created when members of an interdependent group agree to limit their individual claims on a resource in the expectation that the other members of the group will do likewise. Rules of conduct in the use of a given resource are maintained to which all members of the interdependent group subscribe" (Gibbs and Bromley 1989:25).

If new institutions, that is, sets of rules and norms of cooperation, are imposed from outside, it has to be made sure that they are adaptable to existing norms that motivate people's social and economic behavior and should also reflect felt needs of the people in question. These institutional arrangements will eventually be universal.

Preservation of traditional leadership

The existing structures of authority and tradition should be reinforced and fostered rather than weakened during the process of displacement and resettlement. Communal management of CPRs is most effective in societies where the moral authority of traditional leaders and elders is intact. In traditional societies, resource-regulating institutions are based on a set of rules and norms of cooperation based on kinship, customs, taboos, and social mores. The presence of traditional leaders and elders commanding reverence among their constituencies makes enforcement of such institutional arrangements less costly and more effective. This is because pressure could easily be brought to bear on "free-riders" and conflicts over resources could easily be resolved using existing mechanisms of conflict resolution, including through the use or threat of force.

One way of reinforcing and fostering the moral authority of traditional leaders and elders is to involve them from the beginning in the process of negotiation concerning compensation, site selection, preparation for transfer, mobilization for community action, resource allocation at the destination, dispute resolution, and so forth. Community leaders and elders should also play a central role in negotiating the conditions of entry into host societies at the destination, if relocatees are to be resettled in existing villages.

The need to maintain continuity in this regard may conflict with the need to improve the conditions of women and other underprivileged groups, because some of these traditional leaderships may perpetuate social injustices and economic inequalities. Even though it may be inappropriate to use displacement and resettlement to engineer social changes, there may still be a possibility to negotiate for some moderate changes without fundamentally affecting the sociocultural structure of the relocatees. Generally, however, lasting changes can only come from within, and outsiders should guard against imposing changes from without.

Maintenance of group cohesion

Traditional communal property resource management systems are most effective among culturally homogenous groups related by common ancestry or residence. Policy makers and planners should, therefore, aim at maintaining the cultural identity and moral integrity of relocatees by guarding against placing them with "strangers" originating from different villages during the physical transfer between the old and the new "homes" and during resettlement. As far as possible, village units should be preserved during transfer and relocation. Not only does this ease the trauma of the process of displacement, socialization, and adjustment in an unfamiliar environment, but it also tends to maintain community institutions and cohesion which are *sine qua non* for cooperative and collective action in the interest of the common good.

A case study of Eritrean refugees in the Sudan shows that one of the factors that contributed to the breakdown of community cohesion, and consequently to the weakening of traditional resource management systems previously based on mutual cooperation, was the intermingling of groups who originated from different parts of Eritrea and who met for the first time in the resettlement sites. This gradually led to a breakdown of community organizations and amoebic proliferation of leaders competing for power and the material benefits associated with it. This made cooperative solutions to common problems virtually impossible (Kibreab 1996b). Thus, resettlement should, as much as possible, aim at maintaining community cohesion and relocatees' homogeneity.

There is a tendency among authorities to relocate displaced people to existing villages. This is done for various reasons such as an effort to minimize establishment costs in infrastructure or because of lack of unoccupied land for resettlement. It is important to note, however, that unless there are ties between the relocatees and the local residents based on common ethnicity or "good neighborliness," transfer of uprooted and alien populations into already established villages is highly undesirable and fraught with serious problems that prevent successful reestablishment of the new residents. The available evidence on communities relocated to existing villages shows that relocatees were subjected to painful and humiliating experiences at the hands of local residents, including loss of land and other resources (Ganguly Thukral 1992).

If dictated by force of circumstances, such as lack of unoccupied land, the rights and duties of both communities should be negotiated through government mediation resulting in a binding contractual agreement. Mechanisms should also be put in place that draw on existing structures from both communities to enforce such agreements. These agreements should also be enforceable at law. The available evidence from refugee studies suggests that the degree that refugees are well received in host communities is a function of the benefits refugees bring to the affected areas (Kibreab 1987). By the same token, host communities' attitudes toward relocatees can be influenced by investments made in the affected areas' social and economic infrastructures to create capacity of absorption. If relocatees are not accompanied by such investments, their presence is likely to be resented by host populations (unless there are kinship or ethnic ties that outweigh these costs), because of increased competition posed by relocatees for CPRs; strategic commodities such as food crops, sugar, kerosene, salt, and so on; and employment.

Expanding the scope of the risk model

Until now the extent of the relevance of the risk model to situations other than development-related displacements and resettlements has not been explored. There is, however, no doubt that any government or agency concerned with the welfare and viable reconstruction of sustainable livelihoods among displaced communities — the cause of displacement notwithstanding — could gain pivotal insights and inspiration from the risk model in the task of conceptualizing and formulating the resettlement policies which guide and inform the processes of planning, designing, and implementing viable development programs that eliminate or minimize detrimental consequences.

The dismal performance of resettlement projects is not only limited to resettlement schemes established for populations displaced by development-related projects.[21] The record of refugee resettlement schemes, for example, is equally replete with examples of dis-

---

[21]   T. Scudder's (1997:8) inventory shows that only a few have performed relatively well. These are Nigeria's Kainji Dam project and Egypt's relocation of the 50,000 Nubians from the Aswan High Dam.

mal failures.[22] In fact, failure seems to be the rule rather than the exception with regard to refugee resettlement schemes. Between 1962 and 1985, about 155 refugee resettlement schemes[23] were established in Africa (including those that closed down because of repatriation), and only a few have been able to achieve the minimal goal of self-sufficiency. The overwhelming majority of the settlement schemes are still dependent on external assistance for their survival. Some of these schemes have been in existence for more than three decades and there is still no ground for optimism.

Generally, there are no substantive differences between the problems faced by refugees and relocatees in resettlement schemes. The problems faced by refugees in resettlement schemes are more or less the same as those embodied in the risk model. The major problems facing refugees in resettlement schemes are landlessness, unemployment or underemployment, especially during trough seasons, overcrowding, marginalization, increased morbidity and mortality, food insecurity, lack of access to CPRs as compounded by lack of communal tenurial security, and social disintegration. It is true that in the case of refugees, most of these losses are suffered in connection with flight, but this is immaterial because the declared aim of any refugee resettlement scheme is to rectify these losses and to avoid risks of further impoverishment rather than to consolidate and exacerbate such detrimental processes. Instead, failed refugee resettlement schemes have resulted in reinforcing the losses and the risks of impoverishment.

It is important to note, however, that the problems facing refugees, as enumerated above, are effects, rather than causes, of failure of self-sufficiency projects. At the heart of this dismal performance lie misguided host government resettlement strategies and ill-conceived approaches adopted by the international aid regime. The problems of landlessness, unemployment, overcrowding, marginalization, increased vulnerability to disease and mortality, food insecurity, lack of access to CPRs, and social

---

22   See Kibreab (1987; 1989; 1990; 1994; 1995). See also Refugee Policy Group, 1986, Older refugee settlements in Africa, Washington D.C.

23   In refugee studies the term settlement is used rather than resettlement. The latter term is usually used in connection with resettlement of refugees in third countries in Europe, North America, and Australia. In this paper the term resettlement refers to local settlement of refugees in first countries of arrival. For the purpose of this paper there is no substantive difference between the two terms. In the interest of consistency, the term resettlement is used throughout.

disintegration experienced by refugees in resettlement schemes are inevitable outcomes of resettlement policies whose primary pre-occupation is to keep refugees in spatially segregated remote sites so that they do not integrate into host societies. Consequently, they are disabled from competing with host populations for scarce resources and employment opportunities. The second reason for putting refugees in spatially segregated sites is to shift the responsibility of meeting their needs to the international donor community indefinitely or until safe return home is possible.

This bleak situation would undoubtedly have been avoided, or at least mitigated, if host government policies and donor responses were to be informed by the risk model. In the context of a favorable political will and international donor support, the thinking embodied in the risk model could enable host governments and agencies concerned with refugee self-sufficiency issues to design resettlement programs which overcome losses and avoid risks of impoverishment. Thus, the direct relevance of the risk model to post-emergency refugee situations is not a moot point.

Resettling oustees and refugees: the differences[24]

There are differences between refugees' and oustees' situations, rights, and entitlements, as well as in third parties' responsibilities. It is important, therefore, to examine these differences closely in order to determine whether or not they limit the scope of the risk model with regard to formulation of refugee resettlement policies and to the planning and implementation of economic activities aimed not just at enabling refugees to become self-supporting, but also to contributing to economic growth and social progress in the resettlement areas.

The aim here is not to spell out and analyze the similarities and dissimilarities of refugees and oustees in detail. Only the differences that may at first glance appear to have a bearing on the immediate

---

[24] Sometimes self-settled refugees could be forcibly ousted by host governments and relocated to a formal resettlement. For example, the Eritrean refugees in the wage-earning settlements at Es Suki were forcibly ousted from Wad Hileu against their express will and amid bitter resistance. See G. Kibreab (1990). The term oustee can be used to describe those in such a situation. Here, the term oustee refers exclusively to those whose displacement is caused by "development projects."

relevance of the risk model as applied to resettlement of refugees are discussed. It is argued here that in spite of the ostensible dissimilarities between oustees' and refugees' situations, a closer examination of the issues reveals that the so-called differences do not limit the scope of the model, but, rather, make it compellingly relevant.

Planned versus sudden events

First, development project-related displacement is a planned event; as such it is amenable to planning. Refugee movements are often sudden and are therefore not easily amenable to forward planning. It is important to note, however, that this difference is not significant because refugees are invariably held in transit/reception centers or camps before they are transferred to agricultural settlements (generally known in the literature as "local settlements"). The duration of the transition period between relief camps and self-sufficiency projects varies from one country to another, but, in most cases, between five and eight or even more years are spent in preparatory activities before refugees are transferred to a resettlement site. These activities include negotiations (between UNHCR and host governments, between central governments and regional/provincial/local governments, and sometimes between the latter and populations at the potential resettlement sites); fund-raising; conducting of socioeconomic surveys to determine population size, demographic structures, skill profiles and social organization; reconnaissance surveys; site identification; feasibility studies; setting-up of administrative structures; recruitment of personnel; and so forth. There are many situations in which relief camps and transit or reception centers, that have been established en route to durable solutions, have been institutionalized (see Kibreab 1989; 1994; 1996;1991).

Thus, in refugee situations it is only the emergency phase that is sudden and unpredictable and consequently not easily amenable to planning. In this regard, resettlement of refugees is not different from resettlement of populations displaced by development projects, except that in the former the loss has already occurred in the country of origin and what is needed is remedial rather than preemptive action. Nevertheless, in the context of favorable host-government policy and donor response, it is still possible to formulate a refugee resettlement program aimed at enabling refugee communities to reverse the losses suffered as a result of social and economic uprooting and preventing further impoverishment. The losses are, in most cases, identical with those envisioned by the risk model.

Permanent versus temporary displacement

Second, population displacements caused by development projects are permanent, whereas refugee-hood is perceived (reality notwithstanding) by refugees, host populations, host governments, and international organizations concerned with assisting and protecting refugees as being a transient phenomenon. Refugees are protected and assisted in anticipation of voluntary repatriation, which is expected to take place in response to the elimination of the factors that prompted flight. Consequently, refugees are accepted as temporary guests in most developing countries without any opportunity for naturalization. This condition has a bearing on host governments' resettlement policies and practices, on the one hand, and on refugee attitudes and incentives, on the other.

Because refugees are received on a temporary basis, most governments in developing countries impose limitations on their freedom of movement and residence; that is, refugees are required to live in spatially segregated sites, and departure from such sites without permission is a punishable criminal act. For example, the Asylum Act in the Sudan states, "[N]o refugee shall ... depart from any place of residence specified for him. The penalty for contravening this subsection, shall be imprisonment for not more than one year" (see Government of Sudan [1974] *The Regulation of Asylum Act*). This is the rule rather than the exception in most Asian and African countries. The consequence of this limitation on refugee welfare is dramatic. Without freedom of movement and residence, refugees cannot leave their residential areas in search of employment or other forms of income-generating opportunities. They cannot sell their produce outside the designated areas at competitive prices in the marketplace, nor can they import goods for sale from elsewhere.

In agriculturally based refugee settlements, this leads to overcultivation of holdings. Because host governments expect refugees to return within a short period, they tend to allocate inadequate land, disregarding future needs. History is never made to order. Thus, more often than not, the conditions that prompt flight tend to persist irrespective of the wishes of host governments, and refugees have no choice but to overstay. One of the consequences of this is that refugees cultivate their plots continuously without any fallow periods or application of fertility-boosting inputs.[25] This leads to depletion of soil nutrients resulting in invasion by noxious weeds

---

[25]   The failure to apply fertilizers is due to lack of resources, and assistance packages to such communities do not include such inputs.

and dramatic decline in crop yields (Kibreab 1996b). In some countries, refugees are also not allowed to travel beyond designated areas either to graze their animals or to gather firewood. This concentrates animal grazing and human activities over a limited area, and the consequence is overgrazing and deforestation of the local environment.

In addition to causing poverty and environmental degradation, these policies render a long-standing and viable system of traditional resource management inoperative. In traditional societies, the problems of overcultivation (depletion of soil nutrients caused by overcropping) and overgrazing (depletion of palatable and nutritious vegetation and their replacement by less palatable and less nutritious vegetation) are countered through the practice of fallow periods and rotational grazing, respectively. These are impossible in most refugee situations because refugees are prohibited by law from bringing new areas into the production process in response to increasing demands caused by human and animal population growth and immigration. More often than not, when refugees overstay, no additional land is allocated to meet the needs of new families.[26] Most parents have no choice but to share their aging plots with the families of their married sons. This leads to overfragmentation, reducing most plots below sustainable levels.

In most developing countries, refugees are also not entitled to obtain business licenses to engage in profitable economic activities outside settlements. These limitations have a tendency to exacerbate the conditions of impoverishment set in motion by exile.

Hence, it may be argued that these unfavorable policy environments would render the risk model automatically inoperative. As long as refugees are placed in a state of physical confinement, it may be impossible to formulate and implement program activities which, on the one hand, reverse the losses that are already suffered in connection with flight, and, on the other, prevent further deepening of the process of impoverishment associated with involuntary displacement. By the same token, however, it could be argued, more forcefully for that matter, that the *raison d'être* of the risk model is not to sanction existing misguided policy environments and practices, but rather to change them. If instead of reinforcing and con-

---

[26] The only exception in Africa has been Tanzania. When the refugees in Ulyamkulu and Katumba settlements did not return as hoped by the government of Tanzania, and the settlements became over-crowded, the government of Tanzania identified a new site and transferred the surplus population to Mishamo settlement in 1976.

solidating the conditions of impoverishment set in motion during flight and exile, refugee resettlements were designed to overcome and change these conditions by eliminating the formal and informal institutional constraints that perpetuate social and economic vulnerability, the direct relevance of the risk model would not be subject to controversy. Thus, the fact that host governments pursue resettlement policies that reinforce the risks of impoverishment is in itself a compelling reason to urge host governments, UNHCR, and national and international NGOs to draw insights from the model in formulating and implementing their (postemergency) refugee resettlement policies.

Nationals versus aliens

Third, populations displaced by development projects are often nationals, whereas refugees are aliens. This has a direct bearing on rights of ownership and usufruct over arable land, CPRs, and other entitlements that may preclude formulation and implementation of programs that serve long-term needs of refugee communities. Some may argue that this would reduce the relevance of the model. It is argued here, however, that these conditions are reflections of myopic policies pursued by host governments, rather than inherent in refugee situations. One of the most important causes of resource depletion and deterioration of living conditions among refugee communities in resettlement schemes is lack of secure rights of usufruct over arable land and CPRs (Kibreab 1987; Kibreab 1996b). Not only do secure rights of usufruct here refer to security against arbitrary eviction, but they also include security of tenure reflected in the power to exclude nonsettlers or outsiders (including neighboring nationals) within the duration of the refugees' stay. Such tenurial security would generate willingness on the part of refugees to commit their resources and their efforts, as well as to revitalize their resource-regulating institutions (which might have been in abeyance during the process of relocation) in order to manage the said resources sustainably and equitably. Access to natural resources without control is a recipe for environmental tragedy. Nothing incites people to deplete forests, soils, or water supplies faster than fear that they will soon lose access to them (Darning 1989:42). Granting rights of ownership to refugees may be unacceptable to most host governments, but there is no reason why such governments should hesitate to grant to refugees secure rights of usufruct. This kind of institutional arrangement would conserve and foster sustainable land-use practices and improve living standards. When the refugees go home they will leave a sound rather than degraded environment.

In most refugee resettlement projects, refugees lack secure rights of usufruct over land and renewable resources; as a result the CPRs within the schemes become "open-access" resources. Refugee settlers are unable to stop interlopers (commercial farmers, charcoal producers, and local residents) from thoughtlessly overexploiting the natural resources within and in the environs of resettlement schemes. This inevitably generates careless land-use practices among refugees. They cut trees before outsiders cut them and fail to engage in conservation activities because they are unable to protect their local resources against outsiders. One of the central aims of the risk model is to empower disenfranchised groups, and one of the most effective methods of empowering refugees in resettlement schemes is to entrust them with control over local resources. Thus, the fact that refugees are strangers or "temporary guests" does not reduce the direct relevance of the risk model.

Gap in existing mandates

Fourth, even though the question of resettlement of populations displaced by development projects or by political or other events is essentially developmental, in the case of populations displaced by development projects, the government of the country concerned (whose decisions cause displacement) is ultimately responsible for their rehabilitation, reestablishment, and development. There is no corresponding body, in the form of a government, an intergovernmental, or a nongovernmental organization, that is charged with responsibility for refugees' reestablishment and development. This is still a gray area. The experiences of the last three decades have indisputably demonstrated that the problems posed by refugee aid and development are such that neither the UNHCR nor the United Nations Development Programme (UNDP) is equipped or mandated to deal with.

In spite of the endless rhetoric, which began in the 1960s,[27] on the need to make interventions in refugee situations developmental

---

[27] See, for example, the proceedings of the Conference on Legal, Economic and Social Aspects for the African Refugee Problems, sponsored by the Economic Commission for Africa, the UNHCR, and the Dag Hammarskjold Foundation, 1967. In this conference, it was agreed to link refugee aid to regional and national development planning. Since then this call has been made in all relevant international fora, but with no measurable advance.

(rather than limiting such interventions to care and maintenance) from the outset, very little or no progress has been achieved up to now. This is to some extent due to—besides unfavorable host government policy—the gap existing in the constitutional mandates of the intergovernmental organizations concerned with, on the one hand, humanitarian aid (for example, UNHCR) and, on the other, development aid (for example, UNDP).[28] Hitherto, the traditional, and often arbitrary, division of mandates of the United Nations sister organizations have blocked any lasting interagency cooperation.

In the absence of creative rethinking about the existing organizational and bureaucratic structures and redefinition of current international arrangements or the creation of an international or regional organization charged with clear responsibility for meeting short- and long-term (development) needs of refugees, it may be difficult to formulate and implement refugee resettlement policies aimed at reversing and preventing further acceleration of the losses and risks for impoverishment envisioned by the risk model.

It is noteworthy to state here, however, that this does not in any way limit the pertinence of the risk model in the formulation of refugee resettlement policies. The model is not designed to function in an already existing favorable policy environment. Its *raison d'être* is to stimulate development of strategies designed to fill existing policy or organizational vacuums. The model warns governments, intergovernmental organizations, and nongovernmental organizations of the dangers involved in the failure to develop policies and organizational structures that allow them to plan ahead and to implement corrective measures that counteract or rectify (as in the case of refugees) negative consequences associated with their actions or inaction. With regard to resettlement of refugees, if the model is embraced, it could stimulate fresh and innovative conceptualization, which could, over time, shift the frontier of the existing deficient approaches to refugee resettlements.

Conclusion

CPRs play a key role in the livelihoods of the rural poor. This notwithstanding, they are neglected by policymakers and planners in

---

[28]   For more elaborate discussion on these issues, see papers written under the auspices of the research project "Toward the Reformulation of International Refugee Law," Centre for Refugee Studies, York University, May 1995.

resettlement of populations displaced by development projects, and political or other events. The task of reconstructing livelihoods and restoring or augmenting the socioeconomic statuses of relocatees is unachievable without physical replacement of common property and without recreating the conditions that allow the revival of informal institutions that regulate access to, and use of, such resources at the destination. People who depend on CPRs are accustomed to collective action and adherence to certain rules, customs, and traditions that promote common interests. This experience represents an asset and provides favorable grounds for participation in development planning, implementation, and management of projects or program activities. Every effort should be exerted to preserve, revive, and revitalize such institutions.

The risk model is primarily designed to prevent the conditions of impoverishment from unfolding in development-related population displacements. As stated earlier in this chapter, "development projects" are understood to include even those that expand commercial agriculture and production of charcoal and firewood, which in most developing countries are among the major causes of population displacement. The deprivation and suffering experienced by populations who lose access to sources of livelihoods, such as arable land and CPRs, could be avoided if agricultural and resettlement policies were formulated with clear awareness of the detrimental consequences of involuntary displacement as conceptualized in the risk model.

An attempt has been made here to expand the scope of the risk model to include resettlement of refugees. The failure of host governments to formulate refugee resettlement schemes aimed both at making good on the losses experienced by refugees and at preventing further losses has hitherto been one of the major causes of failure of self-sufficiency schemes. This is further compounded by sluggish international responses to programs that require long-term financial commitments. These successive failures could be avoided or minimized if host governments, UNHCR, and funding and development agencies take seriously and draw insights from the risk model.

Acknowledgment

The author is grateful to the Swedish Authority for Research Cooperation with Developing Countries (SAREC/SIDA) for funding the research project, within which this chapter is written, generously.

CHAPTER 13

The effects of resettlement on access to common property resources

Dolores Koenig and Tiéman Diarra[1]

Although we have learned much about what makes for good re-settlement practice, the negative experiences of relocatees are none-theless better documented than the positive ones. Reconstituting livelihoods after resettlement remains problematic, especially for those who live mainly from collectively held resources. We saw this ourselves in Manantali, Mali, where 10,000 people were resettled in conjunction with dam construction. Here, as elsewhere, access to common property resources (CPRs) declined considerably after re-settlement, despite significant attention to the problem during the design of the resettlement project. How could project planners, among whom Koenig was one, show sensitivity to some of the is-sues involved in access to these resources, yet fail so badly to pro-cure adequate livelihoods for people during post-resettlement?

---

[1] The inspiration for the themes in this chapter came from our own re-search in Manantali, Mali, during several different periods. A first group of studies there was funded by the Manantali Resettlement Project (USAID No. 625-0955) during the mid- and late 1980s. Further research in 1993-1994 was funded by a U.S. National Science Foundation Grant. We would like to thank the other members of the various research teams, as well as the Malian Direction Nationale de l'Hydraulique et de l'Energie for their assistance during research. For assistance then, as well as logistical support during preparation of this paper, we would like to thank Dr. Klena Sanogo, Director of the Institut des Science Humaines, Bamako, and the personnel of the U.S. Agency for International Development, Bamako. We retain all responsibility for the views expressed herein.

As the literature discussed in this chapter will show, Manantali was only one case among many. There are few examples of successful strategies for reconstituting livelihoods based on CPRs. Even where there has been some "success," there has often been considerable controversy about whether ultimate developments have been positive or not.

This chapter approaches the problem in three major sections. We begin with a discussion of the general impacts of contemporary social change on access to CPRs. We then turn to some of the problems specific to resettlement, and the final section offers some suggestions for better practice. A single theme runs throughout: *a failure to appreciate the political dimensions of access to common property resources.* Although restoring the livelihoods of those who depend on these resources must go beyond politics, recognition of the profound political issues involved in access to common property resources appears to be the first necessary step in creating development opportunities.

Common property resources in the contemporary world

International environmental concerns brought general attention to CPRs. Hardin's (1968) discussion of the "tragedy of the commons" raised the question of whether it was possible to manage CPRs sustainably, stimulating significant literature. In contrast to Hardin, others argued that, under certain conditions, communally held resources could be managed as sustainably as those held under private, individual tenure regimes. These issues are discussed in some detail in Kibreab's chapter in this volume; for the purposes of this chapter, we will concentrate on a few issues relevant to resettlement initiatives.

First, the distinction between CPRs and open-access resources is important. An open-access resource is one that allows use to anyone who can get to the resource. Since use is not regulated, there are problems in excluding users. Since each new or bigger user can subtract from the welfare of other users, open access carries the potential for "resource mining" and degrading the resource (Berkes and Farvar 1989:7), especially as the number of users or intensity of use increases. Common examples of open-access resources are the high seas, many other waterways, and the atmosphere; less commonly cited are public parks, radio wavelengths, genetic resources, and geosynchronous orbit.

However, true open-access resources have been relatively rare. Much more common have been common property regimes under some type of collective management (Berkes and Farvar 1989:8), which can restrict access, granting use rights to some but excluding others, through a variety of direct and indirect means (Lino Grima and Berkes 1989). These management techniques have permitted common property regimes to avoid the tragedy of the commons and environmental degradation. Moreover, in many "traditional" common property systems, resource endowments among the owners are roughly similar, and management decisions likely to benefit one are likely to benefit others as well (Quiggin 1993:1129). Resources managed collectively include farmland, pasture, hunting and gathering territories, waterways, and irrigation systems (Berkes and Farvar 1989:8). Communities may also collectively manage institutions such as markets, schools, and religious centers (Fisher 1995:32).

Although Berkes and Farvar (1989:9) identified communal property as one of four basic property regime types,[2] there is much variation in the way collective regimes work and many kinds of communal property. Rights to use may be transferable or not, exclusive or nonexclusive, and more or less formally defined (Lino Grima and Berkes 1989). Moreover, many property regimes exist as a mix of ideal types (Berkes and Farvar 1989). Community management may be integrated with either individual or small group use in various ways, and in "traditional" systems, collective use as such appears to be relatively rare (Quiggin 1993). For example, farmland held under common property regimes is usually farmed by households or individuals. Pasture, hunting territories, and fishing areas may be managed and used by groups, but, in other cases, individuals may have the right to grant access: among Quebec's James Bay, Cree hunting territories have individual "owners" from whom permission must be secured when another individual wishes to hunt there (Salisbury 1986). The methods used to exclude access may be either direct or indirect, as in the West African savanna, where access to wells for watering animals provided a means to control access to theoretically open-access grazing. What these various systems have in common is a negative attribute: a lack of formal title at the individual level and usually at the group level as well.

Although many systems worked well under relatively stable conditions, change has indeed brought stress. In some cases, growing populations on a stable land base led to resource degradation, especially among pastoral groups. Overgrazing has occurred among the

---

[2]   The four types are common property, open-access, state-owned, and private property.

Navajo (Scudder 1982) and East African pastoralists. Among the latter, populations and grazing areas used to be kept in balance by periodic epidemics among both humans and animals, long-distance movement, and sometimes aggressive confrontation between different groups. Contemporary conditions (better health care, better internal arrangements, and border policing) have disturbed this balance, leading to pasture degradation (Dyson-Hudson 1991:237). In contrast, arable farming has often been better able to cope with growing populations by manipulating access rules, such as increasing the importance of inheritance systems (Bruce 1988). Although population growth has put stress on common property systems, it has not been the most important factor.

Far more disruptive have been actions by central governments. The imposition of a centralized government authority on top of local groups has decreased their ability to enforce access rules. When Cree could no longer keep Euro-American hunters off their lands in the 1930s and 1940s, they trapped out animals first before the others came in (Berkes 1989; Feit 1982). In Mali, while villagers retained control over who could cultivate fields, they had minimal control over who might cut wood in the local forest, since the government granted permits. Similarly in the Côte d'Ivoire, Senufo farmers wanted to refuse Fulbe herders the right to use their pasture, but the government would then invoke its right to dispose of unused land (Bassett 1993).

Government actions also created overlapping land claims. For example, some governments recognized customary control over cultivated fields, but claimed ownership rights over "vacant" lands. As people became aware of national laws, more people used them to get access to land. The Fulbe refused to ask permission of Senufo to use their pastures and simply came in with their herds. Rural Malian migrants claimed "unoccupied" lands for farms, even taking locals to court if necessary (Diarra and others 1992). These claims were relatively few where not many knew the national laws, but those who were aware were not reticent to use them to increase land access (Goheen 1988; Traoré and Clément 1985).

The fear of losing land to overlapping claims could lead to overexploitation. For example, many Bedouins in Israel's Negev desert wanted to move, but they continued to cultivate farms, often unsustainably, because of fears that they would otherwise lose their customary rights (Marx 1988). Around the Selingue dam in Mali, indigenous farmers carried out extremely extensive cultivation, in part to ensure that their customary claims were respected and to keep other claimants away (Fofana and others 1992). In general, the coexistence of informal and formal tenure systems brought tremendous uncertainty into land use practices (Bassett 1993; Lavigne Delville 1999). It appears that in Africa, at least, much of the desire on the part of farmers for individual tenure came from a desire to decrease the abuses of political and administrative power rather than from dissatisfaction with the rules of indigenous tenure systems (Bruce 1993:40,50).

Sometimes, governments have intervened more directly to try to change common property systems. Most common property regimes involve relatively extensive use by small populations (low productivity per unit of land), as opposed to intensive resource use by larger groups (high productivity per unit of land). Hunting, gathering, and pastoralism are all quite extensive, as are most farming systems based on common property regimes. Governments appear to be constantly tempted by the potential of intensive land use to create higher national productivity, and they often view resettlement projects as a chance to intensify production systems. For example, the administration at the Selingue-irrigated perimeter in Mali consistently manipulated tenure rules in their attempts to increase productivity. They ultimately decreased the size of parcels until it was difficult for farmers to produce enough for subsistence. Similarly, other government attempts at "rationalizing" resource use were also problematic. When the Norwegian government gave subsidies to reindeer herders in the hope that they would decrease their herd size, numbers increased instead as herders met monetary needs with the subsidies instead of butchering animals (Paine 1994).

Governments also held lands clearly defined as state property, such as Crown lands and classified forests. Rights to use these lands were often not clear, and to the extent that they became open-access resources, overexploitation was not uncommon. Saami herders legitimately pastured their reindeer on Norwegian Crown lands, but did not have exclusive access. Increased use by the military, industry, national parks, and recreation for city dwellers, pushed by a powerful lobby arguing for opening the tundra to all users, created growing competition for these lands (Paine 1994). Nonlegal use of public lands is also common. People live in classified forests in Thailand (Eudey 1988), India, Africa (Cissé et al. 1989), and elsewhere, and pasture their herds in them. A World Bank project that planned to undertake community forestry on Crown land and village commons in Pakistan found it to be impossible because people were already living there (Cernea 1991). Governments show varying degrees of tolerance of use of government lands. When local use of these lands is tolerated, people may manage them similarly to lands that they fully hold as common property. For example, many groups have created community rights in fisheries, even counter to laws declaring the sea an open-access resource (Pollnac 1991). However, it is difficult to sustain management regimes when governments do not tolerate local use. In fact, many recent resettlement projects involve the relocation of groups making use of government property, for example, moving farmers and herders out of national parks (Feeney 1998; Mustafa 1997).

Despite the problems, community-based tenure remains viable. Access to farmland in most of rural Africa is still determined by indigenous tenure systems, many of which have community management aspects (Bruce 1988). Grazing land, forests, and hunting areas are managed as commons in both developing and developed countries. Theorists suggest that community-based systems have the potential to solve the commons dilemma by internalizing high information and transaction costs. Community survival offers a built-in incentive to obey rules, and communities often have coercive mechanisms to ensure compliance as well (Lino Grima and Berkes 1989). But communities must be allowed to manage their resources. Assertion of state control without effective management often leads to "resource mining"(Arnould 1990:340), and outside pressures that have led to replacement of community management by open access have indeed created environmental problems (Lino Grima and Berkes 1989:49). To the extent that resettlement compounds existing problems by moving more people onto fewer resources and exerting new forms of government control, these problems only become more acute.

The effects of resettlement on common property resources

Understanding the major obstacles to reconstituting livelihoods among users of CPRs is a first step toward positive actions. The problems include insufficient recognition of political relationships between local populations and the national government as well as among host and resettler groups; continued lack of knowledge about patterns of resource use among groups using CPRs; constraints against effective organization among low-density populations; and post-resettlement problems.

The need for government recognition

The foremost problem is the lack of recognition of common property rights by governments. Few legal systems provide compensation for taking common property, even where those displaced depend on it for their livelihoods (Shihata 1993:47). This is so even though many national laws recognize that people hold property through various forms of customary tenure (see GRM 1987; Adu-Aryee 1993). Thus, governments have often simply asserted their rights over lands. For example, the Indonesian government did not pay compensation to those who relinquished land held under customary rights to the transmigration program, even though the law recognized these rights (World Bank 1988:91). Governments were even less likely to consider compensation when farmers were using open-access public lands. At Sobradinho in Brazil, there was no compensation for lands held de facto rather than de jure (Hall 1994:1795). In India, tribal groups that farmed in forests were considered "encroachers" on national lands (A. Patel 1995:180).

Some governments claimed to be willing to recognize farm lands held as common property, but they often faced what they considered insurmountable problems in valuing them, deciding on amounts for replacement, or calculating compensation (Fisher 1995:30). They were concerned about creating compensation precedents that would have to be followed elsewhere (Gill 1995:237; Robinson 1986). Assumptions were often made about either the "low" productivity of old lands or the "enhanced" productivity of replacement lands that justified allocating relatively small amounts of new land (IER 1984; Robinson 1986). Even when compensation was agreed upon, payments were often delayed for long periods (Adu-Aryee 1993; Robinson 1986).

The situation is even worse for lands used for activities other than farming. Grazing lands have often been simply taken, for example, for irrigation and development schemes in the Sudan (Bascom 1990; Salem-Murdock 1989) and to settle agricultural migrants in Mali (Fofana and others 1992). The importance of forests for hunting, gathering, fuel wood, and timber and the contribution of these activities to the incomes of the very poor have often been ignored (Cernea 1996; Mustanoja and Mustanoja 1993), as has their use as a complement to agriculture (see Hakim in this volume). The use of water courses for fishing and other needs, often in the form of open-access resources, has frequently been overlooked as well. Dam projects often create a significant new water-based resource in the reservoir, but affect negatively, through increasing, decreasing, and/or fluctuating water levels, downstream water resources (Charest 1982; Salem-Murdock and others 1994; Waldram 1988). The Sobradinho dam, for example, displaced 50,000 people from flooded rice lands downstream, as well as 70,000 people from the reservoir (Hall 1994).

If governments and planners fail to recognize that these resources exist and contribute to people's livelihoods, they are not likely to consider compensation, replacement, or rehabilitation. Therefore, the first necessary step is that governments recognize the legitimate claims that people have over CPRs. There are, however, two major obstacles to doing so.

Many of the groups that continue to manage resources collectively are considered "marginal" by their states and the dominant cultures within them.[3] They include the Indians of the Americas, the "tribals" of India, the Saami of Scandinavia, and pastoralists and foragers in general. Dominant cultures often express a "thinly veiled evolutionary determinism," which considers these economic strategies outmoded ways of life destined to disappear (Funk 1985:125). They often believe that these resources could be exploited more effectively, that is, with greater benefits, if traditions were changed. Modern infrastructure development, moreover, could speed the evolution from a traditional to a modern way of life (Funk 1985:125). In this light, persuading nomads to become sedentary can be seen as progress (Salem-Murdock 1989:5).

Moreover, modern nation-states have a difficult time accommodating cultural distinctiveness, despite the fact that some countries have legal provisions for certain rights of "indigenous" peoples (for example, Brazil, India, the United States, and Canada).[4] The Norwegian social democratic state, for example, supported livelihoods based on primary resources, but on the condition that production be carried out under similar conditions of economic rationality and efficiency among all groups (Paine 1994:157,159). Thus, they were willing to support reindeer pastoralists, but were uncomfortable with expression of a unique "Saami" as opposed to general "Norwegian" identity and, more importantly, privileged access to open-access tundra pastures by any group. Similar difficulties were encountered by North American Indian groups that wanted privileged hunting rights, and among those who wanted different rules of land access for South Asian tribal groups. As C. Patel (1995:75) claimed, tribals were no less Indian than anyone else.

---

[3]   A major exception is Africa, where much land in rural areas, including farmland, is held as a common property resource.

[4]   These special statuses do not necessarily carry distinctive property rights. Although members of scheduled tribes do have specific rights under the Indian constitution, they have no separate property regime (Gill 1995:237; Patel 1995:181).

Groups (such as Navajo, Cree, Indian tribals, and the Bobo of Burkina) that exploit resources collectively often do express their relationship to the land in spiritual as well as economic terms and use social identities to claim access to resources (Berry 1988; Deegan 1995; Salisbury 1986; Saul 1993; Scudder 1982). Thus, national governments are often forced to deal with questions of ethnic distinctiveness as well as with the economic and legal questions of distinctive property regimes. They have historically hesitated to do so. As Gibson (1993) noted, both national governments and donor agencies tend to be "integrationist" in orientation, even in light of contrasting policies, such as the World Bank's policy to safeguard tribal peoples. In general, groups with distinct values and institutions have been disproportionately at risk of displacement, in part because the way in which they use resources is judged inappropriate (for example, not sufficiently efficient) by development planners (Gibson 1993:23).

The link to cultural autonomy is one reason that the issue of access to common property resources remains intrinsically political. However, there are practical advantages to letting distinctive cultural groups retain common property regimes. It may decrease ethnic tension, since one factor among many in contemporary ethnic conflict appears to be the resistance of minority groups to the imposition of dominant state culture — especially the cultural aspects with negative economic impact, including interference with existing tenure regimes. Moreover, common property regimes often permit people to make a living in marginal environments where resources vary so much over time and space that it would be difficult to do so in other ways.

A second obstacle to government recognition of common property regimes stems from reluctance to give up overlapping state claims to potential income and resources, particularly on lands believed to contain mineral resources of value. Most developing country governments claim all subsurface rights, and in Africa, many governments also claim ownership of virtually all lands (Shihata 1993:43). Although many of these governments also recognize customary use by existing populations in some way, they are reluctant to give control of extensive parcels to local groups by turning lands over to community ownership, since this would affect their future ability to use resources for national development. Many African countries are trying to decentralize as a part of democratization initiatives, but the process has been slow and halting (Hall and others 1991). If devolution of power is difficult under ordinary circumstances, it becomes even more difficult in involuntary resettlement, where the effort always begins "from above" and where the first local response is almost universally resistance.

Relations between hosts and resettlers

Political issues exist not only between relocatees and their national governments but also between relocatees and host populations. When populations in host areas hold property under common property regimes, their rights are often ignored when resettlement occurs. For example, at New Halfa in Sudan, Nubians were resettled on an irrigation scheme that displaced Shukriyya from their grazing land. While Nubians could obtain freehold land on the scheme, Shukriyya had rights only to tenancies. Not surprisingly, this led to ethnic conflict as the Shukriyya faulted the government for settling strangers on their land, while the Nubians argued that the Shukriyya should not have rights on the scheme (Salem-Murdock 1989:170). In the Mwea irrigation scheme in Kenya, management created a myth that the lands had been unoccupied before irrigation development. Although parts had been underpopulated some years earlier because they lay on an intertribal frontier, there had been much recent immigration. Some immigrants had even begun large-scale tractor farming on land later taken by the scheme. Because their rights were only usufruct, they were ignored (Moris 1973a; 1973b).[5] Disregard for the rights of hosts can cause waves of dispossession, as resettlement of new people displaces current users.

Where host populations retained some political leverage vis-à-vis relocatees and government agencies, they often resisted accepting new residents, refusing them access to necessary resources. Navajo relocated from the former Navajo-Hopi Joint Use Area to other reservation areas often found it impossible to get grazing land because hosts were reluctant to share already overgrazed pastures. People were reluctant to accord even home-site leases to relocatees because they feared that new residents would ultimately want to graze sheep (Scudder 1982:87). At Akosombo in Ghana, planners recognized the principle of customary law that all land had an owner (Sagoe 1970), but they bypassed traditional procedures to request

---

5   The Mwea situation is even more complicated because there were two sets of hosts, the original land owners and recent immigrants, with conflicting notions of land rights. It appears that land owners saw the scheme as an opportunity to divest themselves of immigrants, even though this meant loss of access for themselves as well (Moris 1973a; 1973b).

land. Some indigenous landowners continued for years to deny access to resettlers, and the Volta project was able to get only 15,000 acres, when it had planned on 54,000 (Adu-Aryee 1993:138; Chambers 1970:234). Moreover, some who had ceded land in the early 1960s forced settlers off these lands after a 1966 coup changed the political context (Chambers 1970:237). At Manantali, customary landowners were contacted by project officials and agreed to cede a certain amount of agricultural land to relocatees. As settlers began to place this land into fallow and wanted new fields, however, hosts hesitated to lend more. Some settlers simply cleared new fields without host permission, at times leading to conflicts (Diarra and others 1995). Administrators tended to resolve conflicts by referring to maps of new fields drawn by the resettlement authority, thus creating a sort of cadastre, even though these maps had no legal status (Traoré 1996).

Both hosts and resettlers perceived a risk to common property rights, since by definition resettlement led to larger populations on a common resource base. Moreover, hosts and settlers each tended to be jealous of the others' benefits. Navajo relocatees envied the stock of hosts and local employment, while hosts envied relocatees' new, improved housing (Aberle 1993:178). Hosts appeared especially reluctant to accept resettlers when the resettling population potentially outnumbered them, thus carrying the potential for political dominance (Adu-Aryee 1993:139; Moris 1973a; Saul 1988). Second relocations also accentuated problems. Although many Cree saw advantages to the first James Bay agreement, they spoke out against a second series of dams in the 1990s, in the belief that the remaining land would simply not support the same level of hunting and trapping (McCutcheon 1991:152).

Sometimes, to avoid problems between hosts and relocatees, resettlement planners have tried to place resettlers on public lands, but this can create legal problems when the lands have been reserved for other purposes (Shihata 1993:52). Initial plans for Narmada resettlement included giving forest land to relocatees, but a 1980 national conservation law forbade this, forcing resettlement agencies either to buy land or to request a legal waiver to allow forest resettlement (C. Patel 1995).

Knowledge of resource utilization

In part, the competition over resources between hosts and guests comes from poor planning. Few resettlement projects have correctly evaluated the quantity, quality, or diversity of resources used before resettlement. Since these have commonly been underestimated, planners have in turn tended to underestimate the resources needed post-resettlement.

It is indeed difficult to estimate the quantity of resources needed by many of the groups using CPRs. There are rarely records of the resource bases of specific groups (other than the entire reserves of some North and South American Indian populations). Where larger bounded territories are divided among individuals and groups, interior boundaries tend to be "fuzzy" and flexible. Farmers often have significant amounts of land in fallow, which is much more difficult to measure than cultivated land. The customary-use-right areas that Navajos used for grazing often overlapped one another. Transhumant herders may pasture animals on harvested fields, or use forests simultaneously used by hunters or collectors. Saami reindeer pastoralists would adjust herd sizes to pasture availability. A herder with claims over much pasture and few animals would enter into a temporary partnership with another who needed pasture. If a part of his pasture was left empty, neighbors would be tempted to encroach (Paine 1994:108). Activities at some distance can also affect resource access. For example, in Bolivia, agricultural colonists relatively far away from foraging groups nonetheless had a negative impact on animal availability (Stearman 1990). Moreover, when people consume rather than sell the resources they procure, they often find it difficult to estimate quantities produced.

Rather than actually measuring the resources that potential settlers were using, planners sometimes estimated on the basis of "comparable" figures. At Manantali, feasibility studies appear to have estimated farm sizes and length and size of fallows using other studies in adjoining regions, rather than measuring existing fields and fallows (IER 1984). Since land use was much more extensive in Manantali than in adjoining zones, this led to a gross underestimate of the amount of land needed. Advocates of the Mackenzie Valley pipeline and the Dene Natives who lived in the zone had quite different estimates of their dependence on bush resources versus welfare and transfer payments; in general, local estimates of bush resource use were higher than those of planners (Funk 1985:122).

Analyses of the quality of resources used prior to resettlement and the effects of changing quality have also been poor. Dam resettlement in particular often destroys some of the most productive alluvial land. Rich flood plains, with good agricultural land, lush forests, and rich animal habitats are flooded. People often move to reservoir perimeters, almost always less fertile (Berman 1988 on North Dakota; Hall 1994 on Brazil; Wali 1993 on Panama; Charest

1982 on Quebec; Colson 1971 on Zambia). Hence hectare-for-hectare replacement of lands is often insufficient. Even more generous replacement, for example, twice as much land at Easterville in Manitoba, may prove problematic if the quality is inferior (Waldram 1988:104).

Finally, when estimated resource use has been calculated, it has tended to concentrate on the most important uses of the most important resources. Yet groups often use a portfolio of resources, under a variety of tenure arrangements. Even when resettlement projects have paid attention to primary resources (whether held individually or collectively), they have often underestimated subsidiary ones, especially those held as common property. At Manantali, for example, the resettlement project tried to estimate future needs for farmland, but paid much less attention to pasture, wild fruit, and medicinal and animal forest resources. At Akosombo, rights of inhabitants to collect snails, firewood, and other forest products and to hunt were not calculated because planners decided that these rights were not sufficiently determined to justify attempts at valuation (Sagoe 1970:64). Among the Karelians in Finland, timberland and other forest rights were ignored (Mustanoja and Mustanoja 1993). Among the discussions of Canadian Natives, there is much information on men and hunting, but little on women, processing, or gathering.

In many places, these seemingly subsidiary resources are most important for the livelihoods of the most vulnerable parts of the population, the poor and women, especially female-headed households (Cernea 1996; Guggenheim and Spears 1991). In India, for example, poor artisans (such as mat makers and basket weavers) depended on forest resources for raw materials (Agarwal 1986). In Zimbabwe, while husbands claimed rights on resettlement scheme land, women used forest resources outside the scheme for firewood, fruits, herbs, and crafts. They also cleared off-scheme plots to plant crops to sell for personal incomes (Moore 1993). In general, access to a diverse resource base is important for reestablishing post-resettlement livelihoods; access to "secondary" resources may make the difference between adequacy and inadequacy (Cernea 1996). Furthermore, while projects may encourage hosts and resettlers to settle differences over primary resources, there may be outstanding conflicts in regard to secondary ones. In several farming areas in Mali, host populations accused settlers of abusive forest use (Diarra and others 1992; Traoré and Clément 1985).

Resettlement projects need to carry out fairly detailed studies of resource use and users prior to resettlement to estimate accurately resource needs in resettlement sites. They need to consider as many resources as possible and not just the most obvious one or ones.

Underestimation of the resources necessary after resettlement has often been exacerbated by overestimation of the resources available in the sites where relocatees plan to move. Sometimes receiving areas are already overexploited. Even though many recognized that overgrazing was a problem on the Navajo reservation, original relocation plans did not include the purchase of replacement land. When this provision was later changed, the plan was to replace 900,000 acres with only 250,000, although a bit more was added later (Aberle 1993:165–178). In other cases, the existing claims of host populations on land and their willingness to let others use it were ignored. The project plan for the Manantali resettlement project found 97,200 hectares of land for pasture, new fields, and foraging, estimating that this was 25 times the amount relocatees needed (USAID 1984:Annex 7.9:3). It ignored the fact that these resources belonged to hosts who might not want to cede them. In the same vein, Sagoe (1970:64) suggested that "undoubtedly" Akosombo resettlers would be able to get similar rights to collect and hunt in new settlements or their adjacent hinterland, which would constitute satisfactory compensation. Resettlement authorities have tended to perceive as open-access resources those that the hosts perceive as common property under their collective control.

Moreover, authorities have tended to underestimate the changes in natural resource exploitation patterns likely to occur because of the resettlement. In Manantali, higher water levels in the Bafing River below the dam meant that transhumant pastoralists could cross it only at a few bridges, and they could not cross the lake at all. This made the Manantali bridge a prime crossing place, and increased dramatically the number of transhumant herders sojourning in neighboring villages. Discord between farmers and herders increased substantially after the resettlement, as herds and farming villages had greater contact with one another (Maiga 1996). In general, insufficient attention has been paid to the effects of increased populations using a single resource base, an inevitable result of resettlement, especially in conjunction with dams, where a reservoir occupies much of the former resource area. As Fisher (1995:32) noted, "with resettlement, land is no longer an unlimited resource but becomes a severely limited commodity." Clearly this is why hosts are so often reluctant to share resources with resettlers.

The development component of resettlement initiatives should look explicitly at ways to intensify resource use. Both hosts and resettlers will need to exploit complementary resources to make up for losses. Yet formal programs to intensify farming have often showed a naive belief in the superiority of untested new agricultural techniques. Irrigation (especially when dams have gravity-feed perimeters) and mechanization have proven especially popular, but the latter has been a particular failure (Adu-Aryee 1993; DeWilde 1967). Resettlers themselves appear to be aware of the need to intensify, but some settler attempts to gain more remunerative resources have been refused by authorities. For example, attempts by Easterville relocatees in Canada to get a fish processing plant and a highway intersection with the potential for store or tourist income as a part of their replacement land failed when the provincial government failed to approve these choices (Waldram 1988).

Many programs have been planned without a serious study of the existing mode of resource exploitation, its relationship to the new activities proposed, and the changes that would likely need to be encouraged to move successfully from one economic strategy to another. The end result has been that many people have been unable to carry out economic activities sufficiently remunerative to restore livelihoods after resettlement under common property or other tenure regimes. As has been said before (see Cernea 1993; Scudder 1991), every resettlement project needs to include a well thought-out economic development component. For people who live primarily on the basis of common property resources, it is especially important that both hosts and relocatees be included in development initiatives. Moreover, in-depth research about the property systems used before resettlement and the changes proposed might help avoid naive assumptions about the profitability of resource replacement and rehabilitation.

Organizing for positive change

Despite efforts of donors and national governments to improve resettlement and rehabilitation, top-down efforts are insufficient. Local groups need to organize to demand better conditions, but they are often in a very disadvantageous position. Except for some severely disadvantaged groups relocated multiple times, resettlement was a singular event in the lives of people who often had little experience with government organizations. People who exploit common property resources, often with low population densities and relatively isolated from mainstream national events, have tended to be even more isolated and to find it even more difficult to organize in the face of compulsory resettlement (Dharmadhikary 1995; Hall 1994; Waldram 1988). Although many groups did organize and even go to court, they often found legal battles to be very drawn out, discouraging some and making it difficult to remain unified (Robinson 1986; Waldram 1988). People who knew something about dam construction and resettlement (because, for example, it had happened to neighbors) appear to have been better able to organize than those who were subjected to the first dam construction in the area (Hall 1994).

Although some groups have successfully organized on their own, they have been most successful in gaining a voice when they were able to combine efforts with others who had overlapping interests. Environmentalists have often perceived a common cause, especially when reservoirs would flood wildlife habitats and fragile biological resources (Chernela 1988; Eudey 1988). Northern Canadian Natives, for example, became a symbol of the Canadian environmental movement in the belief that greater control by Native peoples would lead to fewer environmental problems (Waldram 1988; McCutcheon 1991:157).

Yet these coalitions often proved fragile. Larger outside organizations have often had their own agendas that threatened to overtake those of relocatees. For example, Narmada became the symbol of destructive development for many international activists, and they used it to question World Bank approaches (Udall 1995). This led to a split among local nongovernmental organizations. Although some were equally interested in these issues, others remained more concerned about immediate problems of resettlement and rehabilitation (A. Patel 1995; Patkar 1995).

Often coalitions of environmentalists and local resource users broke down as their divergent interests became clear. While Saami pastoralists and conservationists allied against government hydroelectric development in the early 1980s, the publication of the Brundtland Report at the end of the decade drew environmentalists closer to the government, and they began to criticize pastoralists for allowing pasture erosion (Paine 1994). At Narmada, some NGOs working with resettler groups worked hard to get the Indian government to release forest areas for resettlement, while others continued to denounce the negative environmental consequences of such a move (A. Patel 1995). In the Canadian north, environmentalist and Native coalitions fell apart in disagreement about continued Native fur trapping and whaling (McCutcheon 1991:157). A coalition of ranchers and conservationists blocked the transfer of some of the land Navajos wanted to purchase, arguing that Navajo grazing practices posed an ecological threat (Scudder 1982; Aberle 1993).

Many of these coalitions have been more successful at stopping infrastructure development than at procuring better conditions for resettlers. In general, social movements often have greater power to disrupt than to bring about positive change (Hall 1994:1804). The problem of bringing about improved conditions remains.

Post-resettlement issues

Issues over access to common property do not stop once the resettlement is over. First, resettlement projects often introduce new collectively owned resources without well-thought-out management plans. Second, resettlement often leads to either natural or migrant population growth, accentuating problems of resource access.

Governments inspired by socialist principles or interested in achieving economies of scale often attempted cooperative schemes in resettlement areas. Many times, these proved to be dismal failures, in terms of both agricultural productivity and farmer income and satisfaction. In Zimbabwe, for example, cooperative resettlement has consistently shown inferior results compared to those of family farms (Akwabi-Ameyaw 1990; Jacobs 1989), as have earlier attempts in Tanzania (Brain 1976). At Akosombo, farmers linked cooperatives to exploitation by political party officials and few were successful (Chambers 1970:235). To the extent that cooperative ventures were directed by government authorities, members often had little real power or ability to direct their own affairs (Chambers 1970). Even when rights to manage community-owned systems were formally vested in a collective, there was a tendency for state-sponsored systems to be run like private firms, with management directing the activities of laborer-owners (Quiggin 1993:127). Laborers tended to perceive their interests as workers rather than owners.

Other, more limited forms of cooperation also had problems. At Mwea, tenant committees had little power, so tenants created client-patron relations with managers as a way to influence outcomes instead (Moris 1973b). In Norway, since foremen of government-created pastoral districts served primarily as liaisons to the administration, they were usually chosen for their Norwegian language ability rather than leadership skills (Paine 1994). In Manantali, the resettlement project failed sufficiently to prepare villagers for the effort that would be involved in maintaining village water pumps. Several years after resettlement, many pumps had ceased to function (Diarra and others 1995).

Resettlers have often considered new infrastructure and equipment the property of the resettlement organization and held the organization responsible for maintenance. Preparing people to take over and manage resettlement infrastructure has not generally been a major focus of resettlement programs. Moreover, the assistance offered by these agencies during the resettlement period has often created a spirit of dependency among relocatees, who begin to expect that the resettlement organization should solve all their problems.

Collective management systems require that the group of owners establish a procedure for making and enforcing decisions on their own. These may have evolved slowly in existing systems, but if the environment is complex or is subject to rapid social change, always the case in resettlement, rules and procedures need to be more explicit (Quiggin 1993:1128). Just because people managed one set of CPRs before resettlement does not mean that they can transfer those procedures to new groups or new resources post-resettlement.

The second problem that has often arisen after resettlement is population growth. One of the successes of resettlement programs has been the increased provision of public health services to previously isolated populations. Despite increased morbidity from stress at resettlement (Scudder and Colson 1982), populations may show substantial natural enlargement afterward. For example, the Cree population grew significantly, leading to an abundance of youth, with more than 65 percent of the people under the age of 25 (Salisbury 1986:125). By the early 1990s, many were boarding at the single local high school in Chisasibi without adequate adult supervision; it was also questionable if the economy was growing sufficiently to provide enough jobs for them (McCutcheon 1991). At Manantali, many families used compensation payments to pay bride wealth for marriageable sons. A spurt of marriages plus better health conditions led to a mini-population boom less than a decade after resettlement.

In addition, successful economic activities around the dam site can attract immigrants, who sometimes benefit disproportionately in comparison to either indigenous hosts or resettlers. This is especially true if new roads to the dam area ease movement into previously isolated areas. At Bayano in Panama, extension of the Pan-American Highway and dam development led to growth of commerce, logging, and cattle ranching. Government and local elites benefited, but these activities led to siltation and environmental degradation, for which poor colonists and their insecure tenure rights were blamed. With nowhere else to go, they began to encroach on

Indian lands, leading to further ethnic tension (Wali 1993). At Selingue in Mali, fishing and irrigation projects attracted migrants, who nonetheless were unable to get land for complementary rain-fed farms. Hosts resisted lending land to these new migrants, and carried out highly extensive farming with the potential for land degradation as a way to solidify their land claims (Fofana and others 1992). In some areas close to roads, Cree hunters saw increased competition from non-Native sports hunters. Although they did not object to use by outsiders, they wanted priority for their hunting rights (Salisbury 1986).

The record is not encouraging. In the face of erosion of rights to common property resources, both resettlers and their hosts have often faced environmental degradation and decreasing economic prospects. While one solution may be new forms of individual tenure, adapted forms of common property regimes can also work. However, the local group must be able to retain control, to exclude access to some, and to enforce rules. In other words, the resources must be treated as collective property and not become open-access resources.

Improving post-resettlement outcomes

The suggested improvements follow directly from the problems discussed. Because there have been so few resettlement successes, some of the suggested initiatives come from contexts other than resettlement. Three main areas need to be considered: political, economic, and organizational.

Increasing political rights and participation

Resettlement initiatives that recognize the political rights to participation, distinctive cultural and social organization, and property ownership of both relocatees and hosts work better than those that do not. Efforts need to come from two directions. National governments and donors need to do what they can to ensure recognition of rights and participation of affected populations. Hosts and resettlers also need to organize themselves to ensure rights and representation.

The first step is for national governments and international donors to recognize the rights of those groups who own and use common property resources. Where relocated groups are cultural minorities, those with explicit legal recognition have been better able to negotiate satisfactory resettlement conditions than those without. For example, the 1982 version of the Canadian constitution included the concept of aboriginal rights, which in turn led to de facto recognition of First Nations (Funk 1985). In the Americas, where Native and Indian groups had formally demarcated reserves or reservations, this provided a clearly bounded area over which to begin negotiations. The fact that the province of Quebec was required by law to negotiate a treaty with the Cree provided the impetus for the James Bay and Northern Quebec Agreement that gave the Cree Indians much control over local development (Salisbury 1986). The Kuna Indians of the Bayano region of Panama were able to negotiate better resettlement conditions than their neighbors, the Embera, because the former had had a recognized reserve since the 1930s, while the latter did not (Wali 1989).

Recent efforts by international donors have encouraged national government recognition. It is now World Bank policy to compensate for customary tenure (Cernea 1993), and the Inter-American Development Bank (IDB) has also made efforts in this direction. For example, an IDB loan for regional agricultural development in Bolivia required that the Yuqui Indians be assured sufficient land to continue traditional subsistence (Stearman 1990).

Yet legal recognition is not the only top-down effort worth pursuing. Some governments have provided relocatee groups direct funding. The Canadian federal Indian agency provided one Native group more than Canadian $500,000 to research their claims and finance negotiations with the local hydro-power company (Waldram 1988:113); others have received funds to hire lawyers (Salisbury 1986; Waldram 1988). Canadians also funded mediating umbrella groups like the Committee for Original People's Entitlement (Funk 1985:124). Many developing countries may not have similar resources, but they may have existing organizations whose skills can be lent to relocatee groups, for example, legal aid organizations such as *La Clinique Juridique* in Mali or other community action groups.

Equally important are government efforts at transparency. Although infrastructure development groups—sometimes with the collusion of government agencies—are often tempted to limit the availability of information, transparency of procedures and open decisionmaking does seem to facilitate equitable resettlement (Shas 1995:321). Virtually no population accepts resettlement without resistance, and it is simply much less costly to encourage transparency from the beginning, since corrective action to deal with adverse impacts later on usually has high economic, social, and political costs (Fernandes Serra 1993:79). Some (see Funk 1985) have argued that the public inquiry model, by airing many points of view, has self-correcting mechanisms within it. Some governments have moved in this direction; in southern Brazil, for example, state legislatures organized public forums (Hall 1994:179). Fernandes Serra (1993) suggests that governments need to go beyond furnishing information on specific projects to publicize overall sector policies.

While top-down efforts are extremely important and provide the legal basis for many resettlement improvements, they are rarely sufficient in and of themselves to guarantee adequate and timely resettlement and rehabilitation practices. The Canadian Department of Indian Affairs, for example, only began to consider that it should be more active in defending Native rights at Easterville after agreements had already been signed between Native groups and the hydro-power company (Waldram 1988:99). Early and effective attention to resettler concerns seems to have come only when groups organized and participated politically to make their voices heard. Even then, progress might be slow. National policy reforms creating local resource rights in Niger came about only after five years of negotiations between project personnel, local farmers, the Forest Service, and the national administration (Arnould 1990:311).

As noted above, groups using CPRs were not often among dominant political players, and they did not always know what political procedures were available to them. Thus, in most cases where groups were able to organize for better resettlement conditions, they had help and technical assistance from local elites, often scholars or community activists. For example, Cree organization was assisted in part by the public outcry of anthropologists and ecologists (Salisbury 1986:54). Groups at Itaparica in Brazil got help from the Catholic Church and Oxfam in forming community and trade union movements to secure better resettlement (Hall 1994). A group of concerned scholars and planners worked with the Bedouins to forestall takeover of the Negev desert by the Israeli army (Marx 1988). Yavapai Indians in Arizona called on one of their own, Dr. Carlos Montezuma, a physician in Chicago, who helped them find a lawyer for water rights negotiations (Coffeen 1972). In Narmada, NGOs were formed with the participation of urban community activists. As Dhagamwar and others (1995:283) noted, there was little way that tribal and nontribal oustees at Narmada could have challenged and stalled construction as effectively as the *Narmada Bachao Andolan*, a regional group with established organizing skills and international links.

Outsiders were able to help in several practical ways. They often provided funds that allowed groups to do things not otherwise possible. For example, the Arctic Institute of North America provided the initial funding that brought Cree chiefs from different bands together — the kernel of a regional organization for all Cree (Salisbury 1986). Links to the larger world were also useful in providing information to local groups. Both the Dene of northern Canada and Cree hired social scientists as advisers, although they made their own decisions about topics for studies (Funk 1985; Salisbury 1986). The Berger Inquiry on the Mackenzie Valley pipeline in Canada collected and listened to community testimony, permitting sociocultural issues to influence policy (Funk 1985:131). In turn, links to the outside world were useful in making a larger public aware of the problems of relocation, and gave local social movements more leverage on governments (Hall 1994). Activists in Arch-Vahini, one of the Narmada NGOs working on resettlement, attribute their success at getting rights for oustees without formal land tenure to links with Thayer Scudder and Oxfam (A. Patel 1995:186).

However, as noted above, the collaboration of national and international groups has also had the potential to overwhelm local concerns with outside agendas. While international and national input was useful in getting the worst abuses stopped, for example, through the World Bank guidelines (Hall 1994:1805) or the Mackenzie Valley Pipeline Inquiry (Funk 1985), it was not very good at helping relocatees to organize themselves, to develop their own priorities, or to increase control over their own resource base. For this, alliances with local activists and elites appear to have been more useful. The goal should be to decrease dependency of relocatees on all outside organizations, not simply to replace dependency on government agencies with dependency on NGOs.

Local organizations for resettlement and rehabilitation should include both host and resettler groups. We have found no case where hosts were involved on much more than a pro forma basis. For example, the Finns selling land to the government for Karelian resettlement formed the "League of Land Surrenderers" to look after their interests (Mustanoja and Mustanoja 1993:93), and chiefs and elders of host villagers at Manantali were invited to meetings to choose new village sites for relocatees and formally cede their land. Tangible benefits, such as new wells, help hosts accept settlers. However, hosts not only need to get benefits but also to be directly involved in planning and implementation. Where hosts and relocatees are of similar cultural background, they may be able to use existing institutions for new purposes, but the new task and its larger scale will often require new institutions. Where hosts and relocatees have different cultural traditions, they will surely need to develop a formal framework for working together.

While political representation for local populations so that they can effectively lobby for their own priorities is a necessary precondition for good resettlement, it is hardly sufficient. Attention also needs to be given to the creation of new forms of economic activity that will allow people to earn decent livelihoods. Often these will require new organizations as well.

Economic changes

While common property regimes can still be a viable alternative, pre-resettlement common property forms rarely can continue to exist without change. As discussed above, many existing common property systems are already stressed by natural population growth or government moves to turn them into open-access resources. In any case, when the number of people using a resource base is increased through resettlement, the potential for overexploitation and host-resettler competition and conflict grows. The economic development component of resettlement must look at possibilities for changing the ways in which people earn their living, in the present and the future.

The most obvious mechanism is classic intensification of land use, that is, changing technologies to increase the return per unit of land. This possibility is most feasible in farming, where there are a number of well-tested strategies to increase security of tenure while introducing new technologies to increase production. However, the evidence suggests that although planners are often tempted to pin hopes for increased production on irrigated agriculture, they ought to look seriously at tested techniques for intensifying rain-fed production. There are many cases of successful efforts to increase agricultural production in Africa, including but not limited to programs carried out in conjunction with voluntary resettlement (Akwabi-Ameyaw 1990; Dione 1987; McMillan and others 1990). In addition to the use of chemical inputs such as fertilizers, many include agroforestry components or organic techniques that can increase environmental sustainability.[6]

These programs do not need to change tenure systems, although some attempts to increase productivity and security of tenure through the introduction of private farmland have been at least

---

[6]   Examination of these possibilities is beyond the scope of this chapter. In any case, we found very limited information on the continuation of rain-fed agricultural common property regimes in conjunction with involuntary resettlement.

partly successful. Although Narmada resettlement has been highly controversial, some of those working with relocatees have argued that the provision of two hectares to resettling families, including landless, adult sons or different segments of joint families, etc., has given tribal families the degree of security they very much wanted (A. Patel 1995; Gill 1995). In Zimbabwe, the voluntary settlement of residents on family farms has led to increased production and incomes for many who were previously landless (Akwabi-Ameyaw 1990; Jacobs 1989). Some Nubians who received freehold lands on the New Halfa scheme also did very well (Salem-Murdock 1989).

In contrast, short-term tenancy arrangements have been a singular failure. These new tenure arrangements have not given farmers fundamental control over land, but only access to use it as the state or parastatal deemed appropriate (Grayzel 1988:324). African irrigation schemes often retained scheme or state ownership and gave farmers only temporary tenancies (for example, Selingue and the Office du Niger in Mali, Mwea in Kenya, and some parts of New Halfa in Sudan) in an effort to persuade farmers to follow prescribed cultivation rules. This increased tenure insecurity among farmers, who were often unable to make a living by following the scheme rules because administrators often discounted farmers' real costs and held an inflated perception of benefits (DeWilde 1967; Fofana and others 1992; Kamuanga 1982; Moris 1973b). Moreover, farmers were often unable to use holdings as security for loans, and sometimes could not even subdivide for their heirs, as at Mwea (Moris 1973b:318).

Land use intensification for foragers or pastoralists has proven even more difficult, in part because successful models are few. Attempts to make these activities more productive in non-resettlement contexts have been far from successful, especially in Africa (Horowitz 1979; Dyson-Hudson 1991; Shazali and Abdel Ghaffar M. Ahmed 1999). Also problematic have been attempts to encourage people to change completely their livelihoods, as in efforts to encourage pastoralists to become farmers. Yet, if populations grow or the resource base decreases, it is difficult for people to continue extensive patterns of land use.

Successful adaptation to resettlement seems to have occurred when people could continue their old activities, but added new ones to increase incomes and productivity. One example is the James Bay Cree, who continued to hunt and trap after dam construction, creating an income support program for hunters as a way to valorize traditional livelihoods. Registered successful hunters could get a lump sum payment at the beginning of the winter hunting season that would allow them to buy needed equipment and pay for transport to hunting camps for themselves and their families. After dam construction, the amount of food and furs produced by hunters remained the same, although it formed a smaller proportion of income, as people began to earn income from a number of new activities. The Cree created a new social formation, where hunters and wage earners continued patterns of generalized reciprocity, with hunters sharing meat with wage earners and those with cash income helping to buy snowmobiles and other equipment for kin who continued to hunt (Feit 1982; Salisbury 1986; Scott 1984). At Manantali, faced with the loss of bush resources for collecting, a few farmers experimented with planting trees formerly found only in the wild, such as *shea (Butyrospermum paradoxum)* and *néré (Parkia biglobosa)*. Others looked to commercial activities to replace lost agricultural ones. One village created a dynamic new market while individuals formed small groups that undertook agricultural labor for cash to invest in trade. Blacksmiths began to make new tools (such as plows and peanut shellers) alongside their standard hoes.

Other successful examples are few, but ideas abound. For example, Asch (1982:363) suggested that the Dene of northern Canada could retain hunting as a major part of their livelihood if they could increase the value added through local processing. They could tan furs and process fish, manufacture garments and other handicrafts, and perhaps begin fur farms using fish as a feeder stock.

Infrastructure development often brings new jobs as well. Dam construction creates lakes that stimulate the fishing industry (Adu-Aryee 1993; Sissoko and others 1986). Sometimes industries are created around dam sites to take advantage of electricity or other infrastructure (Adu-Aryee 1993). The opening up of isolated areas also brings new services, particularly education and health care, to resettlement zones. Yet immigrants, often more experienced or better prepared to take advantage of the opportunities, may take the most remunerative jobs, creating even more pressure on existing resources. Resettlers end up as a labor reserve, getting only the worst-paid and most ephemeral work (Diarra and others 1995; Charest 1982; Robinson 1986).

The resettlement plan can take steps to increase the relocatees' chances to profit from new opportunities. At Kariba in Zambia, fishing was closed to all except locals for the first six years, from 1958 to 1964 (Scudder, personal communication). Training people in the necessary skills for new jobs is even more important. Cree had access to adult education courses that allowed them to learn such new skills as snowshoe manufacture, economic development, and office support (Salisbury 1986:77). Again, decentralization and local autonomy allow people to structure services to take advantage of old as well as new skills. After resettlement, the James Bay Cree ran their own schools and were able to adapt the curriculum to local needs. They decided to teach early grades the Cree language and to integrate information on Cree culture (such as animal behavior, weather conditions) into the curriculum. Older Cree were hired to teach these topics (Salisbury 1986:118).

Successful new income-earning opportunities create spread effects as increased incomes allow people to purchase consumer goods. Successful farmers can stimulate processing industries and agricultural input providers, rural markets, and consumer goods artisans. Fisheries create income not only for fisher families, but also for market intermediaries, canoe builders, and other support services; by 1975 an estimated 87,000 earned income from Lake Volta fisheries (Adu-Aryee 1993:148). It is useful to think of the resettlement region as a whole, hosts and relocatees together, with possibilities for small business, industry, tourism, and/or mining (Scudder 1982:109). Although growth will take on a dynamic of its own, the economic development component of the resettlement project should include training for likely post-resettlement alternatives.

There is plenty of evidence that people are willing and able to learn new skills. Many have used new technologies to help continue old ways of life. Saami pastoralists used snowmobiles, all-terrain vehicles, portable burlap and wire netting, and field telephones; they had herds ferried to summer pastures on Norwegian naval landing craft (Paine 1994:145,146). Cree began to use snowmobiles, rifles, and radios and to freeze fish instead of smoking it (Salisbury 1986:64). Northern Canadian lifestyles had been quite labor-intensive, and Cree hunters used mechanization to allow a little more leisure. Communications technology clearly made bush travel safer and allowed more Cree to move as families to winter hunting camps (Scott 1984:79). Other technologies may prove useful as well. In Brazil, local people have used satellite photography to document the effects of increased settlement and clearing on land use patterns (Brown and Stone 1989).

Using new technologies to continue old ways of life, and training for new skills and opportunities are both expensive propositions. Although donors and national governments will often fund short-term economic development in conjunction with resettlement, they are often unable or unwilling to do so over the lengthy time period that may be necessary to make sure that economic development is under way. The James Bay Cree, for example, have continued to get significant funding from federal and provincial governments; however, earnings on their substantial compensation generated only one-tenth of the costs to run their many activities (McCutcheon 1991:124). Clearly, one outstanding issue is how to generate funds for long-term development initiatives. For relocatees who continue to manage a collectively owned resource, one option is to consider ways that the property can earn income to fund future activities, perhaps along the model of some United States Indian tribes. The Navajo Nation, for example, earns substantial sums from leases on coal and other minerals on the reservation. A part of the Navajo-Hopi relocation plan involved using compensation to purchase Paragon Ranch, which had significant coal reserves; the money earned was to be used to fund programs for relocatees. Although the ranch had not yet earned much at the time Aberle (1993) was writing, it provides a possible model. The CAMPFIRE program in Zimbabwe encouraged people living in game parks to make decisions about hunting, user fees, rangers, and disposition of meat and fees, with the goal that they would use the funds generated to become self-sufficient (Bonner 1993). Following these models would require many governments to give up overlapping claims over common property resources, but may offer possibilities for locally funded economic development initiatives over the long term.

Better feasibility studies would increase these options. Many of the classic studies of resettlement have been done during and after implementation to look at effects rather than as part of planning (see Colson 1971). Many feasibility studies are unpublished reports and are hard to find (see IER 1984). However, the Navajo-Hopi experience provides evidence that good studies can improve the resettlement process. Although many anthropologists (see Scudder 1982) initially got involved to try to stop the relocation, their findings were also instrumental in securing improvements to the original relocation plan, once it became clear that relocation would proceed. The improvements included moving people as groups rather than families, improving the physical layout of new communities, and increasing the quantity of replacement lands (Aberle 1993).

While people will usually need to adapt the ways in which they earn their living after resettlement, they do not always need to change their property regimes. In fact, continuation of collective property ownership may, in some cases, offer greater possibilities to fund long-term economic development. The major issue is local control of the tenure regime, not its form. New economic activities need to be accompanied by forms of control that put real power in local hands. To be successful, these, like economic activities, will usually demand some adaptation of existing institutions. The final section of this chapter turns to issues of institutional development.

Institutional development

If people choose to retain collective tenure, they will need to create new institutions to address the situations they find after resettlement. It is not always easy to create truly representative and responsive grassroots institutions, especially when the stimulus is a condition, such as resettlement, that is imposed from above (Jacob and Lavigne Delville 1994). Moreover, it is not necessarily education and training that develop leadership skills, but as seen among Native groups in Canada, the long and painful process of negotiation, confrontation, and conflict (Waldram 1980:177). Nonetheless, we would like to offer a few suggestions about the kinds of institutional change that appear to be useful.

Creating new organizations can be quite time consuming. Poor people who spend much time simply earning their subsistence often do not want to spend even more time in meetings, especially when several institutions make multiple demands (McCorkle 1986). Therefore, people must be able to see the benefits from their institutions.

Decentralization and allowing the group to create and implement its own priorities are important. Too often, government agencies create community organizations as entry points to pursue their own agendas and are unprepared to accept rejection of their plans (Grayzel 1988:325). Moreover, certain aspects of plans may lead to greater government control rather than less. In Manantali, for example, the fact that the resettlement project distributed land meant that people began to go to local authorities rather than their own chiefs to solve land conflicts, thus concentrating authority in government hands (Koenig and Diarra 1998). Chiefs were unwilling to resolve conflicts because they thought they might be overruled. If the new organizations are to work, they must have the power to make and enforce their decisions. Sometimes their choices may be quite different from those of the dominant culture; the Cree, for example, decided to keep administrators' salaries low to avoid creating significant economic differences between leaders and others (Salisbury 1986).

People need to be prepared to accept the increasing responsibilities that decentralization and new forms of organization require.

Involving local populations in running their own affairs should not be limited to the resettlement phase alone, but this phase should prepare the population to solve problems that arise post-resettlement. This requires a decentralization of knowledge and skills to manage new infrastructure and the social resources generated by resettlement as well as the natural resource base.

Creating new forms of organizations, in a conscious manner, sometimes allows people to solve continuing problems that may otherwise seem unresolvable. Navajo who settled on replacement lands began to experiment with different range management schemes to solve overgrazing problems. Although these schemes involved co-ordination and agreement among families who would not have co-operated before the move, the new situation permitted them to experiment in ways that existing social groups would have found impossible. It was not clear at the time whether this would work, but Aberle (1993) thought that it might because the Navajo themselves had significant say in setting up these schemes.

Some people will likely welcome the chance to change traditional institutions to meet new challenges. Many forms of local organization are quite inequitable, and simple duplication of existing organizations may fail to address the concerns of women, lower castes, or other poor segments of the population (Grayzel 1988; Guggenheim and Cernea 1993; Koenig 1995). While creation of new organizational structures may be easier when a group is culturally homogeneous or when most of its members have similar resource endowments (Quiggin 1993; Salisbury 1986), the challenge for many resettlement projects is to create new institutional structures that allow all interested parties to participate.

Although people will often begin by creating local organizations, resettlement creates a need for overarching regional institutions as well. Where these were successful, they offered people the potential to restructure their relationships with larger national institutions, giving them more leverage (Feit 1982). The major example is again the Cree, whose umbrella organization, the Grand Council of the Crees of Quebec, allowed them to negotiate more effectively the James Bay and Northern Quebec Agreement. After the resettlement, Cree ran their own Cree Regional Authority, which provided health services, social services, education, housing, police, courts, and so on in a decentralized format that gave them much control (Salisbury 1986). The importance of regional umbrella organizations has been demonstrated elsewhere as well, for example, Senegalese villages involved in resource conservation efforts. Larger intermediary organizations facilitated information transfer among local groups and increased the possibility for gaining outside funding (Arnould 1990:343).

Again, there is much literature on how to create representative institutions that respond to local needs (see Bagadion and Korten 1991; Freeman and Lowdermilk 1991; Cernea 1991). Resettlement planners and local groups ought to turn to it for ideas on such issues as creating participatory organizations, and instituting formal charters, leadership structures, and norms in areas where they had not previously existed.

Conclusion

Common property resources and the activities pursued in conjunction with them are not artifacts of the past, but retain the potential for viable resource management in the present. Although some relocatees will want to change their form of resource tenure, many will want to retain some form of collective management. This ought to be facilitated rather than discouraged by the development initiatives that accompany resettlement . As the chapter suggests, these need to occur at three different levels: political, economic, and institutional.

At the national level, governments need to recognize collective tenure as a legal possibility; in some cases, this will need to be accompanied by political recognition of the distinctive status of cultural minorities. Legal recognition will help facilitate negotiation for compensation and replacement of collectively owned and managed resources. Political efforts cannot remain top-down, however, and efforts at self-organization by affected groups need to be encouraged and facilitated. Although governments and hydropower organizations may see these organizations as threatening over the short term, they are essential if people are to take development into their own hands after project completion.

Political power without resources to actualize development objectives is useless; therefore, any plan ought to consider how resettled people will get the resources necessary to escape impoverishment. Since involuntary resettlement usually involves more people using a single resource , it is naïve to believe that resettlers can simply replicate their pre-resettlement way of life. Some sort of intensification of resource use needs to be planned for. However, projects can introduce new resources that are collectively owned and new activities that build on old ones, rather than obliging resettlers to undertake completely new activities with resources owned under new tenure regimes. Of particular importance would seem to be strategies that add value to traditional products through transformation activities, such as processing of animal and tree products. This not only increases the amount that comes from a particular resource, but also offers new employment. Projects ought to include training programs that will equip resettlers to compete successfully for the production and social service jobs that often develop after resettlement.

Even though local people have often done better than state institutions in managing existing natural resources (see Kibreab, this volume), new forms of political action and new uses of resources demand the development of new local institutions. This is especially true when people are called upon to manage collectively a resource that was open access prior to resettlement, as was the case with the brick makers of Yacyretá, described by Mejía in another chapter of this volume. Local organizations must also include representatives of both host and resettler populations. Grassroots and local organizations need to be complemented by intermediate or umbrella organizations that allow local organizations to learn from one another and give groups greater leverage in negotiating with government and more powerful groups. As Cernea suggests earlier in this volume, planning adequately for both the resource and institutional aspects of involuntary resettlement can create a kind of development synergy. Well-organized groups can argue more effectively for adequate resources, while access to adequate resources can facilitate institutional development. Development planners and governments ought to encourage this synergy toward positive change rather than the downward cycle toward impoverishment so common in involuntary resettlement.

PART EIGHT

Toward social re-articulation

Editors'   The social re-articulation of displaced communities is,
Note   arguably, the most complex part of reconstruction, as it
brings together, at the group level, many of the processes addressed individually in the previous sections.
The four chapters included in this section offer original empirical testimonies of great interest about re-articulation.

It is well documented that forced displacement tears apart existing communities and social structures, interpersonal ties, and the
enveloping social fabric. Kinship groups often get scattered and life-
sustaining informal networks of mutual help, local voluntary associations, and self-organized service arrangements are dismantled. The
unraveling of spatially and culturally based patterns of self-organization, social interaction, and reciprocity represents loss of valuable
social capital that compounds the loss of both natural and man-made
capital. It should take therefore a multisided effort, by all concerned —
people, project agencies, state institutions, or donors — to reconstruct
the social fabric of the relocatees and foster community reestablishment and development.

The chapter by Jonathan Brown focuses on the institutional mechanisms and patterns of cooperation and consultation required for successful relocation. Good interagency cooperation is not, unfortunately,
a very frequent characteristic, and this makes the positive experiences reported by Brown a rather rare and very useful source of ideas
and effective approaches. The study demonstrates that reestablishment of viable communities depends not only on the communities
themselves but also on whether the macro institutions and the outside agencies involved in such processes follow a correct path in their
work and interactions.

The study by Renée Hirschon helps deflate a widespread but er-
roneous assumption about the relationship between economic recovery and social re-articulation at the community level. Through
in-depth empirical ethnographic analysis, Hirschon found that so-

cial solidarity and reconstruction of community ties between the members of a relocated group do not directly depend on the reestablishment of the community's full economic life. Hirschon studied community reestablishment in Kokkinia, an urban refugee settlement in Greece, which arose out of the compulsory exchange of populations between Greece and Turkey in 1923. Hirschon's chapter underscores the relative independence of socio-cultural variables, and suggests that community re-articulation can and must be aimed at even when full economic recovery is not achieved or achievable.

Wolde-Selassie Abutte examines the consequences of the Ethiopian Derg regime's politically mandated emergency resettlement program undertaken in the mid-1980s, which relocated some 600,000 people after a succession of droughts and famines. Based on extended research and involvement in assistance work in the Beles Valley resettlement areas, Wolde-Selassie describes and accounts for the gradual and painful reestablishment of socio-cultural life. Many resettlers deserted the sites. Those who remained went through a difficult process of readaptation. What made a profound difference during this readaptation, shows Wolde-Selassie, is precisely the reconstruction of community associations, be they informal or formal, the revival of patterns of solidarity and mutual help among people, the reaffirmation of community life-norms, and the recreation of interfamily and intergroup ties. This "social reconstruction" propelled the economic recovery.

The final chapter in this section takes a somehow different approach. Based on field investigations over a period of 10 years, L. K. Mahapatra and Sheela Mahapatra explored how the same social unit (a village affected by the dam on the Ramial River) experienced all the impoverishment risks highlighted in Cernea's IRR model and how integrated reconstruction overcame these risks. The process has not been smooth by any measure, but the point the authors emphasize — somehow different than the point emphasized by Hirshon — is that community reestablishment and re-articulation is the product of a multifaceted process of healing and recovery, depending on the convergence of several premises: land; income-generating employment; services; access to common resources; and others.

The dimensions of social reconstruction are, in fact, analyzed not only in these four studies, but also in many other chapters of the volume such as those by Sørensen, Fernandes, and Kibreab. Together they show that the reknitting of delicate community tissues, the re-formation of social capital, the initiation of collective actions by communities once disrupted by displacement, can amount, in time, to social re-articulation and to the resumption of the development process.

CHAPTER 14

Postconflict reconstruction in Azerbaijan: a user's perspective on social assessment and stakeholder consultation

Jonathan C. Brown

The way we listen will affect how we conduct the music.

Susan Devanny Wyner
Orchestra Conductor

The primary motivation for donors to become involved in post-conflict reconstruction should be to assist people in reestablishing their lives in a sustainable way within a framework of supportive institutions. Soliciting the views of the affected people on the nature of the postconflict society and on what they need to arrive at it would seem a natural and vital part of the process by which donors establish their assistance programs. In reality, however, the process of listening to those affected — by using professional "interpreters" — is not always done in a systematic way. And when "the act of listening" does occur, peoples' views are not always heard. And even if their views are heard, they are not always acted upon since donors have a variety of motivations for defining programs as they do. The motivations are laudable, but are also mixed with political, economic, commercial, bureaucratic, and, perhaps, even arbitrary considerations.

But what happens when the people are listened to and heard? What are the implications for their leaders and for the donors? This paper looks at one case of postconflict reconstruction — Azerbaijan — and investigates what happened when there was a real attempt to listen to the affected people, to hear what they had to say, and to act on what was heard. One question is what lessons can be learned? If the people conduct the orchestra, what music emerges? And will the donors and government buy tickets to the concert?

The social assessment process—the analysis of social development issues and stakeholders' views in an active research manner that promotes all actors' participation—is the way in which donors (and recipient governments) should make decisions about what investment projects to undertake and how to fund them. The results of the social assessment process are not considered in isolation but evaluated together with more traditional economic, financial, technical, institutional, and environmental criteria.[1] The social assessment process is unique, however, in that it attempts to convey in a systematic, quantified way the relative importance of issues for different social groups. In the case of Azerbaijan reconstruction, the social assessment process played an important role for donors, and for government, in decisionmaking. The author, who is not a social scientist, shared responsibility with other colleagues at the World Bank for shaping the Bank's response to the postconflict situation in Azerbaijan, and looks at the social assessment process from a "user" perspective.

Background

The problem of population displacement in Azerbaijan stems primarily from civil strife over the area in and around Nagorno-Karabakh in the late 1980s and early 1990s. Under the former Soviet Union, Nagorno-Karabakh was a semi-autonomous republic near the Azeri-Armenian border. The dominant population group in this area was ethnic Armenian, although there was a substantial Azeri minority as well. In 1992, tensions resulted in ethnic riots in both countries that led to an exodus of Azeris from Armenia and of Armenians from Azerbaijan. Military conflict caused large-scale population movement as ethnic Azeris left Nagorno-Karabakh and as territories surrounding the original conflict were mined and occupied. Since an ad hoc cease-fire in 1994, an estimated 30,000 internally displaced people returned home to areas around Nagorno-Karabakh that had been liberated by the Azeri military,

---

[1]   The results of social assessment can also have an impact on understanding these criteria; for example, the views of different stakeholder groups on financial issues can shape approaches to cost recovery, bill collection, willingness to make private investments, and so on.

but about 600,000 of the internally displaced were not able to return to Nagorno-Karabakh or other occupied areas. These displaced persons are currently living in temporary homes throughout Azerbaijan, a substantial number in urban areas in the vicinity of Baku, the capital of Azerbaijan. It is estimated that about 53 percent of the internally displaced live in urban areas and the rest in rural areas.[2] The living conditions of these populations are often deplorable, despite considerable efforts by the government of Azerbaijan and the international community to provide relief.

As a result of the conflict, large areas of Azerbaijan have been devastated, and years of occupation and neglect have led to considerable damage to the physical and social infrastructure, the environment, and the economy in general. The liberated areas, which run from Fizuli in the south in a crescent to Khanlar in the north and border the occupied areas, suffered various degrees of mining and of damage, from light bombardment to complete devastation, as they were fought over and occupied by opposing forces. By 1996 it became evident that the security situation would permit an additional 36,000 people to return to their original homes in the liberated areas.

The government of Azerbaijan decided at that time to request assistance from the World Bank in preparing a program of support for three target groups in the liberated areas: (1) those who had remained in their homes but whose lives had been disrupted by the conflict and would benefit from improved social and physical infrastructure and income-generating activities, (2) the 30,000 internally displaced who had already returned to their original homes but needed support in restoring their livelihoods, and (3) part of the 36,000 displaced people living in temporary homes around Azerbaijan who might choose voluntarily to return to their original homes and who required assistance in resettlement and reconstruction to do so.

The origin of the social assessment process

The social assessment process actually began before 1996. In 1994, the government of Azerbaijan and the World Bank were preparing an investment project to rehabilitate the urban water supply production and distribution system in Baku. Part of the project preparation involved a sociological analysis to identify the behavior

---

[2]   State Committee for Refugees, October 1998.

patterns and views of Baku residents with regard to urban water supply.[3] One element of the social assessment dealt with internally displaced populations since they constituted an important segment of the urban water supply market. The social assessment, based on qualitative consultations of World Bank social scientist Ayse Kudat and Azeri social scientist Ahmed Musayev, revealed that the displaced people were not integrated into the local economy, were dependent on humanitarian assistance, were becoming isolated from the rest of the economy, and, despite the best efforts of the government and the international community, were living under very difficult conditions. A focus group meeting with members of the National Women's Organization (Kadinlar Cemiyeti) from all around Azerbaijan gave numerous examples of widespread destitution among displaced persons in general and extremely low morale among those who were injured during the fighting.

In 1995-1996 the World Bank carried out a poverty assessment of Azerbaijan that had a special section on the plight of internally displaced populations. The poverty assessment was based in part on a special survey of 450 displaced people conducted by Kudat and Musayev and was complemented by work done by the United Nations High Commissioner for Refugees, the World Food Programme (WFP), and nongovernmental organizations. The results confirmed the 1994 indications from the Baku water supply survey and explored in more detail the plight of the displaced population. Even for a country where poverty was widespread, this population included a disproportionately large segment of the "poorest of the poor," who were further impoverished by their forced displacement. In addition, "the breakdown of income on average among internally displaced population households showed an almost equal weighting of income from employment, aid in cash and from government and NGOs, and from the sale of (personal) assets."

Since it was not the government's policy to assimilate the displaced into the rest of Azerbaijan, the only sustainable solution was to return them to their original homes, beginning with those who

---

3   Kudat, Ayse. 1997. "Shaping the Future of Baku's Water Supply." In Michael M. Cernea and Ayse Kudat, eds., *Social Assessment for Better Development.* Washington, D.C.: World Bank.
4   The policy of wanting internally displaced persons (IDPs) to return to their original homes was a matter of not only territorial integrity for the government but also practicality, given that IDP (and other refugees) represented 15 percent of the country's total population and the territory they had left represented about 20 percent of the country.

could return to the liberated areas.[4] The poverty assessment noted that "programs for reconstruction ... need to take into account the varying economic bases of each (district)." The assessment, which had input from World Bank staff with experience in postconflict situations, urged the Bank to move quickly on reconstruction and made five recommendations that were important in shaping the Bank's approach:

1. Reconstruction of the liberated areas of the Fizuli[5] district as a pilot project
2. Investment in income generation and community capacity-building to prepare other internally displaced still in camps for returning home
3. An assessment of reconstruction needs for the internally displaced, who could return to liberated areas
4. Building a base for donor coordination and specifying roles for implementing agencies, donors, and local and national government
5. Establishing a reliable institutional capacity for reconstruction in the Azerbaijan government

These early social analyses convinced the World Bank that part of its country assistance strategy for Azerbaijan with regard to poverty alleviation should be to investigate what could be done for the displaced populations. Since humanitarian organizations were supporting them in their temporary camps and since the mandate of the World Bank in the framework of postconflict situations is to focus on sustainable reconstruction, the Bank suggested to the government that a reconnaissance mission be sent to Baku for discussions with government and donor representatives and, if possible, go to the Fizuli district.

The terms of reference for the reconnaissance mission were: (a) to visit Fizuli, if possible, to determine if the security situation permitted implementation of World Bank-funded activities and, if so, to assess implementation capacity at the district level; (b) to design a "needs" assessment survey, to be carried out by Azeri social scientists, to obtain in a quantified and systematic way the views of the internally displaced persons who had returned to Fizuli, those from

---

5   By this time, nongovernmental organizations and U.N. specialized agencies were making reconnaissance trips and initiating small pilot projects in Fizuli, which appeared to have the largest area of liberated land where IDPs had begun to return on their own.

Fizuli currently living in camps outside the district, and the displaced populations in general. This needs assessment would then be used to identify priority sectors to be included in a pilot reconstruction project for potential World Bank funding; (c) to explore possible partnerships with local and international organizations interested in reconstruction; and (d) to discuss with government the lessons learned by the Bank from reconstruction efforts in other countries, in particular in terms of preparing reconstruction programs to attract donor financing and establishing reconstruction institutions. One of the members of the three-person Bank team[6] was a social scientist, Steve Holtzman, who at the time was involved in writing a new World Bank policy paper on the social dimensions of postconflict reconstruction.

The July 1996 reconnaissance mission

The July mission began its work in Baku with meetings with the government, which was extremely interested in moving forward with a reconstruction program in Fizuli and wanted very specific advice on establishing a reconstruction agency. The government indicated its desire to create such an agency by Presidential Decree within two weeks. The Bank mission also explicitly set out to see as many of the stakeholders involved in providing assistance to the displaced as possible, especially in Fizuli. This task was facilitated by UNHCR, which organized a group meeting with U.N. specialized agencies and local and international NGOs. The group meeting revealed the difficulties these agencies were having in gaining regular and effective access to Fizuli, which was administered by an ad hoc combination of military and civilian authorities with a permit system for nonresidents, including representatives of the donors working in the district, that seemed to change from day to day. The NGOs suggested that instead of focusing on its own agenda of longer-term reconstruction, the Bank should concentrate on the immediate problem of the relief agencies — access to Fizuli. The Bank mission agreed, and a field visit to Fizuli became an early

---

6   This reconnaissance mission was not tasked to come up with a preliminary list of sector priorities for reconstruction, as is often the case in postconflict situations, where speedy decisionmaking by international civil servants is seen as a virtue and which can result in project identification mirroring the technical expertise of the mission members. The Azerbaijan reconnaissance mission focused on establishing a process of stakeholder consultation to identify needs "from the bottom up."

test of the ability of actual and potential donors to operate effectively in this postconflict situation.

The Bank mission, accompanied by a deputy prime minister, along with representatives of the donors and of international and local NGOs, visited Fizuli and two other districts and confirmed that access, even in seemingly secure areas, was a problem because of the way the permit system was implemented. The government recognized this problem, and access improved substantially over the next few months, albeit with "ups and downs."

By the end of the July mission, the following had been accomplished:

The Reconstruction Agency. The Azerbaijan Reconstruction and Rehabilitation Agency (ARRA) was established by Presidential Decree outside the normal governmental bureaucratic structure to ensure flexibility in recruitment and operations. ARRA was placed under the supervision of a deputy prime minister with direct access to the head of state. ARRA was designed with its clients in mind. Its supervisory board was composed of all key government stakeholders as well as representatives of local NGOs, the first time that local NGOs had a direct role in such an organization in Azerbaijan. The Presidential Decree also established an International Advisory Group (IAG) to be chaired by the European Union (EU), the United Nations Development Program (UNDP), and the World Bank, with open membership to donors and international NGOs. This was a formal forum for international NGOs to express their views to government and the donor community. ARRA's mandate was to prepare and coordinate implementation of a resettlement and reconstruction program. The organizing decree did not solve, however, the overlap of responsibility for the physical resettlement of internally displaced people between ARRA and a State Committee that coordinated humanitarian assistance.[7] ARRA's internal organization was headed by a director general with departments for pro-

---

7   The recruitment of ARRA's staff and its initial operations were funded by UNDP, the World Bank, and the government of Azerbaijan; ARRA was up and running by the fourth quarter of 1996 as a result of the demonstrated commitment of the government (suitable offices, usually a problem, were given to ARRA very quickly) and the leadership among the donors in Baku of the UNDP Resident Representative, Paolo Lembo. World Bank funding for ARRA's establishment and operations, some small-scale

(Note continues on the next page.)

gram planning and for implementation. It was considered important for ARRA to gain experience rapidly in implementation of projects financed by different donors given the wide range of procedures and systems of accountability in use.

Needs assessment. Local social scientists, led by Musayev, were hired to undertake a needs assessment in order to provide input toward identification of priorities for a pilot project in Fizuli and as a key part of the social assessment process.[8] The needs assessment initially began with a household survey of 500 respondents, later increased by 1,000, supplemented by focus group discussions to follow up on some of the main findings of the quantitative data collected in the household surveys. National NGOs were involved by Musayev in the needs assessment.[9]

Coordination. The task of coordinating the donor community was left to the resident representatives of UNDP and the World Bank. Among the donors, effective coordination was hampered by the fact that UNDP and the World Bank believed in supporting ARRA as the appropriate institution for coordinating planning and implementing resettlement and reconstruction, while other donors and NGOs preferred to work directly with government ministries and local representatives. This was understandable since ARRA had to

---

pilot projects to gain implementation experience, preparation of a de-mining capacity, social needs and damage assessments, and overall resettlement and reconstruction program preparation was provided through both a PHRD grant and an advance from the Project Preparation Facility (PPF). Similar support from UNDP, and the flexibility in the use of funding between UNDP and the World Bank, allowed ARRA to begin functioning quickly.

[8]   Musayev's team was assisted from Washington by Kudat, who had created the Central Asia and Azerbaijan network of social scientists with funding from the Swiss government, by Holtzman, and by Bulent Ozbilgin and Paolo Caputo from the Bank's social development unit.

[9]   As international NGOs and other donors began to be interested in the Fizuli area, they did not always establish regular contact with ARRA or with the Musayev group, preferring instead to rely on foreign experts for assessing the local situation on the basis of a range of questions limited by the donors' interest. Local NGOs were rarely consulted. The Musayev group produced results based on quantitative surveys across a broad range of issues, while other donors produced results with more limited foci. The results could not be compared, and thus a number of social assessments processes were established that almost competed with each other. Neither ARRA nor the World Bank was sufficiently aware of this situation.

prove itself as an effective and transparent agency. In addition, one major donor was prevented by its national legislation from dealing with any Azeri government agency on "non-humanitarian" projects.

Lessons learned in other countries. The mission was able to compare the situation of internally displaced persons in Azerbaijan with that in other countries. The Azeri displaced shared some of the same characteristics of those elsewhere: (a) they had left their homes in a hurry and had lost most of their capital and possessions; (b) many were living in dreadful conditions and were dependent on humanitarian relief that, over time, results for many in a "dependency syndrome," and (c) the longer the population is displaced, the more difficult it is for those returning to settle into the mode of life they left behind, especially in the absence of substantial assistance from the government and international donors.

However, the Azeri displaced population had some different characteristics that were generally positive: (a) unlike many populations in similar circumstances, the displaced Azeri had remained within their own country during the entire period of displacement; (b) they were better educated and possessed more economic skills; and (c) even though dispersed throughout Azerbaijan, family units had remained largely intact, mostly living in close proximity with other families from the same village.

The lessons drawn from experience worldwide were (a) the importance of providing whatever was necessary and reasonable to allow those who could return to their homes to do so as quickly as possible, and (b) the establishment of mechanisms for "listening to people" since displaced populations are much more conscious of their own needs and problems than are planners or development officials.

In the fall of 1996, the European Union announced it would fund certain specific interventions in parts of the Fizuli district in order to concentrate its assistance on infrastructure and agriculture. As it was unclear at the time what the extent of these projects would be and what the future plans of the EU were, ARRA and the World Bank agreed to widen project preparation beyond Fizuli. ARRA initiated a second needs assessment for the liberated areas outside of Fizuli and a damage assessment of all the liberated areas. The most important findings of the needs assessment began to appear at the beginning of 1997 and concerned both the characteristics of the displaced persons and their views about resettlement and reconstruction. These results were presented at the IAG's first meeting near the end of the first quarter of 1997.

Results of the needs assessment of internally displaced persons[10]

The main characteristics of the internally displaced people that are relevant to resettlement and reconstruction are:

- While unemployment is widespread among these groups (50 percent unemployment on average), the internally displaced in Baku, who have higher education levels, also have higher employment rates.

- The displaced populations are among the poorest of the poor in Azerbaijan; their average incomes, regardless of whether they live in urban or rural areas, are less than the average rural income for the country. Those who have returned to Fizuli have higher incomes even though they no longer receive international assistance on a regular basis.

- Most displaced people spend a very substantial portion of their income on food and have inadequate access to public services.

- While families may be intact—85 percent have integrated households in their temporary homes, versus 95 percent before displacement—community structures are deteriorating more than had been indicated by previous surveys.

- Displaced households were unable to take away many assets at the time of displacement and had sold much of what they did take to sustain themselves. For example, whereas 75 percent owned cattle in their original homes, only 10 percent had cattle in their temporary homes. Few had access to agricultural land in their temporary homes and were dependent on food aid to sustain themselves.

The most positive characteristic was that the families remained largely intact. The rest of the findings confirmed that these were people who were not restarting their lives, but were in a status of increasingly desperate "waiting" to return to their homes.

---

[10]   A detailed report of the needs assessment is available for interested researchers by writing to the author of this chapter.

The most important findings of the needs assessment with regard to resettlement and reconstruction concerned the relative importance of factors that would cause displaced people to leave their temporary homes throughout Azerbaijan, where they were receiving different levels of assistance, and resettle in their original homes. Figure 1 shows the views of Fizuli's displaced persons.

FIGURE 1: FACTORS FOUND IMPORTANT FOR INTERNALLY DISPLACED
PERSONS IN DECIDING TO RETURN TO THEIR HOMES

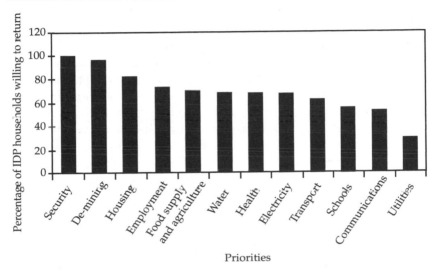

Priorities

Source: Household Survey with IDPs, 1996.

The needs assessment showed three main stimuli for Fizuli's displaced to return: first, security, including de-mining, and the provision of shelter; second, assistance for food and income generation, in particular in the agricultural sector; and third, assistance across a wide variety of physical and social infrastructure sectors.[11] When relocated, returning populations continue to be concerned about land mines, but they begin to express greater interest in having access to food as well as education and health services.[12]

---

[11]   Focus groups subsequently provided information that IDPs prefer a minimum level of services across most sectors rather than having to make choices among sectors.

[12]   The second needs assessment, carried out in fall 1997, concentrated on IDPs who could return to liberated areas other than the Fizuli district, showed that IDPs who had returned to their homes began to give more priority to housing and to monetary allowances from government.

The needs assessment indicated that the institution trusted the most to solve their problems by those displaced was the national government, followed by the district executive officer. The displaced people expressed less trust in local administrators, managers of state-owned farms and companies, *aksakals* (the traditional village elders), and NGOs.

Reliable information is a problem for those returning. They rely as much on informal, oral channels for information as they do on formal sources such as radio, television, newspapers, or official communications.[13]

While housing was an extremely important factor in the decision to resettle as well as after resettlement, the exact nature of the housing preferred was difficult to gauge. Housing destruction varied widely and the needs assessment did not show any correlation between the degree of destruction of housing and the willingness of the displaced to return, perhaps because most had unclear ideas of the current condition of their original homes. It was also not easy to determine the type of assistance the affected persons required — the provision of housing materials, for example, with either the returnees providing labor or the reconstruction of housing by contractors. As part of humanitarian efforts, donors used three very different construction standards, with different cost implications, for temporary housing, ranging from mud brick to limestone to prefabricated housing. Early provision of housing by donors in Fizuli to those returning also varied, both with regard to the size of houses and to construction standards.

The needs assessment had some major messages for government and for the donor community. First, the decision to focus institutional development initially on a national organization was supported. While the World Bank and UNDP continued to favor this approach and worked through ARRA, other donors were less convinced. Concerned about efficiency and ensuring that there was no leakage of funds, and based on the more limited surveys of their own staff, they often decided to work directly with beneficiaries or through international NGOs, especially when ARRA expressed a clear preference for hiring local consultants rather than foreign technical assistance that ARRA considered too expensive.

Furthermore, the decision to assist government with establishing a civilian de-mining capacity was supported. The experience of the

---

[13]   In contrast, IDPs still living in camps rely more on the mass media, especially on television for the nearly 50 percent of IDPs living in and around Baku.

donor community has been that the range of de-mining activities — from surveys of the scope and nature of the "mine" problem and public awareness programs to the actual demarcation of "mine-free" areas and physical de-mining of high-priority locations — is best done through civilian institutions, not through the military. Military standards of acceptable conditions of de-mining for military operations are obviously not the same as civilian standards of what is acceptable.

The needs assessment also indicated the importance of a "comprehensive" approach to resettlement and reconstruction that required substantial project preparation, implementation capacity, and concern with cost recovery.[14] An alternative approach — moving rapidly with a World Bank pilot project in one or two sectors — was rejected primarily because of the needs assessment findings on priorities. Moreover, the findings that the displaced people required support for resettlement at the same time as they required assurance about the availability of longer-term reconstruction meant that donors would have to make sure that resettlement and reconstruction programs were prepared and implemented simultaneously. This finding did not correspond to the views of those donors that wanted to provide assistance to one or two specific sectors, leaving government and other unidentified donors to fund other needs. Even within government the reasoning of the displaced may have been understood, but many officials were used to taking whatever assistance was given, if on a grant basis.

The priority given to housing was understandable, as was the desire of those displaced to return to the large houses (that is, more than 75 square meters) they had had before displacement. However, the choice for the donors was clear: either large houses for a small number of resettlers or more modest houses for a much larger number who wanted to resettle. Housing standards were discussed in the framework of the size and cost of housing provided for in other countries' resettlement programs. The agreed-upon initial housing for those returning whose previous shelter had been destroyed would be 24 square meters for a family of four, with lesser assistance, perhaps in the form of material, for those

---

14   Within the comprehensive approach, however, the needs assessment process showed variability as to sector priorities and within sectors, depending on community-specific circumstances and concerns. This meant that any resettlement or reconstruction program would have to respond to very specific community preferences, making the continuation of the social assessment process essential during program implementation.

whose needs were less. Housing assistance would be in the form of a grant with the homes individually owned. The funding of housing became an issue since those who had substantial funds for housing, such as the World Bank, had a policy that privately owned housing should be funded through a commercial institution that recovered full costs.[15] No commercial housing funding institution existed in Azerbaijan, even if those returning could afford to repay their housing, which, under any reasonable family budget forecasts, they could not. And while government was prepared to make a contribution to housing, it had insufficient resources to cover all the costs of resettlement, initial provision of food and other essentials, start-up income-generation activities, and housing — all on a grant basis.

Results of the damage assessment

By the end of the summer of 1997, ARRA and its consultants had completed the physical assessment of damages in all the liberated areas. Damage to physical and social infrastructure and losses in productive activities during and after the period of conflict amounted to several billion dollars. ARRA estimated that about $500 million would be needed to restore basic infrastructure, social services, and employment to a "minimum" of the preconflict situation.

The physical assessment had been overwhelmingly oriented toward the rebuilding of physical and social infrastructure without assessing adequately the needs of associated equipment, material, supplies, and trained personnel or the recurrent cost implications to keep everything running. The proposed $500 million program was largely a list of buildings to be replaced rather than a strategy, sector by sector, to provide a framework for delivering services with maximum efficiency in the context of constrained resources. In

---

[15]   The World Bank's rationale was that funds provided to government by the World Bank should be used for public goods that would benefit the country as a whole. Publicly owned housing would thus qualify. In the event that governments wanted to use World Bank funds for private housing, there should be cost recovery through a commercial financial institution on real terms, to ensure that the case did not arise that some people benefited while others did not. Government's initial reaction was, with a deliberate sense of irony, to offer to nationalize the private housing of returning IDPs, a suggestion neither in line with its own policy nor with the World Bank's support for private sector development.

addition, the $500 million did not correlate well with the findings of the needs assessment, except for the priority it gave to housing. A quick review of donor views by UNDP and World Bank in October 1997 indicated that raising even $100 million in total financing from all sources would be a challenge, especially in the absence of a comprehensive peace agreements being implemented for all affected parts of the region—Nagorno Karabakh and the surrounding "occupied" and "liberated" areas. The review also showed that only the government of Azerbaijan, the European Union, and the World Bank were prepared to make pledges for reconstruction larger than $5 million. There was hope, however, that a Consultative Group meeting for Azerbaijan scheduled for early 1998 in Tokyo might raise funds for resettlement and reconstruction.[16] It also appeared that a number of donors might be willing to make contributions of $1 million to $5 million, preferably channeling their funds through NGOs or such United Nations agencies as UNHCR and UNDP or through the World Bank.[17] Some humanitarian donors felt it was within their mandate only to assist displaced persons in their temporary homes rather than providing assistance for their resettlement.

Donors in general did not give Azerbaijan a high priority in comparison to other countries in need around the world, partly because they expected Azerbaijan to have large streams of oil revenues after the turn of the century. And for those donors that were prepared to assist Azerbaijan, financing the transition to a more market-based economy for the country as a whole had higher priority than dealing with resettlement and reconstruction in the liberated areas, despite the financial burden that displaced populations placed on government and the international community.

There was, in addition, a partial mismatch between what those donors who had funding for resettlement and reconstruction were prepared to finance, in the choice of sectors as well as between "hardware" and "software," and what the needs assessment or stakeholder consultation process indicated were peoples' highest priorities. Even within the government, there was a strong tendency

---

[16] In the event, the Consultative Group raised substantial funds for Azerbaijan, but with nothing earmarked for resettlement and reconstruction.

[17] The World Bank suggested to donors that funds for de-mining and housing be channeled through UNDP and UNHCR, respectively, while funds for reconstruction be channeled through ARRA or NGOs.

to finance "hardware" — rebuilding housing and infrastructure to generous standards — while leaving the accompanying "software" for later. Education and health were sectors for which physical facilities were already being rebuilt to larger-than-necessary sizes in the liberated areas without appropriate attention to equipment, supplies and material, and training, housing, and salaries for staff needed to make them function effectively.

In the face of this situation, the government, UNDP, and the World Bank in the fall of 1997 were faced with several possible approaches for moving forward with assistance to Azerbaijan for resettlement and reconstruction.

Traditional donor approaches to resettlement and reconstruction

Donors have traditionally approached the preparation of programs to fund postconflict resettlement and reconstruction around the world in at least four different ways:

Separating resettlement and reconstruction. Resettlement — the transport of displaced populations back to their original homes, the cost of initial housing, a subsistence allowance until returnees can begin earning their own income — is often provided as grants by the national government, international humanitarian organizations, and bilateral donors. Reconstruction — investment and working capital for early income-generation activities, the provision of medium- and long-term physical and social infrastructure, access to employment opportunities, and reconstruction of viable communities — is usually beyond the grant-giving mandate of humanitarian organizations and is provided instead, often as loans, by governments and international financial organizations. Physical relocation and reconstruction are coordinated through ad hoc arrangements by donors and government agencies. The advantage of this approach for the donors is that it allows each one to remain within the framework of its specialized expertise or interest. The main disadvantage is that, if coordination between resettlement and reconstruction fails, the results can be disastrous — either the people resettled physically may have no long-term reconstruction framework to sustain them, or a reconstruction program may be implemented in an area where fewer people than expected are inclined to resettle.

Sector concentration. Sector concentration allows a donor to fund reconstruction for a sector, or sometimes several sectors, in which the donor has expertise or interest, thus facilitating implementation for the donor. In addition, it is easier to implement coherent policies on cost recovery, technical standards, and so on with only one donor and the government involved. The potential pitfall is that some sectors will be funded, and others will not, and sometimes the sectors not funded are essential to the sustained recovery of the affected populations. Even within a sector, concentration can be dangerous, as happens when a donor funds electric power production but leaves power distribution to "government counterpart resources" that may then not be forthcoming.

Geographic concentration. Some donors want to finance many visible reconstruction activities in one geographic area, an approach sometimes labeled as "planting the flag." The advantage for the donor is that concentration of resources in a limited area theoretically makes it more likely that project objectives will be achieved. In addition, coordination with other donors appears unnecessary. The disadvantage is that no donor has the mandate or interest in funding the full spectrum of activities that the people require. What is left out remains for government to fund, and the funding may not be available when needed.

The comprehensive approach. The comprehensive approach combines resettlement with reconstruction. It addresses not just one or another separate dimension of displacement and reconstruction— such as housing, employment, or healthcare—but deals with them in their interlinkages. It concentrates on the risks to which the displaced are exposed and covers all the sectors that the needs assessment and stakeholder consultation process have identified as important to the returnees.

It is almost impossible for any one donor to adopt a comprehensive approach with its own financing, but it is feasible to join with other donors. The comprehensive approach requires a strong decisionmaking mechanism in government and effective coordination among donors. This approach works best when there are many donors interested in providing financing, and there are donors— sometimes international financial institutions like the World Bank— that are prepared to fund the "gaps" after other donors with strong interests have funded their "preferences." The comprehensive approach can look like a "Christmas tree"; the many interrelationships require a degree of coordination and cooperation[18] that is difficult in the best of times, but often more than a "reasonable challenge" for governments coming out of a postconflict situation. However, the comprehensive approach, in principle, most often does respond to the expressed needs of the affected populations. It also deals with such difficult issues as technical standards, cost recovery, and targeting of benefits, and works better than piecemeal approaches if the security situation is favorable. The Bank team working in Azerbaijan had as models of the comprehensive approach Sri Lanka in the late 1980s, the emergency flood-relief program in Sudan in 1988, and the example of Bosnia, where more recently a series of more than a dozen sector-concentration efforts resulted, in fact, in the implementation of a comprehensive approach.

The low level of donor interest in Azerbaijan compared to the needs even of the liberated areas; the lack of enthusiasm among donors for using a government institution like ARRA for planning and implementation in a country where implementation was not easy in any sector; the mismatch between the needs assessment, especially concerning security and housing, and the interests or preferences of donors; and the support in the donor community for "simple" projects (with limited inputs and clear outputs) — all these suggested a small pilot project in one region, probably Fizuli, which would build on EU funds already committed and would focus on the reconstruction needs of the displaced persons who had already returned to that area. Government, UNDP, and the World Bank decided *not* to pursue this reasoning but instead to adopt the comprehensive approach and combine resettlement with reconstruction, which was a high-risk approach, basically because of the findings of the needs assessment and stakeholder participation process:

- ■ The longer the displaced remain away from their original homes, the harder resettlement becomes. Therefore, they should resettle as soon as possible.

---

[18]   The most difficult examples of coordination, by no means atypical, are when coordination becomes interdependence, for example, in the education sector, when one donor funds hardware, such as repair of school buildings, another funds operational expenditures such as equipment, textbooks and material, an NGO provides teacher training, and an international financial institution assists government with financing teacher salaries on a declining basis. This kind of coordination requires a commitment to building strong local institutions that will supplement, and eventually replace, donor coordination by the donors.

- Some 36,000 people could be resettled, restoring their lives and building institutional capacity for resettlement and reconstruction for the future as the peace process evolves.

- Affected people clearly stated through the social assessment process that resettlement and reconstruction had to be funded together with access to a broad range of minimum levels of support in social and physical infrastructure and in income generation.

- No reconstruction assistance would be useful without providing minimum levels of housing on a grant basis to families who would own their individual homes.

The adoption of a comprehensive approach was a matter of some debate in government. One faction felt that moving forward immediately with a "hardware" project would show the "impact on the ground" that the displaced had been waiting. For years, as the European Union was doing. Even those sympathetic to the comprehensive approach had real doubts that funding beyond what the World Bank was prepared to put in would be forthcoming. And why build up ARRA, if some donors were not prepared to use it? And, if the World Bank would not fund housing, who would?

Given the decision of the government, UNDP, and the World Bank to proceed with the comprehensive program combining resettlement and reconstruction, a number of actions were taken:

1. The proposed resettlement and reconstruction program that came out of the physical damage survey needed to be reshaped to meet the results of the social assessment process. In November 1997, government, assisted by the World Bank, created in November 1997 sector working groups for agriculture and irrigation, education, energy, infrastructure, housing and resettlement, income-generation including public works projects, and water supply and sewerage. The working groups were composed of ARRA staff and its consultants, representatives of the donors, NGOs, and local experts. The terms of reference for each sector working group was to put forward a sector strategy for reconstruction that (a) was based on the results of the social assessment process, in particular, the needs assessments; (b) took account of government's reform program; and (c) presented a program of priority investments and an estimation of operational support including

recurrent cost implications. The total investment needs for all sectors were to be limited to $100 million.

2. The linchpin to the comprehensive program was finding a mechanism for mobilizing financing for resettlement, especially for initial housing. UNHCR agreed to lead the sector working group on resettlement and housing and to establish a formal partnership with the World Bank to ensure that resettlement and reconstruction in Azerbaijan would be considered as one program. The World Bank said that while it could not disburse its own funds for grants for private housing, it had no objection to government using its counterpart funds in the World Bank project for this purpose.

3. UNDP agreed to take the lead in assisting government with the technical preparation and resource mobilization for a de-mining agency, taking over the role played by the World Bank during the previous year, since the World Bank had neither the resources nor internal technical expertise to give this effort the priority it deserved. Government indicated it would request that part of any investment funding from the World Bank be earmarked to assist in the initial operations of the de-mining agency.

The sector working groups completed their draft sector programs in January 1998,[19] with each group's report then discussed with key stakeholders, including local government officials, local and international NGOs, and representatives of a joint World Bank–UNHCR mission and of a EU mission that had come to Baku to review its future assistance for reconstruction. The sector reports were then integrated into an overall Azerbaijan Resettlement and Reconstruction Program that was discussed in draft in government and with the main donors, then presented by government to a meeting of the International Advisory Group in March 1998 called by the three co-chairs: the European Union, UNDP, and the World Bank. Based on the outcome of the IAG meeting and the intention

---

[19]   The Consultative Group meeting in Tokyo in January, co-chaired by the government of Azerbaijan and the World Bank, had a special session on reconstruction in which the Government gave an overview of its approach to resettlement and reconstruction. Since the specific resettlement and reconstruction program was still under preparation, this was intended to sensitize the donors to the impending request for support rather than as a specific "pledging" session.

of the EU to move forward with sector investments in the Agdam and Terter districts, UNHCR agreed to launch a special appeal to the international donor community for resettlement and housing aid, while UNDP and the World Bank moved forward on the demining and reconstruction fronts.

UNHCR's special appeal

The partnership between UNHCR and the World Bank was based, as UNHCR stated, "on the joint recognition that for return to be sustainable, short-term resettlement activities should go hand-in-hand with longer-term efforts aimed at rebuilding the physical and social infrastructure and of income generation possibilities." This recognition came, as UNHCR also stated in its appeal, from the results of the social assessment process. In April 1998, following the IAG meeting, UNHCR launched a "special appeal" to the donor community for funds to cover resettlement on a grant basis, in particular for initial housing that would be privately owned. The 1998 objective was to raise $5.5 million for the first phase of a multiyear program with an estimated total cost of $12 million. "The initial appeal will be followed by a further funding submission in 1999 for the second phase subject to a World Bank/UNHCR evaluation of the 1998 achievements. Furthermore, UNHCR and the World Bank agreed to combine their efforts to inform the international community about the progress made in resettling returning displaced persons and on the resettling financial requirements as and when implementation proceeds." By October 1998, more than half of the 1998 funding target had been mobilized from Canada, the United States, and the private sector.

World Bank pilot reconstruction project

Following the IAG meeting, the World Bank proceeded to appraise a $54.2 million "pilot project" as the first phase of the $100 million Resettlement and Reconstruction Program. The objectives of the pilot project were to:

- Support the return of displaced persons to the Fizuli, Agdam, and Terter districts when it was safe for them to do so, as well as to assist those who had already returned and those who had never left but had suffered from the conflict.

- Provide a link between resettlement and reconstruction of

livelihoods by funding the costs of resettlement, initial housing and income-generation activities, and a comprehensive
package of minimum services in physical and social infrastructure and in income-generation activities.

■   Enhance the capacity of governmental and nongovernmental institutions to implement the resettlement and livelihood
reconstruction program as well as to create a national determining capacity.

The World Bank's own funding would be used to (a) complement and supplement the funding of the European Union already
committed in the Fizuli district and promised for Agdam and Terter,
(b) cover the longer-term reconstruction for areas in which UNHCR
was assembling financing for resettlement and housing, and (c) permit the government to give initial funding for the de-mining agency
to supplement the approximately $1 million already raised by UNDP.
The pilot project components and its financing are shown in Tables
1 and 2 below.

In addition to its comprehensive coverage, the Pilot Reconstruction Project contained a number of other items that the social analysis process had highlighted. Among ARRA's specific responsibilities
would be establishment of capacity to (a) seek continuous feedback
from the displaced and other stakeholders on the adequacy of the
project's response to their needs, (b) establish close liaison with national and local agencies on implementation of the various project
components,[20] (c) inform the population about the resettlement and
reconstruction program and the potential benefits for those displaced, and (d) assist the IAG in coordinating the assistance of international donors.

The social analysis process also attempted to broaden the process of stakeholder consultation, and the donors themselves were
a key stakeholder group. The pilot project was shaped by their
concerns about institutional capacity. ARRA was provided with funds

---

[20]   The emphasis on community-based project definition and implementation and the use of nongovernmental organizations as one means of assisting local initiatives came more from the experience of donors in other
countries than with the Azerbaijan situation, since the needs assessment
had clearly shown the peoples' overwhelming trust in the national government to meet their needs. This is one example of the peoples' views not
being accepted by the donor community.

TABLE 1: PILOT PROJECT COMPONENTS AND FINANCING

Component	Category	Cost in millions of US$	% of total	Bank financing in millions of US$	% of Bank financing
Relocation	Inst. bldg.	1.8	3.3	—	—
Shelter	Physical	14.0	25.8	—	—
Income generation:					
Agriculture	Physical	9.4	17.3	6.0	30.0
Microcredit and grants	Credit	1.1	2.0	0.4	2.0
Public works, env. mitigation	Physical	0.4	0.7	0.4	2.0
Health and education:					
Health	Physical	0.9	1.7	0.9	4.5
Education	Physical	4.2	7.7	1.9	9.5
Infrastructure and energy					
Infrastructure	Physical	2.4	4.4	0.4	2.0
Energy	Physical	12.1	22.3	7.2	36.0
Institutional support					
ARRA	Inst. bldg.	1.6	3.0	1.4	7.0
Agricultural support	Inst. bldg.	0.4	0.7	0.4	2.0
De-mining agency	Inst. bldg.	2.9	5.4	0.6	3.0
Project Preparation					
Facility (PPF)	Inst. bldg.	0.4	0.7	0.4	2.0
Recurrent costs		2.6	4.8	—	—
Totals		54.2	100.0	20.0	100.0

Source: Azerbaijan Pilot Reconstruction Project, Project Appraisal Document, 1998.

TABLE 2: FINANCING PLAN (IN MILLIONS OF $)

Source	Local	Foreign	Total
Government	9.4	—	9.4
Parallel financing			
UNDP	—	3.2	3.2
UNHCR	6.1	6.0	12.1
EU	4.1	5.4	9.5
IDA	4.9	15.1	20.0
Total	24.5	29.7	54.2

Source: Azerbaijan Pilot Reconstruction Project, Project Appraisal Document, 1998.

to build special capacity in project implementation, particularly with regard to procurement, accounting and auditing, financial management, and sector technical expertise. It was agreed that NGOs, both national and international, would be used as implementation channels, especially at the community level, where government agencies and the private sector had not developed an effective presence.

The social assessment process also had a major impact on how the World Bank saw its own role, which was less concerned with the implementation of its own funding as measured by the rate of disbursements. "As it has through project preparation, the Bank would play an important role in donor coordination for reconstruction activities (UNHCR plays this role in voluntary resettlement and housing, and UNDP for the De-mining Agency) in ensuring that all stakeholders, especially representatives of the internally displaced persons and the local and international NGO community, are involved in the monitoring, evaluation, and inevitable re-engineering during implementation. As one of the three chairs of the IAG, the Bank will assist ARRA and the Government in ensuring that the program is implemented effectively and transparently in partnership with UNDP and UNHCR. As the 'lender of last resort,' the financing of the World Bank is being used to supplement and complement other donors to ensure that affected people receive a comprehensive package of essential services. The Bank's worldwide experience in post-conflict reconstruction operations will continue to be a source of knowledge, especially with regard to technical standards, financial sustainability, and institutional development, on which Azerbaijan can call through frequent supervision which a program this complex requires."

Conclusions

The Pilot Reconstruction Project represents the completion of one phase, admittedly a partial one, in the attempt by the government of Azerbaijan and the donor community to deal with the postconflict situation in the area insofar as the security situation permits. The social assessment process had a major impact in at least three areas:

- ■ Resettlement and reconstruction were combined more easily into a comprehensive approach because of the findings of the needs assessment. But peoples' needs evolve and the program will remain relevant to affected peoples in direct relationship to how well the social assessment process continues in the future.

■ The government and donors focused on developing the country's institutional capacity to deal with resettlement and livelihood reconstruction as much as on the program itself, in part to increase donor coordination. This was due to the inclination by some donors to "go it alone." ARRA now has to tackle its double mandate of (a) implementing the parts of the program for which it is directly responsible, and (b) developing an outward-looking, inclusive, people-oriented approach to donor coordination.

■ The development of the program made new demands on the donors and on government to work together in partnership for the good of the people, listening to the people, hearing their voices, and letting the people lead. The donors, and the various parts of government, have internalized this new approach to different depths, and even those who have worked together best have to constantly renew the process of social assessment, stakeholder consultation, and partnership.

The social analysis carried out during the entire process has generated some lessons that are applicable beyond the case of Azerbaijan:

■ First, it is extremely difficult for the social analysis carried out as action research to operate effectively if it is not supported by a broad range of groups within government and the donor community. Mobilizing and maintaining this support group is as important as the quality of the social assessment process itself. Having some donors prepared to go ahead without an in-depth social analysis puts the government and the donors that favor social analysis in a very difficult situation.

■ Second, the social assessment process needs to have sufficient support and funding so that it can do what is required, when it is required; the failure of the process in Azerbaijan to come up quickly with answers concerning peoples' views on housing standards and techniques or on the real ability of those returning to contribute to cost recovery should have been avoided.

■ Third, the social assessment process needs to be carried out in a systematic, quantifiable manner by professionals and not by more qualitative techniques, which are open to conclusions which lack substantiation. In addition, the social assessment process may need, in some cases, assistance from abroad, but it can, and should, be done in great part by local experts. The social scientists need to ensure that the social assessment process passes the so-called "ASR" test — Art, Science, and Relevance. The *art* refers to the need for the process to remain faithful to what the people really say without too much external interpretation that can cloud the basic truths.[21] The *science* is the ability of the process to understand differences within "the people" and to find useful patterns to which donors can respond with assistance. In addition, the process needs to be *relevant* to the requirements of the donors. The process may well reveal many interesting things of importance to the communities and to government, but it should not neglect the objective of securing money from donors to help people.

■ Fourth, many decisionmakers, in government and in the donor community, simply do not find the social assessment process very useful. They assume that the needs in a postconflict situation are so obvious to experienced practitioners, the resources available are usually so inadequate, and the challenge so immediate and overwhelming that rapid project preparation and implementation is the best approach. Their reaction to what became the final program in Azerbaijan would be that the comprehensive approach took too long to develop and its implementation is too risky, as compared to an approach more limited in sectors and in geographic coverage. This position is narrow and discourages rapid analysis without justification. There is no evidence that the social analysis takes more time than engineering or other parts of project preparation.[22] And, if started before technical studies, social assessment can *reduce* project preparation costs by ensuring that the reconstruction program fits better with peoples' real needs, expectations, and abilities.

■ Fifth, it is clear that basing assistance programs on peoples' needs and not on institutional "preferences" solves the insti-

---

[21]   The Azerbaijan social assessment process probably made the subject of housing techniques and standards too murky to be useful, for example.
[22]   A sound social assessment process requires involvement of Bank social scientists and of local social scientists.

tutional boarding issue mentioned by Voutira and Harrell-Bond in this volume.

- Sixth, there are points in the social assessment process when one needs to make sure that everyone is "on board." In particular, all the key actors have to be involved in the needs assessment and in the stakeholder review of its results, and all the major donors need to be involved in the discussion of the results of the social assessment process. If not, the social assessment process may be relevant as to its substance but irrelevant with regard to its impact. In the case of Azerbaijan, if government and local NGOs were sufficiently involved in the process, more attention should have been paid to establishing a permanent mechanism that would take the initiative to involve *all* the donors, including international NGOs, on a regular basis in the social assessment process, instead of just reporting on the results during IAC meetings. This process of inclusion was attempted with only limited success during the sector working group process, to which donors and international NGOs responded unevenly.[23]

- Seventh, there are instances in which the peoples' views as expressed through the social assessment process are not accepted by the donors, perhaps for good reasons. The peoples' views may conflict with donors' policies – the housing sector in Azerbaijan being a case in point – or with donors' strong inclinations – for example, the use of multiple implementation channels in Azerbaijan instead of just the national government in which the people had expressed the strongest trust.

- Finally, the social assessment process also represents a way of democratically "sharing power" between the displaced people, otherwise largely powerless, and government officials, the donor community (including international NGOs), and civil society. If empowering the people is uncomfortable to some, let them remember that it also means that the people are not there just to share the risks but, in a very real sense, must conduct the orchestra. A good social assessment pro-

---

[23] Particularly helpful among the international NGOs was the role of the SOROS Foundation in the education sector and Medecins sans Frontiers in the health sector.

cess allows the opportunity for all the stakeholders to move forward together, listening and learning, advocating and compromising, assessing and acting.

The way in which donors "listen" and learn about the people does have a major impact on the form and content of the assistance provided. Professional sociological analysis makes "listening" more accurate in relation to peoples' real needs and more relevant to their futures.

Acknowledgments

This chapter is dedicated to the memory of Professor Ahmed Musayev, Sorgu Sociological Research Center, Azerbaijan (1949–1997) and Salem Ouahes, Senior Power Engineer, Europe and Central Asia, Energy Department, World Bank (1943–1997), both of whom played critical roles in the work in Azerbaijan on which this article is based.

This chapter is the result of a collaborative effort involving individuals from various organizations to set in motion a process of social assessment and stakeholder participation for postconflict resettlement and reconstruction in Azerbaijan. Ayse Kudat, currently the social development sector leader for the ECA region in the World Bank, began the process in 1994 and has guided it ever since, in addition to preparing many of the social assessment instruments, draft reports, and participatory framework. Also involved were Elmir Abdullayev and Ali Mamedov of the Azerbaijan Reconstruction and Rehabilitation Agency; Professor Ahmed Musayev of the Sorgu Sociological Research Center; Professor Rasim Ramazanov, SIGMA Strategic Research Center for Development and International Collaboration; Janis Bernstein, Paolo Caputo, Kutlay Ebiri, Steven Holtzman, Ishrat Husain, Kanan Najafov, Salem Ouahes, Bulent Ozbilgin, Peter Pollak, and Tevfik Yaprak of the World Bank; Guido Ambroso and Didier Laye of UNHCR; and Paolo Lembo and Ercan Murat of UNDP.

The social assessment team gratefully acknowledges the collaboration of many internally displaced people of Azerbaijan as well as of the government of Azerbaijan, international organizations, and NGOs (local and international). Deputy Prime Minister Abid Sherifov's support for the social assessment process was particularly critical.

CHAPTER 15

The creation of community: well-being without wealth in an urban Greek refugee locality

Renée Hirschon

Kokkinia, an urban refugee settlement in Greece and the subject of this chapter, was established as part of a massive settlement program that resulted from the compulsory exchange of populations between Greece and Turkey in 1923. This historic event deserves to be better known among those concerned with the treatment of forcibly displaced populations and their resettlement, particularly because of its scale and the variety of solutions that were employed, as well as its duration (more than 70 years) within defined parameters.[1] It could, therefore, provide a useful test case for various models that have been developed—for the stages or the risks and reconstruction dimensions, in well-known frameworks associated

---

[1]   The original paper presented at the Second International Conference on Development-Induced Displacement, University of Oxford, was an overview, covering both the rural and urban settlement program in Greece (Hirschon 1996). It also confronted, at a general level, the central question of "what constitutes success," a problematic issue in the context of development schemes in many parts of the world where different cultural criteria and values exist. In the case study presented here, a number of paradoxes exist, challenging both the criteria used in evaluating success and the models that underlie the whole enterprise of development and resettlement. Voutira and Harrell-Bond (this volume) have taken up this issue and advance our understanding by analyzing diverse cases, both development-induced and refugee-generating, in terms of factors that promote "success."

with Scudder and Cernea. The need for long-term approaches to the evaluation and study of resettlement schemes has been emphasized repeatedly by Scudder and Colson, who have undertaken longitudinal research in this important area. Kokkinia presents a valuable case study for the analysis of the long-term effects of resettlement.

This is not, however, my aim here. Instead, my contribution to this volume is aimed to raise some questions posed by a specific urban case, that of Kokkinia, one of the many settlements established in the 1920s as part of the international effort to deal with resettlement under a compulsory population exchange program. For the purposes of this chapter, I outline the main features of social life there, and attempt to account for some of the patterns that run counter to the commonly held wisdom and expectations of development theory and of development agencies. The evidence from this particular case presents a paradox, since it directly contradicts the notion that economic welfare is essential for the reconstitution of community life. On the contrary, impoverished urban refugee quarters in Greece developed into localities well known for their neighborhood life, despite the absence of economic welfare and of even the most basic physical provisions. Community life developed out of destitution and disruption, and these quarters were marked by a high degree of social integration and identity, even though by most "objective" and measurable criteria they constituted slums. This chapter addresses the problematic relationship between the social and the economic, and the question of the link between the development of a community and the economic and infrastructure provisions that are widely assumed to be its necessary precondition.

Given that the original resettlement program took place in the 1920s, the locality of Kokkinia and others established at the time cannot be studied by the longitudinal method as an ongoing situation, but only through extrapolation, as an historical example of the resettlement process. I have sought empirical evidence for my attempt to reconstruct past phases of the process of settlement from written sources, contemporary observation, and people's accounts and memories.[2]

---

[2]   The monograph resulted from my fieldwork in the 1970s in Kokkinia, part of the metropolis of Athens-Piraeus. It is an analysis of social life in a poor urban locality of refugee origin based largely on social anthropological methods of intensive participant observation, and included research into documentary records, published and unpublished (Hirschon 1989).

An intrinsic point of interest is that Kokkinia is a rare European example. Too few of these have been considered or incorporated into the current conceptual approaches, which tend to concentrate on developing-country contexts. It could well be argued that the two countries involved, Greece and Turkey, in the period from the 1920s right into the post–World War II era, fell into this category. Too often, however, it is assumed that Europe is somehow exempt from the contemporary problems of forcibly displaced people. But the violent breakup of the former Yugoslavia and the consequent refugee problems have shaken this complacency. However different they might appear, the consideration of such examples is essential in the building of adequate and inclusive models for such complex political, social, cultural, and economic processes. Although every case is unique, each one has dimensions that relate to more general or universal patterns.

History and context: the settlement program in Greece

In the few years immediately following World War I, the political map of the eastern Mediterranean was radically changed. The Ottoman Empire, a vast imperial state incorporating many societies and linguistically, religiously, and culturally differentiated peoples, was split into states. Out of it was created the modern state of Turkey. The military campaign of the Greek Army into the interior of Asia Minor resulted in its total defeat in the summer of 1922 and, along with it, the panicked flight of hundreds of thousands of Christian families from their homes to arrive destitute at ports and harbors of the small and poorly endowed Greek state. Within months, the Convention signed in Lausanne in January 1923 stipulated the compulsory exchange of populations between Greece and Turkey. This was because the precondition for a peace settlement was the removal of the main religious minorities from each country. "Turkish subjects of the Orthodox Christian religion and Greek subjects of the Muslim religion" were forced to leave their homelands and were settled in a new country and environment. Thus, the first massive influx of destitute refugees was augmented by the hundreds of thousands of forcibly exchanged peoples. In terms of contemporary Britain, for example, with a population of some 58 million people, this would mean the absorption of around 13 million refugees in a couple of years. Greece was in a severely depleted state after being at war for more than 10 years (Clogg 1979:105ff). The country was economically drained and in political disarray and, adding to the magnitude of the problems, the majority of those requiring provisions were destitute and psychologically shocked and in rapidly deteriorating health.

The early phase clearly constituted an acute emergency. The League of Nations responded by authorizing an independent body, the Refugee Settlement Commission (RSC), to deal with the immediate needs of this mass of people. However, it also had to develop long-term solutions. Funded on an international basis by loans at surprisingly high interest given their humanitarian purpose, the RSC operated for six years. In that time it accomplished an impressive settlement program, a "success story," known internationally at the time and visited by officials from many countries.[3] Many unresolved issues remained, however, not the least of these being the situation of the urban refugees.

Parameters of the Greek case

The significance of the compulsory Greco-Turkish population exchange for studies of resettlement lies in several features. The massive settlement program entailed emergency relief measures as well as long-term solutions, it covered urban and rural areas and it incorporated development as well as national policy dimensions. It is a fascinating and little-examined case that could provide valuable insights if related to contemporary practice. The main parameters presented here provide the context in which to understand the process of resettlement, and its consequences within the Greek state.

First, the scale of the operation was considerable. The Lausanne Convention (1923) was unique in specifying an internationally sanctioned compulsory exchange of populations. In terms of absolute figures for the times, it was a major event and, in proportional terms, placed a very great burden on Greece. The influx of destitute refugees and exchanged persons into Greece numbered well over 1 million, equivalent to a quarter of the total population of the country at that time (Greece's population was about 5 million, and the influx was estimated at 1.25 to 1.4 million refugees) (Kitromilides and Alexandris 1984–1985). The resulting settlement program had pro-

---

3   The success of this rural settlement policy in the north became widely known: "The whole region served as a laboratory for the development of practical methods of settling and uplifting the morale of a war-torn and expatriated people; it was visited by officials from Egypt, Sudan, India, China, Burma and South Africa" (Pentzopoulos 1962:111). The time factor must not be neglected in this evaluation, however, as Scudder and Colson have rightly insisted.

found consequences, changing the demographic, economic, and political character of the country.

Second, it is important to note that the exodus and exchange of populations was not a repatriation exercise, of Greeks to Greece and Turks to Turkey, as is sometimes mistakenly thought. It was an unprecedented forcible removal by international treaty of two religious minorities from their places of origin.[4] The exchanged populations had long histories in their respective homelands and did not view their move as a return home. On the contrary, their expulsion was seen as an "exile," so that the situation represented by this case is comparable to those of involuntary international displacements in many other parts of the world.

Third, this case is particularly interesting in social terms. The two population groups — incomers and hosts — were very similar in many respects, but they did not blend as easily as might have been expected, given the long time period involved. Constituting almost a limited case of "ethnic" differentiation in the Greek context, the refugee and the host populations shared most features usually invoked to explain distinctions based on ethnic difference. Here, the receiving population and the incomers had many cultural features in common and were of the same religion, and the majority spoke Greek. However, the refugees expressed a well-developed sense of separate identity after several decades and generations (Hirschon 1989). This is, therefore, a highly suggestive case. It provides insights that could advance our understanding of how the experience of displacement is expressed in different means of adjustment and integration, and how it affects the formation of group identity.

Fourth, the exchanged peoples and refugees were settled in both rural and urban areas, so that different provisions and priorities were applied in various localities. These different contexts and settlement solutions could provide interesting test cases for the study of various approaches to resettlement and their effectiveness (for example, many villages were reconstituted and set up from scratch, while elsewhere displaced people were settled in existing villages with an already established local population).

Fifth, the settlement program was influenced also by national policy concerns that reflected contemporary geopolitical issues. States were being consolidated. In Greece this was effected through a process of demographic homogenization with a concentrated pro-

---

[4]   Prior to this, an exchange of populations had taken place between Greece and Bulgaria, but on a voluntary basis and on a much smaller scale (see Pentzopoulos 1962).

gram of settlement in the newly acquired northern provinces, where a diverse mix of populations coexisted. The settlement policy tipped the ethnic balance so that the Greek element became numerically predominant (Pentzopoulos 1962:125ff; Clogg 1979:120). The settlement plans in the north of the country, as in other rural areas, were akin to development schemes, and this provides another dimension of potential and valuable comparative material.

Sixth, this case is valuable in its historical depth. It is now more than 70 years since this mass of refugees fled to Greece and the religious minorities were exchanged. Over this long time span, and within the different types of settlement, a variety of processes can be traced and inferred as they unfolded through time.

Urban refugee settlements in Greece

Despite the early realization of the RSC that the majority of displaced people were not agriculturists but urban dwellers, the emphasis was nonetheless given to settlement in rural areas (League of Nations 1926:15–17). This is a continuing theme in (re)settlement programs right through to the present day, the goal being a rapid path to self-sufficiency (Harrell-Bond 1986). However, given that a large proportion of the incomers in Greece were urban dwellers, such a policy could only have limited overall success. Many of the objectives were accomplished for the rural program of settlement, but this achievement contrasts with the intractable problems that confronted the RSC in dealing with the mass of urban displaced peoples.

Right into the 1980s, 60 years after the exodus of populations from their homeland and their arrival in Greece, numerous sections in the cities and towns of Greece were still known as "refugee quarters." They were marked by a lack of amenities, inadequate housing, overcrowding, and poverty. By all measurable criteria (density, housing type, and water and sewage provisions), large sections of these quarters were slums. Notably, however, these areas were attractive and well kept, displaying the great degree of care and effort made by the residents to maintain the infrastructure, however inadequate. The urban refugee quarters constituted the lowest income category, and the inhabitants of such areas were economically at the bottom of the ladder (Hirschon 1989). This situation contrasts with the widely known stereotype of the successful Asia Minor business man—indeed many of the incomers were entrepreneurs and contributed greatly to the economic development of the country by establishing new industries and businesses, as shown even in the earliest reports (League of Nations 1926:83–191).

At the outset, the enormity of the problem was recognized by the RSC. Bearing out the observation of Cernea (1990), who pinpoints two key issues in the resettlement of urban peoples (the relative importance of housing provisions as opposed to income generation), the RSC recognized that provision of accommodation alone would not be an adequate response. However, there simply was not enough money to deal with the demand for shelter as well as for economic support, and the RSC decided to deal only with housing needs (League of Nations 1926:17–18,162ff). An intensive program was instituted in the main cities and provincial towns. Within a few years, 16,700 apartments had been built, and "22,337 houses, wooden huts and moveable dwellings" had been provided (League of Nations 1926:18). By conscious decision on the part of the agency, the urban provisions entailed low-cost housing, not always of a permanent kind, as well as some community facilities.

In the 1926 report, the RSC described an auspicious beginning. Basic communal facilities were provided in the urban quarters — water supply, school premises, and dispensaries — and in some of the larger settlements, crèches and a hospital (League of Nations 1926:168–169) were provided as well. Churches were planned, built largely by contributions from the residents themselves (see below). These constituted minimal and basic infrastructural provisions since, on its dissolution in 1930, the RSC had spent only one-fifth of its total budget on the urban quarters. This disparity in investment meant that, when the RSC was disbanded, more than 30,000 families were still in need of permanent housing in urban centers, while 12,000 housing units were required in agricultural areas (see Hirschon 1989:36–45).

The parallels with development programs in general can be seen, for the extensive program of housing resulted in the establishment or enlargement of many rural settlements as well as many settlements on the edges of existing towns and villages throughout the country. The population influx resulted in a vast increase in the urban population, the introduction of new skills and products, and an increase in the market and labor force (League of Nations 1926:183–191). In the vicinity of Athens-Piraeus, for example, in the eight years from 1920 to 1928, areas that were entirely uninhabited in 1920 had become substantial residential quarters, housing thousands of families (see Table 1).

The issue of housing, a central feature of any settlement program designed for the urban displaced, was never fully solved in Greece and, in fact, became an ongoing problem that marked the experience of the urban refugees. During the 1930s, limited efforts were

TABLE 1: POPULATION INCREASE IN REFUGEE SETTLEMENTS
IN ATHENS AND PIRAEUS, 1920 AND 1928

Areas	Numbers	
	1920	1928
Athens: Kaisariani	11	15,357
Vyrona	0	7,723
Nea Ionia	79	16,382
Nea Philadelphia	110	6,337
Kallithea	4,940	29,446
Piraeus: Nea Kokkinia	0	33,201
Drapetsona	0	17,652
Keratsini	0	10,817
Peristeri	123	7,268

Source: Kayser and Thompson 1964:2.07.

made by the Greek government to address the problem, but the situation deteriorated, exacerbated by the events of the 1940s. World War II, the German occupation, the civil war (1944–1949), and large-scale rural-urban migration in the postwar period all contributed to a chronic state of hardship and deprivation in the urban refugee quarters.

As Cernea (this volume) and others have noted, the relative importance of land and shelter is a crucial distinction in the experience of displacement of urban as opposed to rural dwellers. For the urban refugees and their descendants, housing problems continued to be a particular cause for grievance, a focus of claims for compensation (legally ratified and justifiable; see below), and a node around which the sense of difference and of separate identity of these two sections of the population—the "refugees" and the "locals"—was centered. This sense of a distinctive identity had developed in the early days and was evident even in the 1970s and afterward. In the past it probably fluctuated in its expression and was intensified at different times by the prevailing political and economic conditions. Whatever the strength of this phenomenon, the existence of a sense of difference after two to three generations, even into the fourth, is both remarkable and instructive.[5]

---

[5] Tsimouris's study of the village in Limnos settled by exchanged people reveals a continuing sense of separate identity into the fourth generation (Tsimouris 1998).

The settlement of Kokkinia

The urban quarter of Kokkinia, studied some 50 years after its establishment, is an illuminating case, revealing many features of the urban program in Greece. In 1920, this open area north of the harbor of Piraeus was used as a rubbish dump, but by 1928 it housed a population of 33,000, increasing to 40,000 by 1933. In the 1970s, Kokkinia (population of 86,000 within the municipality boundaries covering some four square kilometers) was part of the metropolis of Athens-Piraeus, and had been fully integrated into the economic fabric of the city, an urban complex of more than 3 million people at that time.[6] As one of the first and largest urban refugee settlements, it passed through various phases of organization and development (Hirschon 1989:49ff). My detailed analysis focused on one section of the municipality, a poor district called Yerania, where standardized prefabricated housing, intended for temporary use in 1928 when it was established, was still largely in use (83 percent of the original housing still remained in 1972). The character of Yerania, and of other districts within Kokkinia, had many features in common, which allow general statements to be made about the locality. Specific references are also made because some of these patterns are thrown into sharp relief by the particular characteristics of life in Yerania in the early 1970s.

Political and economic factors

A central paradox was evident simply by looking at Yerania and other parts of Kokkinia. The attractive and well-kept appearance of the locality, with its colorfully painted houses, whitewashed pavements, and swept streets immediately struck the observer. However, indications of deeper problems also were clear. Laundry hanging between lampposts, children playing in streets, and extensions of the houses onto and under pavements, filling up yards, all indicated high population densities and overcrowding. Houses were shared by several families through a process of subdivision in order to provide a dowry for daughters on marriage, a practice which continued into the third generation (Hirschon 1983). This was even more noteworthy since, in Yerania, the original dwellings were unsubstantial, of prefabricated panel board intended for temporary

---

[6]   A full description of the settlement program and the original provisions of housing in Kokkinia is contained in Hirschon 1989:36–63.

residence. But "temporariness" became continuous occupation for more than 50 years.

The urban settlement of Kokkinia was noted in the 1926 report for its auspicious start. The basic provisions (schools, crèches, a hospital) were made, but the settlement was neglected by successive administrations. The public provision of facilities was inadequate for decades: piped water was introduced to Yerania houses only in the 1960s, roads were unpaved until 1972, and a central sewage system was provided only in 1983.

State policy and housing conditions had significant effects on the responses of the members of this urban population to their position in society. In many areas they were provided with shelter in temporary housing in order to alleviate their plight, and they were awaiting the compensation guaranteed them by the conditions of the Lausanne Convention. In 1930, the signing of an accord between Greece and Turkey canceled out the outstanding claims for compensation owed to Greece in order to promote better relations between the two countries. This was a turning point. Many displaced people saw this as a betrayal of their interests. As time passed and the situation was never fully addressed, they became increasingly disaffected, with far-reaching political consequences for the country (see Mavrogordatos 1992; Hirschon 1989: 45-8, 53).

An additional problem of considerable importance was the issue of the refugees' legal rights. Full legal rights of tenure were not conferred automatically to the occupants of the prefabricated dwellings in Yerania. The requirement of a nominal payment caused severe grievance and contention, and became an issue about which refugees complained publicly decades after their settlement (Pentzopoulos 1962:204ff; Hirschon 1989:45–55).

It is clear therefore that certain aspects of the government's policy played a significant role in shaping the process of integration into the host society and in the perpetuation of the refugees' sense of a "separate identity." Over time, successive governments ignored their grievances. Despite their large numbers, however, they failed to become a pressure group. Thus the mass of urban refugees lived in a state of long-term political marginality and, for Greece as a whole, in spite of their substantial numbers, the refugees were never represented in Parliament in proportion to their electoral strength. Indeed, the gerrymandering of districts and patron-client networks handicapped the refugee vote (Hirschon 1989:44).

This situation in the political and economic spheres had two results. First, because of the expectation of compensation and of further government intervention, people remained in a state of dependency as claimants upon the state. Their expectation for compensation continued right into the 1960s and acted to perpetuate their identity as "refugees" as it gave them a vested interest in a status that carried the potential for material benefits.

Second, their political orientation shifted to left-wing policies and concerted recruitment into the Communist Party, evidenced in long-term trends in voting patterns in the poorer urban areas, including Kokkinia. The civil war of the 1940s marked these localities with particular intensity. This had the effect of further marginalizing the population as they failed to connect with the mainstream political parties and their "clientelist" networks.

Over the long term, poverty and economic and political marginality characterized this and other similar localities. Networks of influence passed them by, especially as, with the passage of time, more successful residents moved away into better areas of the city. Neglect by successive governments resulted in inadequate educational facilities, low educational standards, poor morale, and disaffection. The residents of Kokkinia, overall, became a radicalized proletariat with a strong sense of a separate cultural identity vis-à-vis the local society. Another interesting and contradictory facet of life in this locality was that intense support for the Communist Party coexisted with a marked degree of religious observance, in both formal and informal spheres of life (Hirschon 1989:192–3,219ff).

Social and cultural factors

In contrapuntal distinction with the disadvantaged aspects of the settlement process framed by wider political and economic factors are the integrated social and cultural patterns that developed within the urban quarters.

The pronounced sense of difference, already noted in political economic terms, and expressed in an enduring sense of identity as "refugees," or *mikrasiates*, also had a social and cultural basis. This can be seen to have a connection with the settlers' previous position and the historical tradition of their homeland. In the Ottoman Empire, of which they had been citizens until 1922, peoples were differentiated on grounds of religion into separate "nations" (the millet system). Arguably, the strong sense of identity in relation to the host society derived in part from a proclivity to maintaining boundaries between themselves and "others," based on their experience as a subject people in the multi-ethnic society from which they had been uprooted.

In overall cultural terms, the similarities were great. The receiving population and the incomers had the same religion and largely shared the same culture, and most spoke Greek or, if not, had some sense of "Greek" identity. This led some observers to state that these were Greeks returning "home." However, that was not the way the displaced saw their relocation. Many statements of both populations showed the demarcation of boundaries very early in the process of settlement. The newcomers' perceptions of having a separate cultural tradition within Greek society could not be expressed in terms of gross or obvious differences, however, given the many cultural features common to both groups. Instead, it was focused on minutiae of conduct and detail, so that fine differences were emphasized (Hirschon 1989:4–6,12–14). Soon, the destitute incomers formed critical and unflattering views about the local people that they expressed vividly in derogatory terms, and thereby replicated in a curious way their sense of being "superior subordinates," a stance they had collectively held in their previous homeland (Hirschon 1989:30–35).

This process of boundary demarcation was, therefore, an interactional one. It was probably also a response to the social barriers that soon became apparent. Given the scale of the influx with its resultant competition for scarce resources in the impoverished Greek state, it was inevitable that friction would arise between the two groups. Local people soon began to reveal resentment of the newcomers, expressing negative views, and using a term of nationalist discourse — *tourkospori*, translated as "Turkish seeds/offspring." In the process of contact between the incomers and the host society, mutual prejudices were soon expressed, as many reports (both oral and written) witness. Thus, a crucial factor in the process of settlement and experience of adjustment in this case, as in many others, was the interaction of the newcomers with the locals. It is a factor that needs to be considered as a central part of the integration process in all resettlement programs.

Community, identity, family values, and the neighborhood

In the context of debates regarding the outcomes of various settlement priorities and strategies, most striking are the findings regarding social life in this urban quarter. Although the urban refugee quarters lacked public facilities and infrastructure and were marked by poverty and deprivation, they did not develop into slums with the attendant social problems (such as social and individual pathologies, crime, and drugs). On the contrary, community life was strong, the social networks developed in neighborhoods became highly integrated, and family life was intense. Public areas were well cared for, and localities developed a distinct sense of collective identity.

Here, the crucial role of cultural factors can be discerned. I argue that cultural values provide a template for action, and that the maintenance of cultural practices and values was an essential element in the resilience displayed by these uprooted people. In Kokkinia, cultural imperatives were translated, adapted, and again given expression in the new conditions of life. Central to these were the maintenance of family structure and stability and of the values pertaining to men's and women's roles, and the role of religion and ritual, which endowed life with a meaning even in the face of traumatic disruption and loss. The hiatus created by the expulsion was breached because these people's central values were upheld, creating a bridge between the loss of homeland and the unfamiliar situation into which they had been unwillingly thrust. Through a process of adaptation of traditions and norms of conduct, it is possible that a coherent community and lifestyle can be reconstituted, as this case study bears out.[7]

In short, in response to the new conditions of life in the urban quarters, a highly cohesive society gradually developed out of a mixture of very different peoples. It is noteworthy that the locality was characterized by its coherence and by highly integrated relationships, since the elaboration of social bonds developed through time from scratch, in the face of severe economic deprivation. At the time of Kokkinia's establishment, residents came from various regions of Asia Minor and from different economic backgrounds. The population was heterogeneous, differentiated and disrupted by conditions of their flight. Family members had been lost in the first wave, and, even after settlement, there was much movement from one locality to another as people tried to settle in conditions that better suited their needs and capacities. In very few cases did relatives or friends have houses near one another in Kokkinia. Usually,

---

7 Cf. Scudder's and Colson's suggestion that "conservatism" may be a response in the transition period (stage two of their relocation model). Downing (1996) develops a concept of "social geometry," in which he identifies the key coordinates constituting the basis for everyday social integration. It offers a potent analytical tool for addressing the problems of "social impoverishment" and "social disarticulation" (Cernea 1994 and this volume). The reconstitution of social life in Kokkinia illustrates the applicability of Downing's model.

adjacent houses were allotted to strangers—people whose past in different regions in the homeland did not provide them with an immediate basis for common identity, especially since there were strong regional differences and prejudices. However, a common sense of identity must have developed quite rapidly in relation to the host society (for the reasons outlined above). Exclusion and isolation turned the residents of these quarters inward, and they were left to make the best of their situation.

Some of the factors that promoted local integration included the overall lack of mobility, which itself was due to poverty and was reinforced by the tenure conditions under which housing was granted. The preference for marriage within the group of origin, also an aspect of the cultural tradition, tended to promote a pattern of endogamy with people from Asia Minor and thus within the locality. Consequently, ties of godparenthood and friendship supplemented the overlapping bonds of kinship and marriage. The resulting tight fabric of relationships was further reinforced by the norms of neighborhood conduct. These emphasized egalitarian relationships based on reciprocal exchange and cooperation between households, and they counterposed the emphasis on the family as the focus of individual loyalty.[8]

As already noted, slum-like conditions could easily have resulted and could surely have been expected, given the many obstacles faced by these people. In fact, by all objective criteria, the locality constituted a shantytown in terms of physical facilities. Nonetheless, it was well kept, clean, and attractive. Though not of solid construction, the dwellings endured high-density occupation for more than five decades. Upkeep of the houses was a constant preoccupation: walls and shutters were painted twice a year (before the religious festivals of Easter and Christmas), while details such as steps, flower pots, and even lampposts and pavement edges were whitewashed every few weeks. Indeed, such areas constituted "spotless slums" (Hirschon 1989:3–4).

This can be explained by a set of cultural values emphasizing the importance of the house and family, the power of neighborhood opinion, and the housewife's role. Thus, cultural values associated with family prestige and interfamily rivalry in the community were an important pressure to conformity, since social reputation mattered greatly, and depended on assessments of neighbors. An important force for maintaining standards of order in the public spaces

---

8   It is not possible to describe all the interlocking patterns of social life in this summary overview. The full discussion is to be found in Hirschon 1989.

outside the home was the emphasis on observing neighborhood norms of good conduct. These norms specified collaborative and cooperative activities between households through contacts between the women, thereby promoting integration between households. A further contributing factor was the emphasis on a woman's virtue, a sense of self-esteem associated with her housekeeping abilities. The high standards of cleanliness and upkeep in the locality can be attributed to these cultural values. (Hirschon 1978, 1985).

Space and place, landscaping and meaningful artifacts

One observation, pertinent to the understanding of how Kokkinia became a community despite being so disadvantaged in material terms, relates to the physical environment as a social setting. In the course of my research it became clear that the inhabitants of this locality had created a mental landscape imbued with meaning, a "perceived geography" (see Downing 1996). The neutral territory of the newly established housing settlement was soon transformed into differentiated areas, with landmarks and discrete neighborhoods perceived to have specific characteristics. This process involved re-creating a familiar mental landscape out of an unknown, uncharted expanse. By the construction of a kind of "social landscape geography" in the new settlement, "space" becomes "place." Most interesting is that subdistricts in Kokkinia were characterized in terms of regional stereotypes that related to their previous homeland, attributing to them supposed "typical" characteristics. For example, the district of Yerania was said to be noisy, quarrelsome, and lower in moral tone characteristics that were attributed to the predominance of people from the Smyrna region, who were held to have these negative attributes.[9]

The importance of religion and the sacred was also reflected in this creation of a meaningful landscape. Among the most treasured possessions saved in flight were the icons from churches and from homes. Shortly after arrival, places of worship were designated in tents or sheds, for the construction of churches was a priority for the displaced peoples. The church embodied community life in social as well as in spiritual terms. It provided a concrete point of orientation where specific links with their past life could be expressed. Churches were dedicated to the particular saints of their former homes. In Kokkinia, several churches contain specially venerated

---

[9]   For a fuller description of the process and for other examples, see Hirschon 1989:22-26, 67-68.

icons from Asia Minor, saved in the flight or brought afterward in the exchange. One church built in the 1970s incorporated some stones imported from its namesake in the town of Nicaea (now Iznik, Turkey). The strength of the sentiments relating to the places of past existence is clearly evidenced in the widespread desire to return to visit former homes, even 50 years after their departure, and in the requests of those who could not go for some soil or water to be brought back to them. Abundant empirical evidence from this urban quarter supports Downing's proposals (1996) regarding the importance of reestablishing a "social geometry" for displaced peoples, and De Wet's suggestion that the sociospatial factors are a critical element in the processes involved in resettlement.

What constitutes success?

The word "success" is widely used in the literature, but often without any critical examination. A few cautioning remarks, deriving from cross-cultural skepticism are, therefore, in order. Implicit assumptions about what constitutes a "good life" underlie the notions of success in undertaking any development scheme where the welfare of the displaced population is taken into consideration. First, therefore, the criteria employed in setting up any scheme of assessment or evaluation should be made explicit. The position expressed by Scudder is that "success is improving resettler living standards in ways that they, as well as researchers, acknowledge, and that are culturally sustainable environmentally, economically, institutionally and politically." Since values and priorities are not easily expressed, nor are they universally accepted, the virtue of this definition is that it includes the recipients' as well as the outsiders' evaluations in assessments of success.

Second, several agents may be involved in development projects. Each of these agents, whether from private or public sectors, holds a set of underlying assumptions and premises. The particular views and predispositions of each need not be articulated clearly, if at all. Indeed they may not even coincide and may diverge widely. In any evaluation procedure, therefore, it is important to consider these different sets of interests and approaches, and the degree to which a coordinated approach exists. The evaluation process cannot purport to be an objective measure, existing outside of its own social and moral context.

Further than this, though, a challenging question needs to be faced: to what degree is the development program itself a "closed system"? Since it is based on development aims — and on goals and outcomes related to this paradigm—and insofar as it is evaluated for success in terms of internally defined values, it does constitute a "closed system." Indeed, the evaluation of resettlement projects in many development schemes may constitute an exercise in tautology, especially if based only on economic criteria. The contribution of Cernea's model (see this volume) is its multifaceted nature, encompassing a range of criteria including physical, economic, cultural, and social parameters.

The case of Kokkinia reveals that a viable and integrated community developed despite inadequate physical provisions, poor living standards, and long-term economic hardship. In Cernea's terms, impoverishment did result since economic and political marginalities became a permanent condition. But Kokkinia also clearly demonstrates some of the ways in which cultural values override material deprivation, economic disadvantage, and marginalization. The lives of people in Kokkinia bear witness to a triumph of the human will over the inadequacies of the physical environment, a determined commitment to maintenance of standards in the face of great obstacles. Despite the minimal provision of basic facilities and the neglect that marked the population's experience through the decades, a lively community developed. Life in this locality, therefore, challenges common assumptions about the necessary link between the economic and the social sphere, assumptions that underlie resettlement projects and plans for successful integration.

This raises the question of how to assess the linkages between "economic transformation" and "sociocultural disarticulation." Downing's expressed reservations (1996) indicate that social disarticulation may, to a degree, be independent of economic disruption. He suggests that the spatial-temporal framework is the critical underlying common ground, and needs to be given more consideration. This is borne out by my observations of the ways in which "space" was transformed into "place" in Kokkinia by the transference of meaning into a new landscape, and can also be demonstrated with regard to time patterns (Hirschon 1989:167–69,195ff).

However, it is not only the relative weighting of various factors in a synchronic framework that require assessment. As Scudder has so forcefully argued, the dynamic element must also be included. Allowing for the time factor is crucial, because, in many cases, the desired results may take longer than expected; in others, an auspicious start may founder as time passes and the initial prediction of success may be betrayed. Evaluation of success should be made at various moments in time in order to assess the longer-term benefits or problems that have occurred.

Undoubtedly, the difficulty for long-term longitudinal studies is how to incorporate, or account for, factors extraneous to the settlement provisions themselves. The overall context is not constant but itself changes, and in doing so may have either positive or negative effects on the resettlement scheme. The political and economic context, the regional and national frameworks, therefore, need to be taken into account in understanding results, since these macro-scale factors affect the resettled populations and their communities.[10]

The value of this case study, and of the many other settlements that were part of the program in Greece, is clear. The Greek experience of resettlement in the 1920s provides a showcase, a variety of case studies where different parameters apply and where we could assess the particular constituent processes through time. It could, therefore, also provide a testing ground for assessing what constitutes success, as well as permutations of various degrees of success as a differentiated notion, over a period of more than 50 years.

Conclusion

The case study of Kokkinia, just one of thousands of Greek settlements established in the 1920s, challenges some of the assumptions underlying accepted procedures in resettlement schemes. The widely held picture of the Greek experience of settlement for the forcibly displaced in the 1920s was that of success. But this overall assessment masks a far more complex and differentiated process. For a large number of the dispossessed, however, and for the Greek state itself, the obstacles to a smooth integration into Greek social, political, and economic life were to prove insurmountable. At the macro-scale, far-reaching consequences exacerbated political divisions in the country (Mavrogordatos 1983) and the economic effects were by no means all positive (Mazower 1991). Assessed from this perspective, the question of success is problematic. At another level, however, the urban settlement program reveals two aspects: a lack of physical provisions, on the one hand, but notably, on the other, the development of intense community life based on common cultural values and practices, on family-centered action, and on a separate sense of identity.

---

[10]   Kokkinia provides scope for this kind of long-term assessment, which could not be explored in this summary overview. At periods in the past, the community may have been more or less integrated, depending on conditions in the wider society (dictatorship in the 1930s, the German occupation followed by civil war in the 1940s, the 1967–1974 junta).

Scudder notes that his model has been constructed for the experience of rural resettlement without systematic consideration of urban situations, but contends that many features will be similar in both cases. Certainly, the disruption that affects the forcibly resettled has profound and different effects on all aspects of individual and social life, on power structures and patterns of leadership, both in towns or in the countryside. We should aim, therefore, to develop models that frame resettlement processes to encompass a variety of settlement types. Though a number of urban studies exist, they have not been incorporated into the models and frameworks of analysis. This inevitably limits the degree to which the processes of resettlement can be conceptualized in their full complexity.

The experience of resettlement in the urban locality of Kokkinia does not conform with the common expectations of the development model, and it challenges some of the unexamined preconceptions about the processes as well as the criteria by which we assess them. This chapter aims to add to the body of knowledge by presenting an urban case of long duration, in order to provide insights into some of the intangible aspects of resettlement that might not always receive enough attention. Specifically, it casts doubt on any predetermined relationship between material and economic provisions and the intangible social forces that may lead to the desired end — the creation of a community.

CHAPTER 16

Social re-articulation after resettlement: observing the Beles Valley scheme in Ethiopia

Wolde-Selassie Abutte

Resettlement operations involving the planned and controlled transfer of people from one area to another are undertaken throughout the developing world in response to a range of causal agents, including population pressure, natural catastrophes, man-made disasters, poverty, unemployment, agricultural and industrial development, and, sometimes, political reasons. According to Tadros (1979), there are two types of land settlement, conceptualized as "spontaneous" and "paternalistic." The former, he argues, includes individual initiatives in resettlement, while the second is characterized by imposed, planned, and controlled relocation. This chapter explores resettlement operations in Ethiopia during the 1980s. These belong to the second type, because they were state-motivated and - imposed, and driven by a mixture of motives related to famine and drought prevention, food production, national security, and population control.

Premises for social re-articulation

Success and failure in resettlement schemes depends on a combination of factors. The most important, perhaps, is proper planning, based on adequate pre-investment surveys of the physical and human resources, the social setting, and the human values that affect successful resettlement implementation. Advance planning of resettlement operations in emergency situations is often poor (see

Harrell-Bond and Voutira in this volume); however, Mathur believes, based on his broad experience of resettlement in India following planned development, that, in many instances, resettlement in nonemergency situations is often no better. Indeed, when viewed from the perspective of the resettlers, "no trauma," he argues "can be more painful for a family than to get uprooted from a place where it has lived for generations and to move to a place where it may be a total stranger" (Mathur 1995:17; Varma 1985). He is critical of the lack in many countries of sound policies and legal frameworks that do not fully take into account the rights of resettlers and hosts affected by state-sponsored resettlement schemes.

The relocation of resettlers involves adaptation to new land and new communities. Involuntary displacement threatens to destroy the previous way of life of resettlers. A community's social, political, and religious leaders are often powerless to prevent the disruption and disorder that occurs. Downing has described in some detail the social impoverishment that affects the fabric of relocatees' collectivities. He argues that, for many societies, the impact of resettlement is to weaken or dismantle vital social networks and life-support mechanisms for families. "Authority systems," he wrote, "are debilitated or collapse. Groups lose their capacity to self-manage. The society suffers a demonstrable reduction in its capacity to cope with uncertainty. It becomes qualitatively less than its previous self. The people may physically persist but the community that was, is no more" (1996:34). This is why resettlement should be considered only after all other alternatives are exhausted. If resettlement is absolutely necessary, it should be carefully planned so as to reconstruct better the livelihoods of the resettlers, preventing them from painful socioeconomic and cultural impoverishment.

Cernea (1993) has emphasized that programs that entail displacement as a by-product often produce long-term benefits. However, as he puts it, these benefits do not lessen the disruptions or lighten the hardship for those who have the misfortune to be uprooted. His social analyses and advocacy have helped the World Bank to become the first international development agency to adopt and publish explicit policies based on social science knowledge about resettlement. He points out that the two most important effects of this policy to date have been more systematic planning for relocation and more resource allocation to the resettlers for a broad spectrum of projects. Above all, he holds the view that the magnitude of the adverse effects of resettlement schemes can be reduced, provided that political commitment, fair legal frameworks, and adequate resources are put in place (see Cernea 1997, and this volume).

In this chapter, I attempt to explain how reconstruction and so-cial re-articulation have taken place after a process of impoverish-ment caused by the "politically mandated mass relocation" program initiated by the Derg regime in Ethiopia after the 1984–1985 drought and famine. My particular emphasis is on the Beles Valley resettle-ment scheme. First, I will analyze the initial painful sociocultural disintegration experienced by the resettlers. Nonetheless, at their new sites the resettlers worked hard to restore their livelihoods and community life. Therefore, based on my 10-year work in the resettle-ment areas of Beles Valley, I will describe the recently observed sociocultural re-articulation of the resettled farmers, in light of the "risks and reconstruction model" (Cernea) that postulates the re-constitution of community life as part of reconstruction after dis-placement. I will focus on the successful, innovative, and industrious adaptive strategies pursued by the farmers to restore their liveli-hoods.

The Ethiopian emergency resettlement program

Ethiopia has attempted several large-scale resettlement schemes. The policy motives underlying Ethiopian resettlement have been both developmental and (implicitly) political. According to Dessalegn (1989), pre-1974 Ethiopian resettlement was ad hoc and based on "rationalizing" land use on "government-owned" land in order to raise state revenues and transfer additional resources to the hard-pressed northern peasantry. After the collapse of the imperial gov-ernment in 1974, however, resettlement was broadened in both its scope and application beyond its original purpose, in order to pro-vide long-term rehabilitation of famine victims. Resettlement was adopted as a key policy to tackle a whole range of social problems. Justification for its application included provision of assistance to poor and landless peasants; relief of unemployment in the urban areas; acceleration of the settlement of transient populations; pro-motion of resource conservation and modernization of agricultural practices in densely populated areas; and cultivation of "underutilized" lands. In addition to rehabilitating returning Ethio-pian refugees and displaced persons, resettlement was used by the Derg regime to establish a paramilitary defense force on the Ethiopia-Somalia border (1989: 684).

After the 1984 and 1985 drought and famine, the Derg govern-ment launched a massive emergency resettlement program, consid-ering it a lasting solution for the problems facing Ethiopia's poor.

The government's initial plan was to resettle 300,000 families, around 1.5 million people, in two phases. Because of the sheer expense and logistical challenges of the program, initial plans were scaled down, leading to the eventual relocation of some 600,000 people within 18 months. The program resulted mostly in the long-distance movement of resettlers into areas of the country where the sociocultural and environmental conditions were quite different from their previous locations. The resettlement had an enormous influence on the physical, biological, and sociocultural systems in the new locations that affected the relocated people themselves, the host population, and the environment. The costs of the Derg's experiments in resettlement are still being counted today.

As a result of hasty decisionmaking, the planning of the emergency resettlement was inadequate. It was disorganized and plagued with confusion and mismanagement. Professional assessment of the environmental, economic, and sociocultural features of resettlement was neglected. The participation of the resettlers in the decisionmaking was almost nonexistent. They were not given true information about the program. Recruitment undertaken at the height of the famine in the relief camps and feeding centers was conducted in an unethical way that did not allow an opportunity for rational decisionmaking. As a result, the inadequately planned scheme was accomplished at severe human cost. The resettlers underwent a painful and traumatic experience that caused the breakup of long-established social structures, dismantling of production systems, and population dispersal.

At the time, the Derg embarked on a propaganda exercise describing a glorious image of resettlement as a permanent break with the hardships of the past. Drought-affected people of north-central Ethiopia and land-hungry people of the southwest abandoned their normal ways of life and sought assistance in relief centers. The promises and guarantees offered by government officials persuaded them to join the scheme. But the expectations raised by the propaganda quickly turned to disappointment in the new locations.

The author was an eyewitness (Wolde-Selassie 1991b) during the recruitment stage, when resettlement was promoted by the local authorities with promises of abundant fertile land, so appealing to the chronically land-hungry southwestern Kambaata and Hadiyya peasants. They were told that the lands in the new locations would be cultivated by tractors, that already built and fully furnished corrugated iron-roofed modern houses would be awaiting them, and that they would receive plenty of food, clothing, and necessary implements. Above all, some would even be exempted from the debt of various government levies. Deceived by high expectations, many peasants sold their domestic animals, grain, household furniture, dwellings, garden plants, and other valuables at very low prices. While waiting to leave for the promised land, many of the recruits spent the cash they had raised through the sales.

The promise and the great expectations turned out to be completely unfounded at the new locations. Upon arrival, people found the new context entirely different from what they were promised before their departure. Following the instructions of the political cadres, they were obliged to build their own houses, because the "false huts" built by university students, staff, and professors during the 1985 summer campaign were crumbling (see Pankurst 1992). The lack of infrastructural facilities, together with lack of adequate knowledge about the new setting, aggravated the dissatisfaction, resentment, and discontent of resettlers. Malaria, cattle sickness, and other health problems made the situation worse. Resettlers lamented their decision to leave, and recalled with sadness the lives left behind.

In the hastily organized and executed resettlement, families broke apart. The sites in the new areas were selected superficially, without a thorough analysis of their development potential. At the local level, resettlement planning was delegated to the crude initiatives of the political cadres who were assigned responsibility for each new village. Moreover, in the haste of carrying out the resettlement scheme, the indigenous host populations were completely neglected.

The emergency resettlement was also criticized for its implicit political motives. Many argued that the true purpose behind the program was to remove people from insurgency areas and relocate them in areas where they provided a buffer for the government against insurgency. The controlled resettlement schemes were full of social injustice and human rights violations. Coercion was used during recruitment, and at all times resettlers were heavily guarded to prevent them from escaping. The scheme increased state control over the resettlers. Religious holidays were not freely observed. Free travel was absolutely impossible, as resettlers were strictly forbidden to travel out of the area, and village-to-village travel was possible only with pass letters obtained from the village authorities.

Moreover, collectivization was imposed on the resettlers, and their labor time was strictly controlled according to the point system devised for Producers' Cooperatives. Private trade was restricted and the right to sell shares of grain was curtailed. Resettlement allowed the government to recruit abundant military personnel easily from the controlled, planned, open villages in the new locations. Furthermore, resettlement threatened and violated the rights of the indigenous, host populations by marginalizing and displacing them from the land and other resources that belonged to them by tradition.

As reports produced by the Comitato Internazionale per lo Sviluppo Popoli (CISP) describe, the environmental impacts of the scheme in the new locations has been disastrous. Large areas of forests were indiscriminately cleared, accelerating soil erosion, extinguishing the flora and fauna, and creating an imbalance in the ecosystem of the receiving areas.

A summarized account of the death and desertion of the resettlers in the receiving areas (excluding deaths in transit) during the years 1985 to 1987 was provided in 1988 by the National Study Committee of Receiving Provinces (NSCRP), under the auspices of the Derg. According to this report, out of 594,190 resettlers involved, 116,768 deserted or died (the number of desertions was estimated to be 83,800 and deaths, 32,800). After the 1991 political change in Ethiopia, based on RRC's archival data on the operation of the emergency resettlement scheme, a former Deputy Commissioner of the Relief and Rehabilitation Commission RRC, Ato Elias Negassa, looked again at the statistics. He described the disastrous impacts and horrific scenes of resettlers deserting the new areas: "52,000 households deserted the large-scale farms; of these, 7,000 people died and the rest trekked to their areas of origin or crossed international borders to become refugees. From the integrated settlements, 4,000 heads of households escaped and 4,000 died" (1992:4).

I will turn now to a local, in-depth case study of the impacts of the resettlement program in western Ethiopia.

The Beles Valley resettlement scheme

The Beles River is a tributary of the Abbay (Nile) River located southwest of Lake Tana in the Metekel Zone. The region involved is located in the far western part of Ethiopia, and stretches from the northwest to the southwest of the country in a long narrow strip. At present, it is bordered by the regions of Amhara in the north, Oromia in the east, and Gambella in the south, and, to the west, it shares a border with the Republic of the Sudan.

The Beles Valley conventional resettlement scheme was one of the largest resettlement programs in Ethiopia. The scheme covers an area of 220,000 hectares at a lowland altitude of between 1,000 and 1,300 meters above sea level, with a subhumid tropical climate. The annual average rainfall is about 1,600 millimeters and the rainy season usually lasts from April to the end of September. The topography is slightly undulating from the hilltops toward the rivers. Most of the farmland is relatively gentle and flat, and the soils are generally 47 percent nitosols and 53 percent vertisols. Originally, a forest of various arboreal species and bamboo covered the area. It is also considered to be the most important water source base, offering a considerable amount of untapped perennial water resources both from the main Beles River and a number of its small tributaries that flow throughout the year. Before the arrival of resettlers, the Beles Valley was inhabited by an indigenous ethnic group called Gumz with a population between 15,000 and 20,000 people who formerly practiced shifting cultivation, hunting, gathering, and fishing.

The Beles Valley was chosen to host resettler populations of both famine victims from northern Ethiopia and resettlers from areas in southwestern Ethiopia that were overpopulated and that suffered from cultivable land shortage. At the peak of the resettlement scheme in 1987 and 1988, the population involved in the program reached 82,106 people (household heads among them numbered 21,994; family members, 60,112). The displaced were resettled along the left and right banks of the river in 48 villages with an average of 500 households in each village.

The ethnic composition of the resettled population was heterogeneous and included people originating from Amhara (from Wello, North Shoa, Gojjam, and Gondar), Kambaata, Hadiya, Oromo (from North Shoa and Wello), Wolaita, Tigre, and Agaw (from Wello-Tigray and Sekota). Northern resettlers were mainly intensive cereal cultivators, while the southwestern resettlers were mainly *enset* (false banana plant) and root crop cultivators with additional specialization in a range of nonagricultural activities. These different ethnic groups with diverse backgrounds represented a microcosm of the mixture of the cultures of the entire country.

The stated purpose of the resettlement scheme in the Beles Valley was to achieve surplus agricultural production through highly mechanized farming and application of high-technological inputs by means of collective organization of the agricultural labor force. Agricultural work in the new location, therefore, was collectively organized on a cooperative basis. Since their initial arrival, the resettlers had been working in collective farms whose products were stored in the village warehouses. Rations were supplied during the initial phase by the RRC and later by the village authorities, and were distributed according to a point system classifying their labor efforts. No freedom of initiative or possibility of independent decisionmaking was left to the resettlers with regard to the production process and use of the produce. Resettlers' household economy in the agricultural sector was limited to the management of a 0.1-hectare homestead plot of land assigned to each household.

Social disarticulation at the resettlement site

As already described, almost all resettlers originated from mid-altitude and high-altitude areas of Ethiopia in which agro-ecological conditions were suited to mixed cultivation, including vegetables. Resettlers from the northern parts of the country were generally cultivators of cereal crops, with their main staple food being *injera* (a bread made from *teff* grain) usually served with a vegetable sauce. Resettlers from southwestern Ethiopia were mainly *enset* and tuber crop cultivators, with their main staple food being *qotcho* (made from the *enset* plant and usually served with cabbage), tuber plants, and dairy products. Land in the resettlers' previous locations, though small in size, was "privately" owned and the household was the main unit of production and consumption. Animal husbandry was practiced and a range of complex, informal institutions managed reciprocity and redistribution in agricultural and other production, and operated as well as in the social sphere.

In their places of origin, resettlers belonged to similar ethnic groups and lived in dispersed villages that were further subdivided into hamlets. Institutional arrangements included *idir*, which provided both the legal framework and insurance of the local village community. People in their original areas were known under their respective parish, mosque, clan, or village groups, and kinship ties in the home areas were highly intricate and interwoven through the ancestral lineages. Above all, the community members in the previous home areas had a sense of belonging and spiritual ties through a common origin that many resettlers referred to as "a root area where one's umbilical cord is buried."

In displacement and resettlement, this way of life was ruptured. The new location was far from home (some 1,000 kilometers); it was hot and inhospitable, and infested with several lowland diseases. Resettlers fell victim to the new conditions, many people died, and, for the first time, orphanages opened.

As earlier described, the villages in the resettlement area were located in one place, with groups of residential houses constructed in planned rows with only a 0.1 hectare homestead plot for each household. Unlike their previous experience, the inhabitants of the new villages were now part of a diverse ethnic community with many religions and cultural traditions. During the initial phase, resettlers did not have proper community village institutions, such as *idir* and other religious or secular mutual associations. The observation of religious holidays was constrained because of the difficulties encountered. Long-established kinship ties that had performed multipurpose functions were altered in the new location, and there existed no kinship-based leadership. The complex web of social networks, which had previously formed the intricately interwoven intra- and interhousehold and group relationships of the communities, no longer functioned. In other words, from the early days of resettlement the various communities' close bonds and webs of relationships along several lines, such as neighborhood, kinship, religious beliefs, work groups, land exchange, bond-friendship, fictive and godparenting, were either lost or in abeyance. The new villages were, using Cernea's terminology, socially disarticulated.

Resettlement affected the basic setup of family couples. On the one hand, partners abandoned spouses right at the very initial stage of opting for resettlement by either joining the scheme or remaining with consanguineous kin (mostly true for women because of local marriage). On the other hand, after tasting the bitter experience of resettlement, many resettlers with no children or fewer dependents abandoned their partners partly for similar reasons. Thus, resettlement brought about the breakup of many families. Marriages that were established were rather loose and often resulted in abandonment and separation. Through my own research, I observed that many of the abandoned or separated women found it very difficult to secure a new partner in the resettlement sites. Their chance of remarriage after having many children or being postmenopausal is very small. Men, however, had a higher chance of remarriage after divorce, compared to women. In this sense it could be argued that resettlement has worsened the situation of women more than men.

Resettlement in the Beles Valley disrupted the resettlers' previous way of life in other ways. Religious beliefs and practices were curtailed, and the roles of priests, *qadis*, and ritual leaders were undermined. The deep-rooted and long-established ritual process before, during, and after the burial of the dead for the salvation of the soul was, for example, interrupted. Spiritual festive associations like *Mahber* and *Senbete* in the calendar of the Orthodox church were barely recognized. Resettlers practiced marriage without the usual ceremonies. The role of respected elders and religious leaders as facilitators of the whole process of marriage was disrupted. The crucial role of elders in the overall village community life was largely absent. The traditional administration of the village was replaced by formally elected Peasant Associations through which the committee members were charged with the executive and judicial tasks of administering the new village.

In line with the change of the type of crops produced in the new context, food habits also changed. Resettlers from southwest Ethiopia — for whom *enset* and tubers were their principal foods — were unaccustomed to food derived from lowland cereal crops, and their inability to grow *enset* in the new location meant the loss of an intricate web of relations dependent on *enset* production. As a result, all *enset*-related rituals became only a memory. However, the northern Ethiopian resettlers were also obliged to adjust to the kinds of food prepared from lowland crops. Both the southern and northern resettlers were equally critical of feeding maize porridge to their wives during maternity as opposed to barley porridge, which was common practice in the north, and *bu'illa* porridge (the best part of *enset* foods), the practice of the southern farmers. According to the respective resettlers, both *bu'illa* and barley were of higher nutritional value.

The Beles Valley has only one harvest cropping season a year. The rainfall in the new area is abundant, though erratic, with frequent thunder, hailstorms, and wind that often result in severe crop damage. The heat during the dry season is also intense, resulting in common wild bush and forest fires that frequently destroy field crops. These conditions had adverse effects on the adaptive adjustments of highland peasants. Resettlers explained the enormous climatic difference between the original areas and the new context as:

Agaraachin balten inniwozallen, sawunnetaachin muuz yimaslaall; izzih, balten anniwozam, sawunnetaachinim kasal yimaslaall.
(In our home areas, with what we eat, we used to have a lively and bright look like a banana fruit; whereas, here, we rather look like a charcoal.)

More than anything else, resettlement brought resettlers into direct contact with new communities. Resettlers were amazed by their first contact with the indigenous inhabitants of the new location known as Gumz. The traditional Gumz way of life differed markedly from that experienced by the highland farmers. Partly because of the culture clash that occurred, but also as a result of the competition over resources that had traditionally been under the custodianship of the Gumz people, fierce rivalries led to conflict and loss of life on both sides. This was the most bitter experience brought about by the inadequately planned resettlement scheme for both hosts and resettlers.

For many resettlers, the Beles Valley did not become a permanent home because of the difficulties of adaptation to the inhospitable environment, new dietary habits imposed by the scheme, suffering caused by the prevalent diseases (malaria, tuberculosis, and asthma), lack of incentives to undertake agricultural activities, and nostalgia for reunion with separated families and relatives in their homeland. The size of the resettled population dropped from 82,106 in 1987 and 1988 to 26,660 in 1993 and 1994. The rates of desertion were higher among those resettlers who joined the resettlement scheme in search of better opportunities following government recruitment than among those who joined as a direct result of horrific famine. Moreover, after the 1991 political change in the entire country, ethnic conflicts erupted in many resettlement areas in general, and in the Beles Valley in particular, adding political insecurity to already pressing problems of socioeconomic survival. Although the precise desertion figures from Beles Valley are not known, Elias (1992) calculated that approximately 103,000 resettlers returned to northern Ethiopia from different resettlement sites in the country, including Beles Valley, and another 34,000 resettlers returned to the southern Shoa regions of Kambaata and Hadiya. Ironically, however, after a while, because of even worse conditions in some of the original areas, a number of resettlers subsequently returned to the resettlement sites.

After the 1991 political changes in Ethiopia, which brought about the downfall of the Derg regime and the formation of a new coalition government, a number of the resettlers in the Beles Valley moved within the scheme area. In addition, new populations searching for opportunities moved to the valley. Despite the adversities, however, a substantial number of resettlers did remain in the Beles Valley resettlement scheme area. The present resettlers could be characterized as those who have no alternative place of settlement either in their area of origin or elsewhere in the country, those who are incapacitated or weak, and those who still see better opportunities in the resettlement areas compared to elsewhere and who believe there is a livelihood to be made.

The emerging sociocultural re-articulation

After the initial phase of emergency, illnesses, and transition, many resettlers in the Beles Valley began adapting themselves to the new context. Entrepreneurial activities such as trade and market exchange were, in my own view, one of the best and effective adaptive strategies. The markets signaled economic activity in the new context. However, the markets were initially highly controlled by authorities because of concern that market activities would detract from the cooperative effort in the fields. But despite the repeated effort of the authorities to curtail them, markets emerged and displayed significant economic dynamism. Another important adaptive strategy pursued by the resettlers was the production of handicrafts as an additional means of earning a living in the new location.

In March 1986, one year after the resettlement scheme in the Beles Valley began, the Italian government funded the Tana-Beles Project that provided assistance for the development of a self-sustained economy for the region, in addition to emergency aid. The assistance was aimed at economic self-sufficiency and self-management. The first part of the project activities included the supply of personal items to the resettlers, the implementation and development of rain-fed agriculture and introduction of irrigated agriculture, and the construction of infrastructure. As a result, a number of villages today have access to facilities that are not available to most rural Ethiopians. These include 300 kilometers of all-weather graveled road network, potable water, grain stores of 10,000-quintal capacity, grain mills with generators, a modern regional hospital and clinics in all villages, a malaria eradication center, new corrugated iron-roofed houses, and primary schools. However, since the project was developed in line with the Derg government's ideology, it emphasized agricultural collectivization through which agricultural work was organized on a cooperative basis. The project's highly mechanized technology and capital-intensive, cooperative agricultural development approach were not appropriate to the attainment of self-sufficiency. Being highly centralized, decisionmaking was top-down, with massive intervention leading to imposed socioeconomic change relying mainly on the strategy of collective production. In addition, the handout mentality created dependency and undermined resettlers' own efforts to achieve self-reliance.

Despite such problems with the assistance offered, the Tana-Beles Project improved the conditions of the resettlement area. The activities attracted a considerable influx of people looking for opportunities and employment. Associated private business activities also brought to the area an injection of cash and investment, leading to increased purchasing power. Through the influx of people for business activities, small towns emerged as exchange centers at different locations in the area.

In the resettlement scheme, only those activities considered by the planners as marginal were left to the resettler households. In the absence of support and encouragement, resettlers showed initiative and independence, managing their activities with a conscious pursuit of benefits and supplementary income. Despite the local authorities' efforts to limit them, periodic markets developed for trading home-gardening products, handicrafts, grain, livestock, spices, and clothing. Resettlers opted for alternative adaptive strategies because the economy of ration was not sufficient to guarantee their survival. Their engagement in exchange, trading, and other comparable socioeconomic activities strengthened their relationships within the resettlement villages and developed emerging networks with neighboring areas.

Rebuilding a social identity was one of the strongest needs felt in the new contexts. Religious beliefs of the different ethnic groups began to reassert themselves. Ethnic identity was felt to be important and attempts were made to maintain it in the resettlement villages. Marriage strengthened, particularly among resettlers who belonged to the same ethnic background. Through the marriage ties of the sons and daughters, affinal kin groups began to develop between the families of the spouses in the new context. Different ethnic groups among resettlers have shown propensity toward integrative relations. However, the relations between the indigenous Gumz and incoming resettlers remained mostly conflictual.

In the present Beles Valley context, resettlers' livelihoods are based on both agricultural production and nonagricultural income-generating activities. The dominant agricultural activity is crop production, together with substantial livestock raising and crop-livestock integration. Horticulture and apiculture are also practiced. Many resettlers undertake on-farm and off-farm income-generating activities in order to diversify household income sources. In agricultural production, resettlers apply diverse but well-correlated production strategies, including cultivation of plots by their own draft animals, manual digging and hoeing, exchange of oxen and labor, exchange of oxen for cash and grain, exchange of land and oxen, exchange of grain and labor, exchange of labor for labor, share-cropping land, renting land, obtaining oxen through social networks, use of household labor, festive and reciprocal labor mobilization, hiring farmer(s) for a cropping season, and hiring labor in peak periods. While some of these practices would have been followed in the areas of origin, the combinations of strategies in the Beles Valley were not formerly considered.

Ten to 12 years after arriving in the Beles Valley, and after having experienced a decade of stagnation or, even worse, decline, resettled farmers are now showing remarkable flexibility and imagination, making the best of their access to and control over such key resources as land, livestock, labor, and cash income. The successful livelihood strategies that act as the basis for the resettlers' adaptive readjustments and eventual socioeconomic differentiation include individually tailored production practices, agricultural intensification, household income diversification, recreated and adapted networks of social relations, remittances, economization, and innovation. However, observations indicate that female-headed households still remain more vulnerable than other types of households. This is due, in part, to insufficient labor resources and social support within the household and an inability to call on social networks beyond the household. Women lacking husbands shoulder the responsibility for managing households alone and are obliged to enter into sharecropping arrangements.

In general, however, as resettlers adjust their social arrangements and their productive activities, one can see the gradual strengthening and re-articulation of communities and community-related activities and events. Marriage ceremonies, which in the early years after resettlement were conducted without the correct rituals and other associated practices, now take the form expected, with respected elders and religious leaders once again playing the significant role in facilitating the process of marriage.

Elders' role. The role of elders has regained importance in other aspects of village life. For example, elders in the respective communities once again play a part in the settlement of disputes arising between households, within households, and at the village level. Increasingly, they advise, guide, and punish defaulters according to custom, and are responsible for teaching the importance of culturally accepted values and norms. Elders encourage and motivate self-support among resettlers, visit the weak and disabled, console families of deceased persons, and perform other vital cultural and social services.

The rebirth of religious associations. Various associations based on the Orthodox, Protestant, Islamic, and Catholic churches in the sites have also emerged. They extend support to their weaker members and in many cases have become the main source of livelihood for those households. Hand-in-hand with the reestablishment of the different churches, the church leadership, composed mostly of the elderly, has also reaffirmed itself. They strongly preach faithfulness to one's own religion and the observation of proper performance of followers with respect to the orders of the religions. They perform the daily routine prayers of their religion, for the salvation of the spirits of the dead. Moreover, they have a key role in consoling bereaved families through their frequent prayers and visits. More than anything else, the very reemergence of the belief systems has rekindled optimism and hope among the resettler communities, contributing to their adaptation.

Idir, which is also known as *seera* among the Southern resettlers, is the strongest multipurpose mutual association within the village communities. It was totally absent at the time of resettlers' arrival. However, as they went through adaptive readjustments, resettlers managed to revitalize *idir*, with the household as the basic unit of membership. The present *idir* of the villages cross ethnic and religious boundaries and are inclusively, rather than exclusively, constituted. Besides the well-established *idir* for burial and mourning, there are now *idir* for oxen (a kind of insuring mechanism) and for transporting the sick to the hospital (the stretcher society). *Idir* are administered by an elected wise and respected *dagna* (chief), and those who fail to make contributions to the funds are punished severely.

Resettlers managed also to reestablish *mahber* and *senbete* – mutual religious festive associations mainly among the followers of the Orthodox Church. The *mahber* members meet once a month, rotating houses, and celebrate the name of a selected saint and enjoy food and drink as well as perform prayers. The *senbete* members meet every two weeks, rotating among members. Feasts are organized and consumed in the compound of the village church, attended also by the disabled and other weak members who come in search of food. At the same time, prayers are performed by priests. Both the *mahber* and *senbete* are formed across ethnic boundaries. Mutual support is extended to and asked for by members as needed, both on auspicious and inauspicious occasions.

Reemergence of labor exchanges. With the reestablishment of smallholder household production systems, resettlers' social organization of production has also reemerged. The social organization of production among resettlers in the Beles Valley is centered around various work groups and labor exchange patterns. These include *dabo* (festive labor), *wonfel* (reciprocal labor), *amicha* (affinal kin-based festive labor), *balnjeera/elfinna qaso* (intimate friendship-based festive labor), *waari/maarfeja* (supportive labor for the weak during the early hours in the morning before resettler farmers go to their daily tasks), and *limmaano* (full-time supportive labor, mostly for the disabled). These local, community-level, self-supportive organizations have reemerged and been further strengthened, mainly based on the reestablishment of the small-holder cultivation, managed by the households that demand mutual support.

In the present Beles Valley situation, resettlers have established complex social relations both within the resettlement area as well as with the neighboring populations through marriage, religion, work groups, land exchange, bond-friendship, fictive parenthood, and godparenting as well as on the basis of the individual's entrepreneurial ability in interacting with others. Individuals within the networks of relations exchange a great deal through their interaction. For instance, resettlers without oxen get support through their relations with those who possess oxen, and those without cash can gain access to loans. Based on established relations, some of the village's resettled traders mobilize village-level grain purchase for merchants and earn commission. In the field of agricultural activities, resettlers who have established better networks of social relations are capable of mobilizing an enormous amount of festive labor, which makes a significant contribution to the success of livelihood strategies. Thus, the reemergence of household economy coupled with individual initiatives, innovations, and industriousness act as key elements in the resettlers' adaptation and revitalization, and in the reconstruction of livelihoods even in the absence of properly established sectoral support.

Conclusions

The politically mandated mass relocation of the Ethiopian peasantry after the 1984 and 1985 drought and famine was a tragedy for the resettlers, their hosts, and the country as a whole. The program failed to alleviate the problems of the sending areas. It was accomplished only at an unacceptably high cost in terms of human life. The impact of the resettlement program in the receiving areas was disastrous because of the lack of thorough investigation of the program's development potential, the marginalization of the indigenous host communities, and the negative environmental impacts. Finally, the politically driven and state-controlled process and the resulting settlement scheme were marred by basic social injustice and violations of human rights. The mass relocation brought people into unfamiliar environments affecting both the relocatees and the host population.

Resettlement in the Beles Valley, as described in this chapter, caused enormous sociocultural disintegration and impoverishment. However, after the collapse of collectivization and reestablishment of individual small-holder production systems, resettlers began the adaptation process, partially readjusting themselves and their livelihood systems to the new context. Individual initiatives and industriousness acted as the main factors of resettlers' adaptive strategies that started the process of sociocultural re-articulation and reconstruction of socioeconomic livelihoods in the Beles Valley resettlement scheme.

Operational lessons can be learned from the Beles Valley resettlement experience in order to improve resettlement processes elsewhere and to counteract impoverishment and the sociocultural disintegration that is a component of this impoverishment. First, politically imposed mass relocation must always be avoided at all costs, and the populations' basic human rights should be safeguarded. Second, fair and far-sighted policy and legal frameworks for those resettlement operations that are unavoidable should be formulated at the national and international level. And third, the formulation of resettlement programs should be based on multidisciplinary professional assessments, with the genuine participation of the affected populations, to minimize the impoverishment risks and quicken the reconstruction of people's livelihoods.

The Beles study also yields conceptual insights. In attempting to understand the multidimensional economic and social impacts of the Derg's emergency resettlement program and the dynamics of livelihood reconstruction, I found the Cernea risks and reconstruction model about resettlement analytically revealing and effective. This model was originally conceived as a diagnostic and planning tool for resettlement operations brought about by infrastructure development investments (see Cernea, this volume). Clearly, the episode of forced resettlement analyzed in this study was different in many respects. However, the Ethiopian resettlement case also provides facts from its own reality that further confirm and enrich this conceptual framework. Whatever the underlying motivations of the Derg leadership, Ethiopian peasants conscripted into this enormous imposed relocation program experienced a set of risks remarkably similar to those experienced by development displacees, captured synthetically in Cernea's model.

Consistent with this methodology, the study discussed in this chapter focused specifically on the social consequences of resettlement: the rupturing of familial, kin, and community relations; the erosion of community management and leadership systems; and the undermining of the legitimacy of the spiritual order. These elements configure and draw out complex processes of *community disarticulation and, indeed, re-articulation*. Many straightforward aspects illustrate this process.

The analysis showed that unsympathetic planning of new home plots obstructed resettlers' attempts to re-create previously informal institutions by, among other things, establishing neighborhoods with different ethnic and social compositions. In addition, insufficient, undesirable, and nutritionally nonbeneficial crops imposed officially on the resettlement scheme undermined the resettlers' ability to defeat rampant and unfamiliar diseases.

The Beles Valley resettlers experienced a set of interconnected risks that, research suggests, tend to be common in development-induced resettlement. This also suggests a considerable degree of commonality between refugees in general and development displacees. This similarity is obvious in two ways: first, in the events surrounding removal, and, second, in the livelihood-reconstruction process.

Certainly, like so many refugees in Africa, Beles resettlers were victims of multiple hazards and inflicted deprivations: they were victims of famine and droughts, of political repression, and of loss of private and common assets. The impoverishment risks were practically the same. People abandoned homes, land, and movable property, with no choice over their future destination, and were incarcerated in temporary camps. They were helpless in the face of the emergency and were forced to relocate in a previously unknown place, among suspicious and hostile indigenous communities. They suffered from psychological trauma for lost homes and split family units. The increased mortality and morbidity rate in the Beles Valley, caused by malaria and other epidemics, intensified their physiological and psychological stress. Above all, they suffered from serious sociocultural disintegration, because their previous livelihood and supporting social networks were disrupted in the new and unfamiliar context. The many other related facts already stated in this chapter concerning social disarticulation undoubtedly reveal the deep-rooted similarities in refugees' and resettlers' experiences.

In the reconstruction phase, there are also similarities. For the rebuilding of resettlers' livelihoods, be they refugees or displacees, there is no single universal panacea. However, evidence from Beles would tend to concur with the refugee literature, and with what other contributors to the present volume have written, that providing the conditions necessary to facilitate rather than hinder people's own initiatives and the development of community associations and institutions is vital in the social re-articulation of a disrupted community. This process is central also for the entire economic reestablishment process.

The case presented here is somewhat more encouraging than others about the possibility, even after profound disruption and dispersal, of re-creating within a reasonable time period not only an economic future but also a social and cultural fabric. As Kibreab also suggests elsewhere in this volume, the risks and reconstruction conceptual framework—in identifying key risks, focusing on their interactions, and pointing to strategies for reconstruction—is a relevant analytical and guiding framework for the domains of both development-induced displacement and refugee-type resettlement.

CHAPTER 17

Social re-articulation and community regeneration among resettled displacees[1]

L. K. Mahapatra and Sheela Mahapatra

To apply the model of impoverishment risks and reconstruction of livelihoods to any specific case of involuntary displacement (Cernea 1996a; 1996b) would require data about conditions in the pre-displacement, actual displacement, and resettlement phases. Such data is woefully incomplete for many projects in India, especially those undertaken between 1960 and 1990. Official sources on re-settlement processes are often found to be ill informed or inaccurate and should be read with care. For instance, the study by Dalua, *Irrigation in Orissa* (1991), published by the Water and Land Management Institute of the government of Orissa, fails to provide, in most cases examined, even basic data on areas of submergence (forest, agricultural, and other land) or the exact number of households affected by displacement.

Given such handicaps, this chapter attempts to present a case study of the Ramial Resettlement and Rehabilitation operation — covering both the impoverishment and the reconstruction of resettlers' livelihoods — through several stages of fieldwork and visits to the area, rather than relying on official data. The first author visited the rehabilitation colonies in 1986 and was impressed with the reconstruction process, especially in terms of reintegration and community

---

1   Mr. Dharmananda Behera ably carried out the field investigations in the colonies in August 1996. Dr Ota, Directorate of Resettlement and Rehabilitation, Department of Water Resources, Government of Orissa kindly provided the secondary sources, and the department deserves our thanks for its assistance.

regeneration. Both authors conducted a new field study in August 1996 to update information on the cumulative reconstruction processes.

The chapter first describes the Ramial project and the rehabilitation operation. Second, by applying the risks and reconstruction model, it examines the impoverishment risks faced by the resettlers and the reconstruction of livelihoods in the resettlement colonies. And last, it concentrates on the process of community reconstruction, as a process in which all the efforts to counteract the risks of impoverishment come together.

The Ramial River Project

Between 1975 and 1990 (though Dalua [1991:102] disputes these dates), a rolled earth fill dam, with a catchment area of 328 square kilometers, was constructed over the Ramial River in the basin of the Brahmani River, Dhenkanal, Orissa State. The construction of the dam resulted in the involuntary resettlement of people living in the Dhenkanal and Keonjhar districts. Though official records disagree about the precise number of affected families and the number of families entitled to compensation, it is clear that of the 22 villages affected, 6 were fully submerged. Official documentation stated that 743 families were eligible for rehabilitation; however (and Dalua's study would seem to confirm this), only 414 families actually received rehabilitation assistance by 1991. The Rehabilitation Advisory Committee (RAC) for the Ramial Irrigation Project maintained that the original figure for the number of families entitled to rehabilitation was correct at 743.

In 1995, a further government report on the rehabilitation operation showed an increase in the number of eligible families by 168. The report stated that, by the end of that year, 389 families had secured full rehabilitation with both homestead and agricultural land, while the remainder had received only homestead land and were awaiting a decision on their right to access additional lands. Average family land allocations included 0.3 acres of homestead land and slightly more than three acres of irrigated and nonirrigated agricultural land, and the majority were relocated within the four colonies set aside.

However, the RAC in its regular reports noted a series of planning oversights and poor decisions that adversely affected the resettlers' ability to rehabilitate their communities. The RAC reported as far back as 1989 that the distribution of irrigated land to resettled families was unequal; in Gabagada village, for example, about half the oustees were allocated rocky and uncultivable land, which was passed off as "irrigated land." In 1994 the RAC reported that a number of community assets had been overlooked when calculating compensation, owing to villagers whose villages were submerged. It revealed also that displaced families were yet to receive land ownership documents for resettlement land.

Against this background the authors now examine in more detail the impoverishment risks that confronted the Ramial displacees in the four colony resettlement sites.

Impoverishment risks and reconstruction of livelihoods in the colonies

Land and agriculture

Official reports on the rehabilitation operation contend that families affected by the construction of the dam received fair land-for-land compensation. However, our research suggests that many displacees (around 17 percent of families in the four colonies) were displaced onto lands that were unsuitable for agriculture. On those lands, for which canal-based irrigation was provided, it was found that the level of the canal was too low to permit adequate irrigation, and no alternative system of irrigation was provided. Oustee leaders have suggested that a water-harvesting structure could be constructed to capture natural stream water and made available to upland lands, benefiting an estimated 40 oustee families.

An official originally associated with the rehabilitation colonies acknowledged that unwanted and unusable lands in Kantapal Village were allotted to resettlers. The fact that many families have returned to their previous village sites along the periphery of the reservoir says much about the inappropriateness of allocated land. Elsewhere in the colonies, families continue to apply to the courts for the provision of replacement land not yet allocated.

It can be seen, therefore, that the procedures for distributing lands in the new sites are unfair and unjust. Some families have benefited: for example, 27 families who occupied rocky, unproductive land in their former village have been allotted good, irrigated land. Others have been able to purchase land over and above their allotted lands. However, in general, it is the better-off farmers who have failed to restore their prosperity and have been disadvantaged through resettlement.

Housing

All displaced families, including those who had not owned their own house plot before displacement, received 0.3 acres of homestead land. On this land the oustees, largely without loans or grants, were required to build their own homes. In general, it can be observed that in the resettlement colonies the houses are larger and in better condition than the houses left behind in the villages. However, a number are in poor shape, mainly because the straw for the thatch cannot be produced in poor-quality agricultural lands and there is no access to forest thatch grass. For those no longer enjoying access to the forest resources, thatching materials are more expensive and the range of other previously available building materials is limited.

Employment

In the previous setting, the agricultural economy provided jobs not only for the cultivating family members, but also for agricultural laborers, annual contract laborers (*halia*), and a range of artisans. These opportunities remain largely intact in the new setting, and when workers are not available people are encouraged to move into the colonies from outside. Fishing in the Ramial River was an important source of food and some cash for the tribal and other groups. Since the 1980s, the Fish Seed Corporation of Orissa has been giving assistance for the acquisition of nets and boats to members of formal fishing societies.

It also appears that day laborers receive a higher minimum wage in the colonies than in their old villages, even accounting for inflation: rupees 20 per day in 1995 to 1996, compared to between rupees 3 and rupees 6 in pre-displacement days. We do not know, however, the average number of workdays per laborer, before and after displacement. Those who in their old villages worked in the Talcher coal mines are now working mostly in the construction industry. The local laborers near the coal mines do not allow outside workers to take up coal mining jobs. Some of the colony inhabitants work also at the Kaliapani and Astapal iron ore mines; seasonal labor attracts many in nearby areas. Such former employees as teachers are newly reemployed after being displaced.

The new settlement colonies have also created new employment opportunities for shopkeepers (11 shops in four colonies), rice hulling (three), and business and machine workers (23) in several types of small businesses, including bread and biscuit making and sell-

ing, rice, vegetables, and ice cream. Some of the richer agriculturalists and others who cannot work their land are employing *halia*.

In conclusion, the retention of the *jajmani* system of socioritual
and economic services coupled with new opportunities in business
and manufacturing have diversified and widened the scope of job
opportunities in the new settlements. Overall, these opportunities
add up to better job placements than in the older villages. But this
conclusion has to be complemented and verified with comparative
data on underemployment and unemployment. It is important also
to note that because of the loss of access to forest resources, many
women have lost a crucial source of independent income, and boys
have forfeited a source of capital accumulation, through the breeding and selling of goats gifted by their fathers.

Restoration and creation of common property assets

In comparison to their situation in their former villages, the resettled
displacees have been deprived of many common property assets.
Among these are the river (a source of water for human and animal
consumption), the forest (a source of food, fodder, fuel wood, and,
as previously stated, building materials), mango groves, common
grazing lands, common cremation grounds, and wastelands (though
72 acres of wastelands have been allotted for common needs). Without these common assets, life in the colonies has become costlier
and lower in standards for the poorer people.

However, within the rehabilitation operation, some common assets have been made available. Community houses (*kothu ghara*),
ritual grounds (*rashu bhadi*), ponds and wells, and village goddess
shrines have been provided for each colony. Temples have been built
in Colonies One and Four, provisions have been made for pond fishing in Colonies Two and Four, and maintenance land provided for
the regional goddess. In addition, the schools are better equipped
with a middle English school, and privately sponsored high school
situated on the land allotted to the regional goddess in Colony One.

Countering poverty and marginalization

In their research, the authors identified 96 families (21 percent of
resettled families) living below or close to the poverty line and
subject to food insecurity. Reasons for this may include the low
productivity of rain-fed agricultural lands and the lack of ownership of bullocks, particularly by the poorer families. Further-

more, because the villages have not yet been officially identified as "revenue" villages, they are not entitled to subsidized rice, and without landholding rights the residents cannot take advantage of government-sponsored or other credit and loan schemes once the five-year lease *patta* provisions have expired.

Moreover, in the old villages, unmarried brothers resided as one joint family; however, on resettlement, unmarried sons 18 years and older were not entitled to land. Consequently, when sons married, families were obliged to subdivide their allocated land, creating uneconomical farming units, despite irrigation.

However, there is evidence that new institutions are arising to assist marginalized families. The Committee Fund, for example, enables poorer households to borrow money or grain in times of need.

The caste system in the resettlement villages is maintained and contributes to the marginalization of some vulnerable groups, notably tribal. For example, a low-caste man continues to be barred from common rights such as drawing well water, and untouchability, in some form, is still practiced.

Health care

In their previous location, the displacees did not have easy access to modern medical facilities and relied instead on village *kaviraj* and *gunia* (medicine men) to provide traditional medicine. In Colony Four, however, a medical center has been constructed and is staffed by a full-time doctor and paramedical staff, a primary health center is 5 kilometers from the resettlement colonies, and a subdivisional hospital is some 45 kilometers away. However, despite improved health awareness and vaccination programs, it is the perception of resettlers that in the colonies new diseases like cerebral malaria, typhoid, and jaundice are on the increase, as is infant and child mortality.

Educational opportunities

One of this chapter's authors has stated previously that loss of educational opportunities for resettled people is a major impoverishment risk (Mahapatra 1997). In their previous villages, children were engaged in tending the livestock, looking after their younger siblings, watching the house, or food production and gathering, and were therefore too busy to attend school. Teenagers were often employed as day laborers. At best, boys may be educated up to primary level, and girls discouraged from attending school altogether. Among members of scheduled tribes there is evidence that education was little valued.

After displacement, the outlook and the ecology changed. There was no stable traditional resource base in the forests, and very limited access to encroachable government or common property lands. There was more cash circulating in the economy, and new economic opportunities were available. Colonies were no longer as isolated as they were previously, and education became increasingly valued. By 1986, schools had been opened at the initiative of the resettlers. Almost equal numbers of boys and girls attend grades one to five in three of the colonies' schools, including children from scheduled castes and scheduled tribes. By 1996, there were 19 male and 6 female matriculants.

It can be argued, therefore, that in resettlement, there was a seizing of educational opportunities by parents and children alike, and when this was the case the incidence of marginalization appeared to be lower.

Community reconstruction

A summary of losses and gains

To recap, we have seen that, despite some counterrisk and compensatory actions, the people resettled as a consequence of the construction of the Ramial River dam have suffered land loss; loss of access to common assets, including sites of cultural and social importance; and loss of some income-generating opportunities, including stocks of domestic animals and of social networks and relationships. They were also more vulnerable to disease. Around 12 percent of resettled families abandoned the resettlement colonies altogether, opting instead to return to their previous villages (for details see Table 1 below). Certainly, these losses would have been much worse without the measures adopted to limit risks and adverse side effects.

However, our research has also uncovered resettlement benefits, as a result of reconstruction assistance and of the resettlers' efforts. These include much-improved communication facilities, medical facilities, educational opportunities, and housing, and diversified employment opportunities beyond the exclusive dependence on land and agriculture. In this section of the chapter, we explore further the ways in which oustees have sought to reconstruct their social and community life, to provide the means to sustainability by absorbing the shocks and stresses of modern life and to take

TABLE 1: FAMILIES IN RESETTLEMENT COLONIES BY ETHNIC GROUP AND VILLAGE OF ORIGIN, 1996

	Number of families in Colonies One to Four in 1996				
Ethnic groups	*Colony One*	*Colony Two*	*Colony Three*	*Colony Four*	*Original village*
Santal Scheduled tribe	19	—	—	2	Raipal Baiganpal Rekuti Sirishpal
Gond Scheduled tribe	25	19	5 outsiders	48	Mandiapada Biripal
Munda Scheduled tribe	6	—	9	—	Munda Sahi Biripal
Sabara Scheduled tribe	—	—	43 but 25 returned to village	—	Rekuti
Bathuli/Bathudi Scheduled tribe	—	2	—	—	Biripal
Brahman Priest	—	2	—	—	Gabagada
Chasa Cultivator	3	14 from Ramial plus 41 from Dadara	—	—	Gabagada Sulgaon Dadara
Gudia Sweetmeat maker	—	1 from Dadara	—	—	Sulgaon
Gouda Cowherd	—	9 from Dadara	6 but returned to village	13	Biripal Nuagaon Rekuti Sulgaon
Khadara Brazier	—	1	—	—	Gabagada
Mahanta/Kurmi	10	9	1	9	Mandiapada Kateni Biripal Nuagaon

(continued on next page)

Table 1 *(continued)*

| Ethnic groups | Number of families in Colonies One to Four in 1996 | | | | |
	Colony One	Colony Two	Colony Three	Colony Four	Original village
Patra/Pana Scheduled caste Weaver	52	—	7 but 2 returned to village	10	Nuagaon Biripal Gabagada
Dhoba Scheduled caste Washerman	—	1	—	14	Biripal Nuagaon
Keuta Scheduled caste Fisherman	1 outsider	—	—	5	Gabagada
Hadi Scheduled caste Basketmaker	—	—	5 but 2 returned to village	—	Biripal Rekuti
Kamar Blacksmith	2	—	1 outsider	6	Biripal Mandiapada
Teli Oilman	—	—	1 outsider	1 outsider	
Bhata Genealogist	—	—	—	2	Munda sahi
Kumbhar Potter	—	—	—	26	Nuagaon
Bhandari Barbar	1	—	—	1	Nuagaon Mandiapada
Sundi Distiller	—	—	—	8	Nuagaon

advantage of new and emerging opportunities for further advancement.

Community regeneration and social re-articulation

Rarely do we come across success stories in India of livelihood reconstruction after resettlement. Rarer still are reports of post-resettlement social reintegration. Cernea notes, "social reintegration processes are among the least addressed in current approaches, both at the operational level and in social research. Constraints result from planners' widespread lack of perception of these socio-cultural and psychological (not just economic) dimensions, and their consequent lack of sensitive planning for rebuilding 'social capital,' for facilitating reintegration within host populations, and for compensating lost community owned assets.... Community reconstruction refers primarily to group level aspects, including formal organizations and formal institutions. ... Differences exist between fully recreating new village settlements or neighborhoods, as new social units, and fill-in operations relocating resettlers as scattered families within other pre-existing communities." (Cernea 1996b:32).

Fully re-creating new village settlements is what is referred to here, by us, as "community regeneration," while "social re-articulation" may refer specifically to social reintegration with host and neighboring communities in the new settlement site. It is extremely difficult to analyze these processes; however, Cernea identifies processes of "community reconstruction" and "social reintegration" in opposition to situations of "social disarticulation," where the "de-stabilization of community life" generates a "typical state of anomie." The remainder of this chapter will examine some of the processes of community regeneration and social re-articulation observed in the settlement colonies.

Social structure of the colonies

The four colonies under the Ramial Irrigation Project cover a little more than 1,580 acres and house displacees from 13 villages in the Keonjhar and Dhenkanal districts. In addition, a further 51 families were settled in Colony Two after a separate water project in Dadaraghati (see Table 1). For the purposes of analyzing the social and economic situation of the displacees, all families residing in each of the four colonies are considered together.

From the table it can be seen that each of the four colonies are multiethnic and heterogeneous and include outsiders who purchased land from those oustees who chose to return to their villages or settled elsewhere. Typically, people from the same caste or tribe from one village tended to settle in the same colony. For example, all 14 displacees of Mandiapada and 21 displacees from Biripal Village settled in Colony One. Such *en bloc* resettlement enables the transplanting of community ties from the original location to the place of new settlement.

Pull factors contributing to community regeneration and social re-articulation

In 1986, on the first visit to the Ramial Project, it was clear that community solidarity was emerging in one or two of the colonies. There was evidence of community-wide concern for the development of amenities and for the provision of grants and services to improve the lives of resettlers. Leadership was emerging to mobilize the displacees, and cultural performances were held to express the symbolic and ritual solidarity of the colonies. The resettlement locations were emerging as distinct social entities through the common struggle to rebuild lives physically, culturally, economically, and socially.

Upon return 10 years later, it was clear that in some senses the re-articulation and regeneration processes were crystallizing, and these processes could be identified at three levels: intracolony community regeneration; pan-colony social reconstruction; and colony-host social re-articulation. These processes were mutually reinforcing, enabling the colonies to fulfill a role in the social ecology of the region. Some of the features of those processes are as follows.

Intracolony community regeneration

Myths, spatial patterns of settlement, and informal and formal institutions facilitated and enabled community regeneration.

In Colony Four the myth of the man-eater, *kukurbhuku*, a ghost who resides in a tree, afforded a special solidarity for ritual and security for its residents. In the same colony, patterns of settlement replicated the Orissan village in essential social hierarchy, forming interrelations based on caste-specific division of labor among all different castes and tribal groups. Emerging out of this were other colony-wide associations and relationships leading to the creation of village institutions.

For example, village committees were formed comprising representatives of important castes and tribes in the village, whose members held office for two years and were entrusted with maintaining peace and harmony. They had the task of resolving petty disputes by imposing fines on transgressors of social, ritual, or other behavior as a means of enforcing moral and social self-regulation in order to help maintain social solidarity. Fines are deposited in the Committee Fund, which is used for the welfare of the colony, including the support of more vulnerable members of the community.

Youth clubs have been organized in each of the colonies, as have women's funds (*Nari Sangha*), to and for which women contribute and manage for the benefit of widows and destitute women, lending money on which interest is only charged to the better off. Such funds perform a very important role in the local community where institutional credit is not available. Community houses, or *kothaghara*, have been established in the new settings, providing a place where colony matters can be discussed.

In addition, there are institutions concerned with cultural and religious matters. Village goddesses are installed and worshipped in the traditional way, and the cult surrounding the goddess becomes the symbolic manifestation of the colony's social solidarity and regeneration. A Shiva Temple was constructed in Colony Four to further promote solidarity, as was a Radhakrushna Temple in Colony Two.

However, community solidarity has been advanced also by conflict between the resettlers and host villages related to access to and control over local resources. For example, there has been a long, ongoing dispute among Colonies One, Two, and Three, and the neighboring village of Kandhara over sharing the waters of the branch canal. In 1989, the situation became so tense that the police were involved, until finally the villagers of Kandhara signed an agreement not to create further difficulties. A further host-settler conflict exists over usage of the Antapura Forest to which the Kandhara villagers have denied the settlers access. However, the colony residents have resorted to exploiting the forest resources under the cover of night. Such incidences, it can be argued, serve to cement pre-existing social bonds, contributing significantly to the process of community regeneration in the colonies.

Pan-colony social reconstruction

Although first founded over a four-year period between 1980 and 1984, by 1986 the colonies had established a firm foundation for the regeneration of community life. Arguably, the ritual-symbolic unity of the colonies was achieved the day *Maa Charchika Thakurani*, the regional goddess from the displacee village of Rekuti, was brought to Colony One. At the beginning of the solar New Year, ritual festivals are celebrated at the Temple of Maa Charchika Thakurani with great enthusiasm and include such activities as fire walking, attracting huge crowds not only from within the Ramial colonies, but also from the Dadara colonies and the villages all around. The festival is organized by a committee through which funds are raised and cultural activities undertaken. Residents of the colonies say that the festival is celebrated today with greater enthusiasm than in the olden days.

The regeneration process has also been facilitated by the establishment and successful running of colony schools, which bring together the students of all the colonies. The schools are sponsored and run by community committees and cater not only to the needs of the colony residents but also to those of surrounding villagers. The emergence in 1989 of a nongovernmental organization dedicated to nonformal education has created a further binding force, encouraging the resettlers to be forward-thinking.

Finally, the functional services of the castes, like Brahmins, blacksmiths, potters, cow herders, and so on are shared among the colonies irrespective of where in the colonies the people live. This has the effect of integrating the colonies and creating goodwill and understanding among the colonies and their residents.

Colony-host social re-articulation

In any resettlement there is high potential for conflict between settlers in a new location and hosts. We have seen in the case of the Ramial oustees that the sharing of canal water, forest resources, grazing lands, burial and cremation grounds, and other scarce resources can lead to conflicts. However, joint participation—of the colonies and of oustees and surrounding villagers—in rituals, fairs, and festivals, and children from outside the colonies attending colony schools, markets, and clinics, all contribute to binding the colonies and the nearby villages in ever-widening networks of interaction. Such interaction may develop into closer cooperation over common development concerns and programs, a process that will accelerate when the colonies are declared "revenue" villages and are integrated into the three-tier Panchayati Raj system. In 1996, the electing of two ward members from the four colonies to the Kantapala Gram Panchayat was a clear sign of closer political integration.

However, all this must be achieved despite misguided planning—which created resettlement colonies without pastureland or access to nearby forests, and with insufficient water for irrigation–that was bound to lead to estrangement between the resettlers and their hosts.

Conclusion

It would be wrong to paint a picture of the colonies as havens of peace and tranquility, which they are not. Our research did not go in search of tensions and community divisions; however, those tensions were apparent.

P.K. Nayak, examining the Rengali Project, noted that powerful and influential families could distort land distribution in resettlement. There was evidence of this in Ramial; a resentment was felt by those who received only rocky and inhospitable lands. Resentment is felt also as a result of the inefficient management of canal waters, and this resentment will increase as the demand for water continues to grow.

In conclusion, the authors would argue that the resettlement colonies do not exhibit obvious anomie, and that the process of community regeneration and social re-articulation are well rooted. The Rehabilitation Advisory Committee with the representation of local leaders, drawn not, however, from the resettlers, has been a great source of strength and has played an important role in addressing the genuine grievances of oustees. A number of issues remain unresolved after nearly 20 years. These include land rights and entitlements of a large number of resettlers eligible for land, the laying of roads and other communication facilities, and the recognition of the colonies as administrative villages. The World Bank's Operational Directive 4.30 requires ongoing supervision and maintenance once the project is complete; in the case of the Ramial Project such continuing inputs are vital for sustainable reconstruction of resettlers' livelihoods.

General Bibliography

Aberle, D. 1993. "The Navajo-Hopi Land Dispute and Navajo Relocation." In M. M. Cernea and S. E. Guggenheim, eds., *Anthropological Approaches to Resettlement: Policy, Practice, and Theory.* Boulder, Colorado: Westview Press.

Adams, J. 1998. "Risk in a Hyper-Mobile World." Geography Department, University College, London.

Adu-Aryee, V. Q. 1993. "Resettlement in Ghana: From Akosombo to Kpong." In M. M. Cernea and S. E. Guggenheim, eds., *Anthropological Approaches to Resettlement: Policy, Practice, and Theory.* Boulder, Colorado: Westview Press.

Agarwal, A. 1986. "Deforestation in India: An End to Traditional Crafts." *Cultural Survival Quarterly* 10 (50).

Agdaw Asfaw and Wolde-Selassie Abbute. 1992. "Utilisation of Horticultural Products in the Beles Valley Resettlement Scheme." In P. Diece and C. Viezzoli, eds., *Resettlement and Rural Development in Ethiopia: Social and Economic Research, Training and Technical Assistance in the Beles Valley.* Milan: Franco Angeli.

Agneta, F. et.al. 1993. "The Dynamics of Social and Economic Adaptation during Resettlement: The Case of the Beles Valley in Ethiopia." In M. M. Cernea and S. E. Guggenheim, S. E., eds., *Anthropological Approaches to Resettlement: Policy, Practice, and Theory.* Boulder, Colorado: Westview Press.

Agnihotri, A. 1996. "The Orissa Resettlement and Rehabilitation of Project-Affected Persons Policy, 1994: An Analysis of its Robustness with Reference to the Impoverishment Risks Model."

In A. B. Ota and A. Agnihotri, eds., *Involuntary Resettlement in Dam Projects.* New Delhi: Prachi Prakashan.

Akwabi-Ameyaw, K. 1990. "The Political Economy of Agricultural Resettlement and Rural Development in Zimbabwe: The Performance of Family Farms and Producer Co-operatives." *Human Organisation* 49: 320–338.

Allen, T. and Morsink, H. 1994. "Introduction: When Refugees Go Home" In T. Allen and H. Morsink, eds., *When Refugees Go Home.* London: James Currey.

Appell, C. N. 1986. "The Health Consequences of Social Change: A Set of Postulates for Developing General Adaptation Theory." *Sarawak Museum Journal* 36: 43–74.

Appleby, G. 1976. "The Role of Urban Food Needs in Regional Development, Puno, Peru." In C. A. Smith, ed., *Regional Analysis: Economic Systems, Vol. 1.* New York: Academic Press.

Appleby, G. 1981. "Las Transformaciones del Sistema de Mercados en Puno, 1890–1869." *Analisis* 8 (9): 55–71.

Appleby, G. 1985. "Marketplace Development in the Gambia River Basin." In S. Plattner, ed., *Markets and Marketing: Monographs in Economic Anthropology, No. 4.* Boston: University Press of America.

Appleby, G. 1988. "Using Central-Place Methods to Evaluate Agricultural Development Projects." *Practicing Anthropology* 10 (3–4): 24–26.

Appleby, G. 1993. "Using Urban Commercial Counts and Marketplace Censuses to Appraise Agricultural Development Projects." In K. Kumar, ed., *Rapid Appraisal Methods.* Washington, D.C.: World Bank.

Areeparampil, M. 1989. "Industries, Mines and Dispossession of Indigenous Peoples: The Case of Chotanagpur." In W. Fernandes and E. Ganguly Thukral, eds., *Development, Displacement and Rehabilitation: Issues for a National Debate.* New Delhi: Indian Social Institute.

Areeparampil, M. 1996. *Tribals of Jharkhand: Victims of Development.* New Delhi: Indian Social Institute.

Armstrong, A. 1991. "Refugees and Agricultural Development in Tanzania." In J. A. Mollet, ed., *Migrants in Agricultural Development.* London: MacMillan Academic and Professional Ltd.

Arnould, E. 1990. "Changing the Terms of Rural Development: Collaborative Research in Cultural Ecology in the Sahel." *Human Organisation* 49: 339–354.

Asch, M. 1982. "Dene Self-Determination and the Study of Hunter-Gatherers in the Modern World." In E. Leacock and R. Lee, eds.,

Politics and History in Band Societies. Cambridge (UK): Cambridge University Press.

Asfaha, S. and Lassailly-Jacob, V. 1994. "Analyse Critique d'une Politique d'Assistance aux Réfugiés: Les Sites d'Installations Agricoles Ouverts pour les Réfugiés Erythréens au Soudan." *Refuge: Canada's Periodical on Refugees* 14 (1): 11–19.

Asian Development Bank. 1998. *Handbook on Resettlement: A Guide to Good Practice.* Manila: Asian Development Bank.

Atteslander, P. 1995a. "Social Destabilisation and the Development of Early Warning Systems." *International Journal of Sociology and Social Policy* 15 (8, 9 and 10): 9–23.

Atteslander, P. 1995b. "Global Development and the Meaning of Local Culture – Reflections on Structural Anomie." *International Journal of Sociology and Social Policy* 15 (8,9 and 10): 221–242.

Baboo, B. 1992. *Technology and Social Transformation: The Case of the Hirakud Multi-Purpose Dam in Orissa.* New Delhi: Concept Publishing.

Bagadion, B. and Korten, F. 1991. "Developing Irrigators' Organisations: A Learning Process Approach." In M. M. Cernea, ed., *Putting People First: Sociological Variables in Rural Development.* Second Edition. New York: Oxford University Press/World Bank.

Bank of Athens. 1930. *Bulletin,* December, Athens.

Bascom, J. 1990. "Border Pastoralism in Eastern Sudan." *The Geographical Review* 80: 416–430.

Bartolome, L., de Wet, C., and Mander, H. 1999. *Displacement, Resettlement, Rehabilitation, Reparation and Development,* Draft Paper. Cape Town: World Commission on Dams.

Bascom, J. 1992. "Reconstructing Households and Reconstructing Home Areas: the Case of Returning Eritreans." Paper presented at United Nations Research Institute for Social Development (UNRISD) Symposium for the Horn of Africa on the Social and Economic Aspects of Mass Voluntary Return Movements of Refugees, Addis Ababa, Ethiopia, September.

Bassett, T. 1993. "Land Use Conflicts in Pastoral Development in Northern Côte d'Ivoire." In T. Bassett and D. Crummey, eds., *Land in African Agrarian Systems.* Madison, Wisconsin: University of Wisconsin Press.

Basu, M. 1994. "The Basic Needs Approach in Displacement Situations." *Mainstream* July.

Bates, R. H. 1989. *Beyond the Miracle of the Market: the Political Economy of Agrarian Development in Kenya.* Cambridge (UK): Cambridge University Press.

Baxi, U. 1983. "Towards a Design of Countervailing People's Power in Forest Law and Administration: Agendum for Democratic Law-Making." In W. Fernandes and S. Kulkarni, eds., *Towards a New Forest Policy: People's Rights and Environmental Needs.* New Delhi: Indian Social Institute.

Beck, U. 1990. "On the Way Towards an Industrial Society at Risk: An Outline of an Argument." *International Journal of Political Economy* 20: 51–69.

Beck, U. 1992. *Risk Society: Towards a New Modernity.* New Delhi: Sage Publications.

Behura, N. K. and Nayak, P. K. 1993. "Involuntary Displacement and the Changing Frontiers of Kinship: A Study of Resettlement in Orissa." In M. M. Cernea and S. E. Guggenheim, eds., *Anthropological Approaches to Resettlement, Policy, Practice, and Theory.* Boulder, Colorado: Westview Press.

Berkes, F. 1989. "Cooperation from the Perspective of Human Ecology." In F. Berkes, ed., *Common Property Resources: Ecology and Community-Based Sustainable Development.* London: Belhaven Press.

Berkes, F., Feeny, D., McCay, B. J., and Acheson, J. M. 1989. "The Benefit of the Commons." *Nature* 340, July.

Berkes, F. and Taghi Farvar, M. 1989. "Introduction and Overview." In F. Berkes, ed. *Common Property Resources: Ecology and Community-Based Sustainable Development.* London: Belhaven Press.

Berman, T. 1988. "For the Taking: The Garrison Dam and the Tribal Taking Area." *Cultural Survival Quarterly* 5–9 (12).

Berry, S. 1988. "Concentration without Privatization? Some Consequences of Changing Patterns of Rural Land Control in Africa." In R. Downs and S. Reyna, eds. *Land and Society in Contemporary Africa.* Hanover, New Hampshire: University Press of New England for the University of New Hampshire.

Berterame, S. and Magni, L. 1988. "Local Markets and Exchanges in the Beles Valley Resettlement Area." Paper presented at Workshop on Famine Experiences and Resettlement in Ethiopia, Addis Ababa University, Institute of Development Research, December 29–30.

Betru Haile and Wolde-Selassie Abbute. 1995. "Diagnostic Study on Household Food Security in Beles Valley." Report, CISP, Addis Ababa.

Bhanot, R. and Singh, M. 1992. "The Oustees of Pond Dam: Their Search for a Home." In E. Ganguly Thukral, ed., *Big Dams, Displaced People: Rivers of Sorrow, Rivers of Change.* New Delhi: Sage Publications.

Bjonnes, I.. 1983. "Socio-Economic Analysis of Effects from the Kulekhani Hydroelectric Project, Nepal." Report, Department of Geography, University of Oslo.

Blaikie, P. et.al. 1985. *The Management and Use of Common Property Resources in Tamil Nadu*. London: Overseas Development Administration.

Bonner, R. 1993. *At the Hand of Man: Peril and Hope for Africa's Wildlife*. New York: Alfred Knopf.

Borup, J. H., Gallego, D. T., and Heffernan, P. G. 1979. "Relocation and its Effect on Mortality." *The Gerontologist* 19 (2): 135–140.

Brain, J. 1976. "Less than Second-Class: Women on Rural Settlement Schemes in Tanzania." In N. Hafkin and E. Bay, eds., *Women in Africa*. Stanford, California: Stanford University Press.

Brauen, M. and Kvaerne, P., eds. 1977. *Tibetan Studies*. Zurich: Volkerkundemuseum der Universitat Zurich.

Brenchin, S. R., West, P., Harzmon, D., and Kutay, K. 1991. "Resident Peoples and Restricted Areas: A Framework for Inquiry." In P. West and S. R. Brechin, eds., *Resident Peoples and National Parks: Social Dimensions in International Conservation*. Tucson, Arizona: University of Arizona Press.

Brennan, F. 1995. "Parliamentary Responses to the Mabo Decision." In M. A. Stephenson, ed., *Mabo: The Native Title Legislation: A Legislative Response to the High Court Decision*. St. Lucia: Queensland University Press.

Brett, E. A. 1994. "Rebuilding Organisation Capacity in Uganda under the National Resistance Movement." *Journal of Modern African Studies* Vol. 32, No. 1.

Brittain, V. 1992. "UN Aid Helps UNITA Defy Peace Terms." *The Guardian* 23 March, London.

Brokensha, D. and Scudder, T. 1968. "Resettlement." In N. Rubin and W. M. Warren, eds., *Dams in Africa: an Interdisciplinary Study of Man-Made Lakes in Africa*. London: Frank Cass and Co. Ltd.

Bromley, D. W. and Chapagain, D. P. 1984. "The Village against the Centre: Resource Depletion in South Asia." *American Journal of Agricultural Economics* 66: 869–873.

Bromley, D. W. 1985. "Resources and Economic Development: An Institutionalist Perspective." *Journal of Economic Issues* XIX (3).

Bromley, D. W. 1989. *Economic interests and Institutions*. London: Blackwell.

Brown, F. and Stone, T. 1989. "Using Satellite Photography for Grassroots Development in Amazonia." *Cultural Survival Quarterly* 13: 35–38.

Brubaker, E. R. 1975. "Free Ride, Free Revelation, or Golden Rule?" *The Journal of Law and Economics* LXVII (1): 153.

Bruce, J. 1988. "A Perspective on Indigenous Land Tenure Systems and Land Concentration." In R. Downs and S. Reyna, eds., *Land and Society in Contemporary Africa*. Hanover, New Hampshire: University Press of New England for the University of New Hampshire.

Bruce, J. 1993. "Do Indigenous Tenure Systems Constrain Agricultural Development?" In T. Bassett and D. Crummey, eds., *Land in African Agrarian Systems*. Madison, Wisconsin: University of Wisconsin Press.

Brugge, D. M. 1993. "The Relocation of Navajos From the Hopi Partitioned Lands." In J. Piper, ed., *Papers from the Third, Fourth and Sixth Navajo Studies Conferences*. Window Rock, Arizona: Navajo Nation Historic Preservation Department.

Brunelli, G. 1993. "The Amerindians Five Hundred Years after Columbus." In W. Fernandes, ed., *The Indigenous Question: Search for An Identity*. New Delhi: Indian Social Institute.

Buchanan-Smith, M. and Maxwell, S., eds. 1994. "Linking Relief and Development." *Institute of Development Studies Bulletin* 25 (4).

Cernea, M. M. 1986. "Involuntary Resettlement in Bank-Assisted Projects: A Review of the Application of Bank Policies and Procedures in FY 1979–1985 Projects." Processed. Agriculture and Rural Development Department, World Bank, Washington, D.C.

Cernea, M. M. 1988. "Involuntary Resettlement in Development Projects: Policy Guidelines in World Bank Assisted Projects." World Bank Technical Paper No. 80, Washington D.C.

Cernea, M. M. 1990a. "Poverty Risks from Population Displacement in Water Resources Development." Development Discussion Paper No. 355, Harvard University Institute for International Development, Cambridge, Massachusetts.

Cernea, M. M. 1990b. "From Unused Social Science to Policy Formulation: The Case of Populations Resettlement." Development Discussion Paper No. 342. Harvard University Institute for International Development, Cambridge, Massachusetts.

Cernea, M. M. 1991. "The Social Actors of Participatory Afforestation Strategies." In M. M. Cernea, ed., *Putting People First: Sociological Variables in Rural Development*. Second Edition. New York: Oxford University Press/World Bank.

Cernea, M. M. 1993a, "Anthropological and Sociological Research for Policy Development on Population Resettlement." In M. M. Cernea and S. E. Guggenheim, eds., *Anthropological Approaches to*

Resettlement: Policy, Practice, and Theory. Boulder, Colorado: Westview Press.

Cernea, M. M. 1993b. "Disaster-Related Refugee Flows and Development-Caused Population Displacement." In M. M. Cernea and S. E. Guggenheim, eds., *Anthropological Approaches to Resettlement: Policy, Practice, and Theory*. Boulder, Colorado: Westview Press.

Cernea, M. M. 1993c. "The Urban Environment and Population Relocation." World Bank Discussion Paper No. 152, Washington, D.C.

Cernea, M. M. 1994. "Population Resettlement and Development." *Finance and Development* September.

Cernea, M. M. 1995a. "Social Integration and Population Displacement: The Contribution of Social Science." *International Social Science Journal* 143 (1): 91–112.

Cernea, M. M. 1995b. "Understanding and Preventing Impoverishment from Displacement." Keynote Opening Address, International Conference on Development-Induced Displacement and Impoverishment, Oxford, January 3-7. *Journal of Refugee Studies* 8 (3): 245–264.

Cernea, M. M. 1996a. "Bridging the Research Divide: Studying Refugees and Development Oustees" In T. Allen, ed., *In Search for Cool Ground: War, Flight and Homecoming in Northeast Africa*. London: James Currey.

Cernea, M. M. 1996b. "Public Policy Responses to Development-Induced Population Displacements." *Economic and Political Weekly* 31: 1515-1523.

Cernea, M. M. 1996c. "Eight Main Risks: Impoverishment and Social Justice in Resettlement." Paper, World Bank Environment Department, Washington D.C.

Cernea, M. M. 1996d. "Understanding and Preventing Impoverishment from Displacement." In C. McDowell, ed., *Understanding Impoverishment: The Consequences of Development-Induced Displacement*. Oxford: Berghahn Books.

Cernea, M. M. 1997a. "Hydropower Dams and Social Impacts: A Sociological Perspective." Paper, Social Assessment Series No. 44, World Bank Environment Department, Washington, D.C.

Cernea, M. M. 1997b. "African Involuntary Population Resettlement in a Global Context." Paper, Social Assessment Series No. 45, World Bank Environment Department, Washington, D.C.

Cernea, M. M. 1997c. "The Risks and Reconstruction Model for Resettling Displaced Populations." *World Development* 25 (10): 1569–1588.

Cernea, M. M. 1998. "Impoverishment or Social Justice? A Model for Planning Resettlement." In H. M. Mathur and D. Marsden, eds., *Development Projects and Impoverishment Risks: Resettling Project-Affected People in India*. New Delhi: Oxford University Press.

Cernea, M. M. 1999a. "Economic Analysis and Knowledge for Resettlement: A Sociologist's View." In M. M. Cernea, ed., *The Economics of Involuntary Resettlement: Questions and Challenges*. Washington, D.C.: World Bank.

Cernea, M. M. 1999b. "Introduction: Mutual Reinforcement: Linking Economic and Social Knowledge about Resettlement." In M. M. Cernea, ed., *The Economics of Involuntary Resettlement: Questions and Challenges*. Washington, D.C.: World Bank.

Cernea, M. M. 1999c. "Development's Painful Social Costs. Introductory Study." In S. Parasuraman, *The Development Dilemma: Displacement in India*. The Hague: Institute of Social Studies.

Cernea, M. M. and Guggenheim, S.E., eds. 1993. *Anthropological Approaches to Resettlement: Policy, Practice, and Theory*. Boulder, Colorado: Westview Press.

Cernea, M. M. and Kudat, A., eds. 1997. "Social Assessments for Better Development: Case Studies in Russia and Central Asia." ESD Studies and Monographs Series No. 18, World Bank, Washington, D.C.

Chad, Ministry of Rural Development. 1996. "Systeme D'Alerte Precoce No. 121, Situation Fin Juin 1996." AEDS/SAP, N'Djavena.

Chambers, R. 1969. *Settlement Schemes in Tropical Africa*. London: Routledge and Kegan Paul.

Chambers, R. 1970. "Postscript and Discussion." In R. Chambers, ed., *The Volta Resettlement Experience*. New York: Praeger/Volta River Authority, Accra and University of Science and Technology, Kumasi.

Chambers, R. and Morris, J., eds. 1973. *Mwea, and Irrigated Rice Settlement in Kenya*. Munich: Weltforum Verlag.

Charest, P. 1982. "Hydroelectric Dam Construction and the Foraging Activities of Eastern Quebec Montagnais." In E. Leacock and R. Lee, eds., *Politics and History in Band Societies*. Cambridge (UK): Cambridge University Press.

Chernela, J. 1988. "Potential Impacts of a Proposed Amazon Hydroelectric Project." *Cultural Survival Quarterly* 12: 20–24.

Cheung, S. N. S. 1970. "The Structure of a Contract and the Theory on a Non-Exclusive Resource." *The Journal of Law and Economics* XIII (1).

Chopra, K., Kadekodi, G. K., and Nurty, M. N. 1989. "People's Participation and Common Property Resources." *Economic and Political Weekly* XXIV (51 and 52) December 23–30.

Christensen, H. 1985. "Refugees and Pioneers: History and Field Study of a Burundian Settlement in Tanzania." United Nations Research Institute for Social Development (UNRISD), Geneva.

Circiacy-Wantrup, S. V. 1971. "The Economics of Environmental Policy." *Land Economics* 47: 43.

Circiacy-Wantrup, S. V. and Bishop, R. C. 1975. "Common Property as a Concept in Natural Resources Policy." *Natural Resource Journal* 15: 713–727.

Cissé, Y., Camara, A., Diallo, A., and Sanogo, Z. 1989. *Etude Socio-Economique en Bordure de la Forêt Classée du Sounsan.* Bamako: Institut d'Economie Rurale.

Clark, L. 1987. "Key Issues in Post-Emergency Refugee Assistance in Eastern and Southern Africa," Volume III, Refugee Policy Group, Washington, D.C.

Clark, L. and Stein, B. 1985. "Older Refugee Settlements in Africa: A Final Report." Refugee Policy Group, Washington D.C.

Coal India Ltd. (CIL).1994. "Resettlement and Rehabilitation Policy of Coal India Ltd." CIL, Calcutta.

Coffeen, W. 1972. "The Effects of the Central Arizona Project on the Fort McDowell Indian Community." *Ethnohistory* 19: 345–377.

Cohen, R. and Deng, F. 1998. *Masses in Flight: The Global Crisis of Internal Displacement.* Washington, D.C.: Brookings Institute Press.

Cohen, R. and Deng, F., eds. 1998. *The Forsaken People: Case Studies of the Internally Displaced.* Washington, D.C.: Brookings Institute Press.

Colchester, M., ed. 1999. "Sharing Power: Dams, Indigenous Peoples and Ethnic Minorities." Draft Thematic Paper, World Commission on Dams, Cape Town, South Africa.

Coles, G. 1985. "Voluntary Repatriation: a Background Study." Prepared for the Roundtable on Voluntary Repatriation, United Nations High Commissioner for Refugees (UNHCR)/International Institute of Humanitarian Law (IIHL), San Remo, July 16–19.

Colletta, N. J., Balachander, J., and Xioyan Liang. 1996. "The Condition of Young Children in Sub-Saharan Africa: The Covergence of Health, Nutrition and Early Education." World Bank Technical Paper No.326, Washington, D.C.

Colletta, N. J., Kostner, M., and Wiederhofer, I. 1996. "War-to-Peace Transition in Sub-Saharan Africa: Lessons from the Horn, the Heart, and the Cape." World Bank Technical Department, Africa Region, Washington, D.C.

Colson, E. 1971. *The Social Consequences of Resettlement.* Manchester (UK): Manchester University Press.

Colson, E. 1991. "Coping in Adversity." Paper presented at the Gwendolyn Carter Lectures, Conference on Involuntary Migration and Resettlement in Africa, University of Florida, March 21–23.

Comeau, P. and Santin, A. 1990. *The First Canadians: A Profile of Canada's Native People Today.* Toronto: James Lorrimer and Company.

Commission for Eritrean Refugee Affairs (CERA)/Government of Eritrea. 1995. "PROFERI Phase One: Operational Plan." Addis Ababa, May.

Commission for Eritrean Refugee Affairs (CERA). 1996 "The Establishment of Food Aid Monetisation System." Paper presented at Workshop on Food Aid Monetisation, Asmara, February.

Cook, C., ed. 1993. *Involuntary Resettlement in Africa.* Washington, D.C.: World Bank.

Costa-Pierce, B.A. 1996. "Sustainable Reservoir Fisheries: An Ecosystems Approach." Draft paper. Processed.

Cox, D. and Jimenez, E. 1990 "Achieving Social Objectives Through Private Transfers: A Review." *World Bank Research Observer* 5 (201).

Cox, S. J. B. 1985. "No Tragedy of the Commons." *Environmental Ethics* 7: 49.

Crisp, J. 1996. "From Social Disarticulation to Social Reconstruction." Paper presented at the 2nd International Conference on Displacement and Resettlement, Oxford, September.

Croll, E. and Parkin, D., eds. 1993. *Bush Base: Forest Farm – Culture, Environment and Development.* London and New York: Routledge.

Crozier, M. 1964. *Bureaucratic Phenomenon.* London: Tavistock.

Daley, P. 1989. "Refugees and Under-Development in Africa: The Case of Burundi Refugees in Tanzania." Unpublished D.Phil. thesis submitted, Faculty of Anthropology and Geography, University of Oxford.

Dalua, A.K. 1991. *Irrigation in Orissa.* Orissa: Water and Land Management Institute.

Damodaran, A. 1988. "Morphology of Grazing and its Crisis in Sedentary Communities." *Economic and Political Weekly* XXIII (13) March.

Darning, A.B. 1989. "Action at the Grassroots: Fighting Poverty and Environmental Decline." Worldwatch Paper No. 88, Washington, D.C.

Das, V. 1996. "Dislocation and Rehabilitation: Defining a Field." *Economic and Political Weekly* 31 (24) June: 1510.

Davis Langodon and Seah International. 1996. *Asia Pacific Construction Costs Handbook*. London: E. and F.N. Spon.

De Boschere, G. 1967. *Autopsy de la Colonisation*. Paris: Aubin Michel.

Deegan, C. 1995. "The Narmada in Myth and History." In W. Fisher, ed., *Toward Sustainable Development? Struggling over India's Narmada River*. Armonk, New York: M.E. Sharpe.

Demsetz, H. 1964. "The Exchange and Enforcement of Property Rights." *Journal of Law and Economics*, 7: 11-28.

Demsetz, H. 1972. "Towards a Theory of Property Right." *American Economic Review* LVII (2).

Deng, F. and Zartman, W. 1991. *Conflict Resolution in Africa*. Washington, D.C.: Brookings Institution.

Dessalegn Rahmato 1988. "Settlement and Resettlement in Metekel, Western Ethiopia." *Africa – Dell'Instituto Italo-Africano* XLIII: 211-242.

Dessalegn Rahmato .1989. "Rural Resettlement in Post-Revolutionary Ethiopia: Problems and Prospects." In *Report of Conference Proceedings Vol. II*, Conference on Population Issues in Ethiopia's National Development, Addis Ababa.

De Waal, A. 1987. *Famine That Kills: Darfur, Sudan 1984-1985*. Oxford: Oxford University Press.

De Waal, A. 1988. "Refugees and the Creation of Famine: the Case of Dar Masalit, Sudan." *Journal of Refugee Studies* 1 (2): 127-140.

De Waal, A. 1990. *Famine Survival Strategies in Wollo, Tigray and Eritrea: A Review of the Literature*. Oxford: Oxfam .

De Wet, C. 1988. "Stress and Environmental Change in the Analysis of Community Relocation." *Human Organisation* 47 (2).

De Wet, C. 1993. "A Spatial Analysis of Involuntary Community Relocation: A South African Case Study." In M. M. Cernea and S. E. Guggenheim, eds., *Anthropological Approaches to Resettlement: Policy, Practice and Theory*. Boulder, Colorado: Westview Press.

De Wet, C. 1995. *Moving Together Drifting Apart: Betterment Planning and Villagisation in a South African Homeland*. Johannesburg: Witwatersrand University Press.

De Wilde, J. C. 1967. *Experiences with Agricultural Development in Tropical Africa, Volume 2: The Case Studies*. Baltimore, Maryland: Johns Hopkins University Press.

Dhagamwar, V. 1989. "Rehabilitation: Policy and Institutional Changes Required." In W. Fernandes and E. Ganguly Thukral, eds., *Development, Displacement and Rehabilitation*. New Delhi: Indian Social Institute.

Dhagamwar, V. 1992. "A Long Way from Home: the Search for a Rehabilitation Policy." In E. Ganguly Thukral, ed., *Big Dams,*

Displaced People: Rivers of Sorrow Rivers of Change. New Delhi: Sage Publications.

Dhagamwar, V. 1997. "The Land Acquisition Act: High Time for Changes." In W. Fernandes and V. Paranjpye, eds., *Rehabilitation Policy and Law in India: A Right to Livelihood.* New Delhi: Indian Social Institute.

Dhagamwar, V., Ganguly Thukral, E., and Singh, M. 1995. "The Sardar Sarovar Project: A Study in Sustainable Development?" In W. Fisher, ed., *Toward Sustainable Development? Struggling over India's Narmada River.* Armonk, New York: M.E. Sharpe.

Dharmadhikary, S. 1995. "Hydropower at Sardar Sarovar: Is It Necessary, Justified and Affordable?" In W. Fisher, ed., *Toward Sustainable Development? Struggling over India's Narmada River.* Armonk, New York: M.E. Sharpe.

Diarra, T., Halimata Konaté, S., and Koenig, K. 1992. "Rapport de Site: Yanfolila, Mali." Report to the Institute for Development Anthropology for Land Settlement Review.

Diarra, T., Koenig, D., Koné, Y.F., and Maiga Fatoumata Maiga. 1995. *Reinstallation et Développement dans la Zone du Barrage de Manantali.* Bamako: Institut des Sciences Humaines.

Diece, P. and Viezzoli, C., eds. 1992. *Resettlement and Rural Development in Ethiopia: Social and Economic Research, Training and Technical Assistance in the Beles Valley.* Milan: Frnco Angeli.

Diece, P. and Wolde-Selassie Abutte. 1992. "The Planning of Home-Gardening Activities in the Beles Valley Resettlement Villages." In P. Diece and C. Viezzoli, eds., *Resettlement and Rural Development in Ethiopia: Social and Economic Research, Training and Technical Assistance in the Beles Valley.* Milan: Franco Angeli.

Dione, J. 1987. "Production et Transactions Céréalières des Producteurs Agricoles Campagne 1985–86." MSU/CESA, Bamako.

Dorfman, R. 1974. "The Technical Basis for Decision Making," In E. T. Haefele, ed., "The Governance of Common Property Resources." Paper presented at forum conducted by Resources for the Future Inc., Washington, D.C., January 21–22.

Downing, T. E. 1996a. "Mitigating Social Impoverishment when People are Involuntarily Displaced." In C. McDowell, ed., *Understanding Impoverishment: The Consequences of Development-Induced Displacement.* Oxford: Berghahn Books.

Downing, T. E. 1996b. Personal communication with M. M. Cernea.

Downing, T. 1998. "Protecting the Widow's Mite: Designing Local Environmental Risk Insurance." Paper presented at the Annual Society for Applied Anthropology Meeting, San Jose, Puerto Rico.

Downs, R. and Reyna, S. eds. *Land and Society in Contemporary Africa*. Hanover, New Hampshire: University Press of New England for the University of New Hampshire.

Drabek, T. E. 1987. *Human Systems Responses to Disasters: An Inventory of Sociological Findings*. New York and Berlin: Springer Verlag.

D'Souza, V. S. 1990. *Development Planning and Structural Inequalities: The Response of the Underprivileged*. New Delhi: Sage Publications.

Duffield, M. 1992. "The Emergence of Two-Tier Welfare in Africa: Marginalisation or an Opportunity for Reform." *Public Administration and Development* 12.

Duffield, M. 1993. "NGOs, Disaster Relief and Asset Transfer in the Horn: Political Survival in a Permanent Emergency." *Development and Change* 24.

Dwivedi, R. 1997. "Why Some People Resist and Others Do Not: Local Perceptions and Actions Over Displacement Risks on the Sardar Sarovar." Working Paper Series 265, Institute of Social Studies, The Hague.

Dyson-Hudson, N. 1991. "Pastoral Production Systems and Livestock Development Projects: An East African Perspective." In M. M. Cernea, ed., *Putting People First: Sociological Variables in Rural Development*. Second edition. New York: Oxford University Press for the World Bank.

Eddy, J. 1992. "Recognition, Reconciliation and History." In F. Brennan, ed., *Reconciling Our Differences: A Christian Approach to Recognizing Aboriginal Land Rights*. Australia: Aurora Books.

Eggerston, T. 1990. *Economic Behaviour and Institutions*. Cambridge (UK): Cambridge University Press.

Elias Negasa 1992. "The Ill-Conceived Settlement Programme and its Consequences." Paper presented at Ethiopian Rehabilitation Campaign Donors' Conference, Addis Ababa, May 25–26.

Entitad Binacional Yacyretá. 1994. "Politica para Oleros Margen Paraguaya." Asuncion.

Entitad Binacional Yacyretá. 1995. "Politica para Oleros Margen Argentina." Buenos Aires.

Eriksen, J. H. 1999. "Economic Planning for Social Processes: Comparing Voluntary and Involuntary Resettlement Projects." In M. M. Cernea, ed., *The Economics of Involuntary Resettlement: Questions and Challenges*. Washington, D.C.: World Bank.

Eudey, A. 1988. "Another Defeat for the Nam Choan Dam, Thailand." *Cultural Survival Quarterly* 12: 13–16.

Fahim, H. 1983. *Egyptians Nubians: Resettlement and Years of Coping*. Salt Lake City, Utah: University of Utah Press.

Feeney, P. 1995. "Displacement and Rights of Women." Oxfam Policy Department, Oxford University.

Feeney, P. 1998. "Global Benefits, Local Costs: Expulsion from the Kibale Forest." In P. Feeney, ed., *Accountable Aid: Local Participation in Major Projects*. Oxford: Oxfam Publishing.

Feit, H. 1982. "The Future of Hunters within Nation-States: Anthropology and the James Bay Cree." In E. Leacock and R. Lee, eds., *Politics and History in Band Societies*. Cambridge (UK): Cambridge University Press.

Fernandes, W. 1991. "Power and Powerlessness: Development Projects and Displacement of Tribals." *Social Action* 41 (3): 243–270.

Fernandes, W., ed. 1993. *The Indigenous Question: Search for an Identity*. New Delhi: Indian Social Institute.

Fernandes, W. 1994. *Development-Induced Displacement in the Tribal Areas of Eastern India*. Mimeo, Indian Social Institute, New Delhi.

Fernandes, W. 1995. "An Activist Process Around the Draft National Rehabilitation Policy." *Social Action* 45, July-Sept.: 277-298.

Fernandes, W. and Ganguly Thukral, E., eds. 1989. *Development, Displacement and Rehabilitation*. New Delhi: Indian Social Institute.

Fernandes Serra, M.T. 1993. "Resettlement Planning in the Brazilian Power Sector: Recent Changes in Approach." In M. M. Cernea and S. E. Guggenheim, eds., *Anthropological Approaches to Resettlement: Policy, Practice and Theory*. San Francisco and Oxford: Westview Press.

Fernandes, W., Das, J.C., and Rao, S. 1989. "Displacement and Rehabilitation: an Estimate of Extent and Prospects." In W. Fernandes and E. Ganguly Thukral, eds., *Development, Displacement and Rehabilitation*. New Delhi: Indian Social Institute.

Fernandes, W., Menon, G., and Viegas, P. 1988. *Forests, Environment and Tribal Economy: Deforestation, Impoverishment and Marginalisation in Orissa*. New Delhi: Indian Social Institute.

Fernandes, W. and Paranjpye, V., eds. 1997. *Rehabilitation Policy and Law in India: A Right to Livelihood*, New Delhi: Indian Social Institute and Pune: Econet.

Fernandes, W. and Raj, A.S. 1992. *Development, Displacement and Rehabilitation in the Tribal Areas of Orissa*. New Delhi: Indian Social Institute.

Fernandez, A.P. 1990. "No Dam is an Island." In *Workshop on Persons Displaced by Development Projects*, ISECS and MYRADA, Bangalore.

Ferraro, K. F. 1982. "The Health Consequences of Relocation Among the Aged in the Community." *Journal of Gerontology* 38 (1): 90–96.

Fisher, W. 1995. "Development and Resistance in the Narmada Valley." W. Fisher, ed., *Toward Sustainable Development? Struggling over India's Narmada River*. Armonk, New York: M.E. Sharpe.

Flammang, R., van Leeuwen, J-H. and Appleby, G. 1988. "Informal Financial Markets: Zaire and Senegal." Private Enterprise Development Support Project II, Agency for International Development, Bureau for Private Enterprise, Washington, D.C..

Fofana, M., Halimata Konaté, S., and Koenig, D. 1992. "Rapport de Site: Selingue, Mali." Report to the Institute for Development Anthropology for Land Settlement Review.

Food and Agriculture Organisation. 1996. "Study on the Nutritional Situation of Children in Armed Conflict: A Report." UN Food and Agriculture Organization (FAO), Rome.

Freeman, D. and Lowdermilk, M. 1991. "Middle-Level Farmer Organizations as Links between Farms and Central Irrigation Systems." In M. M. Cernea and S. E. Guggenheim, eds., *Anthropological Approaches to Resettlement: Policy, Practice, and Theory*. Boulder, Colorado: Westview Press.

Frimpong, K. 1995. "A Review of the Tribal Grazing Land Policy in Botswana." *PULA* 9 (1).

Funk, R. 1985. "The Mackenzie Valley Pipeline Inquiry in Retrospect." In W. Derman and S. Whiteford, eds., *Social Impact Analysis and Development Planning in the Third World*. Boulder, Colorado: Westview Press.

Fürntratt-Loep, E. F. 1995. *Quality of Life: From a Common People's Point of View*. Köln: PapyRosa Verlag.

Gallart-Nocetti, A. and Greaves Laine, P. 1992. "Sistema de Monitoreo de Los Reasentamientos de Los Projector Hidroelectricos Aguamilpa Y Zimapan (Mexico)." Paper presented at the International Workshop on Involuntary Resettlement in the Power Sector, Petrobras and World Bank, Santa Catarina, May 4-14.

Galtung, J. 1994. *Early Warnings: An Early Warning to the Early Warners*. Biel: Swiss Institute for Development.

Ganguly Thukral, E. 1992. "Introduction." In E. Ganguly Thukral, ed., *Big Dams, Displaced People: Rivers of Sorrow Rivers of Change*. New Delhi: Sage Publications.

Ganguly Thukral, E. and Singh, M. 1995. "Dams and the Displaced in India." In H. Mohan Mathur, ed., *Development, Displacement and Resettlement: Focus on Asian Experiences*. New Delhi: Vikas Publishing House.

Gasarasi, C.P. 1987. "The Tripartite Approach to the Resettlement and Integration of Rural Refugees in Tanzania." In Rogge J., ed., *Refugees: A Third World Dilemma*. Ottowa: Rowman and Littlefield.

Gaventa, J. 1980. *Power and Powerlessness: Quiescence and Rebellion in an Appalachian Valley.* Oxford: Clarendon.

Gellner, E. 1983. *Nations and Nationalism.* Oxford: Blackwells.

Ghukral, E.G. 1989. "Introduction." In W. Fernandes and E. Ganguly Thukral, eds., *Development, Displacement and Rehabilitation.* New Delhi: Indian Social Institute.

Gibbs, C.J.N. and Bromley, D.W. 1989. "Institutional Arrangements for Management of Rural Resources: Common Property Regimes." In F. Berkes, ed., *Common Property Resources: Ecology and Community-Based Sustainable Development.* London: Belhaven Press.

Gibson, D. 1993. "Involuntary Resettlement and Institutional Disjuncture." Paper presented at the Meetings of the American Anthropological Association, Washington, D.C. November 17–21.

Giddens, A. 1990. *The Consequences of Modernity.* Stanford, California: Stanford University Press.

Gill, M. S. 1995. "Resettlement and Rehabilitation in Maharashtra for the Sardar Sarovar Narmada Project." In W. Fisher, ed., *Toward Sustainable Development? Struggling over India's Narmada River.* Armonk, New York: M. E. Sharpe.

Gill, M. 1999. "Dams and Resettlement as Development: A Case for Building Good Practice." *Cultural Survival Quarterly* 23 (3): 57–63.

Goheen, M. 1988. "Land Accumulation and Local Control: The Manipulation of Symbols and Power in Nso, Cameroon." In R. Downs S. and Reyna, eds., *Land and Society in Contemporary Africa.* Hanover, New Hampshire: University Press of New England for the University of New Hampshire.

Goldstein, M. C. 1990. "China Briefing." Asia Society, New York.

Good, B. J. 1996. "Mental Health Consequences of Displacement and Resettlement." *Economic and Political Weekly* 31 (24), June 15: 1504-1508.

Goody, J. and Goody, E. 1995. "Food and Identities: Changing Patterns of Consumption in Ghana." *Cambridge Anthropology* 18 (3): 1.

Gopal, G. 1992. "Participation of Women in Involuntary Resettlement in Selected Asian Countries: Operational Issues and Guidelines." Unpublished manuscript.

Gordon, H. S. 1954. "The Economic Theory of a Common Property Resource: the Fishery." *Journal of Political Economy* 62 (2), April: 124–142.

Goumaa, H. M., Zerai, W., and Weldesus, M. 1995. "Alebu Returnee Site — A Contextual Assessment and a Community-Based Credit Scheme Design." Report prepared for ACORD, Eritrea.

Government of Andhra Pradesh. 1996. "Draft Policy for Resettlement and Rehabilitation of Displaced and Affected People of Andhra Pradesh State Highways Project." Hyderabad, July.

Government of Maharashtra. nd. "Report on the Task Force on Policy Framework: Institutional Arrangements and Implementation Strategy for Bombay Resettlement and Rehabilitation Strategy (Second Bombay Urban Transport Project)." Bombay.

Government of the Republic of Mali. 1987. "Code Domaniale et Foncier." Bamako.

Government of Sudan. 1974. "The Regulation of Asylum Act No. 45." *Sudan Gazette*, No. 1162, Legis. Supp. 183.

Government of Tamilnadu. 1995. "STOWAD Affected Persons Rehabilitation Action Plan." Tamilnadu.

Grayzel, J. 1988. "Land Tenure and Development in Mauritania: The Causes and Consequences of Legal Modernization in a National Context." In R. Downs and S. Reyna, eds., *Land and Society in Contemporary Africa*. Hanover, New Hampshire: University Press of New England for the University of New Hampshire.

Green, R. H. 1990. "The Land Question: Restitution, Reconciliation and Livelihood." Association of Agricultural Economists of Namibia, Windhoek.

Green, R. H. 1991. "O Pobreza, O Sector Familiar, E A Terra." Report prepared for Mozambique National Planning Directorate, Maputo.

Green, R. H. 1992. "Reconstrucao: The Road From Emergencia to Developmento – Livelihoods and Macroeconomics." Report prepared for Mozambique National Planning Directorate, Maputo.

Green, R. H. 1992a. "Toward Livelihoods, Services and Infrastructure: The Struggle to Overcome Absolute Poverty." Paper presented at African Leadership Forum, Annual Conference, Ota, Nigeria.

Green, R. H. 1992b. *Sound the Tocsin: The Third Horseman Mounts to Ride; Drought in Southern and South Africa 1991–1993.* Sussex: Institute of Development Studies.

Green, R. H. 1992d. "Southern Africa: that People May be Fed." *Food Policy* December.

Green, R. H. 1993a. "The Political Economy of Drought in Southern Africa, 1991–1993." *Health Policy and Planning* 8 (3).

Green, R. H. 1993b. "Calamities and Catastrophes: Extending the UN Response." *Third World Quarterly* 14 (1).

Green, R. H. 1994. "The Course of the Four Horsemen: Costs of War and its Aftermath in Sub-Saharan Africa." In J. Macrae and

A. Zwi, eds., *War and Hunger: Rethinking International Responses to Complex Emergencies*. London: Zed Books.

Green, R. H. 1995. "Post Famine Challenges and the Role of the International Community." In *Famine in Ethiopia: Learning from the Past to Prepare for the Future*, Government of Ethiopia, Relief and Rehabilitation Commission and the Economic Commission for Africa, Addis Ababa.

Green, R. H. 1995. "Internal Conflicts and Costs to African Development." *African Development Report* (African Development Bank).

Green, R. H. 1996. "Perspectivas de Paz, Reconstrucao, Reabilitacao, e Regionalismo." In M. Bravo, ed., *Angola A Transicao para a Paz, Reconciliacao e Desenvolvimento*. Lisbon: Hugin.

Green, R. H. and Mavie, M. 1994. "From Survival to Livelihood in Mozambique." *Institute of Development Studies Bulletin* 4 (25): 77–84.

Gu, J-G. 1996. "The Process of Rural Industrialization in China." Mimeo. Rural Community and Government, Shanghai Institute of Economic Development.

Guggenheim, S. E. 1993. "Peasants, Planners and Participation: Resettlement in Mexico." In M. M. Cernea and S. E. Guggenheim, eds., *Anthropological Approaches to Resettlement: Policy, Practice, and Theory*. Boulder, Colorado: Westview Press.

Guggenheim, S. E. 1994. *Involuntary Resettlement: An Annotated Reference Bibliography for Development Research*. Washington, D.C.: World Bank.

Guggenheim, S. E. and Cernea, M. M. 1993. "Anthropological Approaches to Involuntary Resettlement: Policy, Practice, and Theory" In M. M. Cernea and S. E. Guggenheim, eds., *Anthropological Approaches to Resettlement: Policy, Practice, and Theory*. Boulder, Colorado: Westview Press.

Guggenheim, S. E. and Spears, J. 1991. "Sociological and Environmental Dimensions of Social Forestry Projects." In M. M. Cernea, ed., *Putting People First: Sociological Variables in Rural Development*, Second Edition. New York: Oxford University Press for the World Bank.

Habte-Selassie, E. 1992. "Reintegration of Returnees: Challenges in Post-Liberation Eritrea." Paper presented at United Nations Research Institute for Social Development (UNRISD) Symposium for the Horn of Africa on the Social and Economic Aspects of Mass Voluntary Return Movements of Refugees, September, Addis Ababa.

Hackenberg, R. A. 1999. "Advancing Applied Anthropology, Victims of Globalization: is Economics the Instrument Needed to

Provide them a Share of the Wealth?" *Human Organization* 58 (4): 438–441.

Hagen, T. 1994. *Building Bridges to the Third World: Memories of Nepal: 1950–1992.* New Delhi: Book Faith India.

Hakim, R. 1995. "The Implications of Resettlement on Vasava Identity: A Study of a Community Displaced by the Sardar Sarovar (Narmada) Dam Project, India." Unpublished Ph.D. thesis, Cambridge University.

Hakim, R. 1996a. "Resettlement and Vasava Identity: Some Theoretical Issues." *Economic and Political Weekly of India* XXX1 (24): 1492–1499.

Hakim, R. 1996b. "Resettlement and Rehabilitation in the Context of Vasava Culture: Some Reflections." In J. Dreze, M. Samson, and S. Singh, eds., *The Dam and the Nation: Displacement and Resettlement in the Narmada Valley.* New Delhi: Oxford University Press.

Haimendorf, C. 1990. *The Renaissance of Tibetan Civilization.* Bombay: Oxford University Press.

Hall, A. 1994. "Grassroots Action for Resettlement Planning: Brazil and Beyond." *World Development* 22: 1793–1809.

Hall, R., Magassa, H., Ba, A., and Hodson, J. 1991. "Decentralization, Service Provision, and User Involvement: Local Level Options in the Republic of Mali." Draft report to the Interstate Committee for the Control of Drought in the Sahel (CILSS) and the Club du Sahel, February.

Hanlon, J. 1991. *Mozambique: Who Calls the Shots?* London: James Currey.

Hansen, A. 1990a. "Refugee Self-settlement *vs.* Settlement on Government Schemes: The Long-Term Consequences for Security, Integration and Economic Development of Angolan Refugees (1966–1989) in Zambia." Discussion Paper No. 17, United Nations Research Institute for Social Development (UNRISD), Geneva.

Hansen, A. 1990b. "Long-Term Consequences of Two Africa Refugee Settlement Strategies." Paper presented at the Meeting of Applied Anthropology, York, U.K.

Hansen, A. 1994. "Baseline Report on Food Security, Social, Demographic, Economic and Political Relationships and Conditions in Gash Setit," Deutsche Gesellschaft für Technische Zusammenarbeit (GTZ), April.

Hardin, G. 1968. "The Tragedy of the Commons." *Science* 162: 1243–1248.

Hardin, G. 1978. "Political Requirements for Preserving our Common Heritage." In H. P. Bokaw, ed., *Wildlife and America.* Washington, D.C.: Council on Environmental Quality.

Harrell-Bond, B. E. 1981. "The struggle for the Western Sahara," Part I: "The Background," No. 27; Part II: "The Legal/Political Milieu," No. 38; and Part III: "The People," No. 39. American Universities Field Staff.

Harrell-Bond, B. E. 1985. "Humanitarianism in a Strait-Jacket." *African Affairs* (334): 3–13.

Harrell-Bond, B. E. 1986. *Imposing Aid: Emergency Assistance to Refugees*. Oxford: Oxford University Press.

Harrell-Bond, B. E. 1988. "Repatriation: Under What Conditions is it the Most Desirable Solution for Refugees? An Agenda for Research." *African Studies Review* 32 (1): 41–69.

Harrell-Bond, B. E. 1996. "The Evolution of Solutions: a History of Refugee Policy." *Oxford International Review* 7 (3): 2–10.

Harrell-Bond, B. E., Howard, A., and Skinner, D. 1978. *Community Leadership and the Transformation of Freetown 1801–1976*. The Hague: Mouton.

Harris D. R., ed. *Human Ecology in Savanna Environments*. London: Academic Press.

Hays, J. 1999. "Participatory Development: Mitigating Against Impoverishment in Involuntary Resettlement." Dissertation, London School of Economics and Political Science, London.

Hendrie, B. 1991. "Prospects for Repatriation from Qala en Nahal, Refugee Settlement, Eastern State, Sudan." ACORD, December.

Heredero, J. M. 1985. "Technical Inputs and People's Participation." In W. Fernandes, ed., *Development With People: Experiments with Participation and Non-Formal Education*. New Delhi: Indian Social Institute.

Heredero, J. M. 1989. *Education for Development: Social Awareness, Organisation and Technological Innovation*. New Delhi: Manohar.

Hirsch, E. and O'Hanlon, M., eds. 1995. *The Anthropology of Landscape: Perspectives on Place and Space*. Oxford: Clarendon Press.

Hirschon, R. 1978. "Open Body/Closed Space: the Transformation of Female Sexuality." In S. Ardener, ed., *Defining Females: The Nature of Women in Society*. London: Croom Held.

Hirschon, R. 1985. "The Woman-Environment Relationship: Greek Cultural Values in an Urban Community." *Ekistics* (52): 15–21.

Hirschon, R. 1989/1998. *Heirs of the Greek Catastrophe: The Social Life of Asia Minor Refugees in Piraeus*. Oxford: Clarendon Press.

Hirschon, R. 1996. "The Compulsory Population Exchange of 1923 in Greece and Resettlement Issues." Paper presented at Second International Conference on Involuntary Displacement and Resettlement, University of Oxford, September.

Hitchcock, R. J., Ledger, Scudder, T., and Mentis, M. 1999. "Lesotho Highlands Water Project, General Review." Report No. 20, prepared for Lesotho Highland Development Authority.

Holborn, L. 1975. *Refugees: A Problem of Our Time: The Work of the United Nations High Commissioner for Refugees, 1951–1972*, Vol. I. Methchen, New Jersey: Scarecrow Press.

Horowitz, M. 1979. "The Sociology of Pastoralism and African Livestock Projects." AID Program Evaluation Discussion Paper No. 6, US Agency for International Development (USAID), Washington, D.C.

Horowitz, M. and Salem-Murdock, M. 1993. "Development-Induced Food Insecurity in the Middle Senegal Valley." *Geo-Journal* 30 (2): 179–184.

Horowitz M. *et al.* 1993. "Resettlement at Manantali, Mali: Short-Term Success, Long-Term Problems." In M. M. Cernea and S. E. Guggenheim, eds., *Anthropological Approaches to Resettlement: Policy, Practice and Theory.* Boulder, Colorado: Westview Press.

Human Rights Watch. 1997. "Uncertain Refuge: International Failures to Protect Refugees." *Human Rights Watch Report* 9 (1) (G).

Infrastructure Leasing and Financial Services Ltd. (ILFS). 1995. "The ILFS Environment and Social Report." Bombay, November.

Institut d'Economie Rurale (IER). 1984. "Récasement des Populations de Manantali: Etude Agro- Socio-Economique." Institut d'Economie Rurale, Bamako.

Jacob, J-P. and Lavigne Delville, P., eds. 1994. *Les Associations Paysannes en Afrique: Organisation et Dynamiques.* Paris: Karthala.

Jacobs, S. 1989. "Zimbabwe: State, Class and Gendered Models of Land Resettlement." In J. Parpart and K. Staudt, eds., *Women and the State in Africa.* Boulder, Colorado: Lynne Rienner.

Jayewardene, R. A. 1995. "Cause for Concern: Health and Resettlement." In H. M. Mathur, ed., *Development, Displacement and Resettlement: Focus on Asian Experiences.* New Delhi: Vikas Publishing House.

Jian-Guang, G. 1996. "The Process of Rural Industrialisation in China: Rural Community and Government." Shanghai Institute of Economic Development, Shanghai.

Jodha, N. S. 1986. "Common Property Resources and Rural Poor in Dry Regions of India." *Economic and Social Weekly* XXI (27), July: 1169.

Johns, K. 1996. "Report on the Resettlement Programme of the Aquamilpa Hydroelectric Project." Unpublished report.

Johnson, O. E. G. 1972. "Economic Analysis, the Legal Framework and Land Tenure Systems." *The Journal of Law and Economics* XV (1).

Johri, A. and Drishnakumar, N. 1991. "Poverty and Common Property Resources: A Case Study of the Rope Industry." *Economic and Political Weekly* XXVI (50), December.

Jolly, A. R., ed. 1996. *Journal of the Society for International Development: Revitalising African Development: An Agenda for Twenty-First Century Reform.* London: Sage Publications.

Joseph, J. 1998. "Evolving a Retrofit Economic Rehabilitation Policy Using Impoverishment Risks Analysis — Experience of Maharashtra Composite Irrigation Project III." In H. M. Mathur and D. Marsden, eds., 1998. *Development Projects and Impoverishment Risks: Resettling Project-Affected People in India.* Oxford: Oxford University Press.

Kaffel, H., Osman, R., and Sorensen, C. 1996. "1995 Annual Report (ERT3) Eritrean Rehabilitation Programme," Asmara.

Kamuanga, M. 1982. "Farm Level Study of the Rice Production System at the Office du Niger in Mali: An Economic Analysis." Ph.D. Dissertation, Department of Agricultural Economics, Michigan State University.

Kane, H. 1995. "The Hour of Departure: Forces that Create Refugees and Migrants." Worldwatch Institute, Washington, D.C.

Kaplan, S. and Garrick, B. J. 1981. "On the Quantitative Definition of Risk." *Risk Analysis* 1 (1): 11–27.

Kar, N. C. 1991. *Social, Economic and Cultural Impact of NALCO on Local Tribal in Damanjodi Project Area.* Bhubaneshwar: Nabakrushna Choudhury Centre for Development Studies.

Karadawi, A. 1995a. "Alebu's Returnees: On the Highway to Reintegration." ACORD, London.

Karadawi, A. 1995b. "A Historical Review of ACORD's Qala en Nahal Programme," ACORD, Addis Ababa.

Karanth, G. K. 1992. "Privatisation of Common Property Resources: Lessons from Rural Karnataka." *Economic and Political Weekly* XXVII (31 and 32), August: 1685.

Karve, I. and Nimbkar, J. 1969. "A Survey of People Displaced through the Koyna Dam." Deccan College, Pune.

Kesmanee, C. 1995. "Moving Hilltribe People to the Lowlands: The Resettlement Experience in Thailand." In H. M. Mathur and M. M. Cernea, eds., *Development, Displacement and Resettlement: Focus on Asian Experiences.* New Delhi: Vikas Publishing House.

Khan, A. 1995. "Planning and Development of Policy Issues of Large Scale Resettlement Programmes: A Case of Delhi Resettlement Policies." *Nagarlok* 27 (3): 60–79.

Khodka, C. 1999. *House Construction after Displacement under Nepal's Kali Gandaki Hydropower Dam Project.* Photostudy, KGEMU, Beltari, Nepal.

Kibreab, G. 1987. *Refugees and Development in Africa.* Trenton, New Jersey: The Red Sea Press.

Kibreab, G. 1989. "Local Settlements in Africa: A Misconceived Option?" *Journal of Refugee Studies,* Oxford, 2 (4): 468–490.

Kibreab, G. 1990. *Wage-Earning Refugee Settlements in Eastern and Central Sudan: from Subsistence to Wage Labour.* Trenton, New Jersey: The Red Sea Press.

Kibreab, G. 1991. "The State of the Art Review of Refugee Studies in Africa." Uppsala Papers in Economic History, Research Report No. 26, Department of Economic History, Uppsala University.

Kibreab, G. 1993. "Prospects for Repatriation of Eritrean Refugees from the Sudan and Responses of the International Donor Community." Paper presented at United Nations Research Institute for Social Development (UNRISD) Symposium for the Horn of Africa on the Social and Economic Aspects of Mass Voluntary Return Movements of Refugees, September, Addis Ababa.

Kibreab, G. 1994a. "The Myth of Dependency among Camp Refugees in Somalia, 1978–1989." *Journal of Refugee Studies* 6 (4): 321–349.

Kibreab, G. 1994b "Refugees in the Sudan: Unresolved Issues." In H. Adelman and J. Sorenson, eds., *African Refugees: Development Aid and Repatriation.* Boulder, Colorado: Westview Press.

Kibreab, G. 1995. "The African Refugee Regime with Emphasis on Northeastern Africa: The Emerging Issues." In H. Adelman, ed., *Legitimate and Illegitimate Discrimination: New Issues in Migration.* Toronto: York Lanes Press.

Kibreab, G. 1996a. "Proceedings of the Conference on Changing Patterns of Settlement and Resettlement in Southern Africa." Rhodes University, Grahamstown, Republic of South Africa.

Kibreab, G. 1996b. *People on the Edge in the Horn: Displacement, Land Use and the Environment.* London: James Currey.

Kibreab, G. 1996c. *Ready and Willing...but Still Waiting: Eritrean refugees in Sudan and the Dilemma of Return.* Uppsala: Institute of Life and Peace.

Kibreab, G. forthcoming-a. "Integration of Refugees in First Countries of Asylum: Past Experiences and Prospects for the 1990s." In R. Rogers and S. S. Russell, eds., *Towards a New Global Refugee System.* Under consideration for publication.

Kibreab, G. forthcoming-b. *Common Property Institutions and State Intervention in the Sudan 1889–1989.* Under consideration for publication.

Kitromilides, P. and Alexandris, A. 1984. "Ethnic Survival, Nationalism and Forced Migration: The Historical Demography of the Greek Community of Asia Minor at the Close of the Ottoman Empire." *Bulletin of the Centre for Asia Minor Studies* (Athens) (5): 9–44.

Kliot, N. and Mansfeld Y. 1994. "Resettling displaced people in north and south Cyprus." *Journal of Refugee Studies* 7 (4): 328–359.

Koenig, D. 1995. "Women and Resettlement." In R. Gallin and A. Ferguson, eds., *Women and International Development Annual, Vol. 4.* Boulder, Colorado: Westview Press.

Koenig, D. and Diarra, T. 1998. "Les Enjeux de la Politique Locale dans la Réinstallées et Hôtes dans la Zone du Barrage de Manantali." Autreport, Cahiers des sciences humaines nouvelle série numéro 5.

Kotari, S. 1995. "Developmental Displacement and Official Policies." *Lokayan Bulletin* 11 (5): 9–28.

Kudat, A. 1997. "Shaping the Future of Baku's Water Supply." In M. M. Cernea and A. Kudat, eds., *Social Assessments for Better Development: Case Studies in Russia and Central Asia.* ESD Studies and Monographs Series No18, World Bank, Washington, D.C.

Kuhlman, T. 1990. *Burden or Boon?: A Study of Eritrean Refugees in Sudan.* Amsterdam: VU University Press.

Lane, C. 1996. *Pastures Lost.* Nairobi: Initiative Publishers.

Lash, S. and Wynne, B. 1992. "Introduction." In U Beck, ed., *Risk Society: Towards a New Modernity.* New Delhi: Sage Publications.

Lassailly-Jacob, V. 1993. "Scheme-Settled Refugees and Agro-Ecological Impact on Host's Environment: A Field Report From an Agricultural Settlement in Zambia." Unpublished report.

Lassailly-Jacob, V. 1994a. "Government-Sponsored Agricultural Schemes for Involuntary Migrants in Africa: Some Key Obstacles to their Economic Viability" In H. Adelman and J. Sorenson, eds., *African Refugees: Development Aid and Repatriation,* Boulder, Colorado: Westview Press.

Lassailly-Jacob, V. 1994b. "Resettlers After 25 years: The Kossou Hydro-Electric Project, Ivory Coast." Paper presented at World Bank Sociological Group Seminar.

Lassailly-Jacob, V. 1996a. "Land-Based Strategies in Dam-Related Resettlement Programmes in Africa." In C. McDowell, ed., *Understanding Impoverishment: The Consequences of Development Induced Displacement.* Oxford: Berghan Books.

Lassailly-Jacob, V. 1999. "The Environmental Impacts of Refugee Settlement: A Case Study of an Agricultural Camp in Zambia."

In B. Baudot and W. R. Moomaw, eds., *People and their Planet: Searching for Balance*. London: Macmillan Press.

Lavigne Delville, P. 1999. "Harmonizing Formal Law and Customary Land Rights in French-Speaking West Africa." Issue Paper No.86, Drylands Programme, International Institute for Environment and Development, London.

League of Nations. 1926. *Greek Refugee Settlement*. Geneva: League of Nations.

Lee, L. 1986. "The Right to Compensation: Refugees and Countries of Asylum." *The American Journal of International Law* 80: 532–567.

Lesotho Highlands Water Project. 1986. "Feasibility Study." Maseru, April.

Libecap, G. 1989. *Contracting for Property Rights*. Cambridge (UK): Cambridge University Press.

Lino Grima, A. P. and Berkes, F. 1989. "Natural Resources: Access, Rights-to-Use and Management." In F. Berkes, ed., *Common Property Resources: Ecology and Community-Based Sustainable Development*. London: Belhaven Press.

Lloyd, F. W. 1977. "On the Checks to Population." In G. Hardin and J. Baden, eds., *Managing the Commons*. San Francisco: Freeman.

Loizos, P. 1981. *The Heart Grown Bitter: a Chronicle of Cypriot War Refugees*. Cambridge (UK): Cambridge University Press.

Low, S. and Altman, I., eds. 1992. *Place Attachment*. New York: Plenum Press.

Luhman, N. 1993. *Risk: A Sociological Theory*. New York: Aldin de Gruyter.

MaCann, J. C. 1995. *People of the Plow: an Agricultural History of Ethiopia, 1800–1990*. Madison, Wisconsin: The University of Wisconsin Press.

Macrae, J. and Forsythe, V. 1995. "Post-Conflict Rehabilitation: Preliminary Issues for Consideration by the Health Sector." Conflict and Health Series No. 2, London School of Hygiene and Tropical Medicine Public Health and Policy Publications, London.

Macrae, J. and Zwi, A. 1994. *War and Hunger: Rethinking International Responses to Complex Emergencies*. London: Zed Books.

Mahapatra, L. K. 1991. "Development for Whom? Depriving the Dispossessed Tribals." *Social Action* 41 (3): 271-287.

Mahapatra, L. K. 1994. *Tribal Development in India: Myth and Reality*. New Delhi: Vikas Publishing House.

Mahapatra, L. K. 1996a. "Good Intentions or Policy are not Enough: Reducing Impoverishment Risks for the Tribal Oustees." In A. B.

Ota and A. Agnihotri, eds., *Involuntary Resettlement in Dam Projects*. New Delhi: Prachi Prakashan.

Mahapatra, L. K. 1996b. "Rehabilitation by the Government and the People: A Case Study of Impoverishment of Salandi Major Irrigation Project Oustees." Paper presented at Training Seminar on Resettlement and Rehabilitation at Gopabandhu Academy of Administration, Orissa, June.

Mahapatra, L. K. 1999a. *Resettlement, Impoverishment and Reconstruction in India, Development for the Deprived*. New Delhi: Vikas Publishing House.

Mahapatra, L. K. 1999b. "Testing the Risks and Reconstruction Model on India's Resettlement Experience." In M. M. Cernea, ed., *The Economics of Involuntary Resettlement: Questions and Challenges*. Washington, D.C.: World Bank.

Maiga, M. H. 1996. "Les Conséquences de l'Implantation du Barrage de Manantali sur la Gestion des Ressources Pastorales de la Zone." Doctoral Thesis, Population and Environment, Institut Supérieur de Formation et de Recherche Appliquée, Bamako.

Mairal, G. and Bergua, J. A. 1996. "From Economism to Culturalism: The Social Impacts of Dam Projects in the River Esera." Paper presented at the Conference of the European Association of Social Anthropologists, Barcelona, July.

Marsden, D. 1997. "Resettlement and Rehabilitation in India: Some Lessons from Recent Experience." In H. M. Mathur and D. Marsden, eds., 1998. *Development Projects and Impovrishment Risks: Resettling Project-Affected People in India*. Oxford: Oxford University Press.

Marx, E. 1988. "Advocacy in a Bedouin Resettlement Program." Paper presented at the Meetings of the International Congress of Anthropological and Ethnological Sciences, Zagreb.

Marx, E. 1990. "The Social World of Refugees: A Conceptual Framework." *Journal of Refugee Studies* 3 (3): 189–203.

Mather, T. H., Sornmani, S., and Keola, K. A. 1994. "Incorporating a Human Health Component into Integrated River Basin Development and Management." Report of mission to the Lower Mekong Basin, World Health Organization (WHO), Geneva.

Mathieu, J. L. 1991. *Migrants et Réfugiés' Que Sais-je?*. Paris: Presse Universitaire de France.

Mathur, H. M. 1995. "The Resettlement of People Displaced by Development Projects: Issues and Approaches." In H. M. Mathur and M. M. Cernea, eds., *Development, Displacement and Resettlement: Focus on Asian Experiences*. New Delhi: Vikas Publishing House.

Mathur, H. M. 1997. "Loss of Access to Basic Public Services." In H. M. Mathur and D. Marsden, eds., *Impoverishment Risks in Resettlement*. New Delhi: Sage Publications.

Mathur, H. M. 1998. "Impoverishment Risk Model and its Use as a Planning Tool." In H. M. Mathur and D. Marsden, eds., *Development Projects and Impoverishment Risks: Resettling Project-Affected People in India*. Oxford: Oxford University Press.

Mathur, H. M. 1999. "The Impoverishing Potential of Development Projects — Resettlement Requires Risk Analysis." *Development and Cooperation* (6), Deutsche Stiftung für Internationale Entwicklung (Frankfurt).

Mathur, H. M. and Cernea, M. M., eds. 1995. *Development, Displacement and Resettlement: Focus on Asian Experiences*. New Delhi: Vikas Publishing House.

Mavrogodatos, G. 1983. *Stillborn Republic: Social Coalitions and Party Strategies in Greece, 1922–1936*. Berkeley, California: University of California Press.

Mavrogodatos, G. 1992. "The Unique Achievement." *Asia Minor Catastrophe and Greek Society, Bulletin of the Centre for Asia Minor Studies* 9 (Special Edition).

Maxwell, S., Buchannan-Smith, M., and Bailey, J. 1991. "Famine in Sudan." *Disasters* 15 (2).

Mazower, M. 1991. *Greece and the Interwar Economic Crisis*. Oxford: Clarendon Press.

Mburugu, E. 1993. "Dislocation of Settled Communities in the Development Process: The Case of Kiambere Hydroelectric Project" In C. Cook, ed., *Involuntary Resettlement in Africa*. World Bank Technical Paper No. 227, Washington, D.C.

McCorkle, C. 1986. *Farmer Associations Study: OHV II*. Washington, DC: Checchi and Company.

McCutcheon, S. 1991. *Electric Rivers: The Story of the James Bay Project*. Montreal and New York: Black Rose Books.

McDowell, C. 1996. "Introduction." In C. McDowell, ed., *Understanding Impoverishment: The Consequences of Development-Induced Displacement*. Oxford: Berghahn Books.

McDowell, C. and de Haan, A. 1997. "Migration and Sustainable Livelihoods: A Critical Review of the Literature." Working Paper No. 65, Institute of Development Studies, Sussex.

McKean, A. M. 1986. "Management of Traditional Common Lands (*Iriaichi*) in Japan." In *Proceedings of the Conference on Common Property Resource Management*. Washington, D.C.: National Academic Press.

McMillan, D. 1995. *Sahel Visions: Planned Settlement and River Blindness Control in Burkina Faso.* Tucson, Arizona: University of Arizona Press.

McMillan, D., Painter, T., and Scudder, T. 1990. "Settlement Experiences and Development Strategies in the Onchocerciasis Controlled Areas of West Africa: Final Report." Institute for Development Anthropology, Binghamton, New York:

McMillan, D. et al. 1998. "New Land is Not Enough: Agricultural Performance of New Lands Settlement in West Africa." *World Development* 26: 187–211.

Meikle, S. and Walker, J. 1998. "Resettlement Policy and Planning in China and the Philippines." Unpublished report, Department for International Development, U.K.

Mejía, M. C. 1992. "Yacyretá: Plan de Accion para el Reasentamiento y Rehabilitacion." *Entitad Binacional Yacyretá,* Buenos Aires.

Mejía, M. C. 1999. "Economic Dimensions of Urban Involuntary Resettlement: Experiences from Latin America." In M. M. Cernea, ed., *The Economics of Involuntary Resettlement: Questions and Challenges.* Washington, D.C.: World Bank.

Merton, R. K. 1979. *The Sociology of Science: Theoretical and Empirical Investigation.* Chicago: University of Chicago Press.

Michard, J. L., Adam, K., and Aziablé, M. 1992. "Le Recasement Des Populations Affectees par la Construction du Barrage de Nangbeto." Unpublished report, Coyne et Bellier.

Mishra, G. K. and Gupota, R. 1981. "Resettlement Policies in Delhi." International Institute for Population Studies, New Delhi.

Monu, E. D. 1995. "The Tragedy or the Benefits of the Commons?: Common Property and Environmental Protection." *PULA* 9 (1).

Moore, D. 1993. "Contesting Terrain in Zimbabwe's Eastern Highlands: Political Ecology, Ethnography, and Peasant Resource Struggles." *Economic Geography* 69: 380–401.

Moris, J. 1973a. "The Mwea Environment." In R. Chambers and J. Moris, eds. *Mwea: An Irrigated Rice Settlement in Kenya.* Munich: Weltforum Verlag.

Moris, J. 1973b. "Tenant Life on Mwea: an Overview." In R. Chambers and J. Moris, eds., *Mwea: An Irrigated Rice Settlement in Kenya.* Munich: Weltforum Verlag.

Mougeot, L. J. A. 1989. "Hydroelectric Development and Involuntary Resettlement in Brazilian Amazonia: Planning and Evaluation." Cobham Resource Consultants, Edingburgh.

Mufune, P. 1995. "Comparing Land Policy and Resource Degradation in Botswana and Zimbabwe." *PULA* 9 (2).

Muggah, R. H. C. 1999. "Capacities in Conflict, Assessing the State's Resettlement of IDPs in Columbia." Unpublished report.

Multiple Action Research Group (MARG). 1987. *Sardar Sarovar Oustees in Madhya Pradesh: What Do They Know? Volumes I-III.* New Delhi: MARG.

Mustafa, K. 1997. "Eviction of Pastoralists from the Mkomazi Game Reserve in Tanzania: An Historical Overview," Pastoral Land Tenure Programme, International Institute for Environment and Development, London.

Mustanoja, U. M. and Mustanoja, K. J. 1993. "The Yacyretá Experience with Urban Resettlement: Some Lessons and Insights." In M. M. Cernea and S. E. Guggenheim, eds. *Anthropological Approaches to Involuntary Resettlement: Policy, Practice, and Theory.* Boulder, Colorado: Westview Press.

Muttagi, P. K. 1988. "Rehabilitation in Bombay." *Habitat International* 12 (4): 71–87.

Muttagi, P. K. 1996. "Problems and Prospects of Land Transfers." Unpublished paper, Mumbai, India.

Nadel, S. F. 1946. "Land Tenure on the Eritrean Plateau." *Africa* XVI (1).

Naik, J. P. 1975. *Equality, Quality and Quantity: The Elusive Triangle in Indian Education.* New Delhi: Allied Publishers.

Nayak, P. K. 1986. "Displaced Denizens of Rengali Dam Project: A Study of Socio-Economic Conditions, Resettlement Problems, and Ameliorative Action Measures." Unpublished paper, Oxfam, Bhubaneswar.

National Center for Human Settlements and Environment (NCHSE). 1986. *Rehabilitation of Displaced Persons Due to Construction of Major Dams: Volume I.* New Delhi: NCHSE.

National Thermal Power Corporation Ltd. (NTPC). 1993. "Rehabilitation and Resettlement Policy." NTPC, New Delhi.

Nayak, R. 1995. "Displacement and Human Rights: The Kisan of Orissa." *The Fourth World: Journal of the Marginalised People* (2): 8–38, National Institute of Social Work and Social Sciences (Bhubaneswar, India).

Ndegwa, P. and Green, R. H. 1994. *Africa to 2000 and Beyond: Imperative Political and Economic Agenda.* Nairobi: East African Educational Publishers.

Nelson, M. 1973. *Development of Tropical Lands: Policy Issues in Latin America.* Baltimore, Maryland: John Hopkins University Press.

Netting, R. M. 1978. "Of Men and Meadows: Strategies of Alpine Land-Use." *Anthropology Quarterly* 45.

Ngaide, T. 1986. "Socio-Economic Implications of Irrigation Systems in Mauritania: The Boghe and Foum-Gleita Irrigation Projets." Unpublished masters thesis, University of Wisconsin, Madison, Wisconsin.

Norbu, D. 1994. "Refugees from Tibet: Structural Causes of Successful Resettlement." Paper for the 4th IRAP Conference, Oxfam, Jawaharlal Nehru University, January 5–9.

North, D. C. 1990. *Institutions, Institutional Change and Economic Performance*. Cambridge (UK): Cambridge University Press.

North, D. C. and Thomas, R. P. 1977. "The First Economic Revolution." *The Economic History Review* XXX (2).

Nowak, M. 1977. "The Education of Young Tibetans in India: Cultural Preservation or Agent for Change?" In M. Brauen and P. Kvaerne, eds., *Tibetan Studies*. Zurich: Volkerkundemuseum der Universitat Zurich.

Ntshalintshali, C. and McGurk, C. 1991. "Resident People and Swaziland's Mololotja National Park: A Success Story." In P. West and S. R. Brechin, eds., *Resident Peoples and National Parks: Social Dimensions in International Conservation*. Tucson, Arizona: University of Arizona Press.

Oliver-Smith, A. 1994. "Resistance to Resettlement: The Formation and Evolution of Movement." In L. Kreisberg, ed., *Research in Social Movements, Conflicts and Change*. Greenwich, Connecticut: JAI Press.

Oliver-Smith, A. and Hansen, A. 1982. "Involuntary Migration and Resettlement: Causes and Contexts." In A. Hansen and A. Oliver-Smith, eds., *Involuntary Migration and Resettlement*. Boulder, Colorado: Westview Press.

Omar. 1997. "Update on Kadhan." Unpublished paper, Documentation Centre, Indian Social Institute.

Operations Evaluation Department, The World Bank. 1993. "Early Experiences with Involuntary Resettlement: Impact Evaluation on Thailand, Khao Laem Hydroelectric Project." Report No. 12131, World Bank, Washington, D.C.

Operations Evaluation Department, The World Bank. 1993. "Early Experiences with Involuntary Resettlement: Overview." Report No. 12142, World Bank, Washington, D.C.

Operations Evaluation Department, The World Bank. 1998. "Recent Experiences with Involuntary Resettlement: Overview." World Bank, Washington, D.C.

Ophuls, W. 1973. *Ecology and the Politics of Scarcity*. San Francisco, CA: Freeman.

Organization for Economic Cooperation and Development (OECD). 1992. "Guidelines for Aid Agencies on Involuntary Displacement and Resettlement in Development Projects." Development Assistance Committee, OECD, Paris.

Ostrom, E. 1986. "Issues of Definition and Theory: Some Conclusions and Hypotheses" In *Proceedings of the Conference on Common Property Resource Management*. Washington, D.C.: National Academy Press.

Ostrom, E. 1988. "Institutional Arrangements and the Commons Dilemma." In V. Ostrom , D. Feeny, and H. Picht, eds., *Rethinking Institutional Analysis and Development*. San Francisco, CA: International Center for Economic Growth.

Ostrom, E. 1990. *Governing the Commons: The Evolution of Institutions for Collective Actions*. Cambridge (UK): Cambridge University Press.

Ota, A. B. 1996. "Countering the Impoverishment Risk: The Case of the Rengali Dam Project." In A. B. Ota and A. Agnihotri, eds., *Involuntary Resettlement in Dam Projects*. New Delhi: Prachi Prakashan.

Ota, A. B. and Agnihotri, A., eds. 1996. *Involuntary Resettlement in Dam Projects*. New Delhi: Prachi Prakashan.

Ota, A. B. and Mohanty, R. N., eds. 1998. *Development-Induced Displacement and Rehabilitation*. New Delhi/Bhubaneswar: Prachi Prakashan.

Padjadjaran University. 1989. "Environmental Impact Analysis of the Cirata Dam." Institute of Ecology, Padjadjaran, India.

Paine, R. 1994. *Herds of the Tundra: A Portrait of Saami Reindeer Pastoralism*. Washington, D.C.: Smithsonian Institution Press.

Palmer, G. B. 1979. "The Agricultural Resettlement Scheme: A Review of Cases and Theories." In B. Berdichewsky, ed., *Anthropology and Social Change in Rural Areas*. The Hague: Mouton.

Pandey, B. 1996. "Impoverishment Risks: A Case Study of Five Villages in Coal Mining Areas of Talcher, Orissa." Paper presented at the Workshop on Involuntary Resettlement and Impoverishment Risks, New Delhi.

Pandey, B. 1998. *Displaced Development: Impact of Open Cast Mining on Women*. New Delhi: Friederich Ebert Stiftung.

Pandey, B. and Associates. 1997. "Development, Displacement and Resettlement in Orissa, 1950–1990." International Development Research Centre, Canada, and Institute for Socio-economic Development, Bhubaneswar.

Pandey, B. and Associates. 1998. "Depriving the Underprivileged by Development." Institute for Socio-Economic Development, Bhubaneswar.

Pankhurst, A. 1990. "Resettlement: Policy and Practice." In S. Pausewang et. al., eds., *Ethiopia: Options for Rural Development*. London: Zed Books.

Pankhurst, A. 1992. *Resettlement and Famine in Ethiopia: The Villagers' Experience*. Manchester (UK): Manchester University Press.

Parasuraman S., 1999. "The Development Dilemma: Displacement in India." Institute of Social Studies, The Hague.

Partridge, W. L. 1989. "Involuntary Resettlement in Development Projects." *Journal of Refugee Studies* 2 (3): 373–384.

Partridge, W. L. 1993. "Successful Involuntary Resettlement: Lessons from the Costa Rican Arenal Hydroelectric Project." In M. M. Cernea and S. E. Guggenheim, eds., *Anthropological Approaches to Resettlement: Policy, Practice, and Theory*. Boulder, Colorado: Westview Press.

Patel, A. 1995. "What Do the Narmada Valley Tribals Want?" In W. Fisher, ed., *Toward Sustainable Development? Struggling over India's Narmada River*. Armonk, New York: M. E. Sharpe.

Patel, C. C. 1995. "The Sardar Sarovar Project: A Victim of Time." In W. Fisher, ed., *Toward Sustainable Development? Struggling over India's Narmada River*. Armonk, New York: M. E. Sharpe.

Pathy, J. 1996. "Hydro-Electric Development syndrome: Dispossession and Displacement of Tribal People." In K. Gopal Iyer, ed., *Sustainable Development: Ecological and Socio-Cultural Dimensions*. New Delhi: Vikas Publishing House.

Patkar, M. 1995. "The Struggle for Participation and Justice: A Historical Narrative." In W. Fisher, ed., *Toward Sustainable Development? Struggling over India's Narmada River*. Armonk, New York: M. E. Sharpe.

Patnaik, G. and Panda, D. 1992. "The New Economic Policy and the Poor." *Social Action* 42 (2): 201-212.

Patnaik, S. M. 1996. *Displacement, Rehabilitation and Social Change: The Case of Paraja Highlanders*. New Delhi: Inter-India Publications.

Pearce, D. W. 1999. "Methodological Issues in the Economic Analysis for Involuntary Resettlement Operations." In M. M. Cernea, ed., *The Economics of Involuntary Resettlement: Questions and Challenges*. Washington, D.C.: World Bank.

Pentzopoulos, D. 1962. *The Balkan Exchange of Minorities and its Impact upon Greece*. The Hague: Mouton.

Persoon, G. 1992. "From Sago to Rice: Changes in Cultivation in Siberut, Indonesia." In E. Croll and D. Parkin, eds., *Bush Base: Forest Farm: Culture, Environment and Development*. London: Routledge.

Picaredi, A. C. and Seifert, W. W. 1976. "A Tragedy of the Commons in the Sahel." *Technology Review* May.

Pokharel, J. C. 1995. "Population Displacement and Compensation Planning in Kulekhani Hydro-Electric Project, Nepal." In H. M. Mathur and M. M. Cernea, eds., *Development, Displacement and Resettlement: Focus on Asian Experiences.* New Delhi: Vikas Publishing House.

Pollnac, R. 1991. "Social and Cultural Characteristics in Small-Scale Fishery Development." In M. M. Cernea, ed., *Putting People First: Sociological Variables in Rural Development,* Second Edition. New York: Oxford University Press for the World Bank.

Potten, D. 1976. "Etsha: A Successful Resettlement Scheme." Botswana Notes and Records No. 8: 105–117.

Poulin, R., Appleby, G., and Quan, C. 1987. "Impact Evaluation of Project Nord Shaba." North Shaba Rural Development Project, U.S. Agency for International Development (USAID) Mission, Kinshasa, Zaire.

Powles, J. and Clark, J. 1996. "Oral Testimony Project, Meheba Refugee Settlement, Zambia: A field Report." Paper presented at Second International Conference on Involuntary Displacement and Resettlement, University of Oxford, September.

PROFERI. 1993. "Joint Government of Eritrea and United Nations Appeal for Eritrea. Vols 1 and 2." Government of Eritrea, Asmara.

PROFERI and Franklin Advisory Services. 1994. "Plan of Operation for Pilot Project of PROFERI." Government of Eritrea, Asmara.

Putsoana, M. M., et. al. 1996. "Making Resettlement a Community Development Project: a Case Study of Katse Dam Resettlement in Lesotho." Paper presented at IAI/ISER Seminar on Understanding Changing Patterns of Settlement and Resettlement in Southern Africa, Grahamstown, South Africa, January.

Quarantelli, E. L. 1980. "Evacuation Behaviour and Problems: Findings and Implications from the Research Literature." Disaster Research Centre, Ohio State University, Columbus.

Quarantelli, E. L. 1981. "Psycho-Sociology in Emergency Planning." *International Civil Defence Bulletin* 2 (28).

Quiggin, J. 1993. "Common Property, Equality and Development." *World Development* 21: 1123–1138.

Ramaiah, S. 1995. *Health Implications of Involuntary Resettlement and Rehabilitation in Developmental Projects in India: Volume I.* New Delhi: Society for Health Education and Learning Packages.

Raval, S. R. 1991. "Gur National Park and the Maldharis: Beyond 'Setting Aside.'" In P. West and S. R. Brechin, eds., *Resident Peoples* and National Parks: Social Dimensions in International Conservation. Tucson Arizona: University of Arizona Press.

Reddy, I. U. B. 1993. Displacement and Rehabilitation. New Delhi: Mittal Publications.

Reddy, I. U. B. 1998. "Marginalisation of Project-Affected People: a Comparative Analysis of Singrauli and Rihand Power Projects." In H. M. Mathur and D. Marsden, eds., Development Projects and Impoverishment Risks: Resettling Project-Affected People in India.New Delhi: Oxford University Press, pp.146–154.

Reddy, P. S. 1995. Displaced Populations and Socio-Cultural Change. New Delhi: Commonwealth Publishers.

Rees, W. E. 1990. "The Ecology of Sustainable Development." The Ecologist 20 (1): 18–23.

Repetto, R. and Holmes, T. 1984. "The Role of Population in Resource Depletion in Developing Countries." Population and Development Review 9 (4): 609–632.

Republic of Cyprus. nd. "The Refugees of Cyprus." Press and Information Office, Ministry to the President, Cyprus.

Rew, A. and Driver, P. A. 1986. "Evaluation of the Victoria Dam Project in Sri Lanka," Volume III – "Initial Evaluation of the Social and Environmental Impact of the Victoria Dam Project," Annex J – "Social Analysis," Annex K – "Environmental Analysis."

Robinson, K. 1986. Stepchildren of Progress: The Political Economy of Development in an Indonesian Mining Town. Albany, New York: State University of New York Press.

Rodgers, G., Gore, C., and Figueiredo, J. B., eds. 1995. Social Exclusion: Rhetoric, Reality, Responses. Geneva: International Institute for Labour Studies.

Rodrigo, M. L. 1991. "Resources and Livelihood: Differential Response to Change and Planned Development: A Case From The Mahaweli Irrigation Project In Sri Lanka." University Microfilms International, Ann Arbor, Michigan.

Rotberg, R. I. and Weiss, T. G., eds. 1997. From Massacres to Genocide: the Media, Public Policy and Humanitarian Crises. Cambridge, MA: World Peace Foundation.

Ruiz, H. 1987. "When Refugees Won't Go Home: the Dilemma of Chadians in Sudan." US Committee for Refugees, Washington D.C.

Runge, C. R. 1983. "Common Property Externalities: Isolation, Assurance and Resource Depletion in Traditional Grazing." American Journal of Agricultural Economics 63 (4): 595–606.

Runge, C. R. 1984. "Institutions and the Free Rider: the Assurance Problem in Collective Action." The Journal of Politics 46:155–181.

Runge, C. F. 1986. "Common Property and Collective Action in Economic Development." *World Development* 14 (5).

Sagoe, K. Amanfo. 1970. "Valuation, Acquisition and Compensation for Purposes of Resettlement." In R. Chambers, ed., *The Volta Resettlement Experience*. New York: Praeger/Volta River Authority, Accra and University of Science and Technology, Kumasi.

Saklaini, G. 1984. *The Uprooted Tibetans in India: A Sociological Study of Continuity and Change*. New Delhi: Cosmo

Salem-Murdock, M. 1989. *Arabs and Nubians in New Halfa: A Study of Settlement and Irrigation*. Salt Lake City, Utah: University of Utah Press.

Salem-Murdock, M., Niasse, M., Magistro, J., Nuttall, C., Horowitz, M., and Kane, O. 1994. *Les Barrages de la Controverse: Le Cas de la Vallée du Fleuve Sénégal*. Paris: Harmattan.

Salini Construttori.1989. "Tana-Beles Project, Ethiopia, 1989." Company Report, Addis Ababa.

Salisbury, R. 1986. *A Homeland for the Cree: Regional Development in James Bay 1971–1981*. Kingston and Montreal: McGill-Queen's University Press.

Salisbury, R. and Tooker, E. eds. 1984. *Affluence and Cultural Survival*. Proceedings of the American Ethnological Society, Washington, D.C.

Sapkota, N. 1999. *Impoverishment Risk and Evaluation among Seriously Project Affected Families in the Kali Gondaki Hydropower Project*. KGEMU, Beltari, Nepal.

Saul, M. 1988. "Money and Land Tenure as Factors in Farm Size Differentiation in Burkina Faso." In R. Downs and S. Reyna, eds., *Land and Society in Contemporary Africa*. Hanover, New Hampshire: University of New Hampshire.

Saul, M. 1993. "Land Custom in Bare: Agnatic Corporation and Rural Capitalism in Western Burkina." In T. Bassett and D. Crummey, eds., *Land in African Agrarian Systems*. Madison, Wisconsin: University of Wisconsin Press.

Scombatti, M. and Carvalho, R. 1995. "Evaluacion del Plan de Reasentamiento y Rehabilitacion Sector Olero: Argentina-Paraguay." Buenos Aires.

Scott, A. D. 1955. "The Fisher: The Objectives of Sole Ownership." *Journal of Political Economy* 63.

Scott Wilson Kirkpatrick & Partners. 1988. "Tanzania: Development in Refugee Settlement Areas." Planning Mission Report, United Nations High Commissioner for Refugees (UNHCR).

Schmidt, A. 1997. "How Camps Become 'Mainstream' Policy for Assisting Refugees." Unpublished research report, Refugee Studies Programme, University of Oxford.

Schoepf, M. 1997. "The Forced Repatriation of Rwandese from Tanzania." Unpublished lecture delivered at the Refugee Studies Programme, University of Oxford.

Scott, C. 1984. "Between 'Original Affluence' and Consumer Affluence: Domestic Production and Guaranteed Income for James Bay Cree Hunters." In R. Salisbury and E. Tooker, eds., *Affluence and Cultural Survival*. Proceedings of the American Ethnological Society, Washington, D.C.

Scudder, T. 1973. "The Human Ecology of Big Projects: River Basin Development and Resettlement." *Annual Review of Anthropology* 2: 45–61.

Scudder, T. 1980. "River-Basin Development and Local Initiative in African Savanna Environments." In D. R. Harris, ed., *Human Ecology in Savanna Environments*. London: Academic Press.

Scudder, T. 1981. "What It Means to Be Dammed." *Engineering and Science* 54 (4).

Scudder, T. 1982. "No Place to Go: Effects of Compulsory Relocation on Navajos." Institute for the Study of Human Issues, Philadelphia, Pennsylvania.

Scudder, T. 1991. "A Sociological Framework for the Analysis of New Land Settlements." In M. M. Cernea, ed., *Putting People First: Sociological Variables in Rural Development*. New York: Oxford University Press for the World Bank.

Scudder, T. 1993. "Development-Induced Relocation and Refugee Studies: 37 Years of Change and Continuity among Zambia's Gwembe Tonga." *Journal of Refugee Studies* 6 (3): 123–152.

Scudder, T. 1996. "Development-Induced Impoverishment, Resistance and River-Basin Development." In C. McDowell, ed., *Understanding Impoverishment: The Consequences of Development-Induced Displacement*. Oxford: Berghahn Books.

Scudder, T. 1997. "Resettlement." In A. Biswas, ed., *Water resources: environmental planning, management, and development*. New York: McGraw-Hill.

Scudder, T. and Colson, E. 1982. "From Welfare to Development: A Conceptual Framework for the Analysis of Dislocated People." In A. Hansen and A. Oliver-Smith, eds., *Involuntary Migration and Resettlement: The Problems and Responses of Dislocated People*. Boulder, Colorado: Westview Press.

Sen, A. 1981. *Poverty and Famines: An Essay on Entitlement and Deprivation*. Oxford: Clarendon Press.

Sen, I. 1992. "Mechanization and the Working Class Women." *Social Action* 42 (4), Oct.-Dec.: 391-400.

Sen, A. 1997. "Social Exclusion: A Critical Assessment of the Concept and its Relevance." Paper prepared for the Asian Development Bank.

Sen, A. and Dreze, J. 1992. *Social Security in Developing Countries: Hunger and Public Action.* Oxford: Clarendon Press.

Sequeira, D. 1994. "Gender and Resettlement: An Overview of Impact and Planning Issues in Bank-Assisted Projects." Draft paper prepared for Bankwide Resettlement Review, World Bank, Washington, D.C.

Serageldin, I. 1995. *Nurturing Development: Aid and Cooperation in Today's Changing World.* Washington, D.C.: World Bank.

Sharma, B. D. 1978. *Tribal Development: The Concept and the Frame.* New Delhi: Prachi Prakashan.

Sharma, B. D. 1993. "Community Control over Natural Resources and Industry: The Significance of the Mavalibhata Declaration." In W. Fernandes, ed., *The Indigenous Question: Search for an Identity.* New Delhi: Indian Social Institute.

Shas, A. 1995. "A Technical Overview of the Flawed Sardar Sarovar Project and a Proposal for a Sustainable Alternative." In W. Fisher, ed., *Toward Sustainable Development? Struggling over India's Narmada River.* Armonk, New York: M. E. Sharpe.

Shazali, S. and Ahmed, A. G. M. 1999. "Pastoral Land Tenure and Agricultural Expansion: Sudan and the Horn of Africa." Issue Paper No.85, Issue Paper No.85, International Institute for Environment and Development, London.

Shepherd, G. 1989. "The Reality of the Commons: Answering Hardin from Somalia." *Development Policy Review* 7.

Shi, G. and Hu, W. 1994. *Comprehensive Evaluation and Monitoring of Displaced Persons Standards of Living and Production.* National Research Centre of Resettlement, Hohai University, Nanjing.

Shihata, I. F. I. 1991. "Involuntary Resettlement in World Bank-Financed Projects." In *World Bank in a Changing World* Amsterdam: Martinus Nyhoff Publishers.

Shihata, I. F. I. 1993. "Legal Aspects of Involuntary Population Resettlement." In M. M. Cernea and S. E. Guggenheim, eds., *Anthropological Approaches to Resettlement: Policy, Practice, and Theory.* Boulder, Colorado: Westview Press.

Singh, C. 1989. "Rehabilitation and the Right to Property." In W. Fernandes and E. Ganguly Thukral, eds., *Development, Displacement and Rehabilitation.* New Delhi: Indian Social Institute.

Singh, K. S., ed. 1994. *The Scheduled Tribes.* New Delhi: Anthropological Survey of India and Oxford University Press.

Singh, S., Kothari, A., and Amin, K. 1992. "Evaluating Major Irrigation Projects in India." In E. Ganguly Thukral, ed., *Big Dams, Displaced People: Rivers of Sorrow, Rivers of Change.* New Delhi: Sage Publications.

Sissoko, N. D., Diakité, S., Haidara, H., Nadio, M., and Sokona1, O. 1986. "Population — Santé — Développement dans la zone du barrage hydro-électrique de Selingue." Institut d'Economie Rurale, Bamako.

Sivini, G. 1986. "Famine and Resettlement Programmes in Africa." *Africa — Dell'Instituto Italo-Africano* XLI: 211–242.

Skinner, Q. 1990. *The Return of Grand Theory in the Human Sciences.* Cambridge (UK): Cambridge University Press.

Slingsby, M. 1995. "An Approach to Relocation in the Integrated Slum Improvement, Health and Community Development Project, Vijayawada, India." In F. Davidson, et.al., eds., *Urban Relocation Policy and Practice.* Rotterdam: Institute of Housing and Urban Development Studies.

Smith, S. 1990. "Front Line Africa: The Right to a Future." Oxfam, Oxford.

Soeftestad, L. T. 1990. "On Evacuation of People in the Kotmale Hydropower Project: Experience from a Socio-Economic Impact Study." *Bistaandsantropologen.*

Sorensen, C. 1995a. "Half-Year Report (ERT3): Eritrean Repatriation Programme." September, ACORD, Eritrea.

Sorensen, C. 1995b) " Half-Year Report (ERT4): Seraye Credit and Savings Scheme." September, ACORD, Eritrea.

Sowell, T. 1996. *Migrations and Cultures: A World View.* New York: Basic Books.

Spiegel, H. 1997. Letter to M. M. Cernea.

Stallings, R. A. 1995. *Promoting Risk: Constructing the Earthquake Threat.* New York: Aldin de Gruyer.

Stanley, W. 1996. "Machkund, Upper Kolab and NALCO Projects in Koraput District, Orissa." *Economic and Political Weekly* 31 (24), June 15: 1533-1538.

Stearman, A. M.1990. "The Effects of Settler Incursion on Fish and Game Resources of the Yuqui, a Native Amazonian Society of Eastern Bolivia." *Human Organisation* 49: 373–385.

Stein B. and Clark, L. 1990. "Refugee Integration and Older Refugee Settlements in Africa." Paper presented at the 1990 meeting of the American Anthropological Association, New Orleans.

Stiglitz, J. E. 1998. "Towards a New Paradigm for Development: Strategies, Policies and Processes." Prebisch Lecture given at the United

Nations Conference on Trade and Development (UNCTAD), Geneva, October 19.

Sugden, R. 1984. "Reciprocity: The Supply of Public Goods Through Voluntary Contributions." *The Economic Journal* 94.

Sundaram, P. S. A. 1993. "Relocation Experience in India," In F. Davidson, et.al., eds., *Urban Relocation Policy and Practice*. Rotterdam: Institute of Housing and Urban Development Studies.

Supreme Court of India. 1982. *Lalchand Mahto and Ors vs. Coal India Ltd.* Civil Original Jurisdiction, MP No.16331 of 1982.

Tadros, H. R. 1979. "The Human Aspects of Rural Resettlement Schemes in Egypt." In B. Berdichewsky, ed., *Anthropology and Social Change in Rural Areas*. The Hague: Mouton Publishers.

Taylor, C. C. 1981. "Archaeology and the Origins of the Open-Field Agriculture." In T. Rowley, ed., *The Origins of the Open-Field Agriculture*. London: Croom Held.

Thangaraj, S. 1996. "Impoverishment Risk Analysis — A Methodological Tool for Participatory Resettlement Planning." In C. McDowell, ed., *Understanding Impoverishment: The Consequences of Development-Induced Displacement*. Oxford: Berghahn Books.

Thangaraj, S. 1998. "Impoverishment Risks in Involuntary Resettlement: An Overview." In H. M. Mathur and D. Marsden, eds., *Development Projects and Impoverishment Risks: Resettling Project-Affected People in India*. Oxford: Oxford University Press.

Thirsk, J. 1964. "The Common Fields." *Past and Present* (29): 3–25.

Traoré, A. M. 1996. "Les Enjeux de la Gestion de l'Espace dans la Zone de Manantali: Réalités et Perspectives." Doctoral Thesis, Population and Environment, Institut Supérieur de Formation et de Recherche Appliquée, Bamako.

Traoré, I. and Clément, F. 1985. "Les Migrations au Mali Sud: Element pour l'Intervention de la CMDT." BECIS, Bamako.

Travers, S. 1993. "China: Involuntary Resettlement." Report No. 11641-CHA, China and Mongolia Department, World Bank, Washington, D.C.

Tsimouris, G. 1998. "Anatolian Embodiment in an Hellenic Context: the Case of Reisderiani Mikrasiates Refugees." Unpublished doctoral thesis, University of Sussex.

Tulugak, H. n.d. *More Than Just Rights*. Unpublished manuscript.

Turner, R. J., Wheaton, B., and Lloyd D. A. 1995. "The Epidemiology of Social Stress." *American Sociological Review* 60: 104–125.

Udall, L. 1995. "The International Narmada Campaign: A Case Study of Sustained Advocacy." In W. Fisher, ed., *Toward Sustainable Development? Struggling over India's Narmada River*. Armonk, New York: M. E. Sharpe.

UNICEF. 1989. "Children on the Front Line: the Impact of Apartheid, Demobilisation and Warfare on Children in Southern and South Africa." New York.

UNICEF. 1992. "Signs of Hope Towards Rehabilitation and Renewed Development for the Children of Southern Africa." Windhoek and Nairobi.

UNICEF. 1993. "Somalia: Toward 1994–1996; Reconstruction, Rehabilitation and Restructuring." Nairobi.

UNICEF. 1994. "That They May be Whole Again: Offsetting Refugee Influx Burdens on Ngara and Karagwe Districts." Nairobi.

UNICEF. 1995. "UNICEF and Somali Survival and Development 1996–1999: Through Shifting Prisms with Missing Pieces." Nairobi.

United Nations. 1991. "South Africa Destabilisation: the Economic Costs of Frontline Resistance to Apartheid." UN Economic Commission for Africa and Inter-Agency Task Force, Africa Recovery Programme, New York.

United Nations. 1995. *Copenhagen Programme of Action Adopted by the World Summit for Social Development*, March.

United Nations High Commissioner for Refugees.1995. *Les Réfugiés dans le Monde: En Quête de Solutions*. Paris: Editions La Découverte.

United Nations High Commissioner for Refugees. 1984. "Coming Home." *Refugees* (9), Sept.: 9–10.

United Nations High Commissioner for Refugees. 1996. "Northern Uganda: Review of Rural Settlement Programme for Sudanese Refugees." PTSS Mission Report 96/08, Geneva.

United Nations Research Institute for Social Development (UNRISD). 1996. "After the Conflict." War-Torn Societies Project, UNRISD, Geneva.

United States Agency for International Development (USAID). 1984. "Project Paper: Mali, Manantali Resettlement." Washington, D.C.: USAID.

United States Committee for Refugees. 1995. "World Refugee Survey." Washington, D.C.

United States Committee for Refugees. 1996. "World Refugee Survey." Washington, D.C.

Van Damme, W. 1995. "Do Refugees Belong in Camps? Experiences from Goma and Guinea." *Lancet* 346: 360–62.

Van Wicklin III, W. 1999. "Sharing Benefits for Improving Resettlers' Livelihoods." In M. M. Cernea, ed., *The Economics of Involuntary Resettlement: Questions and Challenges*. Washington, D.C.: World Bank.

Vaswani, K. 1992. "Rehabilitation Laws and Policies: a Critical Look." In E. Ganguly Thukral, ed., *Big Dams, Displaced People: Rivers of Sorrow, Rivers of Change,* New Delhi: Sage Publications.

Viegas, P. 1992. "The Hirakud Dam Oustees: Thirty Years After." In E. Ganguly Thukral, ed., *Big Dams, Displaced People: Rivers of Sorrow, Rivers of Change.* New Delhi: Sage Publications.

Voutira, E. 1994. "Refugee Greece: a Model for Emulation?" *Istor* 1 (1).

Voutira, E. 1996. "Vestiges of Empire: Migrants, Refugees and Returnees in Post-Soviet Russia." *Oxford International Review* VII (3), Summer: 52–59.

Voutira, E. 1997a. "Population Transfers and Resettlement Policies in Inter-War Europe: The case of Asia Minor Refugees in Macedonia from an International and National Perspective." In P. MacKridge and E. Yiannakakis, eds., *Macedonia: Ourselves and Others.* Oxford: Berg.

Voutira, E. 1997b. "The Language of Humanitarian Emergencies and the Idioms of Intervention." Draft paper for the Wider Project on Complex Humanitarian Emergencies, International Development Centre, University of Oxford.

Voutira, E. and Harrell-Bond, B. E. 1995. "In Search of the Locus of Trust: The Social World of the Refugee Camp." In E. V. Daniel and J. C. Knudsen, eds., *Mistrusting Refugees.* Berkeley, California: University of California Press.

Voutira, E., with Mahmud, N., Oestergaard-Nielsen, E., Urquiola, A., Whishaw-Brown, S., and Yu, H. 1995. "Improving Social and Gender Planning in Emergency Operations." Report submitted to the World Food Programme, Rome, and Refugee Studies Programme, University of Oxford.

Waldram, J. 1980. "Relocation and Political Change in a Manitoba Native Community." *Canadian Journal of Anthropology* 1: 173–178.

Waldram, J. 1988. *As Long as the Rivers Run: Hydroelectric Development and Native Communities in Western Canada.* Winnipeg: The University of Manitoba Press.

Wali, A. 1989. *Kilowatts and Crisis: Hydroelectric Power and Social Dislocation in Eastern Panama.* Boulder, Colorado: Westview Press.

Wali, A. 1993. "The Transformation of a Frontier: State and Regional Relationships in Panama, 1979–1990." *Human Organisation* 52: 115–129.

Weighill, L. 1997. "ICARA II — Refugee Aid and Development." Unpublished paper, Refugee Studies Programme, Oxford University.

Wells, M. and Brandon, K., eds. 1992. *People and Parks: Linking Protected Areas Management with Local Communities*. Washington, D.C.: World Bank/USAID.

West, P. and Brechin, S. R., eds. 1991. *Resident Peoples and National Parks: Social Dimensions in International Conservation*. Tucson, Arizona: University of Arizona Press.

Wilcken, J. 1992. "A Theological Approach to Reconciliation." In F. Brennan, ed., *Reconciling Our Differnces: A Christian Approach to Recognizing Aboriginal Land Rights*. Australia: Aurora Books.

Wilson, K. 1992. "Internally Displaced, Refugees and Repatriates From and To Mozambique." Report No. 1, Refugee Studies Programme, SIDA/Oxford University, Oxford.

Wolde-Selassie Abutte 1991. "The Consequences of Resettlement: the Case of South-Western Shoa Resettlers in the Metekel Resettlement Scheme." Addis Ababa University (text in Amharic).

Wolde-Selassie Abutte. 1993. "The Adverse Effects of Displacement and Density in Kambaata and an Endeavour to Combat the Problem — an Issue for Discussion." Addis Ababa University.

Wolde-Selassie Abutte. 1996. "Assessment of Socio-Economic Context and Community Water Supply in the Metekal Zone." Report for CISP, Addis Ababa.

Wolde-Selassie Abutte. 1997. "The Dynamics of Socio-Economic Differentiation and Change in the Beles Valley (Pawe) Resettlement Area, North-Western Ethiopia." Unpublished masters thesis in social anthropology, Addis Ababa University.

Wolfensohn, J. D. 1995. "Address at the Annual Meeting of the World Bank and IMF." Washington, D.C.

Wolfensohn, J. D. 1997. "Address at the Annual Meeting of the World Bank and IMF: The Challenge of Inclusion." Hong Kong.

Wolfensohn, J. D. 1998. "Address at the Annual Meeting of the World Bank and IMF: The Other Crisis." Washington, D.C.

Wolfensohn, J. D. 1999. "Closing Remarks at the Annual Meeting of the World Bank and IMF." Washington, D.C.

World Bank. 1986. "Operations Policy Issues in the Treatment of Involuntary Resettlement." Operational Policy Note 10.08, Washington, D.C.

World Bank. 1988. *Indonesia: The Transmigration Program in Perspective*. Washington, D.C.: World Bank.

World Bank. 1990. "Involuntary Resettlement." Operational Directive 4.30, World Bank, Washington, D.C.

World Bank. 1993. "China: Involuntary Resettlement." Unpublished report, World Bank, Washington, D.C.

World Bank. 1994. "Resettlement and Development: The Bankwide Review of Projects Involving Involuntary Resettlement, 1986–1993." Environment Department Paper No.32, World Bank, Washington, D.C. (Second Edition, 1996).

World Bank. 1995a. "Kenya — Project Completion Report: Export Development Project." Report No. 13886, World Bank, Washington, D.C.

World Bank. 1995b. "Korea — Project Completion Report Korea: Taigu Urban Transport Project." Report No. 14711, World Bank, Washington, D.C.

World Bank. 1995c. "India — Program Completion Report: Export Development Project." Report 13885, World Bank, Washington, D.C.

World Bank. 1995d. "India — Project Completion Report India: Dudhichua Coal Project." Report No. 13938, World Bank, Washington, D.C.

World Bank. 1996a. "China – Shuikou Reservoir Resettlement, Draft of Completion Report." World Bank, Washington, D.C.

World Bank. 1996b. *From Plan to Market: World Development Report 1996.* Oxford: Oxford University Press.

World Bank. 1996c. "Resettlement and Development: The Bankwide Review of Projects Involving Involuntary Resettlement 1986–1993." Environment Department, World Bank, Washington, D.C.

World Bank. 1998. "Post-Conflict Reconstruction: The Role of the World Bank." Environmentally and Socially Sustainable Development Network, World Bank, Washington, D.C.

Zetter, R. 1992. "Refugees and Forced Migrants as Development Resources: the Greek Cypriot Refugees from 1974." *Cyprus Review* 4 (1):7–38.